MAGILL'S CINEMA ANNUAL

MAGILL'S
CINEMA ANNUAL

1990

A Survey of the Films of 1989

Edited by

FRANK N. MAGILL

SALEM PRESS

Pasadena, California   Englewood Cliffs, New Jersey

∞ The paper used in these volumes conforms to the American
National Standard for Permanence of Paper for Printed Library
Materials, Z39.48-1984.

Library of Congress Catalog Card No. 83-644357
ISBN 0-89356-409-5
ISSN 0739-2141

First Printing

PRINTED IN THE UNITED STATES OF AMERICA

PUBLISHER'S NOTE

Magill's Cinema Annual, 1990, is the ninth annual volume in a series that developed from the twenty-one-volume core set, *Magill's Survey of Cinema*. Each annual covers the preceding year and follows a similar format in reviewing the films of the year. This format consists of four general sections: two essays of general interest, the films of 1989, lists of obituaries and awards, and the indexes.

In the first section, the first article reviews the career and accomplishments of the recipient of the Life Achievement Award, which is presented by the American Film Institute. In 1989, this award was given to the distinguished actor Gregory Peck. Following this initial essay, the reader will find an essay that lists selected film books published in 1989. Briefly annotated, the list provides a valuable guide to the current literature about the film industry and its leaders.

The largest section of the annual, "Selected Films of 1989," is devoted to essay-reviews of ninety-one significant films released in the United States in 1989. The reviews are arranged alphabetically by the title under which the film was released in the United States. Original and alternate titles are cross-referenced to the American-release title in the Title Index.

Each article begins with selected credits for the film. Credit categories include: Production, Direction, Screenplay, Cinematography, Editing, Art direction, and Music. Also included are the MPAA rating, the running time, and a list of the principal characters with the corresponding actors. This introductory information on a film not released originally in the United States also includes the country of origin and the year the film was released there. If the information for any of the standard categories was unavailable, the heading is followed by the phrase "no listing." Additional headings such as Special effects, Costume design, and Song have been included in an article's introductory top matter when appropriate. Also, the symbol (AA) in the top matter identifies those artists who have received an Academy Award for their contribution to the film from the Academy of Motion Picture Arts and Sciences.

The section of the annual labeled "More Films of 1989" supplies the reader with an alphabetical listing of an additional 200 feature films released in the United States during the year. Included are brief credits and short descriptions of the films. These films can be located, along with any cross-references, in the indexes.

Two further lists conclude the text of the volume. The first of these is the Obituaries, which provides useful information about the careers of motion-picture professionals who died in 1989. The second list is of the awards presented by ten different international associations, from the Academy of Motion Picture Arts and Sciences to the Cannes International Film Festival and the British Academy Awards.

The final section of this volume includes nine indexes that cover the films reviewed in *Magill's Cinema Annual*, 1990. Arranged in the order established in the introductory matter of the essay-reviews, the indexes are as follows: Title Index, Director Index, Screenwriter Index, Cinematographer Index, Editor Index, Art Director Index, Music Index, and Performer Index. A Subject Index is also provided. To assist the reader further, pseudonyms, foreign titles, and alternate titles are all cross-referenced. Titles of foreign films and retrospective films are followed by the year, in brackets, of their original release.

The Title Index includes all the titles of films covered in individual articles, in "More Films of 1989," and also those discussed at some length in the general essays. The next seven indexes are arranged according to artists, each of whose names is followed by a list of the films on which they worked and the titles of the essays (such as "Life Achievement Award" or "Obituaries") in which they are mentioned at length. The final listing is the Subject Index, in which any one film can be categorized under several headings. Thus, a reader can effectively use all these indexes to approach a film from any one of several directions, including not only its credits but also its subject matter.

CONTRIBUTING REVIEWERS

Michael Adams
Fairleigh Dickinson University

Michael Banka
Freelance Reviewer

Rebecca Bell-Metereau
Southwest Texas State University

Jo-Ellen Lipman Boon
Freelance Reviewer

Helen Bragg
McLaughlin Library, University of Guelph

Beverley Bare Buehrer
Freelance Reviewer

Norman Carson
Geneva College

Greg Changnon
Northwestern University

Kyle Counts
Freelance Reviewer

R. C. Dale
University of Washington

Bill Delaney
Freelance Reviewer

Susan Doll
Oakton Community College

Thomas L. Erskine
Salisbury State University

Joan Esposito
Nassau Community College

Jeffrey L. Fenner
Freelance Reviewer

Gabrielle J. Forman
Freelance Reviewer

Jordan Fox
Freelance Reviewer

Dan Georgakas
Freelance Reviewer

Douglas Gomery
University of Maryland

Sidney Gottlieb
Sacred Heart University

John Hollwitz
Creighton University

Andrew Jefchak
Aquinas College

William Johnson
Freelance Reviewer

Anahid Kassabian
Stanford University

Jim Kline
Freelance Reviewer

Patricia Ann Kowal
Freelance Reviewer

Steven C. Kowall
Freelance Reviewer

Jo Lauria
Loyola Marymount University

Leon Lewis
Appalachian State University

Janet E. Lorenz
Freelance Reviewer

Blake Lucas
Freelance Reviewer

Darryl Lyman
Freelance Reviewer

Mary Lou McNichol
Freelance Reviewer

Marc Mancini
Loyola Marymount University

Cono Robert Marcazzo
Upsala College

Harriet Margolis
Florida Atlantic University

Joss Lutz Marsh
California Institute of Technology

John J. Michalczyk
Boston College

Robert Mitchell
University of Arizona

Peter Moller
Syracuse University

Robert E. Morsberger
California State Polytechnic University, Pomona

Marilyn Moss
University of California, Riverside

Darrin Navarro
Freelance Reviewer

Chon Noriega
Stanford University

Carl Rollyson
*Baruch College of the City University of
    New York*

Paul Salmon
University of Guelph

Michael Sprinker
State University of New York at Stony Brook

Bob Strauss
Freelance Reviewer

Gaylyn Studlar
Emory University

Gordon Walters
DePauw University

James M. Welsh
Salisbury State University

CONTENTS

Life Achievement Award
Gregory Peck 1

Selected Film Books of 1989 5

Selected Films of 1989
The Abyss 19
The Adventures of Baron Munchausen 23
All Dogs Go to Heaven 27
Always 32
Back to the Future Part II 36
Batman 40
The Bear 44
Bill and Ted's Excellent Adventure 48
Black Rain 52
Blaze 56
Born on the Fourth of July 60
The 'Burbs 65
Camille Claudel 68
Casualties of War 71
Cinema Paradiso 74
Communion 78
Crimes and Misdemeanors 82
Dad 86
Dead Poets Society 90
Do the Right Thing 94
Driving Miss Daisy 99
Drugstore Cowboy 103
A Dry White Season 107
Eat a Bowl of Tea 111
Eighty-Four Charlie MoPic 115
Enemies, A Love Story 119
The Fabulous Baker Boys 123
Family Business 127
Field of Dreams 131
Fletch Lives 135
For Queen and Country 139
Four Adventures of Reinette and Mirabelle 143
Getting It Right 147

Ghostbusters II 151
Glory 155
Great Balls of Fire! 160
Harlem Nights 164
Heathers 168
Henry V 173
High Hopes 177
Honey, I Shrunk the Kids 181
Immediate Family 185
In Country 189
Indiana Jones and the Last Crusade 193
Jacknife 197
Jesus of Montreal 201
K-9 205
Lean on Me 209
La Lectrice 213
Lethal Weapon II 217
Licence to Kill 221
The Little Mermaid 225
Look Who's Talking 229
Major League 233
Miss Firecracker 237
Music Box 241
My Left Foot 245
Mystery Train 249
The Navigator 253
New York Stories 257
Old Gringo 262
Parenthood 267
Pet Sematary 271
Queen of Hearts 275
The Rainbow 279
Roger and Me 283
Say Anything 287
Scandal 291
Scenes from the Class Struggle in Beverly Hills 295
Sea of Love 299
See No Evil, Hear No Evil 302
sex, lies and videotape 306
She-Devil 310
Sidewalk Stories 315
Star Trek V 319
Staying Together 323

CONTENTS

Steel Magnolias 328
Story of Women 332
Talvisota 336
Tango and Cash 340
Tap 344
A Taxing Woman's Return 348
Triumph of the Spirit 351
True Believer 356
True Love 360
Uncle Buck 364
Valmont 368
The War of the Roses 372
We're No Angels 376
When Harry Met Sally 380
Wired 384

More Films of 1989 388

Obituaries 433

List of Awards 445

Indexes
Title 451
Director 453
Screenwriter 457
Cinematographer 462
Editor 466
Art Director 470
Music 477
Performer 481
Subject 510

MAGILL'S
CINEMA
ANNUAL

Life Achievement Award
Gregory Peck

If Gregory Peck had never existed, Hollywood would certainly have been compelled to invent him. With his classically handsome good looks and engagingly sincere manner, Peck could have been a matinee idol in almost any era, but his arrival in Hollywood in 1944 fortuitously coincided with the wartime shortage of leading men. This was not, however, his first sojourn to Hollywood. In 1941, Peck made screen tests for producer David O. Selznick, but Selznick rejected the young Broadway actor for, among other things, an awkwardly unphotogenic, "Lincolnesque" quality to his looks.

In 1944 Peck made a forgettable film debut in RKO Radio Pictures' *Days of Glory*, but he was determined not to return to Broadway as a Hollywood failure. He was then cast as a Catholic missionary in John M. Stahl's prestigious production of *The Keys of the Kingdom* (1944), taken from a best-selling novel. Both Peck and the film were huge hits. He received an Academy Award nomination for his performance, and, in spite of his current priestly screen persona, newspaper columnist Hedda Hopper dubbed him the "hottest thing in town."

In 1989, Gregory Peck was still the "hottest thing" in Hollywood, but judged by a somewhat different standard from that which Hopper had in mind, as the American Film Institute offered him its seventeenth annual Life Achievement Award. In accepting the award from an organization that he helped to establish, Peck criticized trends in recent filmmaking and reaffirmed some rather old-fashioned, individualistic ideals in an industry now dominated by multimedia conglomerates. "Making millions is not the whole ball game, . . . Pride of workmanship is worth more. Artistry is worth more," he said in accepting the award. That Gregory Peck would use such an occasion of Hollywood back-slapping to speak his mind candidly is indicative of a well-known fact, that the decency and moral clarity that he projects on the screen have their origin in the person himself rather than in any acting-school tricks of technique.

The aura of all-American honesty and decency that also characterizes his screen persona quickly separated him from most of his contemporaries. While many of the film vehicles of other postwar leading men were regularly marked by the cynicism and psychosexual malaise evidenced in films such as *Sunset Boulevard* (1950), *Double Indemnity* (1944), *Sweet Smell of Success* (1957), and *In a Lonely Place* (1950), Peck's film persona remained distinctively dependable and relatively free of sexual and psychological uncertainty. Noteworthy exceptions to this trend occurred with *Spellbound* (1945) and *Duel in the Sun* (1946), pictures for producer Selznick (who had changed his earlier assessment of the star), and in *Twelve O'Clock High* (1949), the first of Peck's many collaborations with veteran director Henry King.

For *Spellbound*, Selznick hired Peck to play John Ballantine, an amnesiac who thinks that he is an eminent psychiatrist but may be the actual doctor's murderer. In the end, Ballantine's psychological problems are cured by the revelation of a childhood trauma and the love of Ingrid Bergman. For an actor trained in the Stanislavsky method of achieving external effects through identification with the character, Peck found working with director Alfred Hitchcock somewhat at odds with his own approach to acting. Their differences, however, did not prevent *Spellbound* from being an unqualified critical and box-office success. Although both the film and his romantic costar were nominated for Oscars, Peck was ignored by the Academy. Three years later, Peck would star in another, much less successful, venture with Hitchcock and Selznick, *The Paradine Case* (1948).

The year 1946 saw the release of *The Yearling* and *Duel in the Sun*. A more unlikely pair of film characterizations would be hard to imagine for a young leading man with matinee-idol good looks. In *The Yearling* Peck took on the role of Penny Baxter, a poor dirt farmer who attempts to eke out a living for himself, his wife, and their only living son in the scrub country of Florida, circa 1878. Taken from the Pulitzer Prize-winning novel by Marjorie Kinnan Rawlings, *The Yearling* was a lovingly photographed prestige picture focusing on the emotional relationship between Penny Baxter and his son, Jody (Claude Jarman, Jr.), who captures a fawn and tries to raise it as a pet. Whether arranging a barter with backwoods neighbors or quietly listening to his child, Peck is thoroughly convincing as the father who wants the best for his family but can only provide a gentle edge to a hard life. For his sensitive portrayal, Peck received his second Academy Award nomination.

Curiously, in spite of his sensitivity, Peck did much of his work within "male genres": the Western, the war film, the action-adventure film, and the caper film (ubiquitous in the 1960's). His first screen Western, *Duel in the Sun*, provided one of his most uncharacteristic roles, at least until 1978, when Peck took the part of Nazi doctor Josef Mengele in *The Boys from Brazil*. In *Duel in the Sun*, Peck portrayed Lewt McCanles, the black sheep son of a wealthy California ranching family. A rapist and murderer, Lewt strides through the epic Western grinning slyly as he creates mayhem for Pearl Chavez (Jennifer Jones), the woman with whom he will ultimately be locked to the death in a love-hate relationship.

The next year Peck starred in a controversial exploration of America's lack of social consciousness, *Gentleman's Agreement* (1947). Peck played a writer who exposes anti-Semitism when he pretends to be Jewish as part of his research. The film won the Academy Award for the year's best picture, and Peck was nominated for his own performance. Nevertheless, it was not until *Twelve O'Clock High* that Peck assumed another role of comparable complexity. This film was a grimly realistic account of a true episode from World War II, the daylight precision bombing of enemy targets by American flyers during the early days of the war. Working from a superbly intelligent script and surrounded by a cast of astonishingly good supporting actors, including Dean Jagger, Gary Merrill, Hugh Marlowe, and Millard Mitchell, Peck essayed the role of a young general who takes charge of a demoralized bombing unit. Although Frank Savage (Peck) is a by-the-book officer who succeeds in turning the "hard luck group" into a crack outfit, he mentally collapses under the responsibility of leading them in assignments that are virtual suicide missions. From the brutally shocking opening scene in which a bomber literally skids into base and a staff officer must retrieve a crewman's severed arm from the cockpit, *Twelve O'Clock High* announces itself as a film that refuses to glorify war, even one against the Axis. Its basic premise, as voiced by one of its characters, is "How much can a man take?" The film illustrates this premise through an emotionally affecting revelation of the experience of a number of men, so that the audience's growing identification with the unit parallels that of Savage. For his nuanced portrayal, Peck received the New York Film Critics Circle award and his fourth Academy nomination, but he saw the latter award go to Broderick Crawford for his performance in *All the King's Men* (1949).

Peck and King followed with *The Gunfighter* (1950), a spare, authentically detailed Western telling the story of the last few hours in the life of a gunfighter. In subsequent years, this film would acquire a critical reputation as one of the finest examples of its genre, but its box-office reception was lackluster. In 1951, King and Peck returned with the top box-office attraction of the year, a glossy biblical epic, *David and Bathsheba*.

In the next few years, Peck would star in a number of very popular films, including *Captain Horatio Hornblower* (1951) and *The Snows of Kilimanjaro* (1952), but his most unequivocally successful film was William Wyler's *Roman Holiday* (1953). The romantic comedy starred Peck as Joe Bradley, a down-at-the-heels reporter who falls in love with a princess taking a secret holiday from her overly restricted life. Peck graciously accepted the media attention focused on newcomer Audrey Hepburn, whose first starring role, as the princess, brought her an Oscar, an award still eluding her leading man.

Among Peck's other most notable films of the 1950's are two war films, *The Purple Plain* (1954) and *Pork Chop Hill* (1959). The former is an unassuming but emotionally touching film about a British pilot who crashes in the Burmese jungle. Peck coproduced the latter, one of the best films dealing with the U.S. "police action" in Korea. Directed by Lewis Milestone, who also directed the antiwar classic *All Quiet on the Western Front* (1930), *Pork Chop Hill* is an unrelenting exploration of the infantryman's thankless role in combat.

Peck would return to a variety of military roles in the late 1950's and the 1960's, culminating in his portrayal of General Douglas MacArthur in *MacArthur* (1977), but his most famous role and his own favorite film of his career would hark back to the quiet family drama of *The Yearling*. Like that film, *To Kill a Mockingbird* (1962) is a story told from a child's point of view. In this film, Peck plays Atticus Finch, a widower rearing his young son and daughter in a small Southern town during the 1930's. A lawyer by profession, he is asked to defend Tom Robinson (Brock Peters), a black man accused of rape. In spite of all evidence to the contrary, his client is found guilty, but Atticus' children still face the demented wrath of the man who falsely accused Robinson. Although the dramatic highlight of the film is the trial and its nightmarish aftermath, much of the film lovingly details the casual, day-to-day relationship of Atticus and his children. With his fifth nomination for the Oscar,

Peck finally received the award for a performance that he has characterized as one of the easiest of his life, he so identified with both Atticus and the childhood experiences depicted in this adaptation of Harper Lee's Pulitzer Prize-winning novel.

To Kill a Mockingbird was followed with *How the West Was Won* (1963), a star-studded attempt to capitalize on the box-office draw of a wide-screen system, Cinerama. A string of rather forgettable thrillers and Westerns was punctuated by Fred Zinnemann's *Behold a Pale Horse* (1964), a serious although unsuccessful drama set against the backdrop of Spanish political intrigue. In 1970, Peck starred in John Frankenheimer's interesting *I Walk the Line*, in which he portrayed a small-town sheriff whose mid-life crisis leads to disaster. Peck's excellent performance in this film went unnoticed, and the box-office failure of subsequent Westerns with directors Henry Hathaway and Ted Kotcheff led to his self-imposed retirement from acting. He said that he would rather save his energy than make pictures that "no one goes to see." Peck remained active behind the scenes, however, producing among other films, *The Trial of the Catonsville Nine* (1972), a film that questioned the United States' involvement in Vietnam. Such political activity earned for him a place on the "enemies" list of Richard Nixon, even though President Lyndon B. Johnson had awarded Peck the country's highest civilian medal, the President's Medal of Freedom, for his wide-ranging public service as well as his acting.

Peck's absence from the screen in the 1970's was short-lived: His role in the horror thriller *The Omen* (1976) brought him out of retirement and into the biggest box-office hit of his career, with revenues topping $100 million. Although critical praise for the film was nonexistent, the public loved the supernatural sensationalism of a film about the personification of the anti-Christ in a young boy adopted by an unsuspecting diplomat (Peck). Following *The Omen*, Peck's screen appearances have become exceedingly rare, with *MacArthur* and *The Boys from Brazil* receiving generally mediocre critical reception.

The American Film Institute Award might normally be regarded as the final tribute to a career that is finished, but Gregory Peck continues to work in front of the cameras on occasion. Sometimes that work is a reflection of a political con-science that refuses to be dimmed by the demands of public life, as when Peck appeared in a controversial television commercial questioning the Supreme Court nomination of Robert Bork. At an age when retirement would be no shame, Peck continues to grow as an artist. His appearance as the title character in *Old Gringo* (1989; reviewed in this volume) earned for him plaudits from the critics and inspired one to remark that his portrayal of writer Ambrose Bierce "reveals in Mr. Peck something vigorous and new." Rejecting nostalgia for the challenges of the present, Gregory Peck continues to uphold standards of workmanship, artistry, and human decency that have rightfully made him one of America's most honored actors.

Gaylyn Studlar

SELECTED FILM BOOKS OF 1989

Adair, Gilbert. *Hollywood's Vietnam*. London: Heinemann, 1989. A good survey of famous and obscure Hollywood films that take as their subject the war in Vietnam.

Babington, Bruce, and Peter William Evans. *Affairs to Remember: The Hollywood Comedy of the Sexes*. Manchester, England: Manchester University Press, 1989. A study of male/female relationships in Hollywood comedies (romantic and otherwise), from the 1930's through the 1980's, using prominent actors, directors, and two films (*Bringing Up Baby* and *Pat and Mike*) as examples.

Barrymore, Drew, with Todd Gold. *Little Girl Lost*. New York: Pocket Books, 1989. The harrowing story of Drew Barrymore's life so far—stardom as a preteen in *E.T.: The Extra Terrestrial* (1982), a premature entry into Hollywood's life in the fast lane, and a struggle to come back from alcohol and drug dependence.

Bartlet, Chuck, and Barbara Bergeron. *Variety Obituaries, 1905-1986*. New York: Garland, 1989. *Variety*, the weekly "bible of show business," publishes obituaries for every branch of the entertainment industry and for everyone from legends to obscurities. Despite occasional errors and omissions, the information in this twelve-volume set is often the only biographical data available for the majority of the individuals represented here. The volumes are arranged chronologically, volume 11 indexes the years 1905-1986, and volume 12 is a supplement covering the years 1987-1988.

Benson, Thomas W., and Carolyn Anderson. *Reality Fictions: The Films of Frederick Wiseman*. Carbondale: Southern Illinois University Press, 1989. Wiseman directed *Titicut Follies* (1967) and other controversial documentaries; this book is a detailed scholarly analysis of his work.

Berg, A. Scott. *Goldwyn: A Biography*. New York: Alfred A. Knopf, 1989. Berg is the first Goldwyn biographer to have been granted access to his archives, and the result is the most complete work yet on the Hollywood legend.

Bordwell, David. *Making Meaning: Inference and Rhetoric in the Interpretation of Cinema*. Cambridge, Mass.: Harvard University Press, 1989. Bordwell is a leader among academic film theoreticians. In this volume, he offers a history of contemporary film theory and suggests a new approach, which he calls "historical poetics."

Brady, Frank. *Citizen Welles: A Biography of Orson Welles*. New York: Charles Scribner's Sons, 1989. This well-researched book is an admiring but balanced study of Orson Welles and one of the best studies of a much written about man.

Brakhage, Stan. *Film at Wit's End: Eight Avant-Garde Filmmakers*. Kingston, N.Y.: Documentext McPherson, 1989. Brakhage, himself a distinguished figure in American avant-garde cinema, offers biographical sketches of eight prominent directors in the genre.

Bridges, Herb, and Terryl C. Boodman. *"Gone With the Wind": The Definitive Illustrated History of the Book, the Movie, and the Legend*. New York: Simon &

Schuster, 1989. The first of two similar books celebrating the fiftieth anniversary of *Gone With the Wind* (see also the review of Judy Cameron's work, below), this volume provides copious photographs (most in black and white), examining not only the film but also the phenomenon associated with it.

Brown, Jared. *Zero Mostel: A Biography*. New York: Atheneum, 1989. A good biography of the stage and screen comic actor whose career was interrupted by blacklisting in the 1950's and by health problems in the 1960's.

Buss, Robin. *Italian Films*. London: B. T. Batsford, 1989. A good survey of the portrayal of Italy and Italian life in the national cinema, this volume contains a filmography with analysis of 206 Italian films, many of which are little known in the United States.

Bywater, Tim, and Thomas Sobchack. *An Introduction to Film Criticism: Major Critical Approaches to Narrative Film*. New York: Longman, 1989. This is an excellent survey of the many varieties of film criticism, from the newspaper review through auteurism to the highly specialized academic approaches to cinema.

Cameron, Judy, and Paul J. Christman. *The Art of "Gone With the Wind": The Making of a Legend*. New York: Prentice Hall Editions, 1989. Cameron's work differs from that of Bridges (see above) in that its focus is more on the film itself than on the book and the postfilm hullabaloo, and also in that Cameron was able to use many of the personal papers of producer David O. Selznick in producing the book.

Charyn, Jerome. *Movieland: Hollywood and the Great American Dream Culture*. New York: G. P. Putnam's Sons, 1989. This opinionated and entertaining work by novelist Charyn is a series of pleasantly discursive meditations on the American cinema, principally the golden age of the 1930's and 1940's.

Collins, Ace. *Bette Midler*. New York: St. Martin's Press, 1989. A standard "show biz" biography of the singer/actress, this slim volume adds nothing to our knowledge of Midler's career.

Considine, Shaun. *Bette & Joan: The Divine Feud*. New York: E. P. Dutton, 1989. Hollywood's golden age is the setting for this entertaining but superficial book about the feud between Bette Davis and Joan Crawford.

Cowie, Peter. *Coppola*. London: Andre Deutsch, 1989. This biographical survey of Francis Ford Coppola's career was written with the director's cooperation, and Cowie's extensive use of interview material fills in important gaps in the enigmatic filmmaker's life.

Cox, Stephen. *The Munchkins Remember: "The Wizard of Oz" and Beyond*. New York: E. P. Dutton, 1989. This collection of brief reminiscences from thirty of the "little people" who portrayed Munchkins in *The Wizard of Oz* makes an interesting footnote to the film's fiftieth anniversary celebrations.

Crowther, Bruce. *Film Noir: Reflections in a Dark Mirror*. New York: Continuum, 1989. This illustrated history of *film noir* examines the genre's literary origins, its distinctive cinematography, and the actors who embodied the cynical, world-weary characters that made these films so memorable.

Curcio, Vincent. *Suicide Blonde: The Life of Gloria Grahame*. New York: William Morrow, 1989. A balanced biography of the unhappy actress who specialized in playing hard-bitten blondes in the 1940's and 1950's.

Dawidoff, Heidi G. *Between the Frames: Thinking About Movies*. Hamden, Conn.: Archon Books, 1989. A series of well-written essays on Hollywood films since the golden age of the 1930's, in which Dawidoff contends that the freedom from censorship given contemporary filmmakers has not led to better films.

Dick, Bernard F. *Radical Innocence: A Critical Study of the Hollywood Ten*. Lexington, Ky.: University Press of Kentucky, 1989. A survey of the screenwriting careers of each of the ten writers who were blacklisted by the studios in response to congressional revelations about their sympathies toward the Communist Party. Includes filmographies and bibliographies.

Dietrich, Marlene. *Marlene*. New York: Grove Press, 1989. Written to counteract the published efforts of her unwelcome biographers, Dietrich's autobiography is a disappointing blend of blandness and factual error as the actress reveals little new or interesting about her life and career.

Doherty, Thomas. *Teenagers and Teenpics: The Juvenilization of American Movies in the 1950s*. Winchester, Mass.: Unwin Hyman, 1989. The success or failure of most contemporary films seems to rest largely with their acceptance by the adolescent portion of the filmgoing populace. Doherty traces this phenomenon to the "teenpic" genre that began in the 1950's. Chapters cover rock and roll, teen horror, and other subgenres.

Donaldson, Maureen, and William Royce. *An Affair to Remember: My Life with Cary Grant*. New York: G. P. Putnam's Sons, 1989. Donaldson is a photographer whose affair with Grant spanned the years 1973 to 1977; she portrays the late actor as a man of contradictions, obsessed with both his daughter and his own childhood.

Dunaway, David King. *Huxley in Hollywood*. New York: Harper & Row, 1989. The second book in three years to explore novelist Aldous Huxley's Hollywood years, Dunaway's work is well written but provides little new information.

Ellison, Harlan. *Harlan Ellison's Watching*. Los Angeles: Underwood-Miller, 1989. Ellison, a critic, screenwriter, and novelist, offers this enjoyable collection of two decades' worth of acerbic commentary on films and filmmaking.

Ellrod, J. G. *Hollywood Greats of the Golden Years*. Jefferson, N.C.: McFarland, 1989. Ellrod provides biographical sketches and filmographies for eighty-one actors and actresses of the pretelevision era. Although none of this information is unique, the book does collect a considerable amount of information in a single volume.

Farkas, Andrew, ed. *Lawrence Tibbett, Singing Actor*. Portland, Ore.: Amadeus Press, 1989. Tibbett was an opera singer who made several musicals in the early days of talking films. This book is a collection of essays on his life and career.

Field, Syd. *Selling a Screenplay: The Screenwriter's Guide to Hollywood*. New York: Delacorte Press, 1989. Intended for a specialized audience, this book offers the lay reader a useful glimpse of the relationship between the screenwriter and the agents, lawyers, and studio executives who buy and sell his wares.

Fricke, John, Jay Scarfone, and William Stillman. *"The Wizard of Oz": The Official 50th Anniversary Pictorial History*. New York: Warner Books, 1989. An illustrated history of the beloved film, covering the making of the classic, as well as its critical reception, marketing tie-ins, and its rediscovery as a television perennial. This coffee-table volume is a fascinating document.

Gallagher, John Andrew. *Film Directors on Directing*. New York: Greenwood Press, 1989. Twenty-one interviews with both famous and relatively obscure directors on the art of filmmaking. The quality of the interviews varies, but the filmographies (particularly of the more obscure directors) are useful.

Gil-Montero, Martha. *Brazilian Bombshell: The Biography of Carmen Miranda.* New York: Donald I. Fine, 1989. Although Miranda is remembered now mostly for the exotic headgear that inspired Chiquita Banana, this well-researched biography reminds us that she was both an influential musician (popularizing the samba) and a major star in Twentieth Century-Fox's wartime musicals.

Good, Howard. *Outcasts: The Image of Journalists in Contemporary Film*. Metuchen, N.J.: Scarecrow Press, 1989. Good surveys American films over the past quarter of a century and discovers that journalists tend to be represented as either war correspondents, reporters who will stop at nothing for a scoop, or television executives who are obsessed with ratings.

Goodwin, Michael, and Naomi Wise. *On the Edge: The Life and Times of Francis Coppola*. New York: William Morrow, 1989. Unlike Peter Cowie's book (reviewed above), Goodwin and Wise rely heavily on secondary sources for their information. Thus they provide a different and ultimately more somber perspective on the director's career in this well-written and enjoyable book.

Goulding, Daniel J., ed. *Post New Wave Cinema in the Soviet Union and Eastern Europe*. Bloomington: Indiana University Press, 1989. This collection of scholarly essays on the national cinemas of the Soviet Union, East Germany, Czechoslovakia, Poland, Hungary, Bulgaria and Yugoslavia since the mid-1970's is especially useful in the light of political developments in Eastern Europe.

Grobel, Lawrence. *The Hustons*. New York: Charles Scribner's Sons, 1989. The focus of this lengthy biography of the three-generation film family is actor and director John Huston, although coverage incudes his actor father Walter as well as actress daughter Anjelica and other children.

Grodin, Charles. *It Would Be So Nice If You Weren't Here: My Journey Through Show Business*. New York: William Morrow, 1989. Grodin, best known as an actor but also a writer, director, and producer, offers this enjoyable autobiography.

Grubb, Kevin Boyd. *Razzle Dazzle: The Life and Work of Bob Fosse*. New York: St. Martin's Press, 1989. Grubb, a professional dance critic, evaluates Fosse's film and stage career on a work-by-work basis in this copiously illustrated critical biography.

Hanke, Ken. *Charlie Chan at the Movies: History, Filmography, and Criticism.* Jefferson, N.C.: McFarland, 1989. A chronological review of the forty-four films featuring the famous Chinese detective, along with background information on the series' actors and directors.

Harris, Marlys J. *The Zanucks of Hollywood: The Dark Side of an American Dynasty.* New York: Crown, 1989. Harris sifts through tons of newspaper clippings and court depositions in this exhaustively researched biography of the founder of Twentieth Century-Fox studios and his family. The emphasis here is on the Zanucks' personal lives rather than their contributions to film.

Harris, Thomas J. *Children's Live-Action Musical Films: A Critical Survey and Filmography.* Jefferson, N.C.: McFarland, 1989. Focusing on musicals (excluding animation) that are aimed wholly or partly at children, Harris provides an extended discussion of such films as *Tom Thumb* (1967), *Mary Poppins* (1964), and thirteen other similar titles.

Hayes, R. M. *3-D Movies: A History and Filmography of Stereoscopic Cinema.* Jefferson, N.C.: McFarland, 1989. Although the heyday of the three-dimensional film was the 1950's, the technique is still used for special projects such as the Disney-Michael Jackson short *Captain Eo.* This book contains filmographies of more than two hundred such films, along with extensive technical descriptions of the three-dimensional filming process.

Higham, Charles, and Roy Moseley. *Cary Grant: The Lonely Heart.* New York: Harcourt Brace Jovanovich, 1989. As the book's subtitle indicates, the authors focus their attentions primarily on the late actor's love life. Their allegations that Grant had homosexual affairs with both Howard Hughes and Randolph Scott earned for the book a certain amount of notoriety.

Hitt, Jim. *The American West from Fiction (1823-1976) into Film (1909-1986).* Jefferson, N.C.: McFarland, 1989. This is a historical survey of literature on the American West that has been turned into Western films. Hitt examines the relationship between the books and the films, including changes made in adapting the stories for the screen.

Hollander, Anne. *Moving Pictures.* New York: Alfred A. Knopf, 1989. Combining art history with film criticism, Hollander argues that viewing a painting and viewing a film are in many respects equivalent experiences—that the narrative elements in each are closely related.

Humphries, Reynold. *Fritz Lang: Genre Representation in His American Films.* Baltimore, M.D.: Johns Hopkins University Press, 1989. This translation of a French work (originally published in 1982) is a scholarly analysis of the expatriate German director's American films, emphasizing the lesser-known examples of his work.

Issari, M. Ali. *Cinema in Iran, 1900-1979.* Metuchen, N.J.: Scarecrow Press, 1989. Issari takes pains to place Iranian cinema in its cultural and historical context, and the result is the most extensive study in English of film in Iran.

Jackson, Carlton. *Hattie: The Life of Hattie McDaniel.* Lanham, Md.: Madison

Books, 1989. Jackson uses the details of McDaniel's life and career (she was the first black to win an Academy Award) to lend perspective to the struggles of other black entertainers and their efforts to achieve success while overcoming stereotypes.

James, David. *Allegories of Cinema: American Film in the Sixties.* Princeton, N.J.: Princeton University Press, 1989. This is a scholarly study of non-mainstream film in the 1960's and early 1970's—art film, radical cinema, pornography, among other things. Though the title is somewhat misleading, the book is a useful examination of its subject.

Jordan, Ted. *Norma Jean: My Secret Life with Marilyn Monroe.* New York: William Morrow, 1989. Jordan was Monroe's former boyfriend; his principal addition to the Monroe legend is the assertion that Monroe modeled much of her "love goddess" persona on famous stripper Lili St. Cyr (who married Jordan after his affair with Monroe).

Justice, Keith L. *Science Fiction, Fantasy, and Horror Reference: An Annotated Bibliography of Works About Literature and Film.* Jefferson, N.C.: McFarland, 1989. An annotated bibliography covering approximately three hundred secondary sources on science fiction and related genres.

Kael, Pauline. *Hooked.* New York: E. P. Dutton, 1989. Kael remains one of the nation's most influential film critics. Her ninth book collects her reviews, originally published in the *New Yorker*, from 1985 to 1988.

Kipps, Charles. *Out of Focus: Power, Pride, and Prejudice, David Puttnam in Hollywood.* New York: William Morrow, 1989. A well-researched account of Puttnam's rise and fall as the head of Columbia Pictures. Although famous names play only minor roles, this is a good account of Hollywood as big business.

Lang, Robert. *American Film Melodrama.* Princeton, N.J.: Princeton University Press, 1989. By "melodrama," Lang means conflict within the family. He studies the films of King Vidor, D. W. Griffith, and Vincente Minelli for representations of this conflict, which he traces back to the domination of women by men.

Langman, Larry, and Edgar Borg. *Encyclopedia of American War Films.* New York: Garland, 1989. This is an illustrated history of films on war (not only American wars) made in the United States between 1898 and 1988. Entries for films include cast and credit information, and there are also entries on specific wars, battles, and subjects (for example, documentaries, women in war).

Leaming, Barbara. *If This Was Happiness: A Biography of Rita Hayworth.* New York: Viking Books, 1989. Hayworth, a popular actress of the 1940's, led a stormy life, with marriages to a series of famous men, troubles with alcohol, and finally Alzheimer's disease. The centerpiece of this well-researched biography is the allegation that Hayworth's psychological problems began when she was sexually abused by her father.

Lee, Spike, and Lisa Jones. *Do the Right Thing.* New York: Simon & Schuster, 1989. Lee's film was one of the most memorable of the year. This volume contains the script, production notes, and Lee's by-now trademark journal, in which he recounts his thoughts during the film's production.

Lentz, Harris M. *Science Fiction, Horror & Fantasy Film and Television Credits Supplement: Through 1987*. Jefferson, N.C.: McFarland, 1989. This substantial (936 pages) volume updates the original two-volume work, adding both newer material and references to older works that were omitted from the first set. Lentz' work remains the definitive source for this information.

Lynch, Richard Chigley. *Movie Musicals on Record: A Directory of Recordings of Motion Picture Musicals, 1927-1987*. New York: Greenwood Press, 1989. A very useful listing of information on recordings made from film musicals; indexed by performer, composer, and lyricists but not by song.

MacCann, Richard Dyer. *The First Film Makers*. Metuchen, N.J.: Scarecrow Press, 1989. MacCann uses autobiographical comments from early directors and stars, contemporary comments, and more modern evaluations to convey a sense of the challenges confronting filmmakers in the early days of the medium.

McClelland, Doug. *Eleanor Parker: Woman of a Thousand Faces*. Metuchen, N.J.: Scarecrow Press, 1989. Subtitled "a bio-bibliography and filmography," this is a useful compilation of information about an important actress of the 1940's and 1950's.

McGee, Mark. *Beyond Ballyhoo: Motion Picture Promotion and Gimmicks*. Jefferson, N.C.: McFarland, 1989. From Smell-O-Vision to electrically wired seats, McGee's book is an entertaining study of film promotional stunts that go beyond the call of duty (and sometimes common sense).

McGilligan, Patrick. *Robert Altman: Jumping off the Cliff*. New York: St. Martin's Press, 1989. McGilligan regards Altman as the most important American director of the past two decades. This lengthy and well-written book emphasizes both the filmmaker's personal life and his artistic career.

Maguffee, T. D. *Sigourney Weaver*. New York: St. Martin's Press, 1989. Maguffee's work is a disappointingly brief and superficial biography of the American actress.

Maland, Charles J. *Chaplin and American Culture*. Princeton, N.J.: Princeton University Press, 1989. Maland traces Charlie Chaplin's deliberative cultivation of a "star image," which became the prototype for other mass cultural stars, followed by his subsequent fall from grace.

Mancini, Henry, and Gene Lees. *Did They Mention the Music?* Chicago: Contemporary Books, 1989. Mancini's place in the history of American cinema is assured: He has scored ninety films and won four Academy Awards for his work. This is his autobiography.

Mandelbaum, Howard, and Eric Myers. *Forties Screen Style: A Celebration of High Pastiche in Hollywood*. New York: St. Martin's Press, 1989. In this analysis of the work of Hollywood art directors in the post-Art Deco 1940's, the authors identify a pastiche of Early American, Victorian, tropical, surrealist, contemporary, and period revivalism as the dominant stylistic trends of the decade.

Mank, Gregory William. *The Hollywood Hissables*. Metuchen, N.J.: Scarecrow Press, 1989. Mank reviews the lives and careers of nine actors and actresses from Hollywood's golden age who specialized in playing villains.

Molt, Cynthia Marlylee. *"Gone with the Wind" on Film: A Complete Reference*. Jefferson, N.C.: McFarland, 1989. Complete with a foreword by Butterfly McQueen, this is an immense catalog of information about the film—costumes, set furnishings, bibliographies, discographies, and collectibles, as well as more conventional information on the actors, actresses, and other aspects of the production.

Morley, Sheriden. *James Mason: Odd Man Out*. New York: Harper & Row, 1989. This biography attempts to account for Mason's relative lack of recognition, concluding that his status as both a personal and professional loner accounts for his failure to win an Academy Award and the favor of audiences.

Murphy, Robert. *Realism and Tinsel: Cinema and Society in Britain, 1939-1948*. London: Routledge, 1989. Focusing on lesser-known films of the period, Murphy surveys the social context of British cinema during and immediately after World War II.

Neibaur, James L. *Tough Guy: The American Movie Macho*. Jefferson, N.C.: McFarland, 1989. Neibaur analyzes the screen persona of twelve actors known for their portrayal of tough characters. The emphasis is on stars of the golden age, although more contemporary figures such as Sylvester Stallone and Clint Eastwood are also included.

Nollen, Scott Allen. *The Boys: The Cinematic World of Laurel and Hardy*. Jefferson, N.C.: McFarland, 1989. Nollen focuses not only on biography but also on the duo's working relationships with each other and with the camera—on how they developed their style to suit their medium.

Nowlan, Robert A., and Gwendolyn Wright Nowlan. *Cinema Sequels and Remakes, 1903-1987*. Jefferson, N.C.: McFarland, 1989. The authors provide brief filmographies for 1,025 films that have had sequels or have been remade. Despite its omissions (no foreign-language films, significant gaps in the coverage of Westerns, musicals, and science fiction/horror), this is an important addition to the cinema reference shelf.

Okuda, Ted. *Grand National, Producers Releasing Corporation, and Screen Guild/ Lippert: Complete Filmographies with Studio Histories*. Jefferson, N.C.: McFarland, 1989. The three "poverty row" studios mentioned in the title were responsible for literally hundreds of B pictures from the mid-1930's through the mid-1950's. This reference work provides a history of their output.

Oliver, Charles M., ed. *A Moving Picture Feast: The Filmgoer's Hemingway*. New York: Praeger, 1989. A collection of fifteen essays (originally presented at a conference in 1981) on the subject of Hollywood's adaptation of the works of Ernest Hemingway.

Osborne, Robert. *60 Years of the Oscar: The Official History of the Academy Awards*. New York: Abbeville Press, 1989. Although this volume was written with the cooperation of the Academy of Motion Picture Arts and Sciences, it is not the most comprehensive source of information on the Oscars. It does, however, contain interesting photographs as well as coverage through 1988.

Oumano, Elena. *Paul Newman*. New York: St. Martin's Press, 1989. Intended for the popular market, this is a sympathetic biography of the actor/director. Though it breaks no new ground, it does contain a discussion of Newman's major films and other work.

Palmer, R. Barton, ed. *The Cinematic Text: Methods and Approaches*. New York: AMS Press, 1989. A collection of eighteen scholarly essays, seven of which are devoted to specific films. The remainder are more general attempts to transfer arcane literary theory ("translinguistics" and "cinesemiotics") to film criticism.

Paris, Barry. *Louise Brooks: Her Life, Death, and Resurrection*. New York: Alfred A. Knopf, 1989. This is the first full-length biography of Brooks, the actress whose brief and for the most part undistinguished career was long over when she was made famous by a laudatory profile in *The New Yorker*. This book, which reveals as much as will likely ever be known about this deliberately enigmatic woman, will sustain her allure.

Parish, James Robert, and George H. Hill. *Black Action Films*. Jefferson, N.C.: McFarland, 1989. Subtitled "Plots, Critiques, Casts, and Credits for 235 Theatrical and Made-for Television Releases," this useful reference work collects information on a genre that stretches from *Shaft* (1971) to *Beverly Hills Cop* (1984).

Penley, Constance. *The Future of an Illusion: Film, Feminism, and Psychoanalysis*. Minneapolis: University of Minnesota Press, 1989. Nine scholarly essays on cinema, ranging in subject matter from avant-garde to Pee Wee Herman, all linked by a feminist philosophy and a psychoanalytical approach.

Powell, Dilys. *The Golden Screen: Fifty Years of Films*. London: Pavilion Books, 1989. Powell is an influential British film critic. This book collects her *Sunday Times* reviews, which are reprinted in chronological order.

Randall, Tony, and Michael Mindlin. *Which Reminds Me*. New York: Delacorte Press, 1989. As the title suggests, this is a series of show business anecdotes by the actor, who is a terrific storyteller. It is insubstantial but very entertaining.

Reed, Joseph W. *American Scenarios: The Uses of Film Genre*. Middletown, Conn.: Wesleyan University Press, 1989. A discursive and entertaining look at American film genres, from the Western to the high school picture; Reed's wit makes this book both scholarly and readable.

Rubin, Sam, and Richard Taylor. *Mia Farrow: Flowerchild, Madonna, Muse*. New York: St. Martin's Press, 1989. A superficial biography of the actress, which relies heavily on materials already in print.

Russo, John. *Making Movies: The Inside Guide to Independent Movie Production*. New York: Delacorte Press, 1989. A good, readable account of the process of filmmaking, including brief chapters in which independent filmmakers describe their own experiences. Ostensibly for would-be filmmakers, but valuable for any reader interested in what goes into making a film.

Schickel, Richard. *Schickel on Film*. New York: William Morrow, 1989. *Time*'s film critic revises fourteen long essays, all of which have appeared elsewhere in their original versions, in which he offers his take on various film personalities, including Charlie Chaplin, Humphrey Bogart, and Woody Allen.

Schuchman, John S. *Hollywood Speaks: Deafness and the Film Entertainment Industry*. Urbana: University of Illinois Press, 1989. A scholarly study of the image of deaf persons in American cinema. Concludes that Hollywood's image mirrors society's stereotypes. Includes filmography.

Shipman, David. *Movie Talk: Who Said What About Whom in the Movies*. New York: St. Martin's Press, 1989. An entertaining but (because of lack of documentation) less than totally authoritative compilation of quotations about famous film figures.

Shohat, Ella. *Israeli Cinema: East/West and the Politics of Representation*. Austin: University of Texas Press, 1989. This detailed study of the Israeli national cinema is not a survey of general history. It is rather a scholarly analysis of several important Israeli films from a leftist political perspective.

Sikov, Ed. *Screwball: Hollywood's Madcap Romantic Comedies*. New York: Crown, 1989. This exceptionally well-produced volume is an illustrated history of the screwball comedy genre of the 1930's and 1940's. It covers all major examples of the genre, combining analysis with production stills and excerpts from screenplays. It also has a useful filmography.

Silverman, Stephen M. *David Lean*. New York: Harry N. Abrams, 1989. A lavishly illustrated survey of the career of the British director who made *Doctor Zhivago* (1965) and *Lawrence of Arabia* (1962), with filmographies and an anecdotal chapter on the making of each of his films.

Skorman, Richard. *Off-Hollywood Movies: A Film Lover's Guide*. New York: Harmony Books, 1989. Skorman's book describes 445 films, which have in common only the fact that they are not standard products of contemporary Hollywood — foreign films, American classics, offbeat cult films, among other things. Information includes videotape availability.

Slide, Anthony. *The International Film Industry: A Historical Dictionary*. New York: Greenwood Press, 1989. Complementing his *The American Film Industry* (1986), Slide's useful reference work provides entries on studios, publications, and distributors, among other things, outside the United States. The book includes brief essays on the national cinema of every film-producing country in the world.

Stern, Stewart. *No Tricks in My Pocket: Paul Newman Directs*. New York: Grove Press, 1989. Stern persuaded Paul Newman to let him observe and take notes during rehearsals as Newman directed his wife, Joanne Woodward, in a production of *The Glass Menagerie*. The result offers valuable insight into the making of a film and into the mind of an important American artist.

Taylor, Helen. *Scarlett's Women: "Gone with the Wind" and Its Female Fans*. London: Virago Press, 1989. Taylor is a British scholar, feminist, and fan of *Gone with the Wind*. This is a fascinating account of the impact of the book and film on two generations of women.

Taylor, Robert. *Fred Allen: His Life and Wit*. Boston: Little, Brown, 1989. Though best known as a top radio comedian of the 1940's, Allen made a series of films between 1935 and 1952. This is a good biography, aimed at the popular audience.

Telotte, J. P. *Voices in the Dark*. Urbana: University of Illinois Press, 1989. A scholarly analysis of the narrative techniques of *film noir*, arguing that *noir* films were an attempt to give voice to a sense of anomie that permeated the culture in the aftermath of World War II.

Thomas, Tony. *The West That Never Was: Hollywood's Vision of the Cowboys and Gunfighters*. New York: Citadel Press, 1989. This illustrated debunking of the Hollywood Western is based on the popular Public Broadcasting System television series.

Tomaselli, Keyan. *The Cinema of Apartheid: Race and Class in South African Film*. London: Routledge, 1989. Film in South Africa is complicated by a variety of factors, chief among them is race. This fascinating volume analyzes every aspect of South African national cinema, from government cinema and the role of film critics to distribution and the work of independent filmmakers.

Von Gunden, Kenneth. *Flights of Fancy: The Great Fantasy Films*. Jefferson, N.C.: McFarland, 1989. Von Gunden analyzes fifteen films, ranging from *King Kong* (1933) to *Superman* (1978) which represent one subset or another of the fantasy genre, such as the giant monster, the fabulous journey, the child as hero, among other things. The chapters include filmographies.

Wajda, Andrzej. *Double Vision: My Life in Film*. New York: Henry Holt, 1989. Despite the book's subtitle, this is much less an autobiography of the Polish director than a series of essays on the technical aspects of filmmaking. These insights, while not worthless, are less valuable than a more personal book would have been.

Ward, Carol M. *Mae West: A Bio-Bibliography*. New York: Greenwood Press, 1989. An in-depth study of Mae West as both an actress and an author (she wrote several screenplays as well as novels), which examines her life with an eye to accuracy rather than legend.

Winters, Shelley. *Shelley II: The Middle of My Century*. New York: Simon & Schuster, 1989. Winters published the first volume of her autobiography in 1980; this sequel covers the years from the early 1950's through 1963, during which time she won an Academy Award and had a series of affairs, which she relates with gusto.

Wolf, Leonard. *Horror: A Connoisseur's Guide to Literature and Film*. New York: Facts on File, 1989. Wolf analyzes four hundred examples of horror, both literary and cinematic. The book is particularly useful when comparing the successes and failures of attempts to film horror novels.

Wood, Robin. *Hitchcock's Films Revisited*. New York: Columbia University Press, 1989. Wood's original *Hitchcock's Films* (1965) has long been a standard work on the filmmaker. This volume reprints that work and adds nearly two hundred pages of text in which the now-Marxist Wood describes his revised opinion of Hitchcock and also analyzes additional films in the director's canon.

Zorkaya, Neya. *The Illustrated History of the Soviet Cinema*. New York: Hippocrene Books, 1989. A decade-by-decade survey of film in the Soviet Union; although the title might suggest otherwise, there is much more text than illustrations in the book.

SELECTED
FILMS
OF
1989

THE ABYSS

Production: Gale Anne Hurd; released by Twentieth Century-Fox
Direction: James Cameron
Screenplay: James Cameron
Cinematography: Mikael Salomon
Editing: Joel Goodman
Production design: Leslie Dilley
Art direction: Peter Childs, Russell Christian, and Joseph Nemec III
Set decoration: Anne Kuljian
Set design: Andrew Precht, Tom Wilkins, and Gershon Ginsburg
Visual effects: John Bruno (AA), Dennis Muren (AA), Hoyt Yeatman (AA), and
   Dennis Skotak (AA)
Special visual effects: Julia Gibson
Makeup: Kathryn Miles Kelly
Costume design: Deborah Everton
Sound: Blake Leyh and Lee Orloff
Music: Alan Silvestri
MPAA rating: PG-13
Running time: 136 minutes

> *Principal characters:*
> Bud Brigman . . . . Ed Harris
> Lindsey Brigman . . . . Mary Elizabeth Mastrantonio
> Lieutenant Coffey . . . . Michael Biehn
> Catfish De Vries . . . . Leo Burmester
> Alan "Hippy" Carnes . . . . Todd Graff
> Jammer Willis . . . . John Bedford Lloyd
> Sonny Dawson . . . . J. C. Quinn
> Lisa "One Night" Standing . . . . Kimberly Scott

Well before its delayed release in the extremely competitive summer season of 1989, *The Abyss* had already received many months' worth of press coverage, not all of it positive. A very rigorous physical production, incorporating novel location work, new filming techniques, and much innovative hardware, put this ambitious adventure tale behind schedule and sent the negative cost to more than $40 million. Given the additional $20 million in marketing costs, much attention was focused on the risks to distributor Twentieth Century-Fox and the odds against recouping its investment: a large budget, a late release in a summer dominated by the hugely successful *Batman* (1989; reviewed in this volume), and a marketing challenge because the film lacks major stars. In addition, two other undersea adventures— *Deep Star Six* (1989) and *Leviathan* (1989), both following closely in the familiar footsteps of *Alien* (1979; ironically a film to which *The Abyss'* director had made the well-regarded hit sequel, _Aliens_, 1986)—had recently come and gone with critical lambastings and poor box-office results, further muddying the waters.

Facing these odds was the team of producer Gale Anne Hurd and director James Cameron, who were responsible, in addition to _Aliens_, for the ferociously effective 1984 science-fiction thriller _The Terminator_. Although considerably less than a complete success, _The Abyss_ is clearly a most impressive spectacle and one that expands the boundaries of the adventure film.

While on patrol near the Cayman Trough, a U.S. nuclear submarine encounters a deep-water "bogey" that is far too fast and maneuverable to be any type of known craft. In an attempt to catch the object, which also causes loss of power when it passes close by, the submarine strikes an undersea mountain ridge and sinks, falling into an abyss—a miles-deep crevasse. Because other U.S. naval vessels are too far away and a hurricane is approaching, Deepcore, the prototype of a mobile, seabed oil-drilling station, is requisitioned for the attempt at a rescue and salvage operation. Bud Brigman (Ed Harris), the rig foreman, is unenthusiastic about the company volunteering his crew for this assignment. His estranged wife Lindsey (Mary Elizabeth Mastrantonio), Deepcore's designer and project engineer, is furious about risking "her" facility, in part blaming Bud for acquiescing to the mission. The prospect of having to work together again at close quarters is salt in the wound of their pending divorce.

Early in the film, Bud angrily tosses his titanium wedding ring into a marine toilet and then, with second thoughts, retrieves it. Both are symbolic acts that will later simultaneously keep him from losing a finger (part of himself) and, more important, prevent his being sealed in a flooded compartment; later, these regrets and reversed decisions will be reflected in the fate of his wife and of his marriage.

As the storm sets in above, the Deepcore personnel are joined by a team of Navy commandos, led by Lieutenant Coffey (Michael Biehn), charged with the task of dealing with the sunken submarine's cache of powerful, multiwarhead missiles. Coffey denies his susceptibility to High Pressure Nervous Syndrome (HPNS, a sort of bends of the mind, giving rise to delusions and paranoia), even as he is slipping into its grip. The Deepcore workers narrowly escape a number of disasters—natural, mechanical, and man-made—so perilous in the hostile, unforgiving sub-oceanic environment. Soon, Deepcore is itself cut off from the surface and in need of rescue. Enigmatic encounters with craft and probes of the Non-Terrestrial Intelligences (NTIs, the designation given the abyss-dwelling aliens) intrigue the station crew but feed the paranoia of Coffey, who has his own men seize control of the stricken Deepcore. Intent on the destruction of the NTIs, Coffey arms a warhead retrieved from the submarine. The Brigmans' struggle to thwart his plan carries them both to the brink of death and beyond, to a transfiguring final encounter with the NTIs, and, necessarily, restores and recasts their relationship.

The Abyss is a work of several film genres fused together. While a smorgasbord is more likely to have something to please everyone, as a film it is more likely to engender diffusion and cross-purposes. By far the most successful component is the large-scale spectacle, which does perform that rare feat of transporting the audience to a wondrous, previously unseen realm. Much has been written about the production's use of enormous containment tanks at an unfinished nuclear power plant, with sets placed under millions of gallons of water, and the training of cast and crew for the slow and difficult process of filming in this very real medium. When the actors perform their own hazardous stunts—evincing well-justified dismay—realism is further enhanced. The filmmakers' insistence on maximum authenticity extended to all the functional hardware seen in the film. Only a couple of items, such as the roving Deepcore facility itself and the deep-dive suit filled with breathable liquid-fluorocarbon, are slightly beyond existing technology. This attention to realism pays off in the realization of an awesome, engrossing, and totally convincing undersea world.

On a rough par with the spectacle is the overstuffed adventure film structure. Deadly weather, remnants of Cold War tension, equipment malfunctions, dangers of the deep, derangement, nuclear disaster, and alien visitations all converge on the characters in very short order. Cameron hurls this plethora of perils at them, and the audience, with all the exciting roller-coaster razzle-dazzle that has made him one of the premier action directors. An early sequence has a heavy crane, severed from the floating topside facility, falling straight down toward Deepcore. To very effective shot selection, editing, and sound effects, the situation steadily worsens, ratcheting the tension, until the narrow escape that is not quite escape enough. Another sequence, featuring a grueling, to-the-death combat between the crews of twin submersibles has as strong an edge-of-the-seat quotient as action fans could want. It is immediately followed by a harrowing, ingenious escape—where none seems possible—from the wrecked and flooding minisubmarine that survives. Late in the story, terror combines with a terrible beauty as Bud, alone, freefalls thousands of feet through the inky depths, past undersea mountain walls, with no hope of return.

Dramatically and as a love story, Cameron's script, derived from a story that he wrote at age seventeen, is deeply felt but decidedly uneven. Unavoidably, there is much technical exposition to clear. When dialogue is not jargon-laden, it is apt to be pedestrian. Characters, including the leads (who seem an unlikely couple, at best), offer little intrinsic depth and very little in the way of surprise. Cameron's choice of an antagonist (Coffey) who is not evil, or even responsible, is commendably daring. Unfortunately, he has replaced the usual stock villain with a stock psychotic.

These deficits are partly redeemed by Cameron's assured, imaginative direction and the work of his principal actors. Harris and Mastrantonio invest the Brigmans with enough warmth and humanity to transcend the love story's predictable arc, making their physical/symbolic resurrections truly moving. It is a rare accomplishment for actors to continue to control the screen amid so much technology and towering special effects.

Though seemingly integral, the film's science-fiction component—the mysterious but ultimately beneficent NTIs—is uneasily integrated (conceptually and structurally) with the rest of the film to the point that it seems like a convenient device. Overfamiliarity is part of the problem in the wake of several other alien visitors, such as those of *E.T.: The Extra-Terrestrial* (1982) and *Close Encounters of the Third Kind* (1977). Also, Cameron again has a problem with contractually mandated running times, as he did with *Aliens*. Scenes involving the NTIs, their disgust at and threatened response to human despoilation of the planet in general and the oceans in particular, were deleted. Perhaps this contributes to the film's rushed and insufficiently satisfying conclusion.

Technically, *The Abyss* is a marvel. Leslie Dilley's production design, whether within the claustrophobic confines of Deepcore or outside in the breathtaking seabed terrain, is most impressive and completely convincing at all times. Mikael Salomon's cinematography captures a surprising clarity, although it is—either by directorial choice or underwater conditions—somewhat lacking in chromatic variability. A new radio microphone system developed expressly for the film allowed the clear recording of synchronous dialogue while submerged, a development of great benefit to the actors and the film's sense of immediacy. The special effects work, by an army of leading craftsmen, is exemplary, and earned for the team an Academy Award. The luminous, gossamer NTIs and their city-size mothership (beautifully aglow beneath the water, but disappointingly bland above the surface) are bested, however, by one effects creation—the "Pseudopod." This living, shape-changing tube of water sent by the NTIs to explore Deepcore, was accomplished through groundbreaking computer animation. Almost a character in its own right, it conveys a sense of wonder that the film as a whole works to achieve.

While there is an obvious temptation to judge *The Abyss* in terms of its over-reaching ambitions and serious flaws, it is truly amazing the degree to which all its wildly disparate elements are held within some effective orbit.

Jordon Fox

Reviews

Chicago Tribune. August 9, 1989, V, p. 1.
The Hollywood Reporter. August 7, 1989.
Los Angeles Times. August 9, 1989, VI, p. 1.
The New York Times. CXXXVIII, August 9, 1989, p. C13.
The New Yorker. LXV, September 4, 1989, p. 89.
Newsweek. CXIV, August 14, 1989, p. 56.
Rolling Stone. August 24, 1989, p. 37.
Time. CXXXIV, August 14, 1989, p. 79.
Variety. CCCXXXVI, August 9, 1989, p. 20.
Village Voice. August 15, 1989, p. 61.
Wall Street Journal. CXXI, August 10, 1989, p. A13.

THE ADVENTURES OF BARON MUNCHAUSEN

Origin: Great Britain
Released: 1989
Released in U.S.: 1989
Production: Thomas Schuhly for Prominent Features and Laura Film; released by
    Columbia Pictures
Direction: Terry Gilliam
Screenplay: Charles McKeown and Terry Gilliam
Cinematography: Giuseppe Rotunno
Editing: Peter Hollywood
Production design: Dante Ferretti
Art direction: Teresa Barbasso
Set decoration: Francesca Lo Schiavo
Visual effects: Richard Conway and Kent Houston
Makeup: Maggie Weston and Fabrizio Sforza
Costume design: Gabriella Pescucci
Music: Michael Kamen
MPAA rating: PG
Running time: 126 minutes

> *Principal characters:*
> Baron Munchausen . . . . John Neville
> Sally Salt . . . . Sarah Polley
> Desmond/Berthold . . . . Eric Idle
> Rupert/Adolphus . . . . Charles McKeown
> Bill/Albrecht . . . . Winston Dennis
> Jeremy/Gustavua. . . . . Jack Purvis
> King of the Moon . . . . Robin Williams
>   (uncredited)
> Queen Ariadne/Violet . . . . Valentina Cortese
> Vulcan . . . . Oliver Reed
> Venus/Rose . . . . Uma Thurman
> Horatio Jackson . . . . Jonathan Pryce
> The Sultan. . . . . Peter Jeffrey
> Henry Salt . . . . Bill Paterson
> Heroic officer . . . . Sting

The Adventures of Baron Munchausen represents the final installment in director
Terry Gilliam's ambitious trilogy that began with the children's tale *Time Bandits*
(1981), continued with the adult bureaucratic fable *Brazil* (1985), and culminates
with this parable of an old storyteller, Baron Munchausen. Gilliam has asserted that
in all three films his characters are "dreamers caught in an age of reason, where

there is no room for magic or the extraordinary."

As fantastic as the adventures may appear, Karl Friedrich Hieronymus von Münchhausen (his name was corrupted in English translation to Munchausen) actually lived (1720-1797); as a cavalry officer, he campaigned against the Turks in the service of Frederick the Great. The baron was apparently an accomplished teller of tall tales, and his stories were transcribed, almost certainly embellished, and eventually published by his friend Rudolf Erich Raspe in 1785.

Baron Munchausen and Terry Gilliam are clearly like-minded in believing that the only way to combat the limitations imposed by logic and reason is with fantasy and imagination. A headless statue—seen early in the film—is the first of many symbolic reminders that mind and feeling have often been separated, creating dangerous conflict. This unnecessary conflict provides the basis for the extraordinary adventures that follow.

The saga begins in the late eighteenth century, the so-called Age of Reason, in an unnamed European city besieged by the Turks. Despite the bombardment, a threadbare theater company is staging a production of the exploits of the famous fraud and liar, Baron Munchausen. The sets are intentionally artificial so that the "real" adventures that follow are, by comparison, believable.

These real adventures begin with the appearance of the baron himself (John Neville), tottering down the aisle in his faded uniform and shouting, "Lies! Lies! Lies!" The baron claims that he is the reason for the assault on the city: The Turks are pursuing him because of a bet he won with their sultan years before. Actors and audience alike laughingly dismiss the old joker—with the exception of ten-year-old Sally Salt (Sarah Polley); the relationship between the baron and Sally symbolizes the link between imagination and childlike innocence. The baron promises to prove the veracity of his claim by saving the beleaguered city. To accomplish this feat, he must find and enlist the aid of his four closest friends: Albrecht (Winston Dennis), who is the strongest man on earth; Berthold (Eric Idle), who is the fastest man alive; Adolphus (Charles McKeown), who can see farther than any telescope; and Gustavus (Jack Purvis), who can blow harder than a hurricane.

First, the baron must escape the besieged city. Fashioning a makeshift hot-air balloon out of silken knickers donated by the ladies of the town, the baron sails away (with Sally hiding inside as a stowaway). "He won't get far on hot air and fantasy," sniffs Horatio Jackson (Jonathan Pryce), who governs the town with all the cold calculation one would associate with the Age of Reason (and, by extension, with the modern age). The baron will go farther, however, than the townsfolk or the viewer can imagine.

Relying on his regular company of players and fortified by a cadre of Federico Fellini's visual stylists (production designer Dante Ferretti, cinematographer Giuseppe Rotunno, and costume designer Gabriella Pescucci), Terry Gilliam himself takes the audience on a fantastic journey. The recklessly soaring camera, rapid editing, layering of sounds, and sheer quantity of objects on screen—thousands of costumed extras, hundreds of horses, even numerous fighting elephants—combine to evoke a feeling of audiovisual clutter. Yet, it is the kind of clutter that fills a magic toy chest, where one is not annoyed by the jumble but, rather, afraid of missing one of the prizes buried within. For their contributions to the film's visual impact Pescucci, Ferretti, set decorator Francesca Lo Schiavo, visual effects artists Richard Conway and Kent Houston, and makeup artists Maggie Weston and Fabrizio Sforza all received Academy Award nominations.

Of the film's visual treasures, none is more remarkable than the image of the baron and Sally ascending from the ocean to the stars and on to the moon. Inhabiting the moon, which has longstanding associations with fantasy, emotionalism, and madness, are the Queen (Valentina Cortese) and King (Robin Williams, uncredited). The King is certainly mad but not as a result of his surfeit of imagination and passion; in an ironic twist, the King symbolizes the flaws of Cartesian logic. He is so consumed with thought that he is convinced that everything, and everyone, are simply manifestations of his own mental ruminations. In fact, he twists Descartes's most famous pronouncement into "I think, therefore you are." Portrayed as a disembodied head, the King echoes the film's earlier image of the headless statue. Although Williams' hilarious performance makes this scene arguably the film's most entertaining, it is incongruent with the style prevalent throughout the rest of the picture.

Other inconsistencies, however, are actually consistent with the complex nature of the plot. The constantly changing focus of the narrative enhances the effect of a storyteller spinning a yarn. The alternating points of view—from Sally's to the baron's to a somewhat omniscient overview—add depth and interest. When the baron becomes visibly younger during his adventures, the audience realizes that perhaps fantasy provides an antidote to the aging that results from too much logic. This healing effect of imagination is underscored when the adventurers fall back to earth and linger through zodiac signs, which are themselves a triumph of fantasy over the cold, hard facts of science.

On earth, the group encounters the burly god Vulcan (Oliver Reed) and his young bride Venus (Uma Thurman) in the center of the earth. Vulcan and Venus represent masculinity and feminity taken to their logical, or illogical, extremes. He is hard at work (in what is basically a missile silo) manufacturing weapons. She emerges from a three-dimensional execution of Sandro Botticelli's *The Birth of Venus* and dances in midair with the baron. Their absorption in each other provokes the jealous Vulcan to hurl the baron and his companions completely through the earth. They emerge on an island in the South Seas, which proves to be a monster with a marked resemblance to Godzilla, and they soon find themselves, like latter-day Jonahs, in the sea monster's belly.

Gilliam's continual onslaught of allusions—here brought to a crescendo—has become his personal trademark and underscores how logic-defying associations can enrich motion-picture narratives. His freethinking allows him to draw not only from other films but also from paintings, cartoons, and even his own work as the animator for the Monty Python Flying Circus television series. Of all the recurring images, none is more disturbing than the black-cloaked Angel of Death which shadows the baron. Despite being pursued by such a nefarious presence, the baron and Sally succeed in returning to the battlefield outside the city.

On each part of his journey, the baron is reunited with one of his four friends. Each has grown old and weary: Albrecht falters, Berthold limps, Adolphus is almost blind, and Gustavus has a chronic cough. Through the baron, they renew their faith in themselves (and in imaginative thinking) and are able to summon their incredible powers, save the town, and thus defy aging and death.

When reality and fantasy merge at the end, Sally asks the baron, "It wasn't just a story, was it?" *The Adventures of Baron Munchausen* is not "just a story"; it is also a philosophical rumination and a special effects tour de force. For a necessarily episodic film, there is little redundancy. While there are times when the special effects almost seem to overwhelm what appears to be a simple children's story, the film's very adult issues—reality versus fantasy, logic versus imagination, stagnation versus creativity—warrant complex production values. Moreover, though Gilliam's thinking sometimes may be fuzzy, inconsistent, or obscure, his feelings and flights of visual fancy are impressive, which is precisely the purpose of the film.

Marc Mancini

Reviews
American Film: Magazine of the Film and Television Arts. XIV, March, 1989, p. 34.
The Christian Science Monitor. March 14, 1989, p. 10.
Films in Review. XL, June, 1989, p. 365.
Los Angeles Times. March 10, 1989, VI, p. 1.
Maclean's. CII, March, 1989, p. 55.
Magazine of Fantasy and Science Fiction. LXXVI, May, 1989, p. 60.
The Nation. CCXLVIII, March 27, 1989, p. 427.
The New York Times. March 10, 1989, p. C8.
The New Yorker. LXV, April 3, 1989, p. 103.
Newsweek. CXIII, March 13, 1989, p. 69.
Time. CXXXIII, March 13, 1989, p. 82.
Variety. CCCXXXIII, January 18, 1989, p. 8.

ALL DOGS GO TO HEAVEN

Production: Don Bluth, Gary Goldman, and John Pomeroy for Sullivan/Bluth
   Studios Ireland; released by Metro-Goldwyn-Mayer/United Artists
Direction: Don Bluth
Screenplay: David Weiss
Editing: John K. Carr
Assistant direction: Gary Goldman and Dan Kuenster
Animation direction: John Pomeroy, Linda Miller, Ralph Zondag, Dick Zondag,
   Lorna Pomeroy-Cook, Jeff Etter, and Ken Duncan
Production design: Don Bluth and Larry Leker
Special effects: Stephen B. Moore
Sound: John K. Carr
Music: Ralph Burns
Songs: Charles Strouse and T. J. Kuenster
MPAA rating: G
Running time: 85 minutes

> *Voices of principal characters:*
> Charlie . . . . Burt Reynolds
> Flo . . . . Loni Anderson
> Itchy . . . . Dom DeLuise
> Anne-Marie . . . . Judith Barsi
> Carface . . . . Vic Tayback
> Heavenly Whippet. Melba Moore
> Killer . . . . Charles Nelson Reilly
> King Gator. . . . . Ken Page

All Dogs Go to Heaven, directed by Don Bluth, is an engaging animated feature film that yields amusement and interest for adults and children alike. Like Bluth's earlier films, *The Secret of Nimh* (1982), *An American Tail* (1986), and *The Land Before Time* (1988), *All Dogs Go to Heaven* is characterized by high-quality animation, great attention to stylistic and thematic details, and an emotionally charged narrative that makes use of various archetypal patterns. Billed as a musical, the film uses the voices of several well-known Hollywood actors (often "typecasting" the animated character to match aspects of the actor's persona) and offers several original songs written by Charles Strouse and T. J. Kuenster.

Set in New Orleans in 1939, *All Dogs Go to Heaven* depicts the adventures of a group of gangsterlike canine characters. The main character is a rather raffish German shepherd named Charlie B. Barkin (voice of Burt Reynolds). At the opening of the film, Charlie breaks out of the city pound, aided by his faithful pal, a dachshund named Itchy (voice of Dom DeLuise), who has a disturbing tendency to scratch himself frantically whenever he is nervous or afraid. Charlie returns to the gambling joint that he co-owns with a ferocious bulldog named Carface Malone (voice of Vic Tayback) and regales the clientele with the film's first number, "You Can't Keep a Good Dog Down." Without Charlie's knowledge, Carface had framed Charlie in order to take over the business for himself. Under the pretext of celebrating Charlie's return, Carface, together with his sidekick Killer (voice of Charles Nelson Reilly), arranges Charlie's death. When he arrives in Heaven, Charlie is greeted by the Heavenly Whippet angel (voice of Melba Moore), who tells Charlie that all dogs go to Heaven when they die, because "unlike people, dogs are naturally loyal, good, and kind." The Whippet has Charlie sign the register and proves to Charlie that he is dead by showing him a stopped watch that symbolizes his life. Together, they sing a duet, "Let Me Be Surprised." Unhappy with the prospect of an uneventful sojourn in Heaven, Charlie tricks the Whippet into giving him the watch. He then rewinds it and returns to the earth to seek revenge on Carface. The Whippet calls after him, warning Charlie that he can now never return to Heaven.

Charlie's first objective upon returning to life is to enlist Itchy as a reluctant ally in his revenge plans. Itchy takes Charlie to Carface's hideout, where they discover that Carface is keeping prisoner a small orphaned girl named Anne-Marie (voice of Judith Barsi), whom Carface has kidnapped because of her ability to talk to animals and thereby predict the outcome of betting races. On the pretext of rescuing her, Charlie suavely lures Anne-Marie away from Carface's den, intending to exploit Anne-Marie's talents for his own financial gain. Anne-Marie goes to live with Charlie and Itchy at their home in an automobile dump and elicits Charlie's promise to help find parents for her.

The next day, Charlie and Itchy take Anne-Marie to the horse track, where she discovers from the horses which one of them will win the upcoming race, then places a winning bet. To place the bet, Charlie and Itchy (without Anne-Marie's knowledge) steal a wallet from a young couple, whom Anne-Marie has selected as prospective parents. With the winnings from this and other races, Charlie and Itchy build a prosperous new nightclub. When Anne-Marie accuses Charlie of being as selfish as Carface (he has done nothing to help her find new parents and gives none of their money to the poor), he takes her to visit a beautiful collie named Flo (voice of Loni Anderson), who looks after an unruly pack of orphaned puppies. In an attempt to prove his generosity, Charlie brings pizza to the puppies and tries to teach them a lesson about sharing by doing a Busby Berkeley-type musical number, "What's Mine Is Yours." Anne-Marie becomes angry when she finds the wallet that Charlie had stolen at the racetrack and cries herself to sleep, singing the plaintive "Soon You'll Come Home," a song full of her longing for parents and a home. During the night, she sets out to return the wallet to the young couple, now dubbed the "Wallet family." Charlie awakes to find Anne-Marie gone and pursues her. He arrives at the couple's home to find Anne-Marie comfortably ensconced and on the verge of being adopted by the couple. On the sly, Charlie succeeds in luring Anne-Marie away with him.

Shortly after, having been shot at by Carface's gang, Charlie and Anne-Marie hide in an old Mardi Gras warehouse. They accidentally fall through the floorboards and find themselves in the lair of King Gator (voice of Ken Page). The Gator threatens to eat Charlie but changes his mind when Charlie howls and reveals a melodious voice. After declaring eternal friendship in a long musical number ("Let's Make Music Together"), the Gator releases Anne-Marie (now very sick with pneumonia) and Charlie, who return to Flo's place. As Charlie is leaving to seek a doctor for Anne-Marie, he is confronted by Itchy, who has been beaten by Carface and his cohorts. Itchy accuses Charlie of having "gone soft" on the girl and encourages his friend to flee New Orleans. Charlie denies any sentimental attachment to Anne-Marie, claiming that he is simply using her for financial purposes. Overhearing these words, Anne-Marie flees back to the Wallet family. On the way, she is recaptured by Carface's gang.

Using Anne-Marie as bait, Carface lures Charlie to his hideaway. Itchy and Flo gather reinforcements from among New Orleans' canine population and rush to seek help from the Wallet family. In a fast-paced, rapidly edited climax to the film, Charlie battles with Carface and his gang, but he and Anne-Marie are both tied up and thrown into the river to drown. In a vain attempt to rescue Charlie and Anne-Marie, Flo, Itchy, and their allies rush through the streets of the city. Unexpectedly, it is King Gator, hearing Charlie's howls, who frees Charlie and pursues and kills Carface. In his turn, Charlie rescues the drowning Anne-Marie, leaving behind his precious watch to do so. Anne-Marie is rescued from the river, but Charlie, his watch having stopped, dies.

All Dogs Go to Heaven ends with a touching scene in which a ghostly Charlie returns to the sleeping Anne-Marie to bid her farewell. Charlie is called away first by one of the Satanic spirits (hovering over the city), who had earlier appeared in Charlie's nightmare, and then by the Whippet, who vanquishes the Satanic spirit and informs Charlie that he has earned a place in Heaven again by sacrificing his life for Anne-Marie. Charlie tells Anne-Marie that goodbyes are not forever and obtains her promise to take care of Itchy in her new home with the Wallet family.

In the tradition of Bluth's other films (and of the Disney studios where he and many of the creative people involved in the making of this film were trained), *All Dogs Go to Heaven* is a very creative and highly crafted animated feature. The animation itself is exemplified by detailed backgrounds, creative use of color and shading, and character drawings that are complex, move fluidly, and create the illusion of three-dimensions. The expert use of a multiplane camera technique helps to evoke the dark and seedy milieu of gangster films and classic *film noir*, with many high angle shots (when Anne-Marie is left imprisoned and crying at the base of a ladder in Carface's hideout, and when Itchy and the other dogs race through the streets of New Orleans at the end of the film). Similar mood effects are achieved through tracking shots during the various animal races, and, as the audience follows characters who are fleeing or hiding, the camera frequently seems to pull back from a closeup on a character to reveal a wider context for the action. Detailed backgrounds also help to create depth in the film, providing scenes set in nightclubs, at the racetrack, in various hideouts, and in Flo's home in an abandoned church with a tangible sense of atmosphere.

The thematic content of *All Dogs Go to Heaven* draws heavily upon traditional Hollywood gangster films and upon even more archetypal narrative iconography such as visions of Heaven and Hell, the orphan in quest of a home, heroes and villains, a descent into the underworld, and resurrection through self-sacrifice. Although not a cloyingly didactic film, *All Dogs Go to Heaven* does offer several moral lessons: Friendship and loyalty are ultimately rewarded, sharing is shown to be important, and the virtues of a home and family are extolled.

Although generally successful as a children's film, *All Dogs Go to Heaven* has several problem areas. While providing a level of interest for adults, the film-makers' propensity for inside jokes that rely on a knowledge of Hollywood lore and verbal punning are unlikely to be grasped by younger children. For example, signs seen in backgrounds of the film refer to "Count Bassett," "Bluth's Bakery," and "Don's Auto Wreckers." The canine characters share traits of the actors who lend their voices to them: Killer is a wimp, has a strong aversion to cigar smoke, and wears glasses; Flo is a voluptuous collie; Itchy is a short, squat dachshund with a frenetic personality; and Carface inevitably is reminiscent of the gruff Mel on television's *Alice*. Indeed, the complex and convoluted plot of *All Dogs Go to Heaven* is also likely to confuse and disorient younger viewers; some of the scenic transitions are extremely abrupt (the musical scene with King Gator seems almost extraneous to the film).

While the music in *All Dogs Go to Heaven* is not as integral as one might expect in a film billed as a musical, the musical numbers are not without their charm. The score by Ralph Burns serves well in setting the mood for the story, particularly in the rollicking scene set at the racetrack and in the fast-paced chase through the streets at the end of the film. The film's songs are appealing but not always well-matched to the action of the plot. For example, "Let's Make Music Together" and "What's Mine Is Yours" are only marginally related to the action of the story.

With *All Dogs Go to Heaven*, Bluth and his creative team (most of whom have worked with him on earlier films) add to their roster of high-quality, well-crafted and sophisticated animated films. Although not without its weaknesses, this film is one of a very small and select group of well-made children's films that appeal to audiences of all ages.

Helen Bragg

Reviews

American Film: Magazine of the Film and Television Arts. December, 1989, p. 17.
Boston Globe. November 17, 1989, p. 88.
Chicago Tribune. November 17, 1989, VII, p. 35.
Los Angeles Times. November 17, 1989, VI, p. 6.

The New York Times. November 17, 1989, p. C12.
Newsweek. CXIV, November 20, 1989, p. 72.
People Weekly. XXXII, December 4, 1989, p. 21.
Time. CXXXIV, November 20, 1989, p. 91.
Variety. CCCXXXVII, November 15, 1989, p. 21.
The Washington Post. November 17, 1989, p. D7.

ALWAYS

Production: Steven Spielberg, Frank Marshall, and Kathleen Kennedy for Amblin
   Entertainment; released by Universal Pictures and United Artists
Direction: Steven Spielberg
Screenplay: Jerry Belson and Diane Thomas; based on the film *A Guy Named Joe*
   (1943), screenplay by Dalton Trumbo, adaptation by Frederick Hazlitt Brennan,
   story by Chandler Sprague and David Boehm
Cinematography: Mikael Salomon
Editing: Michael Kahn
Production design: James Bissell
Art direction: Chris Burian-Mohr
Set decoration: Jackie Carr
Set design: Carl Stensel
Special effects: Mike Wood
Visual effects: Bruce Nicholson
Special aerial effects: Joe Johnston
Makeup: James McCoy and Don Cash
Costume design: Ellen Mirojnick
Sound: Ben Burtt
Music: John Williams
MPAA rating: PG
Running time: 123 minutes

> *Principal characters:*
> Pete Sandich . . . . Richard Dreyfuss
> Dorinda Dursaton . . . . Holly Hunter
> Ted Baker . . . . Brad Johnson
> Al Yackey . . . . John Goodman
> Hap. . . . . Audrey Hepburn

Eschewing titles, *Always* plunges the audience straight into action. Pete Sandich
(Richard Dreyfuss) swoops his plane low over a lake to pick up extra water to dump
on a raging fire. Back at firefighters' base, at the controller's mike, Pete's tomboy
girlfriend, Dorinda Durston (Holly Hunter), demands to know how much fuel he
has left. Ignoring the question, Pete runs out of fuel. Although the emergency is
fake, Pete's daredevil charm is genuine: He whistles to steady his nerves and lands
the huge old plane like a glider, trimming the top of the trees near the runway with
his wheels. He is still pulling tufts of fir out of the wheels when Dorinda marches
over to yell at him, before taking off herself for some rather shaky acrobatic flying.
She ignores the arrival of a flying birthday telegram, though she smiles at the flyboy
who attempts to sing it.

Good relations between the scrapping but well-suited pair are restored later that night, in the local bar. Pete has bought her some "girl clothes" for her birthday: a white, bridelike dress and precarious high-heeled shoes. Thrilled that he views her this way, Dorinda exits to change clothes. While Dorinda recostumes, Pete and his pal Al Yackey (John Goodman), discuss the nature of love. When a transformed Dorinda reappears, Pete waves to the band ("It works in the movies," he says) to play their song: "Smoke Gets in Your Eyes." While they dance, he engages in semirough banter, never saying, outright, "I love you." The floor clears, and all the men line up for a chance to dance with Dorinda. While she dances with each man in turn (except the telegram deliveryman, who lingers, smitten, at the edge of the crowd), Al talks to Pete about moving from the front line in firefighting to semiretirement in a teaching job.

At home, Dorinda gives Pete an ultimatum: Either she grounds herself and he takes the teaching job in Flat Rock, Colorado, or she gets a tanker license. It is a bitter decision for Pete, but love wins: He will leave the firefighters. The next day, his day off, Pete is called into action because the team is short. Struck by a premonition, Dorinda races on her bicycle to catch him, to have a last kiss. In the air, Al flies too low, and his engines catch fire. Pete makes a dangerously steep dive to water-bomb Al's plane, pulls out of it by a hair's breadth, and then realizes that his own engines are on fire. His plane explodes. Later, Pete is walking through a fire-devastated forest. He meets a gentle older woman—slim, almost elfin—in an oasis of new greenery. Hap (Audrey Hepburn) tells him that he is dead, and that his new role is to "give something back." He is to guard and inspirit a new flier, who proves to be the telegram deliveryman.

Nearly a year later, Al has taken the job as base commander in Flat Rock. He nearly fires Pete's new boy, Ted Baker (Brad Johnson), on his first day: Pete, invisible to mortals though visible to the audience, has discovered his potential for mischief-making and maneuvers the unconscious Ted, who "hears" him like an inner voice, into supplying Al with an exploding cigar. Later, at target practice, Pete suggests to Ted that Al might make a better target, with more disastrous effect. Ted is sacked, and a disgruntled Al, soaked in colored water, flies off to pick up some new equipment.

Coming in to land in San Diego, Al recognizes the voice of the air-traffic controller. It is Dorinda—a Dorinda dressed in black, doing a dreary job. They later watch *Monty Python's Flying Circus* together in her sterile apartment. "I can't live without him," she says. Al is rough in response: He tells her that she is "quitting" and takes her back to Flat Rock.

Ted is flying out as Dorinda is flying in, but he is forced to land when an electrical storm arises. He takes shelter in a tumbledown shed, where he meets an old hobo who can "read" into Pete's "inspiring" thoughts. Unfortunately, he misses half the message: Speaking aloud, mediumlike, the hobo persuades Ted to head back to Flat Rock and the hope of a love that Pete cannot accept. Ted does just that, and both men come face-to-face with Dorinda by the fastest route possible: Ted (following errant instructions from Pete) follows an out-of-control ground-crew vehicle (labeled "Follow Me") all the way onto Dorinda's porch. Pete senses her presence before she emerges, and the expression on her face tells the audience that she remembers him. Pete recalls their first meeting ("I walked up to you, and I said—") and Ted finishes the sentence for him: "You're the reason I'm here." Al, there to inspect the damage to Dorinda's porch, senses the attraction between them and reinstates Ted. Al soon sends the two to town to buy supplies, and the pair encounter a crisis: a school bus-driver has a heart attack at the wheel, and Ted gives mouth-to-mouth resuscitation, saving him. Dorinda is in love. She cooks Ted a meal but talks about Pete all through dinner. Ted is obviously capable of reviving Dorinda's interest in life, but Pete is there to insist on his claim to Dorinda. After Ted leaves, she puts on her white dress, lights candles, plays "their song," and dances— alone, she thinks, but the audience sees Pete moving in unison with her. In bed, with Pete hovering over, she talks in her sleep.

Hap reappears and upbraids Pete for failing in his task to remove himself from human attachments. *Always* reaches its climax with what at first appears to be a repeat perfomance of the mission that killed Pete. Ted, now acknowledged as the base's most gifted pilot, must fly into a narrow canyon to water-bomb a safe path to the river for some trapped firefighters on the ground. Again Dorinda cycles wildly to the base to see her man before he takes off. Then comes a twist: Dorinda, trying to take Ted's place in danger but trying even more to place herself at risk and thus closer to Pete, takes off in the rescue plane. Pete is in the cockpit with her, furious, but he must help her on her own terms, and at last she seems to hear him as he declares his love for her. She hears his advice too, pulling off the mission by the skin of her teeth in a hair-raising action sequence. Then she, like Pete at the beginning of the film, runs out of fuel. She lands the plane on a lake near the base, and it starts sinking, but she makes no motion to save herself. Then a pale hand, Pete's, pulls her to the surface. She has seen him, but only to say good-bye. Faced with the prospect of her death, Pete has understood that he must release her into life.

For some, *Always* is a nearly perfect "movie," fragrant of popcorn and wet handkerchiefs; for others, it is a mass of sentimentality, overwrought action sequences, and ersatz nostalgia for a heroic time. For the latter, the film is made tolerable only by technical grace and the kind of slick direction they distrust but admire in television commercials. For them, a film such as *Always* exists at too many removes from the reality of Montana firefighters' lives: It is an anachronistic homage, a parasitic attempt to re-create the simplicity and romanticism of the films its director loved as a child. For others, however, the film represents not nostalgic return but continuity. They share Spielberg's beliefs (and Victor Fleming's and Frank Capra's) that the best things in life are simple, not that sentiment can surmount loss and death, that old-fashioned values and romantic love still matter, and that an old-fashioned style of filmmaking is still the best way of representing them, particularly if everything is bigger than it was the first time around. Just as they were not put off by the pop Christianity and guardian angels of *It's a Wonderful Life* and *A Guy Named Joe*, so they took *E.T.* to their hearts and applaud the sentimentalized spirituality of *Always*: "Inspiration," as Hap helpfully explains, means the breathing of one's spirit—"spiritus"—into another.

Regardless of whether one momentarily relinquishes hold on the things of the intellect to indulge in the sentimental pleasures of *Always*, the film has one insurmountable problem: This is not wartime. Fleming's *A Guy Named Joe* offered comfort, catharsis, and uplift to a nation of war widows; Spielberg's heroics exist in an unheroic peacetime vacuum. Firefighting is no substitute for dogfights. The whole character of Al is constructed to mediate and mitigate this very problem, carrying the burden of the film's self-conscious meditations. As Pete dives to waterbomb his burning plane, Al protests (in noticeably updated language), "Hey Pete, this ain't a dog-fight, man," and as his trainees miss their targets, he remarks, "I'm glad we're not at war." As he sits in the bar with Pete, at the very beginning of the film, he remarks, "What this place reminds me of is the war. . . . It's England, man—everything except Glenn Miller," and he laments the fact that no one can make a film called "Firemen Strike at Dawn." All that sustains Pete's position is Spielberg's much-demonstrated belief in a man's right to have adventures. Thus, the film must fight too hard to establish its own alternative premises of heroism and sacrifice, contriving a situation in which Pete has suddenly matured but is required, one last time, to risk himself for the sake of another.

Joss Lutz Marsh

Reviews
America. CLXII, January 20, 1990, p. 42.
Chicago Tribune. December 22, 1989, VII, p. 25.
The Christian Science Monitor. December 29, 1989, p. 10.
Los Angeles Times. December 22, 1989, VI, p. 1.
The New York Times. December 22, p. B1.
The New Yorker. LXV, January 8, 1990, p. 90.
Newsweek. CXV, January 1, 1990, p. 60.
Variety. CCCXXXVII, December 20, 1989, p. 22.
The Wall Street Journal. December 28, 1989, p. A7.
The Washington Post. December 22, p. D1.

BACK TO THE FUTURE PART II

Production: Steven Spielberg, Frank Marshall, Kathleen Kennedy, Bob Gale, and
   Neil Canton; released by Universal
Direction: Robert Zemeckis
Screenplay: Bob Gale and Robert Zemeckis
Cinematography: Dean Cundey
Editing: Arthur Schmidt and Harry Keramidas
Production design: Rick Carter
Art direction: Margie Stone McShirley
Set decoration: Linda DeScenna
Special effects: Michael Lantieri
Special visual effects: Ken Ralston, Michael Lantieri, John Bell, and Steve Gawley
Costume design: Joanna Johnston
Sound: William B. Kaplan
Music: Alan Silvestri
MPAA rating: PG
Running time: 105 minutes

Principal characters:
Marty McFly/Marty McFly, Jr./
   Marlene McFly .... Michael J. Fox
Dr. Emmett Brown .... Christopher Lloyd
Lorraine .... Lea Thompson
Biff Tannen/Griff.................. Thomas F. Wilson
Marvin Berry...................... Harry Waters, Jr.
Terry .... Charles Fleischer
Western Union Man .... Joe Flaherty
Needles .... Flea
Jennifer............................ Elisabeth Shue
Strickland .... James Tolkan
George McFly .... Jeffrey Weissman
                                  Crispin Glover
3-D .... Casey Siemaszko
Match................................. Billy Zane
Skinhead .... J. J. Cohen

After coming in as the eighth most popular film of the 1980's, with $208.3 mil-
lion at the box office, *Back to the Future* (1985) was bound to have sequels. *Back to
the Future Part II* (1989), the second of a trilogy, explores time travel in a way that
relies heavily on its predecessor. Viewers who enjoyed the characterization of the
first film may be disappointed with the second, for it depends on already established
personalities and relationships for its emotional weight. Those who relish mind-
boggling twists inherent in the subject, however, will appreciate the breathless pace

of a film that begins in the 1980's, dashes immediately to 2015, and then whisks viewers back into 1950's scenes from the original film. Gimmicks, commercialism, and technology create a cartoonlike atmosphere, but filmmaker Robert Zemeckis occasionally gets in a few digs against decadent materialism and the ethos of success at any cost.

Zemeckis plays on his strong suit in this film, using the technology with which he first experimented in his tremendously popular *Who Framed Roger Rabbit* (1988). In *Back to the Future Part II*, he employs "Vistaglide," an updated version of the computerized camera that allows actors to talk to themselves in various roles. Screenplay author Bob Gale, who worked with Zemeckis on *Back to the Future*, explores possibilities of time travel in a way that brings characters into contact with different versions of themselves. While this duplication may create problems in logic, it produces a rich field for technical wizardry and self-reflexive in-jokes on the sequels themselves.

The plot of such a tangled series of circumstances serves primarily to put characters in high-tech gadgets and mind-bending paradoxes. The film puts viewers into time warp speed from the very opening, with Doc Brown (Christopher Lloyd) dragging Marty McFly (Michael J. Fox) to 2015 so that he can save future progeny from disgrace and a life of crime. Marty sees his future self—an aging unsuccessful businessman, groveling to his Japanese boss—and his son, who is soon to be the cowardly dupe of a teenage crime gang, headed by Griff Tannen, son of his father's old arch rival, Biff (both played by Thomas F. Wilson). Zemeckis takes the opportunity to showcase Fox's delicate features in a convincing female impersonation of Marty as his own teenage daughter. This segment also reflects on the first film by showing Marty to be as spineless as his father had been.

While the problem of family honor is neatly handled by the clever use of Marty doubling as his own son, the real interest lies in the central character's use of a flying skateboard hovercraft and not in the question of whether Marty Junior is fated to a life of crime. The future is rife with 1980's commercialism with such products as self-tying Nikes, holographic advertisements for *Jaws XIX*, multiple video screens, and dehydrated food discs that instantly expand into large, steaming pizzas. Marty's sojourn into the future offers other tantalizing tidbits of future lore, such as portable telephones that all the teenagers wear around their necks, but the film takes the action back to the past almost immediately.

No sooner has Marty rescued his son from infamy than a more complicated ethical twist puts both the future and the past in jeopardy. Marty decides that a copy of the sports almanac from 2015 would be a harmless enough money-making souvenir, even though Doc Brown has warned him that he should take absolutely nothing from the future for fear of wreaking havoc on the past. When Biff Tanen steals Doc's DeLorean time machine and the sports almanac, Marty gets to see exactly what a future governed by unchecked greed, corruption, and materialism would look like. Marty and Doc return to 1985 Hill Valley (yet another oxymoronic paradox) to discover that it has been horribly altered into a nightmare of pornography shops and gambling casinos. In a scene reminiscent of *It's a Wonderful Life* (1946), Marty sees how a single individual can alter the fate of an entire town. Biff Tannen rules, and he has even managed to kill Marty's father and marry his mother, turning her into an alcoholic. In the dystopian Hill Valley of Biff's creation, corruption and wealth dominate in a casino atmosphere. The world has the smoky aura and sense of greasy menace that are also found in *Blade Runner* (1982). Marty's old house is inhabited by blacks (the racist white nightmare of the worst that could happen to a neighborhood), and the sidewalks are peppered with chalk tracings where corpses have lain. Eventually it is revealed that Biff, in an action not far from Marty's own thwarted plan, had taken the 2015 almanac and had given it to the 1955 version of himself so that he could win a fortune betting on sporting events.

Discovery of this awful turn of events sends Marty and Doc back to the 1950's and into scenes from the previous film. Key sequences appear, shot from a new character's perspective—the point of view of Marty II, who must avoid encountering himself, according to some arcane pseudoscientific explanation given by Doc with delightfully baffling gusto. The climax of this film occurs at the same moment as the high point of the first, when Marty's father wins his mother by punching out Biff. Every joke from *Back to the Future* is recast from a slightly different angle, creating a self-referential parody of the whole filmmaking process.

The film's conclusion leaves viewers hanging, quite deliberately, with the promise of *Back to the Future Part III*, to be set in the Old West. A number of issues are left unresolved, including the future of the McFly family and the future of a society that has vacillated from sinister hedonism to the nostalgia of 1950's innocence. While *Back to the Future Part II* may come across as merely another opportunity for film to advertise everything from Nike shoes to the film itself, as the ultimate product, some critics detect the same kind of satirical bite that appears in *Who Framed Roger Rabbit*. Biff Tannen represents an exaggerated perversion of the wholesome, lovable protagonist—his lust for success is a distorted version of Marty's own cravings and the decadent society he would create is simply an entrepreneurial step or two beyond American society of the 1980's.

Critics do not deny the film its cleverness or flash, but some viewers argue that Zemeckis flaws his work by his obsession with technological play at the expense of believable human characters and interaction. For example, the director's fascination with Vistaglide calls on characters to put on some outlandish makeup so as to appear with themselves at various ages. Getting to see Michael J. Fox as middle-aged or as a girl may satisfy some curiosity, but it vitiates viewers' involvement with the actual characters since it calls attention, once again, to the fact that this is a series of stunts. The film's intricate devices and self-reflexive jokes ("There is something very familiar about this," comments a character) underscore this effect of removing the audience from emotional involvement with the characters.

Another unfortunate side effect of Zemeckis' penchant for gimmicks is in the quality of the cinematography. As dazzling as it is in some of its special effects, the overall look of the film is somber. Some reviewers note that the requirements of harsh lighting and layered images forced cinematographer Dean Cundey to produce a "dulled out" look for the rest of the shooting, resulting in a dark, grainy quality throughout much of the film. While this quality may be appropriate for filming Biff's nightmare 1980's, its darkness diminishes the effectiveness of other scenes, making them morose rather than amusing.

While the actors do their best with improbable situations and limited human contact, the film's script and editing hardly allow them time to take a deep breath and look into one another's eyes, let alone say anything moving. The only remaining hint of the kind of incestuous play that enlivened the original film occurs when Marty encounters his mother, whose breasts have been cosmetically augmented, and comments that he hardly recognized her since she is so "big." Perhaps the filmmakers sensed that adolescents, the primary audience for this film, were somewhat uncomfortable with the interplay between Marty and his mother as a girl in *Back to the Future*.

Whatever the reason for the film's focus on gadgets at the expense of relationships, this shift makes the film less appealing for wider audiences, who often require some emotional resonance in their adventure films. For pure escape fantasy, the film serves its purpose, with a breakneck pace, a wealth of technological gewgaws, and plenty of car chases and scuffles to please viewers addicted to constant movement within each shot. Filmgoers who had appreciated such adventure in the first film came in droves to the opening. After an initial box office response of $4.5 million in the first week, however, the film failed to fulfill the financial promise created by the original *Back to the Future*. *Back to the Future Part II* requires the devotion of the fan of time travel, of Robert Zemeckis, of Michael J. Fox, of pure adventure, and of the original *Back to the Future*. The complicated machinations of time travel in the sequel might be no more bewildering to uninitiated viewers than to fans of the original, but, without having seen the original, viewers might wonder why anyone would care what these people did in the first place.

Rebecca Bell-Metereau

Reviews
Chicago Tribune. November 24, 1989, VII, p. 38.
The Christian Science Monitor. December 4, 1989, p. 10.
Los Angeles Times. November 22, 1989, VI, p. 1.
The New Republic. CCI, December 25, 1989, p. 26.
The New York Times. November 22, 1989, p. C9.
The New Yorker. LXV, December 11, 1989, p. 139.
Newsweek. CXIV, December 4, 1989, p. 78.
Time. CXXXIV, December 4, 1989, p. 101.
Variety. CCCXXXVII, November 22, 1989, p. 19.
The Washington Post. November 22, 1989, p. D1.

BATMAN

Production: John Peters and Peter Guber for Guber-Peters Company; released by Warner Bros.
Direction: Tim Burton
Screenplay: Sam Hamm and Warren Skaaren; based on a story by Sam Hamm and on the characters created by Bob Kane and published by DC Comics
Cinematography: Roger Pratt
Editing: Ray Lovejoy
Production design: Anton Furst (AA)
Art direction: Terry Ackland-Snow and Nigel Phelps
Set decoration: Peter Young (AA)
Special visual effects: John Evans and Derek Meddings
Makeup: Paul Engelen
Costume design: Bob Ringwood and Linda Henrikson
Sound: Don Sharpe
Music: Danny Elfman
Songs: Prince
MPAA rating: PG-13
Running time: 124 minutes

Principal characters:

The Joker/Jack Napier	Jack Nicholson
Batman/Bruce Wayne	Michael Keaton
Vicki Vale	Kim Basinger
Alexander Knox	Robert Wuhl
Commissioner Gordon	Pat Hingle
Harvey Dent	Billy Dee Williams
Alfred	Michael Gough
Carl Grissom	Jack Palance
Alicia	Jerry Hall
Mayor	Lee Wallace
Bob the Goon	Tracey Walter

Even six months before it opened in late June, 1989, *Batman* was the most talked about and anticipated motion picture of the year, if not, as some claimed, the decade. A ninety-second trailer was reputed to draw fans, who would then leave before the main feature. The Bat mania, however, found its greatest catalyst in some three hundred Bat products, especially apparel. In a record summer that featured several sequels to previous blockbusters—*Lethal Weapon II*, *Ghostbusters II*, and *Indiana Jones and the Last Crusade* (all reviewed in this volume)—*Batman* offered something new, but familiar.

Batman broke the opening-day box-office records set earlier in the month, becoming the first film to gross $100 million in ten days. In the next three months, the film would gross around $20 million in the United States. Its success led pop sociologists to delve into the national psyche for an explanation. What went unnoticed is that, after its phenomenal first week, *Batman* earned at the same rate as the summer's other top ten films. Thus, the film's success seems more the result of an extremely well-planned advertising strategy—based on manipulation of the minimalist logo—than of the film itself.

Bob Kane's DC Comics hero had taken enough forms since June, 1939, for the logo to promise something for all tastes and ages. In the 1940's, Batman appeared in the *Superman* radio series and two Columbia Pictures motion-picture serials. In the 1960's, a pop-art-inspired television series and film gave adults a camp version of Batman, while Saturday morning television offered children an innocuous cartoon superhero. In the 1980's, Batman returned to the dark humor and menace of the early comics in such DC "graphic novels" as Frank Miller's *Batman: The Dark Knight Returns* (1986). That *Batman* follows suit reassured the hardcore fans who feared another camp version from Tim Burton, director of the kitsch comedies *Pee-Wee's Big Adventure* (1985) and *Beetlejuice* (1988), and Michael Keaton, the star of the latter film.

The film chronicles the first few months of Batman's career (before Robin), as he irons out his modus operandi and—since he is an ordinary human—his motives. The Writers Guild, however, went on strike during shooting, and screenwriter Sam Hamm was unable to refine the script and compensate for Burton's last-minute changes (Warren Skaaren and others replaced him). As a result, the film narrative jumps from one episode to the next, while the sparse dialogue deflates crucial scenes. *Batman* succeeds on Burton's dark visual wit alone; the film—much like a comic book—has the appearance of successive tableaux, minus word-balloons. Given the emphasis on visuals, it is surprising that *Batman* was not filmed in widescreen format.

Batman combines German expressionism with Art Deco to create an archaic, futuristic world similar to the one in Fritz Lang's *Metropolis* (1927). The allusion, however, is less to the aesthetics of the 1920's than to such contemporary films as *Blade Runner* (1982), *Dune* (1984), and *Brazil* (1985). While *Batman* borrows the look of these films—cinematographer Roger Pratt also shot *Brazil*—it often lacks their political awareness. In its opening scene, *Batman* strives for a broad social panorama, in a tracking shot of what was said to be the largest set since *Cleopatra* (1963). Rich and poor alike crowd downtown Gotham, a metropolis whose architecture, in the absence of a building code, shoots up for miles, with incongruous addenda sprouting out. Gotham's mayor (Lee Wallace), a mirror image of New York City's former mayor Edward Koch, announces a festival that he claims will solve the city's economic and social ills. Meanwhile, Axis Chemical spews out pollutants, while its owner, Carl Grissom (Jack Palance), also runs a mob operation with the help of crooked police. These scenes reveal a city in desperate need of governmental regulation. What it gets, however, is a festival and Bruce Wayne

(Michael Keaton), a disturbed multimillionaire turned vigilante.

Having discovered that his second-in-charge, Jack Napier (Jack Nicholson), has slept with his mistress, Alicia (Jerry Hall), Grissom arranges for the police to capture and kill Napier. Batman foils the ambush but drops Napier into a vat of acid, where he is assumed to have been eaten alive. Napier, however, is swept out into the river. In the next scene, a surgeon unwraps Napier's bandages in a basement surgery; when Napier sees what has been done to his face, he staggers up the basement stairs either laughing or crying—one is unsure, because before Napier had been both maniacal and narcissistic. When he reveals himself, the viewer sees that his mouth has been frozen into a rictus, his skin is bleached white, and his hair is turned green. "Jack is dead," he announces. "You can call me the Joker. And as you can see, I'm a lot happier." His inner self has been released; and the Joker proceeds to take over the mob, and then Gotham.

As in most films, the villain has the juiciest role, and Nicholson—with Keaton constrained as the tight-lipped Bruce Wayne/Batman—becomes the focus of attention. In fact, Nicholson's role was expanded during shooting, and a renegotiated contract gave him a percentage of the gross for film and merchandise income. His earnings, estimated at $60 million, were three times higher than Sylvester Stallone's record income for *Rambo III* (1988).

The film's color scheme is also built around the Joker, by use of a process known as tonal separation. Entire sets were colored in one tone and lit as if black-and-white film stock were being used, so that the Joker's green hair and garish zoot suits stand out in sharp relief. The visual emphasis on the Joker aligns black-suited Batman with the drab monotones of the status quo, making him even less of an alternative vision.

The remainder of the film features photographer Vicki Vale (Kim Basinger) and journalist Alexander Knox (Robert Wuhl) tracking Batman, while Vale and Wayne have an affair. At the same time, the Joker poisons the town's hygiene products and pursues Vale, whom Batman saves several times. As in his earlier films, Burton works best with *mise en scène*. Action sequences and confrontations are underdeveloped and poorly choreographed. In one scene, Wayne—persuaded by his butler and confidant Alfred (Michael Gough)—arrives at Vale's apartment to reveal his true identity. The Joker, however, breaks in, shoots Wayne (who has hidden a silver tray under his shirt), and leaves without Vale. (Since Batman had just rescued Vale from the Joker in the previous scene, it would make more sense for the Joker to have reclaimed her.)

Before the Joker shoots Wayne, he recites a nonsensical question he asks all of his victims. It is this phrase that leads Wayne to realize that it was a young Napier who shot and killed his parents when he was a child, a brutal act that led Wayne to create Batman. When the Joker takes over the media waves and issues a challenge to Batman for the day of the festival, Batman is compelled to accept and exact revenge.

The Joker lures citizens to the festival with the promise of throwing $20 million from his parade float, only to release poisonous gas from parade balloons. Batman, in his Batwing, attacks the Joker's float and snares the balloons. In his next run on the float, however, the Joker shoots the Batwing out of the sky with a long-barreled pistol. While Batman recovers, the Joker grabs Vale and drags her to the top of Gotham's abandoned cathedral.

In a scene reminiscent of Alfred Hitchcock's *Vertigo* (1958), Batman pursues them up the dilapidated staircase. Once at the top, he dispenses with the Joker's henchmen and at last confronts the Joker one-on-one. When the Joker accuses Batman of having made him what he is, Batman responds, "I made you, but you made me first." In this reply lies the crux of comic book myths, in which hero and villain are complicit in each other's existence, and are also revealed to be more alike than not in their unstable makeup. Little, however, prepares the viewer for this confrontation, since the previous near-fights fail to generate the sense of a grudge match. Moreover, the final fight is so one-sided that all residual tension dissipates, especially when the Joker appears to know that he killed Batman's parents. Yet, the Joker cannot possibly know this, because he does not know Batman's identity.

In the end, the Joker falls to his death, and Vale and Wayne agree to continue their relationship. In the last scene, Alfred drives Vale to Wayne Manor, telling her that Wayne will be a little late. Although she previously objected to Wayne's vigilantism—which she identified as a manifestation of psychological problems and conservative individualism—Vale now seems to accept Batman. So too does Wayne, who gives Gotham a Batsignal with which to summon Batman. In the last shot, Batman stands erect atop a building, facing the projection from the Batsignal, awaiting a sequel.

Chon Noriega

Reviews

Chicago Tribune. June 23, 1989, VII, p. 40.
The Christian Science Monitor. June 29, 1989, p. 10.
Life. XII, Spring, 1989, p. 84.
Los Angeles Times. June 23, 1989, VI, p. 1.
The New Republic. CCI, July 31, 1989, p. 24.
New York. XXII, July 17, 1989, p. 45.
The New York Times. June 23, 1989, p. C12.
The New Yorker. LXV, July 10, 1989, p. 83.
Newsweek. CXIII, June 26, 1989, p. 72.
Rolling Stone. June 29, 1989, p. 38.
Time. CXXXIII, June 19, 1989, p. 60.
USA Today. June 23, 1989, IV, p. 1.
Variety. CCCXXXV, June 14, 1989, p. 7.
The Village Voice. July 4, 1989, p. 69.
The Wall Street Journal. June 22, 1989, I, p. 12.

THE BEAR

Origin: France
Released: 1988
Released in U.S.: 1989
Production: Claude Berri for Renn Productions; released by Tri-Star Pictures
Direction: Jean-Jacques Annaud
Screenplay: Gerard Brach; based on the novel *The Grizzly King*, by James Oliver
    Curwood
Cinematography: Philippe Rousselot
Editing: Noëlle Boisson
Production design: Toni Ludi
Art direction: Heidi Ludi, Antony Greengrow, and Georg Dietz
Special effects: Willy Neuner, Uli Nefzer, and Johann Fickel
Makeup: Hans-Jurgen Schmelzle
Costume design: Corinne Jorry and Françoise Disle
Sound: Laurent Quaglio
Music: Philippe Sarde
MPAA rating: PG
Running time: 93 minutes

> *Principal characters:*
> Bill . . . . Jack Wallace
> Tom . . . . Tcheky Karyo
> Dog handler . . . . André Lacombe

Having successfully explored the feelings of primitive man in the internationally acclaimed *Quest for Fire* (1982), director Jean-Jacques Annaud elected to go one step further: to create a film that conveys the thoughts and emotions of animals. He envisioned the project simply as "a big solitary bear; an orphan bear cub; two hunters in the forest; the animals' point of view." Six years, seventeen hundred storyboard sketches, and $24 million later, *The Bear*—based on a 1916 novel by James Oliver Curwood—opened to record box-office success in Europe and State-side success as well. In many ways, the story is as simple as Annaud's original synopsis, though bringing it to the big screen proved to be one of the most challenging productions of its time. This picture harks back to the popular Disney wildlife "docudramas" of the 1950's (a tradition since supplanted by the overt objectivity of modern documentaries). Unlike its predecessors, however, *The Bear* required the most up-to-date special effects, opticals, and animatronic puppetry to simulate its particular brand of realism.

Annaud expressed no interest in making a straightforward documentary: "I determined to do a full fiction film, not a scientific one." As with *Quest for Fire*, this picture includes only minimal dialogue. In fact, the three actors share but 657 words between them. The film relies instead on visual techniques, silent film montages, and the characters' extremes of behavior to tell the story.

It is quite a dramatic story, beginning with the opening scene. Momma Bear is gorging herself on honey from a very large, very active beehive (perhaps a reminder that it is not merely humans who routinely destroy what they consider "lower" life forms), when a rock slide suddenly ends her life and orphans her small cub. Comic relief comes quickly. Suddenly alone in the world, the innocent animal seeks companionship, first playing with a butterfly and then attempting to imitate a hopping frog. The bear seems unaware of exactly what he is until he comes across an enormous male of his own species. The big bear lets junior know in no uncertain terms that he has no intention of staying around to provide a role-model. It is not until a pair of hunters shoot and wound the adult and the youngster helps nurse him back to health that he accepts the role of surrogate father.

The Bear makes a point of revealing its protagonists' most human characteristics—the cub has dreams; Papa Bear has a one-night stand in the woods; the cub (bored with his elders' lovemaking) eats peculiar mushrooms and begins hallucinating. Such endearing interludes, however, while charming, are not really the crux of this tale. The story line, like the bears themselves, goes from occasional sluggishness to full-bore charges into action, complete with genuine fear and quite real violence. One such key moment finds the defenseless cub cornered by a hungry puma. The terrified bear wails louder and louder until the puma suddenly backs away. The cub is understandably pleased with himself; then the camera reveals the real reason for the big cat's retreat—the intimidating figure of the big bear looming behind his small friend.

In contrast to the interesting bears, the human characters are rather boring. From the outset, these hunters are clearly the antagonists, but they cannot be said to be true villains until they tease and taunt the cub after they have captured it. Even at this juncture, they do protect the bear from the dogs, finally releasing the cub altogether. These mountain men, who are so much a part of the bears' world, are, in the end, redeemable. After the big bear—in the film's most astonishing scene— forgoes an opportunity to kill the man who had shot him, the hunter returns the favor by later preventing his partner from killing the great creature.

The camera is used quite effectively to simulate the cub's perspective as these men enter his domain. The low angle shots, especially when the small bear first sees the humans, establish the sense of scale essential to understanding all future emotional interactions. Added to this are pronounced wide-angle, distorted close-ups that convey all the confusion and fear that the vulnerable cub experiences while at the mercy of his human captors.

Besides the bears and men, a third character is indispensable to the cinematic telling of this story—the endless unspoiled wilderness that was British Columbia in 1885 (the fact that most of the film was shot in the Bavarian Alps notwithstanding). Annaud's acknowledged inspiration for the look of this picture was the look of certain landscape painters, especially such romantics as Casper Friedrich and Albert Bierstadt. To maximize the mood, the camera often slows down just long enough to let the scenic vistas linger on the screen (and in the consciousness of the audience). To underscore the immense scale of such an environment, the bear cub himself is often shown as but a dot lost in this vast landscape.

"How did they do that?" This question—asked by virtually every viewer of the film—accounts for much of the film's success. One of the secrets was to have three cameras rolling at all times. Annaud shot one million feet of film, a prodigious shooting ratio of almost one hundred to one. He also assembled a crew of two hundred Americans, English, French, Germans, Italians, Austrians, and Swiss. Add to this the casting of literally dozens of reptiles, hundreds of birds, and thousands of insects in supporting roles, and the enormity of Annaud's achievement becomes even more impressive.

With such a cast, the picture cannot help but become a colossal mime performance, relying on the gestures, postures, and movements of its "stars" to communicate. It must be remembered, however, that the interactions, causalities, and reactions had to be created editorially. If this were not challenge enough, the crew found it impossible to record any synchronized sound while shooting. The filmmakers had to build the entire sound track piece by piece from sounds recorded elsewhere or located in sound libraries, including the bears' "dialogue."

This led to one aspect of the viewing experience not altogether satisfying. There are times when the sound effects seem overdone, defeating the sense of realism that the rest of the picture strives so hard to convey. The adult bear's thundering tread, while perhaps an acceptable psychological impact, is simply unbelievable from a strictly acoustic standpoint.

In the final analysis, the success of *The Bear* rests on whether the audience can accept the film's presentation as being from the cub's perspective. For the most part, this is possible, but excessive anthropomorphism can come across as contrived, especially if the viewer actually stops long enough to think about it. The filmmakers have explained that a bear cub's vocal repertoire is so like a human baby's that it can easily be mistaken for such. Accurate or not, the bear's whimperings in the film are so cute that they often sound exactly like those of a young girl. Too, the big bear's intentional stalking and sneaking up on the hunters seem more like the tactics of a guerrilla fighter than the behavior of a bear. Such lapses do not seriously dampen the overall drama and emotional impact of the film. *The Bear* spins a good yarn while it simultaneously makes some important points about man's relationship with the other creatures with whom he shares his world.

Marc Mancini

Reviews
Chicago Tribune. October 27, 1989, VII, p. 46.
The Christian Century. CVI, October 25, 1989, p. 962.

Commonweal. CXVI, December 15, 1989, p. 706.
Film Comment. XXV, September/October, 1989, p. 2.
The Hollywood Reporter. October 24, 1989, p. 4.
Los Angeles Times. October 25, 1989, VI, p. 1.
New Statesman and Society. II, September 29, 1989, p. 41.
The New York Times. October 25, 1989, p. C15.
The New Yorker. LXV, November 13, 1989, p. 121.
Newsweek. CXIV, November 13, 1989, p. 92.
Time. CXXXIV, October 30, 1989, p. 97.
Variety. October 26, 1988, p. 14.

BILL AND TED'S EXCELLENT ADVENTURE

Production: Scott Kroopf, Michael S. Murphey, and Joel Soisson for Nelson
   Entertainment and Interscope Communications, in association with Soisson/
   Murphey Productions; released by Orion Pictures
Direction: Stephen Herek
Screenplay: Chris Matheson and Ed Solomon
Cinematography: Timothy Suhrstedt
Editing: Larry Bock and Patrick Rand
Production design: Roy Forge Smith
Art direction: Gordon White
Set decoration: Jennifer Williams
Special visual effects: Perpetual Motion Pictures
Makeup: Daniel Marc
Costume design: Jill Ohanneson
Sound: Ed White
Music: David Newman
MPAA rating: PG
Running time: 90 minutes

Principal characters:

Ted "Theodore" Logan	Keanu Reeves
Bill S. Preston	Alex Winter
Rufus	George Carlin
Napoleon	Terry Camilleri
Billy the Kid	Dan Shor
Socrates	Tony Steedman
Freud	Rod Loomis
Genghis Khan	Al Leong
Joan of Arc	Jane Wiedlin
Abraham Lincoln	Robert V. Barron
Beethoven	Clifford David
Captain Logan	Hal Landon, Jr.
Mr. Ryan	Bernie Casey

Bill and Ted's Excellent Adventure is a true Hollywood success story. A youth-oriented comedy about two vacuous high school students who travel through time to prepare their final history report, the film was a virtual orphan when Nelson Entertainment acquired it from the financially troubled De Laurentiis Entertainment group in early 1988. The $8.5 million picture was reworked with the sixteen-to twenty-four-year-old audience in mind: Nelson Entertainment provided the funds with which to reedit it, complete the special effects, and add a heavy-metal-flavored rock-and-roll sound track.

The film opens in 2688, in San Dimas, California, where Rufus (George Carlin), a stylishly dressed emissary of the future, informs the audience that the world has evolved into a place of beauty and abundance. Bowling averages are higher, and San Dimas has more "excellent water slides than any other planet we communicate with." Life on earth, however, was not always as wonderful. Seven hundred years ago, "The Two Great Ones"—as Rufus refers to the protagonists of the film's title—encountered a problem that constituted a threat to the foundation of future society. In order to set the world back on its proper course, Rufus must come to the aid of Bill S. Preston (Alex Winter) and Ted "Theodore" Logan (Keanu Reeves), who are in danger of failing American history.

Though the boys are harmless, ingratiating simpletons, their teacher, Mr. Ryan (Bernie Casey), has no choice but to deliver an ultimatum: If their final oral report, due the following afternoon, is anything less than "very special," he will be forced to give both of them failing grades. Failing would mean the end of their rock-and-roll band, the Wyld Stallyns, because Ted's father (Hal Landon, Jr.) has threatened to send his son to a military academy in Alaska if he fails school.

Enter Rufus and his amazing time-travel machine that resembles a telephone booth. He tells Bill and Ted that he has been sent to help them with their history report. In answer to their questions, Rufus dials a number on the "phone" (a sophisticated interstellar guidance system) as Bill and Ted step aboard. Suddenly the machine is engulfed in a shower of lights and noises; the machine disappears and the trio is whisked through the "circuits of history," a maze of oversized electronic circuitry.

In order to demonstrate the machine's capabilities, Rufus takes the boys to Austria, in 1805, where the French have just invaded. (Clips from Paramount's 1956 version of *War and Peace* fill out the battle footage.) Napoleon Bonaparte (Terry Camilleri) is accidentally sucked into the time machine's vortex as it dematerializes and is transported back to San Dimas, in 1988.

Leaving the diminutive French leader in the protective custody of Ted's younger brother, Bill and Ted embark on a journey to collect other important figures from history. The first stop on their itinerary is New Mexico, 1879. When Billy the Kid (Dan Shor) saunters into the saloon where they are drinking beers, Bill suggests to Ted that they "bag him." Fleeing from an enraged posse after a crooked poker game initiated by Billy, the three renegades zap themselves back in time to ancient Greece, where they meet Socrates (Tony Steedman).

Trying to impress the esteemed philosopher (whose name they mispronounce as "So-Crates"), Ted recites the lyrics from a song by the group Kansas entitled "Dust in the Wind"; he concludes with "All we are is dust in the wind, dude." Mesmerized by these odd-looking lads, Socrates joins them. As each figure is added, the phone booth begins to fill up—a witty visual reference to the fraternity prank of stuffing telephone booths with college students.

A stop in fifteenth century England brings Bill and Ted to the castle of King Henry, where they encounter two princesses (Diane Franklin and Kimberley La-

Belle) and instantly fall in love. Introducing himself as "Ted of San Dimas," Ted asks the ladies to accompany them to the upcoming senior prom. Unfortunately, King Henry seizes the boys and orders his men to put them in chains.

Aided by Billy the Kid and Socrates (posing as executioners), Bill and Ted depart the fifteenth century and travel to the future, where they meet "The Three Most Important People in the World" (played by rock-and-roll musicians Clarence Clemons, Martha Davis, and Fee Waybill), who are the forces behind Bill and Ted's rescue mission. From the interaction that follows, Bill and Ted realize that they are revered by these hallowed figures. Urged by Ted to say a few words to the silent assemblage, Bill elicits gasps of awe when he urges them to be "excellent to each other."

With time running out, Bill and Ted make a few more trips through time, rounding up Sigmund Freud (Rod Loomis), Joan of Arc (Jane Wiedlin), Genghis Khan (Al Leong), Abraham Lincoln (Robert V. Barron), and Ludwig van Beethoven (Clifford David). When they return to San Dimas, Bill and Ted drop off their famous friends at the local shopping mall, while they search for Napoleon, who has since discovered the joys of bowling, ice cream, and water slides. Left to their own devices, the historical personages wreak havoc—Genghis Khan obliterates a dummy in a sporting goods store with a baseball bat, while Joan of Arc takes over an aerobics demonstration—and are arrested. Following a dramatic rescue by Bill and Ted, they race to school, just in time for their final history report.

Bill and Ted astound their teachers and classmates with their oral presentation, which stars their famous friends and is modeled after a rock-and-roll concert, complete with strobe lights and wailing guitars. For their efforts, they are rewarded with an A-plus from Mr. Casey, as well as new guitars and their fifteenth century prom dates from Rufus. Rufus explains the significance of his mission by telling the audience that, in time, the boys' music will not only help put an end to war and poverty but also bring the planets into universal harmony, thus allowing meaningful contact between all forms of life. Though Bill and Ted's musical skills are still debatable, Rufus assures the audience that "they do get better."

Released after a one-year delay by Orion Pictures, *Bill and Ted's Excellent Adventure* became the sleeper hit of the 1989 spring season, despite nearly unanimous negative reviews that criticized the film for its lack of intelligence. Immediate plans were made to produce a sequel and two television series—a Saturday morning animated program and a prime-time situation comedy.

Writers Chris Matheson (son of renowned science-fiction author Richard Matheson) and Ed Solomon developed the characters of Bill and Ted in an improvisational comedy group at the University of California, Los Angeles, where they met as undergraduates. In *Bill and Ted's Excellent Adventure*, Matheson and Solomon have cameo appearances as two obnoxious waiters who work in an ice cream parlor that caters to gluttons.

Director Stephen Herek, who also directed the cult hit *Critters*, makes the most of the script's easygoing, juvenile humor, which was slightly dated when the film was finally released. To his credit, Herek refrains from pandering to the material's lowbrow leanings: Bill and Ted may not be intellectual giants, but they are good-hearted, clean-living teenagers; unlike the character Jeff Spicoli (Sean Penn) in the film *Fast Times at Ridgemont High* (1980), neither uses foul language or drugs. Their experiences instill in them a newfound appreciation of American history; more important, they reap the benefits of increased self-esteem in a world that tends to relegate teenagers to second-class status. Actors Alex Winters and Keanu Reeves capture wonderfully the childlike innocence of these adolescent time-travelers; their body language and precise delivery of colloquial references (such as when Ted makes a comparison between Socrates and the controversial heavy-metal artist Ozzy Osbourne) add immeasurably to the film's appeal. Some of the vignettes, rendered in the style of *The Monkees* television show, are hampered by the film's low budget, whereas others—Billy the Kid and company helping Bill do his household chores and Napoleon's bowling experience—serve as nothing more than filler. Despite its shortcomings, *Bill and Ted's Excellent Adventure* is a diverting, harmless romp.

Kyle Counts

Reviews

Chicago Tribune. February 24, 1989, VII, p. 39.
Cinéfantastique. XIX, July, 1989, p. 54.
Library Journal. CXIV, September 1, 1989, p. 229.
Los Angeles Times. February 17, 1989, VI, p. 8.
The New York Times. February 17, 1989, p. C12.
Seventeen. XLVIII, March, 1989, p. 128.
Teen. XXXIII, February, 1989, p. 42.
Variety. CCCXXXIV, February 22, 1989, p. 18.
Video. XIII, September, 1989.
The Washington Post. February, 17, 1989, p. C7.

BLACK RAIN

Production: Stanley R. Jaffe and Sherry Lansing in association with Michael
   Douglas; released by Paramount Pictures
Direction: Ridley Scott
Screenplay: Craig Bolotin and Warren Lewis
Cinematography: Jan DeBont
Editing: Tom Rolf
Production design: Norris Spencer
Art direction: John J. Moore, Herman F. Zimmerman, and Kazuo Takenaka
Set decoration: John Alan Hicks, Leslie Bloom, Richard C. Goddard, John M.
   Dwyer, and Kyoji Sasaki
Set design: Alan S. Kaye, Robert Maddy, and James R. Bayliss
Special effects: Stan Parks
Costume design: Ellen Mirojnick
Sound: Keith A. Wester, Donald O. Mitchell, Kevin O'Connell, and Greg Russell
Sound effects editing: Milton C. Burrow and William A. Manger
Music: Hans Zimmer
MPAA rating: R
Running time: 126 minutes

Principal characters:

Nick Conklin	Michael Douglas
Charlie Vincent	Andy Garcia
Masahiro Matsumoto	Ken Takakura
Joyce Kingsley	Kate Capshaw
Sato	Yusaku Matsuda
Ohashi	Shigeru Koyama
Oliver	John Spencer
Katayama	"Guts" Ishimatsu
Nashida	Yuya Uchida
Sugai	Tomisaburo Wakayama
Miyuki	Miyuki Ono

Frequently criticized for emphasizing style over content, the films of director
Ridley Scott are visually striking, with the *mise en scène* indelibly linked to character and narrative. *Black Rain* is another from the director's long list of films that use
elements of the *mise en scène*—the set design, lighting, and costumes—to add
meaning to the film. *Black Rain* compares with Scott's other films not only in the
use of visual style to enhance the narrative but also in terms of theme.

A fairly conventional police drama, *Black Rain* borrows aspects of its visual style
from *film noir*, a genre in which an overall dark look symbolizes the despair,
pessimism, and corruption of the characters. The plot revolves around hardened

New York City detective Nick Conklin (Michael Douglas). Conklin, who is under investigation for taking money confiscated in drug raids, is assigned to escort Sato (Yusaku Matsuda), a member of Japan's brutal *yakuza*, back to Osaka. Conklin's partner, Charlie Vincent (Andy Garcia), accompanies Conklin. Once in Osaka, Sato escapes, embarrassing Conklin and Vincent as well as the Osaka police department. Despite some opposition from the local police, the two New York detectives attempt to recover their man as well as their pride. Osaka detective Masahiro Matsumoto (Ken Takakura) is assigned to keep the Americans out of trouble, and he and Conklin clash over the responsibility of a detective to his fellow officers. After Charlie is murdered by the sadistic Sato, Masahiro and Conklin team up to recapture the young mobster and break a *yakuza* counterfeiting ring. Along the way, Nick learns the importance of honor and his responsibility to fellow police officers, and Masahiro discovers the power of individual action.

The stunning look of director Scott's films remains the most overwhelming characteristic of his work. *The Duellists* (1978), *Alien* (1979), *Blade Runner* (1982), *Legend* (1986), and *Someone to Watch over Me* (1987) are best remembered for their sumptuously detailed set designs, their fascination with the tonalities of light, and their emphasis on texture and atmosphere. Scott's oft-repeated comments that the design of a film is its statement, or that the background of a film is as important as the actors, attest the emphasis of the visual elements in the director's overall concept for a film. In *Black Rain*, the rain-soaked, neon-laden streets of Osaka serve a function beyond their superficial beauty. They visually recall the *film noir* genre, establishing expectations for the viewer of a story line involving widespread corruption. Corruption dominates *Black Rain*, from the counterfeiting racket operated by the *yakuza* to the ambivalent character of Nick Conklin. Conklin, the film's protagonist, is guilty of the charges placed against him by the internal affairs department of the New York police, but he defends his actions by blaming the system. He tells Masahiro that all New York is one gray area, referring to the widespread corruption and the consistent bending of the rules that has become the standard operating procedure for maintaining law and order. Conklin's comment recalls Scott's depiction of New York in the opening sequence—a cold and dirty city dominated by neutral tones and perpetually gray skies. Though Conklin is willing to accept the deceit and graft of his job as an inherent part of the system, he is surprised to discover the ramifications of such corruption when it goes unchecked. When Sugai (Tomisaburo Wakayama), an elderly leader of the *yakuza*, tells Conklin that the Japanese mob was spawned from the dishonorable practices of Americans during the occupation of Japan after World War II—that the Satos of Japan are the result of the American predilection for bending the rules—Nick begins to understand how omnipresent corruption can be. The "black rain" of the title denotes the ash that fell across Japan after the atom bombs were dropped on Hiroshima and Nagasaki; it connotes the deceit and corruption resulting from the American occupation that followed Japan's defeat. The pervasiveness of that corruption is visually signified by the rain that continually falls from the night skies of

Osaka during the course of the film.

Compared with New York's gritty gray exteriors and earthy brown interiors, the piercing neon and screaming colors of Osaka's nightscapes seem all the more shocking. The differences between New York and Osaka—that is, between the United States and Japan—provide a major theme of the film, and Detectives Conklin and Vincent are the proverbial fish out of water, trying to do their job in a Far Eastern country. More than simply a plot device, however, the clash of cultures in *Black Rain* echoes the real-life tensions between the United States and Japan over the latter's predominance in certain business practices and the manufacturing of various goods. The assertion by Sugai that the *yakuza*'s counterfeit American currency will be better crafted than the original is a pointed reminder of the reasons behind the popularity of Japanese-made products in America. The opening sequence, in which Conklin wins a motorcycle race on his American-made Harley-Davidson against an opponent on a Japanese-made Suzuki, foreshadows the clash between cultures that will reach its zenith in the characters of Conklin and Masahiro. Conklin, the highly individualistic, quintessentially ugly American, continually bickers with Masahiro, the selfless team player who is dedicated to the group. If it is the function of genre films to negotiate the problems of a society becoming increasingly more complex, then the understanding and friendship that develops between Conklin and Masahiro by the end of *Black Rain* offers a simplified—or at least a cathartic—solution to U.S. tensions with Japan.

A recurring image in the film depicts the main characters as virtually absorbed by the stunning set designs. These scenes, usually shot with a long lens, make full use of Scott's preference for backlighting. The use of a long lens and backlighting makes the characters appear almost as a part of the set. Sato, for example, walks through a huge factory where a meeting of *yakuza* leaders is about to take place. Silhouetted against the factory's huge machines, which billow orange and red flames as well as gray smoke, Sato looks every bit like the Devil in Hell. Vincent and Conklin, particularly in the first half of the film, are repeatedly shown crushed against a backdrop of garish neon signs and Osaka architecture as they struggle to penetrate the culture. The Asian typography on the ultramodern, neon billboards accentuates the alien quality of the cityscape, recalling the production design of *Blade Runner*. Menacing and threatening, the architecture of Osaka swallows Charlie Vincent whole, as the unwitting detective is lured into the bowels of an indoor mall and killed.

The use of the production design to define or reflect aspects of the characters is a common device in Scott's films. The dank, festering, claustrophobic metropolis of *Blade Runner* parallels the feverish desperation of the replicants as they work against the clock to increase their life span. In *Someone to Watch over Me*, the class differences between the main characters are visually indicated by their living spaces. The wealthy witness lives in a luxurious, spacious penthouse bathed in a warm, golden light; the working-class policeman assigned to protect her resides in a small, crowded bungalow in a gritty neighborhood. The futility of their relationship is telegraphed by the opposing nature of their living spaces. In *Legend*, the theme of good versus evil is reinforced not only by the lighting design but also by a color scheme involving white, black, and red. Given Scott's background in art and design, his interest in visually relaying information to the viewer is both understandable and expected.

Aside from the trademark visual style and approach, *Black Rain* provides another example of Scott's typical protagonist: the alienated or embittered hero whose quest becomes an obsession. *Blade Runner*'s Deckard (Harrison Ford) becomes obsessed not so much with finding the missing replicants but with uncovering why they so desperately want to live; Feraud (Harvey Keitel) in *The Duellists* pursues a colleague for years over some minor offense; Jack (Tom Cruise) in *Legend* is so fixated on Lily (Mia Sara) that he allows her to destroy their way of life. In *Black Rain*, Nick Conklin becomes obsessed with capturing Sato, driving him to commit violent acts, break the rules, and pull others into his obsession.

With his reliance on visual elements to convey the personalities of characters, Scott recalls the efforts of the German Expressionist directors to utilize techniques of filmmaking to express inner states of mind or traits of character. Like the films of Friedrich Murnau and Fritz Lang, *Black Rain* draws the viewer into the picture and its characters through its compelling visual style.

Susan Doll

Reviews

Boxoffice. CXXV, November 1989, p. R71.
Chicago Sun-Times. September 22, 1989, p. 41.
Chicago Tribune. September 22, 1989, VII, p. 38.
The Christian Science Monitor. September 22, 1989, p. 10.
Commonweal. CXVI, October 20, 1989, p. 565.
Films in Review. XLI, January, 1990, p. 40.
Los Angeles Times. September 22, 1989, VI, p. 1.
Maclean's. CII, October 2, 1989, p. 65.
National Review. XLI, October 27, 1989, p. 58.
The New Republic. CCI, October 16, 1989, p. 31.
New York Magazine. XXII, October 2, 1989, p. 66.
The New York Times. September 22, 1989, p. C12.
Newsweek. CXIV, October 2, 1989, p. 70.
Time. CXXXIV, October 2, 1989, p. 90.
Variety. CCCXXXVI, September 20, 1989, p. 28.

BLAZE

Production: Gil Friesen and Dale Pollock for A & M Films and Touchstone
  Pictures in association with Silver Screens Partners IV; released by Buena Vista
Direction: Ron Shelton
Screenplay: Ron Shelton; based on the book *Blaze Starr: My Life as Told to Huey
  Perry*, by Blaze Starr and Huey Perry
Cinematography: Haskell Wexler
Editing: Robert Leighton
Production design: Armin Ganz
Art direction: Edward Richardson
Set decoration: Michael J. Taylor and Rosemary Brandenburg
Makeup: Monty Westmore and Christina Smith
Costume design: Ruth Myers
Sound: Kirk Francis
Music: Bennie Wallace
MPAA rating: R
Running time: 116 minutes

> *Principal characters:*
> Earl Long . . . . Paul Newman
> Blaze Starr . . . . Lolita Davidovich
> Thibodeaux . . . . Jerry Hardin
> LaGrange . . . . Gailard Sartain
> Tuck . . . . Jeffrey DeMunn
> Doc Ferriday . . . . Garland Bunting
> *Times-Picayune* reporter . . . . Richard Jenkins
> Red Snyder . . . . Robert Wuhl

Fanny Belle Fleming (Lolita Davidovich), a country girl from West Virginia, has
the body of a Rubens voluptuary and misplaced ambitions as a singer. The first
twenty minutes of *Blaze* chart her move to New Orleans, Louisiana, her professional
"seduction" by the sleazy host of a club full of servicemen caught up in the Korean
War (he persuades her to strip for victory), and her professional development from
blonde ingenue to Blaze Starr, the redheaded "Miss Spontaneous Combustion"
("and I do mean bustion"). She becomes truly a star: In 1959, in real life, she
commanded a salary of $1,500 a week (more than the governor made). One night
that year, in the middle of her act, Blaze catches the roving eye of Earl K. Long
(Paul Newman), governor of the "Great State of Louisiana." She is twenty-eight; he
is sixty-three.

Younger brother of the more famous Huey Long, Earl takes a cheerfully corrupt
view of politics and of the constitutional rules that prevent him from running for
another gubernatorial term. His way around these regulations is to put up one of his

yes-men as candidate; once elected, the stooge will step down, and "Vice Governor" Long will take his place. A weak heart does not deter Long from using physical persuasion on a political opponent whom he encounters on Bourbon Street. Nor does it deter him next from plunging into an indiscretion: He wants Blaze and does everything except advertise his desire. True to the bedrock of disarming old-fashioned dignity in her character, Blaze first examines his intentions, making certain that he will treat her like a person, and not merely a piece of pneumatic equipment. She takes in her stride invitations to dine with him or accompany him on whirlwind motor tours of Louisiana. During one of these, Long neatly circumvents the stratagems of blacks, reporters, and opponents to push him into an outright statement of support for black voting rights and professional opportunities (the kiss of political death to his desire for reelection): Descending unexpectedly on a hospital, he upbraids the director (John Fertitta) for employing whites to "serve" blacks. When the director unwittingly replies that the hospital has no blacks on staff, Long hands him three hundred résumés of black doctors and nurses and secures for the hospital director an unwanted reputation as an innovative social reformer.

Blaze visits Long's run-down farmstead, the Pea Patch. They embark on a Southern-style orgy, complete with watermelon and cowboy whoops. Soon, Blaze has him talking to her as well as making love to her—a novelty in Long's experience and a moment when a newer world breaks in upon his last-of-the-breed, old-style romantic machismo. The course of the affair runs true to his flair for sexual as well as political exhibitionism, eventually posing as great a threat to his reelection as rumors of tax evasion and his position on blacks (*Blaze* is in some sense a parable of a man's simultaneous loss of political and sexual power). Long refuses to rein in the much-publicized affair, dares the tax investigators to do their worst, and grudgingly agrees to "shut up and stay home" when black voting rights are discussed in the state legislature.

Still, Long cannot leave the issue alone. He bursts into the tense session, shouts biblical quotations at a rival, who replies with contradictory lines from the same source, douses another opponent with profanity, and literally throws his weight about. To make matters worse, the whole session is shown on television. Long is snatched, drugged, and committed to the state mental hospital. During this political nadir, Blaze becomes his greatest asset. She not only comforts him, but plots for him as well. Long's next move is outrageously simple: Still technically governor, he fires Dr. Cheeseborough (Harlan Jordan), the director of the hospital. Released by Cheeseborough's successor, Long returns to the campaign trail. Meanwhile, Blaze leaves town, for his sake.

Long loses anyway—resoundingly. Convinced that he has also lost Blaze, he arrives on the stage of the strip club, brandishing a shotgun. Blaze appears, fully dressed, from the wings, and they embrace. It is a moment of melodrama that refuses to take itself seriously yet retains its genuine emotional charge. Blaze and Long retreat to the Pea Patch. Long cooks. Blaze's stockings hang out to dry in the backyard. Yet their domestic bliss does not last long; the former governor does not like being a former governor. Thus, Long runs for Congress, campaigning with the forthright slogan, "I ain't crazy." *Blaze* flags at this point: The final half hour seems like an epilogue—not entirely inappropriate for the film as history but incongruent with the rest of the film's momentum. Amazingly, Long's campaign is successful. On the day of victory, however, he dies, in Blaze's arms, of a heart attack.

Blaze is not simply one of 1989's crop of Southern films, although it does have a superb sound track that mixes tunes such as "Jambalaya" with Randy Newman's "Louisiana, 1927." In its moments of pure rustic Americana, such as the shot—almost primitivist in style—through a barn door of two cows against a brilliant green field, the film places itself in a powerful tradition of painting and photography. The film is well served by veteran cinematographer Haskell Wexler (who garnered an Academy Award nomination for his work on the film), and still more by production designer Armin Ganz, who collaborated on the production design of two other contemporary forays into Americana, *Angel Heart* (1987) and *Tucker* (1988). Visually, *Blaze* revels in all the accoutrements of the strip scene, yet it never quite attains the sleaziness that director-writer Ron Shelton injected into the sex scenes in his *Bull Durham* (1988). Like Long's downfall, sex and love are played perhaps a little too much for laughs; yet, the laughs are good, and the good-time flavor is appealing. Moreover, Long's stubborn refusal to part with Blaze adds an emotional depth.

Blaze has a curious relationship with history and with the conditions of its own production. The real Blaze Starr, who was the production consultant to the film, makes a fleeting appearance, thus playfully blurring the boundary between the past and its reconstruction on celluloid. The character of Long's real-life wife, however, is noticeably absent from the film: The omission, at her insistence, leads to some distortion of the facts. At the end of the film, as the final credits roll, a recording of the voice of Earl K. Long is played, reminding the audience of the gap between fact and "fiction." It is an impudent, affectionate, and quirky final stylistic fling.

The success or failure of the film lies with the two central roles. As Blaze Starr, a performer playing a performer who takes her "art" seriously, Davidovich's performance is engaging, fresh, lighthearted, rounded. As Earl K. Long, Newman does an impressive job of submerging his own powerful star image in the historical personage he is creating. A few details of his performance are distracting: Lines muttered in a gravelly voice can be hard to understand; more important, Newman eschews any hint of tragedy, thereby losing a dimension of Long's personality. Yet, Newman's interpretation offers the best of "character acting" and historical impersonation: His version of Long as showy demagogue gives the impression of being overheard and casually encountered, an impression strengthened in contrast to his discomfort with the whole idea of performing for television, which was becoming a powerful medium. Clumsy, hostile, and bombastic, Long stares into the camera, squaring up to it like an enemy and barking out the wrong anecdote at the wrong time. Constrained and squeezed into a small box, turned into black-and-white, Long looks like a tin-pot dictator. The scene spells the end of his brand of Southern politics—wily, colorful, and crazily "not crazy."

Blaze is a film in the fullest sense. The critics who have commented on the ambiguous presentation of such historical issues as Long's support for black rights do not realize that foregrounding the issue would have confused the film, simplified the psychology, pandered to cheap liberal pressures, and pushed the attempt at filmic portraiture into the background. *Blaze* presents life as episodic, haphazard, and ambiguous, an approach that negates linear history.

Joss Lutz Marsh

Reviews

Chicago Tribune. December 13, 1989, V, p. 1.
The Christian Science Monitor. December 15, 1989, p. 10.
Los Angeles Times. December 13, 1989, VI, p. 1.
The New York Times. December 13, 1989, p. C24.
The New Yorker. LXV, December 11, 1989, p. 136.
Newsweek. CXV, December 18, 1989, p. 68.
San Franciso Chronicle. December 13, 1989, p. E1.
Time. CXXXIV, December 18, 1989, p. 93.
Times-Picayune. December 15, 1989, p. LAG30.
Variety. CCCXXXVII, December 13, 1989, p. 28.
Washington Post. December 13, 1989, p. B1.
Washington Post Weekend. December 15, 1989, p. 65.

BORN ON THE FOURTH OF JULY

Production: A. Kitman Ho and Oliver Stone; released by Universal
Direction: Oliver Stone (AA)
Screenplay: Oliver Stone and Ron Kovic; based on the book by Ron Kovic
Cinematography: Robert Richardson
Editing: David Brenner (AA) and Joe Hutshing (AA)
Production design: Bruno Rubeo
Art direction: Victor Kempster and Richard L. Johnson
Set decoration: Derek R. Hill
Special effects: William A. Purcell
Makeup: Sharon Ilson and Rick Sharp
Costume design: Judy Ruskin
Sound: Tod A. Maitland, Michael Minkler, Gregory H. Watkins, and Wylie
    Stateman
Sound effects editing: Scott Martin Gershin
Music: John Williams
MPAA rating: R
Running time: 145 minutes

Principal characters:
Ron Kovic	Tom Cruise
Charlie	Willem Dafoe
Mr. Kovic	Raymond J. Berry
Mrs. Kovic	Caroline Kava
Donna	Kyra Sedgwick
Steve Boyar	Jerry Levine
Timmy	Frank Whaley

Born on the Fourth of July marks writer/director Oliver Stone's return to the Vietnam War front to expand on the themes that he explosively examined in his award-winning film *Platoon* (1986). As with *Platoon*, Stone won the Academy Award for Best Direction and the film won for Best Film Editing. Although it did not win, *Born on the Fourth of July* was also nominated in the categories of Cinematography, Sound, Adapted Screenplay, Original Score, Best Actor, and Best Picture. By dramatizing the life of Vietnam veteran turned antiwar activist Ron Kovic, Stone once again vividly captures the horrors of the Vietnam experience and then goes on to explore the equally horrific effects of Vietnam on the soul of the United States and, more specifically, the soul of one of its most outspoken veterans.

The film opens with an idyllic yet foreboding scene: eleven-year-old Ron Kovic (Bryan Larkin) playing war games with his friends in the woods of Massapequa, New York, where he grew up. Later, Ron (Tom Cruise) competes on the high school wrestling team under a brutal coach, who demands that his team members worship the winning-is-everything credo, a belief reinforced at home by Ron's fiercely moralistic mother (Caroline Kava). When Ron loses a key wrestling match, he is crushed and believes that he must prove himself in some way; he joins the Marines. While waiting to be officially inducted, Ron finishes his senior year in high school and helps his father run the local family-owned A&P market. He also asks his sweetheart, Donna (Kyra Sedgwick), to the high school prom but is disappointed to learn that she is going with someone else. The night of the prom, Ron, at home preparing to leave for the Marines, impulsively races through the rain to the gymnasium where the prom is being held and passionately embraces and dances with Donna.

The scene dissolves slowly on this last moment of youthful innocence, then fades in on Ron, now a Marine sergeant, preparing to advance his troops on a Vietnamese village. As some of the men dig in to cover the others, the troops suddenly open fire on the village. Ron and others give the command to cease fire, but the damage has already been done. When the troops advance on the village, they find huts filled with dead and dying victims of the gunfire. Before they can attend to the wounded, the Marines are attacked by enemy troops. Ron has to be dragged away from the wounded and ordered to prepare for battle. When he finally realizes the seriousness of the attack, he wildly returns fire and in the chaos accidentally shoots and kills one of his own men. Sickened by his deed, Ron later meets with his superior and admits to killing the soldier. His superior does not want to hear Ron's confession and angrily orders Ron to return to his unit.

The scene then shifts to several months later, in January, 1968. Ron and his men are under attack on the outskirts of another Vietnamese village. The fighting is heavy, and Ron is wounded and taken to an operating room, where he is surrounded by mutilated soldiers, some dead, some a breath away from death. The scene fades in on Veterans Hospital in the Bronx, where Ron is recuperating from his wounds. The conditions in the hospital are atrocious. Although he is told that he will never walk again, Ron is determined to prove his doctor wrong and embarks on an aggressive rehabilitation program. At one point, while he proudly staggers around the hospital on crutches, he suddenly loses his balance and crashes to the floor, breaking one of his already paralyzed legs. He is put into traction and nearly goes mad from the restraint and the despicable conditions.

Finally, Ron returns home in a wheelchair. He tries to maintain a positive disposition, but too many things have changed. Many of his childhood friends are dead, victims of the war. His friend Steve (Jerry Levine) manages a hamburger stand and offers Ron a menial position with the meager promise of eventually managing a stand on his own. Ron, who still supports the war, eventually quarrels with Steve about the war's legitimacy. Later, Ron quarrels with one of his brothers, who has embraced a strong antiwar position.

In the Fourth of July parade that year, Ron rides in his own car, dressed in his finest Marine dress uniform, but is greeted by the curses of the crowd in a fine counterpoint to the opening parade scene. Joining other veterans for a post-parade speech, Ron becomes distracted by the crying of a baby in the audience. Horrible memories of the war overwhelm him, and he has to be carried from the stage. One of the people in the audience is another Vietnam veteran and a childhood friend, Timmy (Frank Whaley). That evening, the two veterans swap stories about their war experiences. Ron confesses that he believes he deserves his fate, because he made some atrocious mistakes while in Vietnam. He also confesses that he would sacrifice everything just to have his body whole again.

A visit to his old girlfriend, Donna, who is organizing an antiwar protest, and the ensuing rally, in which Ron is nearly beaten and arrested by aggressive police troops, further alienates the war veteran. Back home, Ron becomes an excessive regular at a local bar, leading to confrontations at home. Ron travels to Mexico, where there is a gathering of Vietnam veterans, with problems similar to Ron's, who are attempting to escape from the mistreatment that they all received after returning home from the war. They spend their time drinking, gambling, and whoring. One friendly veteran, Charlie (Willem Dafoe), calls the setup paradise and encourages Ron to indulge, which he does. Paradise, however, soon sours, with the veterans all harboring deep resentment about being neglected in the United States.

Ron returns to the United States after a fight with Charlie, which proves to be a turning point in the film and in the young man's maturing process. Still haunted by the incident in which he accidentally shot one of his own men, he decides to travel to the young soldier's home in Virginia, where he meets with the boy's family and relates the events that led to his death. The family cannot forgive Ron, although they empathize.

The scene shifts to a massive antiwar rally outside the 1972 Republican Convention held in Miami. Amid the throng of protesters is a large group of disabled veterans, including Ron. Surrounded by television cameramen and reporters, Ron expresses his anger over the shameful treatment of Vietnam veterans and how the war is an abomination, demanding that troops be pulled out immediately. Ron and his supporters are then taken by guards to a place outside the convention hall, where a battle is in full force between protesters and police. Ron is knocked out of his wheelchair by police and dragged to a wagon, where he is readied for arrest. Supporters rescue him, and he encourages them to storm the convention hall again, which they do with Ron in their midst.

The scene then shifts to another convention, this time the 1976 Democratic Convention, where Ron is preparing to address the crowd. As he is wheeled through a mass of enthusiastic supporters, he stops and signs his newly published book for a fan. The film ends with the image of Ron wheeling himself up the ramp to the speaker's platform, where he is greeted by a thunderous ovation.

Born on the Fourth of July is not an easy film to watch. It is filled with pain, agony, and images of death and degradation. There is hardly a quiet, reflective moment in the film. Even the idyllic early images of Ron growing up are tinged with a foreboding of the violence soon to envelop his life. Director Stone revels in such a volatile atmosphere. He is a master of choreographing chaos, using every cinematic effect at his disposal to create a rich, operatic melee of madness. For example, in the critical scene in which Ron is shot, Stone uses heightened and distorted sound effects, slow motion, and overexposed, bleached-out images to capture the feeling of terror that Ron experiences at the moment near death. Even in an early family scene, in which Ron prepares to leave for military duty, Stone creates tension by shifting from Ron in his room, listening to a baseball game on the radio featuring his hero, Mickey Mantle, to Ron walking down the hall and passing his brother's room, where his brother is playing a guitar and singing Bob Dylan's "The Times They Are A-Changin'," then finally walking into the living room, where his father sits watching a television interview with General William Westmoreland.

By dramatizing the life of a living hero, Stone treads on dangerous dramatic ground. Very few biographical films, especially films about living legends, have managed to capture the subject's unique essence with any depth or honesty, or without lapsing into a superficial series of dramatized vignettes of the person's life. Stone and coscreenwriter Kovic have managed to pick the most emotionally significant events of Kovic's life and give them a logical progression that moves with the dramatic sweep of a well-plotted fictional story. Ron's evolution from gung-ho Marine to disenchanted veteran to heroic antiwar activist is believable. The story is told more with images than with words, which makes the overall effect more honest and less preachy.

Cruise manages to shed his high-profile star persona and embody all the facets of Ron Kovic's evolving character with an intense believability. His natural, boyish charm and good looks are later twisted into a haggard, stringy-haired, emotional wreck of a man. Throughout the transformation, Cruise's Kovic remains a fully developed and sympathetic character. Cruise does have trouble handling the shrill, profane moments, but this is more of a flaw with the script and the staging of the scenes than a reflection of Cruise's acting ability, which overall is emotionally gripping and for which he earned an Academy Award nomination.

The major flaw of the film is its reliance on high-intensity scenes of unrelenting turmoil. Although Kovic went through extreme hardships and beyond before finding peace with himself and acceptance by his country, he could not have sustained such a shrill-pitched fervor for all those years without having gone completely insane. He must have had a few placid moments somewhere in his life. Stone, however, skips over those moments and goes for the gut-wrenching confrontations—the big emotions. This approach leads to an unbalanced and distorted view of an extraordinary man's life. Yet Stone has created a compelling and, at times, overwhelmingly passionate cinematic experience, one that effectively uses all the dramatic techniques exclusive to film to tell the story of a man whose struggle to understand his own conscience ultimately changed the conscience of a nation.

Jim Kline

Reviews
Chicago Tribune. December 20, 1989, V, p. 1.
Los Angeles Times. December 20, 1989, VI, p. 1.
The Nation. CCL, January 1, 1990, p. 28.
National Review. February 5, 1990, p. 58.
The New Republic. CCII, January 29, 1990, p. 26.
The New York Times. December 20, 1989, p. C15.
The New Yorker. LXV, January 22, 1990, p. 122.
Newsweek. CXIV, December 25, 1989, p. 74.
Time. CXXXIV, December 25, 1989, p. 74.
Variety. CCCXXXVII, December 20, 1989, p. 21.
The Washington Post. January 5, 1990, p. B1.

THE 'BURBS

Production: Larry Brezner and Michael Finnell for Imagine Entertainment;
   released by Universal
Direction: Joe Dante
Screenplay: Dana Olsen
Cinematography: Robert Stevens
Editing: Marshall Harvey
Production design: James Spencer
Art direction: Charles L. Hughes
Set decoration: John Anderson
Special effects: Michael Arbogast, Jeffrey Pepiot, Paul Stewart, and Thomas Ward
Makeup: Michael Germain and Daniel C. Striepeke
Costume design: Rosanna Norton
Sound: Michael J. Benavente and Warren Hamilton, Jr.
Music: Jerry Goldsmith
MPAA rating: PG
Running time: 102 minutes

Principal characters:
Ray Peterson	Tom Hanks
Mark Rumsfield	Bruce Dern
Carol Peterson	Carrie Fisher
Art Weingartner	Rick Ducommun
Ricky Butler	Corey Feldman
Bonnie Rumsfield	Wendy Schaal
Dr. Werner Klopek	Henry Gibson
Uncle Reuben Klopek	Brother Theodore
Hans Klopek	Courtney Gains
Walter	Gale Gordon
Dave Peterson	Cory Danziger

The 'Burbs opens on a dark and gloomy night. Ominous opera music booms as the camera travels from the image of a spinning globe to zoom in on a small quiet neighborhood, the cul-de-sac of Mayfield Place. Suddenly lights flash from the deepest recesses of the basement of a dilapidated Victorian house on the block. Accompanying the flashing lights are ear-splitting noises which pierce the air and a mysterious wind, which violently rolls the leaves over the dry earth. Witnessing this suburban turbulence is the pajama-clad Ray Peterson (Tom Hanks), who, unable to sleep, happens to be strolling in his front yard. This weird nocturnal upheaval fires Ray's suspicions: Something strange is happening in this house owned by the Klopeks (Henry Gibson, Brother Theodore, and Courtney Gains), neighbors whom no one on the block has seen since their arrival one month earlier.

The following morning over breakfast Ray communicates his suspicions to his wife Carol (Carrie Fisher). He strongly suggests that they should move. Carol attributes Ray's doubts to paranoia and urges him to reconsider the option of taking the family to the lake; Carol is clearly worried about her husband's mental health. Ray, however, is adamant about spending his week's vacation from work puttering around the house. This domestic exchange is abruptly interrupted by the blast of rifle shots that are coming from the Petersons' backyard. Ray opens his back door to investigate and narrowly misses being shot in the head. Outside, neighbor Art Weingartner (Rick Ducommun), brandishing a rifle, informs Ray that he is in pursuit of the huge crows that mysteriously have descended upon their neighborhood as of late. Ray advises Art to put down his weapon and invites him in for coffee.

During this friendly breakfast chat, Art gives Ray an earful, in between mouthfuls—Art is gobbling everything in sight—of his theory about the Klopeks. Art believes that they are fiendish ghouls who are performing satanic rituals. Ray and Carol's son, Dave (Cory Danziger), give this theory credence when he interjects that he and Ricky Butler (Corey Feldman), the spacey overgrown teenager next door, have been spying on the Klopeks at night through a telescope atop the Petersons' roof. Dave reveals that the Klopeks leave the house only at night and busy themselves digging in their backyard. Having heard this report, Ray and Art believe it is their responsibility as concerned neighbors to investigate.

After much blustering and stalling, Ray and Art bravely stride up the Klopeks' stairs and bang the brass knocker. The banging dislodges the knocker, however, and from behind it emerges a swarm of bees which attack Ray and Art. Mark Rumsfield (Bruce Dern), an unstable former military officer, quickly comes to his neighbors' rescue, spraying them both with a high-powered hose. The stung and stunned Ray and Art are shaken out of their shock by Mark's battle cry: It is time for the men on the cul-de-sac to take action and expose their nocturnal neighbors.

When a human femur bone is dug up by Ray's dog following the disappearance of a neighbor, Walter (Gale Gordon), and Hans is observed surreptitiously stuffing a huge garbage bag into the trash can, the men become convinced that the Klopeks have mutilated and murdered Walter for the purpose of a satanic ritual, throwing some of Walter into the garbage bag and burying the rest of him in the backyard. This interpretation gains further credence when Ray finds Walter's toupée while paying a disastrous social call on the Klopeks.

While the Klopeks are out, Ray and Art climb over the Klopeks' wall and begin digging randomly in the backyard, while Mark maintains a lookout from his roof. Hours pass as the Klopeks' yard begins to take on the configuration of Swiss cheese. Finding nothing, Ray and Art decide to try another tack: They break into the Klopeks' house and head for the cellar. Much to their amazement they find an enormous furnace, the source of the flashing light and piercing sounds. Having concluded that the furnace is a crematorium, Ray frantically starts digging below the furnace to unearth the corpses, which he believes are buried below. At the instant that Ray hits metal, thinking he has found the crypt, the Klopeks return with the police. Unfortunately, Ray has actually hit a gas line; as the police and the Klopeks get out of their cars, they are met by a terrified Art, followed by a thunderous explosion. Miraculously, a singed and blackened Ray walks out of the flames and falls into the hands of the waiting detectives.

Ray goes into a rage, threatening to kill Art for turning him into a raving, paranoid lunatic. Exhausted and spent, Ray flings himself on the ambulance stretcher and cries out to be taken to the hospital. As the doors to the ambulance close, the wicked Dr. Werner Klopek (Henry Gibson) goes after Ray with a hypodermic needle, believing that Ray has found the bones in Dr. Klopek's furnace belonging to the victims he has murdered in the name of research. As Ray struggles with the doctor, the stretcher on which they are fighting falls and runs into the Klopeks' car, forcing the trunk open and revealing a trunkload of corpses. At the end, Ray and Carol, arm in arm, walk away from the fiery scene and discuss their plans for an upcoming vacation.

The 'Burbs suffers from predictability, convention, and campiness. In a neighborhood littered with cardboard caricatures, the only character who appears lifelike is Tom Hanks's Ray. The viewer may be initially interested in Ray's character development but the series of misadventures which comprise the plot reveal no substance to his character.

Despite the anemic plot, director Joe Dante makes a laudable effort, often fooling the audience and thereby extracting unexpected humor. Especially noteworthy is Dante's ample use of camera shots: Reverse angles and closeups, and scenes reflected in windows, for example, sustain visual interest where story movement and involvement are lacking. Adept direction, however, cannot substitute for a good script; thus, *The 'Burbs* is consigned to mediocrity.

Jo Lauria

Reviews

Chicago Tribune. February 17, 1989, VII, p. 21.
Library Journal. CXIV, August, 1989, p. 176.
Los Angeles Times. February 17, 1989, VI, p. 6.
The New York Times. February 17, 1989, p. C12.
Newsweek. CXIII, March 6, 1989, p. 58.
People Weekly. XXXI, March 6, 1989, p. 17.
Seventeen. XLVIII, March, 1989, p. 128.
Time. CXXXIII, February 27, 1989, p. 81.
Variety. CCCXXXIV, February 22, 1989, p. 18.
Video. XIII, September, 1989, p. 91.
The Washington Post. February 17, 1989, p. C6.

CAMILLE CLAUDEL

Origin: France
Released: 1988
Released in U.S.: 1989
Production: Christian Fechner; released by Orion Classics
Direction: Bruno Nuytten
Screenplay: Bruno Nuytten and Marilyn Goldin; based on the biography by Reine-Marie Paris
Cinematography: Pierre Lhomme
Editing: Joëlle Hache and Jeanne Kef
Art direction: Bernard Vezat
Set decoration: Daniele Lagrande, Emmanuel de Chauvigny, and Charles Marty
Makeup: Thi Loan N'Guyen and Dominique Germain
Costume design: Dominique Borg
Sound: Guillaume Sciama
Music direction: Harry Rabinowitz
Music: Gabriel Yared
MPAA rating: R
Running time: 149 minutes

> *Principal characters:*
> Camille Claudel . . . . Isabelle Adjani
> Auguste Rodin . . . . Gérard Depardieu
> Mr. Claudel . . . . Alain Cuny
> Paul Claudel . . . . Laurent Grevill
> Blot . . . . Phillippe Clevenot
> Jessie . . . . Katrine Boorman
> Rose Beuret . . . . Daniele Lebrun
> Young lover . . . . Maxime Leroux
> Limet . . . . Jean-Pierre Sentier
> Morhardt . . . . Roger Planchon
> Louise . . . . Aurelle Doazan
> Victoire . . . . Madeleine Marie
> Madame Claudel . . . . Madeleine Robinson

Camille Claudel culminates nearly a decade of growing interest in the real-life Claudel, the pupil and lover of the great turn-of-the-century sculptor Auguste Rodin and the sister of the celebrated Catholic poet and playwright Paul Claudel. The film has also created an art-world uproar for its denigration of Rodin's genius and its elevation of Claudel's creative status. Camille Claudel was first brought to widespread attention by Anne Delbée through her play *Une Femme: Camille Claudel* (1981) and her biography *Une Femme* (1982). Since then, Claudel has been a French *cause célèbre*, the sculptress being seen by many observers as the real creative force behind some of Rodin's best pieces. Galleries have devoted special exhibitions to her sculptures, and there have been numerous television programs, books, and magazine articles on Claudel's life and work.

The film *Camille Claudel* was a five-year project of the French actress Isabelle Adjani, who bought the rights to the biography by Reine-Marie Paris (Camille's grand-niece), won exclusive access to the Claudel family archives, and helped to produce and write the script for the film. She also stars in the film, which broke French box-office records during the 1988-1989 winter season. It swept the Caesar Awards (the French equivalent of the Academy Awards), winning the categories of Best Picture, Actress, Cinematography, Art Direction, and Costume Design.

The story begins in 1885. Camille Claudel (Adjani) runs away from a girls' boarding school. At a construction site, she scoops up handful after handful of moist clay and stuffs it into a cardboard suitcase. She wants to sculpt. Camille shares her dreams with her brother, Paul (Laurent Grevill), an aspiring poet. Her mother, Madame Claudel (Madeleine Robinson), disapproves of Camille's artistic ambitions, but her father, Mr. Claudel (Alain Cuny), secretly supports her.

Camille becomes an apprentice to Auguste Rodin (Gérard Depardieu), who uses her to boost his faltering inspiration. They begin a tempestuous love affair that causes a scandal and arouses the hostility of Rodin's longtime companion, Rose Beuret (Daniele Lebrun). Camille becomes pregnant and begs Rodin to marry her. Unaware of the pregnancy, he rejects her entreaties. The angry Rose attacks Camille with a red-hot poker. Leaving Rodin, Camille has an abortion, horrifying Paul, who has converted to Catholicism and embarked on a promising career overseas with support from Rodin, whom he hates. Camille resumes her own career with some success. After briefly reconciling with Rodin, she leaves again when he insists that she give up all of her own ideas.

Camille begins to abuse drink and drugs. A one-woman show brings no sales, while Paul, shocked at the change in his sister, abandons her. Becoming totally paranoid, Camille destroys her sculptures. The film ends with her being committed by her family to a mental institution, where she died in 1943.

Adjani dominates the screen as her Camille runs the gamut from amorous to childish and from strong-willed to weepy. Adjani, however, seems, as yet, to lack the depth or range to portray convincingly a woman aging from girlhood to forty-nine and descending from a confident artist to a paranoid drunk. Depardieu sculpts a powerful, economical portrait of Rodin as man and artist. Outshining both Adjani and Depardieu, however, is Alain Cuny, who evokes remarkably subtle resonances in his sensitive characterization as the father of Camille and Paul.

Camille Claudel is the first directorial effort of the fine cinematographer Bruno Nuytten. While the film is too long and sometimes confusingly elliptical about the passage of time, Nuytten does fashion some strikingly well-textured sequences, particularly those illuminating the processes of creativity. In one, for example, Camille allows her model a rest from his pose, whereupon Rodin advises her never to spare a model. In another, Rodin, absorbed in his vision for a sculpture, abstractly contorts a naked female model into a tight ball of anguish.

The technical work on *Camille Claudel* is outstanding. Period feeling is beautifully captured in Pierre Lhomme's cinematography, Bernard Vezat's art direction, and Dominique Borg's costumes. The Paris of the time is carefully reconstituted, with the noises of workers erecting a half-finished Eiffel Tower and laying the city's new boulevards echoing the artists' sounds of chisel and hammer on marble. Sculptures used in the film were created by a team of fine artists headed by Hervé Boutard.

The film's great weakness lies in its script, written by Nuytten, Marilyn Goldin, and, uncredited, Adjani. The story impugns Rodin's creativity and exalts that of Camille, yet the film never clearly establishes her individual artistic identity. Instead, the writers merely evoke sympathy for her by showing her as the victim of her mother's lack of understanding, of Rose's jealousy, of Paul's abandonment, and of Rodin's artistic rape of her by appropriating her ideas ("From now on, I forbid you to do anything without asking my permission!"). At the end of the film, the pathetic face of Camille the overdrawn martyr is seen behind the bars of a horse-drawn wagon taking her to the asylum.

Darryl Lyman

Reviews
The Economist. CCCXI, April 8, 1989, p. 106.
The Guardian. January 17, 1989, p. 36.
Harper's Bazaar. CXXII, December, 1989, 168.
Los Angeles Times. December 21, 1989, VI, p. 11.
Monthly Film Bulletin. LVI, April, 1989, p. 108.
The New York Times. December 22, 1989, p. C20.
Punch. CCXCVI, April 14, 1989, p. 49.
Variety. CCCXXXIII, January 4, 1989, p. 14.
Vogue. CLXXIX, March, 1989, p. 498.
World Press Review. XXXVI, March, 1989, p. 36.

CASUALTIES OF WAR

Production: Art Linson; released by Columbia Pictures
Direction: Brian DePalma
Screenplay: David Rabe; based on the book by Daniel Lang
Cinematography: Stephen H. Burum
Editing: Bill Pankow
Production design: Wolf Kroeger
Art direction: Bernard Hydes
Set decoration: Hugh Scaife
Special effects: Kit West, Yves DeBono, Trevor Neighbour, Trevor Wood, Terry Cox, and John Baker
Makeup: Paul Engelen
Costume design: Richard Bruno
Sound: Gary Wilkins
Music: Ennio Morricone
MPAA rating: R
Running time: 113 minutes

Principal characters:
Eriksson............................ Michael J. Fox
Meserve .... Sean Penn
Clark .... Don Harvey
Hatcher............................. John C. Reilly
Diaz .... John Leguizamo
Oahn .... Thuy Thu Le
Brown .... Erik King
Rowan .... Jack Gwaltney
Lieutenant Reilly...................... Ving Rhames
Hawthorne .... Dan Martin
Chaplain Kirk .... Sam Robards

The treatment of the Vietnam War in film has come a long way since the jingoistic *The Green Berets* (1968). The negative response to this film and the major divisions in American society over the war itself resulted in the absence of any further Vietnam War films until the close of the war. Shortly after the war, there appeared the classic, more metaphorical and less political works such as *Coming Home* (1978), *The Deer Hunter* (1978), and *Apocalypse Now* (1979). Not until *The Killing Fields* (1984), however, did films begin to offer greater insight into the human and political natures of the war. In a sense, it helped create a climate that would later foster productions such as *Hamburger Hill* (1987), *Gardens of Stone* (1987), *Full Metal Jacket* (1987), and particularly *Platoon* (1986). In viewing the plethora of films in this subgenre of the war film, one wonders whether a film such as director Brian DePalma's *Casualties of War* increases one's comprehension of the war.

During an intense firefight in the jungles of Vietnam, Private Eriksson (Michael J. Fox) suddenly finds himself dangling precariously in a caved-in Vietcong tunnel. Literally inches from losing his life to a Vietcong guerrilla, he is saved by his tough squadron leader, Sergeant Meserve (Sean Penn). A short time later, when the squadron's reflexes are relaxed in a seemingly peaceful hamlet, a sniper's bullet mortally wounds one of their comrades, Brown (Erik King). As frustrations mount, the five-man squadron is assigned to a high-powered extensive reconnaissance mission. Although they are told that the nearby brothel is off-limits, their frustrations find a new avenue of release.

Meserve decides to kidnap a young village girl, Oahn (Thuy Thu Le), for portable recreation, much to the surprise of Eriksson. What follows is a gruesome rape of the trembling girl by the four members of the squadron. Eriksson remains helpless to prevent the violent rape. A heavy engagement with the enemy fortunately cuts short their entertainment. Fearing any ensuing problems, they shoot the girl. Once back in camp, Eriksson's guilt drives him to try to bring the squadron members to justice. From all sides he encounters bureaucratic red tape until a chaplain (Sam Robards) finally comes to his assistance. Meserve and his men are subsequently tried, convicted, and sentenced for their crime.

This entire nightmarish scene unfolds in Eriksson's mind as he observes a young Asian girl on the San Francisco subway. His soul remains indelibly scarred by the memory. In the early stages of the Vietnam War, journalist Daniel Lang revealed this tragic episode to the public in an article in *The New Yorker* in October, 1969, and then in a book. When DePalma read this soul-searing work, he believed that it "brought the whole experience of what happens to a group of young boys in Vietnam into focus, and detailed how the experience of the war changes them and how they deal with really strong ethical problems in the field."

Using this basic raw material, DePalma worked closely with David Rabe, a Vietnam War veteran and playwright—he wrote a trilogy of plays about the Vietnam War—in order to craft a very tense, realistic drama. To achieve utter authenticity, DePalma filmed in Thailand, where the jungle climate best resembled that of Vietnam. The director then had the actors put through two intense weeks of military training with retired Vietnam veterans. Only in this milieu and with this preparation could Penn, Fox, and the others begin to comprehend the mind-set of the young men in Vietnam, trapped in moral ambiguity.

The My Lai massacre may have overshadowed any other war crimes in Vietnam, yet the incident graphically depicted in *Casualties of War* is just as serious, although on a smaller scale. The film challenges the viewer to reexamine behavior in war, especially by offering a realistic context in which several human beings must make certain ethical choices.

To portray the opposing sides of the moral issues of rape and murder, DePalma skillfully employs the talents of Sean Penn as the quasi-charismatic leader and

Michael J. Fox as the raw recruit. Both characters evolve very differently over the course of the film in the light of the sexual manipulation of the kidnapped Vietnamese girl. Penn's character, Meserve, evolves from a seasoned and respected squadron leader to a violent, sex-driven psychotic, who eventually must pay for his crimes. The character of Eriksson, remarkably played by Fox, is even more nuanced. Eriksson grows from incredulity to guilt, and then from self-doubt to moral decisiveness as he attempts to bring to justice the man who saved his life. Some may criticize the obvious polarity of the two characters. Considering their gradual development over the course of the film, however, the contrast is a fine, rational choice for the director, since it provides the keen tension and multiple perspectives necessary to elucidate the issue. Furthermore, the film raises questions about ethics in war, questions deeply rooted in Western consciousness since the Nuremberg Trials in 1945-1946. With the inclusion of the ethical dimension in the film, DePalma has created a film that stands apart from the earlier Vietnam War productions, thus seriously advancing this subgenre.

In essence, DePalma states blatantly in *Casualties of War* that Oahn was not the only casualty of the Vietnam War, or even the most significant one in the film. Meserve and his comrades must also be considered victims, for they were not sufficiently trained to face moral dilemmas in the field. Ultimately, DePalma suggests that the United States is the greatest casualty because of the incredible havoc that the war has wreaked upon American society.

John J. Michalczyk

Reviews

Commonweal. CXVI, September 22, 1989, p. 502.
Film Comment. XXV, July, 1989, p. 49.
Films in Review. XL, December, 1989, p. 615.
Los Angeles Times. August 18, 1989, VI, p. 1.
The Nation. CCXLIX, September 4, 1989, p. 252.
National Review. XLI, September 29, 1989, p. 63.
The New Republic. CCI, October 2, 1989, p. 26.
New York Magazine. XXII, August 28, 1989, p. 53.
The New York Times. August 18, 1989, p. C10.
The New York Times Magazine. May 21, 1989, p. 24.
The New Yorker. LXV, August 21, 1989, p. 76.
Newsweek. CXIV, August 21, 1989, p. 58.
People Weekly. XXXII, August 28, 1989, p. 17.
Premiere. III, October, 1989, p. 85.
Rolling Stone. September 7, 1989, p. 31.
Time. CXXXIV, August 21, 1989, p. 54.
Variety. CCCXXXVI, August 16, 1989, p. 20.

CINEMA PARADISO

Origin: Italy and France
Released: 1989
Released in U.S.: 1990
Production: Franco Cristaldi (AA); released by Miramax Films
Direction: Giuseppe Tornatore
Screenplay: Giuseppe Tornatore
Cinematography: Blasco Giurato
Editing: Mario Mora
Production design: Andrea Crisanti
Makeup: Maurizio Trani
Costume design: Beatrice Bordone
Music: Ennio Morricone
Song: Andrea Morricone
MPAA rating: no listing
Running time: 123 minutes

  Principal characters:
    Alfredo . . . . Philippe Noiret
    Salvatore Di Vitto (adult) . . . . Jacques Perrin
    Salvatore Di Vitto (child). . . . . Salvatore Cascio
    Salvatore Di Vitto (adolescent). . . . . Marco Leonardi
    Elena . . . . Agnese Nano
    Young Maria . . . . Antonella Attili
    Anna. . . . . Isa Danielli
    Old Maria . . . . Pupella Maggio
    Father Adelfio . . . . Leopoldo Trieste
    Spaccafico. . . . . Enzo Cannavale
    Bill sticker . . . . Leo Gullotta
    Blacksmith . . . . Tano Cimarosa
    Madman. . . . . Nicolo Di Pinto
    Lia. . . . . Roberta Lena
    Peppino's father. . . . . Nino Terzo

Almost everyone loves films. Giuseppe Tornatore, the writer/director of *Cinema Paradiso*, seems to know that, and he is not concerned with the few immovable people in the world who make up the exception to this rule. *Cinema Paradiso*, the film and the small, Sicilian theater for which the film is named, are filled with people who seem to savor every frame of every film they see, and the films they see seem to be made for everyone. For its celebration of the cinema, *Cinema Paradiso* won the Academy Award for Best Foreign-Language Film.

The attendance at Cinema Paradiso, in the small town of Giancaldo, is never less than standing room only. There are children in the front who take delight in roaring back at the Metro-Goldwyn-Mayer lion and lovers who stand in the back and have sex when they think they can get away with it. Town pranksters do their dirty work on the man who always falls asleep, and the snob in the balcony continually spits on the folks below. The Paradiso is more than a motion-picture house; it is a participatory theater where the personalities and eccentricities of the townspeople are played out.

The film follows the life of Salvatore Di Vittò (played alternately by Jacques Perrin as the adult, Salvatore Cascio as the child, and Marco Leonardi as the adolescent), who is first introduced in his silver-haired middle age but who soon returns, through flashback, to his childhood in postwar Sicily. This was a time when, in this particular town, the cinema was a service of the local church. The pastor, Father Adelfio (Leopoldo Trieste), had the final say over what stayed in every film and what did not; those scenes that were cut were, for example, benign acts of Hollywood violence, and any kiss, however genteel, between two adults.

It was during the pastor's private screening that Salvatore, then called "Toto" (Salvatore Cascio), first befriends Alfredo (Philippe Noiret), the town's only projectionist. Toto hides in the lobby, peeking through the doorway, watching each week's film in its entirety, and then sits with Alfredo as he edits the film to the pastor's demands. In this town of motion-picture fans, no one is more star struck than Toto. He pleads with Alfredo to let him keep the pieces of film that were censored. Alfredo refuses, telling Toto that he has to return the complete film to the company, so Toto manages to satisfy himself with whatever tiny trims he can steal, unnoticed.

As Toto, eight-year-old Cascio is irresistibly endearing. Cuteness can often turn sickening, but Cascio also possesses an intelligence that informs his expression and delivery, and he keeps up bravely with the adults who surround him. According to the film's press notes, Tornatore conducted a huge search in casting the role of Toto, and it paid off remarkably well. The role of Alfredo calls for someone who fits the title "screen veteran." The French Noiret is perfect. Like Sean Connery, Yves Montand, and Robert Mitchum, he displays that mixture of roughness, charm, and, above all, wisdom that makes him invaluable in this kind of role.

The film is set in the days before safety film, which is fire resistant, and, as Toto becomes Alfredo's apprentice, he is warned of how quickly and lethally a reel in the projector can catch fire. The warning proves to be a foreshadowing, for Alfredo himself is later caught in a flash fire, blinding him and leaving Toto the only capable projectionist in Giancaldo. The burned Cinema Paradiso is bought and resurrected by a local lottery winner, and Toto is put at the helm in the new projection room. No longer under the blade of the Church, the Nuovo Cinema Paradiso shows its films uncut, and the audience roars in applause at the first sight of a screen kiss.

As Salvatore grows up, he falls in love while filming a young woman, Elena (Agnese Nano), with a home motion-picture camera. When Toto was young, Alfredo had told him that as he grew older, more mundane, realistic things than motion pictures would become important. Yet, when the adolescent Salvatore seeks guidance in love, Alfredo spins a fantastic, romantic yarn—not unlike a Hollywood film—that even he does not find relevant. Salvatore, however, finds relevance in it and lives out the story in winning Elena's heart.

Eventually, Salvatore leaves Giancaldo, and Alfredo tells him, in his last bit of advice, never to return and that holding onto the past will keep him from going forward. Salvatore finds a successful career as a filmmaker, and he follows Alfredo's advice for thirty years. When Alfredo dies, Salvatore does return for the funeral and finds that the old man has left him something—a dusty film canister. By great, sad coincidence, the Cinema Paradiso has been marked for destruction during Salvatore's visit. He stands among all the old, familiar faces of the town as they watch the demolition of the crumbling theater.

Salvatore returns to Rome and his private screening room, where he has his projectionist play the reel of film left in the old canister by Alfredo. He is treated to a long montage of all the amorous clips that Alfredo had to remove from the films—scores of lovers embracing, kissing, and tumbling over each other, with an occasional, playful flash of breasts. This final sequence plays like Chuck Workman's brilliant short, *Precious Images* (1988), in which only a few, carefully selected frames of a film are used to bring all the emotions of that film rushing back. Hundreds of clips from hundreds of films spliced together make for an almost euphoric experience that reminds the viewer why motion pictures exert such a universal appeal.

More than merely a paean to the filmgoing experience, however, *Cinema Paradiso* is an examination of change. Times change, people change, and so do their priorities. Salvatore's memories of childhood are surrealistically blissful. No townful of people could ever really be this constantly joyous. Yet in these scenes, the audience believes, along with Toto, that going to see films may be the highest purpose for living. The adult Salvatore's complete cycle of change is evident in that, though he appears to be enormously wealthy, he makes no attempt to save the condemned Cinema Paradiso. Though no such thing is ever articulated, the message of the final scenes seems to be that Salvatore has finally internalized Alfredo's advice: He can always indulge in nostalgia, but trying to keep the past alive is fruitless.

In Salvatore's teen years, the film loses its narrative focus. Tornatore is most assured in his direction of the first and third acts. He seems to wait out the insecurities of adolescence to get out of Giancaldo, to Salvatore's more sobering years, when he can bring his story full circle. The shimmering exception is the film's one love scene, in which the teenage Salvatore and Elena meet each other in the rain at a makeshift outdoor theater. Rain drenches the young lovers as they make love atop a Sicilian seawall, while behind them heroic images flicker across an impromptu screen. Every element of the scene is so perfectly conceived that the viewer imagines that it must have derived from Tornatore's own experience or that it has long been his most vivid fantasy.

How much importance does Tornatore actually place on motion pictures? Religion permeates the film: Toto was an altar boy, the Church ran the Paradiso during its early existence, and Toto woos Elena in a confession booth. Yet the Church is hardly revered by anyone in the film; the Paradiso is Giancaldo's most religiously attended gathering spot. Perhaps Tornatore's choice of the name "Salvatore" for his main character is a suggestion by the filmmaker that films can serve as a form of salvation.

Woody Allen used a small-town theater in *The Purple Rose of Cairo* (1985) as the means of escape for his central character, Cecilia, played by Mia Farrow. Cecilia gets involved with both a film character who miraculously steps off the screen to be with her, and the matinee idol who originally portrayed him. In the end, however, the film star has returned to Hollywood without taking her along, as he had promised, and the character has gone back into the film, of which all prints have been destroyed. Allen's film was, by turns, very amusing and very sad, and he chose the more somber as his final note, suggesting that fantasy is wonderful but, sooner or later, everyone must return to reality. Tornatore, with his one-two punch of the Paradiso's destruction and the final montage, proposes the inverse of Allen's film: While the mundane realities of adulthood eventually become necessary, a person can always turn to fantasy, through motion pictures or childhood memories, for escape.

Darrin Navarro

Reviews
Boston Globe. September 16, 1989, p. 9.
Premiere. III, December, 1989, p. 116.
Variety. CCCXXXIII, November 23, 1989, p. 20.

COMMUNION

Production: Philippe Mora, Whitley Strieber, and Dan Allingham for Pheasantry Films, in association with Allied Vision and The Picture Property Company; released by New Line Cinema and the Management Company Entertainment Group
Direction: Philippe Mora
Screenplay: Whitley Strieber; based on his book of the same name
Cinematography: Louis Irving
Editing: Lee Smith
Production design: Linda Pearl
Art direction: Dena Roth
Special visual effects: Michael McCracken, Michael McCracken, Jr., Jim Macpherson, and Steve Frakes
Makeup: Michelle Buhler
Costume design: Malissa Daniel
Sound: Ed White
Music: Eric Clapton and Allan Zavod
MPAA rating: R
Running time: 107 minutes

> *Principal characters:*
> Whitley Strieber . . . . Christopher Walken
> Anne Strieber. . . . . Lindsay Crouse
> Andrew Strieber. . . . . Joel Carson
> Dr. Janet Duffy . . . . Frances Sternhagen
> Alex . . . . Andreas Katsulas
> Sara. . . . . Terri Hanauer
> Dr. Freidman . . . . Basil Hoffman

For those who still swear by the adage that "truth is stranger than fiction," Philippe Mora's *Communion*, based on Whitley Strieber's best-selling 1987 nonfiction book, provides a strong counter-argument. Presented as a narrative rather than a documentary, the film is a somber, almost ill-humored re-creation of Strieber's purported encounters with alien visitors. Unfortunately, the filmmakers, beyond allowing for a few fictional characters, resist using dramatic license or stylistic influence to help them spruce up the production. Because of its documentarylike insistence on a prosaic depiction of factual material, *Communion* exists as a less satisfying work than the other, purely fictional examples of the alien visitation genre. It lacks the backward peculiarity of Tobe Hooper's *Invaders from Mars* (1986), the tongue-in-cheek approach of Michael Laughlin's *Strange Invaders* (1983), and the wondrous enchantment of Steven Spielberg's *Close Encounters of the Third Kind* (1977) and *E.T.: The Extra-Terrestrial* (1982). What it does have, however, is an incredible premise that, if true, is undeniably intriguing.

Author Whitley Strieber claims that, in late December of 1985, he was abducted by nonhuman creatures—a mind-boggling experience that left him suffering from extreme fear and crippling self-doubt. Strieber was later coaxed by his frightened wife and concerned friends to undergo tests by both brain specialists and professional psychologists. After months of therapy that included lengthy sessions of hypnotism, Strieber discovered that throughout his life, he had been experiencing similar alien visits and dismissing them as a product of his subconscious. Meeting with others who claimed to have the same kind of experiences, Strieber began to accept the aliens as a significant, enigmatic power and determined that, in order to comprehend a greater truth, the human population should face these beings with an open mind. Therefore, to deliver his message, Strieber wrote *Communion*, which went on to become the third best-selling paperback of 1988. Wanting to extend his message to a new and greater audience, Strieber decided to write and produce a film version of *Communion*.

The film begins with the usually goofy Strieber (Christopher Walken) suffering from a severe case of writer's block. In an attempt to get his creativity back on track, he takes his wife Anne (Lindsay Crouse) and young son Andrew (Joel Carson) to the family cottage for a quiet weekend. Joining them are friends Alex (Andreas Katsulas) and Sara (Terri Hanauer), who later become eyewitnesses to a night of glowing lights and loud explosions disturbing enough to send them packing the next day. The Striebers quickly dismiss the mysterious evening, but Whitley, days later, finds himself slipping into fits of extreme fear and irritability. For the next several months, Whitley's paranoia begins to eat away at the formerly warm, loving family unit. Anne becomes so exasperated that she begins to think about leaving her husband, and Andrew becomes so frightened that he can hardly stand being near his father.

In the film's first quarter, director Philippe Mora's experience as a documentary filmmaker begins to hinder his ability to convey the inherent drama of the narrative. In the early 1970's, Mora gained considerable acclaim for two award-winning documentaries, *Swastika* (1974) and *Brother, Can You Spare A Dime?* (1975), the latter of which is a compilation of images from the 1930's using excerpts from old motion pictures and newsreel footage. Mora tackles Whitley Strieber's real-life story with the same approach he might take to a non-narrative film; he presents his characters impartially, allowing the audience to take them at face value. Little is revealed about the characters other than their participation in the life of Whitley Strieber. Consequently, none of the participants except for Whitley expands to three dimensions, and, as Whitley's family begins to deteriorate, the viewer develops little compassion or concern for the situation. Strieber's script fares no better; seemingly concerned with reporting only the action, it does not provide commentary. This prosaic inclination becomes quite a problem in the film, which, for much of its first half, resembles a domestic drama rather than a science-fiction thriller.

The troubled Striebers return to their cabin for Christmas and begin to ease back into the comfortable routines of normal family life. Suddenly, on the night after Christmas, Whitley is thrown back into his nightmare when the aliens return to his home. He remembers being taken away by hooded, gnomelike creatures, poked and prodded by strange surgical instruments, and sodomized by a long tube. After the abduction, Whitley remembers only pieces of the horrific experience. He again falls into a panic and, thinking that his wife is yet another alien prowler, he almost kills her. Anne declares that she has had enough, and if Whitley does not seek psychiatric help she will divorce him. Whitley struggles with the fear that he is losing his mind, not accepting the conclusion that he has been victimized by beings from another world.

Back in New York, Whitley confides in his personal physician, Dr. Friedman (Basil Hoffman), who, after a thorough examination, determines that Whitley is not psychotic but the victim of a physical assault. Freidman refers him to Dr. Janet Duffy (Frances Sternhagen), a psychiatrist with experience in dealing with assault victims. Duffy, who believes that many victims are successful in pushing their assault experiences into their subconscious, puts him under several sessions of hypnosis, during which an entire series of alien encounters is revealed. Even as a child, Whitley seems to have been a subject of alien scrutiny. Anne undergoes hypnosis as well, and she is able to corroborate Whitley's claims when she relives her own experiences as eyewitness to the abductions of her husband.

Still unable to accept the reality of the situation, Dr. Duffy urges Whitley to attend an encounter group. During the meeting, the participants describe their own experiences with nonhumans—all remarkably similar to Whitley's own. Whitley then learns that his son Andrew also remembers various nights of strange occurrences, suggesting some kind of twisted family legacy.

Communion gains considerable momentum from the possibility that such alien visits may have become commonplace in the United States. With so many people adding their own tales to the fire, the unquestionable truth of Whitley's experience is overwhelming. The film negates this climax, however, by following the support group sequences with a ridiculous segment in which Strieber, wanting to know more about his own involvement with the creatures, returns to the country to seek them out. Inside the alien lair, he watches a vision of himself mixing socially with the strange beings. Realizing his unique relationship with the aliens, Strieber finally begins to accept the existence of extraterrestrial friends. This episode makes the alien encounters singular only to Strieber and serves to weaken the power given to the film by the idea of communal experience.

Strieber soon reaches the conclusion that there are intelligent nonhumans in the universe and that their existence should not be taken lightly by humankind. Having returned to his normal, sensitive self, Strieber sits down at his computer to work on his book and sees the face of a nonhuman above him. He reaches up to pull the alien mask out of the air, and the film concludes with the communion between the writer and his subject.

The depiction of Whitley Strieber's reluctance to face the truth by Christopher

Walken is solid and believable. An Academy Award-winner for his supporting role in Michael Cimino's *The Deer Hunter* (1978), the actor has made a career of playing strange characters who waver between sanity and psychosis. A brilliant performance is an unusual highlight for a science-fiction film, but Walken's typically pained, evasive performance as Whitley provides *Communion* with several extremely engaging moments. Additional help comes from the sound track, created by popular musician Eric Clapton, which underscores the eerie instability of the Strieber character. Lindsay Crouse as Strieber's wife breathes considerable life into what is no more than a cardboard character.

Although most film critics dismissed *Communion*, Strieber's 1987 book was respected by reviewers. The American public must also have taken Strieber's claims seriously because the writer was able to sell more than two million copies of the book. What works on paper however, does not always work on the screen. In print, Strieber's descriptions of his alien friends may have been both intriguing and horrifying, but when these images are translated so literally to the medium of film, they become silly and absurd. The film's special effects team may have wanted to create frightening space creatures but have produced only another variation of the stereotypical, eggheaded, long-limbed alien. Other members of the extraterrestrial gang appear as mumbling, hooded dwarfs or skinny, hyperactive robots. Given these substandard special effects, *Communion* is forced to rely too heavily on Mora's misguided direction and Strieber's reportorial script. Without a sense of style, the film, desperate for a sense of humor, ends up taking itself much too seriously.

Greg Changnon

Reviews
Boston Globe. November 10, 1989, p. 83.
Chicago Tribune. November 14, 1989, VII, p. 2.
The Christian Science Monitor. November 17, 1989, p. 10.
Cinéfantastique. XX, January, 1990, p. 40.
Los Angeles Times. November 10, 1989, VI, p. 10.
The New York Times. November 10, 1989, p. C8.
People Weekly. XXXII, November 27, 1989, p. 19.
San Francisco Chronicle. November 11, 1989. p. C6.
Variety. CCCXXXV, May 10, 1989, p. 24.
The Washington Post. November 11, 1989, p. C5.

CRIMES AND MISDEMEANORS

Production: Robert Greenhut; released by Orion Pictures
Direction: Woody Allen
Screenplay: Woody Allen
Cinematography: Sven Nykvist
Editing: Susan E. Morse
Production design: Santo Loquasto
Art direction: Speed Hopkins
Set decoration: Susan Bode
Makeup: Fern Buchner and Frances Kolar
Costume design: Jeffrey Kurland
Sound: Frank Graziadei and Bob Hein
Music direction: Joe Malin
MPAA rating: PG-13
Running time: 105 minutes

Principal characters:
Judah Rosenthal . . . . Martin Landau
Miriam Rosenthal . . . . Claire Bloom
Dolores Paley . . . . Anjelica Huston
Cliff Stern . . . . Woody Allen
Lester . . . . Alan Alda
Jack Rosenthal . . . . Jerry Orbach
Ben . . . . Sam Waterston
Halley Reed . . . . Mia Farrow

In the course of the 1980's, Woody Allen emerged as the United States' most prolific and perhaps only genuine film auteur. Immediately upon the release of *Crimes and Misdemeanors*, the nineteenth film he has written and directed, critics hailed it as one of the best films of the year, most definitely a new jewel in the Allen crown, and arguably his best film to date. The film's narrative strategy, hinted at in the title, is to probe the moral nuances of illicit behavior through two independent narratives, one comic and one dramatic.

Crimes and Misdemeanors opens at a dinner honoring Judah Rosenthal (Martin Landau), a socially prominent ophthalmologist and philanthropist. He is flanked by his wife and college-age children, suggesting a model family. The audience soon discovers, however, that Judah has been involved with Dolores Paley (Anjelica Huston), an airline stewardess. She has been led to believe that Judah will leave his family and is now impatiently demanding a face-to-face confrontation with Judah's wife. Judah puts her off, and she reacts with ever bolder initiatives: letters to Judah's wife sent to the Rosenthal home, telephone calls asking for his wife, and threats to appear at the door. Wishing to be rid of Dolores yet unwilling to confess his affair to his wife, Judah is emotionally at sea. At this point, his problem appears to be in the misdemeanor category.

What proves to be a comic narrative centers on Cliff Stern (Woody Allen), an idealistic documentary filmmaker. Cliff's wife berates him for not achieving the success that has come to her brother Lester (Alan Alda), a successful television comedy producer. Cliff spends most of his time playing big brother to his niece, whom he takes to repertory film houses. On one of his visits with his niece, Cliff's sister tells him of a sordid affair she had had with a stranger, an affair that might have become violent. In many ways she is more hapless and lonely than her brother. Cliff's fortunes take an apparent upturn when his wife persuades Lester to let Cliff direct a public television documentary on his career. Cliff's first days on the job confirm that Lester is indeed as shallow and transparent as Cliff had always assumed. He also discovers that Lester uses his stardom to bed attractive young women, whom he promises to put in his next project.

The pressure on Judah intensifies when Dolores threatens to reveal that he has misappropriated charitable funds to keep his own affairs in order. Judah protests that the money has always been returned with interest, but he knows such a revelation will destroy his reputation. He seeks counsel "for a friend" from one of his patients, Ben (Sam Waterston), a rabbi who is going blind. Ben blandly suggests that all will be well if "the friend" will only be truthful. An unconvinced Judah meets with his brother Jack (Jerry Orbach), a man with criminal connections who immediately suggests the use of a professional killer. Judah is aghast but does not reject the idea as unthinkable.

In contrast to Judah, Cliff's life has become more positive. His filming of Lester had led him to meet Halley Reed (Mia Farrow), an attractive public television associate producer. Much to Cliff's joy, she shares his jaundiced view of Lester and his love of old films. Cliff shows her footage from his pet project, a study of Professor Louis Levy (Martin Bergmann), a survivor of the Nazi death camps who vigorously proclaims a loving and embracive view of life. Halley promises to talk to producers about making the film into a public television project.

Across town, Judah has agreed to the murder of Dolores and even summons the nerve to go to the scene of the crime, where, in the presence of her dead body, he removes letters and other materials that might link them. His control is very fragile, however, and he soon succumbs to emotional malaise. He eventually wanders to the house where he lived as a child and, in a haunting flashback sequence, recalls his father evoking Jewish morality at a family holiday dinner. The father warns all that "the eyes of God are on us always." Like the killer in Edgar Allan Poe's "The Tell-Tale Heart," Judah feels the need to confess. His brother reminds him that he is not alone in his guilt. There is a hint that Judah could be eliminated as Dolores was and the ironic insistence that Judah would be morally wrong to jeopardize his brother's well-being.

For Cliff, life continues to be blissful. He becomes so confident of his ability, wit, and new love that he puts together a rough cut of the Lester film that is bitingly truthful, hilariously satirizing Lester's sexual affairs and mocking his philosophical expositions on the nature of humor. Lester is not amused; Cliff is fired. More alarmed by what his wife's reaction will be than the dismissal itself, Cliff is pained only when he learns that his beloved Professor Levy, his apostle of hope, has committed suicide. Cliff turns to Halley, asking her to share his life and art. She shatters his expectations by telling him that she is going to London to accept a new position with exceptional career possibilities. They vow to stay in touch.

The film concludes with a party approximately a year later. Cliff has agreed to attend the party with his wife; it is to be their last public outing before a divorce. Among the guests are the Rosenthals. Lester, just returned from Europe, arrives late, and on his arm is his new wife, Halley. Cliff has not heard from her but has imagined their romance could be renewed. She tries to explain that Lester has better qualities than they had perceived. In the background, Ben, now totally blind, is more insistent than ever about the goodness of the world. A thoroughly disillusioned Cliff retreats to a music room, where he is momentarily joined by Judah, who is seeking some fresh air. Judah announces that no one's eyes are watching anyone. The seducer, embezzler, and murderer is almost serene. He will continue to be honored as an exemplary family man and community leader. Cliff has no way to fathom Judah's cryptic disclosure. All he knows is that the commercial artist has triumphed and the meek neither inherit the earth nor succeed in romantic contests with the powerful and arrogant. It is not surprising that the philosophers of life leap to their deaths.

The great risk and achievement of *Crimes and Misdemeanors* is its dual story line. If the two narratives were presented independently, two vastly different films would result. The comic narrative featuring the lovable but inept Woody Allen figure would reprise elements in films such as *Play It Again, Sam* (1972); the dramatic narrative, however, would have the menace of old *film noir* classics such as *Double Indemnity* (1944) without the confession that results in the victory of morality. The interlocked narratives are more than they would be as separate entities, with the light and dark elements creating an engaging dynamic from the opening to the closing sequences.

Much of the film's success, aside from the astute conception, writing, and direction of Allen, stems from the acting. As Judah Rosenthal, Martin Landau gives his best film performance ever, for which he earned an Academy Award nomination. He holds the audience's contempt at bay, even as he plans the murder, and the audience cares more about whether he will confess than what will happen to Dolores. Orbach submits another first-rate evocation of a tough guy who is not vicious and is more loyal to his own code of honor than his more honored brother is to his. Huston evokes sympathy for the mistress, but at the same time Dolores is so completely hysterical that there is no way she can be placated except through acceptance of her impractical terms.

On the comic side, Alda also delivers what may be his best film performance to date, winning the New York Film Critic's Award for Best Supporting Actor. He is somewhat likable yet despicable. Cliff's view of him is easy to understand, yet he may indeed have qualities to which Halley can genuinely respond. Allen plays the character he has been developing for two decades: a dreamy lover of old films and a charmer of children but an inept lover and an urban misfit unable to deal with the routines of everyday life.

The banality of evil has become a theme of numerous postwar films. Allen has given it a personal and domestic character rather than the usual public and political treatment. The motivations and mechanics of evil are also rendered in essentially mundane terms. Allen's evocation of organized religion via the Jewish faith is at once warm and respectful but dismissive. The rabbi is no less poignant a symbol for being as banal as the crimes and misdemeanors he cannot see, and the director is sorrowful, not gleeful, that it would appear that the eyes of God are not always on us, if ever.

Dan Georgakas

Reviews
Chicago Tribune. October 13, 1989, VII, p. 42.
The Christian Century. CVI, November 1, 1989, p. 991.
Films in Review. XL, December, 1989, p. 613.
Los Angeles Times. October 17, 1989, VI, p. 1.
The Nation. CCXLIX, November 13, 1989, p. 575.
The New Republic. November 13, 1989, p. 22.
New York Magazine. October 23, 1989, p. 124.
The New York Times. October 13, 1989, p. C19.
The New Yorker. LXV, October 30, 1989, p. 76.
Newsweek. CXIV, October 23, 1989, p. 67.
Time. CXXXIV, October 16, 1989, p. 82.
Variety. CCCXXXVI, October 11, 1989, p. 32.

DAD

Production: Joseph Stern and Gary David Goldberg for Amblin Entertainment; released by Universal
Direction: Gary David Goldberg
Screenplay: Gary David Goldberg; based on the novel by William Wharton
Cinematography: Jan Kiesser
Editing: Eric Sears
Production design: Jack DeGovia
Art direction: John R. Jensen
Set decoration: Thomas L. Roysden
Makeup: Dick Smith and Ken Diaz
Costume design: Molly Maginnis
Sound: Ron Judkins
Music: James Horner
MPAA rating: PG
Running time: 117 minutes

Principal characters:
Jake Tremont	Jack Lemmon
John Tremont	Ted Danson
Bette Tremont	Olympia Dukakis
Annie	Kathy Baker
Mario	Kevin Spacey
Billy	Ethan Hawke
Dr. Santana	J. T. Walsh
Dr. Chad	Zakes Mokae

Dad is a film about generational relationships, particularly those between fathers and sons. John Tremont (Ted Danson) is a successful stockbroker, totally consumed by his profession. His father, Jake (Jack Lemmon), and mother, Bette (Olympia Dukakis), have retired in California. The film opens with a bucolic dream scene in which a farmer (played by Lemmon's son, Chris), accompanied by his wife and four children, happily manages his modest farm. The dream dissolves to Jake and Bette preparing to eat breakfast; Bette has virtually assumed custodial care of her seventy-eight-year-old husband, even buttering his toast.

The Tremonts' routine is carefully orchestrated by Bette. Following breakfast they go to the grocery store, where Bette selects the groceries and Jake pushes the cart. The routine is shattered, however, when Bette collapses with a heart attack, turning Jake's carefully controlled world upside down. John, called from a company meeting by a desperate message from his sister Annie (Kathy Baker), flies to his parents' home, intending to stay only a few days. Annie immediately makes it clear that the crisis involves not only their mother but their father as well. The dominance

of his strong-willed wife has sapped Jake's vitality, and John realizes that his father is virtually lifeless—hesitant and dispirited.

John decides that he must revitalize his father, especially if Bette is seriously incapacitated by her attack. Together, John and Jake take over the domestic chores, washing the dishes and doing the laundry. Even though Jake has been an amateur automobile racer in the past, he has allowed Bette to do the driving for some time. John persuades Jake to take the driver's examination and to begin having a good time again. Meanwhile, Bette, who is recovering in the hospital, strives to regain control over Jake. As Jake spends more time with his son, he discovers unpleasant truths about John's business ethics. He is disturbed that John buys unproductive companies and closes them down, without concern for the workers. Jake has always been a worker, and he realizes that the world of work has dramatically changed. Before Jake's metamorphosis is complete, his grandson, Billy (Ethan Hawke), pays a surprise visit. John sees himself in Billy and realizes that the same relational questions will inevitably arise between them that have surfaced between him and Jake. At a subsequent dinner with the family, Bette, now recovered, is her old caustic self, and Jake declares that he is happy because the family is together. Thus, the film returns to the dreamworld of the simple farm life.

This romanticized dream is shattered by the reality of Jake's deteriorating health; when he is hospitalized, he is diagnosed as having cancer, a condition that he has feared almost irrationally. The super-professional attending physician, Dr. Santana (J. T. Walsh), contrary to John's express desire, reveals the fact to Jake. The resulting shock drives Jake into a semicomatose state. Once again he is treated custodially, this time by the physicians. John angrily carries his father from the hospital, declaring that he will care for him at home. John quickly learns, however, that caring for Jake is too much for him. Totally consumed with his father's care, John alienates Billy, who wants to help. Fortunately, John is referred to a specialist, an African physician, Dr. Chad (Zakes Mokae). When Annie asks her brother why he is suddenly so totally committed to his father, John explains that he has to prove that he is Jake's son, to be there when he dies, and to mark that moment. Miraculously, Jake suddenly emerges from his comatose state. Dr. Chad offers a medical reason but insists that loving and caring have also had their effect.

The ensuing weeks reveal a new Jake: Full of life, almost randy, he poses a definite threat to Bette, who sees her control over him slipping away. More disturbing to her, however, is that Jake is slipping into another world. He talks of a truck farm in New Jersey, of four—not two—children, and of a wife who is both sweet and supportive. The dream scenes, which have punctuated the film, are diagnosed as "successful schizophrenia." For years, Jake has escaped Bette's domination by transporting himself into this idyllic world.

Jake assumes leadership in the marriage, introducing himself and Bette to the neighbors and becoming the neighborhood baby-sitter. He decides to learn Japanese, but at the culminating Japanese dinner, complete with kimonos and Japanese phrase books, Bette explodes, crying out that she can take no more. John angrily confronts Bette and tells her that all Jake wants is his life back, that for years he stayed at a job that he hated, that he has loved Bette for fifty years, and that she should now let him enjoy the rest of his life. After pleading with John and Bette not to destroy their happiness, Jake flees to his refuge, the greenhouse, and to his beloved plants. Bette follows, and in a tender scene they are reconciled.

Jake's cancer returns. In their final scene together in the hospital, Jake tells John his favorite baseball story and makes the point that anything is possible if one shows up for work. Following Jake's death, John and Billy dress up once more in the crazy costumes that Jake had insisted on wearing during his last uproarious fling with life and, holding one of Jake's potted plants between them, bid him farewell.

Dad is director Gary David Goldberg's first full-length feature film. Goldberg, a longtime television writer and producer, made his reputation with the highly successful situation comedy *Family Ties*. Family ties are central to the plot of *Dad*, but the overall mood is much darker—almost relentlessly so. Critical opinion was not overly favorable, largely because the critics sensed a partial failure on Goldberg's part to transcend the television situation-comedy formula and provide a viable cinematic experience.

Goldberg was attracted to the novel *Dad*, by William Wharton, when the novel was first published in 1981; in 1983, Goldberg purchased the film rights. A principal reason for Goldberg's interest was the fact that his relationship with his own father so closely paralleled that described in Wharton's novel. In an interview with *The New York Times*, Goldberg describes himself as a wordsmith and stresses the difference between television writing and screenwriting, the latter emphasizing the visual over the verbal. Furthermore, he explains that in filming *Dad*, he had difficulty breaking away from the thirty-minute situation-comedy format to which he was accustomed.

Although Goldberg manages to overcome these difficulties to a large extent, he is not entirely successful. The episodic structure of the film shows in its organization around three major crises: the mother's heart attack, the father's mental and emotional shock upon learning that he has terminal cancer, and the father's subsequent death. The story's parallel with Goldberg's own experience has mixed results. The reality of the aging process, particularly the trauma of discovering one's mortality, is undeniable. John Tremont's feelings of sorrow, frustration, even rage, are realistically portrayed. At the same time, however, these feelings are partially vitiated by a heavy dose of sentiment and cliché. Goldberg has attempted to record genuine feeling, but one wishes that he had been able to distance himself and, consequently, his audience more successfully. One thinks, in this connection, of more satisfying depictions of familial relationships in such films as *I Never Sang for My Father* (1969), *On Golden Pond* (1981), or *A Sunday in the Country* (1984).

Dad succeeds in large measure because of a fine cast. Lemmon again proves himself to be an actor able to play a variety of roles and to melt into the character almost flawlessly. The old Jack Lemmon of the early comedies, such as *Mister Roberts* (1955), *Some Like It Hot* (1959), and *The Odd Couple* (1968), emerges briefly in the "comeback" period before Jake's death; some of the body language and comic delivery that Lemon used in those films appears beneath the aging surface. On the whole, Lemmon's rendering of Jake—whether spiritless and defeated or terrifying in his hallucinations—is genuine and believable. Dukakis plays a role similar to her role in *Moonstruck* (1987): the feisty, take-charge mother who cannot resist controlling others any more than she can hold back her sardonic one-liners.

The film is unexceptional in its cinematic technique. Except for the sepia dream scenes, the photography and camera movement and position are not unusual. The two-shot medium and the close-up photography are the predominant perspectives, and the *mise en scène* consists almost entirely of interior shots. These production values altogether reflect Goldberg's long involvement with television.

Norman Carson

Reviews
Chicago Tribune. October 27, 1989, VII, p. 50.
Cosmopolitan. CCVII, December, 1989, p. 52.
Films in Review. XLI, January, 1990, p. 42.
Los Angeles Times. October 27, 1989, VI, p. 1.
Maclean's. CII, November 6, 1989, p. 82.
The New York Times. October 27, 1989, p. C15.
The New Yorker. LXV, November 13, 1989, p. 119.
People Weekly. XXXII, November 6, 1989, p. 19.
Rolling Stone. XXXVIII, November 16, 1989, p. 38.
Variety. CCCXXXVII, October 25, 1989, p. 29.
The Wall Street Journal. October 26, 1989, p. 12.
The Washington Post. October 27, 1989, p. B1.

DEAD POETS SOCIETY

Production: Steven Haft, Paul Junger Witt, and Tony Thomas for Touchstone
   Pictures, in association with Silver Screen Partners IV; released by Buena Vista
Direction: Peter Weir
Screenplay: Tom Schulman (AA)
Cinematography: John Seale
Editing: William Anderson
Production design: Wendy Stites
Art direction: Sandy Veneziano
Set decoration: John Anderson
Special effects: Allen Hall
Makeup: Susan A. Cabral
Costume design: Eddie Marks
Sound: Charles Wilborn
Music: Maurice Jarre
MPAA rating: PG
Running time: 129 minutes

Principal characters:

John Keating	Robin Williams
Neil Perry	Robert Sean Leonard
Todd Anderson	Ethan Hawke
Knox Overstreet	Josh Charles
Charlie Dalton	Gale Hansen
Richard Cameron	Dylan Kussman
Steven Meeks	Allelon Ruggiero
Gerard Pitts	James Waterston
Gale Nolan	Norman Lloyd
Mr. Perry	Kurtwood Smith

The coming-of-age film occupies a significant position in cinema, primarily in
the light of the turbulent period of human life called adolescence. When the rite of
passage in this nebulous age takes place in a male boarding school, the film can
raise many unsettling questions about such topics as education, sexuality, and
psychology. Director Jean Vigo's *Zéro de conduite* (1933; *Zero for Conduct*),
Lindsay Anderson's *IF . . . .* (1968), and Larry Peerce's *A Separate Peace* (1972),
among others, offer diverse perspectives on the male adolescent often trapped in a
hermetic, suffocating milieu. Peter Weir's *Dead Poets Society* captures not only the
day-to-day, humdrum education of young boys force-fed some of the same "truths"
depicted in these earlier works but also key traumatic moments in their search for
personal truth.

When a freethinking English teacher, John Keating (Robin Williams), lands in

Vermont's Welton Academy in September, 1959, his presence creates a stir. For seven adolescents he becomes the catalyst for radical change in their souls. Whereas the conservative, ancient motto at the one-hundred-year-old Welton is "Tradition, Honor, Discipline, and Excellence," Keating urges nonconformity and creativity. Seduced by his unorthodox and liberating ideas, the young boys create a Dead Poets Society, like the one frequented by their teacher when he matriculated at the academy. The nocturnal gatherings of the secret society, directed by their leader, Neil Perry (Robert Sean Leonard), blend quasitribal music with classic poetry readings that reinforce their mentor's philosophy, illustrated by the Latin adage *carpe diem* (seize the day). Through these clandestine sessions in the cave and the various exercises in nonconformity in the classroom, where Walt Whitman, Robert Frost, and Henry David Thoreau become demigods, the young men evolve into free spirits. They leave behind them the collective masses, who, according to Thoreau, "lead lives of quiet desperation."

Keating's influence upon these youths becomes a major threat to the preservation of the Weltonian ideals. He is chastised by the headmaster, Gale Nolan (Norman Lloyd), for not following the traditional path of education. At the same time, Neil's father (Kurtwood Smith) forbids his dutiful son to perform the role of Puck in William Shakespeare's *A Midsummer Night's Dream*. Aspiring to a career in theater, Neil disobeys his father and creates a sensational Puck. Mr. Perry, however, attends this performance. As a result of his son's defiance, Mr. Perry decides to remove him from Welton and enroll him at a military academy. Mr. Perry thereby hopes to ensure that his son will assume a professional career. Trapped by his father's plans for him, Neil commits suicide. The headmaster blames Keating for corrupting the youth and forces him out of Welton. As he collects his personal belongings, Keating witnesses his most timid student, Todd Anderson (Ethan Hawke), defend him in front of the headmaster.

Dead Poets Society is a striking study in classical unity. Natural dialogue, vivid supporting images, provocative sounds, aesthetic symbols, and interrelated themes are carefully created to illustrate the claustrophobic life in an academy designed to supply society with prominent attorneys, bankers, doctors, and political figures.

The harsh reality and apparent naturalness of the boys' experiences can be readily understood. The clever, layered script—which won the year's Academy Award for Best Original Screenplay—with witty and colloquial 1950's dialogue echoes not only scriptwriter Tom Schulman's personal exposure to a similar institution but also that of director Peter Weir and lead actor Robin Williams, who also attended private schools. Their sensitivity to the material was contagious, quickly absorbed by the young actors in the presence of mentor Robin Williams. Over the ten-week production period at St. Andrew's School in Middletown, Delaware, the relationships developed among the boys filtered through their roles on the screen, creating the convincing rapport of the youths in the film. As their most influential teacher, Williams is radical, brilliant, but also humorous. His comedy, however, is not his usual manic monologue but is fresh, witty, and understated. In a rare moment of mimicry, he reveals how Marlon Brando would have delivered the lines, "Friends, Romans, and countrymen . . ." and John Wayne, "Is this a dagger I see before me?" Williams' performance earned for him an Academy Award nomination for Best Actor.

The visual and aural components of *Dead Poets Society*, rich and at times bordering on the excessively lush, serve as poignant vehicles for the narrative. Within the confines of the English Gothic-style academy, the roaming camera seizes upon the architectural beauty. Outdoors, it records the seasonal charms of New England as well as nocturnal romps through the eerie mist. Weir attributes much of the visual depth of these scenes to his collaboration with cinematographer John Seale; they have worked together since *Picnic at Hanging Rock* (1974).

Music is an integral part of the story and, especially, of the life of the highly cultivated John Keating. On the one hand, Maurice Jarre's compositions recall the lavish and emotional melodies he provided in *Dr. Zhivago* (1965) or *Lawrence of Arabia* (1962) as they link the film's titillating images, but in *Dead Poets Society* they are more understated than in his earlier film scores. On the other hand, in the context of the film, Keating makes use of music to raise the aesthetic level of his students. Incorporating Ludwig van Beethoven's music in the physical education program or in athletic contests appears both alluring and humorous. All these elements are carefully orchestrated to handle, reinforce, and illustrate the thematic core of the film. How successfully these elements hold together is evidenced by the fact that it was nominated by the Academy of Motion Picture Arts and Sciences for Best Picture.

Despite sometimes rigid characterization into representative "types" of students, occasionally overly evocative music and images, and the tragic suicide for which the narrative could have better prepared the viewer, the symbolic importance of the work cannot be discounted. Almost from the outset of the film the dramatic tension can be perceived: the classical conflict of the Dionysian (free-spirited) and the Apollonian (rational). It is only in the cave that the creative and primordial instincts of the youths can emerge. Once back in the traditional classroom, these instincts must be suppressed in view of Welton's cult of uniformity.

In Lindsay Anderson's *IF* . . . . the rebel students are brutally lashed by the upper-class "Whips" in order to make them conform. At the same time an underclassman observes through a microscope the absorption of some smaller bits of protoplasm into the larger organism. The message of the image is all too obvious. *Dead Poets Society* utilizes a vast gamut of similar imagery to reinforce Keating's ultimate attempt to instill in the students' hearts and minds the philosophy of Thoreau—"If a man does not keep pace, perhaps he hears a different drummer."

John J. Michalczyk

Reviews

America. CLXI, July 15, 1989, p. 40.
American Film: Magazine of the Film and Television Arts. XIV, July, 1989, p. 57.
Chicago Tribune. June 9, 1989, VII, p. 40.
Commonweal. CXVI, June 16, 1989, p. 372.
Films in Review. XL, December, 1989, p. 617.
Los Angeles Times. June 2, 1989, VI, p. 1.
Maclean's. CII, June 12, 1989, p. 52.
The New Republic. June 28, 1989, p. 26.
New York Magazine. XXII, June 12, 1989, p. 77.
The New York Times. June 2, 1989, p. C8.
The New Yorker. LXV, June 26, 1989, p. 70.
Newsweek. CXIII, June 12, 1989, p. 67.
People Weekly. June 12, 1989, p. 17.
Rolling Stone. June 29, 1989, p. 28.
Time. CXXXIII, June 5, 1989, p. 78.
Variety. CCCXXXV, May 31, 1989, p. 26.

DO THE RIGHT THING

Production: Spike Lee and Monty Ross for 40 Acres and a Mule Filmworks;
   released by Universal
Direction: Spike Lee
Screenplay: Spike Lee
Cinematography: Ernest Dickerson
Editing: Barry Alexander Brown
Production design: Wynn Thomas
Set decoration: Steve Rosse
Costume design: Ruth Carter
Sound: Skip Lievsay
Music: Bill Lee
Song: Carlton Ridenhour, Hank Shocklee, Eric Sadler, and Keith Shocklee, "Fight
   the Power"
MPAA rating: R
Running time: 120 minutes

   Principal characters:
   Mookie .... Spike Lee
   Sal .... Danny Aiello
   Da Mayor .... Ossie Davis
   Mother Sister .... Ruby Dee
   Vito .... Richard Edson
   Buggin Out .... Giancarlo Esposito
   Radio Raheem .... Bill Nunn
   Pino .... John Turturro
   ML .... Paul Benjamin
   Coconut Sid .... Frankie Faison
   Sweet Dick Willie .... Robin Harris
   Jade .... Joie Lee
   Clifton .... John Savage
   Mister Señor Love Daddy .... Sam Jackson
   Tina .... Rosie Perez
   Smiley .... Roger Guenveur Smith

   Do the Right Thing, produced, directed, and written by the black independent
filmmaker Spike Lee, arrived in theaters on June 30, 1989, amid an avalanche of
publicity and controversy. *The New York Times* ran at least five articles on the film:
three consecutive Sunday feature articles—including one entitled "Spike Lee's
Blacks: Are They Real People?"—and two separate reviews by Vincent Canby. *The
Village Voice* devoted eight separate articles to the film. Lee appeared on the covers
of *Newsweek, American Film: The Magazine of the Film and Television Arts,* and

the conservative *National Review*. In his column in *New York Magazine*, Joe Klein accused Lee of recklessly courting violent reactions from black youth, which Klein believed could jeopardize David Dinkins' race for mayor of New York City, to which Lee replied with a scathing full-page letter entitled "Say It Ain't So, Joe." Before *Newsweek* chose Lee for their cover, they made the almost unprecedented decision to run two reviews of the film, a positive one by David Ansen and a negative one by Jack Kroll. Both *The Oprah Winfrey Show* and *Nightline* devoted entire shows to the film's potential sociopolitical impact.

The controversy focused on Lee's open-ended treatment of racism in *Do the Right Thing*, with many critics stating that the film advocates violence as a means of confronting the problem. When white liberal filmmakers have tackled racism, they have cautiously banked their themes with noble pieties, such as in Alan Parker's *Mississippi Burning* (1988) and Richard Attenborough's *Cry Freedom* (1987). From the very beginning of *Do the Right Thing*, when the opening strains of the 1960's civil rights anthem "Lift Every Voice and Sing" make way for the harshly political urban rap song "Fight the Power," by Public Enemy, and the character Tina (Rosie Perez) wildly and edgily dances and shadowboxes through the film's opening credits, Lee puts his racism theme in the audience's face. What is particularly amazing about *Do the Right Thing*, however, is how Lee maintains sympathy, equanimity, and a slyly comic remove from his film's many characters throughout this entire process. The controversy surrounding the film continued during the award season. Many critics and reviewers had selected Spike Lee as the year's best director and also selected the film as the year's best. For the highly visible Academy Awards, however, *Do the Right Thing* was almost completely overlooked. It won nothing and was only nominated for the categories of Best Supporting Actor and Best Original Screenplay.

After the attention-grabbing title sequence, *Do the Right Thing* introduces its various characters with deceptive casualness. The film is set during one twenty-four-hour period on the hottest day of the summer on one block in the predominantly black Brooklyn neighborhood of Bedford-Stuyvesant. Each character is exhorted to wake up by the twenty-four-hour disc jockey, Mister Señor Love Daddy (Sam Jackson). Da Mayor (Ossie Davis) is the drunken but sweet-natured elder statesman of the block who likes to philosophize to the neighborhood's uninterested youngsters and who attempts to court the block's watchdog, Mother Sister (Ruby Dee). She remains steadfastly contemptuous of this "drunken fool." Mookie (Spike Lee) tries to avoid responsibility by living with his sister, Jade (Spike's real-life sister, Joie Lee), though he has a child by Tina, whom he sees only when looking to have sex. Mookie works just hard enough as a delivery boy for Sal's Famous Pizzeria to earn some much-loved cash, which he then counts religiously. The pizzeria is run by its paternalistic Italian owner, Sal (Danny Aiello), who drives into the neighborhood daily from Bensonhurst, Queens, with his two sons, the virulently racist Pino (John Turturro) and his gentle but dim-witted brother, Vito (Richard Edson).

Stirring things up on the block are Buggin Out (Giancarlo Esposito), an unproductive, rabble-rousing black militant who finds little support for his causes among the neighborhood's denizens; Radio Raheem (Bill Nunn), a quiet but imposing young man whose entire self-image revolves around his enormous ghetto blaster, on which he repeatedly plays Public Enemy's "Fight the Power"; and Smiley (Roger Guenveur Smith), a spastic stutterer, who is constantly hawking hand-colored pictures of Martin Luther King, Jr., and Malcolm X shaking hands. Smiley is an incoherent and embarrassing reminder of the two opposing roads of political action set forth by the two black leaders for these largely inactive blacks to follow. Two groups observe and comment upon the action on the block, a very amusing street-corner trio of sedentary men, ML (Paul Benjamin), Coconut Sid (Frankie Faison), and Sweet Dick Willie (Robin Harris), and a quartet of fun-loving, do-nothing teenagers, Ahmad (Steve White), Cee (Martin Lawrence), Punchy (Leonard Thomas), and Ella (Christa Rivers).

As the intense heat of the day wears on people's nerves, tempers begin to flare and arguments break out. Buggin Out demands that Sal add some photographs of black celebrities to the all-Italian Wall of Fame at the pizzeria; when Sal refuses, Buggin Out attempts unsuccessfully to organize a boycott of the restaurant. Sal berates Radio Raheem for playing his radio too loud in the pizzeria. Interactions between people increase in hostility. The tension increases until, at closing time, Buggin Out and Radio Raheem screamingly demand that Sal integrate his Wall of Fame; Sal, snapping, calls them "niggers" and smashes Radio Raheem's radio with a baseball bat. Radio Raheem attacks Sal and the police arrive to break up the fight; they put a chokehold on Radio Raheem that kills him. The enraged crowd, emotionally spiraling out of control, begins to riot. Mookie, angered by the oppressiveness that Sal's pizzeria has come to represent, throws a garbage can through its front window; the crowd follows his lead, looting, trashing, and burning the restaurant to the ground. Smiley steps through the flames to hang a photograph of King and Malcolm X on the wall. The wall is now integrated.

Spike Lee has remained a director of interest and substance since his hour-long New York University thesis in film, *Joe's Bed-Stuy Barbershop: We Cut Heads* (1982), won the Student Academy Award from the Academy of Motion Picture Arts and Sciences. In this film, a barber is torn between making an honest subsistence-level living and making more money by allowing an illegal bookie operation to use his shop as its headquarters. Lee's *She's Gotta Have It* (1986), made on a shoestring budget, was a stylish sex comedy about a woman trying to make peace with her own desire for sex with multiple partners and the demands that her disgruntled partners place upon her. *School Daze* (1988) was an ambitious attempt to make a musical comedy about the conflict between lighter-skinned and darker-skinned blacks on an all-black college campus, a sensational idea that maintained its fascination even as the film became bogged down with fraternity house antics and bathroom-level humor. With *Do the Right Thing*, however, Lee signals his arrival as an important filmmaker. Lee claims to have been inspired to make *Do the Right*

Thing by the Howard Beach incident in which a gang of white Italian Americans wielding baseball bats chased a black man onto a freeway, where he was killed by a passing car. It is a sure sign of Lee's maturity as an artist, however, that, even with such a volatile incident as his source of inspiration, he maintains a sympathetic and critical distance from his characters in this film. He does not look for scapegoats but is instead fascinated and amused by the color and variety of his characters' contradictory and sometimes hypocritical impulses. Lee's level of expertise as a writer, as a framer of images (with the help of his superb cinematographer, Ernest Dickerson), as a director of actors (who are all first-rate here), and as an actor himself has finally caught up with his always lofty ambition, with thrilling results.

Lee has developed a very personal free-form style. His approach to comedy does not impose a rigid situational structure on his characters (as in Blake Edwards' films) but takes its cues from the characters' own distinctive comic rhythms. Consequently, *Do the Right Thing* has empathy even for its broadest characters; rather than serving as plot functionaries, they instead seem crazily individualistic. Lee also has the confidence to interrupt the forward momentum of his plot with lyrical asides that either enhance the film's thematic power or enrich the film's cultural foundation. The most striking examples include a litany of ethnic slurs as various characters face the camera and unleash a torrent of racist abuse, aimed at every ethnic group imaginable, and a magical incantation by Mister Señor Love Daddy of many of the black musical artists who have influenced American culture. Yet, Lee has the dramatic authority to build this highly entertaining film to a powerful and tragic conclusion that is perhaps the most insightful examination ever put on film of racial conditions in the United States.

It is on this front that Lee has received the most criticism, precisely because he pitches his exploration of contemporary racial and class tension in the most honest way possible—with no easy explanations. As an evidently moral man, Lee presents the racist impulses of his characters, both black and white, as irrational. The violence erupts from matters of trivia and is therefore not morally defensible. Yet the violence is cathartic. Although most white people in the United States would clearly have felt more comfortable with *Do the Right Thing* if Lee had condemned the use of violence, Lee refuses to do so. He understands why his characters erupt into violence and chooses to make the viewer understand as well. Those critics who feared that audiences would be stimulated to violence have ignored the responsible way in which Lee treats the violence in the film. He presents the escalation of tension through petty insults and incidents, details the final eruption of violence that is both tragic and cathartic, and then carries it through to its aftermath, in which anger has been vented and his characters find ways to reconnect with each other and move on. Much attention has been paid to the fact that Lee closes the film with two quotations, one from Martin Luther King, Jr., which contends that violence is immoral and never a satisfactory solution to conflict, and the other by Malcolm X, which argues that violence used in self-defense is a sign of intelligence. Since the quotes (particularly that of Malcolm X) do not comment directly on the circumstances which the film depicts but rather on the themes which the film explores, they are clearly meant as stimulation for the film's dialectic on racial conflict to be carried out by the viewer outside the theater. This imaginative and daring film ends on a note of reflection, not provocation.

Jeffrey L. Fenner

Reviews

Chicago Tribune. June 25, 1989, XIII, p. 5.
The Christian Science Monitor. June 27, 1989, p. 15.
Commonweal. CXVI, July 14, 1989, p. 402.
Films in Review. XL, October, 1989, p. 484.
The Los Angeles Herald Examiner. June 30, 1989, p. 7.
Los Angeles Times. June 30, 1989, VI, p. 1.
National Review. August 4, 1989, p. 45.
The New Republic. CCI, July 3, 1989, p. 24.
New York. June 26, 1989, p. 53.
The New York Times. June 30, 1989, p. C16.
The New Yorker. LXV, July 24, 1989, p. 78.
Newsweek. CXIV, July 3, 1989, p. 64.
Time. CXXXIV, July 3, 1989, p. 62.
Variety. CCCXXXV, May 24, 1989, p. 26.
The Village Voice. July 11, 1989, p. 59.

DRIVING MISS DAISY

Production: Richard D. Zanuck (AA) and Lili Fini Zanuck (AA) for Zanuck Co.;
   released by Warner Bros.
Direction: Bruce Beresford
Screenplay: Alfred Uhry (AA); based on his play
Cinematography: Peter James
Editing: Mark Warner
Production design: Bruno Rubeo
Art direction: Victor Kempster
Set decoration: Crispian Sallis
Special effects: Bob Shelley
Makeup: Manlio Rocchetti (AA)
Costume design: Elizabeth McBride
Sound: Gloria S. Borders
Music: Hans Zimmer
MPAA rating: PG
Running time: 99 minutes

> *Principal characters:*
> Hoke Colburn . . . . Morgan Freeman
> Daisy Werthan . . . . Jessica Tandy (AA)
> Boolie Werthan . . . . Dan Aykroyd
> Florine Werthan . . . . Patti Lupone
> Idella . . . . Esther Rolle

Alfred Uhry never dreamed his play would have such phenomenal success. It was originally scheduled for a five-week engagement in the spring of 1987 at an Off-Broadway theater that seats only seventy-four people. Purely on its own merits, it attracted such attention that it had to be moved to a larger theater. Additional productions were established in Chicago, Los Angeles, Toronto, and Atlanta, with other companies touring the country; amazingly, productions opened in London, Vienna, Norway, the Soviet Union, and other foreign countries. Uhry was awarded the 1988 Pulitzer Prize and was commissioned to write the script for the screen adaptation that has brought the story to added millions.

Daisy Werthan (Jessica Tandy) does not want a chauffeur. She is, however, already seventy-two years old and no longer capable of driving safely, as she proves by crashing her Chrysler into the neighbor's garage. Her son Boolie (Dan Aykroyd) hires Hoke Colburn (Morgan Freeman) and establishes all the future conflict with the following lines: "Hoke, I want you to understand, my mother is a little high-strung. She doesn't want anybody driving her. But the fact is you'd be working for me. She can say anything she likes but she can't fire you." Hoke himself is sixty years old and desperately needs a job. As he tells Boolie, "They hirin' young if they hirin' colored, an' they ain' even hirin' much young, seems like." He offers Boolie rather dubious reassurance about his ability to handle Miss Daisy.

Boolie's mother's resistance to being chauffeured around town is anchored in her own character. She does not like to admit that she is getting old. Although she is fairly affluent, as the widow of a successful Atlanta textile manufacturer, she despises conspicuous displays of wealth. She grew up in poverty and was a schoolteacher before her marriage. Furthermore, she is sensitive about being Jewish in a region traditionally seething with bigotry and has strict ideas about how Jews ought to conduct themselves. In a sense, hers is a more delicate position than Hoke's. Both belong to hated minorities, but hers is a tiny minority whereas his minority is virtually the majority. She tells Hoke that he does not understand her when he is trying to persuade her to make more use of her new Hudson and his services. He agrees, saying that if he had her wealth he would flaunt it. When she explains that she does not want to pretend she is rich, Hoke replies, "You is rich, Miz Daisy," and his fully orchestrated, three-syllable pronunciation of the tiny word "is" brings the house down. He is not merely contradicting her but expressing surprise, protest, envy, reassurance, and incomprehension of the strange ways of white people in general.

Morgan Freeman, who also played Hoke in the original stage version, does such a splendid job that he steals the show even from Jessica Tandy, whose distinguished acting career dates back to 1925. He handles the black Southern dialect, which is the crowning glory of both the play and the film, with consummate virtuosity. He can get more meaning into the words "Miss Daisy" than anybody would suspect such simple words could contain. This is what delights audiences and evokes outbursts of laughter. The bickering between employer and chauffeur is reminiscent of the exchanges between Jack Benny and his factotum Rochester, which made all America laugh in the golden age of radio.

The film, like the play, is a series of vignettes covering twenty-five years in the lives of Daisy and Hoke, from 1948 to 1973. Hoke gradually insinuates himself into her favor through patience, gentleness, and instinctive diplomacy. The most revealing scene comes in the late 1950's, when they take their longest excursion by car and eventually get lost. At one point, they have stopped by the roadside to eat a lunch that the frugal Miss Daisy has prepared, when two Alabama state troopers appear. Though the officers look hardly old enough to be shaving, they make a point of calling the elderly Hoke "boy." They show formal Southern courtesy to Daisy but obviously despise her for being Jewish. After she and her chauffeur drive off, the camera studies Hoke's face and then shifts to a close shot of Miss Daisy in the back. Both are experiencing nearly identical emotions of humiliation, anger, and helplessness. Like oppressed people everywhere, these two individuals are putting on a brave front to hide their fear of a world that respects only power.

This encounter does not occur in the play. It is an example of how the author and director have performed the sensitive task of "opening up" a stage play in order to utilize the greater flexibility of the motion picture camera. In the play, the many activities involving automobiles have to be handled in the inhibited fashion that is unavoidable when large-scale action has to be represented on a stage; however, for cinematic purposes the story provides frequent opportunities to display old residential neighborhoods, the homely Southern landscape, and a succession of classic automobiles. More than the homes, the furniture, the clothing styles, or the old Coca Cola signs, the big, soft, ostentatious American cars of the 1950's and 1960's show that this film is as much about history as *Gone with the Wind* (1939): They are symbols on wheels, epitomizing a way of life that is inexorably evolving into something quite different.

The success of this extremely modest story, both as a play and as a motion picture, proves once again that characterization is the most important ingredient of drama. More specifically, the magic formula seems to be: Take two very different, very strong-willed and incompatible people, confine them together, and wait for the inevitable fireworks. Neil Simon's *The Odd Couple* (1968) is a classic example. Felix Unger's neurotic fastidiousness and hypochondriasis accentuate Oscar Madison's gross slovenliness and animal vitality—and vice versa. Through the age-old artistic device of contrast, each character accentuates the other's uniqueness. In *Driving Miss Daisy*, the two principal characters not only are different in philosophical attitudes but also are further differentiated by sex, race, religion, education, and social status. In the last scene when Hoke, now eighty-five, goes to visit Miss Daisy, who is ninety-seven and confined to a nursing home, the audience understands that these two people who were originally so different have unconsciously taken on each other's best traits. Miss Daisy has become gentle, patient, humble, and less militantly independent; Hoke has become dignified, sophisticated, and relatively affluent. Through their long years of enforced association they have worn each other smooth.

Dan Aykroyd, who is best known as a zany comedian, shows intelligence and restraint in his portrayal of Miss Daisy's son Boolie, a cornfed Rotarian-type who is dutiful toward his "Mama" but not really interested in her concerns. His wife Florine (Patti Lupone), who is only referred to in the play, is brought to life in the motion picture version and is just the sort of nagging, childless, social climber the original dialogue suggested. Daisy's maid Idella (Esther Rolle), who remains offstage in the play, is also incarnated in the film and provides humor as a servant who has grown so stoical under the ceaseless pecking of a fussy mistress that she seems to be carved out of mahogany.

A few critics have found fault with the film on political grounds. They suggest that Hoke is an "Uncle Tom," that it is improper in our enlightened age to portray blacks as nothing but faithful household servants, and they believe that the story tends to flatter Jews as being less bigoted than other whites. Audiences have not had their enjoyment tainted by such quibbles. The notion that every work of art should be or cannot help but be a political statement is thankfully fading into the dustbin of history, just as all the heavy rhetoric of Marxism has become a feeble echo that no longer impresses or frightens people. *Driving Miss Daisy* is not saying how things ought to be but how things were. The love that develops between Hoke and Miss Daisy suggests in a low-key way characteristic of the whole story that, although there is great tension between blacks and whites, there is also the possibility of love, understanding, and laughter. Uhry says, "I wrote what I knew to be the truth, and people have recognized it as such."

In recognition of all the wonderful elements that came together so well in the film, *Driving Miss Daisy* was the most honored film at the Academy Awards. It won the Best Picture, Best Actress (Jessica Tandy), Best Adapted Screenplay (Alfred Uhry), and Best Makeup (Manlio Rocchetti) Awards, and was nominated further for Best Actor (Morgan Freeman), Best Supporting Actor (Dan Aykroyd), Best Art Direction (Bruno Rubeo and Crispian Sallis), Best Costume Design (Elizabeth McBride), and Best Editing (Mark Warner).

Bill Delaney

Reviews
Atlanta Constitution. December 4, 1989, p. D1.
Chicago Tribune. January 12, 1989, VII, p. 22.
Jet. LXXVII, December 4, 1989, p. 51.
Los Angeles. XXXV, January, 1990, p. 181.
Los Angeles Times. December 13, 1989, VI, p. 6.
The New Republic. CCII, January 22, 1990, p. 26.
The New York Times. December 13, 1989, p. C19.
The New Yorker. LXV, December 25, 1989, p. 73.
Newsweek. CXIV, December 18, 1989, p. 68.
Time. CXXXIV, December 18, 1989, p. 91.
Variety. CCCXXXVII, December 13, 1989, p. 28.

DRUGSTORE COWBOY

Production: Nick Wechsler and Karen Murphy; released by Avenue Pictures
Direction: Gus Van Sant, Jr.
Screenplay: Gus Van Sant, Jr., and Daniel Yost; based on the novel by James Fogle
Cinematography: Robert Yeoman
Editing: Curtiss Clayton
Production design: David Brisbin
Art direction: Eve Cauley
Set decoration: Margaret Goldsmith
Makeup: Lizbeth Williamson
Costume design: Beatrix Aruno Pasztor
Sound: Ron Judkins
Music: Elliot Goldenthal
MPAA rating: R
Running time: 100 minutes

Principal characters:
Bob................................. Matt Dillon
Dianne.............................. Kelly Lynch
Rick............................... James Le Gros
Nadine .... Heather Graham
David.............................. Max Perlich
Tom the Priest .... William S. Burroughs

The final sequence of *Drugstore Cowboy*, ostensibly a pastiche of home films of the principal characters mugging for the camera, has Desmond Dekker and The Aces singing "The Israelites" in the background. On the chance that the audience has not made the connection already, the film asserts it unequivocally in the song lyrics: "I don't want to end up like Bonnie and Clyde." Bob (Matt Dillon) and his wife, Dianne (Kelly Lynch), are latter-day reincarnations of the famous couple who bedeviled policemen and bank managers across Texas during the Depression. They were carefree outlaws not only in a technical but also in the more general sense of their living outside the boundaries of straight, normal society. Bob's mother (Grace Zabriskie) makes the relevant identification when Bob and Dianne appear at her home unexpectedly to pick up some old clothes, and she refers to the couple as "my dope fiend thief of a son and his crazy little nymphomaniac wife." The latter character recalls the steamy sensuality of Faye Dunaway's Bonnie Parker, while Bob is as bereft of libido as was Warren Beatty's Clyde Barrow in the film *Bonnie and Clyde* (1967).

Further parallels can be drawn between the two films—including the presence of a second couple, Rick (James Le Gros) and Nadine (Heather Graham), who act as generally helpless sidekicks—but the differences between them are far more significant. First, the historical period presented in each establishes two distinctive social milieus. *Bonnie and Clyde* opposed the glamor of violent crime to the spiritless landscape of the dust bowl. Bonnie Parker, at least in the film, was drawn into her criminal's life in large measure out of boredom. Clyde swept her up in the excitement, first of car theft, then of robbing banks. As innumerable commentators observed when it was first released, the film glorified its outlaw protagonists, portraying the lawmen as sneaking villains and ultimately ruthless executioners. The Texas Ranger who hunts Bonnie and Clyde does so because the couple has humiliated him, not out of any sense of duty or of the need to preserve social institutions. His motive is revenge, pure and simple. *Bonnie and Clyde* thus used the 1930's to promote values consonant with the 1960's, when it was produced: Those who live outside the law are, if reckless, nevertheless heroic. Their victimization at the hands of policemen and greedy capitalists tells a moral fable not unlike that unveiled only two years later in *Easy Rider* (1969), in which the hippie drug dealers played by Dennis Hopper and Peter Fonda fall afoul of a vicious, reactionary society symbolized by the tobacco-chewing farmers who shoot them in cold blood.

By contrast, *Drugstore Cowboy*, which combines *Easy Rider*'s drug dealing with *Bonnie and Clyde*'s robbers, makes no such claims for the glamor of life outside the law. Bob, Dianne, Rick, and Nadine live in seedy apartments and motels, dress in mostly worn and decidedly unfashionable clothes, and drive beat-up used cars. They never really get ahead of the game. They are, in short, petty thieves, robbing small drugstores and breaking into rural hospital dispensaries for drugs, relying on guile more than force. While the naïveté of Bonnie and Clyde might plausibly have been interpreted as tragic, Bob's is merely pathetic when it is not flatly ludicrous. His superstitions, his clumsy effort to rip off a younger dealer, and his braggadocio all mark him as a fool, a young punk who believes that he is tough and smart but who is, after all, a small-time hustler and drug addict with no future other than recurrent stints in prison.

Such a story would seem to have little to recommend it, but Gus Van Sant, Jr., has taken this comparatively unpromising material and turned it into an artful, clever, and ultimately ironic fable that risks sentimentality without finally giving in to it. The film opens with Bob's voice-over, coming, as is shown at the end of the scene, from the ambulance that is carrying him to the hospital after he has been shot by a drug addict whom he had regularly bamboozled. It is unclear whether he will live or die. Bob's voice will provide continual commentary on the narrative, punctuating the film with what seems an authoritative view of his life and its significance.

The story follows the foursome as they plan and execute their many robberies, which are spurred on by their constant physical need to remain high. They are shown shooting up, biding time at their various apartments (they are forced to move frequently because they are constantly harassed by the police) until the next robbery, and causing trouble for the police. Finally, Bob realizes that the watchful eye of the law is shutting down his operation, and so he takes his "crew" on the road.

He orchestrates an operation whereby he and the others steal drugs in a town, keep only enough for themselves for a limited amount of time in the car so that they can ditch the drugs on the road if stopped by the police, and send the rest in a suitcase by bus, with which they rendezvous at regular intervals when they need to get high. On the road, Bob and Dianne alienate Rick and Nadine with their superior attitudes; Bob tells Nadine that certain drugs are too strong for her and that she cannot handle them. In retaliation and to prove that she is as tough as they are, Nadine takes an enormous amount of narcotics and dies. Bob, who is very superstitious and who believes that, for example, hats on beds are bad luck, infers from Nadine's death that his luck has run out and that the hat she left on the bed will curse him for years. He swears that if he can bury Nadine without being caught, he will reform himself.

After successfully burying Nadine, Bob leaves Dianne and Rick, returns home to Portland, Oregon, and is enrolled in a drug rehabilitation program. He gets a job and, more important, gets "clean," declining invitations to get high first from defrocked priest Tom Murphy (played with unexcelled brilliance by William S. Burroughs) and then from Dianne, who visits briefly and leaves Bob a small stash of drugs. Bob, however, has given up his life of crime as he promised. Ironically, his vow to go straight leads to his being shot. David (Max Perlich), an even more small-time drug addict/dealer whom Bob has harassed in the past, and his partner break into Bob's seedy room and demand drugs, which they assume Bob has but of which he has none, having given Dianne's "gift" to Tom. David shoots Bob out of anger, revenge, and blind need for drugs, leaving him bleeding on the floor. A concerned resident calls for help, and, as the ambulance carrying Bob pulls away, Father Tom looks down then curtly closes the shade, doubtless in preparation to shoot up. As Bob had told his drug counselor (Beah Richards) earlier, no drug addict ever thinks about anything for long except getting high.

Drugstore Cowboy is an unpretentious, certainly unromantic, portrayal of the seamy underside of drug culture, its banality, its boredom, and its hopelessness. Set in 1971, it declines any of the spectacular sensationalism that has characterized popular views of drug dealing in the era of television's *Miami Vice* and Ronald Reagan, George Bush, and William Bennett. The film is about lowlifes, their delusions, their marginality, and their basic insecurity and desperation. Probably inspired in part by director David Lynch's *Blue Velvet* (1986), which was also set in the Pacific Northwest, *Drugstore Cowboy* differs from that earlier film by remaining almost exclusively naturalistic. The imitation of home films with which the film both opens and closes seems intended to reinforce this effect. The only exception in the film's imagistic naturalism involves Bob's recurrent fantasies, which interject elements of the surreal. Once, when high, Bob puts his finger on the essential attraction that shooting up holds for the hooked: "Everything took on the rosy hue of unlimited success." This success is temporary, to be sure, but potent and ineluctable. At age twenty-six, Bob knows all there is to know about being a drug addict, an insight for which he may pay with his own life.

Drugstore Cowboy is a timely film, with hysteria about crack-dealing gangs of ghetto blacks and ruthless Latino cocaine barons saturating the media and permeating popular consciousness in the United States. The reality of drug addiction is more mundane, and the inadequacy of treatment is the more pressing concern. (In a fine ironic moment near the end, Father Tom predicts the emergence of an international police force conceived by right-wingers as a means of general repression under the pretense of drug interdiction.) Most important of all, *Drugstore Cowboy* demystifies the drug subculture by depicting ordinary white youth as culprits cum victims in a vicious cycle, not of drive-by shooting and luxury life-styles, but of small-time heists and hustles and of pointless, desperate attempts to stay high and one step ahead of the law.

Perhaps setting the film in the near past is intended to distance that drug culture, a legacy of the 1960's, from the one that screams out from television screens on the evening news and across headlines of daily newspapers. What remains most powerful, however, is less the film's historical accuracy of the drug culture than its typification of the perennial social dimensions of the problem. Neither the law nor the criminals are glamorized—the ineptitude of the former is matched by the hopelessness of the latter. When Bob returns to the straight world, his options are scarcely attractive: a dead-end job operating a drill press, a room in a decrepit residential hotel populated by derelicts and addicts such as Father Tom, an apparently interminable program of methadone maintenance, and the constant danger of becoming a mark for just the sort of petty hoodlum he had once been. Bob Hughes finally does "just say no." As the film graphically demonstrates, that is not enough.

Michael Sprinker

Reviews
Gentleman's Quarterly. LIX, July 1989, p. 59.
Maclean's. CII, November 6, 1989, p. 84.
New York. XXII, October 1989, p. 82.
New Yorker. LXV, October 30, 1989, p. 74.
Newsweek. CXIV, October 23, 1989, p. 84.

A DRY WHITE SEASON

Production: Paula Weinstein for Davros; released by Metro-Goldwyn-Mayer
Direction: Euzhan Palcy
Screenplay: Colin Welland and Euzhan Palcy; based on the novel by Andre Brink
Cinematography: Kelvin Pike and Pierre-William Glenn
Editing: Sam O'Steen and Glenn Cunningham
Production design: John Fenner
Art direction: Alan Tomkins and Mike Phillips
Set decoration: Peter James
Makeup: Magdelin Gaffney and Tommie Manderson
Costume design: Germinal Rangel
Sound: Roy Charman
Music: Dave Grusin
MPAA rating: R
Running time: 97 minutes

Principal characters:
Ben du Toit . . . . Donald Sutherland
Melanie Bruwer . . . . Susan Sarandon
Ian McKenzie . . . . Marlon Brando
Susan du Toit . . . . Janet Suzman
Stanley . . . . Zakes Mokae
Captain Stolz . . . . Jurgen Prochnow
Gordon Ngubene . . . . Winston Ntshona
Emily Ngubene . . . . Thoko Ntshinga
Johan . . . . Rowan Elmes
Jonatha Ngubene . . . . Bekhithemba Mpofu

A Dry White Season is an extremely well-crafted film, based on an equally well-crafted novel, that keeps its risks to a minimum. Among the less traditional decisions the filmmakers made, the casting policy deserves recognition. The black cast members are all highly accomplished South African stage actors, each of whom has overcome harassment and official pressure to help build a black professional acting community in South Africa, and the mass demonstrations are populated by school-children from Zimbabwe. It was encouraging to see the South African struggle being represented by people who have been a part of that struggle, or who have an intimate historical connection with it. The representation of police brutality is also unusual and commendable. It is graphic and vivid and skillfully presented, not only for shock value but also for a sense of the relentless day-after-day nausea of it. The music is very good too—the songs of both Hugh Masekela and Ladysmith Black Mambazo give this film an unusual force, using the sounds of South African popular music to drive important sequences forward. Unlike these aspects of the film, however, the story has nothing as compelling to recommend it.

Ben du Toit (Donald Sutherland) lives in an upper-middle-class suburban home in Johannesburg with his wife, Susan (Janet Suzman), and young son, Johan (Rowan Elmes). Ben teaches school and cheers for Johan at soccer, his daughter visits often with her husband and son, and they all spend Sunday afternoons together playing and barbecuing on their well-manicured lawn. They lead average, contented lives, until one day, when their barbecue is interrupted by Gordon Ngubene (Winston Ntshona) and his son, Jonathan (Bekhithemba Mpofu). Gordon is the black gardener who works at both Ben's school and his home. Jonathan was detained by the police and caned, and Gordon is concerned that the unjust punishment will push Jonathan away from school and toward the more militant young people in the Soweto townships. Ben, who pays for Jonathan's schooling, tells Gordon that the police must have had a reason for beating Jonathan and that there is nothing to be done about it now. As Gordon predicted, however, Jonathan learns a lesson from the caning different from that suggested by Ben. He participates in the peaceful student march protesting the education of blacks in Afrikaans instead of English, a march that in real life drew a violent response from the police and that began what is now called the Soweto Uprising. Jonathan is detained in the melee, beaten, and eventually murdered by the Special Branch police. When Gordon and his wife, Emily (Thoko Ntshinga), try to find him, they search the morgue and the hospital, and the police tell them that they have no record of him—he is simply missing. Later, the police inform the family that Jonathan died in the march and that his body was buried immediately.

Gordon will not accept this response and sets out to discover what really happened to Jonathan, how he died, and where he is buried. Ben again tells Gordon to leave well enough alone, but he cannot. When officials of the Special Branch discover that Gordon is collecting statements from witnesses, they decide to detain and question him, and he eventually dies in custody. Emily asks Ben to help her find out what happened to Gordon, and, slowly, Ben begins to realize that his complacency, his assumptions about the police, and his relationship to the world around him have all been built on a foundation of intentional blindness.

It is at this point that the story becomes wholly Ben's. As Palcy has stated in interviews, she assiduously allowed room for Gordon and his family on the screen—more room, she contends, than a white director would have. Once Gordon dies, however, the story shifts to being about, and exclusively driven by, Ben. The quest is his quest, the heroism is his heroism, and the martyrdom is his martyrdom. Marlon Brando says that scenes were cut from this film, scenes important to the film's message about racism. The film that was released in the theaters, however, focuses quite singularly from the middle onward on the one white adult male, Ben.

The book on which the film was based, on the other hand, takes a very different approach to this question. Palcy's statement that the book is only about Ben is in some ways valid; it is certainly true that he is the protagonist from beginning to end, the consciousness the audience shares, the identification the audience makes, and the recipient of the sympathy of the audience. There is, however, much more time in the book for both Stanley and Melanie. It is disturbing that a role as interesting as that of the Stanley of the book was reduced to flatness and that an actor of Zakes Mokae's stature was then required to make something of it. As *The Nation*'s reviewer generously put it, Stanley is "more an icon than a character when compared with Ben." In the book, however, Stanley fills any room he enters, commands all available attention visually, aurally, and intellectually, and manages an infinite web of information and resources. Stanley's role in the book ends with his disappearance; Ben searches for him, is told by his wife that he has escaped to Botswana, and is beaten by a group of young township men. Stanley's final appearance in the film is the final sequence of the film, in which he shoots Special Branch Captain Stolz (Jurgen Prochnow). While this sequence satisfies every audience member's desire, it can be viewed as gratuitous and insulting. The film becomes the story of two white men—Ben and his white male enemy, Stolz. Then Stanley shoots Stolz. A happy ending and a burst of agency on the part of a black character, while very neat and orderly, do not compensate for an hour of film time and do not change the fact that the film is as much about Ben as the book is.

Similarly, the treatment of women in this film is surprisingly traditional. While it is by no means better in the book, at least there is more space in the film devoted to the development of Melanie Bruwer (Susan Sarandon). The Melanie of the film is as strong and worldly as a progressive English white woman journalist in South Africa would have to be, but there is no sense of how or why she has become so knowing, or at what cost. Melanie attracts by far the most sympathy of any woman in the film. Very little of Gordon's wife, Emily, is presented, which is all the more frustrating since she is played by Ntshinga, another of South Africa's preeminent actors. There are no other important black women in the film. Ben's wife and daughter bear the burden of representing Afrikaaner women, who in this film seem to care only about protecting their homes and families and not about the lives, or the quality of life, of anyone beyond that.

Suzman (the niece of liberal South African politician Helen Suzman) gives a wonderful performance as Ben's wife, making an astoundingly blind and racist character as sympathetic as possible. Susannah Harker as Ben's traitorous daughter Suzette is given little screen time and very little room to move. Andre Brink's women are equally uninteresting and politically offensive, but it would have been possible to alter that, just as Welland and Palcy altered other plot features.

Actually, all the performances in *A Dry White Season* are noteworthy. Weinstein, Palcy, and the casting staff all deserve credit for assembling a talented and committed group of actors. Sutherland's tweedy, nearly shambling, insulated teacher gets visibly tenser in each muscle as the story progresses, and it is possible to believe that he could have been so naïve and unknowing. Prochnow is equally plausible as the Special Branch officer who pairs off against Ben. He is profoundly sadistic and yet manages to avoid painting a cartoon caricature; his Stolz is a real living human being who can bludgeon people to death and still call it a day's work.

Palcy gets further points for being able to elicit and manage such performances. Even Brando, who at first forces attention away from the story by simply being Brando, does not overwhelm the screen. His McKenzie, a weary civil rights lawyer, is sly and calculating for all the right reasons; Brando makes McKenzie the center of the trial's attention without turning him into merely a star cameo. Palcy works him in admirably, giving screen time to all the other players in the courtroom drama without losing a single nuance of Brando's performance.

Similarly, both the editing and the camera work reveal much control and polish, especially for a young director. A number of reviewers have criticized the editing for being too heavy-handed, cutting directly back and forth between white suburbs and black townships, for example, but the technique works. No matter how obvious the idea or how common the device, a scene of white children playing contrasted with a scene of black children being brutalized makes explicit what the audience already knows. Palcy's camera, or perhaps more correctly that of cinematographers Kelvin Pike and Pierre-William Glenn is remarkably still and quiet, never boring, and simply nonintrusive; instead of visual pyrotechnics, they use a controlled technique. The demonstration sequences, for example, do not stoop to a shaky, hand-held, pseudodocumentary camera style or to different stock or texture for effect. The filmmakers appear to be recording what is happening in the most direct way, whether it is marching and singing or beating and shooting.

A Dry White Season is an important film because it can remind its audience of certain aspects of the horrors of state terrorist practices that are sometimes forgotten. Moreover, *A Dry White Season* is a good film—it is well made, carefully conceived, and extraordinarily well acted. It would be an even better film if only the black characters, male and female, had more time, space, and agency.

Anahid Kassabian

Reviews
America. CLXI, November 18, 1989, p. 353.
The Christian Science Monitor. September 22, 1989, p. 10.
Films in Review. LXI, January, 1990, p. 46.
Jet. LXXVII, October 16, 1989, p. 59.
Los Angeles Times. September 22, 1989, VI, p. 1.
The Nation. CCXLIX, October 30, 1989, p. 505.
The New Republic. CCI, October 9, 1989, p. 24.
The New York Times. September 20, 1989, p. C19.
The New Yorker. LXV, October 2, 1989, p. 101.
Time. CXXXIV, September 25, 1989, p. 78.
Variety. CCCXXXVI, September 13, 1989, p. 31.

EAT A BOWL OF TEA

Production: Tom Sternberg for American Playhouse; released by Columbia Pictures
Direction: Wayne Wang
Screenplay: Judith Rascoe; based on the novel by Louis Chu
Cinematography: Amir Mokri
Editing: Richard Candib
Production design: Robert Ziembicki
Art direction: Timmy Yip
Set decoration: Lisa Dean
Makeup: Yam Chan Hoi
Costume design: Marit Allen
Sound: Drew Kunin
Music: Mark Adler
MPAA rating: PG-13
Running time: 104 minutes

> *Principal characters:*
> Wah Gay . . . . Victor Wong
> Ben Loy . . . . Russell Wong
> Mei Oi . . . . Cora Miao
> Lee Gong . . . . Lau Siu Ming
> Ah Song . . . . Eric Tsang Chi Wai
> Ben Loy's mother . . . . Hui Fun
> Mei Oi's mother . . . . Wu Ming Yu
> Bok Fat . . . . Lee Sau Kee
> Aunt Gin . . . . Law Lan

Eat a Bowl of Tea is an exuberant mix of American nostalgia and Chinese traditions. After his previous feature, the slick *film noir Slam Dance* (1987), director Wayne Wang returns in this picture to a subject he explored in his first and second features, *Chan Is Missing* (1982) and *Dim Sum* (1985): how Asian Americans adapt to the American life-style.

The film begins with a series of vignette shots of the Chinatown district of New York City in the 1940's. Wah Gay (Victor Wong), in a voice-over narration, explains how American immigration laws at the turn of the century allowed only the men to emigrate from China because of the high demand for cheap labor in the United States. Once settled, the men adapted to American culture, assimilating certain capitalistic practices, while sustaining customs from their native China. Shots of Chinese men gathered in game rooms and in barber shops and restaurants, as well as waiting in line outside the apartment of a prostitute, are shown as a gravelly voiced Wah Gay explains his plight and the frustration he feels living in a community of old men. He talks of the despair he feels over having been separated from his wife for more than twenty years and of the hopes he has for his son, Ben Loy (Russell Wong), who was recently released from the army. Wah Gay hopes to persuade Ben Loy to travel to China, find a woman to marry, and return to New York to start a family, thus fulfilling a dream that Wah Gay and the majority of the old men of Chinatown themselves have failed to accomplish.

Ben Loy is an easygoing, lanky youth, well adjusted to the world outside his home community. A devoted son, he agrees to his father's wish. Before leaving for China, Ben Loy promises his father's best friend, Lee Gong (Lau Siu Ming), to look up his daughter. Ben Loy travels to a rural Chinese village where his mother (Hui Fun) lives. In direct contrast to the microcosmic world of old men in Chinatown, the village is populated predominantly by old women. After a quietly affectionate reunion with his mother, Ben Loy meets and mixes with the other inhabitants of the village. He is introduced to Lee Gong's wife (Wu Ming Yu), who then introduces him to her daughter, Mei Oi (Cora Miao). Mei Oi is very bold and very knowledgeable about the world outside her village. She speaks English quite well and is even familiar with some American slang. The two develop an immediate rapport. During cinema night in the village—Frank Capra's *Lost Horizon* (1937) is shown on a makeshift screen in the open air—the young couple embrace for the first time. Soon afterward, an engagement is announced, quickly followed by a traditional Chinese wedding and an awkward, yet exuberant, wedding night.

Before the strains of the traditional wedding music have had a chance to fade, Ben Loy and Mei Oi are in New York attending a wedding reception held in a restaurant with big band music blaring. Mei Oi is disoriented at first, confused by the stares of the multitude of old men and the bold advances of one of the few younger men in attendance, Ah Song (Eric Tsang Chi Wai). Ben Loy is promised a job as manager of a restaurant and is given an apartment along with many blessings for a fruitful marriage. During the couple's first night in their new apartment, however, Ben Loy is unable to make love. "I feel like everyone is watching us" he says.

As he plunges into the hectic duties of his new job, Ben Loy becomes increasingly concerned about the expectations of his father and the other men of the community. He realizes that he is expected to succeed where they failed, to create a complete and harmonious family life and father many children to carry on the family traditions. As familial pressures mount and his father's demands for grandchildren increase, Ben Loy decides to seek medical help for his impotency. His doctor's advice is to take a vacation and relax. Ben Loy's boss grants some time off for the couple to vacation in Washington, D.C. Freed from the pressures and prying eyes of the close-knit community, Ben Loy regains his sexual abilities, and the two spend a thoroughly enjoyable vacation. Upon their return home, however, their debilitating problems are renewed.

Mei Oi, who is initially sympathetic to her husband's problems, gradually becomes more frustrated. She feels out of place in her new environment and becomes restless and lonely. Ah Song notices her restlessness and one day follows her home.

Although she rejects his first advances, Mei Oi finally lets him into the apartment, and they begin a secret affair.

When Mei Oi announces to Ben Loy that she is pregnant, he is jubilant, then suspicious. He knows that it has been some time since the vacation in Washington, D.C., which was the last time he was able to perform sexually. He eventually brushes away his suspicions, however, and embraces the good news. The community is ecstatic, and Wah Gay feels fulfilled. A neighbor, however, overhears a loud confrontation between Mei Oi and Ah Song, and soon the entire community knows of the affair. When Lee Gong confronts his daughter with the news and asks for an explanation, she violently denies her involvement with Ah Song. The gossip finally reaches Ben Loy and leads him to a brutal argument with his father and then with Mei Oi. Finally, Ben Loy and Mei Oi decide to live apart, both moving in with their respective fathers.

Ah Song, having been out of town on business, returns and finds himself ostracized by the old men. Spying Ben Loy in a bar, he decides to sneak into their old apartment and rendezvous with Mei Oi, unaware that the couple has split up and no longer lives in the old apartment. Wah Gay, seeking vengeance, follows Ah Song and breaks into the apartment ahead of Ah Song to surprise him. When Ah Song enters the apartment, Wah Gay attacks him with a butcher knife, cutting off one of Ah Song's ears. In the ensuing chaos, Ben Loy is ultimately arrested for attempted murder. By the time the authorities learn that it was Wah Gay who attacked Ah Song, the old man has fled the community. Ben Loy is finally cleared of assault charges and returns to his father's empty house.

Ben Loy decides to start a new life in San Francisco. While he is packing, he runs into Mei Oi. They realize that they still care for each other and decide to try to get back together, this time in San Francisco. Mei Oi shows Ben Loy a gift her mother recently sent her, a package of potent medicinal tea. Mei Oi explains that the tea's potency will be transferred to the person who eats a bowl of tea. Wah Gay's voice-over narration begins again as the scene quickly shifts to a San Francisco suburb where a barbecue is in full force, populated by Wah Gay, Mei Oi, Ben Loy, and a brew of children.

Although flavored with traditional Chinese customs and practices, *Eat a Bowl of Tea* is essentially a celebration of American culture. Primarily filmed in Hong Kong, the film still has the look and texture of a faded American photo album from the 1940's. In stark contrast to director Wang's previous film about Asian American culture clash, *Dim Sum*, in which a somber, almost dirgelike atmosphere permeates the action, *Eat a Bowl of Tea* is upbeat and jazzy, with snappy and sarcastic dialogue. Even in the Chinese village scenes with the old women talking to Ben Loy in Chinese, the subtitled dialogue is spiced with an American flippancy, devoid of traditional Chinese vernacular. Seeing these men and women, with strong ties to their Chinese heritage, talking and acting like characters from a 1940's melodrama is disorienting but ultimately gives the film a unique and fresh vibrancy. Yet, Wang does not want to give the impression that Chinatown in the 1940's was one big jazz party. By concentrating on interior scenes and eliminating all panoramic shots of the city (except for one brief scene of a lone skyscraper glimpsed between a tenement building and some trees), Wang creates a claustrophobic atmosphere for these old men trapped in their community, forced to create a hybrid culture devoid of women and desperate for some semblance of a complete family life. Given such a serious theme, the film admirably manages to sustain its lighthearted tone.

Enveloping the film in a sleek American style that borders on a screwball comedy increases the likability of the characters. Yet, the light tone also makes it difficult to accept the more serious concerns of the young couple. Although Ben Loy feels intense pressure from the community to produce almost single-handedly a new generation, his easygoing manner and initial intense infatuation with Mei Oi make it difficult to believe that he would reject her so quickly and completely. The flippant tone also diminishes Mei Oi's frustrations and makes her decision to take on a lover seem out of character, especially considering her traditional upbringing and the moral temper of the time.

After Mei Oi begins her affair, the film skids into a melodramatic farce. The characters lose much of their initial charm and begin to act like figures in a bad melodrama. Despite this shift, the characterizations are well-rounded and full of life. Russell Wong gives Ben Loy's character an all-American boyish charm that contrasts effectively with Victor Wong's portrayal of the rascally insistent Wah Gay. Cora Miao plays Mei Oi as a fiercely independent woman, headstrong and confused, but ultimately the perfect match for the equally untraditional Ben Loy.

Amir Mokri's cinematography, which enhances the period look of the film by bathing the screen in a golden-yellow hue, deserves special mention. The interior shots are filled with a cluttered attention to detail and, at times, a quiet, still-life snapshot effect. Wang used the still-life technique in *Dim Sum*, but in *Eat a Bowl of Tea* there is more care taken with lighting and camera placement to deepen the ethereal, past-era effect. A better film than Wang's earlier efforts, *Eat a Bowl of Tea* is filled with exuberance, quirky humor, and a love for character and culture, both old and new.

Jim Kline

Reviews
The Christian Science Monitor. September 6, 1989, p. 10.
Los Angeles Times. August 4, 1989, p. 5.
The New Leader. LXXII, August 7, 1989, p. 20.
New York Magazine. August 21, 1989, p. 128.
The New York Times. July 21, 1989, p. C13.
Variety. CCCXXXV, May 24, 1989, p. 27.
The Wall Street Journal. July 20, 1989, p. A12.
The Village Voice. XXXIV, August 1, 1989, p. 67.

EIGHTY-FOUR CHARLIE MOPIC

Production: Michael Nolin for the Charlie MoPic Company; released by New
 Century/Vista Film Company
Direction: Patrick Duncan
Screenplay: Patrick Duncan
Cinematography: Alan Caso
Editing: Stephen Purvis
Art direction: Douglas Dick
Special effects: Eric Rylander
Makeup: Ron Wild
Costume design: Lyn Paolo
Sound: Michael Moore and Craig Woods
Music: Donovan
MPAA rating: R
Running time: 95 minutes

Principal characters:
LT	Jonathan Emerson
OD	Richard Brooks
Easy	Nicholas Cascone
Pretty Boy	Jason Tomlins
Hammer	Christopher Burgard
Cracker	Glenn Morshower
MoPic	Byron Thames

Eighty-Four Charlie MoPic is a low-budget Vietnam War film with a unique
approach to its subject matter. First-time writer-director Patrick Duncan uses a
documentary-style technique, presenting the action as if the audience were watching the making of a military training film. The objective camera becomes a subjective member of the fighting unit as the soldiers and cameraman engage in conversation and all the action is filmed from the cameraman's shaky, hand-held point of
view. This approach gives the film an aura of superrealism, as if the viewer were
experiencing what it really must have been like to fight in Vietnam.

The film begins with the offscreen voice of the cameraman announcing the
date—August 1, 1969—and the name of the training film—"Lessons Learned
Project." The project's leader, Lieutenant Richard Drury, or LT (Jonathan Emerson), stands stiffly in front of the camera and explains his objective: to become part
of a unit of experienced infantrymen, follow them on a reconnaissance mission, and
"record procedures peculiar to this combat situation."

The unit is part of the Eleventh Airborne Brigade and is composed of five men.
During the first half of the film, each man is identified by his nickname and given a
chance to face the camera and talk about himself. Easy (Nicholas Cascone), the

company clown and radio operator, joined the army to escape a jail term. He jokes about his Vietnam experience but later asks in wide-eyed seriousness, "Is it paranoid to think someone's trying to kill you when someone is trying to kill you?" Pretty Boy (Jason Tomlins), a California native, claims he has good luck, having miraculously survived death on numerous occasions. Cracker (Glenn Morshower), is a family man from South Carolina who takes pride in his job, not understanding the reasons for being in Vietnam but merely trying to do the best job he can. Hammer (Christopher Burgard) is a self-described "hard-core dude." He swaggers, talks of the blood brotherhood that exists between the men in the unit and of "taking scalps," and confesses that his reason for joining the army was to prove to his father that he is a real man. LT, new to the bush, sees Vietnam as a chance to prove himself to his superiors and rise quickly in rank. He sees the military as a big corporation with enormous opportunity for advancement and the war as a chance of a lifetime for a career officer. MoPic (Byron Thames), the cameraman (MoPic is short for motion picture), is heard more than seen but has his chance in front of the camera, explaining that his usual duties include filming officer functions and meetings and developing film from other cameramen in the field. He mentions that sometimes he receives film from cameramen killed in the field and that it is unsettling to view the footage knowing anything could be on the reel. Sergeant O'Donnigan, or OD (Richard Brooks), is the only man in the unit who refuses to be formally interviewed. Still, he is unquestionably the soul of the unit, and his presence dominates the film. A black, born and reared in an urban environment, he has adapted to and mastered the ways of the bush and leads his men with a quiet, paternalistic intensity.

OD objects to the presence of MoPic and LT, and tries to prevent them from joining his unit. He is, however, ordered to permit them to film his unit in the field, and the unit boards a helicopter bound for the central highlands. Not long after disembarking and penetrating the bush, LT and OD clash. LT at one point makes unnecessary noise, and OD points his rifle at LT's face to silence him. Later, LT threatens to have OD court-martialed if such an occurrence happens again. OD snaps back that if he has to point his weapon at LT again he will pull the trigger. LT reminds OD of the importance of LT's assignment—to gather information that will ultimately help train troops to adapt better to the unique ways of fighting in Vietnam. OD calms down and agrees to cooperate. After this confrontation, the men freely volunteer "tips of the trail" to MoPic and LT, everything from stringing trap wire to pointing out enemy booby traps to demonstrating how to dry wet socks.

The next day, they encounter enemy troops and hide in the bush as the enemy passes by inches away. LT accidentally impales his arm on a sharpened bamboo stick planted in the brush by the enemy. After a quick patch up, the unit pierces deeper into the field, where they witness the gathering of an enemy artillery unit. Easy radios headquarters with the location of the hostile unit, and soon bombs are raining on the enemy.

Later, the unit encounters more enemy troops. Realizing that it would take too long to go around the troops, the men prepare for a confrontation. OD lobs a grenade, and the rest of the men open fire, wiping out the enemy. Only one wounded survivor remains, and LT demands that the men help carry the survivor back to headquarters for interrogation. The rest of the men heatedly disagree with LT, and while they are arguing they are ambushed by another enemy unit. As the men scramble for cover, Pretty Boy is hit and writhes in the open in full view of both the men and the enemy. Hammer is wounded, the radio pack is destroyed, and Pretty Boy is hit again and again. Finally, OD shoots Pretty Boy to put him out of his misery.

After the battle, OD personally prepares Pretty Boy for transport back to base. Another ambush follows, and OD is wounded in the leg while Cracker is mortally wounded in the chest. OD, later, carefully prepares Cracker's body with the same respectful attention he gave to Pretty Boy. Both Hammer and Easy begin to lose their courage. As the unit prepares to move out, Hammer scouts ahead and is blown up by a land grenade. The men are too weak and scared to prepare Hammer's body properly, and they move on to a Vietnamese village, where a helicopter is scheduled to retrieve them.

When the men reach the village, they find that it has been burned and all the villagers killed. While the unit waits for the helicopter, OD begins to talk deliriously, and Easy recites Hail Marys. LT sets off a flare for the helicopter, and suddenly they are under ambush again. Easy convulses in terror while OD returns fire, and LT scrambles for cover. The sound of a helicopter mingles with the sound of gunfire. LT grabs Easy and drags him to the helicopter. MoPic follows, puts the camera in the helicopter, and returns to the village to help LT carry OD. The camera records the final scene of MoPic and LT dragging OD to the helicopter, MoPic stumbling when he is hit by enemy fire. As LT and OD make it to the helicopter, MoPic struggles to get up but is hit again. He strains to rise, but he cannot make it to the helicopter. The helicopter rises, the leg of a survivor blocks the view of the camera, the film runs out and fades to black.

The use of the subjective camera in *Eighty-Four Charlie MoPic* is both its strongest and weakest attribute. The film is mesmerizing to watch. The interaction between the characters and camera, the way each man speaks to the camera as if he were talking to a fellow soldier, pulls the viewer into the film and makes the audience a participant in the action. The audience learns right along with LT and MoPic how to go about surviving in the Vietnam bush. When the unit is on the move, the viewer clambers along with the rest of the men, cutting through the foliage, running for cover, peering through the bush as enemy troops pass by, and enduring the hostile scowls of OD.

The camera misses nothing. All the action—the ambushes, the deaths, the heated confrontations between the men, Easy's jokes and hysterics—is vividly played in front of the camera. For this reason the attempt at superrealism ultimately rings false. Too much is revealed too quickly in front of the camera. Everything is too dramatic, too well orchestrated, and too neat. The camera is always in the right place to capture the ultimate dramatic effect. For example, when the unit has to dive into the bush to hide from the enemy, the camera placement is such that LT's grimacing face is in the foreground, his arm impaled on a sharpened bamboo stick is in the middle of the shot, and the shadows of the passing troops are in the background. The image is perfect. The documentary look for which director Duncan is striving is, ironically, sabotaged by his insistence on a strong dramatic structure.

Duncan is also obviously trying to make a much more basic, intimate war film than others in the genre. Again his success is only partial. The long, continuous takes from the single point-of-view camera serve to intensify the realism, the gritty, documentary look. Only the natural sounds of the bush are heard—birds chirping, insects buzzing, grass and bushes rustling—as the men trudge across the landscape. The small-scale aura of the film increases the intimacy and emphasizes the interrelationship between the characters. The film is, more than anything, a character study, and the use of the subjective camera gives the film almost a home film intimacy. Unfortunately, the characters themselves are too standard and too recognizable from many other war films to involve the viewer enough to reveal the flesh and blood behind the stereotypes.

Because the film is so intimate, because it is not an epic like *Platoon* (1986), *Apocalypse Now* (1979), or *Full Metal Jacket* (1987), and because there are no symbolic Christ figures or metaphorical madmen or sweeping panoramic scenes of extravagant pyrotechnic battles with a cast of thousands, the success of the film relies on its ability to make the audience identify with these simple, unglamorous, honorable men. The camera-as-character technique is dazzling and innovative. It demands intimacy and involvement. The viewer wants to identify with these men. Yet the constricting dramatic structure and stereotypical characterizations serve to dull the full emotional impact for which Duncan is striving in his otherwise stunning directorial debut.

Jim Kline

Reviews
Chicago Tribune. April 28, 1989, VII, p. 32.
The Christian Science Monitor. March 24, 1989, p. 10.
Film Comment. March/April, 1989, p. 11.
Los Angeles Times. April 7, 1989, VI, p. 1.
The New Republic. CC, April 24, 1989, p. 24.
New York Magazine. April 3, 1989, p. 70.
The New York Times. March 22, 1989, p. C24.
Newsweek. April 3, 1989, p. 67.
Time. CXXXIII, April 17, 1989, p. 83.
Variety. CCCXXXIV, January 25, 1989, p. 15.
The Washington Post. May 27, 1989, p. C7.

ENEMIES, A LOVE STORY

Production: Paul Mazursky for Morgan Creek; released by Twentieth Century-Fox
Direction: Paul Mazursky
Screenplay: Roger L. Simon and Paul Mazursky; based on the novel by Isaac
  Bashevis Singer
Cinematography: Fred Murphy
Editing: Stuart Pappé
Production design: Pato Guzman
Art direction: Steven J. Jordan
Set decoration: Ted Glass
Makeup: David Craig Forrest
Costume design: Albert Wolsky
Sound: Don Cohen
Music: Maurice Jarre
MPAA rating: R
Running time: 119 minutes

Principal characters:
Herman	Ron Silver
Tamara	Anjelica Huston
Masha	Lena Olin
Yadwiga	Margaret Sophie Stein
Rabbi Lembeck	Alan King
Masha's mother	Judith Malina
Mrs. Schreier	Rita Karin
Pesheles	Phil Leeds
Yasha Kotik	Elya Baskin
Leon Tortshiner	Paul Mazursky

Herman (Ron Silver) is a man tortured by the past. It is 1949, and Herman, a Jew who escaped the Holocaust physically unscathed by hiding in a barn, now lives on Coney Island. Out of gratitude, he married the gentile former servant, Yadwiga (Margaret Sophie Stein), who saved Herman's life back in Poland, but Herman longs for a woman who is his equal. Yadwiga adores Herman and smothers him with attention, waiting on his every need. Yet it is only while having brutally intense sex with his beautiful but emotionally unstable mistress, Masha (Lena Olin), a survivor from the camps, that Herman is able to immerse himself in the present. During most of his waking hours, Herman walks like a zombie, a man barely alive, hardly feeling and unable to make a decision.

Herman's life becomes even more complicated when Tamara (Anjelica Huston), his first wife, believed to have been killed in the concentration camp, appears in

New York very much alive—and as feisty as ever. For Masha, the line between reality and fantasy begins to blur as she longs for a child. Masha pleads with Herman to marry her, even though she is still wed to Leon Tortshiner (Paul Mazursky). Masha knows of Herman's marriage to Yadwiga, yet she insists that it would be for the baby's sake. Herman, already a bigamist with the sudden resurrection of Tamara, finally succumbs to Masha's demands and commits polygamy.

Immersed in her pain and deep sense of fatalism following the death of her mother (Judith Malina), Masha pleads with Herman to end their lives together by taking an overdose of pills. Herman is tempted with the promise of an end to his own pain and indecision, yet ultimately Herman cannot go through with it and leaves Masha to commit suicide alone. Instead of returning to Yadwiga, who awaits the birth of their child, Herman has one last talk with Tamara, then disappears. The only word from him is not a letter, but money wrapped in a blank piece of paper, sent to his young daughter, named appropriately, Masha.

Although flawed and at times lethargic in its pacing, *Enemies, A Love Story* is a beautifully conceived bittersweet love story with the feel of a fable. The idea of combining Holocaust survivors with bedroom farce was a very risky undertaking and required the actors and directors to walk a very fine line in order for the film to succeed. Fortunately, Mazursky has the appropriate sense of irony.

The disappointment with *Enemies, A Love Story* lies in its failure to break any new cinematic ground with respect to the depiction of the Holocaust. It is an effective piece of filmmaking, yet, filmmakers have a social and moral obligation to explore different facets of the Holocaust as opposed to merely offering yet another traditional interpretation of the experience. By offering new insights of the Holocaust, Costa-Gavras' *Music Box* (1989; reviewed in this volume) has far more impact as a social document. Furthermore, *Enemies, A Love Story* is forced to labor under the constraints of a relatively inactive main character who is unable, for the most part, to stir compassion within the viewer.

Enemies, A Love Story captured the New York Film Critics Award for Best Director. Paul Mazursky, known affectionately as an actor's director and one of the few to use his work consistently to examine the changing role of American women, is perhaps best remembered for his Academy Award-nominated *An Unmarried Woman* (1978), starring Jill Clayburgh in her Oscar-winning role. His other films include *Moscow on the Hudson* (1984), *Down and Out in Beverly Hills* (1986), and *Moon over Parador* (1988).

Unbeknown to her, Anjelica Huston was, even at the early scriptwriting stages, Mazursky's first choice to portray Tamara, Herman's wry, straight-talking first wife. Huston displays impressive comedic timing and wit and imbues her character with the indomitable spirit one would expect from a woman who has lost her two children in the camps, suffered a bullet wound in the hip that has left her with a severe limp, and has survived the harsh realities of the Soviet Union following her escape. Tamara is by far the strongest character in *Enemies, A Love Story*, a woman of compassion, intelligence, and strength. A woman who refuses to surrender to misfortune, Tamara is a survivor in every sense of the word.

Huston won an Academy Award for Best Supporting Actress for her role as Maerose in *Prizzi's Honor* (1985), a black comedy directed by her real-life father, the incomparable John Huston, and starring her longtime offscreen companion, Jack Nicholson. Her other work includes Francis Ford Coppola's *Gardens of Stone* (1987), *A Handful of Dust* (1988), Woody Allen's *Crimes and Misdemeanors* (1989; reviewed in this volume), as well as her father's last film, the adaptation of the James Joyce short story *The Dead* (1987). Anjelica Huston was awarded the Golden Globe for Best Supporting Actress for her work in *Enemies, A Love Story* and received an Academy Award nomination for Best Supporting Actress.

Swedish actress Lena Olin gained international acclaim for her role as the hedonistic, bowler-hatted Sabina in Philip Kaufman's *The Unbearable Lightness of Being* (1988). With the role of the mercurial Masha in *Enemies, A Love Story*, Olin was afforded the opportunity to display her rapid-fire ability to swing from one emotional extreme to the other with complete motivational understanding of the character and, as a result, received the New York Film Critics Award for Best Supporting Actress, as well as an Academy Award nomination for Best Supporting Actress. Although Masha was the only role out of the three for which the director saw more than one actress, the casting of Olin was hardly a chancy move on Mazursky's part, since the actress is a prominent member of Ingmar Bergman's famed company at the Royal Dramatic Theater in Stockholm.

Margaret Sophie Stein made her American film debut as the gentile Yadwiga in *Enemies, A Love Story*, having worked on both the stage and television in Poland, her homeland. While visiting friends in Paris when martial law was declared in Poland, Stein was forced into exile in 1981. A native of Warsaw, the actress physically resembles the character that Isaac Bashevis Singer sketched in his novel, but their backgrounds could not be more different. Stein trained at the Academy of Drama in Warsaw and the National Theater. Rather than turning Yadwiga into a victim, Stein succeeds at painting a character who grows from the humiliating experience her husband has thrust upon her.

Perhaps the most difficult performance to clearly decipher is that of Ron Silver, in the role of Herman, one of the walking dead. Reviews of the film were consistent in their praise of all three of the women, but critiques of Silver's work ran the gamut from inspired to lethargic. Because the character of Herman Broder is chronically depressed and unable to make any decision that might change his life, it is easy to regard Silver's performance as one-dimensional and lacking in feeling. The actor made his film debut in *Tunnelvision* (1974) and continued to appear in such diverse projects as Mike Nichols' *Silkwood* (1983) and Sidney Lumet's *Garbo Talks* (1985).

Mazursky employs several of the same production people as in past films. *Enemies, A Love Story* marks the eleventh collaboration with producer Pato Guzman, the ninth with Albert Wolsky, Academy Award-winning costume designer, the fifth with editor Stuart Pappé, and the third with executive producer Irby Smith. All cite

Mazursky's receptiveness to experimentation as one of the chief reasons for their return.

Even though *Enemies, A Love Story* contains all the classic elements of sexual betrayal, the story is not about the victimization of women, but rather their strength and ability to survive.

Patricia Ann Kowal

Reviews

American Film: Magazine of the Film and Televison Arts. XV, November, 1989, p. 30.
Chicago Tribune. January 5, 1990, VII, p. 27.
The Christian Science Monitor. January 5, 1990, p. 10.
L.A. Weekly. January 26-February 1, 1990, p. 69.
Los Angeles Times. December 12, 1989, VI, p. 1.
The New Republic. CCII, January 1, 1990, p. 26.
The New York Times. December 13, 1989, p. C22.
The New Yorker. LXV, December 25, 1989, p. 73.
Newsweek. CXIV, December 18, 1989, p. 68.
Time. CXXXV, January 8, 1990, p. 76.
US. CXXI, February 5, 1990, p. 60.
Variety. CCCXXXVII, December 13, 1989, p. 31.

THE FABULOUS BAKER BOYS

Production: Paula Weinstein, Mark Rosenberg, and Sydney Pollack (executive
   producer) for Gladden Entertainment; released by Twentieth Century-Fox
Direction: Steve Kloves
Screenplay: Steve Kloves
Cinematography: Michael Ballhaus
Editing: William Steinkamp
Production design: Jeffrey Townsend
Set decoration: Anne H. Ahrens
Makeup: Ronnie Specter
Costume design: Lisa Jensen
Sound: Stephan von Hase
Music: Dave Grusin
MPAA rating: R
Running time: 113 minutes

> *Principal characters:*
> Jack Baker . . . . Jeff Bridges
> Susie Diamond. . . . . Michelle Pfeiffer
> Frank Baker. . . . . Beau Bridges
> Nina . . . . Ellie Raab
> Monica Moran. . . . . Jennifer Tilly

The plot of *The Fabulous Baker Boys* arouses expectations of a sentimental,
depressing, or banal film. The story of two brothers barely surviving as a twin-piano
lounge act in Seattle, Washington, sounds as if it could drown in the bathos of show
business clichés. Because of the combined excellence of the contributions of writer-
director Steve Kloves, actors Michelle Pfeiffer, Jeff Bridges, and Beau Bridges, and
cinematographer Michael Ballhaus, the film transcends these potential pitfalls.
While not quite fabulous, this combination of romance, comedy, family drama, and
musical is one of a handful of American films of the late 1980's that will probably
remain popular into the twenty-first century.

Frank Baker (Beau Bridges) and his younger brother, Jack (Jeff Bridges), have
been performing pop standards and show tunes in Seattle-area hotels and nightclubs
for fifteen years. During this period, their audiences and bookings have dwindled
and their act has grown stale and pathetic. Frank is determined to keep going and
thinks that adding a female singer can save the act. Following thirty-seven young
women with more enthusiasm than talent, the final singer to audition is Susie
Diamond (Michelle Pfeiffer), a tough-talking alumna of the Triple-A Escort Service. Susie proves to have talent and the potential for more.

The Bakers' new act becomes a hit, earning for them more bookings at larger,
swanker night spots. Their newfound success and the sexual tension between Jack

and Susie build as they move toward a New Year's Eve engagement at a luxurious resort hotel. When Frank must return home after one of his children is injured, Jack and Susie stay behind to continue performing and eventually give in to their passions. Frank has feared the consequences of a relationship between his partners, and this apprehension proves justified when Susie soon leaves to sing in commercials.

Without Susie, the brothers find themselves back where they were. After Frank books an appearance on a third-rate local telethon, Jack's pent-up rage explodes, ending the Bakers' professional relationship. Jack eventually approaches Frank to mend their kinship, but they can never work together again. Jack also attempts to continue his romance with Susie, but she is wise enough to know that they are doomed to be loners.

At least Jack and Susie have a temperament in common; the Bakers share only their genes. Frank is a practical businessman, a husband and father with a house in the suburbs. Jack lives in a sparse apartment with an aging, sick Labrador retriever. Jack is intimate only with his dog and with Nina (Ellie Raab), the girl who lives above him and visits whenever her mother is entertaining a male guest. The self-deluding Frank convinces himself that he is putting on a good show, but Jack knows the act is a joke and is indifferent. Frank delivers trite patter between songs. Jack, with one exception, never speaks on stage.

Although Frank complains about carrying the burden of managing the act, he actually relishes it. Like the title character in *Broadway Danny Rose* (1984), Frank would be a better agent or manager than a performer—but not that much better. One of life's losers, he hides behind a façade of optimism. The black lacquer he sprays on his hair to conceal his bald spot is a perfect metaphor for this man, who will go to any extreme to cover up unpleasantness.

The sullen Jack hides from life itself. Fearing commitment, he never spends more than one night with a woman. He tries to adopt an existential Bogart-like stance toward the world but is more weak than cool, full of self-disgust and barely repressed self-pity. Bored while on stage with Frank, he looks as if he might walk off at any moment. Jack comes alive only when he plays jazz piano (dubbed by composer Dave Grusin) at a black nightclub. He thinks he has wasted his talent and his life by staying with Frank. The one time he interrupts his brother's patter is to say, "I love you, Frank." He is both mocking his partner and admiring Frank's ability to persevere.

Susie's main function is to force the brothers to reexamine their lives, but she is a fully rounded character on her own. The cliché about Fred Astaire and Ginger Rogers is that she gave him sex appeal and he gave her style: Susie provides both for the Bakers. She complains to Frank about having to sing banal tunes such as "Bali Hai" and "Feelings" and then goes out and sings the latter with something approximating "feelings." She resists Jack's advances because she knows that giving in will end the act, but she also knows she can survive without the Bakers. A certain poignancy attaches itself to Susie, however, since she may be glamorous enough to shine in the tawdry world of lounge acts, but in the bigger universe of show business, commercials may be the limit of her career advancement. More self-aware than the brothers, however, Susie knows this.

Jeff Bridges has given several good performances in recent years, including those in *Jagged Edge* (1985) and *The Morning After* (1986). He is also capable of being a bad actor, painting his character in too broad strokes, as in *Tucker* (1988). Jack Baker offers him the opportunity to take an unlikable character and make him sympathetic. Bridges plays Jack with great subtlety, making him a man of quiet frustration and anger.

Beau Bridges is even more impressive. With fat jowls expanding his already round face, Bridges expresses the everyman quality of Frank Baker, a good, decent, likable man despite the mediocrity of his work. Acting with his brother for the first time, Bridges has been given the best role of his long career of mostly dismal parts in undistinguished films. Having such a career no doubt aids in identifying with Frank. Bridges well deserved being named the best supporting actor of 1989 by the National Society of Film Critics.

After such films as *Grease II* (1982) and *Ladyhawke* (1985), Michelle Pfeiffer seemed headed for the same dead end as Susie Diamond. With *The Witches of Eastwick* (1987), *Married to the Mob* (1988), and, especially, *Dangerous Liaisons* (1988), she suddenly displayed an impressive range and maturity as an actress. Susie Diamond superficially resembles the Mafia wife Angela De Marco in *Married to the Mob*, but Pfeiffer's interpretation of Susie, an uneducated but smart woman who has larger goals than might be expected yet recognizes her limitations, has much greater depth.

Pfeiffer sang in *Grease II* but not since. Despite having a small voice, she performs with authority and style. With such standards as "More Than You Know" and "My Funny Valentine," she creates an unusual torch singer—one who clearly enjoys what she is doing. Pfeiffer conveys better than any American actress of her generation (with the possible exception of Kathleen Turner) a mixture of strength, vulnerability, innocence, intelligence, sensuality, and mischief. For this performance, clearly her best so far, Pfeiffer was the winner or cowinner of the best actress awards presented by the National Society of Film Critics, New York Film Critics Association, Los Angeles Film Critics Association, and the National Board of Review.

Much of the credit for these performances goes to the twenty-nine-year-old first-time director. Steve Kloves's only previous credit was his screenplay for *Racing with the Moon* (1984), a look at the problems of young love in the 1940's. That script showed promise but not the potential for the sophistication of *The Fabulous Baker Boys*. Producers Paula Weinstein and Mark Rosenberg spent four years trying to interest a studio in Kloves's screenplay before Twentieth Century-Fox agreed to finance it. After considering such directors as George Roy Hill, Weinstein and Rosenberg decided that Kloves's passion for the script warranted his directing it.

Whereas most films about show business sentimentalize this world or present it melodramatically, Kloves does neither; nor does he patronize or satirize this milieu. By expertly blending the musical, comic, and dramatic elements, Kloves creates an original film even though most of the occurrences are predictable. The most original part of *The Fabulous Baker Boys* is probably the ending, since the characters' problems are left realistically unresolved. This uncompromising conclusion also probably explains the film's failure at the box office, despite critical acclaim.

Kloves is aided in conveying the seediness and romance of show business by the cinematography of Michael Ballhaus, selected as the year's best by the National Society of Film Critics. Best known for his work on such Rainer Werner Fassbinder films as *Die Ehe der Maria Braun* (1978; *The Marriage of Maria Braun*), Ballhaus' American cinematography has been uneven, ranging from the undistinguished *Broadcast News* (1987) and *Working Girl* (1988) to the much grittier *After Hours* (1985) and *The Color of Money* (1986). The darker tones Ballhaus seems to prefer give *The Fabulous Baker Boys* a *film noir* tinge and an appropriate undercurrent of menace, since the characters are perpetually on the verge of disaster.

The efforts of Kloves, Ballhaus, and Pfeiffer shine in the film's climactic scene. After Frank leaves Jack and Susie on their own, they perform "Makin' Whoopee" with Susie, in a revealing red velvet dress, sultrily singing from atop Jack's piano and creating the sexual excitement that will result in the consummation of their affair. The camera work is conservative until Susie joins the act, and in this scene, the camera circles and swoops to express the performers' passion. The result is the most memorable nightclub scene since Rita Hayworth performed "Put the Blame on Mame" in *Gilda* (1946) and one of the sexiest moments in 1980's cinema.

Michael Adams

Reviews
Chicago Tribune. October 13, 1989, VII, p. 38.
Commonweal. CXVI, November 17, 1989, p. 644.
Films in Review. XLI, January, 1990, p. 41.
Los Angeles Times. October 13, 1989, VI, p. 1.
Maclean's. CII, October 23, 1989, p. 66.
The New Republic. CCI, November 20, 1989, p. 28.
New York. XXII, October 16, 1989, p. 73.
The New York Times. October 13, 1989, p. C14.
The New Yorker. LXV, October 16, 1989, p. 107.
Newsweek. CXIV, October 23, 1989, p. 84.
People Weekly. XXXII, October 30, 1989, p. 19.
Time. CXXXIV, October 23, 1989, p. 85.
Variety. CCCXXXVII, October, 18, 1989, p. 25.
The Washington Post. October 13, 1989, p. C1.

FAMILY BUSINESS

Production: Lawrence Gordon for Gordon Company; released by Tri-Star Pictures
with Regency International Pictures
Direction: Sidney Lumet
Screenplay: Vincent Patrick; based on his novel
Cinematography: Andrzej Bartkowiak
Editing: Andrew Mondshein
Production design: Philip Rosenberg
Art direction: Robert Guerra
Set decoration: Gary Brink
Costume design: Ann Roth
Music: Cy Coleman
MPAA rating: R
Running time: 115 minutes

> *Principal characters:*
> Jessie McMullen...................... Sean Connery
> Vito McMullen .... Dustin Hoffman
> Adam McMullen .... Matthew Broderick
> Elaine McMullen .... Rosana DeSoto
> Margie .... Janet Carroll
> Christine......................... Victoria Jackson

Over the past twenty years, director Sidney Lumet has presented film audiences with a series of memorably complex characters involved in compelling emotional or moral predicaments: Al Pacino in *Serpico* (1973) and *Dog Day Afternoon* (1975), Treat Williams in *Prince of the City* (1981), Paul Newman in *The Verdict* (1982). In *Family Business*, however, Lumet has less to work with; the story is flat without any interesting edge to it. The attention is divided among three main characters who never quite connect with one another emotionally, and the result is that the film seems unfocused. There is a void at the center that even its all-star cast cannot fill.

The family's troubles begin when Adam McMullen (Matthew Broderick), a Westinghouse scholar studying molecular biology, suddenly feels trapped, fearing that his life has been planned out for him by others. Wanting something more spontaneous, he drops out of college just shy of graduation in order to "find himself." Finding himself begins with bailing his sixty-year-old grandfather, Jessie McMullen (Sean Connery), out of jail for assaulting an off-duty policeman in a barroom brawl. The incorrigible Jessie, who is clearly Adam's idol, has a lengthy police record stretching back forty years, including some time spent in prison for burglary. Adam, for some reason, has a romanticized vision of his grandfather's colorful past—he believes Jessie is "fun"—and would like nothing more than to follow in his footsteps. He therefore approaches Jessie with a plan to pull off a heist of some experimental plasmids and logbooks from a DNA research facility, that, if successful, will net them a fast million dollars. The stolen goods are to be turned over to a former professor of Adam who developed the plasmids and now claims he is being cheated out of the profits by the research company that has dismissed him.

When Vito McMullen (Dustin Hoffman), who is Jessie's son and Adam's father, learns of the robbery scheme, he is furious at his father for influencing Adam and at Adam for throwing away what he has worked so hard to achieve. Vito, in his own youth, fell under his father's spell and as a result, spent some time in prison, but he has since created a respectable life for himself as a successful businessman who owns a large meat-packing company. Vito tries to talk the two out of the heist, but when he finds that he cannot dissuade them, he decides to go along in order to protect Adam.

On the night of the break-in, their plans go awry when a nervous Adam inadvertently sets off an alarm that brings an immediate response from the police. Adam is caught in the parking lot, but Jessie and Vito escape with the plasmids and logbooks. Adam is offered a deal by the police: If he turns in his accomplices and gives back the plasmids, he will be released on probation; if he refuses, then he will probably not be a free man much before his fortieth birthday. Adam refuses the deal, unwilling to "rat" on his father and grandfather.

Vito, however, cares too much about his son to let him spend time in prison. He returns the plasmids, turns himself in, and tells the police of Jessie's involvement. When the stolen plasmids are analyzed, they prove to be nothing more than tap water. Vito suspects that Jessie has pulled a switch on him, but the more experienced Jessie realizes that they were set up. He finds Adam's former professor, who has mysteriously been rehired by the research company and, under the influence of a stranglehold, gets him to admit that it was all a hoax. With the plasmids supposedly stolen, the company could buy more time from investors who were beginning to grow impatient waiting for results. Jessie extorts a large sum of money from the researcher in return for staying quiet about the hoax; however, he has little time to spend it, as the police arrive at his apartment a short while later to arrest him.

At the trial, Jessie's history works against him, as the judge decides to hold him primarily responsible for the burglary. He hands down a severe sentence, one that essentially amounts to life in prison for a man already sixty years old, in spite of an impassioned plea by Adam, who insists that the theft was all his idea. Adam and Vito are chastised by the judge, who calls Vito a poor excuse for a father, but both are given probation rather than jail time.

After the trial, Adam refuses to speak to his father; he says he will never forgive him for "ratting" on Jessie. He visits his grandfather regularly in prison and watches as his health deteriorates and he is moved from his cell to the prison hospital, where he eventually dies. The reconciliation of father and son takes place when Adam arrives one evening carrying Jessie's ashes; he wants Vito to help him plan a proper Irish funeral. The film's final sequence is their tribute to Jessie: a ceremony on the rooftop of Jessie's apartment, looking down on the Irish neighborhood where he lived all of his adult life. The rooftop is crowded with his old friends, along with Vito and Adam and a couple of kegs of beer. As the mourners break into an emotional rendition of "Danny Boy," Jessie's ashes are scattered by the wind to the street below.

Family Business suffers from what seems to have been an uncertainty on the part of the filmmakers—writer, director, and actors—as to whether they were making a comedy or a drama. (One does not necessarily need to choose—Lumet straddled the line successfully in the aforementioned *Dog Day Afternoon* with an enormous amount of help from Al Pacino's manic performance.) Yet this time it does not work; the tone is somehow off. This is the kind of film that results in much nervous laughter on the part of the audience; they are not sure if what they are laughing at is supposed to be humorous. One example comes in a scene in which Vito, in his office at the meat packing plant, brutally punches and kicks one of his employees, who has been caught stealing meat from the company. When the beating ends, Vito's secretary turns to him and asks if this means that he is having a mid-life crisis. Another example is when Jessie, in the back of a prison van, beats a younger convict nearly senseless for calling him "Pops" and then returns to his seat with a self-satisfied grin on his face. Jessie's overtly physical response seems grossly out of proportion to the offense committed.

Part of the problem is with Jessie's character as written by Vincent Patrick. It is hard to understand just why a supposedly bright young man such as Adam worships him. Jessie is a walking anachronism, a "man's man": a hard-drinking, fist-throwing, tough-as-nails kind of guy who pinches waitresses' bottoms, picks up hookers, and spouts what passes for prison wisdom—repeating tiring axioms such as "If you can't do the time, don't do the crime" and calling anyone who is ashamed to admit to having spent time in prison a snob. If this is what Adam aspires to, then why should the audience feel sympathy for his predicament? With his jailhouse romanticism, it seems Adam has got what he wanted as well as what he deserved.

Another problem is the inconsistency in acting levels. Both Connery and Broderick seem to be playing their roles broadly for comedy, grinning and mugging through virtually every scene. Hoffman, meanwhile, plays for drama, turning in a poignant, finely tuned performance, as he weighs what he has to lose if the break-in goes awry. In a heartbreaking scene just after the bungled robbery, Vito comes home to a dark apartment; his wife Elaine (sensitively played by Rosana DeSoto), already in bed, calls out to him to ask how his poker game went. (She knows nothing about the robbery; he apparently told her that he was merely going out to play cards). Vito answers that he lost sixty dollars. A few moments later, when he wanders into the bedroom, Elaine looks up and sees Vito's long face and his sad eyes. She tells him that he looks depressed, that he must have lost much more than sixty dollars. Vito pauses for a moment and then quietly answers, "Yes, I did."

Hoffman's Vito is a decent man who wants nothing more from life than to be able to give his son the things he never had: a lovely home, a stable family life, the best possible education. Instead, he sees everything for which he has worked coming unraveled before his eyes; even worse, he is partly responsible for the unraveling. If there had been some similar realizations on the part of Adam or Jessie, the film might have worked. Instead there is an unsettling underlying premise: that Vito is somehow responsible for having deprived young Adam of "fun"; Adam envies Vito the "fun" he must have had growing up with Jessie as his father, pulling off robberies together. He actually manages to make his father feel guilty about that and accuses Vito of using his need to provide for his son as an excuse for not having "fun" in his own life. The whole idea sounds, and is, perverse, and it trivializes the pain that Hoffman's Vito feels.

Yet the relentless Adam, to prove his point, asks his father what was the most fun they have had together in the past twenty years. Vito pauses and then answers that it was the robbery. Adam excitedly answers, "Me, too." Judging from the poor box office returns for *Family Business*, the audience did not share their sentiment.

Mary Lou McNichol

Reviews

Boston Globe. December 15, 1989, p. 65.
Chicago Tribune. December 15, 1989, VII, p. 28.
The Christian Science Monitor. February 2, 1990, p. 10.
The Hollywood Reporter. December 15, 1989.
LA Weekly. December 15, 1989.
Los Angeles Times. December 15, 1989, VI, p. 1.
National Review. XLII, January 22, 1990, p. 57.
The New York Times. December 15, 1989, p. C28.
People Weekly. XXXIII, January 8, 1990, p. 11.
San Francisco Chronicle. December 15, 1989, p. E1.
Variety. CCCXXXVII, December 13, 1989, p. 30.
The Washington Post. December 15, 1989, p. D1.

FIELD OF DREAMS

Production: Lawrence Gordon and Charles Gordon for Gordon Company; released by Universal
Direction: Phil Alden Robinson
Screenplay: Phil Alden Robinson; based on the novel *Shoeless Joe*, by W. P. Kinsella
Cinematography: John W. Lindley
Editing: Ian Crafford
Production design: Dennis Gassner
Art direction: Leslie McDonald
Set decoration: Nancy Haigh
Special effects: Robbie Knott
Makeup: Richard Arrington
Costume design: Linda Bass
Sound: Russell Williams II
Music: James Horner
MPAA rating: PG
Running time: 106 minutes

Principal characters:
Ray Kinsella	Kevin Costner
Annie Kinsella	Amy Madigan
Terence Mann	James Earl Jones
Karin Kinsella	Gaby Hoffman
"Shoeless" Joe Jackson	Ray Liotta
Doc "Moonlight" Graham	Burt Lancaster
Mark	Timothy Busfield
Archie Graham	Frank Whaley
John Kinsella	Dwier Brown

Until the 1980's, films about baseball were generally undistinguished. Many have been aimed at children, such as *Roogie's Bump* (1954), in which a child becomes a major league pitcher. Others are slapstick comedies, such as *Rhubarb* (1951), in which a cat inherits a team. Many focus on off-the-field activities: an outfielder with mental problems in *Fear Strikes Out* (1957), a catcher with a terminal disease in *Bang the Drum Slowly* (1973). Biographical films such as *Pride of the Yankees* (1942), about Lou Gehrig, and *The Winning Team* (1952), about Grover Cleveland Alexander, wallow in sentimentality. These films are usually filled with unconvincingly athletic actors and clumsily staged game footage. A few such baseball films manage to transcend these limitations with charm, such as chemistry professor Ray Milland moonlighting as a St. Louis Cardinal in *It Happens Every Spring* (1949), or with scatological realism, such as the profane Little Leaguers in *The Bad News Bears* (1976). The 1980's, however, saw the first truly aesthetically pleasing films about baseball, with believable performers and realistic action sequences. Barry Levinson's *The Natural* (1984), from the novel by Bernard Malamud, is the first film to portray the game's mythic mystique, and Ron Shelton's *Bull Durham* (1988) combines myth, unforced camaraderie, excellent game re-creations, humor, and sex with an understanding of and passion for baseball. Even lesser films such as *Eight Men Out* (1988) and *Major League* (1989; reviewed in this volume) have their moments.

Field of Dreams just misses being the third home run of a baseball film; the film excels in its presentation of the sport's mythic appeal but is weakened by oversentimentality. Based on the 1982 novel *Shoeless Joe* by Canadian writer W. P. Kinsella, who has become the first specialist in baseball fiction for adults, *Field of Dreams* is the story of Iowa farmer Ray Kinsella (Kevin Costner). Living with his wife, Annie (Amy Madigan), and daughter, Karin (Gaby Hoffman), Ray is barely making a living when one day in the middle of his cornfield he hears a voice say, "If you build it, he will come." He eventually decides that the voice wants him to build a baseball field on his farm, even though everyone except Annie and Karin thinks that he is crazy. His effort pays off when the long-dead "Shoeless" Joe Jackson (Ray Liotta) appears, looking as he did in his prime with the Chicago White Sox in the 1910's. Jackson, one of the greatest hitters of all time, was banned from baseball, along with seven teammates, after being accused of throwing the 1919 World Series. These teammates (or at least their ghosts or spirits) eventually arrive to pick up where they left off.

When the voice tells him to "Ease his pain," Ray decides "he" is Terence Mann—a famous radical writer from the 1960's who has become a recluse—because of something Mann once wrote about the glory days of baseball and because a character in one of his stories is named Ray Kinsella.

Ray goes to Boston and tracks down Mann (James Earl Jones), who has holed up in his office/apartment writing computer software. He has become disillusioned because of America's failure to realize the ideals of the 1960's. After fumbling a rather feeble kidnapping attempt, Ray gradually persuades the initially hostile Mann to accompany him to a Boston Red Sox game at Fenway Park. They see a scoreboard message about Archibald "Moonlight" Graham, who played in one game for the New York Giants in 1905 but never batted, and Mann hears the voice say, "Go the distance." They travel to Chisholm, Minnesota, to learn that Graham had become a physician after giving up baseball and died after years of being a beloved small-town doctor. Ray then has a long conversation with the ghost of Doc "Moonlight" Graham (Burt Lancaster), who wishes that he could have hit in a major league game at least once. Driving to Iowa, Ray and Mann pick up a young hitchhiker (Frank Whaley), who tells them he is Archie Graham, a baseball player.

Back at the farm, enough other dead major leaguers have gathered for games to be played, and young Graham finally gets to bat in the big time. These games are watched by Ray, Annie, Karin, and Mann—who finds his cynicism diminishing—but those without the necessary faith cannot see them. Among the "unbelievers" is

Annie's brother Mark (Timothy Busfield), who conspires with the townspeople who want to foreclose on the farm. The film's climax arrives when Karin begins choking on a piece of hot dog and Archie Graham steps off the field, sacrificing his new baseball career to become his adult self and save her. After that, Mark can see the players and decides to help Ray save the farm. Mann suggests that the mythical magic of the field will draw thousands of believers willing to pay to see this miracle.

Field of Dreams ends with the appearance of another player, who is not a former major leaguer. Ray feels guilt for having turned against his father when he was a rebellious youth, symbolized by his never having played catch with the former semiprofessional player. When John Kinsella (Dwier Brown), younger than his son, arrives on the field, Ray makes the first hesitant move toward reconciliation.

Director-screenwriter Phil Alden Robinson is faithful to the spirit of W. P. Kinsella's novel, one of the best ever written about baseball, but he does make numerous changes. He eliminates Ray's estranged twin brother and an old man who claims to be the oldest living Chicago Cub and adds a scene in which Annie passionately protests against censorship at a school board meeting as an awkward means of fleshing out her character. Joe Jackson and his fellow Black Sox are at the center of the novel but at the periphery of the film, perhaps because Robinson knew that he would be following John Sayles's depiction of the scandal in *Eight Men Out*. Since Ray's baseball diamond is, in a sense, the central character, *Field of Dreams* is a more appropriate title than *Shoeless Joe*. Robinson's major alteration is to create Terence Mann to replace the real-life J. D. Salinger, the reclusive author of *The Catcher in the Rye* (1951), because portraying the latter would have resulted in legal problems.

Field of Dreams works well in conveying the mythical appeal of baseball. Having long-dead greats return to their youthful forms to play once again expresses the innocence and optimism associated with baseball's past. Allowing the players involved in the game's greatest scandal to play again indicates how a player can try to vindicate himself for past failures with his next at-bat, pitch, or fielding chance. The idea of the novel and the film also shows the timelessness of the sport: Because there is no time limit, a baseball game can go on forever (as in T. Coraghessan Boyle's wonderful short story "The Hector Quesadilla Story"), and the exploits of major leaguers acquire a legendary quality larger than that in other American sports. Robinson assumes his audience will bring these feelings to the film; like jazz, baseball cannot be explained. *Field of Dreams* works on an emotional level, exulting in baseball's folklore, bemoaning America's loss of innocence, and expressing the need to believe in something to keep from drowning in cynicism.

While entertaining and moving as a whole, *Field of Dreams* is ragged around the edges. Robinson likes the exchange "Is this heaven?" "No, this is Iowa" so much that he uses it twice. The Black Sox are joined not only by players from their era but also by later players such as Mel Ott and Gil Hodges for no apparent reason. That Ray Liotta is smaller than and looks nothing like Joe Jackson is immaterial, but Liotta bats right-handed and throws left-handed—exactly the opposite of Jackson and like only a handful of players in major league history. Changing the alienated writer from Salinger to the fictional Mann creates some awkwardness, since a black man is thereby made to express longing for a time when blacks were not allowed to play in the major leagues. The solution to Ray's financial difficulties, inherited from *Shoeless Joe*, leaves a somewhat bitter taste: The magic of Ray's dream is cheapened by charging people money to share it.

Robinson, who cowrote another fantasy film, *All of Me* (1984), and wrote and directed another piece of nostalgia, *In the Mood* (1987), clearly intends *Field of Dreams* to be a life-affirming film in the tradition of Frank Capra's *It's a Wonderful Life* (1946). While Robinson's film lacks the universality of Capra's, it successfully walks the thin line between charm and silliness until the end, when the meeting between Ray and his father sinks the film into unabashed sentimentality.

Robinson is a visually conservative director at his best in handling his actors. Madigan, Hoffman, and Liotta do well with underwritten parts, and Costner, given a less flamboyant role than in *Bull Durham*, has an everyman quality necessary for the audience to want to share Ray's quest. Jones and Lancaster, two great actors, give one of their best performances ever as supporting players. The weight provided by their self-assurance and dignity keeps this delicate fantasy from floating away into absurdity. If the film's message is that baseball can make dreams come true, the film itself is an example of such a dream. Despite its shortcomings, the film was considered one of the best of the year and received an Academy Award nomination for Best Picture.

Michael Adams

Reviews

American Film: Magazine of the Film and Television Arts. XIV, May, 1989, p. 62.
Chicago Tribune. March 21, 1989, VII, p. 31.
Commonweal. CXVI, May 19, 1989, p. 303.
Film Comment. XXV, May, 1989, p. 78.
Films in Review. XL, August, 1989, p. 420.
Mademoiselle. XCV, July, 1989, p. 66.
The Nation. CCXLVIII, May 15, 1989, p. 678.
The New Republic. CC, May 8, 1989, p. 26.
New York. XXII, April 24, 1989, p. 96.
The New York Times. April 21, 1989, p. C8.
The New Yorker. LXV, May 1, 1989, p. 75.
Newsweek. CXIII, April 24, 1989, p. 72.
Sports Illustrated. LXX, May 1, 1989, p. 81.
Time. CXXXIII, April 24, 1989, p. 78.
Variety. CCCXXXIV, April 19, 1989, p. 24.
Vogue. CLXXIX, May, 1989, p. 204.

FLETCH LIVES

Production: Alan Greisman and Peter Douglas; released by Universal
Direction: Michael Ritchie
Screenplay: Leon Capetanos; based on characters created by Gregory McDonald
Cinematography: James McPherson
Editing: Richard A. Harris
Production design: Stephen Hendrickson
Art direction: Cameron Birnie, Jimmie Bly, W. Steven Graham, and Donald B.
  Woodruff
Set decoration: Gary Fettis and Susan Bode
Special effects: Gintar Repecka, Eric Roberts, and Scott Fisher
Makeup: Tom Miller and Michael Mills
Costume design: Anna Hill Johnstone
Sound: Jim Alexander
Music: Harold Faltermeyer
MPAA rating: PG-13
Running time: 93 minutes

Principal characters:
Fletch . . . . Chevy Chase
Calculus . . . . Cleavon Little
Ham Johnson . . . . Hal Holbrook
Becky Culpepper . . . . Julianne Phillips
Jimmy Lee Farnsworth . . . . R. Lee Ermey
Frank . . . . Richard Libertini
Ben Dover . . . . Randall "Tex" Cobb
Gillet . . . . George Wyner

Fletch Lives, like its 1985 predecessor, *Fletch* (also directed by Michael Ritchie), serves primarily as a vehicle for the attractive talents of popular comic actor Chevy Chase. *Fletch Lives*, like *Fletch*, effectively exploits a detective-story framework within which Chase, as the film's title character, dons a variety of disguises, takes a few of his signature pratfalls, and moves constantly from one throwaway verbal gag to another. Along the way, writer Leon Capetanos mocks clichés of Southern culture, satirizes television evangelists, and gives the plot further topical dimension by briefly alluding to the evil side of toxic waste disposal.

As the film opens, Irwin Fletcher (Chevy Chase), known to all as "Fletch," is working undercover for a Los Angeles newspaper, trying to expose corruption in city sewage contracts. He longs for a vacation, which his editor, Frank (Richard Libertini), refuses to give him. One evening, Fletch receives a phone call from a lawyer named Amanda Ray Ross (Patricia Kalember), who informs him that his Aunt Belle has died, leaving Fletch her Louisiana antebellum estate. Fletch enthusiastically informs Frank that his days as a browbeaten reporter are over, and he boards a plane for New Orleans.

During the flight, Fletch dreams of himself as a pre-Civil War patriarch. He is surrounded by buxom Southern belles and humble servants—among them Frank and Fletch's nemesis, Gillet (George Wyner), the attorney for his former wife. The highlight of the dream sequence and an interlude which represents the tone of the film is Fletch's own rendition of "Zip-a-Dee-Doo-Dah."

Ross meets Fletch at the airport, and as they drive into plantation country, the film's hero expects the best, but he finds the worst: Belle Isle, his late aunt's mansion, is a shambles. The only servant left on the estate is Calculus (Cleavon Little), who plays the role of a shuffling, Stepin Fetchit sort of retainer. Ross informs Fletch that she is acting as negotiator for an unnamed party who wishes to buy Belle Isle for $200,000. As an added incentive, she seduces the intrepid investigative reporter but is murdered during the night. Fletch is arrested by an archetypal sadistic Southern sheriff (Don Crockett), who forces Fletch to share a cell with Ben Dover (Randall "Tex" Cobb), a barely human biker who is serving a sentence for molesting a dead horse. Fletch is bailed out of jail by Ham Johnson (Hal Holbrook), a patrician lawyer who appears sympathetic.

Later, Becky Culpepper (Julianne Phillips), a real-estate agent, appears to make another offer—this time for $250,000—for Belle Isle. By this time, Fletch has become quite curious as to why mysterious figures would be so anxious to buy a decrepit shell of a house and apparently worthless land. Posing as an insect exterminator named Billy Gene King, he enters Ross's home and searches her business records. Fletch discovers that his aunt had once intended to leave her estate to television evangelist Jimmy Lee Farnsworth (R. Lee Ermey), but for some reason had changed her mind.

Thus Fletch begins investigating the empire of Farnsworth, who is clearly modeled on real-life preachers such as Jerry Falwell, Jimmy Lee Swaggart, and Ernest Angley. Fletch gains Farnsworth's confidence by posing as one of the minister's gullible, zombielike followers. Farnsworth takes Fletch on a tour of his major project, Bibleland, a laughable quasi-religious theme park, which features such attractions as a Heavenly Hilton hotel and convention complex and a Jump for Jesus trampoline center. On the other hand, Ham Johnson, whose family estate is adjacent to Farnsworth's Bible circus, tells Fletch that he aims to expose the preacher because Farnsworth had cheated Johnson's mother out of a considerable amount of property.

At this point, Johnson appears to Fletch and the viewer as acting in good faith. The plot thickens, however, when Fletch suspects that his sidekick Calculus may have taken a shot at him during a raccoon hunt. Furthermore, Fletch discovers that Becky Culpepper is Farnsworth's daughter. Fletch is confused, but all signs of foul play point to Farnsworth. Disguised as Guest Faith Healer Claude Henry Smoot, Fletch returns to Farnsworth's television studios in order to investigate further. Not only does he find additional examples of the preacher's shady show-business façade, but he also gains access to the operation's computer records. In addition, Fletch makes love to Becky and thereby acquires another source of support and information. Becky insists that her father is fundamentally a sincere, honest man.

Fletch learns that the land that Farnsworth wants to acquire exudes toxic waste. Fletch poses as a chemical company executive named Elmer Fudd Gantry to discover the details of the waste disposal. Following this lead, Fletch dresses as a Confederate Army officer, identifies himself as Bobby Lee Swartz, and crashes a costume ball at the home of Ham Johnson. Johnson realizes that Fletch has stumbled onto the truth: Johnson, out of an obsessive love for his mother, has vowed to sabotage Farnsworth's ministerial empire by drowning it in toxic chemical sewage. Holding Fletch and Becky at gunpoint, Johnson also admits that he poisoned Ross because she knew too much. The film's climax, according to formula, involves a chase which ends when FBI agents, led by Calculus—who is, in reality, an FBI agent named Goldstein—descend on Johnson's home.

The case having been solved, Fletch heads back to Los Angeles, where he is welcomed with open arms by Frank but is ambushed by Gillet. The latter has heard of Fletch's inheritance and demands that Fletch's former wife, the millstone around Fletch's neck, get her fair share. With a final smirk, Fletch signs over the deed to the remains of Belle Isle.

A simple plot summary does not do justice to the many amusing interludes in *Fletch Lives*, the results of Capetanos' keen wit and Chase's comedic skills. Because of Chase's background in improvisational comedy, it is difficult to tell just where scripted material ends and Chase's own spur-of-the-moment, inspired gags begin. Chase is equally at home with broad, burlesque-style comedy and with material usually associated with a sophisticated night-club stand-up routine. Often Chase's verbal delivery, gestures, and mugging are so swift or muted that the film really merits at least a second viewing to appreciate thoroughly Chase's work.

Fletch Lives is a parody of hackneyed detective thrillers—complete with frequent voice-over passages in which Fletch keeps the audience abreast of developments—and thus permits a variety of comic possibilities. For example, Fletch resorts to at least eleven disguises in order to carry out his investigation, many of these improvised. Fletch writes for the Los Angeles newspaper as Jane Doe. Early in the film, wearing a silver-blonde wig and a maid's costume, he calls himself Peggy Lee Zorba as he looks for incriminating evidence in the Kakakis Brothers seafood house. Later, so that he can park his car in a no-parking zone, he slips a "clergy" card behind the windshield wiper. During the flight from California to Louisiana, Fletch identifies himself as Nostradamus to an annoying fellow passenger, and when he is arrested, he tells the sheriff that he is Victor Hugo. Given all Fletch's disguises, it is not surprising that Calculus is not who he had appeared to be either.

Few critics would argue that *Fletch Lives* is serious cinema, but many would agree that Capetanos, Ritchie, Chase, and excellent supporting performers such as Cobb and Little have succeeded in creating an enjoyable, entertaining film.

Gordon Walters

Reviews

Chicago Tribune. March 17, 1989, VII, p. 44.
Films in Review. XL, June, 1989, p. 367.
Los Angeles Times. March 17, 1989, VI, p. 8.
The New York Times. March 17, 1989, p. C17.
Newsweek. CXIII, March 20, 1989, p. 83.
People Weekly. XXXI, February 27, 1989, p. 11.
Punch. CCXCVI, May 26, 1989, p. 42.
Variety. CCCXXXIV, March 15, 1989, p. 13.
The Wall Street Journal. March 16, 1989, p. A14.
The Washington Post. March 17, 1989, p. D7.

FOR QUEEN AND COUNTRY

Origin: Great Britain
Released: 1988
Released in U.S.: 1989
Production: Tim Bevan for Working Title; released by Atlantic Releasing
Direction: Martin Stellman
Screenplay: Martin Stellman and Trix Worrell
Cinematography: Richard Greatrex
Editing: Stephen Singleton
Production design: Andrew McAlpine
Art direction: Charmian Adams
Special effects: Arthur Beavis
Makeup: Morag Ross
Costume design: Sandy Powell
Sound: Simon Fraser and Martin Jackson
Music: Michael Kamen, Geoff MacCormack, and Simon Goldenberg
MPAA rating: R
Running time: 106 minutes

Principal characters:
Reuben James	Denzel Washington
Fish	Dorian Healy
Stacey	Amanda Redman
Bob	Sean Chapman
Colin	Bruce Payne
Lynford	Geff Francis
Kilcoyne	George Baker
Challoner	Craig Fairbrass
Harry	Brian McDermott

The structure and atmosphere of *For Queen and Country* have the qualities of one of the grimmer Thomas Hardy novels updated to the 1980's, urbanized and accelerated. Reuben James (Denzel Washington) is the doomed protagonist, a black British army volunteer who—as shown in the film's opening vignettes—has risked his life in Northern Ireland and the Falklands. Now he has returned to civilian life and to his flat in a brutalized London high-rise project, where most of his old acquaintances, both black and white, are involved in larceny or the drug trade. They are under the constant surveillance of the police, who range from friendly Harry (Brian McDermott) and Reuben's former schoolmate Bob (Sean Chapman) by way of fair but stern Inspector Kilcoyne (George Baker) to racist and sadistic Challoner (Craig Fairbrass).

The only good things that happen to Reuben are his reunion with army buddy

Fish (Dorian Healy), who had saved his life in an ambush by the Irish Republican Army, and his encounter with Stacey (Amanda Redman), whose young daughter he catches stealing from his flat. Shadows, however, soon fall on both relationships, and on Reuben's hopes in general. Fish, who lost a leg in the army, is emotionally unstable and perpetually short of money. When Reuben applies for a passport in order to take Stacey to Paris, he discovers that he is no longer a British subject, because his birthplace, St. Lucia, is now an independent nation. Unable to find a regular job, Reuben reluctantly serves as a backup man in a drug deal for a white acquaintance named Colin (Bruce Payne), and then gives his pay to Fish. Meanwhile Stacey, whose former husband was a gun-carrying criminal, breaks with Reuben when she finds him carrying a gun; a black acquaintance, Lynford (Geff Francis), has brought police suspicion on Reuben by citing him as an alibi for a robbery charge; and the police are angry because Harry has been killed and no one nearby, including Reuben, will admit to having seen the killer (who turns out to have been Lynford). As tension builds between the project residents and the police, Reuben decides to get away from it all and go to St. Lucia. Before he can leave, however, the tension erupts into violence: Fish is shot dead by trigger-happy Challoner, and Reuben shoots Challoner. Bob, as the police marksman, has Reuben in his sights but hesitates to shoot until Kilcoyne prompts him. The film ends with a blackout on the sound of the shot.

For Queen and Country is one of many British films that have focused on the social problems of Great Britain in the 1980's. The most obvious comparison is with another Working Title production, *Sammy and Rosie Get Laid* (1987), in which the shooting of a black woman by the police touches off a riot. *Sammy and Rosie Get Laid*, however, zigzags through a variety of issues and throws off continual sparks of humor. The American release of *For Queen and Country* coincided with that of *High Hopes* (1989; reviewed in this volume), whose downbeat view of the gap between rich and poor in Margaret Thatcher's Great Britain was relieved by continual humor. Even a filmmaker as long on social indignation and as short on humor as Kenneth Loach, however, knows that a light touch can be more effective than a hammering. In his *Looks and Smiles* (1981), which dealt, incidentally, with the problem of young (white) men who have served in the British army in Northern Ireland, many scenes had a casual, improvised tone that preempted any concern with advancing the plot. In *For Queen and Country*, only one scene stands out with this kind of lightness and unpredictability: a man dancing at a party with a television set balanced on his head. Every other scene is insistently solemn and nudges Reuben closer to his eventual doom.

Where Thomas Hardy sometimes resorts to an obvious contrivance to ensure a tragic end to his narratives, Martin Stellman and coauthor Trix Worrell transfix Reuben with a whole series of unlucky coincidences. Despite contacts, Reuben cannot find a job; he happens to be on hand when Harry is shot; he happens to be present when the police question Lynford about the robbery; he loses his British citizenship; Stacey happens to call when he is leaving as Colin's backup, and she happens to feel the gun he is wearing when they embrace; and amid the clash between blacks and police, the racist Challoner happens to shoot Fish, an innocent bystander. No doubt Stellman and Worrell wanted to emphasize Reuben's plight by making the conditions he faced as stark and relentless as possible. Certainly the filmmakers' credentials suggest that opportunism played little or no part in their contrived plot. Stellman spent several years running a school and then a theater for inner-city youth; Worrell, who later took over the theater, is a black Londoner born in St. Lucia. Moreover, since Stellman collaborated on several commercial scripts and had sole credit for *Defense of the Realm* (1985) before making his directorial debut on *For Queen and Country*, he may also have seen the unlucky coincidences as dramatic devices that would tighten the film's hold on its audience.

The casting of Denzel Washington as Reuben reflects an understandable need to find that audience not only among Great Britain's declining population of filmgoers but also in the United States. Washington has presence; he can command attention even when speaking quietly or standing still. In this way, and to some extent in his looks, he resembles Sidney Poitier, in the years when the latter almost single-handedly portrayed black dignity on the motion picture screen. It may be more than a coincidence that the two actors played leading roles in films about South Africa— Poitier in *Cry the Beloved Country* (1951) and Washington in *Cry Freedom* (1987). Like Poitier, Washington tends to hold a pose too long; in *For Queen and Country*, this tendency conflicts at times with Reuben's characteristic impatience. Although the instability of Washington's Cockney accent is unlikely to bother American audiences, the effort to maintain it may have been a distraction to Washington himself. In any event, he gives a generally strong performance in a role that requires him to be on screen in almost every scene.

The other roles are played at the very least with competence; except for Fish, however, they are little more than cameos or plot devices. The script and direction place similar constraints on the key technical contributions: photography, editing, and music score. Although the climactic riot sequence takes place at night, there is neither an overall progression from light to dark nor any dramatic alternation between them; cinematographer Richard Greatrex simply does the best he can with individual scenes, providing crisp outlines and a wide tonal range. Furthermore, there is no apparent attempt to use the resources of editing for rhythm or contrast. Michael Kamen, the chief composer, has provided intense scores for such films as *The Dead Zone* (1983), *Brazil* (1985), and *Mona Lisa* (1986), but the only notable music in *For Queen and Country* is a pounding march that accompanies the opening military vignettes.

For Queen and Country is a worthy attempt to deal with one aspect of racism; it is competently made and interesting. Yet, its effectiveness is undermined both by overuse of narrative contrivance and by underuse of cinematic resources.

William Johnson

Reviews

The Hollywood Reporter. May 15, 1989, p. 3.
Interview. XIX, July, 1989, p. 86.
Los Angeles Times. May 19, 1989, VI, p. 13.
The New Leader. LXXII, May 1, 1989, p. 21.
New Statesman and Society. II, January 27, 1989, p. 40.
The New York Times. May 19, 1989, p. C14.
Punch. CCXCVI, January 27, 1989, p. 54.
Variety. CCCXXXI, May 25, 1988, p. 18.
The Village Voice. May 23, 1989, p. C14.
Vogue. CLXXIX, March, 1989, p. 274.
The Washington Post. June 23, 1989, p. WW37.
Washington Times. June 23, 1989, p. E3.

FOUR ADVENTURES OF REINETTE AND MIRABELLE (QUATRE AVENTURES DE REINETTE ET MIRABELLE)

Origin: France
Released: 1986
Released in U.S.: 1989
Production: C.E.R. and Les Films du Losange; released by New Yorker Films
Direction: Eric Rohmer
Screenplay: Eric Rohmer
Cinematography: Sophie Maintigneux
Editing: Miria-Luisa Garcia
Production design: Françoise Etchegaray
Sound: Pierre Camus and Pascal Ribier
Music: Ronan Girre and Jena-Louis Valero
MPAA rating: no listing
Running time: 95 minutes

> *Principal characters:*
> Reinette .... Joëlle Miquel
> Mirabelle .... Jessica Forde
> Neighbors .... The Housseau Family
> Waiter .... Philippe Laudenbach
> Kleptomaniac .... Yasmine Haury
> Hustler .... Marie Rivière
> Inspector .... Béatrice Romand
> Inspector .... Gérard Courant
> Tourist .... David Rocksavage
> Cadger .... Jacques Auffray
> Charitable Lady .... Haydée Caillot
> Picture Dealer .... Fabrice Luchini

Director Eric Rohmer shot *Four Adventures of Reinette and Mirabelle* as a low-budget, sixteen-millimeter film at the same time that he was working on *Le Rayon vert* (1986; *Summer*). Rohmer had free time on his hands while waiting for the phenomenon of the green ray that figures so prominently in *Summer*'s plot, and so he worked simultaneously on this charming, minimalist film improvised around stories told him by Joëlle Miquel, who plays the film's main character, Reinette, and who did her own paintings.

Four Adventures of Reinette and Mirabelle differs in several respects from other recent Rohmer films. Devoid of romantic interest, it portrays the developing friendship between two vibrant young women who debate nature and ethics rather than men, makeup, or clothes. Unlike the protagonists of *Summer* or *L'Ami de mon amie* (1987; *Boyfriends and Girlfriends*), Reinette and Mirabelle (Jessica Forde) bristle with ideas and arguments. Not since *Ma nuit chez Maud* (1969; *My Night at Maud's*) has a Rohmer film contained such interesting conversation or such self-sufficient heroines.

In the first of the film's four episodes, "L'Heure bleue" ("The Blue Hour"), Reinette and Mirabelle meet when Reinette offers to help Mirabelle fix her flat tire. They go to Reinette's place, a converted barn in the wild, unspoiled countryside, where she paints in solitude. Though Reinette is rather plain, her paintings are maturely sensual, full of provocative naked women. A rapport slowly develops between the two women, and Reinette invites Mirabelle to sleep overnight so that they can rise before dawn to experience the Blue Hour, a minute of perfect silence between night and day. They rise early and go outside, but just as the "Blue Hour" is about to begin, a neighbor cranks up his raucous farm machinery, a dog barks, and the moment is ruined. Mirabelle promises the desolate Reinette that she will stay another night to try again. That day Reinette takes Mirabelle around and shows her the animals of the Housseau family, a real farm family who play themselves. They eat ripe farm strawberries, pet goats, and wander among the cows at pasture. Later, at dinner, Mirabelle invites Reinette, who plans to study art in Paris, to become her roommate. The two dance after dinner, and the next morning they witness the Blue Hour.

In the second episode, "Le Garçon de café" ("The Waiter") Reinette, now in Paris, agrees to meet her roommate Mirabelle at a café after school. An insufferable waiter (Philippe Laudenbach) demands immediate payment in exact change, refuses her larger bill, and accuses her of both wasting his time with her inexpensive order and intending to leave without paying. Furthermore, he does not believe that she is waiting for a friend and tries to take the other chair from her table. Reinette notices that he is making change for another group and confronts him, but he derides her even further. When Mirabelle finally arrives, she too is harassed. Fed up, she persuades Reinette to leave without paying when he turns his back. The next morning Reinette rises early to go back and pay the waiter—thereby denying him the satisfaction of thinking himself right about her—only to discover that he was a one-day substitute.

The third adventure is a combination of three short vignettes: "Le Mendiant, la cleptomane, l'arnaqueuse" ("The Beggar, the Kleptomaniac, the Hustler"). Walking down the street with Mirabelle, Reinette gives some coins to a beggar. She scolds Mirabelle for not giving, and that starts an argument over when one should give. Reinette claims that one should give always as much as one can, though she admits that if a beggar seems to be faking or is playing disagreeable music, she passes him by. Mirabelle, who gives only if the beggar appeals to her, retorts that Reinette should become a medical missionary and go to Africa if she is that serious and committed.

In the second vignette, Mirabelle sees two store detectives (Béatrice Romand and Gérard Courant) watch a young woman (Yasmine Haury) shoplift. After paying at the checkout counter, Mirabelle grabs the woman's second bag, which contains the stolen merchandise, and runs out the door with it. When the woman is apprehended by the store detectives, they find nothing on her. At home, Reinette is setting a meager table for herself. Mirabelle comes in unexpectedly and sets down on the table some lemons, a bottle of champagne, a can of duck confit, and a package of smoked salmon. Initially, Reinette thinks the bounty is for her birthday; when Mirabelle recounts in detail the story of how she acquired the delicacies, however, Reinette rejects the meal, and the two argue vehemently about whether Mirabelle did the right thing. Mirabelle thinks that one never knows the motive for the crime and that people should be protected from the law. Reinette argues that this attitude merely encourages them to repeat their crimes. They should be cured, rather, for that is the real way to help other people—their victims.

In the third vignette, Reinette gives money at a train station to a well-dressed woman (Marie Rivière) who claims that her purse was stolen. As a result of her generosity, however, Reinette misses her train. Trying to solicit correct change for a phone call, Reinette is rebuffed by everyone she approaches and is even robbed by a cadger (Jacques Auffray) whom she asks for change. Walking around looking for change, Reinette overhears the same woman whom she had helped earlier asking another woman (Haydée Caillot) for the same sum with the same story. After trying unsuccessfully to talk the victim out of giving, Reinette scolds the hustler, reducing her to tears. When the repentant woman tries to return the money, the sympathetic Reinette gives back the majority of it and tells her to buy herself a cup of coffee and cheer herself up.

In the fourth and final adventure, "La Vent du tableau" ("Selling the Picture"), Reinette decides to sell one of her paintings to pay the rent. Mirabelle, irritated by Reinette's incessant chatter, tells her that she talks too much and repeats herself. Reinette wagers that she can go through the entire next day without talking. When the gallery owner calls and sets up an appointment for the next day, Mirabelle offers to postpone the bet, but Reinette wants to keep her word. Mirabelle offers to accompany Reinette to the gallery and pretend not to know her. In the gallery, the owner (Fabrice Luchini), intrigued by Reinette's portfolio of paintings, offers her two thousand francs for a painting but only two hundred in advance. Mirabelle saves the day for the tearful Reinette by pretending to discover that she is a deaf-mute and then reproaching the art dealer, whom she shames into advancing Reinette the entire two thousand francs. He has the last laugh, however, when he prices Reinette's painting at four thousand francs after the two women leave.

Early in the film it becomes apparent that Reinette is in many ways a stand-in for the director. Reinette's paintings mirror the film's episodes. For example, two of her paintings, entitled "The Escape" and "The Refusal," foreshadow, among other things, Reinette's dashing out of the café and her refusal to speak for a day. In describing one of her paintings, she explains to Mirabelle that she centers the nude's derrière because it is the woman's most beautiful part. The importance of this remark is underscored by the fact that the art dealer repeats it at the end of the film, adding that Reinette's paintings resemble the sexual fantasies of a very mature male.

The film itself has a circular structure, beginning and ending with an interest in silence. To explain the simplicity and the naïveté of her paintings, Reinette admits only two influences, both fairy-tale authors: the brothers Grimm and Charles Perrault. The remark again points to Rohmer, with his penchant for tales, proverbs, and the like. The odd-looking Reinette, in fact, resembles a character out of a child's story, with her chubby figure, schoolgirl outfits, and long, straight hair with bangs. Like classic fairy tales, Rohmer's film is multilayered, capable of sustaining the most sophisticated interpretations of its artless surface.

Rohmer has been called a moralist in the broad sense, a student of human personality and foibles. In this film he deals with morality in the narrow sense, as Reinette and Mirabelle engage in their lively arguments. His interest in these conversations is not merely in who is right but also in the contradictions between how each woman argues and how she acts when her ideas are put to the test. For example, though she scolds Mirabelle for not turning in the shoplifter, Reinette is herself so moved by the hustler's sob story that she gives the woman money for a cup of coffee. Mirabelle, on the other hand, though she studies law, denies that one should help store detectives do their work and talks Reinette into leaving the café without paying. Rohmer seems to say that there are no obvious answers. Taking an ironic, Socratic stance, he throws the questions back to the viewer, while laughing ironically to himself and—in this film—at himself.

Joan Esposito

Reviews
Chicago Tribune. November 24, 1989, VII, p. 38.
The Christian Science Monitor. August 21, 1989, p. 11.
Connoisseur. CCXIX, October, 1989, p. 66.
Insight. V, August 14, 1989, p. 62.
Los Angeles Times. August 11, 1989, VI, p. 15.
The New Republic. CCI, August 28, 1989, p. 26.
New Statesman and Society. CXV, February 5, 1989, p. 25.
The New York Times. July 21, 1989, p. C10.
People Weekly. XXXII, August 14, 1989, p. 18.
Variety. CCCXXVI, April 1, 1987, p. 14.
The Washington Post. August 25, 1989, p. D7.

GETTING IT RIGHT

Origin: Great Britain
Released: 1989
Released in U.S.: 1989
Production: Jonathan D. Krane and Randal Kleiser; released by Management
   Company Entertainment Group
Direction: Randal Kleiser
Screenplay: Elizabeth Jane Howard; based on her novel
Cinematography: Clive Tickner
Editing: Chris Kelly
Production design: Caroline Amies
Art direction: Frank Walsh
Makeup: Sue Black
Costume design: Hazel Pethig
Sound: John Midgley
Music: Colin Towns
MPAA rating: R
Running time: 102 minutes

Principal characters:
Gavin Lamb	Jesse Birdsall
Minerva Munday	Helena Bonham Carter
Mr. Adrian	Peter Cook
Joan	Lynn Redgrave
Jenny	Jane Horrocks
Harry	Richard Huw
Mr. Lamb	Bryan Pringle
Mrs. Lamb	Pat Heywood
Sir Gordon Munday	John Gielgud
Lady Munday	Judy Parfitt

Getting It Right is one of a growing number of "small" British films that began to make their way into the international market in the late 1980's. Helped in this case by the presence of American director Randal Kleiser—whose credits include *The Blue Lagoon* (1980) and *Big Top Pee-Wee* (1988)—the film is reminiscent of the quirky British comedies that were popular during the 1950's and 1960's. Adapted by Elizabeth Jane Howard from her novel of the same name, *Getting It Right* tells the story of a shy London hairdresser's first hesitant encounters with love and romance.

Gavin Lamb (Jesse Birdsall) is a popular hairstylist in a West End hair salon. Mild-mannered and amiable, he is also a thirty-one-year old virgin living at home with his mother (Pat Heywood) and father (Bryan Pringle). Paralyzed by his insecurities where women are concerned, Gavin carries on a running internal conversation with himself in which he fantasizes about possible romantic encounters and attempts to rationalize the reasons for his nonexistent love life. When he is taken by his gay friend Harry (Richard Huw) to a trendy party thrown by the wealthy, middle-aged Joan (Lynn Redgrave), Gavin's life undergoes a much-needed upheaval that sets him on the sometimes rocky path toward adult relationships.

Joan takes an immediate interest in Gavin, who finds himself first confiding in his hostess and later entering into his first affair with her. Also at the party is Lady Minerva Munday (Helena Bonham Carter), a deeply neurotic young aristocrat who persuades Gavin to take her back to his parents' house for the remainder of the night. Minerva invites Gavin to lunch at her parents' country estate, where he discovers to his amazement that she has told her family that they are to be married.

After a confusing and hilarious encounter with the disagreeable Sir Gordon Munday (John Gielgud) and his unhappy wife (Judy Parfitt), Gavin returns to London and his job, where his growing self-confidence unnerves the salon's snobbish owner (Peter Cook). For the first time, Gavin begins to take notice of his quiet, sweet-natured assistant, Jenny (Jane Horrocks), and the two begin a tentative romance. Jenny is a single mother who longs to "better" herself; at her request, Gavin becomes her private cultural tutor, sharing with her his love of literature, music, and art.

The entanglements of Gavin's now-convoluted romantic life begin to unravel when Joan, who is married, leaves London after a confrontation with her husband, while Minerva crosses the shaky line between madcap eccentricity and emotional collapse. When Jenny tells Gavin that her mother, with whom she lives, is remarrying and leaving England, and that she and her child will be forced by financial circumstances to leave with her, Gavin realizes that he is in love with her, and she agrees to remain in England with him.

Getting It Right is an offbeat comedy that draws its humor from its characters. Gavin is an appealing figure: shy, kindhearted, and possessed of a gently ironic sense of humor that is felt most distinctly in his passages of voice-over narration. The film relates his gradual metamorphosis from overaged adolescence to emotional maturity, a transition that he survives with all of his best instincts intact. At the heart of his relationship with each of the three women who become an important part of his life is his ability to care for them and respond to their needs. All three suffer from their own particular forms of insecurity, which, in the case of both Joan and Minerva, is finally revealed to have a crippling effect on their lives. Jenny's quiet self-doubts, however, find their antidote in Gavin, even as her admiration for him helps to build his own self-confidence. Jesse Birdsall provides Gavin with the necessary combination of innocence and bemusement, both at himself and at the women he meets.

In Lynn Redgrave's hands, Joan emerges as an intriguingly complex character. Wealthy, witty, and somewhere between the bohemian and the trendy in her taste and style, Joan represents for Gavin a decidedly exotic older woman in whose experienced arms he receives his first lessons in love. She is also a woman in deep emotional pain, and Redgrave gives a sure and convincing performance in a difficult role.

The flighty, troubled Minerva undergoes a more drastic shift in the viewer's perception than do any of the other characters. When she is first introduced, she appears to be one in a long line of delightfully eccentric, upper-class British characters. As the story unfolds, however, it becomes clear that her early behavior offers only a hint of the convoluted twists of her psyche, and Minerva is revealed as a desperately confused and self-destructive young woman. Actress Helena Bonham Carter is best known for her role as the young Englishwoman abroad in *A Room with a View* (1986). Her character here is quite different, and she is well cast in a very contemporary and often touching part.

Jenny is the least eccentric and most subdued of the three women in Gavin's life, yet her character is crucial to his eventual success at "getting it right." Although it is clear from the start that it is Jenny with whom Gavin will finally fall in love, there is much quiet pleasure to be had in watching the gradual development of their relationship. Whereas Joan's and Minerva's problems often seem far outside the scope of most ordinary lives, Jenny is facing problems that place her squarely in the mainstream: single parenthood, financial difficulties, and a limited education. Her earnest desire to expand her cultural horizons and her loving dedication to her child's welfare are qualities which endear her to both Gavin and the audience.

In the tradition of the classic British comedy, *Getting It Right* also has a wide assortment of first-rate performances in offbeat supporting roles. Chief among them is that of John Gielgud, who provides the film with many of its most amusing moments as Minerva's vile-tempered father, Sir Gordon Munday, a man who earned his vast fortune, and his title, manufacturing seatbelts. In one of the film's best scenes, Sir Gordon, under the assumption that Gavin intends to marry his daughter, takes the unsuspecting young man to his study and proceeds to question him in the rudest possible manner regarding his prospects and intentions. Gielgud is superb in this brief but memorable role. Also excellent is Peter Cook as Gavin's haughty, officious employer. Cook is an expert at characters with a distinctly nasty undercurrent, and the tyrannical Mr. Adrian is one of the film's more humorous offerings.

Gavin's friend Harry is played on a more serious level by Richard Huw, and he, too, emerges as one of the film's more interesting characters. Harry is at ease with his homosexuality, and the film never treats his sexual preference as an issue. His problems with his lover provide Gavin with an object lesson in the risks involved in falling in love, and Gavin proves himself a loyal friend, responding with compassion to Harry's unhappiness just as Harry had tried to help Gavin overcome his shyness with women.

One of the uses to which the film puts its supporting characters is a clever satire of class-consciousness in Great Britain. Beneath their wealth and sangfroid, the upper-class Mundays display all the symptoms of a garden-variety dysfunctional family, while Gavin's own middle-class parents, despite their protestations of democratic attitudes, are so overcome by the presence of a titled young woman at their breakfast table that they react as if the queen had come to call. Mr. Adrian, on the other hand, makes no pretense of egalitarian attitudes; deference to the aristocracy—and arrogance of everyone else—is central to his philosophy of life.

In its themes and its execution, *Getting It Right* is markedly different from most stories of a young man's humorous struggle toward emotional maturity. That Gavin is physically beyond adolescence and has already established a career sets the tone for the film and for his own ability to cope in an intelligent and adult manner with the situations he encounters. Those situations and the characters he meets along the way make *Getting It Right* an engaging and unusual comedy.

Janet E. Lorenz

Reviews
Chicago Tribune. May 19, 1989, VII, p. 23.
Commonweal. CXVI, June 2, 1989, p. 337.
The Hollywood Reporter. May 5, 1989, p. 4.
Los Angeles Times. May 5, 1989, VI, p. 14.
New Woman. XIX, June, 1989, p. 25.
The New York Times. May 5, 1989, p. C15.
Rolling Stone. June 1, 1989, p. 38.
Variety. CCCXXXV, May 10, 1989, p. 19.
The Village Voice. XXXIV, May 9, 1989, p. 68.
The Washington Post. June 9, 1989, p. C7.
Washington Times. June 9, 1989, p. E1.

GHOSTBUSTERS II

Production: Ivan Reitman; released by Columbia Pictures
Direction: Ivan Reitman
Screenplay: Harold Ramis and Dan Aykroyd; based on characters created by Ramis and Aykroyd
Cinematography: Michael Chapman
Editing: Sheldon Kahn and Donn Cambern
Production design: Bo Welch
Art direction: Tom Duffield
Set decoration: Cheryl Carasik
Special effects: Chuck Gaspar, Joe Day, and Dick Wood
Special visual effects: Industrial Light and Magic
Makeup: Stephen Abrums, John Elliott, and Robert Arrollo
Costume design: Gloria Gresham
Sound: Gene Cantamessa
Music: Randy Edelman
Song: Ray Parker, Jr., "Ghostbusters"; L. A. Reid, Babyface, and Daryl Simmons, "On Our Own"
MPAA rating: PG
Running time: 102 minutes

Principal characters:
Dr. Peter Venkman	Bill Murray
Dr. Raymond Stantz	Dan Aykroyd
Dr. Egon Spengler	Harold Ramis
Dana Barrett	Sigourney Weaver
Louis Tully	Rick Moranis
Winston Zeddemore	Ernie Hudson
Janosz Poha	Peter MacNicol
Janine Melnitz	Annie Potts

In 1984, *Ghostbusters* became a huge box-office success by captivating audiences with its catchy theme song phrase: "Who you gonna call?" The film made "Who you gonna call?" a culturally ubiquitous query. The answer was a resounding "Ghostbusters!"—a foursome who appeared as the comic answer to all possible supernatural problems. The ghostbusters used a distinctly American form of exorcism, protonpacks wielded like combination shotgun-lassos that efficiently dealt with everything from relatively demure ghosts floating in the stacks of the New York City Library to a giant Stay Puft Marshmallow Man terrorizing the streets of Manhattan. Not only did the film, its heroes, and its theme song all prove to be an unprecedented comic hit, but it also spawned a children's cartoon series and millions of dollars in sales from tie-ins, mainly children's toys which made "sliming" (the ghostly dousing of humans with a jellylike substance) the national pastime for millions of ten-year-olds.

Ghostbusters II returns to its heroes' lives five years after the paranormal triumph that won New York City's grateful adoration of their peculiar talents. The Ecto-mobile still squeals through the streets, but the ghostbusters are no longer on a mission to stop a haunting. Ray Stantz (Dan Aykroyd) and Winston Zeddemore (Ernie Hudson) make ends meet by entertaining at children's parties. The ghostbus-ters are under an injunction not to participate in any paranormal activity. Unfor-tunately, the children at this party begin chanting for "He-Man," the new children's cartoon hero. This clever intertextual reference emphasizes the ghostbusters' status as former celebrities. Even as Ray and Winston are coping with the fickle behavior of "yuppie larvae," the other ghostbusters are also coping with their now marginal social status. Peter Venkman (Bill Murray) hosts a local television program, *World of the Psychic*. Boycotted by "real psychics," he wryly deals with an odd assort-ment of guests including a woman who claims to have met an alien at the bar of a Holiday Inn. Egon Spengler (Harold Ramis) experiments with the effects of human emotions on the immediate environment. When not attempting to entertain chil-dren, Ray also runs a dusty occult bookstore in Manhattan.

While the ghostbusters are prevented from performing exorcisms, Dana Barrett (Sigourney Weaver) suddenly finds herself the unwilling participant in supernatural activities. In *Ghostbusters*, Dana was courted by Peter and then possessed by a demon. Five years later, Dana is back to normal as a divorced mother with an infant named Oscar. While she is walking to her apartment building one day, the baby carriage begins to roll on its own power and careens into the street. Dana desper-ately attempts to catch it; when she retrieves her baby, she immediately realizes that supernatural forces are at work.

Dana goes to Egon for help. He enlists Ray's assistance but avoids involving Peter, whose romantic relationship with Dana ended badly several years before. Peter mildly tortures Ray to learn the truth of the situation, and Peter joins Ray and Egon in examining Dana's baby, Oscar. They also begin examining the street across from Dana's apartment after discovering ghost slime, the telltale aftermath of any encounter with a supernatural presence of that type. Peter also works to rekindle his romance with Dana.

While Peter works on Dana, Egon and Ray disguise themselves as road workers. They discover an old, abandoned transit system beneath the street. The transit tunnel contains a river of slime that bubbles up into menacing figures. In the course of their exploration, however, the ghostbusters' masquerade is discovered by the New York City police. In an attempt to exit the shaft under the street, Ray inadver-tently cuts an electric cable, and all of Manhattan is thrown into darkness.

As New York City sits in the dark, Dana receives an unexpected visit from the art historian, Janosz Poha (Peter MacNicol), who supervises her restoration work at the Manhattan Museum of Art. Janosz appears to Dana as no more than a lecherous, if rather harmless, nuisance, but the audience already knows that Janosz is being used by Vigo, Scourge of Carpathia (Wilhelm von Homburg), the ghost of a genocidal emperor whose spirit inhabits an immense painting at the museum. Vigo is waiting for the right moment in which to assume a new life within the body of a child: He chooses Dana's Oscar.

Dana resists Janosz's slight charms even as the ghostbusters are appearing in court to face charges related to plunging the city into darkness. Their lawyer, Louis Tully (Rick Moranis), incompetently defends them in front of a hostile judge who refuses to hear evidence concerning the supernatural. The judge rails against them, but as his diatribe intensifies, a jar of slime, gathered as evidence by Ray from the underground river, begins to bubble. Egon has theorized that the slime is sensitive to human emotion and feeds on New York City's negative energy. The slime bursts into a spectral spectacular. Ghosts terrorize the courtroom and specifically target the judge, who sent many of them to their death. Finally, the ghostbusters are allowed to bring out their protonpacks and zap the ghosts into submission. The judge retracts the ghostbusters' sentences, and the foursome is back in business; soon, their advertisements are blanketing the airwaves.

Continuing to experiment, Egon and Ray discover that the slime they discovered can also be positively energized by affirmative encouragement and the right music. Egon's research also reveals that the painting of Vigo in the museum, which Dana finds so repulsive, is that of a powerful magician who terrorized his own country during the Middle Ages and died at the age of 105, only after being "killed" by numerous methods including hanging and quartering. Dana and Oscar are attacked by slime rising out of their apartment bathroom, but the ghostbusters have yet to figure out the connection between the painting of Vigo and the river of slime. They examine photographs of the painting and detect a living presence in it. Just as quickly as they make this discovery, they are almost incinerated by a mysterious force. Ray, Egon, and Winston go to the sewer to trace the source of the river of slime. After a series of ghostly encounters, they find that source at the museum. With Peter, they then attempt to warn the city's mayor of the imminent danger to all New Yorkers, but he rejects the idea that Manhattan's residents could or should give up their well-known habits of rudeness and indifference to stop some hypothetical flow of negative energy. A scheming assistant to the mayor has the ghostbusters confined to a psychiatric ward. While they are incarcerated, Janosz kidnaps Dana's baby, takes him to the museum and prepares him to become the vessel for the spirit of Vigo at midnight, on New Year's Eve.

Just as the ghostbusters thought, ghosts begin to appear all over the city as the negative energy flow can no longer be controlled. The *Titanic* docks at New York Harbor, and the mayor himself is haunted by the ghosts of past mayors. Released by the mayor, the ghostbusters learn from their secretary, Janine (Annie Potts), that Dana has followed Janosz to the museum to rescue her baby. When the ghostbusters arrive at the museum, they find it covered with an impenetrable wall of slime. In order to combat the negative slime, the foursome use positively energized slime to bring the Statue of Liberty to life. By parading the statue along the streets, the ghostbusters hope to encourage the city's residents to produce a positive energy flow. When the statue uses its torch to break through the museum roof, Vigo materializes and quickly immobilizes the ghostbusters. He is on the verge of taking over Oscar's body when singing is heard from outside: New Yorkers are celebrating New Year's Day. Their positive force field provides the necessary emotional power for the ghostbusters to put Vigo back into the painting. Once again, the ghostbusters become the saviors of New York City.

Although *The New York Times'* film critic Vincent Canby praised *Ghostbusters II* for its more relaxed pace, most critics viewed this change as proof of the film's lack of energy and inventiveness in comparison with the original. Many critics also noted that scenes appeared to lack narrative drive and, more surprising, the film failed to capitalize on its main premise. The notion that New York City, infamous for its ill will to tourists and natives alike, should be feeding a river of negative energy contains enormous potential for a broad range of joke material. Yet, as critics noted, the film hardly exploited this comedic gold mine. Lacking both the narrative energy and the spectacular special effects of the original, *Ghostbusters II* does manage to achieve some measure of the original's offbeat charm, mainly through the charismatic presence of its principal actors. In particular, Bill Murray's knowing grin and smart-guy assurance as Peter Venkman are counterpointed nicely by Dan Aykroyd's sweetly simple Ray. As critics were quick to point out, actress Sigourney Weaver was wasted in the role of Dana, but the new addition to the cast, Peter MacNicol, provides the film with its most amusing moments as the lispingly lecherous art historian, Janosz Poha.

In spite of its flaws, *Ghostbusters II* ranked fifth at the box office by the end of summer and was anticipating some $34 million in tie-in sales. The positive energy of its audience could not be defeated by the film's own lack of either supernatural or comic resonance.

Gaylyn Studlar

Reviews
Chicago Tribune. June 16, 1989, I, p. 28.
Los Angeles Times. June 16, 1989, VI, p. 1.
Maclean's. CII, June 26, 1989, p. 50.
The New York Times. June 16, 1989, p. C5.
The New Yorker. LXV, July 10, 1989, p. 85.
Newsweek. CXIII, June 26, 1989, p. 68.
People Weekly. XXXII, July 3, 1989, p. 14.
Time. CXXXIII, June 26, 1989, p. 89.
Variety. CCCXXXV. June 21, 1989, p. 24.
The Wall Street Journal. June 20, 1989, p. A14.
The Washington Post. June 16, 1989, p. B1.

The New Republic. CCII, January 8, 1990, p. 28.
The New York Times. December 14, 1989, p. C15.
Newsweek. CXIV, December 18, 1989, p. 68.
Time. CXXXIV, December 18, 1989, p. 91.
Variety. CCCXXXVII, December 13, 1989, p. 30.

GREAT BALLS OF FIRE!

Production: Adam Fields; released by Orion Pictures
Direction: Jim McBride
Screenplay: Jack Baran and Jim McBride; based on the book by Myra Lewis with
    Murray Silver, Jr.
Cinematography: Affonso Beato
Editing: Lisa Day, Pembroke Herring, and Bert Lovitt
Production design: David Nichols
Art direction: Jon Spirson
Set decoration: Lisa Fischer
Set design: Kathleen McKernin and Lauren Polizzi
Makeup: Richard Arrington
Costume design: Tracy Tynan
Choreography: Bill Landrum and Jacqui Landrum
Sound: Petur Hlidall
Music editing: Sally Boldt
Song: Otis Blackwell and Jack Hammer, "Great Balls of Fire"
MPAA rating: PG-13
Running time: 102 minutes

> *Principal characters:*
> Jerry Lee Lewis .... Dennis Quaid
> Myra Gale Lewis .... Winona Ryder
> J. W. Brown .... John Doe
> John Phillips.................... Stephen Tobolowsky
> Sam Phillips .... Trey Wilson
> Jimmy Swaggart .... Alec Baldwin
> Steve Allen............................... Himself
> Lois Brown........................... Lisa Blount
> Dewey "Daddy-O" Phillips .... Joe Bob Briggs

At first *Great Balls of Fire!* might have seemed a reasonable investment. Targeted as a summer film, it deals with the life and career of a rock-and-roll icon, Jerry Lee Lewis, known to his fans as the "Killer." Dennis Quaid was cast as the flamboyant rocker, and the piano work and vocals were performed by the Killer himself, who also served as adviser and creative consultant to the project. The music, therefore, is absolutely authentic, but the film fell short of becoming a summer hit.

The title of film critic Richard Schickel's review in *Time* perhaps explains the reason the picture slumped at the box office: "Whole Lotta Irony Goin' On." Director Jim McBride was more interested in the cultural significance of Lewis' career and in the legend of Jerry Lee Lewis than in a literal account of the man's life. Quaid was encouraged to play Lewis flamboyantly, which might have been appropriate to a certain extent, but Quaid pushed the limits of caricature in his performance. In general, neither the fans nor the literal-minded reviewers were impressed or amused.

The screenplay establishes a parallel between Lewis and his God-fearing cousin Jimmy Swaggart (Alec Baldwin). As children, the two cousins sneak off to a black honky-tonk to listen to the music. For young Jimmy (Ryan Rushton), this is the devil's music, but young Jerry Lee (Bert Dedman) is fascinated and presumably inspired by it. As he grows up, Lewis learns how to combine a black left hand with a white right hand to create his own distinctive pounding piano style.

Both Swaggart and Lewis are natural performers. While Swaggart preaches the Bible on street corners standing on the hood of his car (looking like one of Flannery O'Connor's fictional characters), Lewis records his music, becoming very successful as an energetic and inventive rock-and-roll musician and eventually challenging Elvis Presley as the king of rock-and-roll.

The film sketches Lewis' career broadly, following him from Ferriday, Louisiana, his hometown, to Memphis, Tennessee, where Sam Phillips (Trey Wilson) signs him with Sun Records, the same record company that launched Presley's career. As Lewis' records are played, his popularity increases. When Presley is drafted into the army, Lewis is recognized as the heir apparent. At the crest of his popularity, however, Lewis decides to marry his thirteen-year-old cousin Myra (Winona Ryder). After the wedding, Lewis insists that Myra accompany him on a London concert tour. The British tabloids reveal the story and have a field day, creating a scandal that ultimately damages Lewis' career at home, as well as abroad. Myra Williams, the former Myra Lewis, told the Associated Press that Lewis "went from making $10,000 a night to $200 a night" as a result of the scandal.

Based on Myra Lewis' autobiography, the screenplay ignored the darker details of the book. Film critic Caryn James noted in *The New York Times* (June 30, 1989) that Myra had been raped by a neighbor at the age of twelve and therefore "jumped at the chance to marry" because she thought "no one else would want her." In the film, Ryder plays Myra as an innocent teenager still fond of teddy bears.

Director McBride turns Lewis into a mythic figure, made larger than life by his flamboyance and musical energy. Producer Adam Fields and McBride agreed that the film should concentrate on the legend rather than the person. McBride described the screenplay he wrote with Jack Baran as being "loyal to the legend—a story we essentially invented, based on the facts we knew." The screenplay sliced three years (1956-1959) out of a long and determined career and was criticized for being incomplete and truncated. McBride was apparently uninterested in the dark side of Lewis' life: Of his six marriages, his fourth wife drowned in a swimming pool, and his fifth wife died after an apparent drug overdose. Myra was actually his third wife. One of Lewis' sons, seen briefly in the film, died at age three in a swimming pool; another son was killed in a traffic accident at the age of sixteen. None of these tragedies is suggested in the film. The film entirely ignores Lewis' later life, with its problems relating to deaths, divorces, drugs, drinking, threats of bankruptcy, and investigations by the Internal Revenue Service. The film passes over the last thirty years of the performer's life. Lewis tried to clean up his image for the two years prior to the film's release, and, as a result of publicity surrounding the film, played a three-week stint in Las Vegas during the early summer of 1989.

The late film director King Vidor once stated that the public does not want to see the truth. One must applaud director McBride's honesty in making clear his intentions from the film's outset. The film's focus on the legend of Jerry Lee Lewis sometimes creates a cartoonish and unrealistic effect that is, most likely, intentional. Thus, the excesses of the film are a function of the excesses of the legend.

The American public apparently wanted a more realistic treatment than McBride provided, something perhaps resembling *La Bamba* (1987), an absolutely sincere and even reverential biography of Ritchie Valens (born Richard Valenzuela; played by Lou Diamond Phillips), who died in an airplane accident at the peak of his singing career. *La Bamba* was a popular hit during the summer of 1987, but *Great Balls of Fire!*, which also treated a rock star and traded on 1950's nostalgia, was unable to attain an equivalent success in 1989.

Despite the sentimental treatment, the life story of *La Bamba* is a curiously empty tale of teen aspiration and anguish. *Great Balls of Fire!* had the potential to offer much more. A closer analogue than *La Bamba* to the Jerry Lee Lewis film is Francis Ford Coppola's *Tucker: The Man and His Dream* (1988), which recounted the life of the automotive genius Preston Tucker. In Coppola's film, actor Jeff Bridges played the maverick entrepreneur as a legendary hero who personified the American dream. The film's style was slyly satirical, offering a flamboyant and adamantly nonrealistic Preston Tucker. *Great Balls of Fire!* utilizes a similar style, presenting an exaggerated cartoon of Jerry Lee Lewis and exploring the man's image rather than his life. The music, McBride's superior direction, and Quaid's outrageous performance created a more energetic film than *La Bamba*. In particular, Quaid's bumpkinesque impersonation, which often approached caricature, was effectively comic. In the film, Lewis constantly attempts to outclass Presley and other rock-and-roll stars. In one concert scene, he manages to upstage Chuck Berry. Berry insists on having the final performance at a New York concert, even though Lewis' record is at the top of the charts at the time. In response, Lewis douses his grand piano with gasoline and torches it for his finale. Leaving the stage, Lewis remarks: "It's all yours, Chuck."

That type of satirical overstatement, which is reminiscent of *Tucker*, transforms *Great Balls of Fire!* into an allegory of ego and greed, on the one hand, and a splendid satire of the American Dream, on the other. In a sense, Jerry Lee Lewis is the perfect American hero, naïve and sensual, split between sexuality and Fundamentalist religion, greedy, materialistic, vain, egotistical, and yet, somehow innocent. This is the stuff of satire, perfectly executed.

James M. Welsh

Reviews

American Film: Magazine of the Film and Television Arts. XIV, June 1989, p. 26.
Chicago Tribune. June 30, 1989, VII, p. 36.
Films in Review. XL, October, 1989, p. 491.
Los Angeles Times. June 30, 1989, VII, p. 1.
Maclean's. CII, July 10, 1989, p. 46.
The New York Times. June 30, 1989, p. C8.
Newsweek. CXIV, July 10, 1989, p. 72.
Rolling Stone. August 10, 1989, p. 33.
Time. CXXXIV, July 10, 1989, p. 67.
Variety. CCCXXXV, July 5, 1989, p. 18.
The Washington Post. June 30, 1989, p. B1.

HARLEM NIGHTS

Production: Robert D. Wachs and Mark Lipsky for Eddie Murphy Productions; released by Paramount Pictures
Direction: Eddie Murphy
Screenplay: Eddie Murphy
Cinematography: Woody Omens
Editing: George Bowers
Production design: Lawrence G. Paull
Art direction: Martin G. Hubbard and Russell B. Crone
Set decoration: George R. Nelson
Costume design: Joe I. Tompkins
Sound: Gene S. Cantamessa
Music direction: Herbie Hancock
Music: Herbie Hancock
MPAA rating: R
Running time: 118 minutes

Principal characters:

Quick	Eddie Murphy
Sugar Ray	Richard Pryor
Bennie Wilson	Redd Foxx
Phil Cantone	Danny Aiello
Bugsy Calhoune	Michael Lerner
Vera	Della Reese
Sunshine	Lela Rochon
Crying man	Arsenio Hall
Annie	Berlinda Tolbert
Jack Jenkins	Stan Shaw
Dominique La Rue	Jasmine Guy
Richie Vento	Vic Polizos
Willie	Uncle Ray
Jerome	Robin Harris
Jimmy	Charles Q. Murphy
Tommy Smalls	Tommy Ford
Max	Michael Goldfinger
Joe Leoni	Joe Pecoraro
Man with broken nose	Miguel Nunez
Young Quick	Desi Arnez Hines II
Gambler	Reynaldo Rey
Crapshooter	Howard "Sandman" Sims
Bouncer	Roberto Duran
Prince C. Spencer	Himself

When it was released during the Thanksgiving weekend, Eddie Murphy's *Harlem Nights* was greeted with contempt and derision by the critical establishment. Some reviewers were offended by it. *Variety* declared it "overdone, too rarely funny and, worst of all, boring." *Variety*'s critical scorecard indicated that none of the New York critics had responded favorably to the film; four were ambivalent (including Vincent Canby of *The New York Times*); five reviewed the film unfavorably. The script was so bad, the lines so vulgar, and the situations so tasteless that no self-respecting writer would have willingly taken credit for them; but Eddie Murphy took the credit, as writer, star, director, and producer, along with Robert Wachs, the Harvard-educated lawyer who has been Murphy's manager for the past ten years. Meanwhile, *Harlem Nights* became the top-grossing film of the Thanksgiving week-end and was still holding onto the number ten position by Christmas weekend, a month later.

The main action of *Harlem Nights* is set in an imaginary Harlem in 1938. Sugar Ray (Richard Pryor) and his adopted son Quick (Eddie Murphy) co-own a success-ful casino that, in a way, resembles the atmosphere of *The Cotton Club* (1984); *Harlem Nights*, however, does not measure up to that comparison either, despite Herbie Hancock's music. The film is episodic and nearly plotless. What there is of a narrative plot line begins in flashback in the early 1920's and establishes Sugar Ray, who runs a floating craps game at the time, and the boy who shoots a surly gambler who threatens Sugar Ray with a knife (that boy grows up to be Quick, played by Eddie Murphy, and to be Sugar Ray's partner) as the main characters.

Next seen, Sugar Ray and Quick are running the Harlem casino and are doing reasonably well. Mob boss Bugsy Calhoune (Michael Lerner) wants to muscle in on Sugar Ray's success and demands two-thirds of his profits. He sends his top goon, a policeman on the take named Phil Cantone (Danny Aiello), to deliver his ul-timatum. Sugar Ray realizes that the only way to deal with Bugsy is to outwit him or to murder him. A gangland war erupts as Sugar Ray cheerfully executes his scheme.

After Bugsy makes his move against Sugar Ray, underworld warfare quickly reduces the situation to chaos. Bugsy sets up one of his molls (Jasmine Guy) to seduce Quick and then murder him, but Quick senses the setup, has sex with the woman, and then murders her instead. Sugar Ray and Quick have an oddball support "family," which creates roles for Della Reese, who plays Vera, the woman who runs the family whorehouse and who is much like a mother to Quick, and Redd Foxx, who plays a blind croupier named Bennie.

Quick and Sugar Ray are smart enough to realize that they cannot win against Bugsy's mob, and so they work a scam to cheat Bugsy out of enough money to make their getaway to safer territory in another city. They use a comely whore named Sunshine (Lela Rochon) to seduce and set up one of Bugsy's gunsels, a money runner for Bugsy's numbers game. They outsmart Cantone in order to steal the money by bribing two other white policemen. They leave town at the end, free and clear.

As Canby pointed out, *Harlem Nights* is a black variant of *The Sting* (1973), with Murphy and Pryor standing in for Robert Redford and Paul Newman; that film, however, avoided being violent and nasty. *The Sting* was like a puzzle, broken down into its component parts. It was enjoyable to see Henry (Newman) outwitting his opponents at every turn. In *Harlem Nights*, Sugar Ray does the outwitting, but Murphy cannot resist writing in a violent, macho-heroic role for himself, while also trying to play the comedian. He wants to have it all, but he is not enough of an all-round talent to make it work. *The Sting* had two advantages in this comparison to *Harlem Nights*: a much better and more carefully crafted script and originality.

As Spike Lee has done with his films, Murphy is pitching this film to black audiences. Maybe the story is poorly constructed, consisting mainly of comedy skits stitched together by a revenge plot that enables the black heroes to turn the tables on the stupid and dominant white mobsters, humiliating some of them and murdering others. Seeing a man or woman shot to death is no one's idea of a promising comic spectacle. The revenge motif and the violent action are at odds with the comedy, often stripping it of humor.

Other aspects of the film proved offensive to reviewers. Hal Hinson of *The Washington Post* called *Harlem Nights* a "progressively off-putting exercise in star ego," given the fact that Murphy's name appears five times in the credits. Hinson described the tone as "ugly, misogynistic and outrageously profane." Baltimore critic Stephen Hunter of *The Sun* agrees with Hinson in regard to the film's misogyny. In fact, every female character in the film is a prostitute. The most fully developed of these, Vera, is a madam. One of the more awkward comic sequences finds her fighting with the cocky Quick, who hits her in the face and then attempts to get laughs by shooting off one of her toes to teach her a lesson. In his review, Hunter wonders where "the millions of strong, brave black women who have held families together on nothing more than guts and love" have gone. Perhaps he was expecting *The Color Purple* (1985). In fact, *Harlem Nights* might be seen as a black, macho response to *The Color Purple* which made black women appear to be saintly and black men appear to be brutes. The problem is that the brutishness is also present in *Harlem Nights*.

Hunter was also outraged by the film's "pernicious values, cruelty and smugness." He was offended by the portrayal of brutal violence, as seen in the opening sequence, in which the young Quick (Desi Arnez Hines II) shoots the man who is threatening Sugar Ray in the head, as being "cool." The *Variety* review managed to find at least one positive message in the film in a lecture that Sugar Ray gives to Quick concerning the "merits of avoiding conflict."

Yet Murphy surely knows his audience and is out to please them by packing his cast with black celebrities. Murphy and Pryor are well matched and seem to enjoy working together, as do Foxx and Reese, who represent the older generation. Arsenio Hall, who went on to his own show on television after starring with Murphy in *Coming to America*, has the weakest and silliest role as a grief-stricken assassin out to avenge his brother's death (he believes, wrongly, that Quick is responsible for the murder). Berlinda Tolbert, who played Jenny Willis on the hit television series *The Jeffersons*, has a small role as does tapdancer Howard "Sandman" Sims, who plays the belligerent crapshooter who is murdered in the first reel by young Quick. Boxer Roberto Duran also appears in a cameo as a bouncer.

Despite the film's tasteless vulgarity, its awkward plotting, and its clichés, *Harlem Nights* apparently reached its target audience. It is not Murphy's worst film, as anyone who saw *The Golden Child* (1986) would realize. *Variety* judged Murphy's direction to be "competent, if unevenly paced." Ultimately, however, the film may be more significant as a sociological artifact than as general entertainment.

James M. Welsh

Reviews
Chicago Tribune. November 17, 1989, VII, p. 35.
The Christian Science Monitor. November 24, 1989, p. 10.
Jet. LXXVII, November 20, 1989, p. 56.
Los Angeles Times. November 17, 1989, VI, p. 8.
The New Republic. CCI, December 18, 1989, p. 24.
New York Times. November 17, 1989, p. C19.
Newsweek. CXIV, November 27, 1989, p. 92.
The Sun. "Maryland Live" Section, November 17, 1989, p. 15.
Time. CXXXIV, November 27, 1989, p. 88.
Variety. CCCXXXVII, November 22, 1989, p. 19.
The Washington Post. November 17, 1989, p. D1.

HEATHERS

Production: Denise Di Novi; released by New World Pictures in association with
Cinemarque Entertainment
Direction: Michael Lehmann
Screenplay: Daniel Waters
Cinematography: Francis Kenney
Editing: Norman Hollyn
Production design: Jon Hutman
Art direction: Kara Lindstrom
Special effects: Marty Bresin
Makeup: Julie Hewett
Costume design: Rudy Dillon
Sound: Douglas Axtell
Music: David Newman
Song: Big Fun, "Teenage Suicide Don't Do It"
MPAA rating: R
Running time: 102 minutes

Principal characters:
Veronica Sawyer	Winona Ryder
J. D.	Christian Slater
Heather Duke	Shannen Doherty
Heather McNamara	Lisanne Falk
Heather Chandler	Kim Walker
Pauline Fleming	Penelope Milford
Father Ripper	Glenn Shadix
Kurt Kelly	Lance Fenton
Ram	Patrick Labyorteaux
Martha Dunnstock	Carrie Lynn
Betty Finn	Renee Estevez

It is difficult to imagine David Lynch's having any progeny. Films such as the cult classic *Eraserhead* (1978) and the later stylish parody of *film noir*, *Blue Velvet* (1986), strike one as *sui generis*, inimitable achievements of an eccentric genius. Nevertheless, two 1989 Hollywood releases seem to be cut from the same bolt of warped and twisted imaginative fabric as Lynch's masterpieces: Both *Parents* and *Heathers* aim at the same blend of perverse, wicked satire and the macabre that marks Lynch's major films. Of the two, *Parents* is the more relentless and bizarre. Its premise of a child who suspects his mother and father are cannibals—he turns out to be right—almost guarantees it. Yet, by finally giving up on its own negativity, *Heathers* was more successful at the box office.

The key to *Heathers* lies in the moral conflict aroused in the heroine, Veronica

Sawyer (Winona Ryder), an intelligent teenager torn between her sense of justice and her desire to be a member of what Heather Chandler (Kim Walker), ringleader of the group, describes as "the most popular clique in school." The plot's moral force is generated by Veronica's ambivalence over having abandoned her childhood friend, Betty Finn (Renee Estevez), for the more secure social position occupied by the girls who give the film its title: Heather Chandler, Heather McNamara (Lisanne Falk), and Heather Duke (Shannen Doherty).

The film opens with the three girls lounging on wrought-iron lawn furniture, dressed to the nines, sipping soft drinks, and about to commence their regular croquet match in Veronica's back garden. This first sequence is brilliantly staged: As the credits roll to the tune of an unconventional rendition of "Que Sera, Sera," the three Heathers quarrel over whose turn it is to play, explaining the origin of the title as they name each other. Heather number one (Chandler) asserts her predominance from the outset, putting the other two in their respective places and making the one effectual shot—which turns out to be aimed at a hapless Veronica, buried up to the neck. Struck by Heather number one's red ball (the Heathers are each color-coded, both in dress and in croquet equipment), Veronica becomes a talking head, complaining in her diary about her impossible position in the clique, as the film cuts to her sumptuous, though tasteful, bedroom, where she is writing furiously, a monocle on her right eye (a symbol of her confusion, which she will shed by film's end).

The scene quickly shifts to the following day at school, where Veronica is summoned to the cafeteria from her isolation on the stairway by Heathers number two and number three, emissaries of Heather number one. This and subsequent encounters among the principal female figures are punctuated by a variety of teen slang— "Come on, Veronica," Heather number one goads her to play a cruel joke on Martha Dunnstock (Carrie Lynn), nicknamed "Dumptruck." "It'll be very"— broken up by somewhat random profanity. These girls are teenagers of the 1980's, more sophisticated and hip, the film argues, than their spiritless parents (symbolized by Veronica's unperceptive mother and father, played by Jennifer Rhodes and Bill Cort), and more in tune with reality than are their befuddled teachers. As in the countless teenage romances which *Heathers* mercilessly pillories, the adults merely frame the action; crises and their resolution remain the sole province of the youth.

The cafeteria depicts a site of social stratification: "Geeks" eat together, suitably distant from the "in crowd," and Heather number one exercises her tyranny over everyone, especially Veronica. Near the end of the scene, Veronica, having eyed him several times, introduces herself to the new guy in school, J. D. (Christian Slater), whose manner of speaking is as distinctive as his looks, piquing Veronica's interest and arousing the envy of the two resident senior jocks, Kurt Kelly (Lance Fenton) and Ram (Patrick Labyorteaux). When the latter two harass J. D., he pulls out a .44 magnum and shoots them—with blanks, it turns out, but this incident proves a prelude to the real violence.

Dragged to a local fraternity party by Heather number one, Veronica coldly resists the advances of a dull college boy, vomits in the hall, and is summarily denounced by the imperious Heather. Veronica returns home to confide her bitterness and her wish for Heather's death to her diary. Suddenly, J. D. appears. After successfully challenging Veronica to a game of strip croquet, he suggests they visit Heather number one and obtain Veronica's desired revenge. In a marvelous sleight of hand, J. D. (juvenile delinquent/James Dean—both meanings are operative in the film's tissue of allusion) slips Heather a cup of drain cleaner mixed with milk; she keels over onto a glass coffee table. Seemingly appalled at his mistake, J. D. recovers when he notices the Cliff Notes to Sylvia Plath's *The Bell Jar* (1963) on the floor. He convinces Veronica to stage Heather's death as a suicide, complete with a suitably ridiculous note ("I die knowing no one knew the real me") penned by Veronica, a master forger who can imitate anyone's handwriting.

It soon becomes clear that the film's major premise is its making light of teenage suicide. J. D. and Veronica embark on a killing spree—she reluctantly—that claims the loutish Kurt and Ram and aims at Heather number two (Duke). In addition, the hapless Martha Dunnstock unsuccessfully tries to take her own life, and Heather number three (McNamara) is only narrowly foiled in a similar attempt by the repentant Veronica. At this point, Veronica disentangles herself from the increasingly frightening J. D., only to discover that he is perfectly willing to pursue the game to the end by staging her suicide as well, setting up the act by warning her insouciant parents about her recent depression. Veronica, disenchanted with J. D.'s nihilism, fools him by pretending to have hanged herself from the beam in her bedroom—a scene that ends with a hilarious exchange between Veronica and her mother reminiscent of another famous macabre comedy, *Harold and Maude* (1971).

In *Heathers*, J. D. represents the mad alter ego first conjured up in Veronica's diary, the figure who enables her to act out her secret desires. As Veronica remarks to Heather number three: "I can't get him [J. D.] out of my head." She can get him out of her life, however, and does so in the final, apocalyptic sequence.

A bald plot summary cannot do justice to the visual and verbal cleverness that punctuates *Heathers* and constitutes its real genius. Often teetering on the edge of banality, it consistently recovers with a deflating self-conscious irony or a wicked swipe at conventional pieties about the ultimate good sense of teenagers. (If the adults in this film are vacuous, venal, or silly, the majority of their progeny are well on their way to a similar emptiness.) The mood of the film swings from the surreal—in the zany and sick dream sequence of Heather number two's funeral—to the deadpan—in the patio scenes with Veronica and her guileless parents—to the screwball—in the fruitless attempt by the police to solve the mystery of Kurt's and Ram's deaths. Camera angles, lighting, and slick editing all mark the film as knowing and sophisticated about both its subject matter and the tricks of the filmmaker's trade. In nearly every way, *Heathers* is a product of smart, mature cinematic technique.

The film is less self-aware, however, in structuring its essential ideological materials and in resolving its narrative contradictions through the plot. The film turns on the transformation of Veronica from confused camp follower into moral leader, the "new sheriff in town" who will make Westerburg High "a nice place." From the beginning, the film codes her as possessed of a troubled conscience—the main theme of her diary. Her nemesis is the unconscionable Heather Chandler, whose character is defined by her unapproachable popularity, which even the geeks acknowledge. The geeks are Heather's polar opposites, just as J. D. proves to be Veronica's, playing the nihilistic Nietzschean Superman to her ostensibly weaker moral heroine. In this system of contradictory values, various characters combine the basic polarities of conscience/popularity and unpopularity/nihilism: Betty Finn represents moral conviction and unpopularity; Martha Dunnstock is the very embodiment of the unpopular wallflower but flirts with J. D.'s nihilism by attempting suicide; and Kurt and Ram act out J. D.'s cavalier rejection of any ethical principle while representing the male equivalents of the popular Heathers.

As a solution to the moral conflict created by the contradictory values, *Heathers* offers the transformed Veronica at film's end, who redeems Martha Dunnstock in an act of charity while proclaiming herself the new queen, arbiter of Westerburg's mores and savior of its inhabitants. The self-conscious reference to melodramatic Westerns (Veronica as the "new sheriff") would seem to undercut the seriousness of the narrative resolution. In a film so determinedly suspicious of conventional social values and mercilessly parodic of standard film genres, can anything be taken seriously?

The film's comic resolution finally tilts the balance in favor of the positive qualities that Veronica has always possessed but that her fascination with J. D. temporarily suspended. *Heathers* turns away from its more outrageous potential conclusion to reaffirm the basic sanity and moral conviction of even the most jaded of teenagers. Thus *Heathers* ultimately becomes a pleasant, reassuring fable, proving that America's "troubled youth" are really decent and sensible, and that, left to their own devices, they will sort out the good from the bad, the valuable from the worthless.

In this way, *Heathers* recoups the fundamental values of the films it ostensibly satirizes—teenage screwball comedies such as *Ferris Bueller's Day Off* (1986) and *Risky Business* (1983)—repudiating the threatening possibilities it has mobilized. Adult audiences can watch with impunity, savoring the film's flirtation with nihilism while being reassured in the end that their world is secure against the anarchic violence of youth. Teenagers may find it rather less comforting, for they are less likely to accept the proffered salvation of Veronica's triumph. They know only too well that geeks remain geeks, that fat girls are unpopular and generally unhappy, and that the Veronicas rarely possess the courage and clear-sightedness to abandon the Heathers. For all of its intelligence and sly artfulness, *Heathers* remains a conventional film—in other words, a success.

Michael Sprinker

Reviews

American Film: Magazine of the Film and Television Arts. XIV, January, 1989, p. 10.
Chicago Tribune. March 31, 1989, VII, p. 34.
Cinéfantastique. XIX, July, 1898, p. 54.
Films in Review. XL, September, 1989, p. 423.
Gentleman's Quarterly. LIX, April, 1989, p. 123.
Los Angeles Times. March 31, 1989, VI, p. 1.
The Nation. CCXLVIII, April 17, 1989, p. 530.
New York Magazine. XXII, April 3, 1989, p. 68.
The New York Times. March 31, 1989, p. C8.
The New Yorker. LXV, April 17, 1989, p. 113.
Newsweek. CXIII, April 3, 1989, p. 67.
Rolling Stone. April 20, 1989, p. 38.
Time. CXXXIII, April 17, 1989, p. 83.
Variety. CCCXXXIV, January 25, 1989, p. 15.
Video. XIII, September, 1989, p. 88.

HENRY V

Origin: Great Britain
Released: 1989
Released in U.S.: 1989
Production: Bruce Sharman for Renaissance Films; released by Samuel Goldwyn
  Company
Direction: Kenneth Branagh
Screenplay: Kenneth Branagh; based on the play by William Shakespeare
Cinematography: Kenneth Macmillan
Editing: Michael Bradsel
Production design: Tim Harvey
Art direction: Norman Dorme
Special effects: Ian Wingrove
Makeup: Peter Frampton
Costume design: Phyllis Dalton (AA)
Sound: David Crozier
Music direction: Simon Rattle
Music: Patrick Doyle
MPAA rating: PG
Running time: 135 minutes

Principal characters:

Henry V	Kenneth Branagh
Katherine	Emma Thompson
Chorus	Derek Jacobi
Pistol	Robert Stephens
Fluellen	Ian Holm
French King	Paul Scofield
Dauphin	Michael Maloney
Constable	Richard Easton
Mountjoy	Christopher Ravenscroft
Exeter	Brian Blessed
Mistress Quickly	Judy Dench
Falstaff	Robbie Coltrane
Canterbury	Charles Kay
Alice	Geraldine McEwan
Bishop of Ely	Alec McCowen
Burgundy	Richard Innocent
Bardolph	Richard Briers

Henry V is the fourth in William Shakespeare's series of English history plays. In
the first, *Richard II*, the king is deposed by the usurper Henry Bolingbroke, who
becomes Henry IV and has Richard murdered. In *Henry IV, Parts I* and *II*, Prince

Hal, who will become Henry V, is a scapegrace, consorting with the tavern knight Sir John Falstaff and his cronies Pistol, Bardolph, and Nym in a series of thieving and boozing pranks. Yet when rebellion is afoot against his father, Hal turns heroic in each play and helps defeat the rebels. At the end of *Henry IV, Part II*, the king dies, and Hal, becoming Henry V, casts off his old ways and rejects Falstaff and his company.

Henry V opens with the Archbishop of Canterbury (Charles Kay) and the Bishop of Ely (Alec McCowen) hoping for a war to deflect a pending law that will strip the church of half its possessions. King Henry (Kenneth Branagh) asks them to explain whether the Salique Law justifies his claim to France, warning them at the same time to take heed how they "awake our sleeping sword of war that shall shed much guiltless blood." They assure him that he is entitled in good conscience to claim the crown of France and that they will take any sin upon themselves, and they urge him to remember the warlike blood of his ancestor the Black Prince, and promise to raise money for the venture. The nobles agreeing, Henry is resolved, and his resolution is sharpened by a message from the French ambassador, bringing from the Dauphin a gift of tennis balls to taunt him with his youth. In France, Charles VI, the French King (Paul Scofield), is grim about the prospects of war, but the hot-headed Dauphin is eager for the glory of battle. Sir Laurence Olivier, in his version of the play for film, had Charles VI portrayed as a doddering, half-senile monarch and most of the French nobles as decadent fops, but Branagh makes them formidable adversaries.

After a conspiracy to murder Henry is uncovered, Henry has the conspirators executed. While Henry is preparing to sail, Falstaff (Robbie Coltrane) dies, and his cronies Pistol (Robert Stephens), Bardolph (Richard Briers), Nym (Geoffrey Hutchins), and his serving boy (Christian Bale), formerly the king's boon companions, join the army. In France, Henry first attacks and captures the port city of Harfleur. As his expeditionary force marches through rain and mud, an enormous French army masses and prepares to attack him at Agincourt, near Calais. Though greatly outnumbered (the historical estimates vary from five against one to ten against one), Henry refuses to surrender. On the night before the battle, he goes in disguise among his troops to check their morale, and in the morning, St. Crispin's Day, he challenges their mettle with a rousing speech. As the armored French cavalry attack, the English longbowmen wait until Henry signals and then shoot volley after volley of arrows that strike havoc among the massed French. According to Shakespeare, the French suffer ten thousand deaths, the English a mere twenty-nine. These figures are exaggerated, but it is certain that the French casualties were in the thousands, those of the English in the hundreds. After the spectacular victory of Agincourt, Henry negotiates with the French and woos the French Princess Katherine (Emma Thompson) in a comic scene, in which neither can speak more than a smattering of the other's language.

In 1944, Olivier's *Henry V* was a landmark film, the first screening of a Shakespearean play to succeed brilliantly as a cinematic work of art. Olivier's *Henry V* became the standard by which all subsequent Shakespearean films have been measured. Accordingly, when Kenneth Branagh, a young actor in his late twenties with limited screen experience, undertook to make a new film of *Henry V*, numerous skeptics proclaimed him audacious for daring to compete with Olivier. When the new *Henry V* was released, it confounded the skeptics and received universal acclaim as a new masterpiece, not competing with Olivier but reinterpreting the play in a way meaningful for the late 1980's. Made during World War II to boost the morale of the troops, Olivier's film is full of spectacular pageantry and heroic panache. To achieve this effect, Olivier cut the ambiguous elements of the play and of King Henry's character. Branagh's version, made after the disastrous wars in Suez and Vietnam, is much darker, retaining the ambiguities that Olivier cut. In Branagh's *Henry V*, the cause for war is not just, and it is by no means certain that Henry is "the mirror of all Christian kings."

Olivier's version begins and continues for several scenes in the Globe Theatre, where *Henry V* is having its first performance. Branagh's version begins in darkness. As he speaks his opening line, "O for a Muse of fire," the Chorus (Derek Jacobi) strikes a match, dimly lighting a deserted soundstage, littered with props from the film. Whereas Olivier's Chorus is a heroic figure full of rousing rhetoric, Branagh's more contemporary Chorus implies that this could be any war, any time. Olivier, working with a low budget, made a virtue of necessity by having obviously painted backdrops and cardboard castles that not only are reminiscent of the artificiality of the theater in which the audience is seated, working upon its imagination, but also resemble the medieval paintings in Books of Hours. Branagh, working with a relatively lower budget, minimizes pageantry and gives a much darker, more realistic film, visually as well as dramatically, with many scenes set in windowless, dimly lit rooms, where the characters are filmed in extreme close-up.

As his Chorus leads the audience to the end of the soundstage, double doors open into the world of Henry V. Olivier plays the following scene for laughs, having a simpering, clownish Ely continually dropping manuscripts while Canterbury criticizes him. Branagh presents these characters not only straight but also as sinister conspirators provoking war. First walking toward the audience out of darkness, Henry allows the clerics to poison his mind, one on each side whispering to him. Throughout the film, Henry repeatedly says that everything is God's will, but the audience has cause to doubt him as he threatens to break France to pieces and make "many a thousand widows."

Olivier gives his rallying "Once more unto the breach" speech at Harfleur in bright daylight and goes galloping back into battle after it; Branagh gives it at night before a burning gate and afterward grimaces with pain and fatigue. In lines that Olivier cut, Branagh's Henry threatens the defenders with the rape of their women and the murder of their infants, "spitted upon pikes," unless they will surrender. Whereas Olivier has the quarrel between the Welsh Fluellen (Ian Holm) and the Irish Macmorris (John Sessions) as a comic interlude in the sunny field, Branagh gives it in the rain in a muddy trench reminiscent of World War I. Branagh, unlike

Olivier, includes the hanging of Henry's friend Bardolph, an act to which the king assents, though he weeps at the sight. Branagh's Henry, a much younger, less assured monarch, must make tougher decisions than the Henry of Olivier.

Olivier's Henry is a matinee idol, handsome and dashing. Branagh's is plainer, a bantam, with less panache and bravura. Olivier and company act on a grand scale, performing almost operatically, while Branagh and company avoid swashbuckling and are more conversationally realistic. More self-questioning, Branagh's Henry has some of the doubts of *Hamlet*, which was written the next year.

A classic highlight in Olivier's film is the charge of the French knights at Agincourt. Rather than try to compete with it, Branagh leaves it out altogether and gives the effect of the charge in reaction shots of the appalled English soldiers as the audience hears the charge, louder and louder like a tidal wave. Olivier's battle, in bright daylight, is exhilarating; Branagh's, in the rain and mud, is appalling, with ghastly deaths, slaughtered horses, and corpse robbers. At the end of the battle, Branagh's Henry, muddied and covered with blood does not even know which side has won.

After the battle, Henry goes directly to the French court, where Burgundy (Richard Innocent) gives a speech pleading for peace that is juxtaposed to a flashback of the horrors of battle, in contrast with Olivier's version, which juxtaposes the speech to pastoral scenes of France. At the end, Olivier's Henry returns to the Globe and has the Chorus end on a wholly positive note, giving only part of the closing speech praising "this star of England"; Branagh, on the other hand, includes the whole speech, with its statement that Henry's successors "lost France, and made his England bleed" and that, in short, nothing was achieved except needless slaughter.

Both versions of *Henry V*, that of Branagh and that of Olivier, are superb films, cast with some of Britain's greatest actors. Branagh calls *Henry V* "a political debate inside an adventure story." Olivier stressed the adventure; one critic even called Olivier's version "Robin Hood versus the Nazis." Branagh presents the more provocative political debate, which is appropriate after Vietnam, Afghanistan, and the dismal wars of the Middle East and Latin America. Olivier's version is more colorful and exciting; Branagh's is more somber and thoughtful. Branagh's *Henry V* is a film for its time.

Robert E. Morsberger

Reviews

Los Angeles Times. November 8, 1989, VI, p. 1.
The New Republic. CCI, December 4, 1989, p. 28.
The New York Times. November 8, 1989, p. C19.
The New Yorker. LXV, November 27, 1989, p. 104.
Newsweek. CXIV, November 20, 1989, p. 78.
Time. CXXXIV, November 13, 1989, p. 119.
Variety. CCCXXXVI, September 20, 1989, p. 29.

HIGH HOPES

Origin: Great Britain
Released: 1988
Released in U.S.: 1989
Production: Simon Channing-Williams, Victor Glynn, and Tom Donald for Film
    Four International, in association with British Screen; released by Skouras
    Pictures
Direction: Mike Leigh
Screenplay: Mike Leigh
Cinematography: Roger Pratt
Editing: Jon Gregory
Production design: Diana Charnley
Art direction: Andrew Rothschild
Costume design: Lindy Hemming
Music: Andrew Dixon
MPAA rating: no listing
Running time: 110 minutes

> *Principal characters:*
> Cyril .... Philip Davis
> Shirley .... Ruth Sheen
> Mrs. Bender .... Edna Dore
> Martin .... Philip Jackson
> Valerie............................ Heather Tobias
> Laetitia Boothe-Braine .... Leslie Manville
> Rupert Boothe-Braine .... David Bamber

High Hopes is yet another film from Great Britain that illustrates and examines the various social maladies that face contemporary British society. Like *My Beautiful Laundrette* (1986), *Sammy and Rosie Get Laid* (1987), *Letter to Brezhnev* (1986), and *Dance with a Stranger* (1985), *High Hopes* depicts the state of a nation riddled with class tensions and ruled by a government that, for many, has delivered far less than what was promised. What distinguishes this film from its neighbors, however, is the involvement of director/writer Mike Leigh, one of Great Britain's most important television and stage directors. *High Hopes* is Leigh's second attempt at feature films, and by using his unique method of project development, which includes the nurturing of both character and plot through improvisation, he has fashioned a film that not only is another entrant in the current British film invasion but also stands alone as an intensely innovative and original creation.

Leigh's first effort at filmmaking was 1971's *Bleak Moments*, which, after winning rave reviews at the London Film Festival, was released only briefly in New York nine years later. In the almost two-decade period between his two feature films,

Leigh has spent most of his creative time conceiving and directing plays of the English stage and television films for the British Broadcasting Corporation (BBC) and Channel 4, which ultimately funded *High Hopes* as well as *A Room with a View* (1986) and *My Beautiful Laundrette*. Leigh had difficulty securing financial backing for the film because of his rather unusual artistic procedure. He typically comes into a film without a script, with only actors whom he handpicks and with whom he then works individually to choose and develop characters. In isolation, Leigh and a single actor develop the qualities, peculiarities, and histories of a specific character, often creating an entire life history. Leigh then pulls together his cast and supervises improvisations between the actors, given a predetermined environment. After weeks of developing situations and outcomes, Leigh's camera begins to roll, capturing a highly structured narrative piece. Leigh's innovative procedure results in a film (*High Hopes* being no exception) that contains performances that are both utterly convincing and beautifully poignant and situations that are both strikingly ordinary and intensely compelling.

Leigh's favorite topic is the unyielding rigidity of the class system in Great Britain and the desultory and hopeless life of Great Britain's lower class. In Leigh's films, a Tory government allows for the rich to keep getting richer and the poor to flourish only in poverty and pessimism. He portrays the upper and middle classes as self-absorbed buffoons and even casts a cynical eye on the lower class. The members of Great Britain's less fortunate social group are often stupefied despondents whose only activity is maliciously harping on others who share their woes. Even Leigh's depiction of the revolutionary Left who struggle philosophically with the Thatcher government is viciously satirical; a minor character in *High Hopes* is a would-be radical, who nervously chain-smokes, mispronounces the buzzwords of her leftist viewpoint, and, in the same breath, speaks of both her anticapitalist leanings and her desire to open a jewelry shop.

If Leigh finds one type of Briton favorable, it is the member of the lower class who holds onto a small amount of optimism while existing within the restrictive English economy and facing the prejudicial eyes of the fortunate upper class. It is the life of one such couple that makes up the focal point of *High Hopes*. Cyril (Philip Davis) and Shirley (Ruth Sheen) are two long-haired bohemians who live together as companions in a paltry, cramped apartment in King's Cross. Cyril, who works as a messenger, complains about the current political state of London—a city where an economic boom of the rich has dulled political protest from all. Shirley, who plants trees for the city, longs for the chance to rear and nurture a child despite Cyril's constant refusals to father it. In the course of the film, Cyril and Shirley's relationship is interwoven with the relationships of two other couples, both of whom are economically well-off and one of whom belongs to the upper classes. Yet it is Cyril and Shirley (and their sturdy, loving, and hopeful relationship) who are ultimately applauded by the film.

As *High Hopes* opens, Cyril and Shirley visit Cyril's mother, Mrs. Bender (Edna Dore), an elderly woman who has long held onto her council apartment despite the almost total gentrification of the neighborhood. She experiences fits of forgetfulness and delusion that signal the onset of Alzheimer's disease and raise the concerns of Cyril and Shirley. A few days later, Mrs. Bender locks herself out of her apartment and asks her upper-class neighbor, Laetitia Boothe-Braine (Leslie Manville), for help. Laetitia reluctantly agrees to let Mrs. Bender inside her home and calls Mrs. Bender's daughter, the screechy, social-climbing Valerie (Heather Tobias), asking her to come fetch her mother. Soon, Rupert Boothe-Braine (David Bamber) returns home bearing opera tickets and gossips with his wife as Mrs. Bender, alone at the kitchen table, sips tea. Valerie arrives and appears more concerned with Laetitia's decorating than helping her mother. She then discovers that she, too, has forgotten the keys and must call for brother Cyril, who arrives just after the exasperated Boothe-Braines cancel their pre-opera dinner plans.

After successfully gaining entrance to Mrs. Bender's apartment, Valerie reminds Cyril and Shirley about the seventieth birthday party that she and Martin will be throwing for Mrs. Bender. As Shirley and Cyril get ready for bed that evening, Shirley brings up the subject of a baby, and Cyril again refuses to bring up a child in such a hopeless environment as London. A child deserves a place where he can have a job, a place to live, and enough to eat, Cyril says uncomfortably. In a bittersweet moment, Shirley points out Cyril's naïveté and proclaims that the world will never be perfect.

On the day of Mrs. Bender's seventieth birthday party, Valerie's cigar-chomping, entrepreneur husband, Martin (Philip Jackson), picks up Mrs. Bender and stops for a quick liaison with his mistress while Mrs. Bender waits in the car. Cyril and Shirley arrive at Valerie's on their motorcycle, closely followed by the despicable Martin and the helpless Mrs. Bender. Martin begins an incessant lecture on the benefits of capitalism directed toward Cyril, and Valerie forces her mother to gulp champagne and eat cake. When things do not proceed as planned, Valerie turns into a loud drunk, finally retreating to her bubble bath. In the commotion, Mrs. Bender slips into the past and begins to sink into delusion. Cyril and Shirley then take Mrs. Bender to their apartment, where Shirley suggests that Mrs. Bender needs to be looked after for a while. Cyril agrees, and, after a brief period of reminiscing, Mrs. Bender spends the night. The next morning, the threesome take to the roof of the apartment building, and, as the film ends, Cyril and Shirley show Mrs. Bender what London looks like from above.

The final image of *High Hopes* is extremely effective in that it restructures the family unit and provides the main characters with some reward for their refusal to give up hope in a world that casts them as misfits. Cyril and Shirley stand arm-in-arm looking out over the rooftops of the city, and the camera situates Mrs. Bender so that she sits lower and directly between the couple. At the end of the film, Shirley has finally found a "child" to nurture and take care of: Cyril's elderly and incapacitated mother. The potential of Cyril and Shirley's loving relationship (the only one in the film not legitimized by marriage) has been fully realized by the addition of Mrs. Bender, and its flourishing is suggested in the final scenes by the optimistic way in which the couple faces their gray future. The irony of the film's title is eased by the way in which Shirley and Cyril refuse to give up the fight in a London that is filled with dead ends for the lower class.

The technical devices within *High Hopes* remain virtually invisible; Roger Pratt's camera and Andrew Dixon's music serve only to highlight the film's remarkable script and performances. If the film has a fault, it is the inconsistent tone of the film's dramatics, Heather Tobias' Valerie is a hugely satirical portrayal of a desperate social-climber; she blithers across the screen, shrieking and preening. The snobby, impatient Boothe-Braines are played much the same way. Although these hilarious performances account for much of the film's wacky black humor, it often seems that they exist in an entirely different film from that occupied by the observed performances of Davis and Sheen. Leigh combines naturalism and caricature without reservation, and the result is a film that awkwardly stitches together two disparate parts. Yet the subtle wisdom of Davis' performance as Cyril and Sheen's as Shirley, along with Mike Leigh's intelligent and uniquely developed script, makes *High Hopes* stand out among British films of the late 1980's.

Greg Changnon

Reviews

American Film: Magazine of the Film and Television Arts. XIV, March, 1989, p. 12.
Chicago Tribune. April 14, 1989, VII, p. 38.
The Christian Science Monitor. April 7, 1989, p. 11.
Commonweal. CXVI, April 7, 1989, p. 212.
The Guardian. September 1, 1989, p. 23.
Los Angeles Times. March 9, 1989, VI, p. 1.
The Nation. CCXLVIII, March 13, 1989, p. 352.
New Leader. LXXII, February 20, 1989, p. 22.
The New Republic. CC, March 13, 1989, p. 26.
New Statesman and Society. II, January 13, 1989, p. 44.
New York Magazine. XXII, February 27, 1989, p. 142.
The New York Times. September 24, 1988, p. A12.
The New Yorker. LXV, February 20, 1989, p. 96.
Newsweek. CXIII, February 27, 1989, p. 69.
Time. CXXXII, March 20, 1989, p. 72.
Variety. CCCXXXII, September 7, 1989, p. 25.

HONEY, I SHRUNK THE KIDS

Production: Penney Finkelman Cox for Walt Disney; released by Buena Vista
Direction: Joe Johnston
Screenplay: Ed Naha and Tom Schulman; based on a story by Stuart Gordon, Brian
    Yuzna, and Ed Naha
Cinematography: Hiro Narita
Editing: Michael A. Stevenson
Production design: Gregg Fonseca
Art direction: John Iacovelli and Dorree Cooper
Special vocal effects: Frank Welker
Makeup: Del Armstrong
Costume design: Carol Brolaski
Sound: John Reitz, David Campbell, and Greg Rudloff
Music: James Horner
MPAA rating: PG
Running time: 86 minutes

      Principal characters:
      Wayne Szalinski . . . . Rick Moranis
      "Big" Russ Thompson . . . . Matt Frewer
      Diane Szalinski . . . . Marcia Strassman
      Mae Thompson . . . . Kristine Sutherland
      "Little" Russ Thompson . . . . Thomas Brown
      Ron Thompson. . . . . Jared Rushton
      Amy Szalinski . . . . Amy O'Neill
      Nick Szalinski . . . . Robert Oliveri

Toward the end of *Honey, I Shrunk the Kids*, a mother, fearful that she may never see her children again, admits to her husband that their search for money and fame has destroyed their family. As the golden light of a new day fills their backyard, both vow to love each other and repair their broken lives. Such sober moments give this Walt Disney comedy a seriousness that its whimsical title obscures. Unquestionably a product of the Disney studios, *Honey, I Shrunk the Kids* is slick, amusing, colorful, and clever. With an old-fashioned approach to filmmaking and storytelling, the film entangles inept fathers, competent mothers, and vulnerable children in a dangerous adventure. Their struggle to triumph over staggering odds leads to a clearer understanding of who they are and what they might become. Like many other Disney fantasies, the film takes its audience on an impossible journey into an inaccessible dimension of space. In *Honey, I Shrunk the Kids*, the journey is to the backyard of the American home.

    Honey, I Shrunk the Kids opens with an aerial view of a middle class suburban neighborhood: The lawns are mowed, there are two cars in each garage, bicycles and skateboards lie in the driveways, and the birds are chirping. In the home of Wayne (Rick Moranis) and Diane (Marcia Strassman) Szalinski, however, there is no domestic tranquillity. Mom and Dad are estranged. Their professional lives leave them little time for parenting. She is a real-estate agent, and he is an absentminded maverick inventor. On this particular summer's morning, Mom has left home, and Dad is upstairs tinkering with his latest invention, a room-sized laser gun that will shrink objects to microscopic size. His son Nick (Robert Oliveri), who wants to be just like his father, is downstairs perfecting a piece of his own homespun inventiveness. Daughter Amy (Amy O'Neill) struggles to make breakfast among the chaos of Dad's homemade gadgetry: an automatic dog feeder, a mechanical telephone pickup, and a remote-controlled lawn mower. In this first glimpse of the Szalinski home, the audience sees a cartoon version of contemporary America: absentee, workaholic parents, who have turned over the running of the household to appliances and the children.

Next door to the Szalinskis is another version of the American family: the Thompsons. Their house is obsessively neat and tidy, quiet and orderly. Russ (Matt Frewer) and Mae (Kristine Sutherland) Thompson are preparing to take the children on a weekend fishing trip. Whereas the Szalinski kids are unable to get their parents' attention, the Thompson boys, Russ (Thomas Brown) and Ron (Jared Rushton), suffer from too much parental concern. Russ is pushed by his father to play football, lift weights, and "act big." Ron, a carbon copy of his father, is set the difficult task of being the model son.

The Szalinskis and the Thompsons may be neighbors, but they dislike and distrust each other. The children, who attend the same school, regard each other as strangers. It takes an accident, believable only in the world of Disney, to force the families together. When Ron Thompson hits a baseball through the attic window of the Szalinskis' home, the baseball lands on Wayne's unattended shrinking machine. The machine sputters to life and zaps a nearby sofa, and the four kids. Later, when Wayne comes to the attic to do some housecleaning, he unknowingly sweeps the kids into a dustpan and tosses them away.

After almost thirty minutes of background and exposition, the delicious promise of the film's premise is finally delivered: Tiny humans will be threatened and perhaps killed in the backyard. Blades of grass become towering trees. Drops of water fall like bombs, threatening to wash away the four miniatures. The enemies they must defeat are nature, human excess, and the ineptitude of their own parents. The journey takes them over the now-treacherous backyard landscape in their quest for home and reunification with their families.

Honey, I Shrunk the Kids is not the special-effects extravaganza one would expect from a Disney film directed by Joe Johnston, who was an art director with George Lucas' Industrial Light and Magic. The film makes no pretense of real-life situations; for example, the miniaturized kids' bizarre encounters—with a scorpion, a bee, or an oatmeal cookie—are sometimes terrifying but mostly humorous. The opening credits appear in a raucous cartoon of tiny children terrorized by oversized letters that spell the names of stars, producers, and the director. The music, a pastiche of funky jazz, early rodeo, and Muzak has no connection to the narrative, thus neither intruding on nor supporting the story. The film's focus remains on the four kids' struggle toward home and a return to normality.

In a climactic moment derived straight from the Old Testament and Greek mythology, Wayne Szalinski almost eats his own son, who clings to a piece of breakfast cereal in a spoon poised at his father's lips. Having discovered his children's whereabouts, Wayne fires up the shrinking machine. Before zapping the children, however, the parents decide to test the machine's ability to shrink and grow objects. As the guinea pig, the elder Russ Thompson allows Wayne to shrink him and attempt to bring him back. While the tiny children and giant parents look on, the bombastic father is reduced to the size of an ant. When the process is reversed seconds later, he discovers that his hat is a little too large for his head. Even though he has grown imperceptibly smaller, the crisis of losing his children and finding them again makes him realize how foolish he has been.

Honey, I Shrunk the Kids is a parable about size, where characters define themselves by bigness. Diane Szalinski works so hard at being a big real-estate saleswoman that she forsakes children and home. Wayne Szalinski, obsessed with being a world-renowned physicist, brushes aside his son Nick in his rush to win the next grant. Russ Thompson, who believes that big is always better, has alienated his sons because he tries so hard to impose his distorted view of the world on them. In the end, after bigness has been vanquished, a tranquillity settles over these middle-class American homes, and the audience senses that all these "little" people have grown in a dimension that has nothing to do with size.

In a marketing scheme reminiscent of the 1940's and 1950's, *Honey, I Shrunk the Kids* is preceded by a cartoon called "Tummy Trouble." A violent, noisy, and unamusing derivative of the 1988 animation hit, *Who Framed Roger Rabbit*, "Tummy Trouble" follows the further adventures of Roger Rabbit (voice of Charles Fleischer), as he babysits Baby Herman (voices of April Winchell and Lou Hirsch), who is actually an aging, cigar-smoking character actor in diapers. Chasing each other at the speed of light through the corridors of an ultramodern hospital, they are threatened by oversized hypodermic needles, ghoulish doctors, and amazon nurses. Although "Tummy Trouble" has the energy and frenzy of a cartoon starring the Road Runner, Tom and Jerry, and Bugs Bunny, audiences familiar with live-action cartoons such as *Star Wars* (1977)and *The Empire Strikes Back* (1980) will find little to thrill or amaze them in the two-dimensional world of Roger Rabbit.

Peter Moller

Reviews
Chicago Tribune. June 23, 1989, CII, p. 50.
The Christian Science Monitor. August 18, 1989, p. 10.

Cinéfantastique. XIX, July 1989, p. 14.
Los Angeles Times. June 23, 1989, VI, p. 12.
The New York Times. June 23, 1989, p. C17.
People Weekly. XXXII, July 10, 1989, p. 13.
Rolling Stone. August 10, 1989, p. 31.
Variety. CCCXXXV, June 28, 1989, p. 16.
The Wall Street Journal. June 20, 1989, p. A16.
The Washington Post. June 23, 1989, p. F1.

IMMEDIATE FAMILY

Production: Sarah Pillsbury, Midge Sanford, and Lawrence Kasdan; released by
    Columbia Pictures
Direction: Jonathan Kaplan
Screenplay: Barbara Benedek
Cinematography: John W. Lindley
Editing: Jane Kurson
Production design: Mark Freeborn
Art direction: David Willson
Set decoration: Kimberley Richardson
Set design: Byron Lance King
Makeup: Irene Kent
Costume design: April Ferry
Sound: Larry Sutton and Bruce Carwardine
Music: Brad Fiedel
MPAA rating: PG 13
Running time: 95 minutes

> *Principal characters:*
> Linda Spector . . . . Glenn Close
> Michael Spector . . . . James Woods
> Lucy Moore . . . . Mary Stuart Masterson
> Sam . . . . Kevin Dillon
> Lawyer Susan Drew . . . . Linda Darlow
> Michael's mother. . . . . Jane Greer
> Bessie . . . . Jessica James

The tragic circumstances of infertility have long been standard fodder for television films and for episodes of series television. The subject has, however, rarely seen the light of a motion picture screen, perhaps because it is hardly typical escapist film fare. The idea of a couple's potent desire to procreate and their subsequent failings probably does not qualify for the type of grand-scale entertainment that ensures box-office profits. In recent films such as *Baby Boom* (1987), *Three Men and a Baby* (1987), and *Look Who's Talking* (1989; reviewed in this volume), it is usually single men and women, busy with careers, who become saddled with children for which they simply have no room. One must look back to 1983's *The Big Chill* to find a mainstream film that concerned itself with a woman's all-consuming urge to bear a child. It is no surprise, therefore, that the director, the writer, and one of the stars of *The Big Chill* have joined forces once again to create *Immediate Family*, a film devoted to the story of a barren Seattle couple. Unfortunately, the film, with its hackneyed characters and all-too-familiar narrative line, plays too much like a television film. If it were not for a stunning supporting performance, *Immediate Family* would simply be a forgettable and unconvincing melodrama.

Married for eleven years, Linda and Michael Spector (Glenn Close and James Woods) are a happy and successful couple, but their inability to have a child has raised the concerns of their friends and sparked their own feelings of inadequacy. Linda becomes susceptible to fits of excessive drinking and smoking when another month goes by without conception, and Michael is getting bored with his many mornings collecting sperm samples for the fertility clinic. Finally, the Spectors decide on adoption, and, acting on advice from lawyer Susan Drew (Linda Darlow), they decide to allow themselves to get close to their prospective child's mother. Linda and Michael complete questionnaires and applications and wait for an expectant mother who likes them to respond.

When a response comes, it is from unwed, seventeen-year-old Lucy Moore (Mary Stuart Masterson), who then travels to Seattle to meet and get to know the Spectors. At first, the Spectors are shocked at the questionable nature of the uncouth and penniless Lucy, but soon the young woman's rustic decency wins them over. The threesome begin to spend a considerable amount of time together, and, when Lucy's boyfriend Sam (Kevin Dillon) arrives, the two couples tour Seattle and discuss the adoption. Lucy and Sam understand that the only way that they could make their relationship successful would be to give up the child they would have trouble rearing. The Spectors are impressed by the young couple's special devotion to each other, and, when Sam goes back home to Ohio, they invite a distraught Lucy to stay with them in their home.

Soon Lucy is ready to deliver the baby, and the Spectors hurry her to the hospital like expectant parents. Once she gives birth, Lucy refuses to hold her baby and is taken to another wing of the hospital to convalesce with patients recovering from other types of procedures. The Spectors, however, are allowed to spend unlimited time with the newborn, and at home they hurry to complete the nursery. Arriving at the hospital one morning to see their new son, Linda and Michael are met by their adoption lawyer, who tells them that Lucy has had a change of heart. Michael tries to talk Lucy out of her sudden decision, but Lucy is adamant; she believes that the baby will be better off with his natural mother. Lucy packs her things and returns to Ohio with her child, while a heartbroken Linda returns home without a baby for the nursery.

In Ohio, Lucy and Sam find that rearing a child as teenagers is as hard as everyone has said it would be. They struggle to spend time together as a family, even though they live in two separate, broken homes. Lucy's lazy stepfather and Sam's angry mother offer no help, and the sudden burden of responsibility has taken its toll on the happy-go-lucky attitudes of the young parents. Back in Seattle, Linda and Michael are faced with yet another failure, and their unhappiness begins to corrode the stability of their marriage. Late one night, their doorbell rings, and Michael discovers Lucy, Sam, and the baby at the doorstep. The young duo has come, in effect, to return the baby to its more proper parents, and, after Lucy bids a sweet farewell to her son, she and Sam disappear into the night.

As is evident in *Immediate Family*, director Jonathan Kaplan has a considerable talent for depicting strong female characters from various sectors of the social stratosphere. In fact, Kaplan's most important films before *Immediate Family* have been similar narratives concerning admirable women. *Heart Like a Wheel* (1983), which may be one of the most underrated films of the 1980's, provided a sympathetic yet tenacious portrait of real-life figure Shirley Muldowney, and in it actress Bonnie Bedelia gives a remarkably complex performance as the professional drag racer fighting for her moral validation, enhancing Kaplan's reputation as a director able to coax a fascinating performance from a marginal screenplay. In *Immediate Family*, Kaplan patiently lets his camera capture the emotions and reactions of his two female leads and allows for one of them, Masterson, to produce a beautifully realized performance despite the limitations of a clichéd, mediocre script.

Masterson, by her early twenties had already produced a list of quality performances that are easily the best element in the films that contain them. She brought a wide-eyed innocence and honesty to the otherwise brutal *At Close Range* (1986), and she provided the only sophisticated and mature note to Howard Deutch's hopelessly sophomoric *Some Kind of Wonderful* (1987). The same is true for her superior work here (in several scenes, she overshadows the unusually subdued Glenn Close), for which she has collected a mass of rave reviews and the National Board of Review citation for Best Supporting Actress. Masterson is at her best in the film when she has nothing to say. When the Lucy character shows snapshots of her mother to Linda and Michael, Masterson's face lights up with pride, but, at the same time, her cloudy, sad eyes signal her own joyless future as an absent mother. Immediately after she gives birth, Lucy is asked if she wants to hold the baby, but the exhausted girl refuses, afraid to touch what she must relinquish. It is a powerful moment made unforgettable by Masterson's wounded yet defiant expression. At the film's end, when Lucy and Sam leave the Spectors' house, Lucy reads the farewell message she has left for her child, and Masterson's haunting voice, crackling with pain, concludes the film with an emotional wallop that allows one to forget the many sluggish and unremarkable sections that comprise the majority of the picture. Perhaps Masterson's greatest accomplishment is making a white-trash teenager who steals another woman's legal son an entirely sympathetic character.

As Linda Spector, Glenn Close underplays her role so severely that her performance comes across as half-baked and lifeless. Close has said that after her riveting, intense performances in *Fatal Attraction* (1987) and *Dangerous Liaisons* (1988), she wanted to play a sympathetic character, but her Linda Spector is so ordinary, one would hardly be inclined to share her story. Close is only effective when she can play off Masterson; a scene in which the two women dance together to a Van Morrison song may be the film's sweetest moment. James Woods is able to provide some light comedic relief but little else in his thankless role as Linda's husband. Usually a provocative, exciting performer, Woods is mostly bland here. Kevin Dillon is both appealing and convincing as the film's fourth leading player, Lucy's boy-friend Sam.

As good as Masterson is, she simply cannot save a film that is overloaded with situations much too familiar to audiences who have seen more than a night's worth of television. Screenwriter Barbara Benedek, with her scripts for *Immediate Family* and *Men Don't Leave* (1990), seems to be resurrecting the woman's picture, but, unfortunately, these two films follow the same well-trod narrative paths of most of the melodramas of the 1940's and 1950's. Director Kaplan, in adapting Benedek's material to the screen, makes most of the film too obvious to be interesting. When Lucy returns to Ohio with her child, her working-class life-style is so horrendous that it is clear that the baby should be with the Spectors. Cigarettes are waved in the baby's face, most of his formula is spilled on the floor, and his diaper is changed on a table cluttered with cassette tapes and dirty tools. The only parental role models that Lucy has are angry, single mothers and lazy widowers. To be poor, according to Kaplan, is to be unhappy, resentful, and neglectful. Yet, if Lucy's life-style were as safe and luxurious as that of the Spectors, Kaplan would not be able to provide the typically upbeat ending his film ultimately contains.

Greg Changnon

Reviews

Chicago Tribune. October 27, 1989, VII, p. 48.
The Christian Science Monitor. November 10, 1989, p. 10.
Commonweal. CXVI, December 1, 1989, p. 670.
Los Angeles Times. October 27, 1989, VI, p. 4.
Maclean's. CII, October 30, 1989, p. 98.
New York Magazine. XXII, November 6, 1989, p. 102.
The New York Times. October 27, 1989, p. C18.
People Weekly. XXXII, November 13, 1989, p. 17.
Time. CXXXIV, November 6, 1989, p. 84.
Variety. CCCXXXVII, October 18, 1989, p. 25.
The Washington Post. October 27, 1989, p. B7.

IN COUNTRY

Production: Norman Jewison and Richard Roth; released by Warner Bros.
Direction: Norman Jewison
Screenplay: Frank Pierson and Cynthia Cidre; based on the novel by Bobbie Anne
 Mason
Cinematography: Russell Boyd
Editing: Antony Gibbs and Lou Lombardo
Production design: Jackson DeGovia
Art direction: John R. Jensen
Set decoration: Thomas L. Roysden
Special effects: Tom Ward
Makeup: David Forrest
Costume design: Aggie Guerard Rodgers
Music: James Horner
MPAA rating: R
Running time: 120 minutes

Principal characters:
Samantha Hughes	Emily Lloyd
Emmett Smith	Bruce Willis
Irene	Joan Allen
Lonnie	Kevin Anderson
Tom	John Terry
Mamaw	Peggy Rea
Anita	Judith Ivey
Grampaw	Richard Hamilton
Pete	Stephen Tobolowsky
Dwayne	Dan Jenkins

Norman Jewison, one of Hollywood's most honored and prolific directors, usually divides his creative time directing intense issue dramas or romantic slice-of-life
comedies. Some of his most acclaimed films are undaunting depictions of racial
and religious prejudice, such as *In the Heat of the Night* (1967), *A Soldier's Story*
(1984), and *Agnes of God* (1985), or angry examinations of institutional corruption
such as *And Justice for All* (1979). He has also dabbled in bittersweet smaller works
from the pure fluff of the 1964 Doris Day vehicle, *The Thrill of It All*, to the
multilayered *Moonstruck* (1987), starring Cher. In 1989, Jewison seems to have
attempted to make a film that pulls together these two conflicting types of stories,
but his success is questionable. *In Country*, a look at both the troubled lives of
Vietnam War survivors and the coming-of-age of a jolly Kentucky teenager, is a
near miss worth noting.
Images of newly trained troops boarding transport planes bound for the war open

In Country. The troops are comprised of soldiers at the crossroads of their military lives; their days of instruction are over, and they are ready to face the challenges of combat. The film quickly moves to the high school graduation of Samantha (Sam) Hughes (Emily Lloyd) many years later. The commencement exercises represent a crossroads in the life of this effervescent teenager as well; she must now decide whether to continue her education in a university atmosphere or to stay in her hometown of Hopewell, Kentucky, and continue her role as sweetheart of Lonnie (Kevin Anderson), the local sports star. It is a summer of decision and growth for Sam, a girl who has yet to discover who she is and what her place is in the world. Sam's father died in Vietnam before she was born, and Sam's mother, Irene (Joan Allen), has remarried and moved away. Sam has remained in Hopewell to finish high school and care for her uncle Emmett (Bruce Willis), a Vietnam War veteran who has failed to adjust to civilian life. Emmett's lethargic attitude and sudden fits of unexplainable anger lead Sam to suspect that he suffers from the aftereffects of Agent Orange. Her attempts to get him help all come up fruitless: To Sam, this is merely another example of how the veterans have been forgotten by the American people.

Somewhere inside the dilapidated home in which she and her uncle live, Sam finds a cache of letters written by her father, Dwayne (Dan Jenkins), during his tour of duty in Vietnam. The discovery sparks her search to find out all she can about the father she has never seen and about how he died in a place she does not know. Emmett unsuccessfully tries to discourage her many requests for information, and her mother ignores her questions as well. In an attempt to get closer to the other veterans in town, Sam helps to organize a dance and solicits the townspeople to come and show their support for the former servicemen. The dance is ignored by most in the town, and the few veterans who do attend notice how their neighbors have forgotten what they have done for their country. Sam, however, uses the dance to seduce the town mechanic, Tom (John Terry), a physically scarred veteran who is later unable to perform sexually.

After the unsuccessful dance, Sam asks her mother to tell her all she can about Dwayne, but Irene suggests that Sam forget the past and move on to a future. Still unsatisfied, Sam goes to the farm of her paternal grandparents, Mamaw (Peggy Rea) and Grampaw (Richard Hamilton), and peppers them with questions. Mamaw can only tell her granddaughter about her father's childhood but gives her Dwayne's diary that was returned with his body. Sam, in an effort to get closer to her father's spirit, spends the night in the Kentucky wilderness and reads the diary. Sparked by the revelation that her father may have murdered the enemy without reservation, Sam suffers a loss of faith and imagines the horrible circumstances of his death. After a night of calling into question everything she knows about her father and herself, Sam is discovered by a worried Emmett, who, in a tearful confession, reveals his own still-festering emotional war wounds.

What follows is a powerful coda in which Sam and Emmett, together with Mamaw, travel to Washington, D.C., to visit the Vietnam Veterans Memorial. There,

Sam and Emmett begin to come to terms with their lingering memories of the Vietnam War. These final minutes comprise the most eloquent and moving sequence in the film; the images of the war survivors gathering together before the imposing, black granite monument to remember the dead are strikingly beautiful. Their power is intensified by the crisp cinematography of Russell Boyd's camera and the haunting music of James Horner's original score. The narrative effectiveness of the grandiose finale, however, is another matter entirely. Although it may move audiences to tears, the Washington trek does not provide a satisfactory resolution to the conflicts developed throughout the film. A visit to the memorial seems too simple a cure for Emmett's twenty years of suffering and Sam's complete loss of faith. *In Country* quickly ends, though, as the threesome walk arm-in-arm away from the monument and into a brighter future.

Having once been a Kentucky teenager herself, novelist Bobbie Ann Mason has a wondrous ear for dialogue and a keen understanding of small-town life. Veteran screenwriter Frank Pierson and teammate Cynthia Cidre retain much of the gritty dialogue in their screenplay, but the writers fail to translate Mason's knack of portraying the ordered randomness of country life. Randomness to the screenwriters means the inclusion of several subplots that fail to amount to anything significant. By the time Sam makes it to Washington at the end of the film, she has broken up with her boyfriend, Lonnie, bought her first used car, counseled her pregnant schoolmate, run many miles on the Hopewell roads, and decided to attend college. Mason was able to tie all these incidents together and suggest the emergence of Sam Hughes's adult psyche, but the film treats them as typical, slice-of-life episodes in country living. At the end of the novel, Sam is deeply moved when she sees her own name on the Vietnam Veterans Memorial and comes to the understanding that she, like all Americans, can also be considered a veteran of the war experience. Mason ends her novel with the suggestion that Sam has suffered the same loss of innocence and faith that many of the young soldiers, including Emmett, suffered during their time in Vietnam. Even the title of the work suggests this theme; the term "in country" was used to describe a soldier's tour of duty and also describes the condition of Sam's life. By eliminating the finale of Mason's book, the script and consequently the film fails to drive home a message that would have made for a more effective narrative.

Transcending the limp script are the exceptional performances of the film's principal actors. Emily Lloyd's Sam is a vibrant young woman barely able to hold back her tremendous spirit. It is hard to believe that *In Country* is Englishwoman Lloyd's third role; she turned heads in David Leland's *Wish You Were Here* (1987) and held up what little there was in Susan Seidelman's *Cookie* (1989). Although her accent slops at times and her energy level occasionally overflows, Lloyd, at age seventeen, gives the performance of a much older, more accomplished actress. Former television actor Bruce Willis, after *Blind Date* (1987), *Sunset* (1988), and *Die Hard* (1988), expands his dramatic range with his sympathetic portrayal of Emmett Smith. He dirties his image with oily hair, a Fu Manchu beard, and an ever-present cigarette, but his performance, especially during a third-act monologue, is more than merely costume and props. Willis still has a considerable way to go as a dramatic actor, but his capable work in the supporting role was good enough to be nominated for a Golden Globe Award by the Hollywood Foreign Press Association. Joan Allen, a Tony award-winning stage actress, provides the film's finest performance as Sam's mother, Irene. Appearing in only a handful of scenes, Allen brings to the screen several poignantly realized moments. When Irene urges Sam to forget the past, Allen's misty-eyed delivery expertly signals her own bitter memories. The rest of the cast is filled with accomplished actors who work together as a convincing ensemble: especially Peggy Rea as Sam's grandmother, John Terry as the sexually dysfunctional veteran, and Judith Ivey as Emmett's lively former girlfriend.

In a decade in which the Vietnam film became a crowded genre, *In Country* is unique in its emphasis on the survivors of the conflict: the daughters who lost fathers, the women who lost husbands, and the veterans who are still emotionally wounded. *Born on the Fourth of July* (1989; reviewed in this volume) also depicts the struggle of a Vietnam veteran, but the film's centerpiece is a lengthy battle sequence detailing the tragic circumstances of veteran Ron Kovic's debilitating injury. Jewison's film includes only a short sequence of jungle fighting, and that exists only as the imaginings of Sam Hughes as she reads her father's war diary. Unlike the other Vietnam films of the 1980's, such as *Platoon* (1986), *Full Metal Jacket* (1987), and *Casualties of War* (1989; reviewed in this volume), *In Country* depicts not what its viewers think the war must have been like but what they know it has left behind.

Greg Changnon

Reviews

Chicago Tribune. September 29, 1989, VII, p. 37.
Commonweal. CXVI, November 3, 1989, p. 591.
Films in Review. XL, December, 1989, p. 622.
Los Angeles Times. September 15, 1989, VI, p. 1.
Maclean's. CII, September 18, 1989, p. 75.
The Nation. CCXLIX, October 9, 1989, p. 396.
The New Republic. CCI, October 16, 1989, p. 30.
New York Magazine. September 25, 1989, p. 129.
The New York Times. September 15, 1989, p. C6.
Newsweek. CXIV, October 2, 1989, p. 70.
People Weekly. XXXII, September 25, 1989, p. 16.
Rolling Stone. October 19, 1989, p. 27.
Time. CXXXIV, October 2, 1989, p. 90.
Variety. CCCXXXVI, September 13, 1989, p. 31.

INDIANA JONES AND THE LAST CRUSADE

Production: George Lucas and Frank Marshall (executive producers) and Robert
   Watts for Lucasfilm; released by Paramount Pictures
Direction: Steven Spielberg
Screenplay: Jeffrey Boam; based on a story by George Lucas and Menno Meyjes
   and on characters created by Lucas and George Kaufman
Cinematography: Douglas Slocombe
Editing: Michael Kahn
Production design: Elliot Scott
Art direction: Stephen Scott, Richard Berger, Benjamin Fernandez, and Guido
   Salsilli
Set decoration: Peter Howitt, Ed McDonald, and Julian Mateos
Special effects: George Gibbs and Michael J. McAlister
Makeup: Peter Robb-King
Costume design: Anthony Powell and Joanna Johnston
Sound: Ben Burtt, Gary Summers, Shawn Murphy, and Tony Dawe
Sound effects editing: Ben Burtt (AA) and Richard Hymns (AA)
Music: John Williams
MPAA rating: PG-13
Running time: 127 minutes

> *Principal characters:*
> Indiana Jones . . . . Harrison Ford
> Professor Henry Jones . . . . Sean Connery
> Marcus Brody . . . . Denholm Elliott
> Dr. Elsa Schneider . . . . Alison Doody
> Sallah . . . . John Rhys-Davies
> Walter Donovan . . . . Julian Glover
> Young Indy . . . . River Phoenix
> Vogel . . . . Michael Byrne
> Kazim . . . . Kevork Malikyan
> Fedora . . . . Richard Young

In a summer filled with sequels, perhaps none fulfilled original expectations as
well as the third installment of the Indiana Jones saga. Executive producer George
Lucas and director Steven Spielberg reassembled many of the filmmakers who
worked on the first two films to work on the third, including composer John
Williams, cinematographer Douglas Slocombe, editor Michael Kahn, production
designer Elliot Scott, costume designer Anthony Powell, stunt co-ordinator Vic
Armstrong, and special effects supervisor George Gibbs at Lucas' Industrial Light
and Magic.
   After two films, the mythic nature of Indiana Jones is further cultivated when he

finally receives a background treatment in the third. The film begins with young Indy (River Phoenix), who lives near Monument Valley, Utah. On a Boy Scout outing in 1912, he spies looters stealing a valuable archaeological object, the Cross of Coronado. Young Indy steals the cross and is chased through the desert, across the tops of the cars in a circus train, and into his own home. Once there, he proudly presents the cross to his father (Sean Connery), who promptly returns it to the alleged legal owners, the looters. From this introduction, filmgoers finally learn the origins of many of Indiana Jones's trademarks: his whip, his loathing of snakes, his chin scar, and his brown fedora. Before the film ends, audiences will also know the derivation of his name.

Twenty-five years later, the adult Indy (Harrison Ford) is teaching archaeology and, as in the two previous films, is entangled in vigorous extracurricular adventures in the field. A wealthy businessman, Walter Donovan (Julian Glover), who has contributed to the school's museum and has an obsession for ancient artifacts, hires Indiana to find the Holy Grail and the man Donovan had originally hired to find it, Professor Henry Jones. Henry, a professor of medieval literature with a lifelong interest in the Arthurian legend and the Holy Grail, also happens to be Indiana's estranged father.

Indiana follows the trail to Venice, Italy, where he meets Austrian art historian Dr. Elsa Schneider (Alison Doody). After finding clues and escaping from rats, a fire, and thugs in a speeding boat, Indiana makes his way to a castle near the Austrian-German border. There he finds his father and his father's kidnappers, the Nazis. The Nazis want the Holy Grail because it is supposed to give eternal life to anyone who drinks from it.

The Nazis and the Joneses engage in a series of exciting chase sequences to see who will find the Holy Grail first. Old friends Sallah (John Rhys-Davies) and Marcus Brody (Denholm Elliott) are enlisted to help, and other friends turn out to be enemies. After finding the Holy Grail, the Joneses outmaneuver booby traps and defeat the Nazis. In the process, Indiana and his father not only have found and protected the Holy Grail but also have found each other.

After the enormous success of *Raiders of the Lost Ark* (1981), audiences eagerly awaited Indiana's second adventure. When *Indiana Jones and the Temple of Doom* came out three years later, it set box-office records. Unfortunately, the film was a disappointment. It had a decidedly darker tone and a giddy heroine; moreover, the film's violence provoked censure from critics and parents and led ultimately to the establishment of a new PG-13 film rating.

In this latest installment, Indiana Jones returns to the excitement, entertainment, and unadulterated fun of the first film. Scriptwriter Jeffrey Boam—whose credits include cowriting *Innerspace* (1987) and *The Lost Boys* (1987)—provided a screenplay as humor-packed as *Raiders of the Lost Ark*, with a renewed emphasis on the characters and their complexity.

The appearance of Indiana's father provided a new source of humor and depth. As originally written, the character was a crotchety old man similar to Henry

Fonda's character in *On Golden Pond* (1981). When Sean Connery was cast for the part, however, the character changed. Though Henry Jones is still cantankerous, under Connery's control he becomes slightly more eccentric and much more intimidating. Indiana admires and has obviously been influenced by his father, yet he has never been able to please him. "We never talked," Indiana says to his father. "You left just when you were becoming interesting," his father replies.

Just as many do in the presence of a parent, the competent, heroic Indiana with whom audiences are familiar suddenly reverts to hilariously childish mannerisms when his father is around. Only his father can call the famous Indiana Jones the rather deflating "Junior." Although Indiana is constantly trying to prove himself to his father and rescues him a number of times, he still cannot gain his father's respect and love.

Connery and Ford are an inspired duo. Their teasing, competitive, almost Oedipal father-son rivalry enhances the high jinks and makes the dialogue sparkle with tension and wit. The scholarly Professor Jones, Sr., seems totally unimpressed with his son's energetic, inventive, and death-defying methods for dealing with his archaeological enemies. This antagonism provides suspense as well as humor. As Indiana flees the Nazis on a motorcycle with his disgruntled father in the sidecar, the two stop at a crossroads to argue whether they should go right and save Marcus or go left to pursue the Holy Grail.

Like its two predecessors, *Indiana Jones and the Last Crusade* is packed with breathtaking, careening chase sequences and stunts. Every form of transportation that was available in 1938 becomes a vehicle of adventure for Indiana and/or his father. Trains, planes, boats, motorcycles, horses, and camels are only the beginning. The filmmakers applied the same standards of authenticity to creating exact replicas of an International Mark Seven tank as they had to obtaining genuine Latin inscriptions on the secret-laden tablets. Even a zeppelin found its way into the film. The special effects department had to produce a thousand imitation rats, some mechanically articulated, for a scene in a Venetian catacomb, as well as re-create a complete Middle Eastern town in Spain. The filming of *Indiana Jones and the Last Crusade* took place not only in Spain but also in England, Italy, Utah, Colorado, New Mexico, and the stunning three-thousand-year-old city of Petra in Jordan.

Indiana Jones and the Last Crusade is estimated to have cost close to $40 million. It opened over the Memorial Day weekend and accounted for more than 50 percent ($37 million) of the total box-office gross for the four-day weekend. It grossed a record-breaking $46.9 million on 2,327 screens in the United States and Canada in its first six days. The previous record, $42.2 million, was held by *Indiana Jones and the Temple of Doom*. *Indiana Jones and the Last Crusade* became the first film to sell $10 million in tickets in a single day. These records would fall several weeks later, however, when *Ghostbusters II* (1989; reviewed in this volume) was released, only to be felled by the release of the highly advertised *Batman* (1989; reviewed in this volume).

Audiences may have an emotionally difficult time allowing the mythic Indiana

Jones to ride off into the sunset. Despite its formulaic plot, *Indiana Jones and the Last Crusade* is a highly entertaining film. As in the best of Spielberg's works, the pace never lets up and humor gleefully spikes the experience.

Beverley Bare Buehrer

Reviews

America. CLX, June 17, 1989, p. 591.
American Film: Magazine of the Film and Television Arts. XIV, May, 1989, p. 28.
Chicago Tribune. May 24, 1989, V, p. 1.
Commonweal. CXVI, July 14, 1989, p. 403.
Los Angeles Times. May 24, 1989, VI, p. 1.
The Nation. CCXLVIII, June 19, 1989, p. 862.
The New Republic. CCI, June 19, 1989, p. 28.
New York Magazine. June 5, 1989, p. 58.
The New York Times. May 24, 1989, p. C15.
The New Yorker. LXV, June 12, 1989, p. 103.
Newsweek. CXIII, May 29, 1989, p. 69.
People Weekly. XXXI, June 5, 1989, p. 13.
Rolling Stone. June 15, 1989, p. 31.
Time. CXXXIII, May 29, 1989, p. 82.
Variety. CCCXXXV, May 24, 1989, p. 25.
The Wall Street Journal. December 1, 1988, I, p. 12.

JACKNIFE

Production: Robert Schaffel and Carol Baum for Sandollar/Schaffell; released by
   Cineplex Odeon Films
Direction: David Jones
Screenplay: Stephen Metcalfe; based on his play *Strange Snow*
Cinematography: Brian West
Editing: John Bloom
Production design: Edward Pisoni
Art direction: William Barclay and Serge Jacques
Set decoration: Robert J. Franco and Gilles Aird
Special effects: Richard Johnson, John Elliot, and Dan Kirshoff
Makeup: Joan Isaacson
Costume design: David Charles
Sound: Don Sharpe
Music direction: Patricia Peck
Music: Bruce Broughton
MPAA rating: R
Running time: 102 minutes

Principal characters:
   Megs .... Robert De Niro
   Martha .... Kathy Baker
   Dave .... Ed Harris
   Shirley .... Sloane Shelton
   Bobby Buckman .... Tom Isbell
   Tiny .... Jordan Lund
   Jake .... Charles Dutton

The scene has lost none of its impact: Michael (Robert De Niro) sits across from
his friend Nick (Christopher Walken) in a "game" of Russian roulette, as Vietnamese place bets on which man will blow his own brains out. In an attempt to
coax the amnesiac Walken back from the grave, Michael offers words of friendship
and love. For a moment, Nick seems to hear his plea, but then he lifts the gun to his
head and pulls the trigger. In the years since Michael Cimino's *The Deer Hunter*
(1978), there has been a seemingly endless string of films about Vietnam throughout
the 1980's. Whatever their differences, they have shared one aspect: They all end on
a note of despair. Its uplifting coda notwithstanding, even Oliver Stone's *Platoon*
(1986) conveys an overwhelming sense of profligate waste. Who among its viewers
can forget the overhead shot of the corpse-strewn battlefield or that the young hero,
in murdering his sergeant, had succumbed to the same ruthless impulses he had so
loathed?

In this respect, David Jones's *Jacknife* represents a breakthrough. It is one of the first Vietnam films to suggest that the Vietnam veteran can build on the emotional rubble of the past. Unlike Cimino, Jones does not film Stephen Metcalfe's drama (based on his play *Strange Snow*, 1982) on a vast canvas of the time before, during, and after the war, nor does he dabble in the kinds of ethereal metaphors that reduced the war to little more than a *tabula rasa* backdrop in Francis Ford Coppola's *Apocalypse Now* (1979) and Stanley Kubrick's *Full Metal Jacket* (1987). The film relies wholly on its characterizations, and the performances by lead actors Robert De Niro, Ed Harris, and Kathy Baker give *Jacknife* a poignancy that few Vietnam dramas possess.

Joseph "Megs" Megessey (De Niro), a war veteran with a heavy beard and long hair, appears one morning at the house of a former army friend. He tells Dave Flanagan (Harris), an alcoholic who wakes up to the rattle of beer cans in his bed, that the two of them have a long-standing fishing date. Dave is not thrilled by the idea but reluctantly goes along. Accompanying them is Dave's live-in sister Martha (Baker), an unmarried high school biology teacher. The tension between the two supposed friends escalates when Megs and Martha fall in love and Dave fears he will be left alone.

Although *Jacknife*'s situations parallel those in *Coming Home* (1978), Vietnam is not the omnipresent issue it was in that earlier Hal Ashby film. Jones makes clear that many of Megs's and Dave's social difficulties stem from their war experiences, but he does not press the point. Once it gets beyond the Vietnam trappings, *Jacknife* is not so different from domestic difficulties dramas such as *Ordinary People* (1980) and *Terms of Endearment* (1983). Like those films, not much happens in the way of plot but much occurs in terms of character evolution.

Jones does not steer completely clear of cliché. (Bruce Broughton's saccharine score does not help; it has a way of underlining the obvious.) He also digs into the grab bag of Vietnam banalities: wartime flashbacks, the alcoholic veteran, group therapy sessions, soul-searching confrontation scenes. In one over-directed sequence, Megs recklessly barrels down the highway in a tractor-trailer and berates Dave for feeling sorry for himself. The point is that Megs may or may not be another in a long line of Vietnam psychopaths.

Yet, just when the film seems about to sink under the weight of a cliché, it is buoyed by the cast. In their scenes together, De Niro and Baker are like two chords in a well-orchestrated symphony of psychic recovery: Their exchanges have the hesitant stop-flow rhythm of two people acclimating themselves to each other, and they never hit a false note. There is an especially evocative moment when Megs explains that it was Martha's smile that first attracted him to her. The words are commonplace, but Megs utters them with such affecting conviction that they seem an original sentiment. In a scene of equally subtle impact, Megs asks Martha if she and Dave ever eat together. "Sometimes I eat with Dave," she answers. "Dave always eats alone."

Jones demonstrated a flair for directing conversation in *Betrayal* (1983). As in that film, he knows how to manipulate his camera to get the maximum emotional mileage from the dialogue: when to use a one-shot to communicate a character's isolation; when to resort to a two- or three-shot to convey the characters' growing fraternity. He uses silence just as eloquently. At one point, in a rage after Martha spurns his advances, Megs puts his fist through a window. As Martha comforts him, Jones cuts to a close-up of their hands; Megs's bandaged fingers lose themselves in Martha's, and he surrenders to her gesture of support.

In the role of Megs, De Niro lends the film a resonance it would not have possessed with another actor. Watching him, it is impossible not to recall the man he played in *The Deer Hunter*. In that film, his Michael was an almost mythical superman, complete with dashing D'Artagnan mustache and beard. Yet like Megs, he was from the working class, wore a cap, and had an appetite for the outdoors. Megs might just as well be Michael fifteen years after Vietnam but stripped of the latter's taciturn invulnerability and with a pressing need for companionship—the results of his war experiences. Then again, Harris' Dave could just as well be Walken's Nick. Disillusioned and bitter, he is what Nick might have become had Michael saved him from an early death; he is Nick with a second chance.

As with other recent Vietnam films such as *Platoon*, *Gardens of Stone* (1987), *Full Metal Jacket* (1987), and *Hamburger Hill* (1987), *Jacknife* recalls the progressive attitudes of the first wave of Vietnam films, among them *The Boys in Company C* (1978), *Coming Home*, *The Deer Hunter*, and *Apocalypse Now*. The machismo and comic-book heroics of *Rambo: First Blood Part II* (1985), whose hero returns years later to the jungle and kills the enemy who was so elusive in the real Vietnam, have been replaced in these films by the notion that the war was morally suspect from the start and thus, at least ideologically, never winnable. The often-articulated claim from the Right that the United States would have won the war if U.S. soldiers had only not withdrawn is thus smartly undercut.

With the consensus being that *Platoon* provided the last word on battlefield horrors, Hollywood in the late 1980's began turning out a spate of films that explored the impact of the war at home. Francis Ford Coppola's *Gardens of Stone* told the story of two army veterans assigned to Arlington National Cemetery who despise the war because they believe it had no purpose. Norman Jewison's *In Country* (1989; reviewed in this volume) and Franklin J. Schaffner's *Welcome Home* (1989) both examine the difficulties faced by veterans in adjusting to domestic life. By far the most ambitious film of this sort was Oliver Stone's *Born on the Fourth of July* (1989; reviewd in this volume) which, like *The Deer Hunter*, has a tripartite structure of before, during, and after the war. What distinguishes Stone's film from its predecessors is its implicit conviction that the devastated veteran, in this case true-life paraplegic Ron Kovic, could find emotional and spiritual release by protesting the war in arenas both public and private.

As with another stage-to-screen adaptation of 1989, *Driving Miss Daisy* (reviewed in this volume), which barely touches on the civil rights movement in telling the story of an elderly Jewish woman and her black chauffeur, *Jacknife*'s sociopolitical impact is diluted by its hermetic narrative. Megs and Dave ultimately resolve their differences and, by the final fadeout, are well on their way to putting the ghosts of Vietnam behind them; their peace of mind, however, springs from a solipsistic acceptance of the terrible things the war did to them, not from large-scale activism, as was the case with Kovic. *Jacknife*'s political subtext is thus virtually nil, yet there is no denying its sincere and powerful appeal to the emotions.

Michael Banka

Reviews
Chicago Tribune. March 24, 1989, VII, p. 38.
The Christian Science Monitor. April 14, 1989, p. 11.
Cosmopolitan. CCVI, May 1989, p. 48.
Los Angeles Times. March 10, 1989, VI, p. 6.
Maclean's. CII, April 10, 1989, p. 41.
The New Republic. CC, March 6, 1989, p. 24.
The New York Times. March 10, 1989, p. C10.
People Weekly. XXXI, April 3, 1989, p. 17.
Variety. CCCXXXIV, March 1, 1989, p. 18.
Video. XIII, October, 1989, p. 80.
The Wall Street Journal. March 2, 1989, p. A14.
The Washington Post. March 24, 1989, p. C1.

JESUS OF MONTREAL
(JÉSUS DE MONTREAL)

Origin: Canada and France
Released: 1989
Released in U.S.: 1989
Production: Roger Frappier and Pierre Gendron for Max Films International and
   Gerard Mital Productions; released by Orion Classics
Direction: Denys Arcand
Screenplay: Denys Arcand
Cinematography: Guy Dufaux
Editing: Isabelle Dedieu
Art direction: François Séguin
Costume design: Louise Jobin
Sound: Patrick Rousseau and Marcel Pothier
Music: Yves Laferrière, François Dompierre, and Jean-Marie Benoit
MPAA rating: no listing
Running time: 118 minutes

Principal characters:
Daniel Coulombe	Lothaire Bluteau
Mireille	Catherine Wilkening
Constance	Johanne-Marie Tremblay
Martin Durocher	Rémy Girard
René	Robert Lepage
Father Leclerc	Gilles Pelletier
Lawyer	Yves Jacques

Denys Arcand's film *Jesus of Montreal* is an impassioned exploration of the spiritual exhaustion and artificiality of the modern age and of the urgent human need for spiritual fulfillment and sincere artistic expression. In a rich blend of social realism and religious allegory, Arcand has woven a modern-day parable susceptible to interpretation on many levels. Thematically and stylistically, *Jesus of Montreal* succeeds in integrating a serious social critique, poignant human drama, sophisticated humor, and a wealth of rich allusions to the history of Western culture.

In the film, Daniel Coulombe (Lothaire Bluteau) is asked by Father Leclerc (Gilles Pelletier) to "modernize" and perform a Passion play on the life of Christ. The performance of the play had been an annual tradition for forty years but in recent years had ceased to attract an audience. Daniel recruits a group of four struggling actors: Constance (Johanne-Marie Tremblay), Martin (Rémy Girard), René (Robert Lepage), and Mireille (Catherine Wilkening). The outdoor play that the troupe performs proves to be both popular with its audience and a critical *cause célèbre*, but, after its first performance, Father Leclerc warns the actors that his superiors in the Church hierarchy are bound to deem it blasphemous.

Despite her commitment to both the new play and her fellow performers, Mireille has to fulfill a previous obligation to audition for a beer commercial, which is being directed by her former lover. She asks Daniel to accompany her. He does so, and, in an outburst of anger at the manner in which the auditioning actors are being treated, he destroys camera equipment and physically assaults a woman who is overseeing the auditions. As a result, in the midst of a performance of the Passion play, while he is playing Christ on the cross, Daniel is arrested by two policemen. At his preliminary hearing, Daniel is interviewed by the court psychologist, who finds him "better adjusted than most of the judges in this court." Shortly after, Leclerc tells Constance, Mireille, René, and Martin that the Church bureaucracy demands substantial alteration to their play and proposes as a "compromise" that the actors go back to the original script for the play.

As the troupe doubtfully contemplate their own fate, Mireille, with tears welling up in her eyes, passionately insists that they cannot quit and intimates that she has been redeemed by her association with her committed colleagues. Despite a security guard's insistence that the play has been cancelled, the troupe undertakes a final performance. Security guards interrupt the proceedings, but members of the audience are as angered by the disruption as the cast themselves. During an ensuing scuffle, the cross bearing Daniel is knocked over, seriously injuring the actor and rendering him unconscious. Attended by Constance and Mireille, Daniel is rushed to an overcrowded Catholic hospital, where Constance tries unsuccessfully to find help for him. Daniel, however, regains consciousness and appears to have recovered. Upon exiting the hospital, he raves/prophesies like an abandoned Christ, accosts people waiting for the subway, and then again collapses. At the Jewish hospital where he is taken, medical staff fail to revive him. Constance and Mireille grant a doctor's request for the use of Daniel's body, and, in a form of modern resurrection, Daniel's eyes and heart are used in transplants.

The dominant structuring principle of *Jesus of Montreal* involves an elaborate and extended parallel between the modern narrative and traditional biblical events. Daniel Coulombe (whose name signifies both the ability to prophesy and the spiritual symbolism of a dove), embodies both the calm assurance and the spiritual insight of a prophet, along with the sacrificial and inspirational aspects of a Christ figure. Daniel plays the part of Christ on a literal level, but the linking of Daniel and Christ on the allegorical level is also rich and varied. Like Christ, Daniel gathers a group of disciples about himself. Although steadily gaining in public notoriety, Daniel retains the basic Christ-like qualities of commitment to ideals (he will not "sell out" by doing commercials), material poverty (he apparently owns no property or possessions), human kindness and tolerance (he loves children and refuses to judge Constance when he finds that Leclerc is sleeping with her), and the ability to inspire and convert others (he "saves" Mireille from debasing herself through doing sexually exploitative commercials).

At times, the parallel between Daniel and Christ is quite specific and detailed.

The scene in which Mireille auditions for the beer commercial invokes a direct comparison with the Gospel descriptions of Christ in the Temple. The association between advertising and the worshipping of false gods is underscored by such lyrics in the beer commercial as: "The young crowd's here/ We worship beer," and "Nothing's sacred to you/ But a good glass of brew." Daniel's destructive rage is at least sparked by the realization that even Mireille's human dignity is for sale in the name of advertising, as she is asked by the directors to remove her clothing. Later in the film, there is a reenactment of the temptation of Christ by Satan, as a lawyer and public relations specialist (Yves Jacques) attempts to entice Daniel with the prospect of exploiting his acting talent and public fame for material gain, intimating to Daniel that all the city of Montreal (visually spread before them as they look out the window of a skyscraper) could be his for the taking.

Jesus of Montreal simultaneously broadens and deepens the propensity for social critique so powerfully displayed in Arcand's *The Decline of the American Empire* (1986). Using Montreal as his example, Arcand offers a generalized depiction of the ills of modern society. For example, Arcand alludes to the problem of urban poverty when Daniel recruits Constance from the soup kitchen where she works and when Father Leclerc describes the desperately impoverished parishioners who seek solace in the Church. Spiritual poverty is equally well depicted through the figures of Father Leclerc and of the lawyer, through the cliché-ridden pretentiousness of several theater critics in the film, and through the manner in which the film foregrounds the omnipresence of advertising (with its concomitant exploitation of human sexuality) in modern society.

Again, like *The Decline of the American Empire*, *Jesus of Montreal* is a serious but by no means solemn film, which makes good use of satiric comedy. When Daniel and Constance first seek Martin, he is doing voice dubbing for a pornographic film. The fraudulence and absurdity of this process is underscored by the fact that Martin is trying to do the voices for two different males in the film and is rushing frantically between two different microphones (and two different female actors). Some of the humor in the film arises from the secularization of religious terms and concepts; for example, when one of the policemen arresting Daniel (who is, at the time, hanging from the cross) realizes that he has forgotten one of the forms that he needs, he instinctively exclaims, "Christ! I forgot it again!" One of the film's most hilarious moments occurs when the actors mock Father Leclerc's suggestion that they return to the original script by giving an impromptu send-up of the play, using several different acting styles, including Comédie Française, New York Method acting, street slang, and Kabuki.

Besides its intrinsic humor, this foregrounding of theatricality relates to one of the film's central thematic concerns. As well as using religious allegory to explore serious social issues, the film explores the relationship between human drama and theater. The film opens in the midst of the performance of a play, and only retrospectively, several minutes into the film, is the viewer aware that the "real" events of the film have yet to begin. Similarly, the troupe's interactive theatrical approach to the Passion play is itself designed to break down barriers between audience and players and to present a historically accurate depiction of Christ, which challenges the superficially theatrical representations of traditional Passion plays. Theatrical language and terms are used frequently in the film to describe real-life relationships.

The end of the film sees the blurring of distinctions between life and theater, when Daniel's portrayal of Christ seems to have provoked his transformation into a Christ-like figure as he preaches in the subway. Throughout the film, art has been shown to be capable of serving either higher spiritual values or crass material purposes—it rescues Mireille, but, in prostituted form, it becomes the means through which human beings are degraded and exploited. The final scene of the film, which shows two young singers in the subway (singing underneath a billboard advertising men's cologne) makes this point clear. The singers had earlier been seen auditioning for the beer commercial, and the actor adorning the cologne advertisement had been the gifted performer in the play that opens the film.

Jesus of Montreal is both allegorical and moral, without being pretentiously didactic. Although rooted in an unmistakably Quebecois sensibility, it offers a powerful exploration of universal human concerns. Though the ending of the film raises doubts about the degree of salvation attained by specific characters, the ongoing human need to seek salvation and the ability of art to express those urges is demonstrated by the artistic integrity and unity of the film as a whole.

Paul Salmon

Reviews

Chatelaine. LXII, November, 1989, p. 14.
The Christian Century. CVI, September 27, 1989, p. 836.
Cinema Canada. June, 1989, p. 16.
Los Angeles Times. May 16, 1989, VI, p. 1.
Maclean's. CII, September 18, 1989, p.74.
The New York Times. May 18, 1989, p. C23.
Saturday Night. CIV, November, 1989, p. 103.
Sight and Sound. Autumn, 1989, p. 234.
Variety. CCCXXXV, May 17, 1989, p. 32.
The Village Voice. XXXIV, December 12, 1989, p. 109.

K-9

Production: Lawrence Gordon and Charles Gordon for Gordon Company; released by Universal
Direction: Rod Daniel
Screenplay: Steven Siegel and Scott Myers
Cinematography: Dean Semler
Editing: Lois Freeman-Fox
Production design: George Costello
Art direction: Jay Burkhardt
Set decoration: Marla Caso
Makeup: Charles Balazs
Costume design: Eileen Kennedy
Sound: Richard L. Anderson
Music: Miles Goodman
MPAA rating: PG-13
Running time: 102 minutes

Principal characters:

Dooley	James Belushi
Tracy	Mel Harris
Lyman	Kevin Tighe
Brannigan	Ed O'Neill
Jerry Lee	Himself
Halstead	Daniel Davis
Freddie	John Snyder
Benny the Mule	Pruitt Taylor Vince

Like *Turner and Hooch* (1989), *K-9* is an unusual "buddy" film about a man, in both cases a policeman, and his proverbial best friend. Neither *K-9* nor *Turner and Hooch* is a "dog film," either aesthetically or generically, though the canines are the real stars of both films, despite the considerable comic talents of James Belushi and Tom Hanks. Like Hooch, Jerry Lee is no Benji, Lassie, or even Spuds McKenzie; Jerry Lee is to Benji what Clint Eastwood is to Roy Rogers. Through the expert handling of trainer Karl Lewis Miller, Jerry Lee's "human" persona is thoroughly urban, street-smart, and irreverent, and the exchanges between Jerry Lee and partner Dooley (James Belushi) are reminiscent of those between Reggie Hammond (Eddie Murphy) and Jack Cates (Nick Nolte) in *48 HRS.* (1982).

As the opening credits roll, director Rod Daniel establishes Dooley as an unpredictable maverick, who is the target of several predictably unsuccessful assassination attempts by the thugs of the wealthy and socially accepted drug lord, Lyman (Kevin Tighe). When his police car is riddled by bullets fired from a helicopter, Dooley cannot get another vehicle (this is not the first one he has lost) primarily because he cannot get another partner, who would theoretically be more responsible than he. The remainder of the film concerns the developing partnership of Dooley and Jerry Lee, who are both independent loners unaccustomed to following orders. After the helicopter sequence, Dooley catches Freddie (John Snyder), a small-time hoodlum who has set Dooley up. Ignoring the restrictions on police brutality, Dooley makes Freddie reveal that Lyman is the cocaine dealer behind the assassination attempt. As a favor to a superior, Brannigan (Ed O'Neill), Dooley apprehends—in his unconventional way—another criminal. In return Dooley receives Jerry Lee, a drug-sniffing dog, as his partner.

The relationship gets off to a rocky start: Jerry Lee heeds only Dooley's kill command, and their first search of Lyman's warehouse produces a single marijuana cigarette. Jerry Lee proves his mettle, however, when Dooley subsequently enters a tough bar and is threatened by Benny the Mule (Pruitt Taylor Vince). Jerry Lee routs the thugs and then holds Benny by the front of his pants while Dooley gets the necessary information.

When Dooley takes Jerry Lee home to meet his girlfriend, Tracy (Mel Harris), further complications ensue as the presumably jealous Jerry Lee first prevents the lovers from kissing and then, accompanied by the ominous musical theme from *Jaws* (1975), sneaks into bed with them. Not appeased by the frozen steak Dooley offers him, Jerry Lee extracts his revenge when Dooley steps in dog manure. Despite the partners' retaliatory gestures, they are coming together as a team. When Dooley, in a four-footed, head-to-head "talk" with Jerry Lee, asserts that they are "both members of the animal kingdom," he not only is pleading for cooperation but also is implicitly acknowledging that he is slightly animal-like while Jerry Lee is slightly human.

Because he will not or cannot "listen" to Jerry Lee, Dooley barely averts another assassination attempt. Lyman then kidnaps Tracy in order to prevent Dooley from foiling the drug sale to Halstead (Daniel Davis). A manic Dooley invades Lyman's dinner party, accuses Lyman of kidnaping and drug dealing, and proceeds to destroy the furniture and food; he and Jerry Lee are taken away by the Long Beach police, apparently leaving Lyman free to complete the drug sale. Dooley's madness, however, was merely a ploy to deceive Lyman: When Jerry Lee "deliberately" breaks wind in the police car, Dooley and Jerry Lee escape when Jerry Lee is let out of the car. Dooley subsequently takes Halstead's place, with the aid of Jerry Lee, and drives the tractor trailer that carries the drug-laden car to meet Lyman.

When he meets Lyman, Dooley, whose priorities have been subtly shifting, offers to trade the drugs for Tracy and to let Lyman go. Earlier, his pursuit of Lyman had seemed an obsession, but Dooley is becoming more human. Dooley's trump card is a computer game, which he claims is an explosive device, but the ruse is revealed when he ironically wins the game and the machine emits even more ironic applause. In the ensuing melee, Dooley saves Tracy; meanwhile, Jerry Lee pursues the escaping Lyman. Just before the dog knocks him over, Lyman wounds Jerry Lee. Distraught over Jerry Lee's wound, Dooley cannot express his elation about Lyman's long-awaited capture.

Having comforted Jerry Lee with the words, "It's all right, buddy," Dooley takes his wounded partner to a hospital to be treated by a physician rather than a veterinarian. He tells the doctor, "He's not just a dog. He's my partner," and forces the doctor to treat Jerry Lee. When he has time to reflect, however, Dooley speaks the language of logic and convention: "He took the hit. That's what they're for. He's just a dog." Dooley's actions belie his words when he rushes to see Jerry Lee, who is in the recovery room. Convinced of Jerry Lee's impending death, Dooley reveals his true feelings to what he believes to be a dying dog who can neither hear nor comprehend his words: "Lyman wasn't worth it. You could have been killed." At this point Jerry Lee opens his eyes and then closes them, suggesting he intends to deceive Dooley and prolong his partner's apologetic, affectionate speech, which ends with a promised trip to Las Vegas.

When Jerry Lee does obviously recover, Dooley attempts to recant: "Forget it. I thought I was talking to a dead dog." The concluding sequence, however, shows two couples—Dooley and Tracy, Jerry Lee and his mate, a white poodle—in a car en route to Las Vegas. In a sense, Dooley and Jerry Lee have both been domesticated, but the final image also implies the equality of the man and the dog. Viewers should perhaps be thankful that director Rod Daniel, recognizing that there are limits to credibility, did not have the talented Jerry Lee behind the wheel.

K-9 marks the worthy feature screenwriting debut of Steven Siegel and Scott Myers—through their work on this film, they became affiliated with Lorimar. Rod Daniel, on the other hand, has an extensive background in television, most notably in crime shows and comedies: He has directed episodes of *Magnum, P.I.* and *Newhart*; in addition, he not only produced *WKRP in Cincinnati* but also directed many episodes of that popular series. From television Daniel moved to feature films, among them *Teen Wolf* (1985) and *Like Father Like Son* (1988).

K-9 and *Turner and Hooch* represent a real departure from the hackneyed buddy films and television series featuring two warring but likable law enforcement personnel. Although the original model concerned two males, television began exploiting the male/female chemistry, implicitly attributing the friction to the woman's increased assertiveness and not to her manipulative, passive behavior. The contemporary male lead has correspondingly softened, and the tough cop with a heart of gold has become a cliché. Dooley behaves outrageously because he cannot trust others; he must consciously repress his real desire for commitment. All he needs is the love of a good woman and the love of a good dog, though Jerry Lee seems more essential than Tracy.

Thomas L. Erskine

Reviews
Boston Globe. April 28, 1989, p. 35.

Chicago Tribune. April 28, 1989, VII, p. 45.
Los Angeles Times. April 28, 1989, VI, p. 17.
The New York Times. April 28, 1989, p. C19.
People Weekly. XXXI, May 22, 1989, p. 13.
USA Today. April 28, 1989, p. D4.
Variety. CCCXXXV, May 3, 1989, p. 12.
The Wall Street Journal. June 20, 1989, p. A16.
The Washington Post. April 28, 1989, p. D7.
Washington Times. May 1, 1989, p. E3.

LEAN ON ME

Production: Norman Twain and John G. Avildsen (executive producer); released by Warner Bros.
Direction: John G. Avildsen
Screenplay: Michael Schiffer
Cinematography: Victor Hammer
Editing: John Carter and John G. Avildsen
Production design: Doug Kraner
Art direction: Tim Galvin
Set decoration: Caryl Heller
Makeup: Toy Van Lierop
Costume design: Jennifer Von Mayrhauser
Sound: Tom McCarthy and Burton M. Weinstein
Music: Bill Conti
Song: Bill Withers, "Lean on Me"
MPAA rating: PG-13
Running time: 108 minutes

Principal characters:

Joe Clark	Morgan Freeman
Ms. Levias	Beverly Todd
Dr. Frank Napier	Robert Guillaume
Mayor Don Bottman	Alan North
Leona Barrett	Lynne Thigpen
Mrs. Elliott	Robin Bartlett
Mr. Darnell	Michael Beach
Mr. Rosenberg	Ethan Phillips
Thomas Sams	Jermaine Hopkins
Kaneesha Carter	Karen Malina White

Lean on Me is the second film in a less than two year period (the first is the 1988 film *Stand and Deliver*) to generate its narrative tension from the academic improvement of high school students. Whether the students' test scores are acceptable becomes as momentous as whether Rocky Balboa (Sylvester Stallone) in *Rocky* (1976) knocks out his opponent. Scenes of adolescent boys and girls concentrating on the words of their knowing and dedicated teacher or on a difficult question on a national achievement test and then triumphantly jotting down the correct answer become as stirring as seeing the victorious Rocky dancing over a fallen Apollo Creed (Carl Weathers). Considering the greater importance of the educational conquest, the shots of the students are more gratifying.

Both *Stand and Deliver* and *Lean on Me* are based on actual events: The earlier film relates the achievements of Jaime Escalante (Edward James Olmos), a mathematics teacher in East Los Angeles, California, whose once-inferior students gain national recognition for excelling in calculus; *Lean on Me* depicts the exploits of Joe Clark (Morgan Freeman), the principal of Eastside High School in Paterson, New Jersey, who is embroiled in controversy over his dictatorial, often sledgehammer tactics aimed at improving the school. Shortly after his appointment, Joe Clark declares a state of emergency and announces to his faculty and staff that his word is law. In his first dramatic act, he expels three hundred underachievers, thereby bringing under control one of the most raucous school assemblies depicted on screen. In subsequent days, he shouts his orders from a bullhorn, chains the school doors in violation of fire regulations to keep out the drug dealers, and fires a music instructor during an altercation over her desire to teach Mozart's music instead of the school song. It is one of the pluses of the film that Clark's behavior and methods are portrayed as sometimes unreasonable and even reprehensible.

Yet Joe Clark cares. His emotional intensity becomes the galvanizing force for change. In the persuasive performance by Morgan Freeman, Joe Clark—regardless of the truth about his real-life counterpart—is a dynamo who must take extreme steps to deal with nearly irremediable conditions. In the sweep of emotion that accompanies his courageous battle and victory, one tends to overlook the injustice of some of his actions.

John G. Avildsen, who also directed *Rocky* and *The Karate Kid* (1984), is a master at manipulating audience response through his depictions of men (or boys) struggling against great odds. Some critics have attacked Avildsen's sacrifice of intellectual values to purely emotional ones. Opponents of the real Joe Clark, and the severest critics of this film, see it as a mindless tribute to a man who employs neofascist behavior to control the unruly students. Most viewers, however, will find *Lean on Me* a satisfying tale of a man who does what is necessary. Sympathetic viewers will focus on the redeeming characteristics that tend to humanize Joe Clark: his kindly concern for an unwed student who becomes pregnant, his willingness to give a troublesome but repentant boy another chance, and his affectionate regard for individual students. Excused or, perhaps, forgotten will be his peremptory and unfair dismissal of two teachers, his failure to give credit to members of his staff for their earnest efforts, and his violation of the rights of the students whom he dismisses without a hearing.

The fact that events in the film differ substantially from what actually happened at Eastside High School has also caused heated debate. Opponents of Joe Clark are quick to point out that, from his tenure as principal up to the time that the film was released, the percentage of students from the school who went on to college was 22 percent, whereas the year before he arrived, it was 35 percent. In addition, it is argued that the improvement in test scores after he arrived was slight and probably more a result of his dismissal of underachievers than of any actual improvement in the remaining students' education. The film's conclusion, however, implies that Joe Clark was indisputably successful. Questions arise as to whether such poetic license is advisable, or even ethical, when a film deals with events that were still making news at the time of the film's release and involving the sensibilities of a large number of people. When *Lean on Me* was released, Joe Clark was sitting in the principal's chair at Eastside High, still at the center of a storm, still winning advocates and riling opponents. In fact, the film was shot on location at the school with the cooperation of Joe Clark himself. Should Avildsen's work be examined as simply a film, or must the film's context be considered, thereby holding the artist accountable for providing an objective view of the situation?

If one could ignore the controversy surrounding the film, including concerns over what is fictional and what is factual, *Lean on Me* is a moving story of a man of mettle who instills in seemingly unsalvageable students a sense of purpose and pride in their high school and themselves. The climactic scene outside the jail, where thousands of students demonstrate their support of the tough principal they have grown to love, is rousing drama; the impassioned pleas of individual students on his behalf let Joe Clark know how much his efforts have mattered. An earlier scene, shortly before the students take a crucial basic skills test that will determine whether the state will take over the school, becomes a rousing celebration by the students, teachers, and principal of their newfound, proud identity. It is difficult to resist sharing their feeling as the swaying assembly lift their voices in song, and Joe Clark beams his love to the reciprocating throng.

Avildsen is assisted by some incisive characterizations. Responsible for Joe Clark's appointment is a colleague from twenty years earlier, now the school superintendent, Dr. Frank Napier (Robert Guillaume), who becomes caught in the cross fire between the warring factions. Guillaume is outstanding at revealing the character's conflicting feelings as he tries to reconcile his friend's dream with the legitimate gripes of Clark's opponents. Mrs. Carter (Regina Taylor) is the mother of one of the students at Eastside High School. Clark visits her shabby apartment to find out why she has put her daughter out of the house. Taylor's performance, even though it is confined to this brief scene, provides one of the film's most moving moments as she explains that she does not want her daughter, whom she loves more than herself, to see her for what she is. Taylor makes the woman's desperation heartbreakingly palpable. Certainly, the film's underpinning is the charismatic performance of Morgan Freeman. As Clark moves through the school's corridors barking orders, reprimanding a teacher, or disciplining students, he possesses the strength that comes from conviction, and he is believably the center of a storm. When he tousles the hair of a pudgy boy who is trying to steer clear of trouble, one believes in Clark's ability to win the love and loyalty of thousands of students.

Issues such as the opportunity for a good education and values such as instilling productive discipline in young people are easy to endorse; the methods employed by Joe Clark to attain them, however, will continue to be debated. Director Avildsen's treatment of Joe Clark's story will remain a subject of dispute: Some will continue to label the film simplistic and fraudulently manipulative; many, perhaps a vast majority, will continue to find in *Lean on Me* a source of inspiration.

Cono Robert Marcazzo

Reviews

Chicago Tribune. March 3, 1989, VII, p. 39.
Commonweal. CXVI, April 21, 1989, p. 245.
Films in Review. XL, June, 1989, p. 361.
Glamour. LXXXVII, April, 1989, p. 226.
Los Angeles Times. March 3, 1989, VI, p. 4.
New York Magazine. XXII, March 20, 1989, p. 73.
The New York Times. March 3, 1989, p. C16.
People Weekly. XXXI, March 20, 1989, p. 19.
Seventeen. XLVIII, April, 1989, p. 117.
Time. CXXXIII, March 13, 1989, p. 82.
Variety. CCCXXXIV, February 1, 1989, p. 18.
The Washington Post. March 3, 1989, p. D4.

LA LECTRICE

Origin: France
Released: 1988
Released in U.S.: 1989
Production: Rosalinde Deville; released by Orion Classics
Direction: Michel Deville
Screenplay: Rosalinde Deville and Michel Deville; based on *La Lectrice* and *Un Fantasme de Bella B. et autres récits*, by Raymond Jean
Cinematography: Dominique le Rigoleur
Editing: Raymonde Guyot
Production design: Thierry Leproust
Art direction: Ysabelle Van Wersch-Cot
Makeup: Joel Lavau
Costume design: Cécile Balme
Sound: Philippe Lioret
Music: Ludwig van Beethoven and Quentin Damamme
MPAA rating: R
Running time: 98 minutes

Principal characters:
Constance/Marie	Miou-Miou
Jean/Philippe	Christian Ruché
Eric	Régis Royer
General's widow	Maria Casarès
Businessman	Patrick Chesnais

Michel Deville's two previous works, *Péril en la demeure* (1984) and *Le Paltoquet* (1986), were playful, visual pun-filled exercises in cinematic reading disguised as whodunits. With *La Lectrice*, he switches genres to comedy, and, although the film pretends to offer a romp through literary reading, it actually offers its viewers a joyous and extremely rich *lecture de cinéma*.

A person is in bed reading a book. From the viewer's vantage point in the middle of the room, the reader's face cannot be seen, but her identity is naturally inferred to be that of the film title's lectrice, or (female) reader. She lies on the right side of the bed, reading a book whose cover obscures her face. The left side of the bed remains invitingly open, ready for her partner to snuggle down beside her. The bed and most of the lower part of the room are decorated in muted, late autumnal tones with highly pronounced linear graphic motifs—stripes, bars, squares—that seem to clash and harmonize at the same time. The angles and shapes of their seemingly disordered and heterogeneous conjunctures are magically tamed and rendered homogeneous by the color scheme's severely limited palette and the graphic, linear conceptual basis they share.

The upper sector of the room features a largely monochromatic wall, on which is set another striking composition—a large painting of much the same description just made. The painting echoes rather than duplicates the decor of the lower portion of the room, formalizing what might pass as informal, containing in its own frame the more open diegesis of the relatively less contained room below it. The picture's forms, while remaining abstract, reveal the lower decor's disguised representational core: the shapes of books piled and stacked in heaps. Although it remains far more abstract than representational, the picture somehow looks like a *trompe l'œil* window into another world, a passageway into a distilled echoland of the chamber in which the viewer stands.

The central horizontal portion of the room, literally the bed's sheets and pillows, graphically form a white separating band between the two other sectors. The bright white bedclothes, stridently sprinkled with bold black wavy scribbles, draw the viewer's gaze back to the reader, and the camera now begins to approach her. She is reading a book called *La Lectrice*. She puts down the book and rubs her eyes, but, surprisingly, the viewer now sees that the reader is not *une lectrice* but rather *un lecteur*, a male reader. Once the viewer recovers from the surprise generated by misreading the scene, a woman, the real *lectrice* of the film's title, jumps into bed alongside the *lecteur*. Constance (Miou-Miou) cuddles up to Jean (Christian Ruché) and begins her *lecture* (reading of the book aloud).

While puckishly playing with the everyday concept of an establishing shot as a locator of the film's action, Deville immediately promises—and begins to deliver—an amazingly rich textual and textural narrative. In effect, he lays out the tools and materials with which he means to work and confidently offers them for our inspection, just as a cardplayer must offer to explain the rules of a new game to his fellow players. The game he is going to play is essentially one of narrative legerdemain, and he invites the viewer to try to follow his sleight of hand. According to his rules so far, he will be manipulating color, graphic motif, *mise en scène*, representation, identity, and language in literary, cinematic, semiotic, and narrative terms.

As Constance reads *La Lectrice* to Jean, she is projected into the role of the novel's protagonist, Marie, and Jean plays Marie's friend Philippe. Both couples live in Arles and seem indistinguishable from each other. Encouraged by her friends, Marie decides to put her love of reading to work, so she advertises her services as a reader. Her subsequent encounters with various clients form the balance of the film's plot, but the narrative intertwines them with occasional revisits to Constance and Jean. (This episodic structure leads to occasional lapses in dramatic tension, probably the film's greatest weakness.)

Marie meets the mother of her first client in their family room, a space made not rich but rather luxuriant, lush, and verdant by its green and rose strongly figured flowery wallpaper. The mother explains that her teenage son, Eric (Régis Royer), has been confined to a wheelchair as the result of a serious accident, and that he needs more human contact. Marie enters Eric's room. Instead of echoing the riotous vigorous growth of the outer chamber (Eric as he was and ought to be), his bedroom is dimly lighted and painted a dark, black-infused green with only a few stark, uncompromisingly linear blackened red bookshelves to relieve its expressionistically monastic decor.

Within only a few scenes, Deville has made it quite clear that he will be using decor not only expressively but also expressionistically, somewhat in the manner of French filmmaker Fritz Lang. Lang employed elements of set design to broadcast and reify the inner emotions of his characters—to make his characters' emotional states legible. Lang and his coworkers were perhaps inclined by the monochrome nature of black-and-white film stock to rely heavily on graphic motifs to write their expressionist *lecture*, but *La Lectrice*'s production designer, Thierry Leproust, also incorporates the expressive possibilities of color to enhance the reading of his film. Each character in the film has his own highly expressive, stylized, and individualized decor, and the cheerful boldness of Leproust's visual imagination lends to the film great charm.

As Marie walks through the door into Eric's room, she immediately asks him if she may address him in the familiar *tu* form. Although he acquiesces, he addresses her in the formal, respectful *vous* person throughout their association. While she speaks to him in a normal, middle-class, conversational mode, he always responds in measured, polished phrases, couched in the most refined level of French. He speaks the language as if he were a *littérateur* of the eighteenth century, a person highly educated in the ways of the language. Royer plays this difficult role skillfully, tempering Eric's polite correctness and intensity (matching the level of the language) with a quiet earnestness and humility that steers Eric quite free of the shoals of affectation or stuffiness.

Marie begins her *lecture*: erotic, passionate nineteenth century poetry by Guy de Maupassant and Charles Baudelaire, poetry quite at odds with the linguistic reserve of her auditor. Eric listens intently as she reads, but soon his attention rests more on Marie's legs than on the writers' images. When she notices this, she obliges Eric by letting her skirt ride up as it pleases. Not one to draw lines between fiction and reality, she will oblige virtually all of her eventual clients in their own idiosyncratic readings of her readings.

A few clients down the line, Marie encounters a businessman (Patrick Chesnais), who is highly successful financially but gruff and bluff and totally unpolished. His apartment—all white, lean, sparse, almost a minimalist decorative joke in its incompleteness—looks like a place longing for someone to move in and occupy it. Linguistically, the businessman is at an equally far remove from young Eric. He mutters, slurs his speech, speaks in short unfinished phrases, inarticulately and artlessly blurting out whatever is on his mind. Like all Marie's male clients, he has sex on his mind, and Marie obliges him, while reading to him in bed. In a series of hilarious scenes, she reads him provocative passages from Marguerite Duras and Raymond Jean—the latter the author of the story from which the film was adapted.

The central pun, "La lectrice lit au lit" (the reader reads in bed), although never verbally articulated, remains in vigor through most of the reader-client relationships in the film, regardless of whether sex is involved. For example, Marie reads revolutionary theory to the aging widow of a Hungarian general (Maria Casarès) in her bed, without the slightest hint of anything besides feminine camaraderie to put her there.

As Marie comes to represent a spirit of literary liberty, a trio of male authority figures (a judge, a medical professor, and a police inspector) attempt to intimidate her by obliging her to read the nastiest works of the Marquis de Sade to them, removing the locus from the bedroom to a figurative courtroom. Marie rises to their implicit threat and reads the scatological obscenities in the same unaffected cadences she has used for all of her *lectures*. She leaves the judge's home triumphant but realizes that her *lecture* will probably bring her reading career to an end. Constance, putting down the novel, tells Jean that she has decided to place an ad.

R. C. Dale

Reviews
Atlanta Constitution. June 2, 1989, p. F1.
Boston Globe. May 26, 1989, p. 44.
Commonweal. CXVI, May 5, 1989, p. 278.
Connoisseur. CCXIX, June, 1989, p. 48.
Films in Review. XL, October, 1989, p. 488.
Los Angeles Times. May 12, 1989, VI, p. 4.
The New Leader. LXXII, April 3, 1989, p. 21.
The New York Times. April 21, 1989, p. C10.
Variety. CCCXXXII, August, 24, 1989, p. 86.
The Washington Post. May 19, 1989, p. D7.
Washington Times. May 23, 1989, p. E3.

LETHAL WEAPON II

Production: Richard Donner and Joel Silver for Silver Pictures; released by Warner Bros.
Direction: Richard Donner
Screenplay: Jeffrey Boam; based on a story by Shane Black and Warren Murphy and on characters created by Black
Cinematography: Stephen Goldblatt
Editing: Stuart Baird
Production design: J. Michael Riva
Art direction: Virginia Randolph and Richard Berger
Set decoration: Marvin March
Sound: Robert Henderson and Alan Robert Murray
Music: Michael Kamen, Eric Clapton, and David Sanborn
MPAA rating: R
Running time: 114 minutes

Principal characters:
Martin Riggs . . . . Mel Gibson
Roger Murtaugh . . . . Danny Glover
Leo Getz. . . . . Joe Pesci
Arjen Rudd . . . . Joss Ackland
Peter Vorstedt. . . . . Derrick O'Connor
Rika Van Den Haas. Patsy Kensit
Trish Murtaugh . . . . Darlene Love
Rianne Murtaugh . . . . Traci Wolfe
Captain Murphy . . . . Steve Kahan

Batman (1989; reviewed in this volume) was extensively merchandised and initially analyzed as a film version of a comic-strip character; of all the films released during the summer of 1989, the one that is most closely drawn to the style and sensibility of the conventional comic-book hero, however, is *Lethal Weapon II*. Following the pattern of adventure combined with character interaction that emerged in *The Great Escape* (1963) and grew into a kind of subgenre with *The Dirty Dozen* (1967) and *The Longest Yard* (1974), *Lethal Weapon II* appeals to the same desire for action and idealism that made those films so successful. In *Lethal Weapon II*, however, the story has become almost irrelevant, serving primarily as a pretext to have the endearing and heroic Los Angeles police partners Martin Riggs (Mel Gibson) and Roger Murtaugh (Danny Glover) perform a reprise of their odd-couple antics from *Lethal Weapon* (1987). Unlike many sequels, as Riggs and Murtaugh avoid almost constant peril while dispatching various small-time villains on their way toward the final confrontation with the premier villain, *Lethal Weapon II* improves on most of the entertaining aspects of the first film. Director Richard

Donner also directed the first *Superman* film, and his ability to present what is ostensibly romantic fantasy in the guise of realism suits the situation very well. The violence, detailed destruction of mechanical objects, stylized romantic encounters, excessive sonic effects, blazing color, frantic pace, and use of broad physical and verbal comedy make *Lethal Weapon II* the cinematic equivalent of a comic strip. At the same time, both Gibson and Glover endow their characters with a depth that reaches beyond comic-strip flatness to achieve plausible and engaging humanity.

The realistic contours of the film derive from its location in a contemporary, urban setting and from its organizing plot which involves the pursuit of a gang of South African criminals who are an obvious but effective analogue for the quintessential modern menace, the unreconstructed Nazi. Led by the always competent Joss Ackland playing the ultimate fascist/racist incarnation of evil, their sneering contempt for other races (especially and not coincidentally the black Murtaugh), their lobotomized, guttural snarling, and their perverse pleasures turn the apparent seriousness of their activities into a display of comic exaggeration. The elaborate shoot-outs and car chases are further exaggerated by sound and special effects; at the same time, the hard-edged lighting, gritty street scenes, and aura of danger surrounding the heroes keep the narrative plausible enough that the threat of death cannot be dismissed. Riggs is still capable of completely off-the-wall behavior when he recalls his wife's death, and Murtaugh continues to express dismay at Riggs's wild forays beyond the law while trying to serve out his career sensibly and honorably; less is made of these traits than in *Lethal Weapon*, however, because their relationship moves past the point of comic banter while maintaining an essentially lighthearted tone. This deepening and widening of their relationship is at the heart of *Lethal Weapon II* and is the source of its appeal beyond the context of cleverly staged action scenes.

The concept of the unlikely friendship is one of the staples of the adventure film. Two people of very different personalities, plunged into a situation of tension and pressure in which their survival depends on mutual cooperation, is one of the most fundamental formulas for dramatic interest. The pairing of opposites, however, goes beyond action. In films, teams such as Stan Laurel and Oliver Hardy developed the comic potential inherent in the clash of disparate outlooks as did Dan Aykroyd with Eddie Murphy in *Trading Places* (1983) and with Tom Hanks in *Dragnet* (1987). In the comic-book realm, there have been a host of partnerships, usually of unequal stature or social class, including Batman and Robin, the Lone Ranger and Tonto, and the Green Hornet and Cato, who brought their individual backgrounds together in a team effort. *Lethal Weapon II* manages to utilize elements of all these combinations, goes beyond some of the more familiar arrangements to enliven the form, and then transcends them by demonstrating the depth of feeling beneath the superficial differences. Continuing the basic setup of *Lethal Weapon*, Gibson and Glover comfortably slide into the same characters. Since all the details have already been explained, *Lethal Weapon II* avoids unnecessary exposition and laborious explanations and develops a natural flow from the start. The real advance is not only that the first film laid everything out but also that most of that kind of establishing material is irrelevant. Ever since the films of Jean-Luc Godard and the introduction of the French movement *nouvelle vague* (new wave), it has been clear that film can jump over excessive explanation without the audience really missing anything. In the thoroughly commercial *Lethal Weapon II*, this implicit assumption explains many of the film's gripping qualities.

The film begins in the middle of a car chase, with the cautious Murtaugh driving his family station wagon and the hyperactive Riggs calling for more speed and daring. The focus of the pursuit is unclear, but the Riggs/Murtaugh partnership is set at the film's center. From this point, director Donner begins to reach for the subtle reality of a relationship in which comfortable assumptions of ethnicity are revealed as excuses employed to avoid the complexity of people's real lives. First, the tacit racist convention of an ethnic subordinate's inferiority is fractured, as Murtaugh is obviously Riggs's equal, and then the convention is shattered as the minority character is presented with the features usually reserved for Waspish stereotypes—solidity, caution, conservative dress and morale, and an abiding personal reserve. Then, the standard-issue handsome Caucasian hero is presented as wild, unstable, irrational, anarchic, and charged with the sexual energy often associated with bestial lower-class types. Glover has the more difficult role to make interesting, but a genuine sweetness shines through his portrayal of a lovable square. He plays the stolid Horatio to Gibson's dazzling, antic Hamlet, a foil for Gibson's japes; and he has some delightful moments when he tentatively tries a few of Gibson's lines and bits. Gibson, whose personal charm is actually enhanced by the element of psychic distress that makes him unpredictable and dangerous, is excellent as the soulful scamp. His romantic allure is both wholesome and exciting, and his athletic skills make his feats convincing.

While the principals dominate the film, the supporting parts are intelligently cast, particularly Ackland as Arjen Rudd, the incarnation of malignancy, capable of unspeakable acts and completely devoid of conscience. His offhand disposal of an underling who botched an assignment and his insinuating glance at his secretary suggest horrors beyond even those he commits. As Rika Van Den Haas, the South African whose revulsion for Rudd validates her credentials as a human being, Patsy Kensit does as much as possible with an underwritten, practically nonexistent role, and her romantic interlude with Riggs reopens emotional areas that Riggs has tried to seal away. The most diverting character is Leo Getz, the accountant-turned-informer, who is played with a manic zest by Joe Pesci. He becomes a kind of endearing but troublesome pet for Murtaugh and Riggs. Getz's penchant for minor physical disasters has elements derived from the Three Stooges (an interest of Riggs in *Lethal Weapon*) and the cartoon character who is blown apart with no apparent damage.

In addition to its action, much of the film's considerable commercial success is the result of the escapism it offers. The heroes are supported in their struggles by strong family structures: the family of police who are a team dedicated to civil order; the loving Murtaugh family, straight out of middle American myth, which has expanded to include Riggs; and the family of love that is revealed in the film's two strongest scenes. As Riggs and Murtaugh face death together, first from a booby-trapped toilet and then amid a blaze of bullets in the film's bloody finale, their intense affection for each other becomes clear both to them and to the audience. In a rather daring exposition of the exceptionally powerful feeling at the core of a male-bonding relationship, *Lethal Weapon II* shows that a man does not have to be cold to be strong and that the essence of humane decency is a respect for diversity, singularity, and individuality.

Leon Lewis

Reviews

Chicago Tribune. July 7, 1989, VII, p. 35.
The Christian Science Monitor. July 7, 1989, p. 10.
Films in Review. XL, October, 1989, p. 483.
Los Angeles Times. July 7, 1989, VI, p. 1.
The New York Times. July 7, 1989, p. C18.
Newsweek. CXIV, July 17, 1989, p. 53.
People Weekly. XXXII, July 24, 1989, p. 12.
Time. CXXXIV, July 24, 1989, p. 53.
Variety. CCCXXXV, July 5, 1989, p. 18.
The Wall Street Journal. July 6, 1989, p. A1.
The Washington Post. July 7, 1989, p. D1.

LICENCE TO KILL

Origin: Great Britain
Released: 1989
Released in U.S.: 1989
Production: Albert R. Broccoli and Michael G. Wilson for Danjaq and United
    Artists; released by Metro-Goldwyn-Mayer/United Artists
Direction: John Glen
Screenplay: Michael G. Wilson and Richard Maibaum; based on the character
    James Bond, created by Ian Fleming
Cinematography: Alec Mills
Editing: John Grover and Carlos Puente
Production design: Peter Lamont
Art direction: Michael Lamont and Ken Court
Set decoration: Michael Ford, Richard Helfritz, and Frederick Weiler
Special effects: Neil Corbould and Daniel Dark
Special visual effects: John Richardson
Makeup: Norma Webb
Costume design: Jodie Tillen
Sound: Edward Tise
Music: Michael Kamen
Song: Narada Michael Walden, Jeffrey Cohen, and Walter Afanasieff, "Licence to
    Kill"
MPAA rating: PG-13
Running time: 133 minutes

Principal characters:

James Bond	Timothy Dalton
Pam Bouvier	Carey Lowell
Franz Sanchez	Robert Davi
Lupe Lamora	Talisa Soto
Milton Krest	Anthony Zerbe
Sharkey	Frank McRae
Killifer	Everett McGill
Professor Joe Butcher	Wayne Newton
Q	Desmond Llewelyn
Felix Leiter	David Hedison
M	Robert Brown
Della Churchill	Priscilla Barnes
Miss Moneypenny	Caroline Bliss

While on holiday in Florida, James Bond (Timothy Dalton) resigns the British
Secret Service after having his licence to kill revoked by his superior, M (Robert

Brown), and goes underground to avenge the mutilation of his longtime friend, former Central Intelligence Agency agent Felix Leiter (David Hedison), and the death of Felix's new bride (Priscilla Barnes). Both are victims of the ire of Latin drug lord Franz Sanchez (Robert Davi), a man who prizes loyalty above money and has a penchant for revenge when he is betrayed.

Aided by one of Felix's informants, former Army pilot Pam Bouvier (Carey Lowell), and the Secret Service gadgetry wizard Q (Desmond Llewelyn), Bond tracks down Sanchez in his native Isthmus City; using Sanchez's own drug money as collateral, Bond offers his special services as a former British agent. Despite an initial rebuff, Bond succeeds in ingratiating himself with Sanchez and infiltrates the cocaine operation, eventually destroying the laboratory. After a harrowing chase with state-of-the-art tanker trucks, Bond finally extracts his revenge by killing Sanchez, but not before he informs Sanchez that his vendetta was "strictly personal."

Licence to Kill is the first 007 adventure in twenty-seven years that bears an original title, one not used for any Ian Fleming novel or short story. Originally entitled *Licence Revoked*, the film's name was changed primarily because of a negative response to "revoked"; however, it was also a logical attempt to capitalize on some implicit Bondian iconography: his licence to kill. Furthermore, *Licence to Kill* is only the second Bond adventure that has been filmed on sound stages other than Pinewood Studios in England. *Moonraker* (1979) was the first, done in studios near Paris. With the exception of some locale work in Florida, *Licence to Kill* was shot in its entirety in Mexico and at Mexico City's Churubusco Studio in an attempt to produce the film at the same budget as that of the previous Bond film.

Timothy Dalton brings considerable strength as an actor to the character of James Bond, with an extensive Shakespearean theater background that includes roles in *Romeo and Juliet*, *Richard II*, *King Lear*, and *Henry IV*. Dalton made an auspicious film debut as the young King Philip of France opposite Peter O'Toole and Katherine Hepburn in *The Lion in Winter* (1968) and later appeared in such films as *Wuthering Heights* (1970), *Cromwell* (1970, with Alec Guinness and Richard Harris), and *Mary, Queen of Scots* (1971, with Vanessa Redgrave). His film credits also include his first outing as James Bond in *The Living Daylights* (1987) and roles in *Flash Gordon* (1980) and *Hawks* (1988).

Unfortunately for the 007 series, Dalton's strength as an actor may also become the weak link between this film and the other fourteen films of the series (excluding *The Living Daylights*, which was originally conceived before Dalton was named as the fourth incarnation of 007). Dalton brings an exciting blend of self-assurance, tense impatience, and wounded vulnerability to the character. Though a welcome change from the lighthearted frivolity brought to the series by his predecessor, Roger Moore, Dalton's intensity and determination to return 007 to Ian Fleming's original conception of the superspy has created an enormous chasm between the character of Bond and the inherent peculiarities of the Bond scripts themselves. If Bond is to be humanized to capitalize on the dark angst that Dalton brings to the role, there needs to be a shift in emphasis away from big-budget special effects and outrageous hijinks back to the central character of James Bond himself.

Despite the fact that the previous Bond film, *The Living Daylights*, was the second most popular film in 1987 outside the United States, it barely reached the top twenty in the country. With decreasing audience attendance in the United States, it was foremost in the producers' minds that Bond be taken in a different direction from previous films. Dalton's intensity and seriousness have afforded the opportunity to return to Ian Fleming's original conception of 007 as a cold-blooded operative for the British government. The problem arises, however, when the issue of commerciality enters into the scripting of a Bond adventure. If one strips away the Secret Service from Bond, as the writers have done in *Licence to Kill*, there remains little to distinguish Bond from other similar film heroes, most notably Mel Gibson's character, Martin Riggs, in *Lethal Weapon II* (1989; reviewed in this volume). It is particularly disconcerting to see Bond lose control, since it is so out of character for a man with such high ranking. Surely Bond has seen coworkers and friends killed before, either directly or indirectly as a result of his chosen profession. One need only recall the anguish suffered by Bond with the death of his wife in *On Her Majesty's Secret Service* (1969).

The issue then becomes one of Bond's own identity, or rather nonidentity. If the character is to lose his identity from year to year, or decade to decade, he becomes nothing more than a pawn in the game of commercial filmmaking, a character that becomes whatever the public appetite demands at the time of scripting. It seems obvious that the series' producers have chosen to go after commercial viability rather than pulling the audience back to Bond, and that choice proves to be problematic. James Bond is too well defined at this point in his existence to be thrust so far off-center that he would be willing to surrender his patriotism to his country so quickly and so easily. The suave, imperturbable professional superagent with the enviable double-zero prefix has been turned into an emotionally out-of-control, slightly crazed revengemonger. While this transformation may result in a solid action-adventure film, it strays far off course from audience expectations for a Bond adventure.

Perhaps by virtue of his long-term relationship with the feminist actress Vanessa Redgrave, Dalton seems uncomfortable with the remaining vestige of the sexism that was an inherent part of the Bond tradition in the 1960's and 1970's. His scenes with his female costars never ring true. There is an aura of boredom whenever he is forced to interact with the women in the story. One obvious remedy might be to provide Dalton with a female sparring partner who is his equal, a grown woman with worldly experience. One never believes former fashion model Carey Lowell as an ex-Army pilot. She tries to imbue the character of Pam Bouvier with a tough resiliency that should help to explain Bond's attraction to her, but Lowell never seems to be able to transcend acting tough, as opposed to being tough. As for Talisa Soto as Lupe Lamora, the love of Sanchez's life, she remains a throwback to the multitude of Bond women who have come and gone without making a significant contribution to the film series. In recent years only Barbara Bach remains memorable as the strong female Russian counterpart of 007, Major Anya Amasova, in *The Spy Who Loved Me* (1977).

The accomplishment of this Bond film is that the writers, Richard Maibaum and Michael G. Wilson, have finally acknowledged one extremely important aspect of Bond that was for the most part ignored prior to *Licence to Kill*. Ian Fleming created Bond with the clear understanding of the duality of good and evil that exists in espionage, particularly during peacetime. For the first time the villain of a Bond adventure is sketched as a *Doppelgänger* of 007, the flip side of the same coin, the only difference between the two being a predetermined right and wrong. Both men prize the same quality: loyalty. Each man kills because it is part of his respective job. Bond happens to have the blessing of his country—except in this film, where Bond is stripped of his patriotism and merely indulges in a round of personal revenge.

Reviews of *Licence to Kill* ran the gamut from utter disdain to effusive praise— not unlike the continuing debate among fans as to which actor will be forever the quintessential James Bond.

Patricia Ann Kowal

Reviews

Chicago Tribune. July 14, 1989, VII, p. 41.
The Christian Science Monitor. July 18, 1989, p. 11.
Cinéfantastique. XIX, July 1989, p. 17.
Los Angeles Times. July 18, 1989, VI, p. 1.
The New Republic. CCI, August 7, 1989, p. 27.
New York Magazine. XXII, July 24, 1989, p. 52.
The New York Times. July 14, 1989, p. C8.
Newsweek. CXIV, July 17, 1989, p. 52.
People Weekly. XXXV, July 17, 1989, p. 11.
Time. CXXXIV, July 24, 1989, p. 53.
Variety. CCCXXXV, June 14, 1989, p. 7.
The Wall Street Journal. July 13, 1989, p. A8.

THE LITTLE MERMAID

Production: Howard Ashman and John Musker for Walt Disney Pictures, in
association with Silver Screen Partners IV; released by Buena Vista
Direction: John Musker and Ron Clements
Screenplay: John Musker and Ron Clements; based on a story by Hans Christian
Andersen
Editing: John Carnochan
Animation direction: Mark Henn, Glen Keane, Duncan Marjoribanks, Ruben
Aquino, Andreas Deja, and Matthew O'Callaghan
Art direction: Michael A. Peraza, Jr., and Donald A. Towns
Special visual effects: Mark Dindal
Music: Alan Menken
Songs: Howard Ashman and Alan Menken, "Under the Sea" (AA), "Kiss the
Girl," "Part of Your World," "Poor Souls," "Les Poissons," "Fathoms Below,"
and "Daughters of Triton"
MPAA rating: G
Running time: 82 minutes

Voices of principal characters:

Ariel .... Jodi Benson
Eric...................... Christopher Daniel Barnes
Sebastian .... Samuel E. Wright
Triton .... Kenneth Mars
Ursula .... Pat Carroll
Scuttle............................ Buddy Hackett
Flounder .... Jason Marin
Grimsby .... Ben Wright
Flotsam and Jetsam................... Paddi Edwards

Although the Disney company has long been synonymous with animated fairy
tales, *The Little Mermaid* is their first feature-length venture into such lore in nearly
three decades. Here the source is Hans Christian Andersen's story about a world in
the depths of the sea. As transformed by the writing-directing team of John Musker
and Ron Clements, with songs by Howard Ashman and Alan Menken and brilliant
animation, *The Little Mermaid* becomes a rare film that gives some kind of joy to
small children, senior citizens, and everyone in between. The fantasy of it allows for
pure escape, but the story nevertheless manages to promote parental understanding
and tolerance and to suggest the values of persistence and sacrifice.

The Musker-Clements adaptation begins with a sea shanty sung by the crew of a
roving clipper. On board is Eric (voice of Christopher Daniel Barnes), the handsome young prince of a nearby kingdom. It is Eric's birthday, and his stuffy old
mentor Grimsby (voice of Ben Wright) reminds him that he must find a proper

bride soon. Many fathoms below, a deep-sea concert is about to begin in the kingdom of the mer-people, presided over by a splendid, white-haired merman named Triton (voice of Kenneth Mars). Yet Sebastian (voice of Samuel E. Wright), the small red crab who serves as the community's musical director, is forced to cancel his production shortly after it starts because of the absence of the star singer, Triton's own daughter, Ariel (voice of Jodi Benson). The latter is less rebellious than curious, for she collects artifacts from the surface world—forks, belts, wagon wheels, pipes, and the like—and stashes them away in a secret underwater cave.

Back at the undersea kingdom, Flounder (voice of Jason Marin), a shy fish and friend of Ariel, happens to mention his and Ariel's visit with Scuttle (voice of Buddy Hackett), a seagull. Triton immediately erupts in anger, for he has forbidden his daughter to go to the surface. Exasperated, Triton tells Sebastian to look after Ariel. The calypso-talking shellfish accepts the order with regret, for he too knows how uncontrollable the beautiful sixteen-year-old mermaid can be. Sebastian follows her to her hiding place, where she sings "Part of Your World," a ballad expressing her desire to go where people are; she also sings portions of it from time to time during the rest of the picture. At the end of the song, she looks up to see the huge shadow of Prince Eric's ship as it passes through. She swims to the ship, reaching it in time to overhear the prince's conversation with Grimsby about finding not merely a wife but "the right girl."

As Ariel hides just beneath the rail of the boat, smitten by Eric's good looks and pleasant demeanor, a violent storm surges forward; big waves rock the ship and lightning ignites one of its masts. Soon the entire ship is burning in the rough sea. All escape to lifeboats, but when Eric returns to retrieve his dog he is knocked unconscious into the water by flying debris. Ariel saves him, then sings him awake on the beach of his kingdom. As the sun's glare momentarily blinds him, she rushes back into the water before he can see that she is a mermaid.

At this point, the tale's antagonist makes known her evil presence in dramatic fashion. The classic Disney villain-woman here takes the form of an obese octopus named Ursula (voice of Pat Carroll). The shape of her eyes constantly changes, and through her heavily rouged lips come the deep-toned sounds of vengeance. Having endured years of Triton's proclamations, she sees in Ariel's giddy love of the human prince possibilities for seizing the undersea throne and shrinking the hated king to the size of a guppy. She keeps, in fact, a kennel full of deformed creatures who had been proud and beautiful until they allowed themselves to be hoodwinked by Ursula.

Following her secret heroism with the prince, Ariel displays all the expected strange signs of a girl in love. Even her pompous father notices. At first he is happily taken with the idea, but Sebastian accidentally blurts out that the object of her affection is a human being. The king roars like a land beast and goes directly to Ariel's secret place. There he not only berates her and forbids her to go again to the surface but also destroys all of her trinkets from the world above. Worse still, he does not allow her to defend herself verbally.

Taking advantage of Ariel's vulnerability at this point, Ursula sends her two lackeys, eels named Flotsam and Jetsam (Patty Edwards), to introduce a deal to the unhappy girl. Ariel instinctively resists them at first but then changes her mind, since her father has shown himself to be so closed-minded. Ursula's scheme is explained by way of a spectacular musical express called, ironically, "Poor Souls." She sings in her throatiest tones and swirls her black tentacles hypnotically. She is a multilimbed Mephistopheles, seeming to barter for Ariel's soul but actually needing it only as a means to get at Triton himself.

The octopus-witch gives Ariel legs but takes away her voice, as temporary payment. Ariel's dream of bliss with the prince will come true only if she can get him to kiss her before sundown on the third day of her surface adventure. Ursula feels confident of success, because Eric's memory of the precious creature who saved his life can only be triggered by the latter's beautiful voice.

As Ariel walks unsteadily ashore, her slender new limbs tremble and buckle like those of Bambi shortly after birth. Yet she masters walking when the prince approaches her, impressed by her beauty, which seems familiar but made slightly forlorn by the fact that she cannot speak. Even without a voice, however, Ariel's effect on the prince is strong. By the end of the second day, she has made great romantic progress, helped along in a dim moonlight boatride by Sebastian's mood song called "Kiss the Girl." Eric's lips in fact almost come together with hers, but Ursula's eels tip over the boat and break the romantic spell.

Having narrowly missed defeat, the witch then takes charge and creates a spell of her own. Disguised as a beautiful maiden, she wins over Eric with the lilting voice she has commandeered from Ariel, who sleeps late that fateful day. Almost as if hypnotized, Eric quickly forgets Ariel and decides to marry the mystery woman, whose speech and song are the thing for which he has been waiting. Yet just before the wedding, which is to take place at sea, Scuttle invades her privacy and sees that her mirror reflects the evil Ursula.

The final sequence of *The Little Mermaid* is too predictably raucous, overly influenced by such examples of the preposterous-adventure genre as the Indiana Jones series. Yet, despite its excessive noise and protracted climax, the ending fulfills each of the fantasy requirements suggested from the start. Triton, having been briefly shrunk and deformed, returns to his position of might, wearing his sea crown; Ursula, after a wild few minutes of conquest, is resoundingly defeated; and, finally, Ariel and Eric are joined together in matrimony, with a bittersweet blessing from the entire mer-kingdom, including Triton.

It is likely that *The Little Mermaid* will eventually become the biggest of the Disney moneymakers as well as a feature to which audience members—especially the youngest ones—will respond positively for decades to come. Though not as dazzling in animation as *Fantasia* (1940) or as emotionally endearing as *Pinocchio* (1940), it will survive for future generations because of its youthful charm and wit. The whole production comes across as free-spirited as its central figure. Even its scattered moments of sadness or disappointment are tempered by the kind of ticklish animation that has always marked the best of Disney. An example of the latter occurs just before the final sequence, when the leggy but voiceless Ariel quietly weeps at her dim prospects. The tear in her eye develops in classic Disney fashion, from thin trickle to fully grown bubble, then hesitates for an instant before its melancholy yet musical fall into the sea.

More exciting examples of animated humor involve the lovable but cantankerous crab, Sebastian. In the best of these, "Under the Sea," the small red creature orchestrates a highly disciplined group of snails, seahorses, blowfish, darters, and dolphins, to say nothing of the schools of unidentified but very rhythmic fish, in a geometric spectacular that must please the spirit of Busby Berkeley. As *Time*'s Richard Corliss expressed in an early review, "if ever a cartoon earned a standing ovation in mid-film, this would be it."

Generally speaking, shenanigans take clear precedence over emotional manipulation in *The Little Mermaid*. This is just as well, for the film's impressive animation seems most evident, in its depth and smoothness of movement, when the characters are at their silliest.

Andrew Jefchak

Reviews

American Film: Magazine of the Film and Television Arts. XV, December, 1989, p. 17.
Chicago Tribune. November 17, 1989, VII, p. 35.
Cinéfantastique. XX, January, 1990, p. 30.
Commonweal. January 12, 1990.
Los Angeles Times. November 15, 1989, VI, p. 1.
The New Republic. December 25, 1989.
The New York Times. November 19, 1989, p. B17.
The New Yorker. LXV, December 11, 1989, p. 140.
Newsweek. CXIV, November 20, 1989, p. 72.
Time. CXXXIV, November 20, 1989, p. 91.
Variety. CCCXXXVII, November 8, 1989, p. 32.
The Washington Post. November 17, 1989, p. D7.

LOOK WHO'S TALKING

Production: Jonathan D. Krane for Management Company Entertainment Group;
 released by Tri-Star Pictures
Direction: Amy Heckerling
Screenplay: Amy Heckerling
Cinematography: Thomas Del Ruth
Editing: Debra Chiate
Art direction: Graeme Murray
Set decoration: Barry W. Brolly
Costume design: Molly MacGinnis
Sound: Ralph Parker
Music: David Kitay
MPAA rating: PG-13
Running time: 90 minutes

> *Principal characters:*
> James . . . . John Travolta
> Mollie . . . . Kirstie Alley
> Rosie . . . . Olympia Dukakis
> Albert . . . . George Segal
> Grandpa . . . . Abe Vigoda
> Mikey . . . . (voice of Bruce Willis)

On the surface *Look Who's Talking* seems to be simply another Hollywood comedy demonstrating how much trouble men and women have dealing with one another. In this version, beautiful Mollie (Kirstie Alley) loves her already married boss, Albert (George Segal), who, not surprisingly, keeps spurning a permanent relationship. After an accidental pregnancy, Mollie takes a heroic stand and keeps her child. She abandons Albert and spends the second half of the film struggling to find a father for her son, Mikey. Only in the end does she find the right man right under her nose, the earnest young cab driver, James (John Travolta), who helped get her to the hospital during labor.

What makes *Look Who's Talking* different and appealing is that baby Mikey has audible thoughts that can be heard only by the audience. Through the narration of Bruce Willis, sometimes sweet, sometimes wise-cracking, Mikey seeks to change the world around him. He assists his mother in "finding" James, in a delightful change in a conventional romantic comic plot.

At first glance, *Look Who's Talking* seems to fit into the 1980's yuppie genre of adults dealing with parenthood. *Three Men and a Baby* (1987), *Baby Boom* (1987), *She's Having a Baby* (1988), and *For Keeps* (1988) offer but four obvious examples of seemingly related titles. *Look Who's Talking*, however, is very different. In *Three Men and a Baby* and *Baby Boom*, audiences saw intelligent adults who were unable to make two pieces of diaper tape work. *Look Who's Talking* is not about parents dealing with a baby but with what it means to create and maintain a family.

Look Who's Talking is a throwback to the screwball comedies of the 1930's. Indeed, from the opening sequence, during which the sperm of Albert is tracked down Mollie's Fallopian tubes and is shown fertilizing her egg, the offbeat, quirky nature of this film's look at love and life in the 1980's becomes apparent. Mollie is not the hip, in-control woman of the 1980's; in fact, she seems to be totally overwhelmed by her choices and responsibilities. The film does not preach, however, and her affair with Albert, a married man, is taken as something ordinary. Although Mollie is a professional, this does not make her life ideal; rather it simply complicates it further. Being single in New York City in the age of the female executive is difficult.

It is not surprising, therefore, to find that *Look Who's Talking* was written and directed by a woman. The film is certainly an auteurist effort from the pen and camera of Amy Heckerling, a rare successful female Hollywood filmmaker. Heckerling made her directorial debut with *Fast Times at Ridgemont High* (1982), one of the few films to treat teenagers as complex individuals. A critical and financial hit, Heckerling was a rare female director on Hollywood's fast track. *Look Who's Talking* certainly presents a woman's point of view of the hardships of life and of necessary compromises. *Look Who's Talking* will probably be remembered for its high grosses, but it ought to be remembered as a unique look at the complexities of being a successful woman.

What was unexpected was how successful *Look Who's Talking* became at the box office. In the spring of 1977 no one predicted that George Lucas' *Star Wars* (1977) would make millions of dollars. On a smaller scale, *Look Who's Talking* did the same thing during the fall of 1989, once again proving that making hit films cannot be turned into a predictable, formulaic assembly-line industry. *Look Who's Talking* was considered so ordinary, so much routine fluff that *Newsweek*, *Time*, and *The New Yorker* did not bother to review it. Those in the daily press who took a look most often came to the same conclusion as Chris Willman of the *Los Angeles Times*, who warned that filmgoers fed up with the plethora of cute toddlers should steer clear of *Look Who's Talking*. *Variety*, the leading film industry trade paper, could find little box-office potential for such an obvious, ill-conceived comedy.

Yet audiences flocked to American theaters. *Look Who's Talking* took in more than $12 million in its first weekend of release, setting a record for a fall weekend. It then accumulated more than $14 million the following weekend, thus setting yet a new record by a staggering $2 million. *Look Who's Talking* did so well that it remained in U.S. theaters through the Christmas season, despite the influx of new films.

Tri-Star Pictures, then still a subsidiary of a struggling Columbia Pictures— before Columbia was purchased by Sony a few weeks later—sold *Look Who's Talking* around an unexpected cast of adult characters. The film's male lead, John Travolta, who had not made a hit film in years, was cast against his long-held macho image. Kirstie Alley, who played Mikey's mother, was known principally for her role as an uptight, ambitious bar manager on the hit NBC-television series *Cheers*. Noted character performers Olympia Dukakis and Abe Vigoda played off-beat grandparents.

Only the most knowledgeable of film fans recognized the independent film company that developed *Look Who's Talking*. Management Company Entertainment Group (MCEG) had never had a motion picture hit and was known throughout the film industry as simply another struggling independent company, sponsoring inexpensive films such as *The Chocolate War* (1988) that usually ran in art houses to small audiences. Yet, as has been regularly the case in Hollywood since feature filmmaking became a big business, the unexpected happened. *Look Who's Talking*, made for about half the cost of the average feature film of the 1980's—about $9 million—turned into the top-grossing film in the nation for the month after its release, generating more than $100 million at the box office before the close of 1989.

Suddenly business magazines were praising the career plans of Krane, MCEG's thirty-seven-year-old president. "Overnight" he seemed on his way to fulfilling his dream of fashioning a media conglomerate that distributed films abroad, lent money to independent filmmakers, sold videos, and packaged film deals such as *Look Who's Talking*. Yet a Hollywood-based media conglomerate has never been built on a single blockbuster, even one that earned more than $100 million. The 1980's were littered with failed instant success stories: Cannon, Vestron, and New World could not do it, could MCEG?

Look Who's Talking, however, does provide a good example of how a small company with a single feature film can compete at the margin with the big studios. For *Look Who's Talking*, Krane struggled to keep costs to a minimum. He agreed to go over his $6 million budget only because he was able to persuade Tri-Star, then desperate for product, to help with financing and distribution. Still, he landed Travolta for half of what the actor originally sought, because Travolta needed work. Krane moved the film's production to Vancouver, British Columbia, to avoid the added expenses of a union shoot in the film's setting of New York City. Krane also cut ten days from the shooting schedule by limiting the number of outdoor scenes and set changes. *Look Who's Talking* is minimalist filmmaking by 1980's Hollywood standards and gives hope to all aspiring independent filmmakers who search for that one, unexpected hit.

Douglas Gomery

Reviews

Boxoffice. October, 1989, p. R61.
Chicago Tribune. October 13, 1989, VII, p. 49.
The Christian Science Monitor. November 17, 1989, p. 10.
Los Angeles Times. October 13, 1989, VI, p. 12.

The New York Times. October, 13, 1989, p. C12.
People Weekly. XXXII, October 30, 1989, p. 14.
Rolling Stone. October 19, 1989, p. 29.
Time. CXXXIV, November 20, 1989, p. 98.
USA Today. October 13, 1989, p. 5D.
Variety. CCCXXXVII, October 18, 1989, p. 28.
The Wall Street Journal. October 26, 1989, p. A14.
The Washington Post. October 13, 1989, p. C7.

MAJOR LEAGUE

Production: Chris Chesser and Irby Smith for Morgan Creek/Mirage; released by
  Paramount Pictures
Direction: David Ward
Screenplay: David Ward
Cinematography: Reynaldo Villalobos
Editing: Dennis M. Hill
Production design: Jeffrey Howard
Art direction: John Krenz Reinhart, Jr.
Set decoration: Celeste Lee
Makeup: Joann Wobisca
Costume design: Erica Edell Phillips
Sound: Susumu Tokunow
Music: James Newton Howard
MPAA rating: R
Running time: 107 minutes

Principal characters:
Jake Taylor	Tom Berenger
Rickie Vaughn	Charlie Sheen
Roger Dorn	Corbin Bernsen
Rachel Phelps	Margaret Whitton
Lou Brown	James Gammon
Lynn Westland	Rene Russo
Willie Mays Hayes	Wesley Snipes
Charlie Donovan	Charles Cyphers
Steve Harris	Chelcie Ross
Pedro Cerrano	Dennis Haysbert
Pepper Leach	Andy Romano
Harry Doyle	Bob Uecker
Clu Haywood	Pete Vuckovich

The spate of baseball films released in the 1980's all share one common characteristic: Each makes at least passing reference to the mythology or lore surrounding
the game. From the bawdy comedy of the made-for-cable film *Long Gone* (1987) to
the mysticism of 1989's *Field of Dreams* (reviewed in this volume), these motion
pictures reflect on baseball's identity as the American national pastime. Whether
equating the game's history with developments in America's sociopolitical history,
as in *Eight Men Out* (1988), or presenting the players as modern versions of mythic
heroes, as in *The Natural* (1984), baseball films of the 1980's have used nostalgia,
hyperbole, and metaphor to examine human nature through the national sport.
Major League, released during the first week of the 1989 baseball season, continued

this tendency by celebrating the game's history and rituals and by fostering the myth that baseball unites people in a spirit of eternal youth and optimism.

The story line of *Major League* parallels those of *Long Gone* and the 1988 baseball comedy *Bull Durham* in that the central character is a veteran athlete who plays one last season before ending his career in a private moment of glory. Tom Berenger plays Jake Taylor, a former star catcher who suffers from the pain caused by spending too many years behind the plate. Despite his aging bones, Jake agrees to catch for the beleaguered Cleveland Indians in order to spend "one more year in the sun." He leads a team of misfits and losers assembled by the new owner of the Indians, former showgirl Rachel Phelps (Margaret Whitton), who has no understanding of the game or its traditions. She wants to move the Indians to sunny Miami, but she can break her stadium lease with the city of Cleveland only if attendance falls to new lows. By putting together what she believes to be a losing team—one stocked with faded has-beens and untested newcomers—she is sure that attendance will plummet.

The ragtag group of ballplayers who make up the Indians provide most of the humor in this daft comedy. Featured among the players are Rickie Vaughn (Charlie Sheen), a young pitcher straight out of the penitentiary whose wild pitches and punk hairstyle earn for him the nickname "Wild Thing"; Roger Dorn (Corbin Bernsen), a handsome free agent who refuses to get too close to a fly ball for fear of marring his good looks; Willie Mays Hayes (Wesley Snipes), whose only talent is his baserunning ability; and Pedro Cerrano (Dennis Haysbert), who practices voodoo on his bat because it does not like curveballs. After the players uncover Ms. Phelps's insidious scheme, they overcome their personal weaknesses and pull together to win the playoffs at the end of the season. In doing so, they recover their self-respect.

Of the recent glut of baseball films, *Major League* has earned a reputation for being the favorite among real-life players, perhaps because of its clever weaving of baseball fact and fiction and baseball lore and superstition. Though the players in the story line are entirely fictional, the Cleveland Indians are an actual major league franchise, and—just like the team in the film—they have not enjoyed a winning season for some time. Director/scriptwriter David Ward hails from Cleveland, and he undoubtedly chose the setting and the team for that reason. Yet, because it is set in Cleveland—an industrial city in the throes of a recession—the story of a group of hard-luck losers who work together to pull themselves out of a slump takes on an added connotation.

Cleveland's status as a city generally down on its luck is alluded to in the opening credit sequence. Randy Newman's song "Burn On," which refers to an embarrassing moment in Cleveland's history when the Cuyahoga River was so polluted that it caught on fire, plays as images of Cleveland's rundown factories and empty shipyards fill the screen. This set of images segues to a series of headlines detailing the Indians' fall from grace after their last pennant win in 1954. Before the narrative even begins, an association is made between a humiliating moment from Cleveland's past, its hard-luck status as a city hit by economic hardship, and its losing baseball team.

The real-life world of baseball is also effectively blended with the fictional world of *Major League* through the appearance of former ballplayers in fictional roles. Bob Uecker, who parlayed his mediocre baseball career into a more lucrative vocation in show business, appears as jaded Indians announcer Harry Doyle. Harry's inebriated remarks while broadcasting the games are absurd yet somehow accurate. Former Milwaukee Brewers pitcher Pete Vuckovich appears briefly as a mean-looking New York Yankee slugger named Clu Haywood, who serves as Rickie "Wild Thing" Vaughn's nemesis.

More than with any other type of athlete, baseball players are known for their offbeat superstitions and bizarre rituals—a legacy inherited from the game's beginnings in the nineteenth century. Baseball literature and lore make reference to the superstitious nature of the players. *Major League* exaggerates this aspect of the game through the character of Pedro Cerrano, who practices voodoo on his bat. Before each game, Pedro prays in front of his locker, which has been transformed into an altar complete with burning candles, exotic statuary, and a live boa constrictor. Pedro asserts that his bat is afraid of curveballs, and he makes offerings of liquor to the god Jobu so that Jobu will take the fear out of his bat. Though some team members scoff at these practices, others take notice. Teammate Willie Mays Hayes emulates Pedro's actions by getting his own reptile—a harmless and frail-looking garter snake—and keeping it in his locker.

As offbeat as Pedro's practices may seem, the exaggeration is only slight compared with the actual superstitions and rituals of real-life players from the past and the present. During the early twentieth century, for example, it was not unusual for major league teams to travel with mascots—usually young black boys or hunchbacked men. It was considered good luck to rub the hair of black boys or the hump of a hunchbacked man before climbing into the batter's box. More specifically, manager John McGraw of the New York Giants often requested that a wagonload of good-luck barrels be hauled around in plain view of his players during a game. George Stallings, manager of the Boston Braves, traveled with a trunk filled entirely with good-luck charms and trinkets, including a ten-cent piece blessed by a Cuban witch doctor. The superstitions and rituals that sluggers have had about their bats loom large in baseball lore: Tony Pena, a former catcher for the St. Louis Cardinals, rubbed a bone on his bat to generate hits; the legendary Ted Williams picked out his own lumber to carve his bat; and lesser-known slugger Pat Kelly used a black bat, which he nicknamed the "Soul Pole," to intimidate pitchers.

How important this knowledge of baseball lore and history is to the enjoyment of *Major League* is ultimately debatable. Yet, the conclusion of the film seems dependent on the audience's awareness of a very cherished moment in baseball lore—at least in terms of an emotional impact if not for practical understanding. *Major League* culminates in a crucial game between the Indians and the New York Yankees, which goes down to the last inning. Throughout the game, each ragtag player has faced his personal demons and come out on top: Pedro finally belts a curveball; the Wild Thing strikes out big, bad Yankee Clu Haywood; and Roger Dorn fields a great catch. At the bottom of the ninth, with the winning run on base, Jake Taylor comes up to the plate. Taylor points to the upper deck of the stadium in a gesture that directly recalls the famous moment in baseball lore when Babe Ruth "called his shot" before slamming a home run in the 1932 World Series. The opposing team, like the film audience, expects Taylor to hit a home run just as Ruth did. Instead, Jake bunts. The Yankees are caught off guard, Willie Mays Hayes scores the winning run, and the Indians win the one-game playoff. Jake's sacrifice hit is just that: Eschewing the glory of a Babe Ruth-style homer, Jake sacrifices his last chance for personal fame for the sake of the team. Knowing that the man on base can score the necessary run, he bunts to make that possible.

Throughout the film, short scenes illustrating fan reaction to the team's winning season serve as a Greek chorus to the events in the narrative. The team has succeeded in uniting the diverse peoples of the city of Cleveland in a spirit of optimism. No other baseball film has quite captured the excitement or craziness that occurs when a city is fortunate enough to have a winning sports team. At the end, the fans, the players, and the film audience are united in a celebration of the team's victory. Yet, the celebratory feeling transcends that one game, even that one season. The film celebrates the game itself—not only its history, its lore, and its rituals but also its ability to wrap its audience in a spirit of youthful optimism. Just as Jake Taylor cannot quite let go of his youth and opts for "just one more year in the sun," so the filmgoer looks for baseball to recapture that feeling of youth and glory, for youth passes quickly and the moment of victory is fleeting.

Susan Doll

Reviews
Boxoffice. CXXIV, June, 1989, p. R31.
Chicago Sun-Times. April 7, 1989, p. 39.
Chicago Tribune. April 7, 1989, VII, p. 18.
Films in Review. XL, September, 1989, p. 419.
Jet. LXXVI, April 24, 1989, p. 56.
Los Angeles Times. April 7, 1989, VI, p. 10.
The New Republic. CC, May 8, 1989, p. 26.
The New York Times. April 7, 1989, p. C19.
Sports Illustrated. LXX, Aprpil 17, 1989, p. 84.
Time. CXXXIII, April 24, 1989, p. 78.
Variety. CCCXXXIV, April 12, 1989, p. 21.
The Washington Post. April 7, 1989, p. C1.

MISS FIRECRACKER

Production: Fred Berner; released by Corsair Pictures
Direction: Thomas Schlamme
Screenplay: Beth Henley; based on her play, *The Miss Firecracker Contest*
Cinematography: Arthur Albert
Editing: Peter C. Frank
Production design: Kristi Zea
Art direction: Maher Ahmad
Set decoration: Debra Schutt
Costume design: Molly Maginnis
Sound: Glenn Berkovitz
Music: David Mansfield
Additional music: Homer Denison
MPAA rating: PG
Running time: 102 minutes

Principal characters:

Carnelle Scott	Holly Hunter
Elain Rutledge	Mary Steenburgen
Delmount Williams	Tim Robbins
Popeye Jackson	Alfre Woodard
Mac Sam	Scott Glenn
Tessy Mahoney	Veanne Cox
Miss Blue	Ann Wedgeworth
Benjamin Drapper	Trey Wilson
Missy Mahoney	Amy Wright
Unnamed character	Bert Remsen
Unnamed character	Christine Lahti

Moving beyond its origins as a theatrical production, *Miss Firecracker* joins those relatively uncommon films that capture the quintessential flavor of American life. It does so not through the pickled Technicolor artistry of a Hollywood studio as in *State Fair* (1945), but by blending location shooting in Yazoo City, Mississippi, with outstanding performances by several acclaimed actors against the backdrop of a small town's annual beauty contest. The hopes and frustrations of a spicy collection of personalities simmer together until they erupt in the fireworks of a Fourth of July sky.

Holly Hunter once again plays Carnelle Scott, a role that the Academy Award nominee originated when Pulitzer Prize-winning playwright Beth Henley's *The Miss Firecracker Contest* had a 1984 Off-Broadway run. Carnelle knows that she is referred to as the local "hot tamale," but she wants to break through the typecasting to create another image of herself, both for herself and for those around her. She aims to do so by winning the Miss Firecracker contest, just as her cousin Elain Rutledge (Mary Steenburgen) did years before. She counts on Elain to help her in various ways, including the loan of the red dress that Elain herself wore for her own triumph.

Carnelle also needs other costumes to compete, but when she inquires at the local ladies' shops, she is uniformly turned away, with the salesladies and customers sniggering behind her back as she goes. In desperation, she calls on Popeye Jackson (Alfre Woodard), a black seamstress who stops making bullfrog costumes in order to sew Carnelle's patriotic baton twirler's outfit. Unlike Elain, Popeye does not disappoint Carnelle.

The other major ingredient in this savory stew is Delmount Williams (Tim Robbins), Elain's younger brother, who still loves his sister despite the fact that she had him institutionalized. The film introduces Delmount as he is picking up dead animals from hot county roads for a gimpy old private contractor; the moment inevitably comes when Delmount responds not to the boss's command to get back in the pickup truck but to the call of a passing train. When he arrives back at the old homestead, where only Carnelle now lives, he ransacks it looking for some yet uncovered valuable that his dead mother might have left hidden somewhere.

If Carnelle had not already decided to create a new persona for herself, Delmount would have forced her at least to change her life-style, for he plans to sell the house as quickly as he can. Delmount is not actually unkind to Carnelle, and he cannot hide his vulnerability from Elain, but he is certainly less than Prince Charming to either his relatives or the local ladies. The violence he frequently exhibits threatens to go beyond destruction of property. Yet even such a suspect if not actually reprehensible figure expresses true poetry of the soul as he begins to respond to Popeye's fragile appeal. Delmount's particular weakness is a tendency toward bad dreams, which only Elain knows how to soothe away. As Delmount grows increasingly attracted to Popeye, though, the bad dreams magically disappear; meanwhile, Popeye herself has fallen hopelessly and breathlessly in love. Despite her sturdy outward appearance and unconventional behavior, Popeye gradually takes on an otherworldly charm. Though Delmount and Popeye may be an odd couple, Popeye seems like a fit companion to join Delmount as he goes off to New Orleans in pursuit of a philosophy degree.

While Delmount is plagued by nightmares, Carnelle suffers from memories, or so the film's narrative structure would suggest, for it opens and closes with a disturbing home movie-style image of a parade, which turns out to be the one in which Elain rode triumphant as Miss Firecracker. The key image in this memory shows Carnelle as an ugly little girl in an outgrown cotton dress, minus various teeth and bedecked with a hideous yellow wig hat that makes her resemble a scrawny chicken. Yet the image of Carnelle could only come from Elain's perspective, which means that it is Elain's vision of herself that Carnelle must reject. By film's end, when Carnelle learns that Elain has denied her the use of the red dress and its attendant glory to which she aspired, Carnelle rejects the ugly yellow hat to which Elain would condemn her. Instead, she herself condemns Elain to the entrapment that the red dress represents and which Elain has thus far willingly accepted as her role in life.

Ultimately, only Elain, the shallowest of the four protagonists, remains unchanged, ready to return to her wealthy husband and their suburban life-style despite her announced intention of divorcing him. The lure of expensive beauty creams apparently cannot be denied, nor does she really wish to escape from her "life as a beauty," a topic she actually expounds upon in her keynote speech to the appreciative audience watching the beauty pageant.

Clearly *Miss Firecracker* evokes various concepts and perceptions of beauty, playing off the superficial and the spiritual, the external and the innate. Carnelle is not unloved; apart from Delmount, a carnival worker named Mac Sam (Scott Glenn) also hates to see her make herself unhappy in her pursuit of an unattainable and unworthy goal. He instead urges her to aspire to "eternal grace," however it may come to her. As Carnelle gives herself a chance to shake off the imposed images of her upbringing, she learns to appreciate herself and Elain for what they are each worth. Carnelle's strength of character is what makes Mac Sam love her; in contrast, Elain is loved for the aura of character that she projects. The casting of Alfre Woodard as Popeye also quietly but insistently challenges the audience to realign its measure of attractiveness—despite Woodard's precariously balanced performance that, in marked contrast to her other appearances, often threatens to overstep the bounds of dignity. Together, Popeye and Delmount do achieve dignity and the beauty that comes with it.

Miss Firecracker, in other words, takes a typically feminist issue and deals with it from a different point of view, downplaying the issue as such. Inevitably, though, the oppression of stereotyped concepts of beauty makes itself felt. Carnelle's escape, however, comes from her individual struggle. The fact that she does escape in spite of her lack of support from the woman she most admires and whom she most trusts adds to the story's potential for feminist analysis, but such an analysis comes very much from outside the film, which sticks subtly but insistently to the particularities of Carnelle's situation.

Miss Firecracker not only is director Thomas Schlamme's first feature film but also is the first film released by Corsair Pictures, a new production company led by experienced film director Frank Perry. Schlamme was surrounded by friends during this project; his wife, Christine Lahti, has a cameo, while his partner Fred Berner acts as producer, and he and Hunter have been friends for years. Still, for Schlamme, more accustomed to working in New York City and with past experience directing Bette Midler for the cable station Home Box Office (HBO), *Miss Firecracker* must have presented a major change of pace.

Hunter not only had played Carnelle on stage for a year but also has been friends with Henley for several years and has performed in most of Henley's plays. Yet even Hunter acknowledged that, however well she knew Carnelle from the theater, she herself was older, and that combined with the ability to take the play off the stage and on location changed things for her interpretation of the character. Among her film roles, Hunter's performance in *Miss Firecracker* is her most poignant and her most satisfying thus far, yet she does not overpower the whole. The locale's authentic flavor and the general mix of the acting ensemble would prevent that even if her own restraint did not. Hunter and Steenburgen are native Southerners, which certainly gives them an edge both on accents and on understanding the characters they play. Steenburgen, an Academy Award winner, and Woodard, an Oscar and Emmy award nominee, had already played together in *Cross Creek* (1983). With Delmount, Robbins adds depth to the sort of half-baked character he played in *Bull Durham* (1987). The smaller parts—Trey Wilson's slightly sleazy emcee and Veanne Cox and Amy Wright as two of the more pathetic contestants—are also handled with expertise.

The viewer sees Carnelle begin her quest for the beauty title when she walks off her job at a catfish processing plant. According to Henley, locale determined the image of Carnelle working with the gut-sucker machine that leaves her mucking about in blood and entrails. Scenes such as this one more and more frequently represent one image of the South, but the *locus classicus* of Southern imagery from Hollywood is without question *Gone with the Wind* (1939). Henley captures one of the especial agonies of small-town Southern beauty pageants when she has the winning contestant perform Scarlett O'Hara's most famous soliloquy; Carnelle trumps this laughably poor play, for the film's audience at least, by responding with sincere tears. Her feet may rest in offal, but her soul sees beyond, aided by both cultural and personal memories, neither of which Henley means to condemn, for ultimately Carnelle derives the strength to face these memories from the memories themselves.

Harriet Margolis

Reviews

American Film: Magazine of the Film and Television Arts. XIV, May, 1989, p. 60.
Chicago Tribune. April 28, 1989, VII, p. 43.
The Christian Science Monitor. May 16, 1989, p. 11.
Los Angeles Times. April 28, 1989, VI, p. 16.
The Nation. CCXLVIII, May 15, 1989, p. 677.
The New York Times. April 28, 1989, p. C12.
The New Yorker. LXV, May 29, 1989, p. 103.
Newsweek. CXIII, May 1, 1989, p. 75.
Time. CXXXIII, May 1, 1989, p. 68.
Variety. CCCXXXIV, April 19, 1989, p. 22.

MUSIC BOX

Production: Irwin Winkler for Carolco Productions; released by Tri-Star Pictures
Direction: Constantin Costa-Gavras
Screenplay: Joe Eszterhas
Cinematography: Patrick Blossier
Editing: Joele Van Effenterre
Production design: Jeannine Claudia Oppewall
Art direction: Bill Arnold
Set decoration: Erica Rogalla
Set design: Bill Fosser
Makeup: Steve LaPorte and Dorothy Pearl
Costume design: Rita Salazar
Sound: Pierre Gamet, Gerard Lamps, and William Flageollet
Music: Philippe Sarde
MPAA rating: R
Running time: 123 minutes

Principal characters:
Ann Talbot	Jessica Lange
Mike Laszlo	Armin Mueller-Stahl
Jack Burke	Frederic Forrest
Harry Talbot	Donald Moffat
Mikey Talbot	Lukas Haas
Georgine Wheeler	Cheryl Lynn Bruce
Judge Silver	J. S. Block
Karchy Laszlo	Michael Rooker

Music Box is a compelling drama of the ultimate test of the love between a daughter and her father. Set within the framework of a courtroom thriller, *Music Box* poses the question of how much people really know about their loved ones. When her father, Mike Laszlo (Armin Mueller-Stahl), is accused of being a Nazi sympathizer who committed heinous war crimes in Hungary, Ann Talbot (Jessica Lange), a tough and gifted criminal lawyer, agrees to defend him, despite her lack of experience in immigration law.

Fiercely proud of his adopted country, Laszlo convinces his daughter that the government's attempts to revoke his citizenship are the result of pressure from the Hungarian government for his past anticommunist protests. Ann has known her father all her life and believes he is incapable of committing such atrocities. All she has to do is witness the love he shares with her young son, Mikey Talbot (Lukas Haas).

The prosecuting attorney, Jack Burke (Frederic Forrest), mounts a formidable case against Laszlo, relying primarily on the testimony of several victims who all identify Laszlo as the dreaded Misha of the special branch of Hungary's pro-Nazi military. Employing her savvy as a criminal lawyer, Ann fights to prove her father's innocence. Yet as witness after witness graphically describes the horrors that were inflicted upon them and their loved ones, Ann grows increasingly suspicious of Laszlo's activities during World War II.

Although emotionally moved, Ann succeeds in negating nearly all the witnesses' testimony and accuracy. The government's final witness is near death back in Budapest and the trial moves to Hungary. Ann's case is aided by the anonymous delivery of condemning court papers against the final witness and Ann succeeds in convincing Judge Silver (J. S. Block) to drop the case against her father because of lack of evidence to justify deportation.

A seed of doubt about her father still remains within Ann, however, and before returning to the United States, Ann decides to visit the sister of her father's friend. Canceled checks and his friend's mysterious death strongly indicate that Laszlo was being blackmailed. The sister asks Ann to take the pawn ticket that was part of her brother's few remaining effects and return the item to her. Ann agrees, but as she prepares to leave the apartment, she sees photographs of the woman's brother. Stunned, Ann realizes that the man in the photographs is the man described in the courtroom testimony as Misha's fellow torturer. Ann's world begins to crumble as she realizes that her father is not the man she thought he was.

Upon her return to Chicago, Ann goes to the pawnshop and retrieves the pawned item, a beautiful nineteenth century music box. As she sits in her car listening to the music box's soothing melody, she discovers, hidden deep within its mechanism, incriminating photographs undeniably identifying her father as the accused war criminal. Crushed, Ann confronts Laszlo at his celebration party thrown by her former father-in-law (Donald Moffat) and forbids her father from seeing his grandson again. Then Ann makes the most difficult decision of her life: She turns over the evidence against her father to Burke, thus ensuring Laszlo's deportation and inevitable punishment.

Music Box is a compelling film that succeeds in breaking new cinematic ground in the retelling of the Holocaust. It is a film that does not concentrate on the horrors of war and the suffering of its victims but instead chooses to explore the devastating effects of such horrendous anti-Semitic activities on the families of the aggressors. This is not to imply that the suffering of Gentiles is more significant than that of Jews. It is merely another perspective, an important one that has been explored rather infrequently in film. Unlike Paul Mazursky's *Enemies, A Love Story* (1989; reviewed in this volume), *Music Box* offers new insights into the Holocaust.

Constantin Costa-Gavras, the film's director, insists that *Music Box* is not about vengeance, not a cry for an individual's punishment for acts of inhumanity that were committed years before, but rather an attempt at understanding and discovering how people could have committed such acts of violence. This outrage at inhumanity is a recurrent theme in the best of Costa-Gavras' work, including *Z* (1969), *État de siège* (1973; *State of Siege*) and *Missing* (1982).

Screenwriter Joe Eszterhas, whose parents were refugees who witnessed wartime atrocities committed against not only Jews but all Hungarians as well, was driven to write *Music Box* after following the real-life trial of the Ukrainian-born Cleveland autoworker John Demjanjuk, the man accused by the Israeli government as having committed countless crimes against humanity as Ivan the Terrible of Treblinka. Eszterhas astutely uses the historical crimes but unfortunately allows himself to fall into the trap of succumbing to clichéd Hollywood plot devices, especially in the latter third of the film. If the film's ending seems at all contrived, it is because Eszterhas loses the focus of the story and resorts to emphasizing the melodramatic suffering of the heroine.

Thanks to Costa-Gavras' superb direction, *Music Box* feels more like a thriller than a mere courtroom melodrama. The scenes within the courtroom have an urgency to them that aids their function as tools of revelation. Costa-Gavras has been criticized in the past for his somewhat heavy-handed approach to filmmaking, but, in the case of *Music Box*, this approach works to the film's advantage to have the main character lag slightly behind the audience in her realizations about her father. That is not to say that *Music Box* is an easy film to view. Information is planted so subtly at times, such as when Ann's father-in-law makes the comment, "Sometimes an apple does fall far from the tree," that unless the viewer follows along carefully, it is possible not to grasp fully the consequences of the outcome.

It is to the director's credit that he chose not to succumb to conventional Hollywood exploitation of depicting wartime violence with the use of flashbacks. The horror of these wartime atrocities is conveyed solely by the courtroom testimony of the victims, thus strengthening their impact. The faces, the eyes, the trembling voices that mark the pain of remembrance are all unforgettable.

Jessica Lange has fought hard against critics' early dismissal of her as simply another pretty, fluffy blonde. In *Music Box*, Lange attempts to make her beauty more accessible than in other films, such as her film debut in the ill-fated Dino De Laurentiis remake of *King Kong* (1976) and her more auspicious turn as the mysterious Angel of Death in Bob Fosse's *All That Jazz* (1979). She has dyed her hair a nondescript brown, and, even though Ann is a successful lawyer, the minimal amount of makeup used, combined with harsh lighting, gives the character a somewhat weary look that is reminiscent of blue-collar workers, a reflection of her immigrant roots. In addition to the character's physicality, Lange imbues Ann with the subtle nuances of a woman caught between Old World tradition and New World influences, between familial expectations and social demands. A simple gesture such as a slight lowering of her eyes when in the presence of her father offers an instant understanding of the character of Ann. Even Lange's voice functions as an emotional Geiger counter, a reflection of Ann's struggle against the gradual realization that her beloved father is a true Jekyll and Hyde character.

Lange has managed to build an impressive career by constantly testing her talents and refusing to give in to the comforts of stardom. She is a demanding perfectionist who has at times been chastised for her on-set seriousness, as if that were a legitimate condemning defect. Lange candidly admits that she is not willing to devote time away from her family to another project like Taylor Hackford's embarrassing *Everybody's All American* (1988). In 1983, Lange became the first actress in thirty-five years to receive two different Academy Award nominations in the same year, one for her starring role in *Frances* (1983) as well as her Oscar-winning supporting role in *Tootsie* (1983). Lange's performance in *Music Box* has garnered the actress her fifth Academy Award nomination.

The acting throughout *Music Box* is consistently impressive, with the sole exception of Michael Rooker as Ann's brother, Karchy. His performance is too theatrical, especially in comparison to the brilliant subtlety of both Lange and the fine German actor, Armin Mueller-Stahl, who brings a reserved Old World texture to the character of Ann's father.

Patricia Ann Kowal

Reviews
American Film: Magazine of the Film and Television Arts. XV, February, 1990, p. 51.
Chicago Tribune. January 19, 1990, VII, p. 31.
The Christian Science Monitor. December 29, 1989, p. 10.
Los Angeles Times. December 25, 1989, VI, p. 2.
Movieline. I, January, 1990, p. 32.
The Nation. CCL, January 1, 1990, p. 30.
The New Republic. CCII, February 5, 1990, p. 26.
The New York Times. December 25, 1989, p. C49.
The New Yorker. LXV, January 8, 1990, p. 90.
Premiere. III, January, 1990, p. 52.
Time. CXXXV, January 8, 1990, p. 76.
Variety. CCCXXXVII, December 27, 1989, p. 10.

MY LEFT FOOT

Origin: Ireland
Released: 1989
Released in U.S.: 1989
Production: Noel Pearson for Ferndale/Granada; released by Miramax Films
Direction: Jim Sheridan
Screenplay: Jim Sheridan and Shane Connaughton; based on the book by Christy
  Brown
Cinematography: Jack Conroy
Editing: J. Patrick Duffner
Art direction: Austen Spriggs
Set decoration: Shirley Lynch
Makeup: Ken Jennings
Costume design: Joan Bergin
Sound: Ron Davis
Music: Elmer Bernstein
MPAA rating: R
Running time: 103 minutes

Principal characters:
Christy Brown	Daniel Day-Lewis (AA)
Mrs. Brown	Brenda Fricker (AA)
Lord Castlewelland	Cyril Cusack
Mary	Ruth McCabe
Dr. Eileen Cole	Fiona Shaw
Mr. Brown	Ray McAnally
Young Christy Brown	Hugh O'Conor

Among films of its genre, *My Left Foot* is one of the most successful because it is one of the least manipulative. Inspirational films about men or women who actualize their human potential despite great physical affliction often tend to be sentimental instead of perceptive and tough. The protagonists' victories in such films as *The Miracle Worker* (1962), *Coming Home* (1978), and *Children of a Lesser God* (1986), among others, can be profoundly affecting if the representations of characters and obstacles are convincing.

In *My Left Foot* there is great pleasure to be had when the young Christy Brown (Hugh O'Conor), trapped in a body that will not do what he wants and perceived as mentally defective by most of those with whom he has contact, through force of will, spells "mother" on the wooden floor with a piece of chalk held between his toes as family members stand by gaping. The adult Christy Brown (Daniel Day-Lewis) goes on to become a successful painter and author.

Such victories would not have the impact they do if character and situation had been romanticized or made more palatable for the general public. As depicted by O'Conor, Day-Lewis, and director Jim Sheridan, the cerebral palsy that afflicts Christy Brown is anything but pretty. Day-Lewis' body twitches, his face contorts into grotesque configurations, his voice produces unpleasant and muddled sound instead of articulate speech, and saliva drips down the side of his mouth and onto his lapel to glisten there conspicuously. The disease's representation is clinically accurate and thoroughly credible.

Possibly adding to the viewer's confidence in the story is the knowledge that Christy Brown actually existed and that the screenplay is an adaptation of his autobiographical first book. Moreover, one is convinced while watching the unfolding narrative that both the author and the filmmaker have been unrelentingly honest in their exploration and expression of the facts.

This veracity is reflected in thoroughly human character portraits, showing flaws that, though severe, do not prevent a loving acceptance of the individuals portrayed. A fine example is Christy's wonderfully clearsighted, although emotional, perception of his father, a sometimes unemployed Dublin bricklayer. Mr. Brown (Ray McAnally), after doubting the existence of intellectual capabilities in his son, witnesses a demonstration of Christy's ability to think and to write; he then throws the boy over his shoulder and carries him into the neighborhood pub to declare proudly that Christy is his son. This same father, upon learning that his unmarried daughter is pregnant, responds with classic callousness, causing Christy to bellow and thrash around in a formidable display of fury. Christy is able to censure his father's arrogant intolerance and at the same time acknowledge the reinforcement and love that he provided.

It is the mother, though, who contributes from his very young years the nurturance that enables him, despite his physical handicap, to believe in his own worth. In an early scene, Mrs. Brown (Brenda Fricker), pregnant and close to term, lifts the grown boy Christy over her shoulder like a sixty-pound sack of potatoes and carries him up the long winding stairway to his bedroom; she sweats and grimaces with the effort but does not reveal even the slightest trace of annoyance. Christy may have been, but was never allowed to feel like, a burden to his mother, who gave him loving attention when he needed it and was the first to take seriously his efforts to communicate with language.

Christy acknowledges other instances of reinforcement. In a game of spin the bottle, when a pretty young girl's spin points to Christy, she may feel revolted by the thought of playing out her turn, but, instead of evading her duty, she rises, crosses to kiss Christy's cheek, and says that he has nice eyes. He is delighted and becomes awakened to sexual possibilities.

Christy's desires become more focused after he meets the doctor responsible for bringing him to public notice. Doctor Eileen Cole (Fiona Shaw), after seeing an example of Christy's artwork, becomes his mentor: She teaches him to speak with greater clarity and to use his body with more skill and arranges an exhibition of his artwork at a reputable gallery. Christy falls in love with this patient, kind, and attractive woman and is devastated when he learns that she is engaged. His inner turmoil thoroughly upsets a celebratory dinner in his honor, at which he attempts to congratulate Eileen but cannot hold back the regret and bitterness that he feels.

The ninth of twenty-two children (thirteen survived), Christy never lacked for companionship: He recognizes the support given by his brothers, who took him with them, allowed him to play their games, and did not make him feel unwanted. One younger brother eagerly agrees to help Christy write his first book. The example of the mother, evidently, had its influence.

Christy's main enemy was not people, or even his Dublin family's often dire poverty, or the Catholic Church, which added its own strictures to those already provided by economic necessity—these all seemed tolerable because of the generally good spirits of the people around him; rather, his enemy was the disease itself, which constantly presented challenges, one of the most significant, perhaps, was the challenge to sexual acceptance. The narrative is framed as flashbacks from a gala benefit at which he will appear; he is being watched by a nurse, Mary (Ruth McCabe), until it is time to present him to the assembly. At first, she is aloof, and he is rude to her; during the long wait, however, she reads his book, gets to know him, and eventually responds to his pleas for the only kind of acceptance he has been denied.

Despite the millstone of an intolerable disease, Christy is eventually able to call Hamlet a cripple, because Hamlet cannot act until it is too late. Christy was not so unfortunate: He lived a life of great accomplishment, experienced a range of feeling beyond the ordinary, and knew the richness of various human relationships. The film is a celebration of his triumphs, and the viewer delights to be a part of it.

The outstanding films about human accomplishment despite physical disability have aroused strong identification with protagonists who suffer from blindness, deafness, cerebral palsy, paraplegia, and the like. Although most people do not know these afflictions firsthand, life offers some form of resistance to everyone, and viewers welcome the opportunity to empathize and to enjoy vicarious victories over forces that are destructive and seem at first irresistible; this is especially true when those victories and obstacles are presented with the accuracy, insight, and skill apparent in *My Left Foot*.

The integrity of this fine film is the result of the splendid work of Irish stage director Jim Sheridan in his directorial debut for the cinema and the inspired performances of his cast. Sheridan has put together an almost seamless film; technique is not obtrusive, and the viewer can focus easily on the extraordinary story. Day-Lewis, who is building a reputation as one of England's most versatile young actors, has never been better. He is meticulous in the way he captures the progressive improvement in Christy's speech, consistent in sustaining the physical characteristics of a cerebral palsy victim, and dynamic in conveying the intense, often explosive, emotional life of the character. His performance in this film was deservedly awarded the Academy Award for Best Actor and Best Actor honors at the Montreal Film Festival and by both New York and Los Angeles film critics.

Outstanding, also, are Fricker (who won an Academy Award for Best Supporting Actress) as the mother, who is a stalwart rock of love, and, in support, Fiona Shaw and Ruth McCabe. Shaw, as Doctor Cole, clearly suffers with her patient and revels in his triumphs. McCabe provides the film's perfect lyric conclusion when, after relative indifference, she comes to accept Christy as the man she loves. *My Left Foot* is one of those rare films that makes audiences, even though they are at the cinema and not the legitimate theater, want literally to applaud its achievement—and they do.

Cono Robert Marcazzo

Reviews

Films in Review. XL, December, 1989, p. 616.
Lancet. September 2, 1989, p. 553.
Los Angeles Times. November 10, 1989, VII, p. 1.
The New Republic. CCI, November 27, 1989, p. 24.
New York Magazine. XX, November 13, 1989, p. 109.
The New York Times. November 10, 1989, p. C10.
The New Yorker. LXV, October 2, 1989, p. 98.
Newsweek. CXIV, November 27, 1989, p. 90.
The Spectator. CCLXIII, August 26, 1989, p. 30.
Time. CXXXIV, November 6, 1989, p. 84.
Variety. CCCXXXVI, August 23, 1989, p. 31.

MYSTERY TRAIN

Production: Jim Stark for JVC; released by Orion Classics
Direction: Jim Jarmusch
Screenplay: Jim Jarmusch
Cinematography: Robby Müller
Editing: Melody London
Production design: Dan Bishop
Set decoration: Dianna Freas
Special effects: Gary King
Makeup: Meredith Soupios
Costume design: Carol Wood
Sound: Drew Kunin, Robert Hein, and Eugene Gearty
Music: John Lurie
MPAA rating: R
Running time: 110 minutes

Principal characters:
Jun .... Masatoshi Nagase
Mitzuko .... Youki Kudoh
Luisa .... Nicoletta Braschi
DeeDee .... Elizabeth Bracco
Johnny .... Joe Strummer
Will Robinson .... Rick Aviles
Charlie........................... Steve Buscemi
Night clerk.................. Screamin' Jay Hawkins
Bellboy............................... Cinqué Lee
News vendor .... Sy Richardson
Man in diner........................ Tom Noonan
Radio D. J. .... (voice of Tom Waits)

Jim Jarmusch's first four films present strong family resemblances together with distinct formal strategies. All of them feature marginal, anomic characters, who drift through various encounters without learning or changing much on the way. The number of these central characters has increased from one in *Permanent Vacation* (1980) to half a dozen in *Mystery Train*, and they have become leavened by more upbeat characters such as Roberto (Roberto Benigni) in *Down by Law* (1986) and, to a lesser extent, Mitzuko (Youki Kudoh) and Luisa (Nicoletta Braschi) in *Mystery Train*. The number of important foreign characters has increased, too: none in *Permanent Vacation*; the Hungarian Eva (Eszter Balint) in *Stranger Than Paradise* (1984); the Italian Roberto in *Down by Law* (together with a brief appearance by Nicoletta Braschi); and, in *Mystery Train*, not only Italian Luisa and Japanese Mitzuko but also Japanese Jun (Masatoshi Nagase) and English Johnny (Joe Strummer). Jarmusch has kept more and more collaborators from film to film, most notably John Lurie, who played a key supporting role in *Permanent Vacation* and central roles in both *Stranger Than Paradise* and *Down by Law*; although he does not appear on-screen in *Mystery Train*, he wrote the music for it, as he did at least in part for the other three films.

The settings of Jarmusch's films have varied from New York City alone in *Permanent Vacation* to New York, Cleveland, and Florida in *Stranger Than Paradise*, New Orleans and other parts of Louisiana in *Down by Law*, and Memphis, Tennessee, in *Mystery Train*. Stylistically, *Permanent Vacation* is the most eclectic of the four films: Shot in color, it opens with slow-motion scenes of busy streets, and it resorts at times to a voice-over monologue from its central character. *Stranger Than Paradise*, in black and white, consists of a series of continuous scenes separated by blackouts. *Down by Law*, also in black and white, contained no reaction shots and, according to Jarmusch, was filmed entirely with a normal focal-length lens. (Other lenses commonly used are short focal-length, or wide-angle, lenses which exaggerate depth; long focal-length, or telescopic, lenses which enlarge objects and compress depth; and zoom lenses, which can range continuously over different focal lengths.) *Mystery Train*, which returns to color, presents in succession three episodes that are gradually revealed to be taking place at the same time.

All three episodes are located in part in the seedy, old Arcade Hotel, disused in reality but revived by Jarmusch for the occasion. (He also revived Memphis' old train station for the film's opening sequence.) The night clerk (Screamin' Jay Hawkins) and bellboy (Cinqué Lee, brother of filmmaker Spike Lee) provide offbeat and pungent interludes throughout. Each hotel room that appears in the film is decorated with a large (and different) portrait of Elvis Presley.

In the first episode, "Far from Yokohama," Jun and Mitzuko arrive in Memphis by train and proceed to tour the city's musical landmarks, walking everywhere with a large suitcase slung on a stick between them. Mitzuko favors Elvis, while Jun prefers Carl Perkins. At nightfall they go to the Arcade Hotel, where Mitzuko tips the bellboy a plum and Jun brings out his camera for the first time—to record their room. Because Jun perpetually looks glum and speaks only in curt phrases, Mitzuko tries to cheer him up by putting lipstick on his mouth and then smearing it with an energetic kiss; he explains, however, that, despite his exterior, he is really very happy inside. They go to bed, and Mitzuko is upset because Jun makes love glumly and curtly. In the morning, Jun insists that Mitzuko make room in the suitcase for the hotel towel, which he says it is the custom to take. They hear a gunshot from somewhere nearby but take little notice.

The second episode, "A Ghost," begins with Luisa at the airport. She was planning to fly back to Rome with her husband's coffin but has to wait a day because of a technicality with the flight documents. She spends the day wandering around the city. In one encounter, she allows a persuasive news vendor (Sy Richardson) to sell her a stack of magazines. Later, in a café, a drifter (Tom Noonan) approaches her with a story of having given a ride to Elvis' ghost, who presented him with a comb that he was to pass on to a "lady from Rome" in return for twenty dollars. Luisa hands over twenty dollars in order to get rid of him, but, when she finds him lying in wait outside the café, she takes refuge in the nearby Arcade Hotel. There she bumps into loquacious DeeDee (Elizabeth Bracco), who has just broken up with her boyfriend and has tried unsuccessfully to persuade the night clerk to let her have a room on the cheap. Luisa invites DeeDee to share a room. DeeDee chatters away, keeping Luisa awake. Then, after DeeDee has fallen asleep, Elvis' ghost appears to Luisa. In the morning, as the still sleepless Luisa tells DeeDee what happened, they hear a gunshot.

The third episode, "Lost in Space," begins with Johnny in a black bar. He is obstreperously drunk and playing with a handgun, having just lost his job and his girlfriend, who turns out to be DeeDee. A customer calls Johnny's black workmate, Will Robinson (Rick Aviles), who arrives at the bar with DeeDee's brother Charlie (Steve Buscemi). They persuade Johnny to go with them in Will's van, but he insists on stopping at a liquor store, where he shoots the clerk and grabs two bottles of bourbon. The three then drive around town taking turns at the bourbon as Will and Charlie try to decide what to do: Johnny is too drunk to care. Eventually they go to the Arcade Hotel, where the night clerk, who knows Will, stows them in a decrepit spare room. In the morning, Johnny is overcome with self-disgust and tries to shoot himself; as the other two men struggle with him, Charlie is accidentally shot in the leg.

In a brief epilogue, Jun and Mitzuko, and then DeeDee, board a train; Luisa is back at the airport; Will and Johnny hoist groaning Charlie onto the back of the van and drive off alongside the railroad tracks on which the train is now departing.

Once again Jarmusch has made an entertaining film out of what seem to be unpromising materials. As in his previous films, there is little narrative continuity: Each episode itself consists of a series of barely connected episodes, and the few bursts of action, such as the two shootings, arise unexpectedly, almost arbitrarily. Most films about anomic characters drifting through life are less accessible—or, from another viewpoint, less ingratiating—than those of Jarmusch. They range from the deliberately fragmentary pseudonarratives of James Benning—*8½ × 11* (1974), *11 × 14* (1977), *Him and Me* (1982)—to such intensely serious works as Wim Wenders' *Im Laut der Zeit* (1976; *Kings of the Road*) Chris Petit's *Radio On* (1979), and Jon Jost's *Bell Diamond* (1986). The one recent film of this type that did offer quirky humor was *Candy Mountain* (1988), directed by Robert Frank and Rudy Wurlitzer, but its deadpan drifter became involved in a quest—an unlikely enterprise for any of Jarmusch's protagonists, who seem unaware of the future and incapable of a sustained plan. When they do break out of passivity to make something happen, they invariably act on impulse. The pattern was already set at the end of Jarmusch's first film when Allie (Chris Parker) suddenly steals a car, sells it, and buys a boat passage to France. This insistence on the present moment, divorced from responsibility to past or future, may account at least in part for the popularity of Jarmusch's films.

Although *Mystery Train* was generally well received by the critics, many of whom were enthusiastic, the film does reveal the weaknesses of Jarmusch's predilection for loosely connected, or entirely disconnected, scenes. However amusing or surprising such scenes may be, their sheer quantity puts them at risk of seeming arbitrary and gratuitous. For example, the scenes involving the persuasive magazine selling and the three men in the decrepit hotel room can cause a viewer to become impatient. At the same time, other scenes stand out with exceptional force and clarity, such as Luisa explaining her delay on the telephone in loud and carefully enunciated Italian. Best of all, perhaps, is the sequence in which Will, Johnny, and Charlie drive aimlessly around Memphis at night, not knowing what on earth to do about the shooting of the liquor store clerk. Paradoxically, this passage of disconnection from past and future is the most sustained sequence in the whole film.

The cast is almost uniformly excellent, since it is difficult to distinguish between one's responses to the players and to their roles. Braschi and Hawkins stand out in large part because their roles are the most poised and positive; yet Steve Buscemi gives a memorable performance as the nervous, vacillating, and unlucky Charlie. It is a tribute to Jarmusch's skill that he manages to bring such a diversity of roles— along with the cityscape of Memphis—into the service of his wry vision.

William Johnson

Reviews
The Christian Science Monitor. December 1, 1989, p. 11.
Film Comment. XXV, July, 1989, p. 19.
The Hollywood Reporter. May 16, 1989, p. 6.
Insight. V, November 27, 1989, p. 60.
Los Angeles Times. December 20, 1989, VI, p. 4.
The Nation. CCXLIX, December 11, 1989, p. 726.
The New Republic. CCI, December 11, 1989, p. 24.
New Woman. XIX, December, 1989, p. 35.
The New York Times. September 29, 1989, p. C16.
Newsweek. CXIV, December 4, 1989, p. 78.
Variety. CCCXXXV, May 17, 1989, p. 33.

THE NAVIGATOR
An Odyssey Across Time

Origin: Australia and New Zealand
Released: 1988
Released in U.S.: 1989
Production: John Maynard and Gary Hannam; released by Circle Releasing
    Corporation
Direction: Vincent Ward
Screenplay: Vincent Ward, Kely Lyons, and Geoff Chapple
Cinematography: Geoffrey Simpson
Editing: John Scott
Production design: Sally Campbell
Art direction: Mike Becroft
Special effects: Paul Nichola
Makeup: Marjory Hamlin
Costume design: Glenys Jackson
Music: Davood A. Tabrizi
MPAA rating: PG
Running time: 92 minutes

> *Principal characters:*
> Griffin.......................... Hamish McFarlane
> Connor .... Bruce Lyons
> Arno.............................. Chris Haywood
> Searle .... Marshall Napier
> Ulf................................... Noel Appleby
> Martin .... Paul Livingston
> Linnet .... Sarah Pierse

To take fantastic story material and make it not only compelling but also highly credible, requires an unusual degree of conviction on the part of its creators. Conviction—or faith—is also at the core of this first Australia-New Zealand co-production, in which the medieval world collides, imaginatively and excitingly, with our own.

An unusual ability to visualize a particular world and mindset, to identify with it seemingly from the inside and bring it all vividly to an audience, are among the qualities that distinguish director Vincent Ward in what is only his second feature film. He brings to bear formal training as a painter and sculptor, and film experience as an art director. Even at this stage of his career, Ward gives every evidence of becoming such a distinctive cinematic stylist—as is, for example, David Lynch—that it becomes unlikely that even the odd scene from one of his films could be confused with the work of any other director. Earlier works by the thirty-three-year-old New Zealander include the dramatic documentaries *A State of Siege* (which he made at the age of twenty-one) and *In Spring One Plants Alone* (1982). Typifying his total immersion in a project, Ward actually lived with a family in their primitive and remote Maori village for two years while making the latter film. He moved into dramatic features with the 1984 release *Vigil*, which saw a harsh New Zealand farming life through the eyes of a withdrawn and vengeful eleven-year-old girl. From the documentaries through *The Navigator*, Ward has amassed an impressive roster of awards and film festival prizes.

As *The Navigator: An Odyssey Across Time* opens, title cards recall how the Black Death decimated entire European populations. It is 1348, and the people of an isolated mining village in Cumbria, England, have good cause to fear that even their remoteness will not save them. A young boy, Griffin (Hamish McFarlane), who is gifted with second sight, has glimpsed darkly puzzling fragments in his seizurelike visions: a cross shimmering underwater, floating coffins, a body falling from a high church steeple. Signs and portents are an accepted part of these villagers' lives, so they do not easily dismiss the boy's account. Then, Griffin's elder brother Connor (Bruce Lyons), a villager widely admired and one of very few to have traveled in the larger world outside, returns from an extended journey with tales of horror and devastation, of roads choked with panic-stricken refugees in desperate flight. His story is soon proven when ships filled with plague victims attempt to land nearby, and the equally panicked Cumbrians believe that they have no choice but to repulse the landing, even to the point of setting ships ablaze and dispatching anyone who tries to swim ashore.

Griffin determines the meaning of his visions to be that the village's salvation will depend upon immediately undertaking a mission to raise a newly forged cross of their Cumbrian copper on the spire of a distant cathedral. Together with the somewhat reluctant Connor, he leads a small expedition into the deep caverns beneath the local quarry. It is at this point that the mitered edges of past and present, reality and imagination, overlap with great visual skill but more than a little story confusion. Such is the force and flow of the cinematic image that audiences take what follows as literal story events, rather than what it is clearly shown and stated to be: products of a longer trance into which Griffin falls. (Despite the transition here from monochrome to color, this point has still been lost on nearly all of the film's reviewers.) Using an unlikely rock-breaking contraption that resembles a horizontal catapult, the miners tunnel deep into the cavern walls, finally breaking through—into the sewers of modern day Auckland, New Zealand.

Upon reaching the surface, they are greeted by a panoramic view of the city, lit up at night by (to their medieval eyes) a hundred thousand candles. Yet this inspiring, heavenly vista soon gives way to a series of hellish, frightening trials that the band must overcome if they are to complete their mission before dawn. For men with no concept of cars or trucks, traversing a busy superhighway at night, in one piece, proves harrowing and nearly fatal. One of the band, a rotund, comical man named Ulf (Noel Appleby) cannot make the crossing and—to his great distress—is instructed to remain behind. The group must then cross a harbor in a pilfered boat, running afoul of a submarine en route, before reaching the city proper. There the band splits up: Connor, on his own, to scout out the sought-for cathedral; the others to locate a forge where they might cast their cross. The miner Searle (Marshall Napier), by now convinced that he must be the unknown figure fated to fall to his death in the boy's (ongoing) visions, becomes a hard, antagonistic taskmaster to Griffin. Averting disaster seems to rest almost entirely in the hands of this clairvoyant child.

Following other encounters, the group is finally reunited to complete its mission, the outcome of which remains in doubt until the very end. Back in the Cumbrian caverns of 1348, Griffin convinces the awestruck miners of their success. It is important to him that the village at large become convinced of this too. Dawn arrives aboveground, and the bell of a distant cathedral tolls. In a "twist" ending that resolves the cryptic pieces of Griffin's dream, the audience learns that the village has indeed been spared, but not without cost.

Contrasts of historical period and point of view in films, especially in a time travel context, are usually served up for easy humor or adventure (for example, 1979's *Time After Time* and the *Back to the Future* series). Occasionally, filmmakers will take a serious and thoughtful dramatic approach, as in the 1984 release *Iceman*. *The Navigator* presents viewers with a more curious combination: It has the style and sensibility of a European "art" film, yet it is often shot and edited like a thriller.

Ward makes expert use of the tricks and techniques of modern cinema: insistent flashback fragments, flash-forwards, quick cuts, repeated shots offering contrasting views on the same action. Effective sound montage underscores action scenes and the way the city must be a daunting information overload to the travelers. At its ninety-two-minute running time, the film feels tight and is composed of standout sequences. The grippingly suspenseful and visually striking action set piece—a perilous attempt to winch the newly forged cross into place atop the high church steeple—in which Griffin's premonitory flashes finally come true, has a subjective camera swerving around corners in a frantic race up church-tower stairs, finding disturbing, height-emphasizing angles on the action along the building exterior, and placing the audience right there with key characters sure to come to grief on the treacherous, rotted-out scaffolding.

The primacy of the visual in the film is played out almost to a fault. Geoffrey Simpson's brilliant camerawork—stark, high-contrast monochrome that gives an old lithographic quality to the medieval scenes (in their depiction of the period, they are as convincing or memorable as anything in Ingmar Bergman's 1958 classic *The Seventh Seal*) and a dreamy, electric palette for the latter-day color scenes—remains the centerpiece. Ward can hold the audience's attention with a shot of merely a burning torch falling, end over end, down a deep canyon wall. He can also show modern machinery seen the way his medieval adventurers see it: as monstrous, malevolent apparitions. (The "battle" with the "sea monster" sub has fear, grandeur, and film poetry to it.) Alternately, in the film's emphasis on design, and in an overstated scene like that of Connor's terrified ride while pinned to the front of an elevated train, Ward leaves himself open to the same criticism that has dogged most of director Ridley Scott's career—that he is willing to subordinate everything else to the achievement of maximum visual impact.

Still, *The Navigator* does have more going for it than the purely visual. The beautiful sequence in which the medievals forge their cross, with the aid of some skeptical foundry workers, is one that even atheists could find inspiring. Themes of faith (transcending any simple specifics of religion), sacrifice, and an enviable sense of community lost to modern man broaden and deepen the travelers' quest. Ward's cast (which includes some nonprofessional actors) convincingly inhabit their roles, building audience interest and identification despite the minimal character definition provided them by the rather thin script. McFarlane's Griffin is perfectly up to the challenge of carrying the film, oddly melding a child's innocence with a preternatural wisdom. His own journey, from the butt of other children's jokes in the opening scene, to someone commanding the full respect of adults, to village savior, parallels the wonders that he sees.

Griffin's visions, so vividly depicted in the film, provide a window to the present. As such, replete with references that can mean nothing to the men of Griffin's time, they are far too detailed and too real to pass for dreams. It is also curious how the modern characters whom they encounter take them (in their hooded robes and candle-powered miners' helmets) unquestioningly in stride; for their part, the medievals react to the modern world with appropriate awe or terror, always accepting it simply on their own terms, but seem to ignore anything that has no immediate bearing on their mission. There are coincidences and stretched believability within the dream and factual gaps outside it. Then again, dreams or visions are generally exempt from such concerns. In the end, Griffin's dreamed quest is shown to be as valid and efficacious as any actual trip across great distances and the intervening centuries. Director Ward has succeeded admirably in his declared goal of creating "an authentic legend."

Jordan Fox

Reviews
Chicago Tribune. August 11, 1989, VII, p. 46.
The Christian Science Monitor. July 21, 1989, p. 10.
The Hollywood Reporter. March 30, 1989, p. 4.
Los Angeles Times. April 5, 1989, VI, p. 5.
The New York Times. June 28, 1989, p. C17.
Newsweek. CXIII, April 17, 1989, p. 72.
Rolling Stone. June 1, 1989, p. 36.
Variety. CCCXXXI, May 11, 1989, p. 28.
The Village Voice. July 4, 1989, p. 72.

NEW YORK STORIES

Production: Jack Rollins, Charles H. Joffe, and Robert Greenhut for Touchstone
   Pictures; released by Buena Vista
MPAA rating: PG
Running time: 130 minutes

"Life Lessons"
Production: Barbara DeFina
Direction: Martin Scorcese
Screenplay: Richard Price
Cinematography: Nestor Almendros
Editing: Thelma Schoonmaker
Production design: Kristi Zea
Art direction: Wray Steven Graham
Set decoration: Nina Ramsey and Dave Weinman
Costume design: John Dunn
Sound: Bruce Pross and Tony Martinez

> *Principal characters:*
> | | |
> |---|---|
> | Lionel Dobie | Nick Nolte |
> | Paulette | Rosanna Arquette |
> | Philip Fowler | Patrick O'Neal |
> | Reuben Toro | Jesse Borego |

"Life Without Zoe"
Production: Fred Roos and Fred Fuchs
Direction: Francis Coppola
Screenplay: Francis Coppola and Sofia Coppola
Cinematography: Vittorio Storaro
Editing: Barry Malkin
Production design: Dean Tavoularis
Art direction: Speed Hopkins
Set decoration: George DeTitta, Jr., and Dave Weinman
Costume design: Sofia Coppola
Music: Carmine Coppola and Kid Creole and the Coconuts

> *Principal characters:*
> | | |
> |---|---|
> | Zoe | Heather McComb |
> | Charlotte | Talia Shire |
> | Claudio | Giancarlo Giannini |
> | Hector | Don Novello |
> | Princess Soroya | Carole Bouquet |

"Oedipus Wrecks"
Production: Robert Greenhut
Direction: Woody Allen
Screenplay: Woody Allen
Cinematography: Sven Nykvist
Editing: Susan E. Morse
Production design: Santo Loquasto
Art direction: Speed Hopkins
Set decoration: Susan Bode and Dave Weinman
Special effects supervision: Stuart Robertson and Joel Hynek
Special visual effects: R/Greenberg Associates, Nancy Bernstein, Joseph V. Iannuzzi, Patrick McDonough, and Bruce Morosohk
Makeup: Fern Buchner
Costume design: Jeffrey Kurland
Music recording: Roy B. Yokelson

> *Principal characters:*
> Sheldon .... Woody Allen
> Psychiatrist .... Marvin Chatinover
> Mother .... Mae Questel
> Lisa .... Mia Farrow
> Treva .... Julie Kavner

In sports, reputations are not very often made in all-star games, they are carried to them. This tends to be true of *New York Stories*, a kind of all-star game of modern film directors, featuring short films (of about forty minutes each) by Martin Scorcese, Francis Ford Coppola, and Woody Allen. The format is intriguing: Each artist contributes an independent segment reflecting his own style and vision of New York City life and people, and the result is an anthology film that shows a wide range of city subjects and also allows the audience to compare some of the strengths and weaknesses of the individual directors. Scorcese's contribution, however, is the only unqualified all-star performance here, and, although the primary purpose of this collective film is not to separate contenders from pretenders, *New York Stories* merely acknowledges the cinematic skills of Coppola and Allen while it confirms and displays those of Scorcese.

Each of the segments focuses on characters who are unpleasant or objectionable in one way or another but who are redeemed—or at least made worthy of the audience's interest and sympathy—by some other trait: desperate humor in Allen's segment, adolescent charm in Coppola's, and intense artistic imagination in Scorcese's. As in so many of his other films, the main character of Scorcese's "Life Lessons" is menacing. Nick Nolte brilliantly portrays Lionel Dobie as a painter in a love-hate relationship with his work, himself, his live-in assistant, and the art world. The suffering of the artist is one of the great clichés of the romantic era, and, much to their credit, Scorcese and Nolte explore as well as adore this image. In some respects, "Life Lessons" is about the bankruptcy of the romantic notion of the artist. Dobie is more than a maker of imaginative fantasies: He is a liar, unable or unwilling to speak honestly with the woman he says he loves. He is more than an energetic action painter: He is an incipient psychopath, ready to attack a canvas or a rival in love. The magnificent erotic obsession that animates him is at least implausible and inscrutable and at worst a degrading fraud. Paulette (Rosanna Arquette) is Dobie's assistant and the object of his servile attention. She does not, however, seem worthy of this attention, being very insecure, immature, often cruel, and, in general, not the type of muse usually associated with a great artist. Dobie wants to prove that Paulette is all-important to him, but she is only an object of manipulation or unfulfilled desire, a source of creative irritation. The closing shot of the film is cool and ironic, showing Dobie moving on to his next pretty young conquest, who will be Paulette's replacement and, as the euphemism goes, stretch his canvas.

Ending the film with a reminder of the capacity of the romantic artist to be a lecher or a Svengali, though, does not completely undermine the sense of Dobie's heroic stature. Dobie is compromised by relentless egotism and intense passion that make him incapable of lasting personal and social attachments, but his artistry is nevertheless a triumph. "Life Lessons" dramatizes the process and the price of a certain kind of artistic creation in extraordinary detail, and the repeated images of Dobie spreading paint on a huge canvas are unforgettable not only because they are visually exciting but also because they are accompanied by almost painfully loud but perfectly chosen musical selections. Procol Harum's mysterious "Whiter Shade of Pale" and a frenetic live version of Bob Dylan's "Like a Rolling Stone" are the auditory equivalents of Dobie's action paintings and also add a subtle nostalgic note to the film. Dobie's work is set in the postmodern world of vapid performance artists (Paulette is in love with one) and art-for-profit collectors (with whom Dobie must deal), but his approach to art and the music with which he surrounds himself recall the 1960's, perhaps the last great flourishing of romanticism. Scorcese identifies himself with Dobie to a certain extent—note, for example, the extremely active camera motion that Scorcese uses to convey but also duplicate Dobie's attack on his canvas—and perhaps shares Dobie's sense of distress, vulnerability, and prideful achievement. More than a lion (as he nicknames himself in the film), Lionel Dobie is Blake's Tiger, "burning bright,/ In the forests of the night," and Scorcese knows and shows that this fire is illuminating and consuming.

"Life Lessons" is much like Scorcese's great earlier films, especially *Taxi Driver* (1976) and *Raging Bull* (1980), both of which it complements by showing that a murderously energetic soul can work on other canvases besides the human body. Coppola's "Life Without Zoe," however, is radically—and no doubt purposely— unlike the earlier films for which he is most well known. Like "Life Lessons," "Life Without Zoe" is at least tangentially about jealousy and the selfishness of an artist, but Coppola sets his tale in an adolescent world of fashion and luxury in which there is all gain and no pain. The story, scripted by Coppola and his daughter

Sofia, centers on young Zoe (Heather McComb), who, in the absence of her mother (Talia Shire) and father (Giancarlo Giannini), a world-renowned concert flutist, lords over a plush apartment in the Sherry Netherland Hotel, draws money daily from an apparently unlimited allowance, and socializes with similarly advantaged young girls and boys at a private school that looks like a finishing academy and at extravagant parties where finished children inevitably congregate.

Insofar as it has a plot, "Life Without Zoe" is about the reintegration of a family composed of three willful individuals. Zoe rescues her father from the consequences of the kind of harmless flirtation to which handsome artists are prone and then not only gives precocious marital advice to her mother but also arranges for the two of them to fly to Europe to join the father on his concert tour. Plot is of secondary importance here, however, and functions primarily as an occasion for Coppola's visual dance on the surface of upscale life. The camera and the characters gaze lovingly on the designer clothes of twelve-year-old girls, the unrelieved splendor of living in a classy hotel, and the carefree excess of a party thrown by the richest boy in the world, and the unstated but inescapable message is that money can buy love and happiness. It would be wrong to take "Life Without Zoe" too seriously. Alfred Hitchcock once said that in his films he offered his audiences not a slice of life but a slice of cake, and Coppola no doubt has something like that in mind here. Still, any viewer of this film older than Zoe should be wiser than she is and feel troubled, even offended, as well as charmed by this not altogether harmless fantasy.

In this anthology of film fantasies, Woody Allen's contribution is in some respects the most difficult with which to identify and enjoy. "Oedipus Wrecks" is witty in places and superbly directed and acted, but it is also laboriously repetitive—the only short film in *New York Stories* that should have been even shorter—in hammering on a somewhat personal and private theme. The film begins with a master stroke by turning Freud upside down. Instead of striving to kill the father in order to have all the mother's love, Sheldon Mills (Woody Allen) wants his mother (Mae Questel) dead so that he will be free to marry his non-Jewish girlfriend Lisa (Mia Farrow) and live and love as he wants. Sheldon's face lights up gleefully when he pictures his mother's coffin, but he knows that even when she is not physically present she will boss him around, a foreshadowing of the central imaginative device in the film and also the concluding message.

When Sheldon's mother mysteriously disappears, fulfilling his fondest wish, he is almost instantly liberated, sexually and emotionally, but the dream quickly turns into a nightmare. In a grotesquely comic representation of what Freud would call the return of the repressed, his mother suddenly appears as a giant face in the sky, hovering over him constantly. Previously his mother was merely a loud, intrusive, domineering woman; now she is a cosmic force, and he is even more deeply embarrassed—about her and about himself. His only refuge, especially after Lisa confirms his worst self-doubts by leaving him, is with Treva (Julie Kavner), a clairvoyant who at first represents the exact opposite of Sheldon's desire to believe that the world is rational and logical. Treva dresses ridiculously, communicates with the spiritual world, and leads Sheldon through a series of nonsensical rituals that he tolerates simply because he has no other options. Yet she also knows how to cook chicken—in one of the funniest and most memorable scenes of the film, Sheldon stares in loving amazement at a leg of her chicken, dripping with luminescent fat— and it is from this point on, for better or worse, that Freud gets turned around again. Sheldon's rueful discovery is, to quote the musical accompaniment that Allen, as usual, uses so well, "I want a girl just like the girl that married dear old dad." His mother returns to the earth once she is assured that her son is finally in good hands. In Allen's view of the tragicomic contest of life, first prize is one Jewish mother, and second prize is two Jewish mothers—Sheldon's fate.

What is ultimately so disappointing about "Oedipus Wrecks" is that it is not as interesting as the above summary appears. A description of the film suggests that it flirts with profundity, which in a few scenes may be the case, but it settles for caricatures instead of characters and paralysis without pathos. Trimmed down into a fantasy sequence integrated into a larger film, "Oedipus Wrecks" might have been a brilliant bit, but alone and unsupported it limps.

Ironically, each of the directors represented in *New York Stories* has had a major role in creating the critical sensibility that will not be entirely satisfied by this film. Only Scorcese's segment is serious, provocative, and technically adventurous. Coppola's story is at best a trifle, and Allen's piece struggles too hard to turn nervous energy into comic delight and philosophical wisdom—something he usually manages to do with much more ease and assurance.

Sidney Gottlieb

Reviews

America. CLX, April 15, 1989, p. 353.
The Christian Science Monitor. March 8, 1989, p. 10.
Commonweal. CXVI, April 7, 1989, p. 212.
Films in Review. XL, June, 1989, p. 362.
Los Angeles Times. March 3, 1989, VI, p. 1.
Maclean's. CII, March 13, 1989, p. 62.
The Nation. CCXLVIII, March 27, 1989, p. 426.
New Leader. LXXII, March 6, 1989, p. 20.
The New Republic. CC, March 27, 1989, p. 24.
New York Magazine. XXII, March 13, 1989, p. 63.
The New York Times. March 1, 1989, p. C17.
The New Yorker. LXV, March 20, 1989, p. 93.
Newsweek. CXIII, March 6, 1989, p. 58.
People Weekly. XXXI, March 13, 1989, p. 15.
Time. CXXXIII, March 6, 1989, p. 68.
Variety. CCCXXXIV, March 1, 1989, p. 16.

OLD GRINGO

Production: Lois Bonfiglio for Fonda Films; released by Columbia Pictures
Direction: Luis Puenzo
Screenplay: Aida Bortnik and Luis Puenzo; based on the novel by Carlos Fuentes
Cinematography: Félix Monti
Editing: Juan Carlos Macias, William Anderson, and Glenn Farr
Production design: Stuart Wurtzel and Bruno Rubeo
Art direction: Scott Ritenour
Set decoration: Tessa Davies
Set design: Steve Saklad and Tom Warren
Makeup: Lee Harman, Peg Schierholz, and Alberto Lopez
Costume design: Enrico Sabbatini
Sound: Simon Kaye
Music: Lee Holdridge
MPAA rating: R
Running time: 119 minutes

Principal characters:
    Harriet Winslow . . . . Jane Fonda
    Ambrose Bierce . . . . Gregory Peck
    Tomas Arroyo. . . . . Jimmy Smits
    Frutos Garcia . . . . Patricio Contreras
    La Garduna . . . . Jenny Gago
    Pancho Villa . . . . Pedro Armendariz, Jr.

Old Gringo is Argentinean director Luis Puenzo's lavish and spectacular dramatization of Mexican author Carlos Fuentes' novel, *Gringo Viejo* (1985; *The Old Gringo*) dealing with the clash between cultures and social classes, and the war that rages within each human heart. Set in Mexico during that country's stormy revolution, the film blends fact and fiction as the action unfolds before the eyes of an American spinster caught in historical and human turmoil.

The film begins in Washington, D.C., in the year 1913. Schoolteacher Harriet Winslow (Jane Fonda) is gathering research material at the Washington Library when she overhears a man addressing a formal assemblage of patrons. Harriet does not know who the man is nor does she ever see his face, but she is impressed by his arrogance, independence, and lack of respect for pomp and formality. The man is the cantankerous and unpredictable writer Ambrose Bierce (Gregory Peck), who has come to dedicate his many volumes of writings to the library. He is old, drunk, and bitter, and eventually insults his audience, throwing his volumes to the floor, and staggering out of the room. Before departing, he tells the gathering that this is the last time anyone will see him alive.

Harriet returns home, where she lives with her mother. Mrs. Winslow is about to go visit the grave of her husband, who was reportedly killed while fighting in the Spanish-American War. Harriet refuses to go with her mother, which leads to an argument. Mrs. Winslow, realizing that she can no longer control her daughter's rebellious spirit, reluctantly retrieves a letter that she has kept hidden from Harriet for several weeks. Addressed to Harriet, it is an affirmative answer to her inquiry into a teaching position in Mexico. After reading the letter, Harriet throws her mother a defiant look and immediately starts packing for Mexico.

The scene shifts to a New Year's celebration outside a lavish hotel, where Harriet is now staying, in Chihuahua, Mexico. One of the people attending the festivities is Ambrose Bierce. As he sits drinking and watching the jubilant crowd, he overhears a group of men talking in Spanish about plans to further the cause of the Mexican rebels in allegiance with the bandit/revolutionary Pancho Villa (Pedro Armendariz, Jr.). At the mention of Villa, Bierce confronts the men and asks them if he can join with them. They scoff at his suggestion.

The next morning, Harriet is escorted to her teaching job by car down primitive roads to the hacienda located deep in territory controlled by Federale troops. She is ignorant of the fact that her escort is made up of the revolutionaries that Bierce has been talking to the night before. Bierce, determined to join with the revolutionaries, follows Harriet and her escort on horseback. When Harriet arrives at the hacienda, which is heavily guarded by Federale troops, the revolutionaries suddenly open fire on the troops. Harriet, still in the car, watches in horror as soldiers and rebels wage a bloody and explosive battle all around her. She is rescued by soldiers and ushered into the palatial building. Bierce helps the rebels, and he is thanked by General Tomas Arroyo (Jimmy Smits).

As the revolutionaries continue to take command of the hacienda, they discover that the owner of the hacienda, Miranda, is away, and thus their ultimate plan to capture the estate and hold him for ransom has only been partially realized. Harriet runs into Bierce whom she does not recognize as the man she saw briefly at the Washington Library. Although Bierce is as cantankerous as ever, they comfort each other, with Harriet finally falling asleep in Bierce's arms. The next morning, Harriet awakens to find Bierce gone. Later, as Harriet plays with some of the children, Arroyo confronts her and tells her that he grew up in this hacienda as the bastard son of one of Miranda's men after the man raped his mother. He tells Harriet that he eventually killed his father for raping his mother. He confesses that he has strong, conflicting feelings for the hacienda, feelings ranging from revulsion to reverence.

As the rebels continue to search the grounds, they discover a pile of papers hidden in the bell tower of the church. Arroyo is elated and calls the volumes sacred, because they are papers written by Spanish ancestors bequeathing the land back to its original occupants, the Indian peasants. A huge celebration is held, and both Bierce and Arroyo try to woo Harriet. She ends up with Arroyo in the master bedroom, where they make love.

Time passes, and Arroyo's men grow restless. Finally, Arroyo's second-in-command, Frutos Garcia (Patricio Contreras), threatens to organize the troops and abandon Arroyo if Arroyo will not desert the hacienda. As Garcia makes his demands, Bierce, in an attempt to provoke Arroyo into action, tells Arroyo that the papers found in the church are worthless and sets them on fire. Arroyo, enraged, acting as if he were coming out of a trance, shoots Bierce, who stumbles out of Arroyo's command post and onto the street. Harriet, who has just discovered who Bierce really is, runs out to comfort him as Arroyo follows and shoots Bierce dead.

The scene shifts to Chihuahua. Harriet, after escaping from the hacienda on horseback, confronts the American consul. She lies and tells him that Bierce is her father, that he has been killed by Mexican revolutionaries, and that she wants to claim the body and return to the United States. She then journeys to the headquarters of Pancho Villa, where Arroyo has finally reestablished his own troops. She tells Villa that Arroyo has the body of her father and that she demands he give it up to her. Villa tells her that she must first sign a paper that not only entitles her to the body but also authorizes the execution of Arroyo. Harriet, shocked at first at the thought of signing Arroyo's death warrant, ultimately signs the paper. She watches in horror as the body of Bierce is strapped against a wall and then Arroyo, after bidding farewell to his fellow revolutionaries, takes his place next to Bierce's corpse and is executed.

Old Gringo has the look and scope of an epic. It is filled with gorgeous natural splendor, wide, sweeping shots of festivals, battles, and elaborate village scenes all populated with hundreds of people swirling through scene after spectacular scene. Its three principal characters are all larger than life, all caught in an extraordinary period of time that compels them to act with dynamic potency. The conflicts that arise among the three principal characters take on a historical as well as symbolic significance. Harriet Winslow is not merely a sheltered American spinster but a representation of bourgeois naïveté, one who is indifferent to the injustices and oppression caused by a rigid social class structure. Tomas Arroyo represents the revolutionary spirit and how that spirit can be tamed by the forces he most despises. Ambrose Bierce also represents the revolutionary spirit but at a later stage— cynical, bitter, tired of fighting injustice, longing for death, yet still possessing the spark of rebellion, even at the moment of death.

The most interesting aspect of the film is how the filmmakers have taken a historical period, peopled it with historical figures, and then created a totally fictional story to illustrate the forces that were in play during that era and, most specifically, that particular revolutionary moment in time. By establishing the three main characters as representations of the conflicting forces of the revolution, the filmmakers are then free to re-create the war on a more intimate, microcosmic scale.

Another interesting aspect of the film is how the viewer's perspective of the action is presented from Harriet's point of view. The most cinematically effective scene presented from her perspective is the first battle scene, in which Harriet literally drives through the action, watching the brutal yet spectacular carnage explode all around her as her car careens out of control. The viewer shares her initial impression of Arroyo, that of an inhumane monster with little regard for human life. Yet, the viewer ultimately comes to understand Arroyo's noble side as well, right along with Harriet.

The problem with the film is that the main characters are never given any real human dimensions and remain merely representations of clashing ideologies. Attempts are made to humanize the characters, but the attempts are never fully successful. For example, in the love scene between Arroyo and Harriet, the scene is played with great romantic gentleness and innocence, the intent being to show Arroyo's sensitive side. Yet the filmmakers overcompensate, and the scene seems jarringly incongruous. Other attempts to illustrate the gentle side of the characters ring just as false. Bierce in one scene is shown reciting one of his most famous stories, "An Occurrence at Owl Creek Bridge," around a campfire to a group of spellbound children, an action that seems totally out of character for the cynical and curmudgeonly old man. Harriet's character never shows any true horror and outrage at events that, most assuredly, would have seemed overwhelmingly appalling to someone of her sheltered, middle-class upbringing. For example, the day after the first battle in which Harriet witnessed a vast array of brutal atrocities, she is shown frolicking with the prostitutes as if she were a young school girl on vacation with some classmates.

The gritty reality of the situation is never established. The film is too slick, too opulent to capture the true, sweaty spirit of the historical setting. For all its scenes of bloodshed and death, the film remains emotionally bloodless, preaching to the audience instead of creating characters with whom the audience can more fully identify. Director Puenzo's previous film, *The Official Story* (1985), which dealt with the political atrocities of his native Argentina and the radicalization of its main character, a middle-class schoolteacher, shares similar themes with *Old Gringo* but possesses what *Old Gringo* completely lacks: full-dimensional characters who are totally integrated within their historical time and place. For all its grandeur and attention to historical detail, for all its explosive action and elaborate re-creation of one of the most dramatic moments in history, *Old Gringo* betrays the revolutionary spirit it tries to illustrate by being too didactic, too bourgeois, and too intent to show off its riches when it should be striving to illustrate the simple verities of the human heart.

Jim Kline

Reviews
Chicago Tribune. October 6, 1989, VII, p. 34.
The Christian Century. CVI, October 25, 1989, p. 961.
Connoisseur. CCXIX, September, 1989, p. 68.
Films in Review. XLI, January, 1990, p. 45.
Los Angeles Times. October 6, 1989, VI, p. 1.

Maclean's. CII, October 16, 1989, p. 60.
The New York Times. October 6, 1989, p. C8.
Rolling Stone. October 19, 1989, p. 27.
The Times Literary Supplement. October 13, 1989, p. 1125.
Variety. CCCXXXV, May 24, 1989, p. 6.
The Wall Street Journal. November 2, 1989, p. A16.
The Washington Post. October 6, 1989, p. C1.

PARENTHOOD

Production: Brian Grazer for Imagine Entertainment; released by Universal
Direction: Ron Howard
Screenplay: Lowell Ganz and Babaloo Mandel
Cinematography: Donald McAlpine
Editing: Michael Hill and Daniel Hanley
Production design: Todd Hallowell
Art direction: Christopher Nowak
Set decoration: Nina Ramsey
Makeup: Fern Buchner and Peter Wrona, Jr.
Costume design: Ruth Morley
Sound: Richard S. Church
Music: Randy Newman
Song: Randy Newman, "I Love to See You Smile"
MPAA rating: PG-13
Running time: 124 minutes

Principal characters:
Gil Buckman	Steve Martin
Karen Buckman	Mary Steenburgen
Helen	Dianne Wiest
Frank Buckman	Jason Robards
Nathan	Rick Moranis
Larry Buckman	Tom Hulce
Julie	Martha Plimpton
Tod	Keanu Reeves
Susan	Harley Kozak
David Brodsky	Dennis Dugan
Garry	Leaf Phoenix
Marilyn	Eileen Ryan
Grandma	Helen Shaw
Kevin	Jasen Fisher
George Bowman	Paul Linke
Taylor	Alisan Porter
Justin	Zachary Lavoy
Patty	Ivyann Schwan
Cool	Alex Burrall
Stan	Lowell Ganz
Lou	Clint Howard

The subject of this film by actor-turned-director Ron Howard is the world's most challenging job, parenthood. Frank (Jason Robards) is the patriarch of the Buckman clan. He is stubborn, gruff, and remote as a father. He has four grown children, and director Howard intertwines all of their stories in this wry, telling film.

The eldest of Frank's children, Gil (Steve Martin), is the focus of the film. As a child, Gil's birthday outing with his father was to a St. Louis Cardinals baseball game. Once there, however, Frank quickly turned his son over to the ushers and went his own way. Now an adult, Gil has three children of his own: two boys, Kevin (Jasen Fisher), age nine, and Justin (Zachary Lavoy), age three, and an eight-year-old daughter, Taylor (Alisan Porter). Gil is determined not to repeat his father's mistakes. He is a perfectionist parent, determined to rear his children correctly. He is a caring, doting father who does his best to interact with his children in a style completely opposite that of his own neglectful father. Often, his chosen method of active parenting conflicts with the more traditional image of a father who needs to spend most of his time at the office in order to advance his career.

Gil is married to Karen (Mary Steenburgen), who is as patient with her husband and children as Gil is anxious. The main problem in their life is their eldest son. Kevin is not doing well at school, where it is suggested that he be placed in a special education class. He is also not doing well on his Little League baseball team, of which his father is the coach. Kevin's fellow team members are permanently angry with him, because he does not play well. Kevin is a high-strung boy who panics easily, especially when his overprotective father unwittingly puts pressure on the boy because of his own guilt over possible parenting inadequacies.

Gil's sister, Helen (Dianne Wiest), is a lonely divorcée with two surly, unpredictable children. Her thirteen-year-old son, Garry (Leaf Phoenix), silently stalks the house with a mysterious bag (which, the audience eventually learns, contains videotapes of pornographic films). Her daughter, sixteen-year-old Julie (Martha Plimpton), who got a combined score of 1,291 on her Standard Aptitude Test, refuses to go to college and instead is having an affair with the not-so-bright Tod (Keanu Reeves). She eventually marries Tod, who then moves into Helen's home with Julie. Helen's children are angry (mostly at their absent father, a dentist), and they vent their anger on their mother.

Another of Frank's children is Susan (Harley Kozak). She and her husband, Nathan (Rick Moranis), are the archetypal Yuppie parents. They are determined to make their daughter, Patty (Ivyann Schwan), into a genius. Nathan has her learning Spanish, reading Kafka, memorizing square roots, and studying karate. Patty, however, is only three years old. While Nathan is expending his energy and time on Patty, he seems unaware that his marriage is in trouble. Susan outwardly proclaims that the family is "power eating" only health foods, but she sits in her closet eating junk food.

Frank's youngest child is Larry (Tom Hulce). He is the prodigal son whom Frank may love the most. Larry disappears for years at a time and seems to come home only when he is in trouble. True to form, Larry suddenly appears at his father's house, bringing with him wild dreams of success, schemes for wealth, an illegitimate mulatto son, Cool (Alex Burrall), and a huge gambling debt that has put his life in danger. Larry wants Frank to take care of Cool as well as his debt, but to do so means that Frank will have to abandon his own plans for retirement.

It is director Howard's job as well as that of writers Lowell Ganz and Babaloo Mandel to weave together the threads of all these stories in a way that will be understandable, empathetic, telling, and amusing without becoming maudlin or overly sentimental. It is a task they take on with great earnestness and sincerity, one that reflects many of their own life experiences. Between the three men, they have produced fourteen children. Many of the scenes in the film and many of the children's antics were taken directly from the lives of the members of the creative team. The result is a film that is true to life, likably charming but also a bit manipulative.

Howard grew up on television as Opie on *The Andy Griffith Show* and then as Richie on *Happy Days*. It was the world of the Cleavers, Donna Reed, and Ozzie and Harriet. *Parenthood* continues this wholesome and idealized tradition and brings it up to date. Howard maintains the magical holiness of the family unit but also manages to throw an acerbic gremlin or two into the works. His film tries hard to please, with its ambitious construction, likable and talented cast, warmly glib script, and wealth of parenting wisdom.

The problems Howard, Ganz, and Mandel throw at the Buckman clan are not earth-shattering. They are the normal difficulties and day-to-day doubts of middle-class parents. It does seem, however, that the main purpose for following the progress of several families instead of one is to allow the writers to delve into virtually every normal problem of parenting. The film tackles uncaring fathers, learning disabilities, communication problems, teenage pregnancy, conflicting goals of parents and children, the attempts by parents to live their children's lives, a parent's inability to prevent a child from following the wrong path in life, and the simple fact that one never stops being a parent. They are challenges that are presented with compassion, perception, and humor.

To execute these stories, Howard repeats a formula that proved successful in his previous feature, *Cocoon* (1985): a first-rate ensemble cast. Several in the cast are Oscar winners. Jason Robards won for *All the President's Men* (1976) and *Julia* (1977), Wiest won one for *Hannah and Her Sisters* (1986), and Steenburgen won for *Melvin and Howard* (1979), for which Robards was also nominated. Hulce, nominated for an Oscar for *Amadeus* (1985), also received acclaim for his work in *Dominick and Eugene* (1988).

Martin, who won praise for his roles in *All of Me* (1984) and *Roxanne* (1987) is more restrained in *Parenthood* but still humorous and sympathetic. His wit and physical antics go a long way in preventing the film from becoming bogged down in sentimentality. He is especially amusing when bailing out his son's birthday party by playing Cowboy Bob, the balloon-twisting entertainer, or doing a victory dance when his son finally catches an important pop fly during a baseball game.

The rest of the cast proves equally adept at realizing the film's intent. Wiest brings a hopefulness and availability to her role of the mother rejected by her children, but she tinges it with more than a bit of cynicism. As a consequence, her performance offers tension along with the humor. When her character finds the pornographic videotapes in her son's room, there is something very sensible and nonjudgmental about her comment: "I assume you're watching these because you're curious about sex—or filmmaking."

This is typical of the candid and articulate dialogue these characters are given. It is a dialogue nicely punctuated by Randy Newman's musical score. If there is a problem, it is the profusion of stated parenting homilies and the way all the stories are neatly rushed to completion in a much too syrupy conclusion.

Beverley Bare Buehrer

Reviews

American Film: Magazine of the Film and Television Arts. XIV, July, 1989, p. 57.
Chicago Tribune. August 4, 1989, VII, p. 34.
Christian Science Monitor. August 18, 1989, p. 10.
Films in Review. XL, November, 1989, p. 549.
Los Angeles Times. August 2, 1989, VI, p. 1.
Maclean's. August 14, 1989, p. 53.
The New York Times. August 2, 1989, p. C15.
The New Yorker. LXV, August 7, 1989, p. 75.
Newsweek. CXIV, August 7, 1989, p. 18.
Rolling Stone. August 24, 1989, p. 38.
Time. August 7, 1989, p. 54.
Variety. CCCXXXVI, August 2, 1989, p. 18.
Vogue. August, 1989, p. 200.
The Washington Post. August 2, 1989, p. D1.

PET SEMATARY

Production: Richard P. Rubinstein for Paramount Pictures
Direction: Mary Lambert
Screenplay: Stephen King; based on his novel
Cinematography: Peter Stein
Editing: Michael Hill
Editing: Daniel Hanley
Production design: Michael Z. Hanan
Art direction: Dins Danielson
Set decoration: Katharin Briggs
Special effects: Lance Anderson and David Anderson
Makeup: Lance Anderson
Costume design: Marlene Stewart
Music: Elliot Goldenthal
MPAA rating: R
Running time: 102 minutes

Principal characters:

Dr. Louis Creed . . . . Dale Midkiff
Jud Crandall . . . . Fred Gwynne
Rachel Creed . . . . Denise Crosby
Ellie Creed . . . . Blaze Berdahl
Gage Creed . . . . Miko Hughes
Victor Pascow . . . . Brad Greenquist
Missy Dandridge . . . . Susan J. Blommaert
Irwin Goldman . . . . Michael Lombard

Stephen King is a gifted storyteller and a more-than-competent craftsman. His publication successes, however, have not been matched by his excursions into film production. A few of his novels, particularly *Carrie* (1974), *The Shining* (1977), and *The Dead Zone* (1979), have been transformed into relatively good films, and *Stand By Me* (1986), adapted from King's story "The Body," was excellent, besides being a popular success. On the other hand, certainly not all of King's material has been translated effectively to cinema. *Cujo* (1981) was one of his better novels, but the film was not successful. *Christine* (1983) also did not work on film. *Pet Sematary* is also a film that fails to capture whatever it was that made the novel an interesting read, even though King himself wrote the script. King's works are read for entertainment, not enlightenment. His novels usually depend on supernatural gimmicks that are farfetched and strain credulity. In the best of them, King's sheer storytelling ability overpowers logic, but the magic he creates on the page often does not translate effectively to the screen, where realism is magnified.

First published in 1983, *Pet Sematary* was a typical Stephen King success, maintaining its place on *The New York Times* best-seller list for more than thirty weeks.

The novel tells the story of Dr. Louis Creed, who moves his family of four from Chicago to rural Maine, where he takes a job at a small college. His first day on the job sees a fatality when a student named Victor Pascow is killed. The ghost of Victor Pascow comes back to haunt Louis when the good doctor is tempted to explore the territory beyond an innocent-looking pet cemetery near his home. The odd spelling of the book's title derives from the children who established this cemetery years ago. This obvious bit of foreshadowing is accurately translated to the film. What the film misses is the psychological terror that is more fully anticipated and described in the novel.

King himself wrote the screenplay for the film, played a brief cameo as a minister at a graveside funeral service, and later hit the publicity trail in order to help promote the film. He told *Entertainment Tonight* that writing the screenplay was difficult because in writing the novel he managed to scare himself, suggesting that the novel represented his very best writing. King claimed that the framework for the story was partly autobiographical. When his daughter's cat, Smucky, was killed by a speeding fertilizer truck on the highway in front of his house near Orrington, Maine, he buried it in a makeshift pet cemetery nearby. Later, his son was almost killed by speeding traffic on the same highway.

In the film, Winston Churchill, the cat belonging to Ellie Creed (Blaze Berdahl), is killed on the road. Ellie's father (Dale Midkiff) goes to bury it with his neighbor, old-timer Jud Crandall (Fred Gwynne), who lets him in on a secret. Beyond the pet cemetery, over the high ground, is an ancient Indian burial ground that has mysterious powers. Whatever is buried there comes back alive but changed, and not for the better. The place is evil. The cat comes back transformed into a snarling beast. After Louis' young son Gage (Miko Hughes) is run down by a truck on that fateful highway, Louis gets an unholy idea that unleashes a spectacular bloody conclusion for a story that turns quite nasty.

The film contains almost all the novel's main action, but the story, humanized to an extent by the novel's technique, seems obscenely grotesque when reduced to its most superficial components on the screen. The details are a bit different at the end. On his final visit to the burial ground at the end of the novel, Louis is accompanied by another man, who is so terrified by the experience that he soon leaves Maine for St. Louis. The film drops this man entirely but reveals more of Louis' unhappy reunion with his wife, Rachel (Denise Crosby), at the very end.

Director Mary Lambert serves up a flat, one-dimensional visual plot summary and fails to bring the characters to life and to make them as interesting as they are in the novel. Perhaps King should share the blame. "This movie is very special to me," the novelist noted. "It's the first screenplay I've adapted from one of my novels, and it's my first book to be filmed in my home state of Maine, where many of my stories are set." Taking the film crew on location to Ellsworth, Maine, surely helped to establish atmosphere, but the problem has to do with internal character development, not external settings.

Veteran actor Fred Gwynne is agreeable as the friendly neighbor Jud Crandall, though *Variety* complained that his "Pepperidge Farm accent makes him sound as if he needs oral surgery." *Variety* described newcomer Dale Alan Midkiff, who played Dr. Louis Creed, as "an appealing if ill-developed lead." His character seems to move without understandable motives, leaving the audience to wonder why the man is such a fool. The problem is with the script. Denise Crosby, the granddaughter of Bing Crosby, at least has an apparent motive for what she does, but her character is ephemeral and little more than an innocent victim of the evil goings-on. Brad Greenquist probably gets the most out of a minor role here, playing the spooky Victor Pascow, who is first seen as a disfigured body and later as a reappearing ghost.

Because *Pet Sematary* was filmed only twenty miles from King's home, King took an interest in the production and visited all the rehearsals. King has said that he considered *Pet Sematary* as a second attempt at *The Shining*, as shaped by the talents of a very strong director, Stanley Kubrick, and a very influential actor, Jack Nicholson. Perhaps King was too close to the project to see its flaws. "If Stephen King (rightly) feels that most of his novels have been botched in their translation to film," the *Variety* review noted (April 26), "at least this time he has to point a finger at himself." *Variety* went on to ridicule the film as "undead schlock dulled by a slasher-film mentality." In a piece in *The New York Times* entitled "Common Sense Seems to Be in Short Supply" (May 7), Vincent Canby dismissed *Pet Sematary* as "a gaudy movie about child abuse." Richard Harrington made essentially the same observation in *The Washington Post*, earlier, on April 22, noting that in the last fifteen minutes the film "turns very ugly indeed, coming close to celluloid child abuse."

Paramount Pictures apparently sensed the film's weaknesses and decided to market *Pet Sematary* directly to the Stephen King fans, declining to preview it for the critics, who caught up with it the week following its release. Joel Siegel gave it a negative review on *Good Morning America* (ABC television, April 28), and Richard Harrington entitled his review in *The Washington Post* (April 22) "An Adaptation with No Bark and No Bite." *Pet Sematary* still did very well on its opening weekend April 21, and was the top-grossing film, earning $12 million and setting a record as "the biggest opening weekend of any movie ever released before Memorial Day," according to Steve Pond's "Dateline Hollywood" column in *The Washington Post* (April 28). Ultimately, however, the film was a decidedly second-rate adaptation, poorly dramatized and populated by two-dimensional characters.

Filmed in garish color, *Pet Sematary* worked well enough as a manipulative scare machine to hoodwink its initial rush of thrill seekers, even though it was not as interesting as the original novel. The violence and nastiness were fairly extreme, as was the premise. It functioned typically as a horror film in which not much attention was paid to character development. Lacking interest, the main characters were little more than human props to be sacrificed merely to advance the plot.

James M. Welsh

Reviews

Boston Globe. April 21, 1989, p. 46.
Chicago Tribune. April 24, 1989, V, p. 2.
Cinéfantastique. XIX, March, 1989, p. 4.
Los Angeles Times. April 24, 1989, VI, p. 5.
The New York Times. April 22, 1989, p. A16.
People Weekly. XXXI, May 15, 1989, p. 13.
Us. III, May 29, 1989, p. 62.
Variety. CCCXXXV, April 26, 1989, p. 26.
The Washington Post. April 22, 1989, p. C1.

QUEEN OF HEARTS

Origin: Great Britain
Released: 1989
Released in U.S.: 1989
Production: John Hardy for Enterprise/TVS Films; released by Cinecom
    Entertainment Group
Direction: Jon Amiel
Screenplay: Tony Grisoni
Cinematography: Mike Southon
Editing: Peter Boyle
Production design: Jim Clay
Art direction: Philip Elton
Makeup: Magdalen Gaffney
Costume design: Lindy Hemming
Sound: Peter Glossop
Music: Michael Convertino
MPAA rating: no listing
Running time: 112 minutes

Principal characters:
Danilo	Joseph Long
Eddie	Ian Hawkes
Rosa	Anita Zagaria
Nonno	Vittorio Duse
Mama Sibilla	Eileen Way
Barbariccia	Vittorio Amandola

As *Queen of Hearts* begins, the camera slowly tracks a nondescript stone wall, finally reaching a breach that suddenly reveals great depths beyond what had appeared to be a monotonous, flat surface. There, before the viewer, lies a medieval Italian town shimmering in sun-drenched, autumnal tones — virtually the last thing the viewer would have expected to lie beyond the forbidding surface of that tracked wall. It is a breathtaking camera movement, offering the viewer a promise of visual daring in what will follow.

In the ancient town, a passionate love story unfolds. Two star-crossed lovers, Danilo (Joseph Long) and Rosa (Anita Zagaria), gaze rapturously but hopelessly at each other through their facing windows. The gulf between them is much wider than the street that separates them. Rosa has been promised to the local butcher, Barbariccia (Vittorio Amandola), who has come to bring his dowry gift. As her mother accepts it on the part of her reluctant daughter, the desperate *innamorato* bursts through the door, grabs the startled daughter, and spirits her away. The vengeful *fidanzato* gives furious chase, relentlessly closing the distance between himself and the fleeing couple as they run up the stairs of the town's highest tower. At the top, they see that they have nowhere to go but down to the cobbles hundreds of feet below. Danilo kisses his beloved's hand, and they leap over the parapet to their certain doom.

Michael Convertino's throbbingly romantic, Verdiesque score, beautifully written to match each twist and turn of the events, lushly overrides what little dialogue the sound track has captured. Director of photography Mike Southon shows an equal mastery of visual tonality as he captures the lovers' plight and eventual flight through the sunbaked town into the dark tower and up onto its dazzling parapet.

Unifying their work, director Jon Amiel virtually reinvents both romanticism and narrative as he goes. Working from an original script by Tony Grisoni, Amiel first reduces his romantic plot to the barest essentials and then tells his story through a series of wonderfully inventive visual essentializations, always sidestepping cliché to find new—and very often astonishing—ways of spinning his tale. Amiel thoroughly understands conventions from their cores on out and can penetrate to the very heart of a genre or a movement while simultaneously sweeping away the hoary patina that has served both to preserve it and to corrode it over the years.

Although this is his first film for the big screen, Amiel had already proven his inventive genius as director of the brilliant *The Singing Detective* series produced by Great Britain's Channel 4 and shown here on public television. Viewed by some as the premier cinematic event of the 1980's (even though it was technically not a cinematic event at all), *The Singing Detective* managed that same simultaneous enhancement and *dépatinage* through its insistence on renewal of genre and refusal to submit to the conventions that have suffocated it.

Yet what of the ill-fated lovers, who have just leapt from the top of the huge medieval tower to their certain doom? As they hurtle toward their destruction, a hay cart lumbers into the street far below, and doom suddenly becomes their salvation. In an instant, the film seems to switch genres from high romantic tragedy to historical swashbuckling comedy, in what the viewer will eventually recognize as merely the first in the countless number of genre switches that seem to inform this film's narrative strategy.

The next switch occurs a moment later, as the camera cuts to the narrator, Eddie Lucca (Ian Hawkes), as a boy, recounting the tale of how his mother and father got married and how Barbariccia subsequently had sworn his revenge on them by slashing his own hand with a knife. At this juncture, the question arises of whether the narrative should be taken as the one that young Eddie heard from his parents, the one that young Eddie has filtered through his imagination, the one that the elder Eddie—the eventual voice-over narrator of the film—is supplying, or perhaps none of the above. Those viewers who like that sort of maze will find this picture utterly delightful in its refusal to sit still and submit to the ordinary rules of the narrative game. In its playful and inviting way, *Queen of Hearts* is as irresolvable a narrative labyrinth as its solemn and forbidding predecessor, *L'Année dernière á Marienbad* (1961; *Last Year at Marienbad*).

Young Eddie's voice-over now brings the story chronologically up to the early 1960's, a time when his father, Danilo, his mother, Rosa, and his *nonna*, Mama Sibilla (Eileen Way), have come to settle in a rainy London room, complete with tents and big umbrellas to protect themselves from the weather. Eddie recalls the story his father told him about a remarkable vision he had when he was first starting his new life as a waiter. The audience is then shown the event. It is Christmas Eve, and the glum, lonely Danilo is serving a pair of tipsy British upper-class twits who offer him a five-pound note if he will only smile. As he sadly obliges them, the roast pig he has just served them suddenly looks up at him and utters a prophecy: "Money is like the sun," it says. "Trust the coins, but beware the King of Swords!"

Danilo immediately translates the pig's oracle into action; he visits an opulently sordid gambling den, where he turns his five-pound note into a down payment on the Lucky Café. Through hard work and good luck, the family prospers in their new enterprise and their new home in the Italian district. Through unflagging inventiveness and ingenuity, the narrative also flourishes, still cheerfully refusing to settle down into any single containable genre, although it seems to be hovering around a gentle sort of immigrant domestic comedy at this point.

Soon, however, Danilo's father decides to come from Italy and live with them. Eddie's *nonno* (Vittorio Duse) is a marvelously problematic figure who has death written all over him and whose arrival marks the beginning of the end of the family's prosperity. Characteristically, the narrative never attempts to explain why Nonno should portend such doom for the formerly happy family as things begin to disintegrate around them and among them. As with the mysteries of its own contours, the narrative simply confines itself to revealing Nonno's fell nature with audacious ellipticity and astonishing invention.

In Nonno's wake, the family's old nemesis, Barbariccia, also materializes. Over the intervening years, Barbariccia has prospered, and now he has come to London to open a few clubs and to carry out his revenge on Danilo. A splendidly diabolical figure, the very picture of nemesis, of palpable and implacable swaggering ill-will, Barbariccia turns Eddie's elder brother into his messenger boy, takes away the Lucky Café's charmed espresso machine, and generally oversees the demise of the café and the family. Danilo desperately turns to another game of cards—this time, with Barbariccia himself. This time, Danilo loses everything. The pig's oracle can now be seen to apply not only to suits of the Italian deck (coins and swords) but also to the king who has cut himself to swear a blood oath, the King of Swords. To gain his final triumph, Barbariccia taunts Danilo into one last wager: double or quits against Danilo's wedding ring. Danilo loses the ring, and with the ring goes the last remaining trace of his honor.

The narrative, which at first seemed so loose and virtually unstructured, has by now revealed its formal strategy: a policy of reversal, in which the film's opening episodes are reiterated, but in reverse order. Following that structural logic, Danilo, in the depths of despair, must now take another leap: this time into the cold, wintry Thames River. Since the narrative has remained so implacably independent of genre, the viewer is refused the comforts of genre predictability insofar as Danilo's fate is concerned. In its complete polarization of the two episodes—one set on a sunny, romantic, autumnal Italian day and the other on a dark, realist, wintry London night, one at the beginning of hope and daring, the other at its end—the logic of form dictates the worst for Danilo.

Once Danilo's fate is learned, the narrative returns to the voice-over of Eddie, now in the present, and the film's opening image of a scanned wall is repeated, but this is a wall in his old London neighborhood, which he says has become lost to him. Return as he will, he can no longer quite locate the precise place where his story occurred.

The voice-over reasserts the difficulties in locating the narrative. Situated somewhere among the visions of the young Danilo and the younger Eddie and the present-day Eddie who is recalling it all, the narrative has twisted and turned and flexed and flowed constantly, eddying between comedy and tragedy in a complex, engaging, and creatively exhilarating fashion, leading back through memory and imagination to a lost place beyond the drab walls of conventional reality.

R. C. Dale

Reviews

Chicago Tribune. October 20, 1989, VII, p. 48.
The Christian Science Monitor. October 13, 1989, p. 10.
Commonweal. CXVI, November 3, 1989, p. 591.
Los Angeles Times. September 29, 1989, VI, p. 8.
Maclean's. CII, November 6, 1989, p. 86.
The New Leader. LXXII, October 2, 1989, p. 21.
The New York Times. September 20, 1989, p. C19.
Rolling Stone. October 2, 1989, p. 90.
Time. CXXXIV, October 5, 1989, p. 36.
Variety. CCCXXXV, September 6, 1989, p. 23.
The Wall Street Journal. September 28, 1989, p. A23.
The Washington Post. October 11, 1989, p. B2.

THE RAINBOW

Origin: Great Britain
Released: 1989
Released: 1989
Production: Ken Russell for Vestron Pictures
Direction: Ken Russell
Screenplay: Ken Russell and Vivian Russell; based on the novel of by D. H.
 Lawrence
Cinematography: Billy Williams
Editin₍: Peter Davies
Production design: Luciana Arrighi
Music: Carl Davis
MPAA rating: R
Running time: 104 minutes

Principal characters:
Ursula Brangwen	Sammi Davis
Anton Skrebensky	Paul McGann
Winifred Inger	Amanda Donohoe
Will Brangwen	Christopher Gable
Uncle Henry	David Hemmings
Anna Brangwen	Glenda Jackson

When director Ken Russell adapted D. H. Lawrence's novel *Women in Love* (1920) to the screen in 1970, it was both damned and praised by critics for its excesses. The film was richly textured and wildly sensual in its imagery. Those who loved it believed its style was a brilliant match for Lawrence's effusive prose; those who did not believed Russell had gone over the artistic edge, creating a film, to borrow from William Shakespeare, "full of sound and fury, signifying nothing."

With *The Rainbow*, Russell has again returned to Lawrence, even to some of the same characters (*The Rainbow*, 1915, precedes *Women in Love* in its narrative chronology of the Brangwen family). Russell's new work, however, is unlikely to create as much controversy as its predecessor; it lacks both the fire and the vision of the earlier film. Russell's style in *The Rainbow* is restrained; he seems to have distanced himself from his material. He gives us Lawrence's words, but this time, unfortunately, without the intensity of feeling.

The Brangwens are a turn-of-the-century farm family in the Midlands of England whose bucolic country cottage is within earshot of the booming coal mines in an era rushing headlong into industrialization. In his adaptation, Russell has chosen to focus on only the final section of the novel—specifically on those chapters that deal with the quest of young Ursula Brangwen (Sammi Davis) for self-identity and her rebellion against the conventions of her age.

Early in the film version, Ursula Brangwen, who is in her final year of school, is asked what she thinks is the most important attribute a person should possess. She answers that it is not intelligence that matters, but courage—courage to do whatever one wants to do in life. As Ursula begins to make a life of her own, she discovers through painful experience the wisdom of her words.

At home, Ursula sees her mother Anna (Glenda Jackson) consumed by the needs of her children, her daily hours spent bathing, feeding, comforting, and coaxing her large brood (five, with Ursula the eldest). Perplexed and somewhat aghast at her mother's total absorption in her family, Ursula wants to know what she had ever wanted for herself. Without missing a beat, her mother replies pointedly, "What I've got."

Domesticity is not, however, what Ursula wants. Headstrong, she longs for adventure and passion, and a chance to be free from the constraints imposed on women by society. Her role model, for a time at least, is her school's athletics teacher, Winifred Inge (Amanda Donohoe), a free-spirited feminist who first introduces Ursula to the joys of lesbian sex while the two are skinny-dipping in the river. Winifred has little positive to say about men, recalling that her own mother did not exist as a person as far as her father was concerned. She warns Ursula that the most a man has to offer is his passion and that even that does not last.

Despite the warnings, Ursula falls in love with a handsome young soldier named Anton Skrebensky (Paul McGann). The two steal their first kiss in an empty church and some weeks later move on to a moonlit bedroom at the estate of Ursula's uncle to consummate their relationship before Anton goes off to war.

With Anton away and her formal education at an end, Ursula decides, against her father's wishes, to try her hand at teaching. Her pupils are poor, the children of coal miners, and the school itself can best be described as Dickensian: damp, gray, cold, and sooty, with a brutal headmaster who seems addicted to randomly caning his charges. In such a dismal atmosphere, Ursula soon finds herself succumbing to the same sort of tyranny as her employer to keep order in her classroom.

The nearest thing to a crisis arises when Anton, after a two-year absence, returns from the war in Africa and begins to talk of their future together. Ursula loves him but believes her own emerging identity to be threatened by the proposed marriage; Anton has made it clear that he would not want her to pursue her teaching once she becomes his wife. This establishes the classic Laurentian conflict between the romantic Ursula, who wants the lovers to stay just as they are, wrapped in each others' arms without need of anyone else, and the pragmatic Anton, who insists on making proper plans for children, servants, and living arrangements. The tensions between the two rise even higher when Anton declares that Ursula should marry him and come away for her own good, to distance herself from Winifred and what he views to be her "unnatural" sexual behavior.

Repulsed by this prim, conventional streak that suddenly shows in Anton, Ursula rejects his proposal only to regret her decision some weeks later when she discovers that she may be carrying Anton's child. This possibility causes a change in heart, and, as she explains to Winifred (who is now married with a child of her own), she has come to the conclusion that if marriage was good enough for her mother, then it should be good enough for Ursula, too. She has written to Anton apologizing profusely for her behavior and asking if he will have her back. Her afternoon with her friend ends on a somewhat sour note, with a hint that Winifred's own marriage has taken an unhappy turn. She sends Ursula home with a warning: that a child binds a woman to a man as surely as if she was handcuffed to him.

Bicycling home at dusk, Ursula is surprised on the road by wild horses, which race toward her threateningly. In her panic, she loses control of the bicycle and falls, and is forced to flee on foot. She is surprised for a second time by a group of miners, who menacingly follow the frightened young woman, forcing her to wade across the river to escape. By the time she arrives home, Ursula is soaked, exhausted, and feverish. The final straw is a telegram waiting for her on the mantle. It is from Anton—he has already married someone else. Ursula collapses into bed, where she dreams deliriously until her father, Will (Christopher Gable), awakens her the next morning, pointing out to her a rainbow arching across the sky outside her bedroom window.

As soon as her father leaves, Ursula leaps excitedly from bed. In the film's last image, she is running off, packed bag in hand, to find the rainbow. This ending echoes the opening scene, in which Ursula, as a toddler, races helter-skelter through the fields toward a distant rainbow, only to be intercepted by her father who saves her from falling into the river. When her father asks what she is doing, she replies simply enough that she wants the rainbow.

One of the chief problems with Russell's film is that, in terms of emotional complexity, Sammi Davis' Ursula never advances much beyond this point. Her Ursula is spirited and headstrong, like the child in the opening scene but without any soul. She fails to give a sense of the inner turmoil through which her character is going. Lawrence's dialogue spills out of her mouth too easily, without any psychological insight or resonance. In Davis' portrayal, Ursula's anger, her tirades against her family, her lover, the mines of her Uncle Henry (David Hemmings), comes across more as rudeness or scrappiness, than as hunger for change.

Another part of the problem is with the script (written by Russell and his wife Vivian), which relies heavily on incident without allowing time for reflection on the part of the characters involved, resulting in a muddle of unclear motivations. Winifred, the feminist, decries the marital state, yet suddenly marries Ursula's Uncle Henry without explanation and without a reaction from Ursula. Ursula harangues her uncle about the plight of the poor miners, yet she quite readily accepts the need to beat their children into submission in the schoolroom, presumably because it allows her to feel like an independent woman earning her own living.

The look of the film marks a radical departure from *Women in Love* (1970), although both were photographed by the superb Billy Williams. Gone are the daring camera angles, the mirror reflections, the intense colors, and dramatic contrasts of the earlier film. The look here is more pastel, more subdued. Williams lavishes attention on the lush countryside with its thatched roof cottages, tree-lined lanes, and cascading waterfalls. In a way, this prettiness works against the film. It all seems so peaceful and idyllic, rather than stifling or claustrophobic, that it makes it even harder to understand the true nature of Ursula's rebellion. Somehow it adds to the impression that Ursula's distress is merely a bad case of postadolescent impetuosity, and that, given time, she will probably grow out of it.

There are some saving graces, especially in the brief but shining performances of Glenda Jackson as Ursula's mother and David Hemmings as her wealthy Uncle Henry. Jackson plays the mother as a woman with a wealth of inner resources. She is not the warrior that her daughter desires to be, but a compromiser, a peacemaker, a woman of remarkable strength and balance. She has few lines in the film, but it does not matter; Jackson has the rare ability to "speak" with a glance, a turn of the head, or a lift of an eyebrow. Every thought registers on her face, rendering words unnecessary. Hemmings' Uncle Henry projects an outward aura of charm and graciousness that covers a heart turned cold by avarice and exploitation. He skillfully blends this contradiction in Henry to create a believably complex character, one worthy of Lawrence's original.

Mary Lou McNichol

Reviews
America. CLXI, July 15, 1989, p. 40.
American Film: Magazine of the Film and Television Arts. XIV, May, 1989, p. 11.
Chicago Tribune. June 2, 1989, VII, p. 38.
The Christian Science Monitor. May 9, 1989, p. 11.
Film Comment. XXV, May/June, 1989, p. 2.
Films in Review. XL, October, 1989, p. 490.
Los Angeles Times. May 18, 1989, VI, p. 1.
The New Republic. CC, May 15, 1989, p. 28.
The New York Times. May 5, 1989, p. C9.
The New Yorker. LXV, May 29, 1989, p. 102.
Newsweek. CXIII, May 8, 1989, p. 70.
Time. CXXXIII, May 15, 1989, p. 75.
Variety. CCCXXXV, May 3, 1989, p. 12.

ROGER AND ME

Production: Michael Moore for Dog Eat Dog Films; released by Warner Bros.
Direction: Michael Moore
Screenplay: Michael Moore
Cinematography: Christopher Beaver, John Prusak, Kevin Rafferty, and Bruce
  Schermer
Editing: Wendey Stanzler and Jennifer Beman
Sound: Judy Irving and Charley Arnot
MPAA rating: R
Running time: 90 minutes

    Principal characters:
      Michael Moore .... Himself

    After making a major splash with audiences and critics alike at the Toronto and
New York film festivals, *Roger and Me*, a rollicking, populist documentary made
for $250,000 by Michael Moore (and purchased for $3 million by Warner Bros.),
opened in December, 1989, to the kind of fanfare reserved for Hollywood's biggest
year-end releases. *Roger and Me* proceeded to spark the hottest media debate since
Spike Lee's *Do the Right Thing* (1989; reviewed in this volume), as critics, political
columnists, and television talk-show hosts offered sharply divided opinions of the
veracity of Moore's filmmaking tactics as well as his public persona. In addition,
animal rights activists condemned Moore for depicting the slaughter of a rabbit on
film, and one of the United States' most powerful corporations, now very nervous,
threatened to pull sponsorship from any program on which Moore appeared. That
corporation was General Motors (GM), and *Roger and Me* is a sardonic, angry, and
outrageously humorous chronicle of how GM's greed (as embodied by the figure of
chairman Roger Smith, the Roger of the film's title) has all but destroyed the city in
which it was founded, Flint, Michigan. Moore uses a nonlinear, unorthodox style to
present a savage, real-life fable of how the outrages of 1980's capitalism in the
United States have betrayed the trust of the working people. In the process, he peels
back the veneer of a Reaganism that uses public relations uplift as a panacea for
deep-rooted social problems.
    Moore makes no pretense for objectivity. From the first line of the film ("I was
kind of a strange child"), Moore himself is front and center; the film is, after all,
called *Roger and Me*. Opening with home films of himself as a child, Moore takes
the audience on a brief tour of his family and boyhood in the 1950's, when Flint was
a prosperous, all-American company town, shows us his abbreviated career as a
magazine editor in San Francisco, and his return home just in time to witness
firsthand Flint's sharp, downward slide into "the worst place to live in America"
(according to *Money* magazine). As GM begins to move its already profitable
operations to Mexico, where workers are paid seventy cents an hour and there are

no pesky unions to cause trouble, plants are closed and thousands in Flint are thrown out of work. As Roger Smith is giving himself a $2 million raise, the city is cutting back to twice-monthly garbage collection and the rat population is growing larger than the human population. As Roger Smith is enjoying his wild game dinner at the Grosse Pointe Yacht Club's Sportsman's Night, Flint's citizens are raising rabbits for "pets or meat," selling their own blood for cash, and taking exciting new jobs at Taco Bell (where, as the manager says, "every time you turn around there's another challenge"). As the city pays Reverend Robert Schuller $20,000 to bring his inspirational message to the local hockey arena (he advises residents to "turn your hurt into a halo") and the Star Theatre of Flint gives discounts to GM employees to see such sterling entertainers as Bobby Vinton, Mitzi Gaynor and Anita Bryant (who advises the unemployed to "go out and do something with your hands"), the Flint post office processes eighty-two thousand address changes, and the city's violent crime rate becomes the highest in the United States.

Moore structures *Roger and Me* around his quest to meet with Roger Smith and convince him to witness firsthand the damage his decisions have wrought on Flint; though Moore is, not surprisingly, unsuccessful, this device becomes a perfect metaphor for the unaccountability of our leaders to the problems that they create. Moore narrates the film with biting sarcasm, while he mercilessly crosscuts between the haves and the have-nots, finding a bitter irony at the heart of every civic improvement and corporate decision. He invades the annual "Great Gatsby" party, for which the city's wealthy thoughtfully hire the local unemployed (mostly black) to be human statues. He presents the city's scheme to turn Flint into a tourist mecca with new construction—a Hyatt Regency Hotel (where citizens are allowed to ride the city's only escalator), the Water Street Pavilion (an upscale shopping center described as having "a major parking ramp" that is conveniently located where "buses can pull up and unload forty senior citizens or so"), and a $100 million theme park called Autoworld (that featured a GM exhibit in which a puppet auto worker sings a song to the robot replacing him on the assembly line called "Me and My Buddy"). All three of these tourist magnets failed. In *Roger and Me*'s cutting climax, Roger Smith is shown reading his annual Christmas message from Charles Dickens (the most famous literary chronicler of industrial abuse), calling Christmas "the one time of year when men and women open their hearts freely," while, in Flint, a family is being evicted from their home on Christmas Eve, tree and all. The satire here is razor sharp.

Moore, like all the best documentary filmmakers, has an extraordinary knack for capturing moments of telling insight from his subjects but, unlike most documentary filmmakers, Moore's "found" moments are invariably bracingly amusing. He holds the camera on his subjects long enough for them to reveal their own evasions. Thus, when GM lobbyist Tom Kay tries to argue that he is sure that Roger Smith "has as strong a social conscience as anybody," he stumbles and mispronounces the word conscience. When Miss Michigan, Kaye Lani Rae Rafko, is asked if she has any message for the downtrodden people of Flint, she blurts "keep your fingers crossed for me as I go for the gold." When a former autoworker tries to explain why he prefers his new job as a prison guard (even though it only pays half as much), he says "it's much nicer in here," but he cannot be heard over the din of an argument that erupts between inmates. When Roger Smith closes a stockholders' meeting before Moore has a chance to speak, pretending not to notice him, Moore's camera and audio capture Smith conspiratorially gloating to a colleague about how they managed to avoid him. The incidents are endless (and priceless).

Upon its release, the muckraking *Roger and Me* not surprisingly began to draw heat from all sides. In particular, animal rights groups were incensed by Moore's decision to show the "pets or meat" saleswoman clubbing a rabbit to death and skinning it on camera. Yet, since the woman explains that the rabbit is going to be her dinner for the evening (and that she sometimes makes only ten or fifteen dollars a week), their outrage seems misdirected. Had Moore stopped filming, would the rabbit be any more alive today? More valid as criticism are the arguments that Moore reorders events to accentuate his points. To create ironic juxtapositions and a compact sequence of events that has cumulative power, Moore implies inaccurately that certain actions were taken as solutions to specific problems that, in reality, were not. The Hyatt Regency Hotel, Water Street Pavilion, and Autoworld were all constructed before the plant closing depicted in the film occurred, Reverend Schuller came to town in 1982, and the thirty-five thousand layoffs described were spread over a decade and not concentrated into the time frame that the film covers. They were, however, caused by General Motors, albeit as a result of layoffs and plant closings that occurred over a less dramatically convenient period of time. While these details reflect a questionable exercise of artistic license on Moore's part (particularly within a documentary format), they do not discredit Moore's essential point that the unimpeded pursuit of unlimited profits by corporations has undercut the working class in the United States during the Ronald Reagan era. They also do not negate Moore's success at satirizing the popular 1980's emphasis on positive thinking and patriotic rhetoric (so supremely embodied by Reagan and corporate heads such as Roger Smith).

The controversy surrounding *Roger and Me*, however, had definite impact. After winning Best Documentary citations from the New York Film Critics, the Los Angeles Film Critics, the National Society of Film Critics, and the National Board of Review, the film was not even nominated for the Academy Award for Best Documentary. The documentary selection committee of the Academy of Motion Picture Arts and Sciences are traditionalists, having similarly shut out the most lauded documentary of 1988, *The Thin Blue Line*, because of its modernist approach. Both Errol Moriss, the director of *The Thin Blue Line*, and Michael Moore have very individualistic styles that do not conform to the long-held view that the proper documentator should be self-effacing and "objective," his individual voice subservient to the thematic material at hand. What is often ignored in this cherished ideal is that all documentary filmmakers, like all fiction filmmakers, begin with a subject they want to explore and points that they want to make, decide what to include in the frame of their camera based on these points, pare down their footage to that which best expresses their intentions, and juxtapose sequences and images to convey their themes with the greatest dramatic (or comic) power. Morris and Moore have merely called attention to this process by being more adept than most at selecting styles that effectively communicate their respective agendas. For Morris, it was a hypnotic obsession with how the details of a crime can shift from varying points of view and how those details can be made to serve political agendas that have very little to do with justice. For Moore, it is an American huckster's appreciation of how political and cultural leaders avoid accountability and divert the energy of the masses from progressive change by purveying fantasy and rhetorical myth. He is an angry absurdist. Not merely a detached chronicler of corporate uncaring and abuse, Moore intends to be the comic ringleader of urban revolt.

Jeffrey L. Fenner

Reviews

American Film: Magazine of the Film and Television Arts. XV, November, 1989, p. 14.
The Christian Science Monitor. December 15, 1989, p. 10.
Detroit News. December 17, 1989, p. E1.
LA Weekly. December 22, 1989, p. 35.
Los Angeles Times. December 20, 1989, VI, p. 1.
The New Republic. CCII, January 22, 1990, p. 26.
The New York Times. September 27, 1989, p. C15.
The New Yorker. LXV, January 8, 1990, p. 90.
Newsweek. CXIV, October 9, 1989, p. 113.
Rolling Stone. January 11, 1990, p. 30.
Time. CXXXV, January 8, 1990, p. 77.
Variety. CCCXXXVI, September 13, 1989, p. 36.
The Village Voice. December 26, 1989, p. 102.

SAY ANYTHING

Production: Polly Platt for Gracie Films; released by Twentieth Century-Fox
Direction: Cameron Crowe
Screenplay: Cameron Crowe
Cinematography: Laszlo Kovacs
Editing: Richard Marks
Production design: Mark Mansbridge
Set decoration: Joe Mitchell
Makeup: Cheri Minns
Costume design: Jane Ruhm
Sound: Patrick Drummond
Music: Richard Gibbs and Anne Dudley
Song: John Betts and Martin Page, "All for Love"
MPAA rating: PG-13
Running time: 100 minutes

> *Principal characters:*
> Lloyd Dobler.......................... John Cusack
> Diane Court .... Ione Skye
> James Court........................... John Mahoney
> Corey Flood........................... Lili Taylor
> D. C. .... Amy Brooks

Say Anything is first-time director Cameron Crowe's fresh and full-dimensional examination of the standard boy-meets-girl story. With his 1982 screenplay for *Fast Times at Ridgemont High*, Crowe created the quintessential teen sex comedy, populated by revamped and updated teen stereotypes. With *Say Anything*, Crowe revamps one of the oldest story lines and creates an amusing, moving portrait of two young lovers dealing with some of the most important questions that life can pose.

The film, set in a suburb of Seattle, begins with Lloyd Dobler (John Cusack) declaring to his two best friends, Corey (Lili Taylor) and D. C. (Amy Brooks), that he is going to ask out Diane Court (Ione Skye). The two young women are skeptical of Lloyd's chances of success, since Lloyd is a marginal nobody and Diane is the most successful and intelligent student at their high school. Lloyd, however, has made up his mind and begins plotting his strategy. Diane is first seen rehearsing the valedictorian speech that she plans to give at her high school graduation ceremony. She rehearses while her father, James Court (John Mahoney), drives her to the ceremony. Mr. Court is Diane's biggest fan, and he listens to her rehearse with rapt attention, offering encouragement and approval with her every word. Diane's speech is received flatly by her classmates. Because of her ambitious efforts to excel, Diane has succeeded in alienating herself from the rest of the student body. Lloyd, however, sitting with the rest of the graduating class, still believes that she is perfection.

After graduation, Lloyd calls Diane but talks to Mr. Court. Right after Mr. Court hangs up with Lloyd, he receives a call that compels him to drive immediately to his business—a nursing home that he owns and operates—and seek out Diane, who works there part-time. Mr. Court informs Diane that she has just won the Reed Fellowship, a prestigious scholarship that will enable her to study abroad in England.

The next day, Diane returns Lloyd's call, and he asks her to attend a postgraduation party with him. She agrees to go, and Lloyd is astounded. When Lloyd arrives to pick up Diane, he is greeted at the door by Mr. Court, with whom he talks briefly, making an unfavorable first impression. When Diane appears, she is dressed in a stunning low-cut, high-hemline white dress, much to the surprise of her father and Lloyd. The party is wild, attended by hundreds of spirited postgraduates, many of whom are friends of Lloyd, none of whom are friends of Diane, but all of whom are stunned when the two arrive together. Lloyd is immediately designated "Key Master," the person who confiscates everyone's car keys and returns them only when the owner is sober enough to drive. As Lloyd assumes his dubious honor, Diane is whisked away by other party members and soon makes acquaintances with people she has always wanted to get to know.

During the festivities, a member of the high school faculty shows up, one of the favorites of the students who is also Lloyd's career counselor. She talks to Lloyd and asks him why he never declared a specific career goal for himself. He tells her that he did not specify anything, because he has no idea what he wants to be and to specify a career would be dishonest. He tells her that his father, who is an officer in the Army stationed overseas, wants him to become a career officer as well. Lloyd says he is not interested in the Army nor is he really interested in attending the local junior college. He says that he is looking for a "dare to be great" situation, one that he will know when he confronts it. Finally, the party winds down. After returning all the keys to their owners and driving a drunken guest home, Lloyd and Diane drive around until dawn. She tells Lloyd about her relationship with her father and about how, when her parents split up, she was forced to choose which parent with whom to live. She confesses that her father is also her best friend.

For their second date, Diane asks Lloyd to have dinner at her house along with her father and some family friends. The dinner progresses relatively smoothly until it is interrupted by the unexpected arrival of two federal agents, who inform Mr. Court that he is under investigation for tax fraud. Mr. Court is outraged by their accusations and angrily tells them to leave.

Later, Lloyd visits with Diane while she works with her father at the nursing home. Afterward, she tells Lloyd that she feels guilty for spending so much time with him and neglecting her father in his time of need. Lloyd agrees and asks that they concentrate on being friends. They spend much of their time together, however, and eventually make love. Diane tells her father that she is in love with Lloyd and reveals that she has second thoughts of leaving for England and abandoning her father when he is obviously in need of moral support. Mr. Court insists that she go to England and that she break up with Lloyd before things progress any further and she starts having more thoughts of giving up the Reed Fellowship. He tells her that she has a strong and successful future ahead of her, while Lloyd does not.

The next day, Lloyd and Diane meet and drive through town. Lloyd tells Diane that he loves her, and Diane is concerned by his words. She tells him that this is a very difficult time for her and that she has to concentrate on concerns other than their relationship. Lloyd pulls the car over and asks if she is telling him that they are breaking up. At first she says no, but then she hands him a pen and tells him to write to her when she is in England. Lloyd is devastated.

Mr. Court becomes more and more concerned about the Internal Revenue Service (IRS) investigation. Witnessing his concern, Diane makes an appointment with the chief investigator and asks him to tell her the reason for the inquiry. The director tells her that her father has been stealing money from his patients at the nursing home for years. Diane cannot believe the accusation is true. Upon returning home, however, she snoops around, breaks into one of her father's locked boxes, and discovers a large stash of hundred dollar bills. Outraged, she drives to the nursing home and asks him point blank if he is guilty. When he says no, she tells him that she found the money. When he tries to justify his motives, telling her that the money is for her future career endeavors, she screams at him that he is a liar and a thief and storms out. She drives to the gym where Lloyd is practicing kick boxing and declares her love for him.

The IRS investigation finds Mr. Court guilty, and he lands in jail. Lloyd visits Mr. Court, telling him Diane has come along also but refuses to get out of the car. Mr. Court asks Lloyd if he is planning to accompany Diane to England when she leaves. Lloyd says yes, that he has found what he wants to do with his life and that it is to be with Diane. Mr. Court explodes, saying that Lloyd is mediocre and that he is not a permanent part of Diane's life, only a distraction. Diane then appears, and Mr. Court asks for her forgiveness. Instead, Diane hands him the pen she had given Lloyd and tells her father to write to her. The film ends with Lloyd and Diane on a plane bound for England.

With *Say Anything*, director/writer Crowe has accomplished a rare feat: He has made a film about teenagers that contains no gratuitous sex, gross humor, or food fights. While his screenplay for *Fast Times at Ridgemont High* contained much of all of the above, Crowe in his new film concentrates on creating fully realized human beings.

With the very first scene of the film—Lloyd's conversation with Corey and D. C. about dating Diane—Crowe plunges the audience into a full-dimensional world peopled by caring, compassionate characters. It is startling to see teenagers, especially teens of the opposite sex, actually relating to one another as friends and not as potential sex partners or as adversaries exchanging crude remarks. Unlike the characters in *When Harry Met Sally* (1989; reviewed in this volume), who demonstrate the impossibility of men and women ever being friends, Crowe takes for granted that such friendships exist. Also, in the first scene of the film, Crowe sets the tone of the film and maintains this aura of heartfelt compassion throughout.

There are no stereotypes and no malicious characters. Even Mr. Court, with his deceits and thievery, is not played as an ogre. On the contrary, his character closely parallels that of Lloyd; both are willing to sacrifice their own future well-being for Diane's sake. Crowe makes the similarities between Lloyd and Mr. Court obvious. Yet he also makes obvious the key difference in their characters. Mr. Court has instilled in Diane the importance of honesty and openness, but then Mr. Court commits the ultimate betrayal by perverting his own philosophy.

While Mr. Court is baffled over why Diane is attracted to Lloyd, it is obvious to Diane and everyone else why Lloyd is so dynamic: He is sincere, honest, and caring. In one scene, Corey tells Lloyd, "I may be a good person, but you, Lloyd, are a great person." In another scene, Corey, D. C., and another female friend pose the question: If you were Diane Court, would you be attracted to Lloyd? They all come to the same conclusion: yes. Cusack's performance as Lloyd is a stunning achievement. His subtle, fast-clipped speaking mannerisms, filled with self-assurance one moment and confusion the next, coupled with his wide-eyed expressions of bewilderment and hope, exude a naïve sincerity. He is totally convincing as a high school graduate who sees that his chance at greatness lies in his ability to love another human being.

Say Anything can be viewed as a subtle, subversive piece of propaganda disguised as a teen sex comedy. After all, it preaches that human worth is measured not by wealth, social position, or even intelligence but by a person's ability to express honesty, sincerity, and compassion. It also insists that men and women are equal. In other words, it goes against all the basic principles of a successful, ultracompetitive capitalistic society. *Say Anything* is very persuasive in its viewpoint because its characters are so appealing, so sympathetic. As he did with *Fast Times at Ridgemont High*, Crowe has once again redefined the teenage character. This time, however, he has endowed his young creations with oversized hearts instead of oversized glands.

Jim Kline

Reviews
Chicago Tribune. April 14, 1989, VII, p. 38.
Cosmopolitan. CCVII, July, 1989, p. 28.
Films in Review. XL, September, 1989, p. 422.
Los Angeles Magazine. May, 1989, p. 72.
New York Magazine. May 8, 1989, p. 80.
The New York Times. April 14, 1989, p. C11.
The New Yorker. LXV, May 15, 1989, p. 121.
Newsweek. CXIII, April 17, 1989, p. 72.
People Weekly. XXXI, April 24, 1989, p. 16.
Variety. CCCXXXIV, April 12, 1989, p. 20.
The Washington Post. April 14, 1989, p. C1.

SCANDAL

Origin: Great Britain
Released: 1989
Released in U.S.: 1989
Production: Stephen Woolley for Palace Pictures; released by Miramax Films
Direction: Michael Caton-Jones
Screenplay: Michael Thomas; based in part on the stories "Nothing But," by
    Christine Keeler and Sandy Fawkes; "Mandy," by Mandy Rice-Davies and
    Shirley Flack; "Stephen Ward Speaks," by Warwick Charlton; "The Profumo
    Affair, a Summing Up," by Judge Sparrow; and "Scandal '63" by Clive Irvind,
    Ron Hall, and Jeremy Wallington
Cinematography: Mike Molloy
Editing: Angus Newton
Production design: Simon Holland
Art direction: Chris Townsend
Set decoration: Maria Djurkovic
Costume design: Jane Robinson
Sound: Eddy Joseph
Music: Carl Davis
MPAA rating: R
Running time: 106 minutes

> *Principal characters:*
> Stephen Ward . . . . John Hurt
> Christine Keeler . . . . Joanne Whalley-Kilmer
> Mandy Rice-Davies . . . . Bridget Fonda
> John Profumo . . . . Ian McKellan
> Lord Astor . . . . Leslie Phillips
> Mariella Novotny . . . . Britt Ekland
> Mervyn Griffith-Jones . . . . Daniel Massey
> Johnnie Edgecombe . . . . Roland Gift
> Eugene Ivanov . . . . Jeroen Krabbe

Given the factually sensational material that inspired it, *Scandal* might easily have deteriorated into relentless sleaziness. With help from an economical script by Michael Thomas and a group of fine acting performances, however, director Michael Caton-Jones manages to control this drama of private pleasure and public turbulence. A thirty-one-year-old Scot, making his directorial debut with this feature, Caton-Jones brings with him an unestablished view and a fairly unopportunistic grasp of the affair. What he ultimately delivers is something personal about troubled, unfortunate people, not reckless reminiscences about the high and mighty.

The events of 1961 through 1963 unfold in tapestry-walled rooms glowing dimly, in smoky hallways and damp back-alleys. The names involved echo through time like sin recaptured: John Profumo, Lord Astor, Christine Keeler, Mandy Rice-Davies, Stephen Ward, Eugene Ivanov. Yet reincarnating the episodes is not dependent here on viewer memory; Caton-Jones and his troupe carefully reconstruct them from deep secrets, beneath all the thick, black headlines of London tabloids.

Scandal begins in the lecherous eye of Ward (John Hurt), a hugely successful osteopath who numbers among his patients Winston Churchill, J. Paul Getty, and Elizabeth Taylor. He enjoys hanging around lords and powerful politicians, the ticket to whose friendship, he believes, is his ability to arrange unthreatening liaisons with beautiful, sexually imaginative girls. His own lusts are a bit confused, certainly unorthodox. He seems to be an untouchable voyeur, yet his capacity for judging beauty is neither cold nor unenthusiastic. When he spies a charming seventeen-year-old showgirl named Christine Keeler (Joanne Whalley-Kilmer) in a cabaret, he decides to play Pygmalion. More than eager for the glamorous life, Christine accepts all the demands made on her by the smooth-talking gentleman. So accepting is she that, after moving into his flat, she does not even ask him why he chooses to sleep alone.

Although he maintains other attractive women in his stable, including the saucy postadolescent Mandy Rice-Davies (Bridget Fonda), Christine is his prize, the only one they all ask for, a sensuous charmer with dark, alluring young eyes who creates manifestations of fantasy for Ward, who nevertheless controls her. "Lick your lips," he tells her as she saunters toward an obviously interested man in an expensive private club. To the approval of her hedonistic mentor, she becomes the delight of businessmen and diplomats, including Ward's Russian friend Eugene Ivanov (Jeroen Krabbe). Knowing that Ivanov is a spy, Ward hopes to use Christine as a source of bedroom information with which he, in turn, will try to impress his friends in high places. Christine's feelings for the Russian naval attaché, however, are not particularly strong. Soon after her conquest of him, she attends a wild party at the estate of Lord and Lady Astor. She runs naked and drunk into the next-door neighbor John Profumo (Ian McKellan), secretary of state for war in Harold Macmillan's Conservative cabinet. Thoroughly fascinated, Profumo pursues her passionately but secretly, for his wife is not as disinterested or broad-minded as Lady Astor. For months the dazzled minister sends Christine notes and gifts and, at least on one occasion, leaves her money. Yet the potential danger in their relationship eventually overcomes his desire, and he stops visiting.

Christine herself becomes restless and unnerved by Ward's voyeurism. She leaves him and, for nearly a year, drifts among providing lovers. One of them is a hot-tempered West Indian named Johnnie Edgecomb (Roland Gift), who, gun in hand and fiercely jealous, arrives one day at Ward's flat, where Christine is staying with Mandy. Johnnie fires several shots at their door; no one is injured, but tabloid reporters cover the story, and the machinery of scandal is set in motion.

Disappointed by the crudeness of the circumstances and fearful that his own name will be ruined, Ward decides to drop Christine completely. When his worried friends Astor and Profumo confer with him on the danger Christine poses, Ward says, "I dreamed her up. I can make her vanish."

Christine, however, does not go away just yet. In need of funds to survive, she decides to sell her story to the *Sunday Pictorial*, which is only too willing to engage in checkbook journalism. Christine's story is called "The Model, the Minister, and the Russian Spy." Publication of it gives birth to further rumor and innuendo, and before long Profumo is compelled to make a personal statement before members of the House of Commons. He denies any impropriety with Christine. No one, it seems, is willing to believe him, and eventually he feels the pressure sufficiently to resign his appointment.

Police begin investigating Ward. They question Christine, Mandy, and all of Ward's clients and friends, especially the more notorious ones, such as Mariella Novotny (Britt Ekland). Not surprisingly, all begin to distance themselves from him as inconspicuously as possible. Ivanov himself is recalled by Moscow. Each of Ward's connections dissolves as a result of the notoriety, which quickly has reached out to international outlets.

After questioning 147 people, the police arrest Ward, whom they accuse of living off the earnings of prostitutes, specifically Christine and Mandy. The trial is a scandal-sheet reporter's dream, featuring nearly constant questions and answers of the most intimate kind, spoken before a noisy audience, with even noisier people in the streets outside the Old Bailey. Mandy seems to thrive on the circus atmosphere, achieving the status of an impromptu entertainer. When asked by Ward's defense attorney, "Are you aware that Lord Astor denies any impropriety in his acquaintanceship with you?" she responds, "Well he would, wouldn't he?" She then pauses like a pro to acknowledge laughter from the gallery. On her way out of the building, she pauses to alter her makeup and fashion the correct smile for the media and the aroused crowd outside.

The tone of the rest of the trial is drastically different. Whereas Mandy came alive in the public spotlight, Christine is extremely nervous, self-conscious, and guilt-ridden. What is worse, she reflects upon the real love she feels for Ward, despite his patriarchal manipulativeness. The prosecution literally reduces her to tears, and ultimately the defendant himself rises to protest sadly on her behalf, "It's not fair!" In the noise of voices and gavel, he and Christine look at each other a last time. Later, before swallowing a fatal dose of barbiturates, Ward writes, "I'm sorry to disappoint the vultures."

Network television would approach a project such as *Scandal* as "docudrama," material volatile enough, despite its age, to be delivered in small, juicy junks before and after commercialized messages. What Caton-Jones, writer Thomas, and producer Stephen Woolley have done is to subordinate historical imitation, though it must be acknowledged that Whalley-Kilmer does indeed look strikingly like old photographs of the young Christine Keeler. Instead of reigniting the explosions of yesteryear, they present visual diary entries about pleasure-seeking individuals who become victims first of their own private ecstasy systems and then of a gaping society that in its ill-spent leisure, searches for what the tabloids constantly provide: dirt to supply conversation and vicarious wickedness. The filmmakers, however, choose not to plow that dirt.

In fact, Keeler and Ward and, to a lesser extent, Rice-Davies are presented here more as results of scandal than they are careless perpetrators of it. Profumo, on the other hand, is soon demoted to the inside pages, since the demand for his thinly haired scalp is comparatively slight. Because the osteopath and his wenches are the variable sacrifice, the minister looks to be a casual risk taker who, once caught, gives up his seat of power with only moderate embarrassment, then retreats quietly off-camera. Obviously, satire is not a high priority here either.

At scattered moments in *Scandal*, viewers are brought into unnerving contact with the pain of isolated punishment, made harsher when dealt by the sufferers themselves. The depth of Hurt's fine performance is measured in full as he prepares Ward's act of death—the inverse of all the acts of love he has previously established. The camera watches him without a blink, coldly recording the friendlessness, the social ostracism, that must torture him. His thoughts are accurate, predictive: No one comes to his funeral. In another instance, the private pain belongs to Christine, and it is presented as acute agony, in black and white, as the whole world watches. She emerges from the court as if from a dark cave, and the masses from the bright of day push forward, to get closeup photographs, to touch her hem, or perhaps to brutalize her. As they surge forward, she cowers against the stone wall, terrified. Whalley-Kilmer's remarkable face, which viewers first see in its youthful lasciviousness at a cabaret, is by now frozen in anxious caution.

Andrew Jefchak

Reviews

American Film: Magazine of the Film and Television Arts. XIV, March, 1989, p. 10.
Films in Review. XL, September, 1989, p. 422.
Los Angeles Times. April 27, 1989, VI, p. 1.
The Nation. June 5, 1989, p. 787.
National Review. June 30, 1989, p. 54.
New Republic. May 29, 1989, p. 24.
The New York Times. April 28, 1989, p. C10.
The New Yorker. LXV, May 15, 1989, p. 121.
Newsweek. May 1, 1989, p. 76.
The Spectator. CCLXII, March 11, 1989, p. 45.
Time. CXXXIII, May 1, 1989, p. 68.
Variety. CCCXXXIV, March 8, 1989, p. 21.
The Washington Post. April 28, 1989, p. D1.

SCENES FROM THE CLASS STRUGGLE IN BEVERLY HILLS

Production: James C. Katz for North Street Films; released by Cinecom
    Entertainment Group
Direction: Paul Bartel
Screenplay: Bruce Wagner; based on a story by Paul Bartel and Wagner
Cinematography: Steven Fierberg
Editing: Alan Toomayan
Production design: Alex Tavoularis
Art direction: Robert Kensinger
Makeup: Cinzia Zanetti
Costume design: Dona Granata
Sound: Trevor Black
Music: Stanley Myers
MPAA rating: R
Running time: 102 minutes

> *Principal characters:*
> Clare Lipkin .... Jacqueline Bisset
> Frank............................... Ray Sharkey
> Juan............................... Robert Beltran
> Lisabeth .... Mary Woronov
> Peter .... Ed Begley, Jr.
> Howard........................... Wallace Shawn
> To-bel .... Arnetia Walker
> Zandra........................... Rebecca Schaeffer
> Willie.............................. Barret Oliver
> Rosa................................ Edith Diaz
> Dr. Mo Van De Kamp................... Paul Bartel
> Sidney .... Paul Mazursky

For director Paul Bartel, having a personal vision that is more often than not considered offensive, vulgar, and tasteless, *Scenes from the Class Struggle in Beverly Hills* was no easy film to have produced in Hollywood. Following his cult classic *Eating Raoul* (1982), which focused on the murder and consumption of wealthy perverts, Bartel was given $2.5 million to make *Not for Publication*, a comedy that died before it got off the ground. Even the sequel to *Eating Raoul* did not do well because of the original's failure in overseas distribution. Only *Lust in the Dust* (1985), starring Divine, made up for its lackluster box-office receipts in its success on videocassette. It was finally an independent studio, Cinecom, that gave *Scenes from the Class Struggle in Beverly Hills* its $4.5 million budget and then wrestled with Bartel during the film's editing.

Raunchy camp, black humor, and foul language surge through every stereotypical role that Bartel has created in *Scenes from the Class Struggle in Beverly Hills*. The two central characters are an aging actress, Clare Lipkin (Jacqueline Bisset), who is recently widowed when her husband befittingly dies during orgasm, and Lisabeth (Mary Woronov) a recent divorcée who is fumigating her home to rid it of the stench of her former husband. Although Clare is constantly beseeched by her dead husband Sidney (Paul Mazursky) from his un-resting place in Hell, she seems pleased that he is gone so that she might have a second chance to resume her career as the soap opera queen she once was.

Clare invites Lisabeth, her son Willie (Barret Oliver), and houseman Frank (Ray Sharkey) to stay with her during their home's fumigation. She suddenly finds herself with more than a full house when Lisabeth's third-rate playwright brother, Peter (Ed Begley, Jr.), breezes into town with his new and trashy black wife, To-bel (Arnetia Walker), who is in the marriage purely for the sex (even Clare's dog tries to bed her) and the advantages of Rodeo Drive. Next returns Howard (Wallace Shawn), Lisabeth's sniveling former husband, who is horrified to run into To-bel, a former pornography star and the primary reason for his divorce. In addition to her guests, Clare has a precocious daughter in heat, Zandra (Rebecca Schaeffer), and her own houseman, Juan (Robert Beltran). Clare's quack diet doctor, Dr. Mo Van De Kamp (Paul Bartel), also appears to be a permanent fixture at the Lipkin house.

If not for the two housemen, there would be no progression at all in the story. The characters, hedonistic and decadent, are required to do nothing but gourmand- ize, dream about fame, prattle about nothing, and fantasize about sex, even to the point of bedding the servants for fun. It is Clare's boyish houseman, Juan, who propels the film into action. Juan has got himself into trouble with a gang of hoodlums over a gambling debt that he is unable to pay. That is the reason he is compelled to make a bet with Lisabeth's houseman, the rakish Frank. Frank con- cocts a game for the two of them in which the winner will be determined by the first one to seduce the other's employer. If Juan wins, he will be given the money to pay off his gambling debt. If he loses, he must submit his body to Frank for a night.

As the entire cast romps between the sheets and betwixt the various bedrooms in the Lipkin house for the sheer pleasure of unadulterated sex, Frank and Juan set out on their mission. Juan longs to be on the other side of the class line. Frank says that he has been on both sides and that there is no difference. Although Clare seems the most likely to submit to one of the servants, her decadence seems to slant more toward rich, dark chocolate cake than to Frank's amorous calls. Juan seems to be the only character who has any ounce of naïveté or innocence, which is displayed in his clumsy courting of Lisabeth.

Juan is also the only character who has any morals—although by uncustomary standards—when he truly falls in love with his quest, Lisabeth, and is willing to forfeit his victory to protect her virtue. Not realizing that Juan has already achieved his victory, Frank shams a night of passion for the benefit of Juan by using a drugged and passed-out Clare. Out of love for Lisabeth, Juan allows Frank to believe that he has won and freely gives his body to Frank. With this encounter,

Juan loses his innocence and comes of age.

It is Juan who really wins in the end, when he leaps over class boundaries. He and Lisabeth are preparing to leave on a trip in her chauffeur-driven car when the thugs return to eliminate Juan. Suddenly Frank becomes Juan's knight in shining armor as he pulls up on his motorcycle and tosses Juan money to pay his gambling debt.

The title, *Scenes from the Class Struggle in Beverly Hills*, is a misnomer. There is no struggle whatsoever. In fact, the classes seem to be relatively the same: greedy, avaricious, decadent, and obsessed with sex. Even Frank tells Juan that he has been on both sides and that there is no difference. Clare's dead husband takes this one step further. He states that there is no difference even in the afterlife and that his lust for passion has only been magnified.

Bartel has made every character in *Scenes from the Class Struggle in Beverly Hills* a stereotype to prove his point that all people are the same—that they are basically base with some good occasionally glimmering through. Of the stereotypes, Clare is the aging soap opera queen trying to make a comeback, Lisabeth is sexually uptight, Peter is an arrogant but terrible playwright, To-bel is the former pornography star prostituting herself for money but with a heart of gold underneath, and Frank is the conniving houseman who comes through for his own just in the nick of time. Only Juan and Lisabeth's cancer-stricken son, Willie (Barret Oliver), who is coming into an awareness of his sexuality, seems to have any childlike innocence.

Juan's naïveté in comparison to Frank's cunning smoothness shines through when he begins his haphazard courtship of Lisabeth. He is the only person whom the audience is allowed to feel for, because he is the only character in this sexual farce who feels. When he does fall into bed with Lisabeth, he falls in love. The only other touching scene in the entire film is when Frank—although he has lied and cheated to get Juan into bed—comes through with Juan's money in the end.

The decadence that accounts for the severe lack of movement in the characters also seems to have affected the cinematography. Bartel plants his camera to absorb the lust around it. It seldom moves until a change of location demands that it move. Were it not for the bet between the two housemen that sets the plot in motion, nothing would stir during the entire film.

Scenes from the Class Struggle in Beverly Hills has been billed a "delightful offensive comedy." Although Bartel has set out to shock his audience, he unfortunately does so in the first five minutes of the film. Audiences were jolted in *Eating Raoul* but without Bartel's self-indulgence. There were things in *Eating Raoul* that were left to the imagination. Although wealthy perverts were murdered by the film's heroes, they were murdered just outside the camera's range. That is not the case in *Scenes from the Class Struggle in Beverly Hills*. Seeing the same copulations from different angles or with different faces and hearing the same licentious prattle becomes boring and tiring.

Steven C. Kowall

Reviews

Boston Globe. June 16, 1989, p. 35.
The Christian Science Monitor. June 2, 1989, p. 15.
Films in Review. XL, October, 1989, p. 489.
Interview. July, 1989, p. 86.
LA Weekly. June 9, 1989.
Los Angeles Times. June 7, 1989, VI, p. 5.
The Nation. CCXLVIII, June 19, 1989, p. 860.
The New York Times. June 9, 1989, p. C13.
Newsweek. CXIII, June 12, 1989, p. 68.
Time. CXXXIII, June 12, 1989, p. 73.
Variety. CCCXXXV, May 10, 1989, p. 27.
Village View. June 9, 1989.
The Washington Post. June 17, 1989, p. D3.

SEA OF LOVE

Production: Martin Bregman and Louis A. Stroller; released by Universal Pictures
Direction: Harold Becker
Screenplay: Richard Price
Cinematography: Ronnie Taylor
Editing: David Bretherton
Production design: John Jay Moore
Art direction: Lucinda Zak
Set decoration: Gordon Sim
Makeup: Irene Kent and Irv Buchman
Costume design: Betsy Cox
Sound: Keith Wester
Music: Trevor Jones
MPAA rating: R
Running time: 112 minutes

Principal characters:
Frank Keller	Al Pacino
Helen	Ellen Barkin
Sherman	John Goodman
Gruber	Richard Jenkins
Terry	Michael Rooker
Frank, Sr.	William Hickey
Serafino	Paul Calderon
Struk	Gene Canfield
Miss Allen	Barbara Baxley

Sea of Love opens with a scene in which Frank Keller (Al Pacino) is doing a routine job. Pretending to be from the Yankees organization, he has filled a hall with criminals expecting to meet team members. Frank takes the stage to tell them that he has good news and bad news: They are all under arrest, but the good news is that the drinks are free. Out on the street he passes up the opportunity to arrest a late arrival when he sees the man has his son with him. These opening scenes show Frank has flair mixed with humor and compassion. At the same time, he is hardly a dedicated cop. He now does his job in a fairly perfunctory manner. He can retire after twenty years of service, but he does not know what to do with himself, so he puts up with what he knows. He is, in fact, somewhat pathetic, getting drunk and telephoning his former wife in the middle of the night. She has married another policeman, Gruber (Richard Jenkins), whom Frank constantly picks on and accuses of stealing his wife.

In many ways, Frank looks like a loser—except that he still has his curiosity, a spark of interest in the cases he investigates, especially in a series of murders of men who have put advertisements in the personals column of a New York City magazine. When a policeman from Queens, Sherman (John Goodman), points out the similar circumstances of the murders, the two men decide to team up on the case, even convincing a skeptical superior to allow them to place their own advertisement in the magazine and lure suspects to meetings at O'Neals', a restaurant across from Lincoln Center.

Al Pacino brings to the role of Frank Keller the intensity, excitement, and craziness that made him a star in *Dog Day Afternoon* (1975). What makes Pacino such a fascinating actor, however, is that he is more than manic; somehow he finds the humor in his characters—in this case, balancing Frank's passion against his experience. Frank knows when he is out of control and can view himself with some skepticism. As Richard Price, the screenwriter of *Sea of Love*, puts it in an article in *Esquire*, Pacino has "years on his face, he's got weight in his face, gravity."

It is the acting and the editing that set *Sea of Love* apart from so many other films that it resembles. It is a buddy film, a crime action adventure, a romance with a suspense plot. Is Helen (Ellen Barkin), one of the suspects Frank meets in O'Neals', a murderer, picking out men in the personals columns who have written poetry as a means of attracting women? She has many of the requisite qualities: She seems hard-boiled and aggressive toward men and secretive about her past. She is passionate and could have a streak of violence in her. It is the edge that Barkin gives Helen, the crookedness of her smile, the cant of her body (Helen almost never stands up straight), that makes it possible to believe she may be guilty.

Frank's complicated emotions keep getting in the way. As a cop he is suspicious and goes berserk when he finds a pistol in Helen's purse, thinking she is indeed the murderer and that he is her next victim. In fact, it is a starter pistol, presumably carried to frighten anyone who might molest her. Frank is the devious one who does not tell Helen, for example, that he is a cop. She discovers his true identity in a riveting scene when two punks come into her shoe shop and quickly spot Frank staring at them. One of them knows immediately that Frank is a cop and says so. Pacino's face is an incredible study as he stares the men down until they leave the shop. It is an unblinking, unflinching stare that is ready for anything—for the punks to leave or for them to start something, a stare that is all cop. At this moment, Frank is not a person; he becomes his job, and Helen knows it. In reply to her outrage at being deceived, Frank launches into a clichéd explanation about how a cop is never free to be himself and always is, in some sense, on duty, seeing things that others ignore and prepared for action. The speech is less convincing than the stare itself. The screenwriter could have taken it from countless films on the subject. It is one of those moments when words fail to convey the character. Pacino does his best, but the writing lets him down.

Sea of Love usually avoids clichés and sentimentality through humor. John Goodman as Sherman, for example, is not merely a fat sidekick but rather a shrewd, amusing middle-aged cop from Queens having a ball in an unusual Manhattan assignment. Like Frank, he shows a certain flair, in one scene exhibiting "some of the finest dancing by a fat guy since Ralph Kramden's mambo lesson," to quote Terrence Rafferty's observation in *The New Yorker*. It is Sherman who often calms Frank, although Sherman is capable of his own momentary craziness when he brings a woman from O'Neals' to Frank's apartment.

Editing and acting enhance each other by not dwelling for too long on any part of the film or on the characters' emotions. There is just enough of Frank's romance with Helen, which is judiciously set off by scenes with his buddies making jokes out of the poetry they offer to Frank and Sherman for the personals ad. Glimpses of Helen's life when she is not with Frank, of her young daughter sleeping, and of her mother meeting Frank at the door raise questions about whether she might be capable of murder. It seems unlikely, but then again she responds so minimally to Frank's personal questions that her motivations are in doubt.

In the end, *Sea of Love* is a love story. The poem Frank places in the magazine is one written by his mother and fondly quoted from memory by his father. Thus Helen responds to an authentic poem, not merely one made up for the occasion by policemen. "Sea of Love" is the song left playing on the stereo of one of the murdered men. It is a nostalgic song about love. It could be a song about a past love, a song that is a memory of falling in love, or both. It was recorded by Phil Phillips in 1959, so it is, in fact, a period piece, a part of Frank's growing up. The record is also in Helen's collection, so that viewers are made to wonder whether the record is meant to identify her as the killer or as the romantic Frank wants to love. The song is a simple but effective device, expressing a yearning to which personals ads speak, a desire to find in love a sweet acceptance of another that Frank and Helen desperately want but distrust. The song makes them feel younger, simpler, and more giving than they have a right to expect from each other. The film has a similar effect on its viewers, making them hope that what Frank suspects about Helen is not true and that somehow there can be a sea of love to wash over them like the sound track bathing viewers in the lush romanticism of the song's lyrics.

Carl Rollyson

Reviews

Chicago Tribune. September, 15, 1989, VII, p. 37.
Commonweal. CXVI, October 20, 1989, p. 565.
Los Angeles Times. September 15, 1989, VI, p. 8.
National Review. XLI, November 10, 1989, p. 61.
The New Republic. CCI, October 9, 1989, p. 25.
The New Yorker. LXV, September 18, 1989, p. 100.
The New York Times. September 15, 1989, p. C12.
Newsweek. CXIV, September 18, 1989, p. 81.
Time. CXXXIV, September 25, 1989, p. 78.
Variety. CCCXXXVI, September 13, 1989, p. 18.

SEE NO EVIL, HEAR NO EVIL

Production: Marvin Worth; released by Tri-Star Pictures
Direction: Arthur Hiller
Screenplay: Earl Barret, Arne Sultan, Eliot Wald, Andrew Kurtzman, and Gene
   Wilder
Cinematography: Victor J. Kemper
Editing: Robert C. Jones
Production design: Robert Gundlach
Art direction: James T. Singelis
Set decoration: George DeTitta, Jr.
Special effects: Connie Brink and William Traynor
Costume design: Ruth Morley
Sound: Gordon Ecker and Bruce Stambler
Music direction: Michael Dittrick
Music: Stewart Copeland
MPAA rating: R
Running time: 103 minutes

> *Principal characters:*
> Wally Karew . . . . Richard Pryor
> Dave Lyons. . . . . Gene Wilder
> Eve . . . . Joan Severance
> Kirgo . . . . Kevin Spacey
> Braddock . . . . Alan North
> Sutherland . . . . Anthony Zerbe
> Adele . . . . Kirsten Childs

See No Evil, Hear No Evil reunites Richard Pryor and Gene Wilder for the first time in almost a decade. Like their earlier films—*Silver Streak* (1976), also directed by Arthur Hiller, and *Stir Crazy* (1980)—*See No Evil, Hear No Evil* relies on liberal doses of blue humor and chase scenes. The premise of the film, however, finds Pryor and Wilder caught between their trademark free-for-all humor and a social message about physical handicaps. Wally Karew (Richard Pryor) and Dave Lyons (Gene Wilder) are a blind and deaf team who become involved in a murder outside their newsstand in New York City. The film revels in good intentions. Pryor and Wilder spent time researching their roles at the Braille Institute in Los Angeles and the New York League for the Hard of Hearing. In a goodwill gesture, Tri-Star made available captioned versions of the film for hearing-impaired audiences.

It is never clear, however, whether the social message was integral to the premise or an afterthought designed to ward off protests. The gratuitous linkage between sensory impairment and drunk driving, divorce, and other social ills causes the film to lose focus. In the end, *See No Evil, Hear No Evil* appears to be a compromise, rather than a synthesis, between the outrageous humor of Pryor and Wilder and a coherent statement on the blind and deaf.

The opening sequence, however, which introduces the viewer to the sights and sounds of New York City that are denied Wally and Dave, promises a much more complex film. Stunning aerial shots of New York City emphasize its visual appeal. Next, a series of ground level shots reveal the unappealing noises of the city. In addition to traffic and construction sounds, these include street corner arguments among various ethnic groups. These shots establish various thematic tensions and divide them into either sight or sound so that they correspond with the two main characters. Dave, who can see, is a calm person who retreats from life, while Wally, who can hear, is confrontational, like the other quarreling ethnics.

In the midst of the street noises, Dave stands off the curb waiting for the light to change, unaware that a truck is honking at him. In a series of close-ups, we see magnified lips mouth insults, the most painful and accurate being, "What are you, deaf?" Dave, able to read lips, responds to these insults, whereupon the blind Wally Karew, who is passing by, believes that Dave is addressing him. Dave, meanwhile, because he is not looking in Wally's direction, is unaware of Wally's counter-challenge.

See No Evil, Hear No Evil is meticulous in setting up these visual and aural gags, even if they are oftentimes predictable and implausible. Despite Wilder's reported research into deafness, the aural gags require that Dave almost never look around to see if he is missing something. Central to these gags is the theme of "passing" as a nonhandicapped person. Wally refuses to use a cane, and so his sister, Adele (Kirsten Childs), often must rescue him. Once, posing as a sighted person, he leads another blind man across the street and into the back end of a truck parked on the corner. Likewise, Dave hides the fact that he is deaf, which results in fractured conversations whenever he looks away from a speaker.

The two men next run into each other when Wally applies for a job at Dave's newsstand. After some confusion, each man owns up to his handicap, and the two agree to work together. While eating ice cream cones in the park after work, Dave admits that his greatest fear about being deaf is making a fool of himself. Wally offers to solve the problem immediately and places his cone on Dave's head. Wally presents himself as having come to grips with his handicap, largely because he is not afraid to make a fool of himself and others. Still, both men are uncomfortable with their handicaps and the resultant discrimination, and continue to devise strategies for passing.

One day, Wally and Dave witness the murder of Wally's bookie outside their newsstand. Dave sees the legs and buttocks of the killer, a woman in red, while Wally recognizes her perfume—Shalimar. Wally and Dave, however, are arrested, since no one else saw the woman and since Wally's outstanding gambling debt provides a credible motive.

Before he was shot, the bookie dropped a rare gold coin into the coin box at the newsstand. The killer, Eve (Joan Severance), and her accomplice, Kirgo (Kevin

Spacey), pose as lawyers in order to get Wally and Dave into their custody and retrieve the coin. Wally and Dave, however, realize that Eve is the woman who killed the bookie. Because the police do not believe them, however, Wally and Dave are forced to escape rather than wait for the killers to return with the bail.

Once outside the jail, Dave and Wally steal a police car and a standard chase scene ensues, with Eve, Kirgo, and Captain Braddock (Alan North) in pursuit. The one twist is that Wally drives since Dave is still handcuffed. Nevertheless, the chase is predictable and ends when Wally propels the car onto a garbage barge headed for New Jersey.

In New Jersey, Wally calls his sister, Adele, and the three set off to find the killers and clear their names. They find Eve and Kirgo at the Great Gorge resort, waiting to meet their boss, Sutherland (Anthony Zerbe). Dave and Wally manage to retrieve the coin, but Adele is kidnapped in the process and taken to the Sutherland estate, a glass-covered mansion atop a cliff.

At the Sutherland estate, Dave rescues Adele from a greenhouse surrounded by Doberman pinschers but sets off the alarm, which he cannot hear. Meanwhile, Kirgo captures Wally and takes him to Sutherland's office. Wally questions Sutherland about the coin, which is peeling, and is told that it is actually a superconductor worth eight million dollars. When Kirgo attempts to renegotiate his contract, Sutherland turns off the lights and shoots him. Wally realizes that Sutherland is also blind and grabs Kirgo's gun. The two blind men stalk each other, shooting at noises, until Wally drops his gun. At this point, Eve walks in with Adele and Dave. When she sees Kirgo on the floor, she aims her gun at Sutherland, who tries to offer her the same deal as Kirgo. This time when he turns off the lights, however, Eve is the first to shoot, sending Sutherland through the wall and down the cliff.

Eve locks Dave, Wally, and Adele in the study and heads for the helicopter. In a sign of his newfound willingness to take risks, Dave throws Wally's jacket over a cable that runs down to the helicopter pad, and he and Wally slide down, dropping on Eve and the pilot. When the police arrive, Dave and Wally are cleared of all charges. Later, Dave and Wally are at the park again, eating ice cream cones. Dave is about to place the cone on Wally's head when Wally preempts. Their two-day experience has made both men realize that neither is handicapped as long as they have each other and are not afraid to make fools of themselves.

See No Evil, Hear No Evil has two major weaknesses: its lame plot and the two-dimensional performances of Severance and Spacey, who were more effective as the evil and incestuous siblings in television's *Wiseguy*. The plot and villains lack either camp or parody, although the inexplicable nervous breakdown of Captain Braddock at the end suggests that Director Arthur Hill—who also directed *The In-Laws* (1979)—might have been aiming in that direction. Similarly, the action sequences, particularly the shoot-out between Wally and Sutherland, are poorly choreographed.

What makes the motion picture succeed, on a limited basis, is the chemistry between Pryor and Wilder, evident in all their films. Pryor is especially effective as a blind person, never once letting his eyes focus. Wilder, as is his style, sometimes seems on the verge of laughing at things he is not supposed to be able to hear. The best scenes in the film have little to do with the plot or action scenes. These involve the few moments when the characters of Pryor and Wilder are allowed to interact with each other alone. The actors' give-and-take and improvisation result in both humor and insight into the ostensible theme of passing.

Chon Noriega

Reviews

Chicago Tribune. May 12, 1989, VII, p. 24.
Films in Review. XL, September, 1989, p. 491.
Jet. LXVI, June 5, 1989, p. 36.
Los Angeles Times. May 12, 1989, VI, p. 6.
The New Republic. CC, June 12, 1989, p. 26.
New York Magazine. XXII, May 22, 1989, p. 71.
The New York Times. May 12, 1989, III, p. C8.
People Weekly. XXXI, May 29, 1989, p. 15.
Variety. CCCXXXV, May 17, 1989, p. 30.
Video Review. X, December, 1989, p. 66.
The Wall Street Journal. May 18, 1989, I, p. 14.
The Washington Post. May 13, 1989, p. C1.

SEX, LIES AND VIDEOTAPE

Production: Robert Newmyer and John Hardy; released by Miramax Films
Direction: Steven Soderbergh
Screenplay: Steven Soderbergh
Cinematography: Walt Lloyd
Editing: Steven Soderbergh
Art direction: Joanne Schmidt
Set decoration: Victoria Spader
Makeup: James Ryder
Costume design: James Ryder
Sound: Paul Ledford
Music: Cliff Martinez
MPAA rating: R
Running time: 100 minutes

Principal characters:
  Graham . . . . James Spader
  Ann . . . . Andie MacDowell
  John . . . . Peter Gallagher
  Cynthia . . . . Laura San Giacomo
  Therapist . . . . Ron Vawter
  Barfly . . . . Steven Brill

Sex, lies and videotape, twenty-six-year-old filmmaker Steven Soderbergh's feature film debut, captured the spotlight at the 1989 Cannes Film Festival when it received not only the Best Picture and Best Actor awards but also the International Critics' award. An offbeat, independent feature, written, directed, and edited by Soderbergh, the film has a spare visual style and an emotional complexity that give it, despite its American director, setting, and cast, a vaguely European sensibility.

The story is set in Baton Rouge, where Ann Millaney (Andie MacDowell) lives with her husband, John (Peter Gallagher), a successful attorney. The film opens with Ann discussing her latest anxieties with her therapist (Ron Vawter). An old college friend of John, Graham Dalton (James Spader), is arriving soon for a visit, and Ann confesses that she is uncomfortable at the prospect of his stay. She also mentions that she is currently unwilling to make love to her husband, and she believes that he has also lost interest in her. Unbeknown to Ann, John is having an affair with her sister, Cynthia (Laura San Giacomo), a sultry, sexually uninhibited young woman who is markedly different from Ann.

Graham arrives and proves to be a quiet, enigmatic drifter with a penchant for black clothes and unflinching honesty. Relieved that he is so unlike her husband, Ann finds herself drawn to him and agrees to help him hunt for an apartment. As the two get to know each other, Graham tells Ann that he is impotent and later shocks her by revealing that his private obsession is videotaping women discussing the most intimate details of their personal lives. While Ann is upset by Graham's revelations, Cynthia is intrigued by her sister's reluctance to discuss him. When she stops by his apartment to introduce herself, Graham invites her to make a video-tape, and she agrees.

Cynthia and Ann's relationship is an uneasy one, filled with hostility and envy on both sides, and Ann is appalled—and perhaps secretly jealous—that Cynthia has made a tape for Graham. She is also beginning to suspect that John is having an affair, and she confronts him with her suspicions, which he denies. When she finds Cynthia's earring in their bedroom, however, Ann realizes the truth and immediately drives to Graham's apartment, where she insists on making a videotape.

John learns that Ann has made the tape when she asks him for a divorce. Furious, he arrives at Graham's door, knocks him down, locks him outside on the porch, and then watches Ann's videotape. Ann talks openly on the tape about her sexual feelings and inhibitions then abruptly turns the tables on Graham by seizing the camera and beginning to tape him. Uncomfortable at finding himself the subject rather than the viewer of the tape, Graham nevertheless explains that he was once a compulsive liar, particularly where women were concerned, and his decision to live with rigorous honesty has led him to withdraw from any sort of intimacy. His only means of achieving sexual satisfaction now is watching his videotapes. Ann, how-ever, has broken through that emotional isolation, and, at the tape's conclusion, they make love.

John leaves, and Graham destroys his collection of tapes; his private world has been invaded and is no longer within his control. In the film's closing scenes, Ann and John separate, Cynthia breaks off her affair with John, John's legal career en-ters a decline, Ann and Cynthia grow closer, and Ann begins a relationship with Graham.

Sex, lies and videotape is a provocative examination of the complexities of emo-tional and physical intimacy. The basic structure of its story is a familiar one: that of an outsider whose arrival disrupts the structure of an existing relationship or group, forcing its members to reexamine their lives and confront long-ignored truths. It is the way in which Soderbergh makes use of this structure—and the twists he gives it—that make the film a compelling and original work.

Ann provides the film with its emotional center. She is a woman who, seen from the outside, would appear to have an enviable life, yet it is apparent from the film's first scene that her inner life is far from placid or content. Graham's arrival brings to the surface the emotions that Ann has suppressed, emotions that have manifested themselves in the obsessive anxieties that she relates to her therapist. Her life with John is a tissue of lies, a hollow fabrication in which a carefully decorated home and an upwardly mobile lifestyle serve as substitutes for a sense of genuine love and commitment.

For John, Ann represents the sort of wife that a successful young attorney ought to have; she is cool, beautiful, and circumspect in her behavior. Yet her loss of interest in him sexually troubles him very little; his interest in her is as a wife, not a lover. It is Cynthia who attracts him and whose uninhibited sexuality excites him, although her lifestyle would no doubt render her unacceptable to him as a wife. It is also clear from a conversation John has with a friend that Cynthia is not the only woman with whom he has betrayed Ann. A wedding ring, he confides, acts like a magnet where women are concerned. John is unquestionably the film's least sympathetic character; he is a self-satisfied hypocrite whose sharp comeuppance at the film's conclusion is emotionally satisfying, if dramatically somewhat weak.

Cynthia is one of the film's most intriguing characters. An independent, outspoken young woman whose physical hold on John is so strong that he repeatedly cancels appointments with an important client for afternoon visits to her apartment, she is a complex mixture of self-assurance and longstanding resentment toward her sister. It becomes apparent that in their childhood relationship, she found herself relegated to the role of "bad sister" next to the pretty, popular, well-behaved Ann, a role she continues to play with both relish and a good deal of bitterness. Shocking Ann with her language, her attitudes, and her behavior is a double-edged sword that brings her both satisfaction and an aura of toughness that will not permit emotional intimacy.

Graham is the story's wild card, a character whose lifestyle and behavior offer a threat to the status quo. Ann and Cynthia are changed by their encounters with him as they confront the truth of their own lives, while John finds his life changed against his will by the decisions of the other characters. What Graham adds to the pattern into which their lives have fallen is honesty, an ingredient missing in the behavior of all three. A one-time compulsive liar, Graham has resolved to live with ruthless honesty—much as an alcoholic resolves to live without drinking, and the effect of his decision is disconcerting. He is a man who says exactly what he thinks and answers even the most intimate questions with a complete lack of dissimulation, a practice that repeatedly takes those around him by surprise. This level of openness is perhaps what has persuaded the women on his earlier videotapes to trust him; it is certainly at the heart of both Ann's and Cynthia's responses to him.

It is the experience of making the videotapes that has a transforming effect on the two sisters. For Cynthia, the extreme emotional honesty and the level of openness and trust that it requires offer her a glimpse of another side of her own nature that gradually begins to appear in her subsequent behavior. Her anger toward Ann begins to subside, and she makes a few hesitant overtures of friendship, while her relationship with John no longer offers her the same degree of satisfaction. For Ann, the confrontation with the emotional emptiness of her own life allows her to see that Graham, too, is living in a state of alienation and prompts her to reach out to him through his own video camera.

The twist that Soderbergh gives his story is that Graham—the outsider, the intruder—is changed by its events as well. When Ann turns the camera on him, he says helplessly, "this wasn't supposed to happen," but he is forced at last to confront his own self-imposed isolation and to recognize that perhaps honesty and intimacy are not mutually exclusive. Despite his seeming self-sufficiency earlier in the story, it emerges during the taping that he may have instigated the changes in his life as a means of proving his worth to a former girlfriend, a ridiculous plan, as Ann is quick to point out to him. Underneath his carefully constructed existence as a loner, Graham is in reality an extremely vulnerable young man, and his brutal encounter with John, who destroys the privacy of his world by viewing Ann's tape, has a devastating effect on him. At the film's close, he has, in effect, reentered society by establishing a relationship with Ann.

Any film that deals so exclusively with issues of emotion and its characters' inner lives must necessarily rely heavily on the skills of its actors for a large measure of its success or failure. *Sex, lies and videotape* has three exceptional performances in the work of Andie MacDowell, Laura San Giacomo, and James Spader. (Peter Gallagher is well cast as John, but the role offers less opportunity for a display of acting talent because of the character's own shallowness.) MacDowell makes Ann by turns amusing, edgy, and dreamily bewildered as her years of self-denial begin to crumble, while San Giacomo brings an underlying humanity to what could have been an unsympathetic role. The character of the enigmatic Graham is a difficult one, and Spader manages, in a quiet, controlled performance, to hint at the troubled emotions that will eventually emerge.

Soderbergh has given his film the look and aura of a documentary, a technical choice in keeping with the theme of Graham's use of videotape as a substitute for emotional intimacy. The film consists almost entirely of conversations between its various characters, and its script is witty, intelligent, and precise in the ways in which it establishes each character's voice. That *sex, lies and videotape* is Soderbergh's first feature makes his accomplishment especially impressive.

Janet E. Lorenz

Reviews
American Film: Magazine of the Film and Television Arts. XIV, April, 1989, p. 76.
Chicago Tribune. August 11, 1989, VII, p. 37.
Films in Review. XL, October, 1989, p. 482.
LA Weekly. August 4, 1989, p. 29.
Los Angeles Times. August 4, 1989, VI, p. 1.
The New Republic. CCI, September 4, 1989, p. 26.
New York Magazine. August 7, 1989, p. 40.
The New York Times. August 4, 1989, p. C12.
The New Yorker. LXV, August 7, 1989, p. 73.
Newsweek. CXIV, August 7, 1989, p. 61.
Time. CXXXIV, July 31, 1989, p. 65.
Variety. CCCXXXIV, February 1, 1989, p. 20.
The Wall Street Journal. August 3, 1989.

SHE-DEVIL

Production: Jonathan Brett and Susan Seidelman; released by Orion Pictures
Direction: Susan Seidelman
Screenplay: Barry Strugatz and Mark R. Burns; based on the novel *The Life and
    Loves of a She-Devil*, by Fay Weldon
Cinematography: Oliver Stapleton
Editing: Craig McKay
Production design: Santo Loquasto
Art direction: Tom Warren
Set decoration: George DeTitta, Jr.
Makeup: Joseph Campayno
Costume design: Albert Wolsky
Sound: Tod A. Maitland
Music: Howard Shore
MPAA rating: PG-13
Running time: 99 minutes

      Principal characters:
        Mary Fisher . . . . Meryl Streep
        Ruth Patchett . . . . Roseanne Barr
        Bob Patchett . . . . Ed Begley, Jr.
        Nurse Hooper . . . . Linda Hunt
        Mrs. Fisher . . . . Sylvia Miles
        Nicolette Patchett . . . . Elisebeth Peters
        Andy Patchett . . . . Bryan Larkin
        Garcia . . . . A Martinez

Housewife Ruth Patchett (Roseanne Barr) is in the beauty parlor. She is mis-
shapen, warty, and frumpy. She weighs 201 pounds, but she has not given up on
feminine fantasy. Under the drier, she gapes first at a romantic miniseries and then
at a *Life Styles of the Rich and Famous* spot on its author, "Her Majesty Mary
Fisher" (Meryl Streep), at home in her pink Long Island palace, a camp monument
to fantasy. Ruth's accountant husband Bob (Ed Begley, Jr.) has given his consent for
Ruth to join him at an elegant business party. Out of place and clumsy, Ruth spills
wine on Mary Fisher. While she leaves at Bob's command in search of salt and
Perrier water to remove the stain, Mary's eyes meet Bob's. A shopping-mall rendition of "Strangers in the Night" strikes up loudly. Bob offers to drive her home.

    Bob's car draws up in a suburban street. Ruth is unceremoniously dumped on the
wet sidewalk: A crane shot emphasizes her loneliness as she walks the last block
home. Mary and Bob, meanwhile, arrive at her palace, seventy miles away, where
Mary makes a pass at Bob, who does not decline. Meanwhile, in the empty bed,
Ruth reads another Mary Fisher romance. By 4:30 A.M. she throws the book away

and bites into a doughnut. She knows that her husband and Mary Fisher are together.

Mary Fisher is pretty, rich, and thin. Her car license plate reads *"L'AMOUR."* She is a walking male fantasy who gets what she wants, but Ruth does not give up easily. She shaves her mustache, tends the home, and plans a gourmet meal for Bob's parents. When she serves a dead gerbil in the mushroom soup, however, Bob explodes, calling Ruth a she-devil. He leaves for Mary's circular pink satin bed. Abandoned, while lightning flashes above, Ruth screams. The next day, she plots her revenge—to take from Bob, one by one, the four assets he has told her he prizes: his home, his family, his career, and his freedom.

The home is easily disposed of: Bob's prized stake in suburbia explodes in flames after Ruth plugs in every gadget they possess, cooks canisters in the microwave, drops cigarettes in the waste-paper basket, crunches appliances in the washer, turns on the gas, blows out the pilot lights, and leaves. The next step costs more heartache: She delivers her two unlovely children, Andy (Bryan Larkin) and Nicolette (Elisebeth Peters), to the palace.

Her revenge rapidly turns romance sour. Nicolette's ghetto-blaster gives Mary a writing block. Bob starts to ogle other women. Meanwhile, Ruth takes a job at the Golden Twilight Nursing Home, where Mary has placed her cantankerous and foulmouthed old mother (Sylvia Miles). When Ruth has substituted vitamins for Valium long enough, Mrs. Fisher agrees that a visit to the palace would be in order. While she is away, Ruth pours urine over her bed, to ensure that a superintendent who cannot endure incontinence will refuse to have her back.

Mrs. Fisher's arrival hastens the demise of Mary's graceful life-style. Her mask slips at family lunch: Mrs. Fisher calls Mary a slut of forty-one, and Mary screams back like a fishwife. Meanwhile, in the parallel world that Ruth inhabits, diminutive Nurse Hooper (Linda Hunt) is won over by an orgy of cream cakes. She asks Ruth what she should do with nearly fifty thousand dollars in savings. The two flee the Golden Twilight together. At the pink palace, *People Weekly* magazine's reporter (real-life talk-show host Sally Jessy Raphael appearing as herself) arrives to interview the Queen of Romance. The session begins with the charge that Mary writes "soft porn for bored housewives," and the situation deteriorates rapidly, with Nicolette posing half-dressed for the photographer and Mrs. Fisher revealing all about Mary's days as a "teenage tramp."

Ruth and Hooper start the Vesta Rose employment agency, dedicated to giving new life and hope to downtrodden women. In turn, the grateful women become Ruth's "personal army" in her campaign of vengeance. She places nubile nymphet computer operator Olivia Honey (Maria Pitillo) in Bob's office, where he promptly proceeds to embark on an affair with her.

While Bob plays, Mary mopes. Her new novel, *Love in the Rinse Cycle*, is rejected by her publishers. Mary walks out of a humiliating meeting only to be confronted with a rack full of copies of *People Weekly* magazine. Home again, she takes pills. A rash has developed on her face (Ruth's wart, meanwhile, has slowly disappeared), and she considers a facelift. Bob is unsympathetic: He takes to spending whole nights in the office. During one of these, he makes photocopies of Olivia's backside, with his hands attached and his signet ring, a first love-gift from Mary, in full view.

Olivia's reign is over the moment she tells Bob at Ruth's suggestion how much she loves him. When Olivia comes to cry on her shoulder, Ruth tells her to teach Bob a lesson by making his thievery from his clients more obvious and to take the money for herself for a fresh start in New Zealand. While the two women fix the frame-up in Bob's office late one night, transferring monies to his Swiss bank account and thence to Olivia's, Ruth discovers the photocopies. When Mary rips open the envelope the next day, she snaps.

Bob is put on probation but not thrown out. When the police arrive, however, he is in for a harsher sentence. The lawyer says not to worry: They will argue that a computer virus caused the unaccountable transfers, which will be easy enough to prove, since the largest transfer was from Mary's own account. This is the last straw: Mary abandons Bob to his fate. He has lost his fourth asset, his freedom.

A year later, it is clear that prison has improved him. He has even learned how to cook. As for Mary, she has become a serious artist and a realist, wearing an all-new uniform of black dress, crystal pendant, and spectacles, and is feted for her new novel, *Trust and Betrayal: A Docunovel of Love, Money, and Betrayal*. At the film's close, Ruth walks toward the audience, alone but happy in the crowd, fat but stylish in a new white outfit, to the tune of Elvis Presley's "Devil in Disguise."

It is not surprising, perhaps, that none of British author Fay Weldon's novels has been filmed before: Weldon inhabits a postfeminist pessimist's world. In *The Life and Loves of a She-Devil*, Ruth Patchett's goal is not to destroy what Mary Fisher stands for—woman as parasite and playmate—but to possess everything that Mary once possessed—lover, riches, palace, and above all power—by destroying her and replacing her with herself, literally. To this end, she endures years of painful surgical operations. Every gruesome detail of this process was dwelt upon in the 1986 Public Broadcasting System/British Broadcasting Company miniseries of *She-Devil*. This adaptation relished the novel's savage cynicism and its potential for Grand Guignol.

Seidelman's film is a horse of a very different color. The novel and the television series were strong meat for a sophisticated adult audience. America, alas, no longer enjoys such an audience. In writers Mark Burns and Barry Strugatz's hands, Mary Fisher rejects frilly romance for self-respect, Ruth is not a devil but an angel in disguise, and the story as a whole aspires to become a parable of feminist revenge, female friendship, and woman's strength. The material, however, proves intractable: A black comedy cannot be whitewashed.

The casting of Barr as Ruth seemed perfect. There was even an inherent similarity between the style of her television show and the feel of the novel. Yet the germs of *She-Devil*'s problems are also present in Barr's show, such as a fondness for the uplifting moment. A deadlier attack of cutesiness cripples Seidelman's *She-*

Devil: Barr plays the role completely straight, presenting herself to the camera as a successful role model for lumpish and unlovely women. Dressed up, toned down, delivering her monologues in a monotone, the gimmick of the straight role turns into a straitjacket from which she has no escape. No stand-up comic or popular icon could turn overnight into a straight actress who could hold her own against Streep's romance queen.

An extraordinarily skilled and disciplined actress, Streep turns her hand to comedy with a deftness of touch that delights; as the reigning Queen of Hollywood, she revels in spoofing her own image in the persona of "Her Majesty Mary Fisher." She delivers a combination of glamour and hilarity hardly seen since the untimely death of Carole Lombard. At one high point, half-drunk and resenting Bob's warning not to stray from the formula, she rises to hands and knees on her pink satin bed to announce, with emphatic waggles of her bottom, that she is an artist. As frilly Miss Fisher, Streep becomes as good an incarnation of constructed fake femininity as one could wish.

She-Devil is to some degree a personal film for Seidelman. Weldon's story has striking similarities to her own *Desperately Seeking Susan* (1985). Both are tales of shape-changing and role-swapping women featuring philandering husbands against a backdrop of consumerist suburban boredom. In both films, Seidelman has the opportunity to play with (and off) two powerful icons of popular culture, Madonna (as Susan) and Roseanne Barr. In terms of style, too, *She-Devil* shares *Desperately Seeking Susan*'s fondness for the camp or bad-taste moment—shock-cuts from Mary fellating Bob to Ruth chopping zucchini, for example, or from Ruth emptying bed pans to Garcia (A Martinez) serving watercress soup. With cinematographer Oliver Stapleton, Seidelman exploits the comic potential of the clichés of romantic camerawork. *She-Devil*'s opening sequence not only bears Seidelman's filmic signature but also deliberately invokes the spirit of her *Desperately Seeking Susan*. The camera lingeringly pans across a beauty parlor before alighting, in monstrous close-up, not on *Desperately Seeking Susan*'s pretty Roberta but on *She-Devil*'s warty Ruth, desperately seeking beauty (the first of many moments when *She-Devil* exploits Barr's overblown body). At moments such as these, Seidelman bares her affinities with Pedro Almodóvar. Both filmmakers' fascination with popular media, and with the politics and paraphernalia of femininity and beauty, is echoed, too, in Michael Caton-Jones's *Scandal* (1989; reviewed in this volume).

Some of *She-Devil*'s relations live closer to home. The film ducks the brutality of Danny Devito's genuine black comedy *The War of the Roses* (1989; reviewed in this volume), but nevertheless bears a family relationship to *Fatal Attraction* (1987); both films show Hollywood still attempting to come to grips with domestic and sexual demons.

Joss Lutz Marsh

Reviews

American Film: Magazine of the Film and Television Arts. XV, December, 1989,
     p. 64.

Chicago Tribune. December 8, 1989, VII, p. 44.

The Christian Science Monitor. December 22, 1989, p. 10.

Los Angeles Times. December 8, 1989, p. F1.

Los Angeles Times. December 13, 1989, p. F14.

Maclean's. CII, December 18, 1989, p. 59.

The New Republic. CCII, January 22, 1990, p. 26.

The New York Times. December 8, 1989, p. B5.

Newsweek. CXIV, December 11, 1989, p. 88.

San Francisco Chronicle. December 8, 1989, p. E1.

Time. CXXXIV, December 11, 1989, p. 93.

Variety. CCCXXXVII, December 6, 1989, p. 32.

The Washington Post. December 8, 1989, p. C1.

The Washington Post Weekend. December 8, 1989, p. 65.

SIDEWALK STORIES

Production: Charles Lane for Rhinoceros Productions; released by Island Pictures
Direction: Charles Lane
Screenplay: Charles Lane
Cinematography: Bill Dill
Editing: Anne Stein and Charles Lane
Production design: Lyn Pinezich
Art direction: Ina Mayhew
Makeup: Lisa A. Johnson
Music: Marc Marder
MPAA rating: R
Running time: 97 minutes

Principal characters:
Artist .... Charles Lane
Child .... Nicole Alysia
Young Woman....................... Sandye Wilson
Father .... Darnell Williams
Mother .... Trula Hoosier
Doorman .... Michael Baskin
Street Partner....................... George Riddick

In a bold and daring move, filmmaker Charles Lane wrote and directed a black-and-white, silent film for release in 1989. Entitled *Sidewalk Stories*, this comedy-drama enjoyed a limited distribution on the art-house circuit through Island Pictures. In an era when black-and-white classics are colorized on video and any appreciation of silent filmmaking is relegated to film history classes, Lane's film is a reminder that the power of the cinema to make relevant statements about contemporary society is not dependent on such pretenses to realism as color and dialogue. The power of *Sidewalk Stories* resides in its use of filmmaking techniques and in its references to film history to convey its message.

Shot on a shoestring budget in only two weeks' time, *Sidewalk Stories* uses actual New York locations to tell the story of a homeless man who earns a meager wage as a street artist in Greenwich Village. Having staked out a piece of sidewalk in order to sketch portraits to sell to passersby, the artist, played by the director, Charles Lane, shares the Village street with magicians, dancers, and mimes. The artist lives in an abandoned building, taking some comfort in a few possessions and pirated electricity. His routine is disrupted when he accepts responsibility for a two-year-old child (Nicole Alysia), whom he discovers in an alley. The toddler's father (Darnell Williams), who was a braggart and a gambler, has been killed in a street encounter. Since the artist does not know how to locate the mother (Trula Hoosier), he assumes the role of parent.

Befriended by a sympathetic young woman (Sandye Wilson), the artist and the child are able to survive despite their humble circumstances. Their luck changes for the worse, however, when their makeshift home is finally torn down. The artist loses his sketching materials, the child loses her stroller, and the two are forced to seek cover in the city's homeless shelters. Sometimes they are able to find a cot to sleep on; often they are closed out when the shelters are filled to capacity. Eventually, the artist sees the child's picture on a milk carton and uncovers the mother's identity and address. Mother and child are reunited.

In the final, most effective scene of the film, the artist—who by this point has lost not only his few possessions and his livelihood but also his "family"—sits with the young woman in a small, grassless park, which is inhabited by dozens of homeless people. As the two sit quietly on a bench with blank expressions on their faces, the viewer becomes aware of naturalistic sound effects and dialogue. The sound gradually becomes louder until the audience is able to hear homeless people of all ages and from all ethnic backgrounds beg passersby for money.

Sidewalk Stories draws heavily on the conventions of the silent comedy genre. Much like the shorts of Mack Sennett, for example, Lane's film features a cast of secondary characters, who are essentially stereotypes broadly depicted for comic purposes. The pair of detectives who try to help the mother find the child include a short, intense officer coupled with a tall, jolly, fat one. Like contemporary Keystone Kops, the two are amusing because their physiques and personalities are opposite. In the library where the artist and the child take refuge from the cold outdoors, the librarian wears the dark-framed glasses and stern hairdo that have come to be associated with her profession. Even the child's father, who is not a sympathetic character, is amusing because his identity as a hopeless gambler and braggart is exaggerated. His gestures are broad and his demeanor loud. As he lies dying in the street, he asks the artist to toss a coin and call heads or tails; he remains a gambler to his dying breath.

Like the silent comedies of yesterday, props are exaggerated in size not only for comic purposes but also to serve a symbolic function. The father's gambling vice is represented through the oversized pair of dice that he tosses. In a dream sequence, the artist envisions being brought before a judge, who pronounces him guilty with a giant gavel, representing both the judge's authority and the artist's fear of authority figures. The film also features certain stylistic elements reminiscent of silent comedy. For example, at one point, the artist looks quizzically into the camera and thus directly at the viewer. Elsewhere, a pair of kidnappers are denoted as sinister through a wide-angled close-up of their shifting eyes. Even the fact that the characters have no names but are known simply as, for example, "the artist" is a convention borrowed from the silent cinema.

Any discussion of silent comedy inevitably brings forth Charlie Chaplin as a source of comparison. Indeed, many of the themes and images in *Sidewalk Stories* are comparable to those found in Chaplin's work. The story line itself seems to be an updated version of *The Kid* (1921). Like a modern-day Little Tramp, Lane's character of the homeless artist is the proverbial outsider looking in—a person who is forced by his economic condition to live outside mainstream society, unable to enjoy even the most basic comforts of a middle-class existence. That Lane's homeless world differs from that of mainstream society is indicated by the opening sequence. The people who participate in the bustle of busy Wall Street are contrasted with the painfully slow-moving homeless, for whom time and destination have no meaning. The urban poor of this opening sequence are presented as though they exist in another dimension.

In addition to being an outsider to society, the artist is an underdog, much like Chaplin's Little Tramp. The artist is first seen sharing his piece of sidewalk with another portrait artist—a large, formidable bully who wants this piece of turf all to himself. The artist's underdog status is visually indicated by the juxtaposition of his small, slight body against that of the tall, broad-shouldered bully. In a comic bit highly reminiscent of Chaplin, the bully pushes the artist to the ground; he gets up; the bully pushes him down again; he gets up; the bully pushes him down one more time. At this point, the artist starts to get up, thinks twice of it, and then pushes himself back down on the sidewalk, saving the bully the trouble. Despite his underdog status, the artist eventually wins the turf by setting the bully's easel on fire.

In a number of scenes, Lane emphasizes the gap between the rich and the poor, just as Chaplin often did in his shorts. The artist takes the child to a small public playground, where a group of yuppie mothers in fur coats share the same set of park benches with a couple of homeless people in rags. When the child pushes down the bratty offspring of one of the mothers, the mothers chase the artist and the child off the playground. The pair are excluded from even the simplest of privileges by their dire economic circumstances. The young woman invites the artist and the child to her comfortable apartment for dinner, but the snooty doorman (Michael Baskin) does not want to let them in the building. Again, their exclusion from events and places most people take for granted emphasizes their exclusion from the rights and privileges afforded mainstream society.

Sidewalk Stories includes a number of tragic events involving the homeless artist, yet the homage to Chaplin, the comic bits, and particularly the silent format weave a magic spell that shields the viewer from any real harshness or discomfort. That spell is deliberately broken at the end, when the camera pulls back and the sound is turned up to make visible and audible dozens of homeless people asking passersby for money and cigarettes. The small bits of dialogue and naturalistic sound reveal the desperate reality of the homeless and the urban poor. Their numbers include men and women, the old and the young, African Americans, whites, and an American Indian, indicating that homelessness knows no boundaries of sex, age, or race. The conclusion offers a bitter alternative to those in Chaplin's films, in which the Little Tramp walks off into the distance twirling his cane to let the viewer know that he will prevail no matter what tragedy may befall him. Lane's technique, in which the dreamlike quality of the silent cinema is disrupted by the harsh reality of sound, confronts the viewer about the homeless; it drops the bleak reality of the problem right in our laps. Never has sound been used so militaristically. The viewer is left with the stunning realization that there are millions of homeless and that they all have a sidewalk story to tell.

Susan Doll

Reviews

Boston Globe. November 24, 1989, p. 107.
The Christian Science Monitor. November 10, 1989, p. 10.
Los Angeles Times. November 23, 1989, VI, p. 21.
The New Republic. CCI, December 18, 1989, p. 24.
New York Magazine. XXII, November 6, 1989, p. 36.
The New York Times. November 3, 1989, p. C14.
Variety. CCCXXXVI, October 4, 1989, p. 34.
The Village Voice. XXXIV, November 7, 1989, p. 67.
The Wall Street Journal. November 2, 1989, p. A16.
The Washington Post. November 22, 1989, p. D4.

STAR TREK V
The Final Frontier

Production: Ralph Winter and Harve Bennett; released by Paramount Pictures
Direction: William Shatner
Screenplay: David Loughery; based on a story by William Shatner, Harve Bennett, and David Loughery, and on the television series created by Gene Roddenberry
Cinematography: Andrew Laszlo
Editing: Peter Berger
Production design: Herman Zimmerman
Art direction: Nilo Rodis-Jamero
Special effects: Michael Wood
Special visual effects: Bran Ferren
Makeup: Wes Dawn, Jeff Dawn, Kenny Myers, and Richard Snell
Costume design: Dodie Shepard and Nilo Rodis-Jamero
Sound: David Ronne
Music: Jerry Goldsmith
MPAA rating: PG
Running time: 106 minutes

Principal characters:
James Kirk . . . . William Shatner
Mr. Spock . . . . Leonard Nimoy
Dr. Leonard "Bones" McCoy . . . . DeForest Kelley
Montgomery "Scotty" Scott. . . . . James Doohan
Pavel Chekov . . . . Walter Koenig
Commander Uhura . . . . Nichelle Nichols
Sulu . . . . George Takei
Sybok . . . . Laurence Luckinbill

In 1966, the hour-long science fiction action series *Star Trek* appeared. Its three-season run on NBC-TV gave no indication that its stars and its rhetoric would be around twenty-three years later. A cult phenomenon, the original television series has inspired books, annual conventions, a second series (*Star Trek: The Next Generation*), and five feature-length films. This fifth film, however, does not bring much that is new. That is not to suggest that screenplay coauthors William Shatner, Harve Bennett, and David Loughery do not take on some big issues, such as the existence of God and Eden, the place of emotions in a rational society, and the meaning of fear and shame in the psychic life of all sentient beings. It is, however, to suggest that the screenplay and Shatner's direction handle these issues even more clumsily and heavy-handedly than the series did back in the 1960's.

The film opens with a "teaser" scene of the Vulcan Sybok (Laurence Luckinbill) performing an act of faith healing on some obviously working-class person in a desert somewhere. The healed man is converted to a disciple of the Vulcan on the spot. This ambiguous sequence is immediately followed by some stunning footage of Yosemite National Park, making a strong statement about the importance of natural resources for the future. Captain Kirk (Shatner) is spending his shore leave climbing El Capitan, a three-thousand-foot sheer cliff face, until Mr. Spock (Leonard Nimoy) appears in levitation boots, hovering beside the physically straining Kirk. When Kirk loses his grip, Spock rescues him in midair, setting up one of the major themes of the film: the importance of friendship. They are joined by Dr. McCoy (DeForest Kelley) and almost immediately called away from shore leave to head an emergency mission.

The planet Nimbus III, the "Planet of Galactic Peace," had been established jointly by Romulans, Klingons, and Federation diplomats to serve as an example of cooperative interplanetary efforts. It has proved to be a failure, however, attracting only the least desirable and least productive members of each civilization. The representatives of each government have been kidnapped, and the *Enterprise* is the only starship available to go there. It is assigned to resolve the problem, in spite of the fact that it is not yet fully operational.

When the *Enterprise* crew arrives at Nimbus III, they find that the hostages are feeling quite cooperative with their captor, and they urge Kirk to listen to him. The captor is Sybok, a renegade Vulcan who has gathered a group of followers by showing them how to rid themselves of shame and fear. Sybok is convinced that the origin myths common to every culture have their source on the other side of the Great Barrier at the center of the galaxy. He has taken the diplomats hostage as a way to bargain for use of a starship to take him and his followers on their quest for Eden. Spock is able to tell Kirk a surprising amount about Sybok, who was a star pupil in the Vulcan schools but who rejected the Vulcan valorization of pure logic and sought a different kind of knowledge and understanding. He is, as the audience discovers later, Spock's half brother.

Kirk and his crew find the hostages, and much to their surprise and chagrin, however, the Romulan delegate betrays them to Sybok, and they are taken prisoner. Sybok and his followers, including all three diplomats from Nimbus III, are now prepared to board the *Enterprise* to begin their journey to the Great Barrier. There is, however, one small problem: While they have been down on the planet's surface, a Klingon starship has engaged the *Enterprise* in combat. The Klingon captain is determined to capture Captain Kirk, both to avenge the deaths of his comrades and to bring great glory to himself. Fortunately, the Klingon has not discovered that Kirk is not aboard the *Enterprise*, which drops its shields just long enough for the shuttlecraft carrying Kirk, Sybok, and the others to crash-land in the shuttle bay. If this plot line seems gratuitous, it is: The Klingons seem to serve much the same purpose in the *Star Trek* films that the Nazis serve for the *Indiana Jones* films. They provide action, particularly combat, at the expense of plot logic.

The *Enterprise* takes off for the center of the galaxy, followed by the Klingon vessel. En route, Sybok continues to accumulate followers by converting crew members. He heals their psychic wounds by helping them to relive their most deeply buried secrets. Apparently this kind of dark secret is at the core of every psyche, be it human, Romulan, Klingon, or something else, and it is through this process that Sybok converts individuals to followers. Kirk, Spock, and McCoy, however, are not converted by Sybok because of the strength of their friendship.

Although no attempt has been made to cross the Great Barrier before this time, both the *Enterprise* and the Klingons get through fairly uneventfully. They see a planet, and the awestruck crew realizes that they have found Paradise. They head for the planet, go into orbit, and send down a landing party, which includes Sybok, Kirk, and Spock. The planet's surface is an inhospitable desert, and Sybok bemoans his failure. This, it seems, is not an appropriate place for God. Suddenly, however, an unusual sort of geological activity begins, with tall rock pillars shooting up and forming a pseudo-Stonehenge around the landing party. A large holographic head of a bearded white man appears, complete with a bass speaking voice. This they believe to be God, until after a short period of time he reveals his real intentions to them. He attempts to threaten them into taking him off his planet, on which he is apparently imprisoned.

To help the landing party escape, Sybok martyrs himself to the head. The *Enterprise*—because of technical difficulties—beams up everyone but Kirk. The Klingon diplomat orders the Klingon vessel to cooperate, the Klingons shoot on the head and beam Kirk onto their ship, and all is once again well. God has not been found, new areas of the galaxy have been explored and new life forms contacted, and the Klingons have once again been forced to succumb to the superior moral and intellectual force of the Federation. The film closes with the crew together again in Yosemite, sitting around the campfire singing "Row, Row, Row Your Boat."

Quite simply, there is little new here. Each of the previous *Star Trek* films had an identity of its own and appealed to fans of different sorts. *Star Trek V*, however, attempted to combine the deep and meaningful philosophical pretensions of *Star Trek: The Motion Picture* (1979) with the corny humor of *Star Trek IV: The Voyage Home* (1986). The humor worked in *Star Trek IV* because it was well written and well directed (by Leonard Nimoy), but its presence in *Star Trek V* seems inconsistent with the film's self-image. Perhaps the film lacks a self-image altogether, wavering among action, philosophy, religion, psychiatry, and humor.

Among the positive aspects of this film, the aging of the characters finally provides a sense of development and passage of time. The friendship among Kirk, Spock, and McCoy has grown and mellowed over the years and is as strong as ever but much more gentle and forgiving than it was in the loud, blustery, and contentious early days. The implication of a romance between Uhura and Scotty was delightful.

In the context of *Star Trek: The Next Generation*, however, *Star Trek V* seems more dated than ever. The new television series has come a long way toward shifting the founding principles onto the terrain of the 1980's. Included among the ship's bridge officers are women; unlike the kind of glorified receptionist that Uhura was. Similarly, the *Star Trek* films have made no advances in affirmative action. There is still no major black or Hispanic character, and Spock remains the only nonhuman on the *Enterprise*. *Star Trek: The Next Generation* has explained this away in one episode by suggesting that the Federation starships are manned by life-forms from one planet at a time. The films, including *Star Trek V*, still present the mission of the Federation as a white male human colonialist one, the Prime Directive notwithstanding.

Visually, *Star Trek V* is nothing spectacular either. Although the special effects are well done, there is nothing particularly imaginative about them. They have neither the self-indulgent splendor of the effects in *Star Trek: The Motion Picture*, nor the tongue-in-cheek self-mocking of the cloaked landing in Golden Gate Park from *Star Trek IV*. The lack of a sure, governing tone for the film stilted the effects by failing to provide identity and direction for the tasks.

Jerry Goldsmith's music is one of the few consistent features of this film. Goldsmith wrote the music for *Star Trek: The Motion Picture* and composes for *Star Trek: The Next Generation*. The theme that first appeared in the films and has permanently replaced the original television theme was cowritten by Goldsmith and Alexander Courage. The music carries the focused tone that the rest of the film lacks: As Goldsmith well knows, all *Star Trek* stories, whether on the small screen or large, are action/adventure shows. His big, Hollywood symphonic style more than suits the film that *Star Trek* could have been.

In short, *Star Trek V: The Final Frontier* is a period piece—set in the future, produced in the 1980's, but perhaps only at home in the 1960's. It may be of some nostalgia or curiosity value to *Star Trek* fans; it may be a hit with science-fiction fans; on its own, however, its orbit decays rather rapidly.

Anahid Kassabian

Reviews

Chicago Tribune. June 16, 1989, VII, p. 44.
The Christian Science Monitor. June 19, 1989, p. 15.
Cinéfantastique. XIX, July, 1989, p. 55.
Films in Review. XL, October, 1989, p. 486.
Los Angeles Times. June 9, 1989, VI, p. 1.
Maclean's. CII, June 26, 1989, p. 52.
New York Magazine. XXII, June 19, 1989, p. 68.
The New York Times. June 9, 1989, p. C10.
Newsweek. CXIII, June 19, 1989, p. 63.
People Weekly. XXXI, June 26, 1989, p. 15.
Rolling Stone. July 13, 1989, p. 75.
Time. CXXXIII, June 26, 1989, p. 89.
Variety. CCCXXXV, June 14, 1989, p. 22.
The Wall Street Journal. June 16, 1989.

STAYING TOGETHER

Production: Joseph Feury; released by Hemdale Film Corp.
Direction: Lee Grant
Screenplay: Monte Merrick
Cinematography: Dick Bush
Editing: Katherine Wenning
Production design: Stuart Wurtzel
Art direction: W. Steven Graham
Set decoration: Elaine O'Donnell
Special effects: Cliff Wenger
Makeup: Christa Reusch
Costume design: Carol Oditz
Sound: Jan Erik Brodin
Music direction: Miles Goodman
Music: Miles Goodman
MPAA rating: R
Running time: 91 minutes

Principal characters:
Brian McDermott	Tim Quill
Kit McDermott	Dermot Mulroney
Nancy Trainer	Stockard Channing
Duncan McDermott	Sean Astin
Eileen McDermott	Melinda Dillon
Jake McDermott	Jim Haynie
Beverly Young	Daphne Zuniga
Denny Stockton	Levon Helm
Lois Cook	Dinah Manoff
Beth Harper	Sheila Kelley

Staying Together presents a portrait of a feisty, fiercely independent yet close-knit rural family and how it deals with a severe identity crisis. Director Lee Grant maintains an intense emotional level throughout the film as the various family members confront one another and struggle to redefine themselves as individuals and as a family unit.

The film opens on a traditional family scene: Eileen McDermott (Melinda Dillon) preparing breakfast for her family. Yet traditional soon changes to wildly atypical as she and her husband Jake (Jim Haynie) call upstairs to awaken their teenage sons Kit (Dermot Mulroney), Brian (Tim Quill), and Duncan (Sean Astin). Only eldest son Kit is upstairs, and he quickly dresses, then quietly sneaks out the window, and dashes around the small, sleepy town in search of his two brothers. He finds middle brother Brian asleep in bed with the leading mayoral candidate, Nancy

Trainer (Stockard Channing). He finds youngest brother Duncan passed out on a park bench after a full night of revelry. All three sneak back home and join their parents around the breakfast table.

While Mr. McDermott leaves to take care of some important business matters out of town, the rest of the family prepares to open the family-owned and run McDermott's Famous Chicken Restaurant. The restaurant is a town landmark, having been in existence for twenty-five years. The brothers are well known and liked by the rest of the townspeople, who frequent the restaurant with great enthusiasm and loyalty. The brothers mingle and joke with the clientele. Duncan tries unsuccessfully for the umpteenth time to get waitress Lois Cook (Dinah Manoff) to cure him of his cursed virginity; Brian takes a break and drives off on his motorcycle to a farmhouse in the woods, where he visits with, and then buys some marijuana from, Beth Harper (Sheila Kelley); and Kit flirts with Beverly Young (Daphne Zuniga), who is engaged to successful building engineer Kevin Burley (Keith Szarabajka) but who still encourages Kit's advances.

After closing down the restaurant for the day, the brothers gather at the Buffalo Gap, a rowdy, after-hours night spot, where they drink and dance with the local women and then stagger home together down the middle of the street, stopping to taunt Kevin when he and Beverly drive by. Later, young Duncan, feeling confident and secure in his miniuniverse, bellows that the town should be renamed McDermottville.

The following morning, however, the confidence that the brothers displayed earlier is shattered when Mr. McDermott announces at the breakfast table that he has sold the restaurant and the land on which it is built. He tells his family that he is tired of the business, has always hated chickens, and is ready to enjoy an early retirement. The brothers are stunned by the news. Brian is outraged that he and his brothers were not consulted about the decision to sell the restaurant. He ends up screaming his outrage at his father, and then storms out, vowing never to return.

Brian races off on his motorcycle, at first directionless, but then he ends up at a construction site, where he asks the foreman for a job. The foreman turns out to be Kevin, whom Brian insulted only the night before. At first Kevin laughs when Brian asks him for a job but later changes his mind when Brian impresses him with his strong-willed determination. Later, Brian returns home to gather his belongings. He ends up moving in with Nancy Trainer, who is in the middle of her mayoral campaign and who seriously doubts there will be any benefits to her campaign if the voters find out she is romantically involved with a teenager. After she wins the election, she tells Brian to move out. He finally ends up living with Beth Harper and her young son.

Kit finds a job in town at the general store run by Denny Stockton (Levon Helm), an old friend of the family and a regular at the Buffalo Gap where he sings and plays in a band. One evening after work, the McDermotts—minus Brian—gather at the Buffalo Gap and listen to Denny and his band. Denny coaxes Mrs. McDermott onstage to sing with the band, something she did on a regular basis when she and Denny attended school together.

In his spare time, Kit trains as a marathon runner with Beverly. Later, the two of them enter an out-of-town race, and Kit places third. Afterward, they drive to a romantic inn and spend the night together. Beverly tells Kit that she is still planning on marrying Kevin, but only because he will be a stable provider, unlike Kit, whom she looks upon as immature and unstable. She insists that Kit attend her wedding, which is forthcoming and which portends to be a gala event. Kit, confused by the relationship, nevertheless agrees to attend the wedding.

Meanwhile, Mr. McDermott becomes more and more aimless. He buys a mobile home, and he and Mrs. McDermott use it to take several short trips. After returning from one of the minivacations, Mr. McDermott gathers some old business records and begins burning them in the backyard furnace. As the records burn, he suddenly collapses. He is rushed to the hospital, where the family gathers and waits for reports of his condition. Brian appears and demands to see his father. He pushes past the hospital staff and bursts into Mr. McDermott's room to find his father dead of a heart attack.

After the funeral, Brian reconciles with the family. He and his brothers help Mrs. McDermott adjust to life without their father. Duncan encourages her to take Denny's suggestion and rejoin his band as lead singer. She is reluctant at first but soon warms to Denny and his affectionate advances. Kit takes his mother's friendship with Denny as an affront to his father's memory. Feeling confused about his own unstable relationship with Beverly and threatened by his mother's new romantic relationship, he lashes out at her one morning during breakfast, accusing her of having an affair with Denny while Mr. McDermott was still alive. Mrs. McDermott explodes with anger and comes close to telling Kit to move out. Kit takes off running. Later, Brian and Duncan look for Kit in the family truck and find him jogging down a dirt road. When they confront him, he sprints off into the brush. They follow him, rumbling through the rugged terrain as Kit attempts to evade their pursuit. Suddenly, the truck crashes through a large barrier of brush and flies over a cliff and into a lake below. As Kit watches from the cliff above, the truck submerges, his brothers nowhere in sight. Finally, they reappear at the surface, and the brothers curse one another over who is to blame for the accident. They come to blows, and Duncan is knocked down. The other brothers at first look worried but then pick up Duncan and attempt to throw him back in the lake if he does not quit faking unconsciousness. The brothers end up horsing around together in the lake before returning home.

The scene shifts to the wedding of Beverly and Kevin. All the principal characters are present: Mayor Nancy Trainer enviously eyes Brian and his new love, Beth; Kit dances with the just-married Beverly and announces that he is planning to run in the Boston Marathon; and Duncan barely manages to contain his excitement when former waitress Lois finally agrees to cure him of his virginity. After the wedding, the brothers gather at the Buffalo Gap to listen to their mother sing with Denny and his band. Kit makes up with his mother, and the three young men end up staggering home together down the middle of the street, once again demanding that the town change its name to McDermottville.

The main theme of *Staying Together*—a family with a well-established identity within the community suddenly stripped of that identity and having to redefine itself—is a classic theme that has been examined in many of the most endearing films ever made. Films such as *The Magnificent Ambersons* (1942), *Gone with the Wind* (1939), *The Grapes of Wrath* (1940), and the two *Godfather* films (1972, 1974) all depict families in the throes of radical change. Yet, unlike the classic films mentioned, the families of which must adapt to the radical changes dictated by their societies, the family in *Staying Together* must deal with a much more private upheaval initiated by themselves. This gives the film a more intimate feel, as does the small-town setting and the common-folk family at the core of the story.

One of the best scenes in the film, the one taking place in the McDermott's restaurant as the brothers serve their famous fried chicken to the townspeople, has a wonderful communal intimacy and serves to illustrate the subtle but powerful influence that the McDermotts have on their community and how crucial their identity within the community depends on the success of their restaurant. When the restaurant closes, their self-assurance and well-established identity vanishes, both in the eyes of the community and in their own eyes. They are no longer the leaders, the aristocrats of their community; they no longer have the right to swagger down the main street of town and demand that the town change its name to suit them. They are directionless, struggling to regain the confidence that comes with a strong self-identity.

Director Lee Grant and scriptwriter Monte Merrick develop an interesting contrast in expectations by setting the story in a sleepy rural community and then centering the action on three brothers whose actions are more commonly associated with urban characters. The brothers are cocky and explosively emotional, engage in illicit affairs, smoke marijuana, and flaunt all traditional heart-of-America values. The contrast in expectations is at first disorienting, then amusing, but ultimately unconvincing. Grant and Merrick want the audience to sympathize with the brothers as they go through their painful identity crisis. Yet the action is so riddled with one crisis situation after another that the brothers are never allowed to display any subtle shading to their characters.

Overall, the film has the tone of a raunchy television sitcom in which a loud, wise-cracking family faces a series of conflicts, all of which are neatly resolved by the end of the program. For all the personal upheaval and turmoil with which the McDermotts must deal throughout the film, they seem completely unchanged and unfazed by any of the action when they once again swagger off together in the final scene. *Staying Together* has an exciting, timeless theme, propelled by dramatic action and dynamic characters, but the lack of subtlety ultimately undermines an otherwise noble and worthwhile undertaking.

Jim Kline

Reviews

Boston Globe. November 10, 1989, p. 82.

Chicago Tribune. November 10, 1989, VII, p. 40.

Glamour. LXXXVII, October, 1989, p. 196.

Los Angeles Times. November 10, 1989, VI, p. 1.

The New York Times. November 10, 1989, p. C15.

People Weekly. XXXII, November 20, 1989, p. 29.

Rolling Stone. September 21, 1989, p, 47.

Variety. CCCXXXVI, September 6, 1989, p. 25.

The Village Voice. XXXIV, November 21, 1989, p. 92.

The Washington Post. November 10, 1989, p. D7.

STEEL MAGNOLIAS

Production: Ray Stark for Rastar; released by Tri-Star Pictures
Direction: Herbert Ross
Screenplay: Robert Harling; based on his play
Cinematography: John A. Alonzo
Editing: Paul Hirsch
Production design: Gene Callahan and Edward Pisoni
Art direction: Hub Braden and Michael Okowita
Set decoration: Lee Poll and Garrett Lewis
Set design: Steven Wolff
Costume design: Julie Weiss
Sound: Al Overton
Music: Georges Delerue
MPAA rating: PG
Running time: 118 minutes

> *Principal characters:*
> Ouiser Boudreaux .... Shirley MacLaine
> Annelle Dupuy Desoto................. Daryl Hannah
> Clairee Belcher..................... Olympia Dukakis
> Shelby Eatenton....................... Julia Roberts
> Drum Eatenton .... Tom Skerritt
> Spud Jones............................ Sam Shepard
> Truvy Jones........................... Dolly Parton
> M'Lynn Eatenton .... Sally Field
> Sammy Desoto .... Kevin J. O'Connor
> Jackson Latcherie .... Dylan McDermott

Herbert Ross's *Steel Magnolias* was a long-running, popular, and financial success near the end of 1989 and into 1990, but the film is a lesson in the difference between aesthetic worth and mass appeal. Producer Ray Stark gathered a cast of first-rank stars, added some talented veteran and youthful supporting players, and accurately gauged the attraction of such an entourage. *Steel Magnolias* is based on the play by Robert Harling, who adapted his own work for the screen. What Harling presents, however, is a pale imitation of James L. Brooks's 1983 film, *Terms of Endearment*, a much more substantial exercise in comedy-melodrama.

The film's narrative focuses on the antics of the Eatenton family, a small-town Louisiana clan headed by father Drum (Tom Skerrit) and mother M'Lynn (Sally Field). As the story begins, it is the wedding day of Shelby Eatenton (Julia Roberts), and the Eatenton home is the scene of bustling activity. Much of the action of the early part of *Steel Magnolias* takes place either in the Eatenton home or in Truvy's Beauty Spot, a salon owned by Truvy Jones (Dolly Parton). Cross-cuts back and forth from these two centers of activity effectively unite the numerous eccentrics who people the story space.

The film's opening shots feature images of the Eatenton house and also introduce Annelle Dupuy (Daryl Hannah), a young misfit who wanders into town. Annelle makes her way to Truvy's beauty parlor, where, awkward, shy, and mysterious though she is, she impresses the buxom proprietor enough to find herself a job as a "glamour technician."

Meanwhile, back at the Eatenton abode, preparations for the wedding festivities continue apace. Most noteworthy of these is Drum's energetic attempts to scare away the flocks of birds that roost in the trees surrounding the house with a pistol. Drum's tactics do not amuse Ouiser Boudreaux (Shirley MacLaine), a cranky curmudgeon who lives next door to the Eatentons. M'Lynn Eatenton intently and intensely works at making sure that everything unfolds smoothly on Shelby's big day. In contrast to Drum's lighthearted and spontaneous demeanor, M'Lynn seems distracted and unable really to enjoy herself. Behind M'Lynn's façade of pleasant smiles and cheerfulness lurk serious misgivings about Shelby's future.

Mother and daughter head for Truvy's shop to have their hair done for the big event, and it is there that the tension that exists between M'Lynn and Shelby surfaces. M'Lynn, Shelby, Truvy, Annelle, and Clairee Belcher (Olympia Dukakis) joke and gossip, but soon Shelby experiences a serious episode of insulin shock. Her mother comes to the rescue, calmly forcing Shelby to drink some orange juice. Yet Shelby—even in view of the fact that she is ill—fiercely expresses her resentment of M'Lynn's attentions. It is soon learned that Shelby's diabetes is not a trifling matter, that her mother has perhaps overprotected her for some time, and that Shelby is determined to have her freedom and live her own life, even if that involves considerable risk.

M'Lynn and Shelby have an angry discussion regarding Shelby's plans to rear a family of her own. M'Lynn reminds Shelby that the doctor has advised against her having children. M'Lynn even goes so far as to criticize nastily Shelby's fiancé, Jackson Latcherie (Dylan McDermott), of ignoring his future wife's welfare. M'Lynn and Shelby discuss the possibilities of adopting children or obtaining them through less formal channels. Shelby points out, however, that adoption officials will never grant a child to someone as fragile as she is and that Jackson has not been successful in arranging a private adoption. At this point in his story, Harling's plotting becomes patently transparent. Given the fact that Shelby has been amply presented as strong-willed but gravely ill, it will come as no surprise that her novel fling at happiness and motherhood is doomed to failure.

The film's next sequence begins at Christmas, when the town is dressed for an annual festival and when Shelby and Jackson come home for the holidays. Annelle has blossomed. Clairee has bought the local radio station and does color analysis for broadcasts of high-school football games. What is most important about this Christmas interlude is that Shelby tells M'Lynn that she is pregnant, and M'Lynn is not amused. Bitter moments of accusation and acrimony spoil the reuniting of mother and daughter.

Harling then moves the plot quickly to Jackson, Jr.'s first birthday, some nineteen months later. The real information surfaces at a gossip session at Truvy's. Annelle has progressed into another stage of development, having been "born again," and Shelby's condition has deteriorated to the point that she now regularly undergoes dialysis. In fact, doctors have told her that she must have a new kidney. No search for a donor is necessary, since M'Lynn heroically comes forth. Shelby undergoes her operation near the end of October, during the Halloween season. She is very brave, helping in the hospital's nursery as she herself recovers from surgery. Shelby's attempts to hide her discomfort go unnoticed by nurses but are quite apparent to the viewer.

Shelby eventually returns home, and a period of some normalcy sets in. Indeed, it is while she is alone one afternoon, playing with Jackson, Jr., that she succumbs to her disease. Her husband arrives to find Shelby lying on the veranda, telephone in hand, unconscious. Shelby's coma will in fact be terminal. The remainder of the film focuses on Shelby's death and the manner in which her family and friends deal with the tragedy. The passage of the film concerning Shelby's death is touching, sometimes genuinely moving. M'Lynn faithfully spends every day at her daughter's bedside, exercising her limbs, talking to her, showing her pictures of her son, knowing that Shelby is not aware of her presence. Field expresses M'Lynn's frustration and anger well when she demands that Shelby open her eyes.

The fact remains that Shelby is being kept alive by support systems, and the family—including the indomitable M'Lynn—eventually sees that they must let her go. Jackson signs the papers that authorize the removal of life-support equipment, and M'Lynn holds Shelby's hand as her child dies. Characteristically, however, it is M'Lynn who immediately takes charge of funeral arrangements, ordering Jackson to ready Shelby's pink suit, the one she wore on her honeymoon trip only a few years before.

Harling does not allow the audience to grieve for long. While M'Lynn voices her bitterness once again at graveside, at the expense of Annelle, Clairee and Ouiser see to it that matters do not become too serious. The film's narrative draws to a close as all the friends and acquaintances presented throughout the film are reunited at the Eatenton home. The tone is now bittersweet—recalling the finale of *Terms of Endearment*—as Jackson and the others acknowledge that life must go on. After all, as Harling rather heavy-handedly makes the point, it is the Easter season, and death should not be in everyone's thoughts.

Steel Magnolias' appeal is founded on two ingredients: humor, which often sinks to levels of questionable taste, and superficial, manipulative melodrama. The film's genuinely moving moments are cheapened by the arbitrary imposition of obscenely colliding comic relief. Childish toilet humor and jokes at the expense of homosexuals all too often define Harling's comic scope, yet the film might have been acceptable as a decent comedy had Harling kept the maudlin tear-jerking to a minimum. Ultimately, therefore, the viewer must ask what the film wants of its audience, since the film is more confusing than enlightening.

Ross's direction too is uncertain. Julia Roberts, whose performance earned for her an Academy Award nomination for Best Supporting Actress, contributes the only work worthy of serious attention. Most of the other players are trapped in caricature roles, which Ross forces them to render very broadly. Such fine actors as Skerrit and MacLaine are reduced to the stature of clowns, and Parton, whose work attracted much attention after the film's initial release, is permitted to overact to a painful degree. Only Sam Shepard, who plays Truvy's ne'er-do-well husband, Spud, seems to remain immune to Ross's demeaning standards and offers a refreshingly low-key interpretation.

Gordon Walters

Reviews

American Film: Magazine of the Film and Television Arts. XV, November, 1989, p. 62.
Chicago Tribune. November 17, 1989, VII, p. 40.
Cosmopolitan. CCVII, November, 1989, p. 52.
Los Angeles Times. November 15, 1989, VI, p. 1.
New Woman. XIX, December, 1989, p. 35.
The New York Times. November 15, 1989, p. C21.
Newsweek. CXIV, November 27, 1989, p. 90.
Time. CXXXIV, November 20, 1989, p. 92.
Variety. CCCXXXVII, November 15, 1989, p. 20.
The Washington Post. November 17, 1989, p. D1.

STORY OF WOMEN
(UNE AFFAIRE DE FEMMES)

Origin: France
Released: 1988
Released in U.S.: 1989
Production: Marin Karmitz; released by MK2/New Yorker Films
Direction: Claude Chabrol
Screenplay: Colo Tavernier O'Hagan and Claude Chabrol; adapted from the book
   Une Affaire de femmes, by Francis Szpiner
Cinematography: Jean Rabier
Editing: Monique Fardoulis
Production design: François Benoit-Fresco
Special effects: Jean-François Cousson
Makeup: Judith Gayo
Costume design: Corinne Jorry
Sound: Jean-Bernard Thomasson and Maurice Gilbert
Music direction: Michel Gamot
Music: Matthieu Chabrol
MPAA rating: no listing
Running time: 110 minutes

Principal characters:
Marie Latour	Isabelle Huppert
Paul Latour	François Cluzet
Lulu/Lucie	Marie Trintignant
Lucien	Nils Tavernier
Mouche 2	Lolita Chammah
Mouche 1	Aurore Gauvin
Pierrot 1	Guillaume Foutrier
Pierrot 2	Nicolas Foutrier
Ginette	Marie Bunel
Jasmine	Dominique Blanc
Father Mourier	Louis Ducreux
Prosecutor Mourier	Michel Blanc

Story of Women is the first film in several years by acclaimed French director Claude Chabrol to be released in the United States. Chabrol, a leading member of the French New Wave and the director of such films as *Les Cousins* (1959; *The Cousins*), *Le Boucher* (1970; *The Butcher*), and *Violette Nozière* (1978; *Violette*), has long been a master of stories that lay bare the hypocrisy beneath the surface of conventional bourgeois life. In *Story of Women*, he expands his focus in an examination of life in France under the Nazi Occupation, during which the Vichy government masked the hypocrisy of its collaboration with Nazi policies by adopting a stance of high moral fervor.

Based on a true story, the film's subject is a provincial French housewife-turned-abortionist who keeps her family supplied with black market goods by assisting local women who find themselves unexpectedly pregnant. Marie Latour (Isabelle Huppert) lives with her two young children in a small village near Dieppe. Her husband, Paul (François Cluzet), is a prisoner of war, and Marie must struggle to make ends meet in a run-down, cramped apartment. When she finds her neighbor attempting to induce an abortion with a hot mustard bath, she offers her assistance and successfully ends the young woman's pregnancy with a solution of soapy water. During a chance encounter with a prostitute, Lulu (Marie Trintignant), Marie mentions her newfound knowledge and offers to help Lulu and any of her friends who might find themselves in similar circumstances.

Word of Marie's skills spreads, and she is soon earning much-needed extra money from her prospering business, which eventually includes renting out rooms in her apartment to Lulu and her friends for use with their "clients." When Paul is released and returns home, Marie is angered by his presence and refuses to sleep with him, viewing his return as a hindrance to her new life. Paul is a gentle, defeated man who at first fears that his wife, too, is a prostitute, but who later tolerates her activities when he discovers the truth from their son and is himself unable to find work.

Marie's growing income enables the family to move to more spacious quarters as her appetite for new clothes and other wartime scarcities increases. She hires an assistant, takes a lover—a handsome young collaborator and informer named Lucien (Nils Tavernier)—and begins voice lessons to fulfill her dream of becoming a singer. Harsh reality intrudes on her successful enterprise, however, when a farmer's wife, desperate to prevent an addition to her large, hungry family, dies after her abortion. Her husband, unable to cope with the loss of his wife, throws himself in front of a train, leaving their orphaned children in the care of his sister, who visits Marie and angrily accuses her of causing both deaths.

Marie grows bolder in her affair with Lucien, and Paul returns home one day to find them together. Furious at his wife's open infidelity, he informs the authorities that she is an abortionist, and Marie is arrested. Sent to Paris for her trial, Marie cannot understand the expressions of outrage from the Vichy officials; she is, after all, living in a society in which black market profiteering thrives, Jews are regularly deported in accordance with Nazi policy, and "respectable" citizens collaborate with their conquerors. The government, however, has taken refuge behind a show of reverence for morality and family values, and Marie is accused of the murder of future French citizens. Although she admits her activities and apologizes for them in court, she receives the death sentence and is guillotined, becoming one of the last women to be executed in France.

Story of Women is a stark, carefully observed portrayal of a woman who is very much a reflection of her time. The film is resolutely unsentimental in its depiction of Marie, refusing to make her either a heroine or a villainess. In Huppert's exceptional performance, Marie emerges as a fundamentally selfish, practical, and amoral woman who performs her first abortion as an act of friendship and all subsequent ones purely for profit. Her greed, her rejection of her husband, and her frequent thoughtless behavior toward her son all serve to make Marie a difficult character to like, yet the film never judges her. Chabrol and his cowriter, Colo Tavernier O'Hagan, place her actions firmly within the context of the society in which she lives, and it is clear that Marie believes that she is simply providing a much-needed service and is profiting from that need in a way no different from those around her who have turned the circumstances of the Occupation to their favor.

The film also makes it apparent that Marie's view of her activities is not an inaccurate one, a fact made painfully clear in the case of the farmer's wife, who has already attempted suicide before visiting Marie. Living under a government that discourages birth control but offers no hope for a family already pushed to the point of despair, the woman confesses to Marie that she feels no love for her children, only the exhausting burden of her daily efforts to feed them. Her subsequent death and her husband's suicide do not invalidate her earlier need for help; rather, they bring a profound complexity to the story. The woman's abortion may have been the immediate cause of her death, but its roots lie in less easily definable social and political issues.

Stylistically, the film also offers a subtle context for Marie's actions. The apartment in which Marie is living when the story opens is dark and claustrophobic, and the difficulties of her daily life as a young mother alone with two children make her desire for the income that the abortions will bring eminently understandable. Later in the film, when her thriving business allows the family to relocate to a larger apartment, the attraction of the comparatively spacious, sunny rooms is almost palpable. At a time when the French government is cooperating with Nazi policies and those who prosper often do so outside the law or at the expense of their fellow citizens, Marie has adopted a course of action entirely in keeping with the society around her.

If the viewer's sympathy for Marie subsequently undergoes a shift as her more disagreeable characteristics continue to emerge, it is a shift accompanied by the realization that the facts of most human issues are neither black nor white but part of a vast gray area in between. If Marie's motives for performing abortions are selfish ones, it is also an inherent part of the film's message that hers is a practical solution to a very real problem faced only by women, a solution opposed by a male government that has been emasculated by its subservience to the country's German conquerors. Her motives and personal flaws are not the reason Marie is condemned to die; she is executed to provide the Vichy government with an opportunity to assuage its own guilt with an outraged show of moral superiority.

Story of Women is a complex and powerful film that sparked enormous controversy in France, and its highly charged subject matter and frank depictions of

Marie's primitive kitchen-table abortions held up its distribution in the United States. Yet Chabrol's film is not, on its most important level, about abortion, and it takes no clear stance on the issue. What is of interest to the filmmaker is the story's unique place in the history of the Occupation and the manner in which it reflects the hypocrisy that made the Vichy government possible. For Chabrol, the outcome of Marie's story symbolizes a phenomenon that he discusses in an October 15, 1989, *New York Times* interview. A quote from that interview expresses both the film's message and the reason for Marie's execution: "Countries become extremely 'moral' — in quotes — when they feel themselves to be weak."

Janet E. Lorenz

Reviews

Chicago Tribune. February 11, 1990, VII, p. 8.
The Christian Science Monitor. October 27, 1989, p. 10.
Film Comment. XXV, September, 1989, p. 16.
The Hollywood Reporter. October 27, 1989, p. 4.
Los Angeles Times. October 26, 1989, VI, p. 10.
LA Weekly. October 27, 1989.
The Nation. CCXLIX, November 13, 1989, p. 575.
The New Republic. CCI, October 30, 1989, p. 24.
The New York Times. October 15, 1989, II, p. 24.
Time. CXXXV, January 15, 1990, p. 52.
Variety. CCCXXXII, September 7, 1988, p. 25.
The Village Voice. October 17, 1989, p. 90.
The Washington Post. November 3, 1989, p. C7.

TALVISOTA

Origin: Finland
Released: 1989
Released in U.S.: 1989
Production: Marko Röhr for National-Filmi Oy and Finnkino Oy
Direction: Pekka Parikka
Screenplay: Antti Tuuri and Pekka Parikka; based on the novel by Tuuri
Cinematography: Kari Sohlberg
Editing: Keijo Virtanen
Production design: Pertti Hilkamo
Art direction: Aarre Koivisto
Set decoration: Raimo Mikkola
Special effects: Esa Parkatti
Makeup: Mila Niemi
Costume design: Tuula Hilkamo
Sound: Paul Jyrälä and David Lewis Yewdall
Music: Juha Tikka
MPAA rating: no listing
Running time: 196 minutes
Also known as: The Winter War

Principal characters:

Martti Hakala	Taneli Mäkelä
Jussi Kantola	Vesa Vierikkö
Pentti Saari	Timo Torikka
Vilho Erkkilä	Heikki Paavilainen
Erkki Somppi	Antti Raivio
Juho Pernaa	Esko Kovero
Arvi Huhtala	Martti Suosalo
Aatos Laitila	Markku Huhtamo
Veikko Korpela	Matti Onnismaa
Paavo Hakala	Konsta Mäkelä
Matti Ylinen	Tomi Salmela
Yrjö "Ylli" Alanen	Esko Nikkari

Talvisota is perhaps the most ambitious undertaking in the history of the Finnish cinema. It is also the first film to be made about the Winter War, Finland's brave, agonizing stand against the Soviet invasion of 1939-1940. In an effort to shore up its own borders against Nazi Germany, the Soviet Union invaded Finland on November 30, 1939, only to meet with fierce resistance from the Finnish army, many of its soldiers recently recruited from among the population at large. During the course of a 105-day siege, the Finns withstood crushing losses and the bitterly cold winter

weather in their attempt to repel the Soviet invaders. *Talvisota* captures their struggle in an unsparing, magnificently filmed chronicle of epic proportions.

The film opens on the Hakala family farm as two brothers, Martti (Taneli
Mäkelä) and Paavo (Konsta Mäkelä), prepare to enlist in the army. Martti leaves
behind him a wife and child, while Paavo must bid farewell to his girlfriend. At the
recruiting station, they are joined by other men from their district, including Erkki
Somppi (Antti Raivio), their illegitimate half-brother by the family's one-time
maid.

So hurried are the preparations for the coming war that the men find themselves
ill-equipped and without a field kitchen, a problem they remedy by appropriating
one from a nearby unit. The company embarks for the frontier by train and then
marches toward the border under cover of night, listening to the battle wisdom of an
older man, a World War I veteran, nicknamed "Ylli" (Esko Nikkari). The company
stops briefly in a small town, where Paavo has a brief romance with a young local
girl and Martti gives assistance to a farm wife whose husband has been sent by the
government to dig trenches.

When the Soviets cross the Finnish border, the village is evacuated and the
company advances toward the front. During their first bombardment, Ylli is killed,
bringing home to the men the reality of what lies ahead for them. After replacing a
battle-weary unit at the front, the company engages in its first round of combat with
the Soviets. The fighting is bloody and terrifying to the men, and the war takes on a
human face when the Soviets enter the Finnish trenches and must be repelled in
hand-to-hand combat. Paavo is wounded during the skirmish, while the battle takes
a heavy emotional toll on Erkki, who snaps while on sentry duty and bolts from his
position. He is found at battalion headquarters and returned to the unit.

Paavo is sent home to recover from his wound and alarms his family with his
changed manner and his comment that "none of us will come back alive." As he
and Martti leave for sentry duty on his first day back at the front, Paavo is hit
directly during the shelling, and Martti finds his brother's body in pieces when he
rounds a corner in the trench. When the bunker is hit, Martti is sent to headquarters
to report on the severity of their losses and the imminent approach of the Soviet
army. During a fierce attack by the enemy, the few remaining Finns hold their
ground and manage to blow up a Soviet tank with a Molotov cocktail. After the
battle, they learn that the company's commanding officer has been killed on his way
to check on their condition.

On Christmas Day, the men celebrate with a service and hymns in the bunker.
They have also built a sauna—an unexpected luxury in the midst of the bloody
fighting. The Soviets drop leaflets by plane urging the men to lay down their arms
and join them in the great proletariat struggle, and one of the Finnish soldiers is
killed on his way to the latrine, where he had intended to use his leaflet as toilet
paper. When the bunker is hit and flooded with water, the men abandon it, and it is
quickly occupied by the Soviets.

The company is replaced and sent to a barracks away from the fighting for some much-needed rest. Martti is granted leave and returns home, where he lies to his family about the details of Paavo's death. He returns to his unit and is sent to the Taipale River to aid in its defense. During a long series of violent attacks, Erkki is killed, and the men see another company slaughtered when they begin their charge too late. With most of the company dead and the Finns losing ground to the advancing Soviets, Martti manages to survive a brutal firestorm of bombings. Confused and numb with exhaustion, he learns that a peace treaty has been signed, and he peers over the hill where he has taken shelter to see the Soviet troops only yards away on the other side, dancing and cheering at the news.

Talvisota is an extraordinarily powerful depiction of a small nation's bitterly fought defense of its independence. The film captures both the spectacle of modern warfare, with its tanks and bombing raids, and the personal face of men subjected to the horrors of battle yet unflagging in their determination to hold out against their country's invaders. Overmatched in both men and equipment, the Finns nevertheless manage to make up in cour.ge what they lack in numbers, repeatedly succeeding in turning back the Soviets in the face of seemingly insurmountable odds. Indeed, the battle statistics for the Winter War attest to their remarkable achievement; while the Soviets lost 200,000 men, the Finnish death toll stood at 25,000.

A key element in the war, and one that is underscored by the film's title, is the bitter Finnish winter. The snow and icy cold are felt throughout the film as the men fight in heavy coats, mufflers, and gloves, wiping the oil from their rifles to prevent the parts from freezing together and carving away at a large frozen block of cheese that constitutes an important part of their rations. The men's hardy constitutions in the face of such daunting weather is evidenced by their use of the sauna, which they follow with a quick roll in a snowbank. Their ability to withstand the cold plays a crucial part in their continued resistance to the Soviets; as one character's father comments, "King Winter is on our side."

Director Pekka Parikka re-creates the battle scenes with an eye for detail and an inherent grasp of the scope and heightened emotion of warfare. The scenes in which Soviet soldiers advance on the beleaguered Finns have an immediacy that brings to life the reality of trench warfare as the Finns face their enemies across barely a stone's throw of ground. Vividly filmed and unflinching in its depiction of the bloody results of battle, *Talvisota* manages to convey both the nobility—and the necessity—of the Finns' struggle and the stark horror of war itself. Harrowingly gruesome shots of lost limbs and bodies torn apart by exploding shells force the viewer to confront the full measure of the toll that war can exact, a toll that makes the Finns' continued grit and courage all the more remarkable.

The film also examines the devastating effect that continued exposure to such brutality has on the men themselves. Unfamiliar with war yet eager to fight to defend their country when the film opens, the men undergo a literal trial by fire when they first reach the front and quickly find their illusions about the glory of war replaced by an increasingly grim realization that the experience of battle will subject them to horrors for which nothing in their lives has prepared them. The ways in which they cope differ from man to man; Martti becomes hardened and numb, Paavo's youthful exuberance gives way to a bleak despair, and Erkki undergoes a breakdown before emerging as a capable soldier.

The men of the unit also form close bonds of brotherhood that are tempered by the heat of battle, making each loss a painful and disheartening blow. One of the things that sets *Talvisota* apart from so many war films is the number of its central characters who are killed in the course of the war. Rather than offering only a few token deaths among the men in the unit, Parikka and his coauthor, Antti Tuuri, shock the viewer again and again with the deaths of almost all the men they have developed as characters in their story. By the film's end, their loss has come to represent the terrible losses that Finland suffered at the hands of the Soviets.

The irony of *Talvisota*—one not stated in the film itself—is that, although the Finnish army's brave defense of its borders earned for the country worldwide sympathy, the peace treaty that brought the Winter War to a close gave the Soviets much of the land that the soldiers had fought so hard to defend. Yet although the country's borders were altered and hard-fought territory was lost, Finland succeeded in retaining its independence from the Soviets through a fierce determination and courage that surprised their giant foe.

Janet E. Lorenz

Reviews
Variety. December 26, 1989, p. 2.
The Hollywood Reporter. December 27, 1989, p. 4.
Los Angeles Times. December 8, 1989, VI, p. 4.

TANGO AND CASH

Production: Jon Peters and Peter Guber for Guber-Peters Company; released by
Warner Bros.
Direction: Andrei Konchalovsky
Screenplay: Randy Feldman
Cinematography: Donald E. Thorin
Editing: Hubert de la Bouillerie and Robert Ferretti
Production design: J. Michael Riva
Art direction: David Klassen and Richard Berger
Set decoration: Marvin March
Costume design: Bernie Pollack
Music: Harold Faltermeyer
MPAA rating: R
Running time: 98 minutes

> *Principal characters:*
> Tango .... Sylvester Stallone
> Cash .... Kurt Russell
> Kiki................................. Teri Hatcher
> Yves Perret .... Jack Palance
> Requin.............................. Brion James
> Quan .... James Hong
> Lopez.............................. Marc Alaimo
> Owen .... Michael J. Pollard

Ray Tango (Sylvester Stallone) and Gabe Cash (Kurt Russell) are rival Los
Angeles detectives with extraordinary successes in thwarting criminals, primarily by
breaking up major drug deals. The two are opposites: Tango, polite and soft-spoken,
immaculately groomed, wearing dark, three-piece European suits, comes to the
office looking more like a stockbroker than a police officer; Cash, in contrast, his
wavy blond hair down to his shoulders, has a wardrobe that seems to consist of
little more than kneeless jeans and torn t-shirts. He has a "living for the moment"
spontaneity about him, a preference for action over thought, and a problem of not
knowing when to keep his mouth shut.

One thing the two do have in common, although they are unaware of it at the
film's start, is a common enemy—crime boss Yves Perret (Jack Palance), who is
tired of being frustrated by Tango and Cash in his unlawful pursuits. Rather than
killing the two, which Perret decides would only make them martyrs and set every
other cop in Los Angeles on his trail, he instead chooses to set them up; he destroys
their reputations by leading them into a trap with a dead man, some heroin, and a
briefcase full of money. Federal agents break in and arrest Tango and Cash, having
as evidence a doctored tape that cleverly implicates the two in a payoff scheme.

Perret's setup is so well orchestrated that both defense lawyers convince their clients to plea-bargain, promising that their sentences will not be more than eighteen months in a minimum security prison (a "country club," as Cash calls it). En route to the "country club," however, something goes wrong. The two prisoners are transferred and end up in a maximum security prison instead—one that seems to be filled with revenge-minded thugs who have their new cell-mates, Detectives Tango and Cash, to thank for putting them behind bars in the first place.

The atmosphere in the prison is reminiscent of one of Dante Alighieri's Circles of Hell: Knee-deep garbage lines the cell block; a half dozen small litter fires burn unattended, giving off a sooty gray-blue light; psychopaths bang on the cell bars, shouting promises of sodomy and torture as greetings to the new arrivals. To make matters worse, Perret has the corrupt warden and most of the guards in his pocket. On their first night in prison, Tango and Cash are beaten by marauding thugs who have access to the cell keys. The two are then dumped down a chute, ending up in the basement laundry—a huge, dimly lit, steamy room, where they encounter more thugs, these slowly coming out of the shadows in dark silhouette, some wielding baseball bats. Perret is there, too, as is his main henchman, a pony-tailed Briton named Requin (Brion James), who has a fondness for knives.

A free-for-all fight ensues, with Tango and Cash, although ridiculously outnumbered, inflicting serious damage on their adversaries before finally being subdued. Perret, who does not want these two back on the street ever, turns their fates over to the avenging inmates, who choose to amuse themselves by lowering the two, one at a time, into a huge tub of water in which a live electrical wire has been immersed. The entertainment ends abruptly when an assistant warden, one of the few honest officials left in the prison, breaks in with a small force of armed guards, and the fun is called off.

The following day, Cash decides he has had enough. He plots an escape through the prison ventilation system, but Tango, believing it is another setup, refuses to go along. Cash goes on his own, only to find en route the body of the sympathetic assistant warden, his throat slit ear to ear. This gruesome discovery is immediately followed by the sound of a barking dog that tells Cash he is being hunted. He finds himself trapped in an air shaft with guards approaching at one end and a huge whirling fan at the other. Cash loses his footing and is about to be sucked into the fan, when Tango arrives on the other side and jams a pipe into the blades, stopping the motion just long enough for Cash to squeeze through.

They proceed with the escape together, climbing, in the pouring rain, to the roof of one of the prison buildings, where they leap for their lives, grabbing onto some sloping electrical wires and sliding on straps to the ground. Once free, the two part company, with Tango giving Cash the name of a woman, "Katherine," to contact if he needs to get in touch.

Back on the streets again, the two separately set out to clear their names—slowly unraveling the trail that leads them to Perret, who is holed up at his headquarters in an abandoned government airfield heavily protected by security. None of this stops

Tango and Cash, however, and with the help of a special vehicle designed by Cash's friend Owen (Michael J. Pollard), a weapons expert, the two succeed in breaking into the compound and fending off scores of would-be assassins. They eventually force their way into Perret's office, where they find a surprise waiting for them: Perret has taken Katherine (Teri Hatcher), who is known as Kiki and who is Tango's younger sister, hostage. Perret stands, holding a knife to the woman's throat, the image repeated in a half dozen mirrors, making it seemingly impossible for Tango and Cash to tell flesh and blood from mere reflection.

Tango pleads with Perret not to hurt her; Perret responds by ordering both men to drop their guns. Tango slowly begins to lower his weapon but then suddenly raises it to take one decisive shot, which pierces Perret's forehead. Glass crashes as Perret and Kiki tumble to the ground. A ring on Perret's hand had been the giveaway; Tango noticed that it was reversed in all the mirror reflections except one.

The two grab Kiki and make it out of the compound just as the building is blown to smithereens from a previously activated (by Perret) time bomb. The film ends with the promise of future liaisons—a romantic one on the part of Cash and Kiki (much to the protective Tango's displeasure) and a professional one for Tango and Cash, as Kiki makes the two sparring cops admit they work well together.

Tango and Cash is less a cop picture or buddy picture than it is a superheroes comic book translated to film. The characters are larger than life—the two protagonists spend much of the film showing off their bulging biceps—and are beaten and tortured with barely more than a bruise to show for it. Cash is wounded in the film's final sequence, but he simply shrugs it off, saying it was a clean shot—the bullet passed through his arm. They wisecrack through life-threatening situations. Stallone and Russell handle their roles with the required physical aplomb, and they banter well together. It is hard to refer to what the two of them do as "acting"; these are not roles that demand much in the way of revealing the interior lives of the characters.

The villains are arch, with kinks and quirks worthy of superhero foes (Perret repeatedly fondles two pet rats, named "Tango" and "Cash"). Perret and his cohorts are diabolically evil, if not psychotic, without any trace of moral complexity. Much of the violence, too, is comic book violence. A car chase of a would-be killer through a parking garage plays like an out-of-control bumper car ride in an absurdist's amusement park; the confrontation at Perret's compound features a dozen "big-wheel" monster vehicles crashing and exploding on the moonscape terrain like some grotesque motorcross event.

The comic book feel of the film may not be entirely accidental. The film's producers, Jon Peters and Peter Guber, were responsible for the blockbuster *Batman* (1989; reviewed in this volume), released only a few months earlier. Peter Mac-Donald, who served as executive producer on *Tango and Cash* as well as directed its very effective action sequences, also directed action sequences for *Batman*. Perennial bad guy Jack Palance made life as difficult for "The Caped Crusader" as he did for Tango and Cash.

Special credit should be given to the film's production designer, J. Michael Riva, and to the cinematographer, Donald E. Thorin, for the look of the film. Riva's design for Perret's windowless world, his high-tech, underground bunker, is both elegant and chilling (like Perret himself); the prison sets, the trashed cell block and the dingy basement laundry where Tango and Cash nearly meet their demise, are also superbly envisioned and richly textured so as to reinforce the feeling that these two framed cops really are caught in the bowels of the prison system. Thorin's photography is especially effective in low light situations, as in the prison laundry, where faces remain hidden in shadows, and menacing figures emerge from silhouettes to take on form in the dim blue-gray light, or in the prison escape scene, in which the two heroes, in a downpour, glide on electrical wires with shooting sparks lighting the night sky around them. The visual excitement that Riva and Thorin bring to the production helps to lift this action/comedy out of the realm of the ordinary.

Mary Lou McNichol

Reviews
Boston Globe. December 22, 1989, p. 45.
Chicago Tribune. December 22, 1989, VII, p. 26.
The Christian Science Monitor. January 12, 1990, p. 10.
The Hollywood Reporter. December 22, 1989.
Los Angeles Times. December 22, 1989, VI, p. 4.
The New York Times. December 22, 1989, p. C16.
People Weekly. XXXIII, January 15, 1990, p. 15.
San Francisco Chronicle. December 22, 1989, p. E1.
USA Today. December 22, 1989, p. D7.
Variety. CCCXXXVII, December 27, 1989, p. 10.
The Washington Post. December 22, 1989, p. D1.

TAP

Production: Gary Adelson and Richard Vane; released by Tri-Star Pictures
Direction: Nick Castle
Screenplay: Nick Castle
Cinematography: David Gribble
Editing: Patrick Kennedy
Production design: Patricia Norris
Art direction: Frank Silva
Set decoration: Leslie Morales
Special effects: Phil Cory
Makeup: Michelle Buhler
Costume design: Patricia Norris
Improvography: Gregory Hines
Choreography: Henry LeTang
Sound: David Stone
Music: James Newton Howard
MPAA rating: PG-13
Running time: 110 minutes

Principal characters:
Max Washington . . . . Gregory Hines
Amy . . . . Suzzanne Douglas
Little Mo. . . . . Sammy Davis, Jr.
Louis . . . . Savion Glover
Nicky . . . . Joe Morton
Francis . . . . Dick Anthony Williams
Sandman . . . . Howard "Sandman" Sims
Bunny . . . . Bunny Briggs
Steve . . . . Steve Condos
Slim . . . . Jimmy Slyde
Spats . . . . Pat Rico
Arthur. . . . . Arthur Duncan
Harold. . . . . Harold Nicholas

Tap is ostensibly a tribute to authentic black tap dancing and features some of the greatest "hoofers" still alive: Harold Nicholas, Sandman Sims, Jimmy Slyde, Arthur Duncan, Steve Condos, Bunny Briggs, and Pat Rico. Actor-dancer Gregory Hines and fourteen-year-old Savion Glover represent the present and future of the hoofer tradition. The problem with *Tap*, however, is that it never looks its subject straight in the face; in the end, the cliché-ridden dialogue and numerous subplots undermine the film's message altogether.

Tap begins with Max Washington (Hines) in jail for grand theft. In a dramatic opening sequence, Max stomps out a furious tap dance to the rhythm of a leaky faucet, while the other prisoners scream at him for waking them. Max is "the best second-story man in the business" but was drunk the night he got caught because it was also the night of his father's funeral. While in jail, Max beat a sadistic prison guard and was put into "purgatory," an isolation box, for three months. It was there that he started to tap again in order to keep from going over the edge.

When Max is released, he stands poised between two courses of action: return to a lucrative, but dangerous, life of crime, or become an impoverished tap dancer like his father. His decision is framed as one between two families. Francis (Dick Anthony Williams), the black mobster for whom Max worked, refers to his operation as a family; while the tap studio, Sonny's Side of the Street, functions as another type of family. The dance studio was founded by Max's father, Sonny, a legendary dancer who taught his son to pick up dance moves from the rhythm of the streets. For most of the film, Max resides at a hotel opposite the dance school, which invokes the obvious pun that he does not live on the "sunny side of the street."

Max visits the dance studio, where he watches his former lover, Amy (Suzzanne Douglas), teach a class and is reunited with Amy's son, Louis (Savion Glover). When Max ventures up to the third floor to practice, he encounters Amy's father, Little Mo (Sammy Davis, Jr.), and the other old hoofers, who do not recognize him at first. Max's youthful arrogance results in a "challenge." The scene is a historical document of sorts, with the hoofers shot in full figure to reveal their still considerable talents. In this and subsequent dance sequences, however, the backlighting often obscures the dancers in its attempt to impart an aura of nostalgia.

Little Mo and Max are in the midst of a tap dance showdown when Amy breaks up the challenge and scolds her father, who is apparently dying. She refuses to forgive Max for leaving her, unaware that he was sent to jail. At this point, the film introduces three new subplots: Max's renewed pursuit of Amy; Amy's new career as a choreographer for a Broadway director's watered-down tap revue; and Little Mo's dying wish to revive authentic tap. Max soon recaptures Amy's heart but cannot follow her career path. which offers hope of the financial success he seeks but requires that he compromise his art. Unable to have both artistic freedom and financial security, Max rejoins Francis' mob "family."

For a film about tap, it is more than ironic that the film's strongest scenes have to do with crime and not dance: the opening scene and Max's robbery of a jeweler's office safe. In the latter scene, Max must scale a building and lower himself down a neon sign to an open window. The street noises rise to a crescendo, while crosscuts reveal the getaway driver, Nicky (Joe Morton), engaged in a frantic scat response to these sounds. The noise comes to an abrupt halt when Max enters the building and shuts the window. He is anxious as he fills a bag with jewels, and, when he stands, he bumps against a water cooler. The cooler begins to drip. Suddenly, the room acquires the visual and aural qualities of his jail cell. The drops become louder, and Max backs toward a wall, where the shadow of the window blinds falls across his face and torso like prison bars. Max replaces the jewels and leaves, telling his accomplices that he is going home.

With the romance and crime plots resolved, the question of tap's past and future remains. One problem with *Tap* is that the dialogue is often stilted and contrived as exposition. Louis, who has spent his entire life at the dance studio—and is quite a good dancer himself—seems shocked when he hears that the old hoofers once worked. His surprising naïveté, however, is just an excuse for a history lesson from the old hoofers. The lesson never materializes, however, and the audience is left with a few grumbled remarks from Sandman blaming rock-and-roll for the demise of tap, an explanation that Little Mo denies out of hand.

Little Mo's denial is curious, since the solution he offers is to team up with a rock-and-roll sound engineer (Timmy Capello) at the Times Square bar he frequents on tap night. Their plan is to create a tap-rock fusion, something—Little Mo claims—that only Max is talented enough to pull off. Thus when Max returns "home," it is to front the house rock-and-roll band of the Times Square bar. He sings for a bit and then begins to tap on special shoes with synthesizer pickups. Max trades riffs with the drummer, struts around the bar, and finishes triumphant. The nature of his triumph, however, is revealed in a brief reaction shot of the exuberant audience: white teenagers in a small bar. In a sense, the film invokes the tap dance tradition in order to kill it off, as it becomes just another black influence on white rock-and-roll culture. Max, who had too much integrity to join the Broadway tap revue, suddenly seems all too willing to become a rock-and-roll sideshow.

Tap is an excuse to showcase Hines and legendary tap dancers, and on that account the film is quite good. Henry LeTang, who taught both Hines and his brother Maurice, choreographs three generations of hoofers, whose presence proves tap much more alive than the film admits. Offscreen, Glover as well as veterans Briggs and Slyde appeared on the Broadway stage within the past year. Despite a cliché-ridden script, Sammy Davis, Jr., won high praise as an actor while he also proved himself still up to a "challenge" after hip replacement surgery.

Even as a showcase, however, *Tap* remains ambivalent about its subject and raises some questions about its racial depictions. Reviewers objected to the crime element in *Tap*, an all-too-common feature of films about blacks and ethnic minorities. There is a blackmail logic to the film: Support your local tap dancer, or he will become a criminal. Yet the film never even makes credible the social constraints that are said to motivate Max, especially since the other tap dancers seem content with their impoverished lot in life. Even worse, Max's criminal tendencies find a strong resonance in the depiction of tap as a composite of "stolen" moves.

The film's ambivalence about its subject reaches a climax with writer-director Nick Castle's brief tribute to his father, a choreographer who worked with Fred Astaire and Gene Kelly. In their reunion scene, Max and Amy perform a jazzed-up version of the Astaire and Ginger Rogers dance to Irving Berlin's "Cheek to Cheek" in *Top Hat* (1934). The impromptu dance on the studio's rooftop never quite develops and is unsuited to Hines, who rarely uses his upper body as did Astaire.

Max and Amy had rehearsed the dance years earlier, but Max backed out of the performance at the last minute. The film, however, never explains whether his reason was aesthetic or—more likely—because he was sent to jail. Their dance is, after all, not a reappropriation of tap as stolen by Astaire, but an updating of Astaire into the rock-and-roll era. Indeed, throughout the film, rather than focus on black tap and the question of its past influence and future directions, Castle uses the idea of black tap as theft to validate its own theft at the hands of white dancers and musicians. Max's decision, therefore, becomes a no-win choice: No matter which direction he turns, he is compromised.

Chon Noriega

Reviews

Chicago Tribune. February 10, 1989, VII, p. 31.
Ebony. XLIV, February, 1989, p. 46.
Jet. LXXV, February 13, 1989, p. 58.
Los Angeles Times. February 10, 1989, VI, p. 1.
The New Republic. CC, March 20, 1989, p. 32.
The New York Times. February 10, 1989, p. C17.
The New Yorker. LXIV, February 6, 1989, p. 74.
Newsweek. CXIII, February 13, 1989, p. 79.
People Weekly. XXXI, February 13, 1989, p. 16.
Variety. CCCXXXIV, February 8, 1989, p. 18.
The Washington Post. February 10, 1989, p. D7.

A TAXING WOMAN'S RETURN

Origin: Japan
Released: 1988
Released in U.S.: 1989
Production: Yasushi Tamaoki and Seigo Hosogoe for Itami Productions; released by New Yorker Films
Direction: Juzo Itami
Screenplay: Juzo Itami
Cinematography: Yonezo Maeda
Editing: Akira Suzuki
Production design: Shuji Nakamura
Lighting: Akio Katsura
Sound: Osamu Onodera
Music: Toshiyuki Honda
MPAA rating: no listing
Running time: 127 minutes

> *Principal characters:*
> Ryoko Itakura . . . . Nobuko Miyamoto
> Teppei Onizawa . . . . Rentaro Mikuni
> Inspector Mishima . . . . Toru Masuoka
> Assistant Chief Inspector Hanamura . . . Masahiko Tsugawa
> Chief Inspector Sadohara . . . . Tetsuro Tanba
> Nekota . . . . Koichi Ueda
> Shorty Masa . . . . Mansaku Fuwa

In director Juzo Itami's films, the underside of Japanese society is clearly displayed. From the treatment of women to corruption in high-level politics, Itami airs all the dirty laundry. Yet, perhaps the most interesting aspect for Western viewers of Itami's films is the tone with which he addresses these serious subjects. The director himself categorizes his films such as *A Taxing Woman* (1988) and its sequel, *A Taxing Woman's Return*, as comedies.

Just as *A Taxing Woman* chronicled the process of stalking and capturing a tax evader, *A Taxing Woman's Return* follows the same formula, though the prey is much bigger—and much more dangerous—this time. *A Taxing Woman's Return* amplifies the original themes of *A Taxing Woman* by bringing them to even higher echelons of government and business, and the sacred domain of religion. Japan has its corrupt religious leaders, just as in Western countries, though the criminal's crime in *A Taxing Woman's Return* almost seems mitigated at times by his unswerving (or insane) belief in his anointedness. The amazing schemes that the characters devise to evade taxes seem as if they must be a product of Itami's fertile imagination (he wrote as well as directed the film), yet he has said that the film has been very well researched: These elaborate subterfuges may be exaggerated but not by much.

In an almost police procedural style that will be familiar to fans of detective thrillers, Ryoko Itakura (Nobuko Miyamoto) relentlessly tracks her man. In the best *film noir* style, *A Taxing Woman's Return* opens with a whitish-gray corpse floating in iron-gray water, with a dull gray sky overlooking the scene. The corpse is evidently an "expendable" cog in the crime world's works, according to the master villain, Teppei Onizawa (Rentaro Mikuni). Onizawa styles himself as the chief elder of a religion called Heaven's Path. Though he and his wife, Kinu Akaha (Haruko Kato), or the "Holy Matriarch," may preach their own special brand of spirituality, in reality they have established a huge land-swindling corporation that is hiding millions of yen from the tax inspectors. While Onizawa is carrying on an affair with a sixteen-year-old named Nana (Yoriko Doguchi), who has been left with him by her father as collateral for a debt, the Holy Matriarch is off buying floor-length fur coats. Itami's view of love is somewhat morbid: Onizawa's tribute of his love for Nana is to buy her a sepulcher near his own, perhaps an allusion by Itami to the "whited sepulcher" that Onizawa has become.

Unbeknown to Onizawa and the Holy Matriarch, however, they are being investigated by the brave and resourceful Itakura. Paired in this film with a young inspector fresh from college, Inspector Mishima (Toru Masuoka), Itakura is driven to be more successful than ever. Itakura and Mishima are opposites, but, contrary to popular American film manipulation, they do not fall in love. Ironically, the only relationship involving love is the tainted affair between the elderly Onizawa and the nubile Nana. Mishima is a by-the-book type, while Itakura will do whatever is necessary to collect the needed proof, including making up her face to pass as an abused wife who is seeking shelter at the Heaven's Path sanctuary. Also involved is a monk (a star turn by Ryu Chishu) who is the supposed head of Heaven's Path yet who knows nothing about the religion that has been founded in his name.

Onizawa is really the main character in the film, and his portrayal as a man insanely convinced of the righteousness of what he is doing (he believes that his wholesale evictions and land swindles free land for development that will aid the Japanese economy) is eerily frightening. At the end, when he locks his young, heavily pregnant mistress and himself into the tomb, it is implied that they will die there together. Itami did not intend *A Taxing Woman's Return* to be taken lightly, despite its tag as a "comedy." Yet, there are some scenes in the film that are done for the comedic effect. While these scenes are definitely humorous, it is indicative of the cultural difference between the Western and Eastern viewer that these films are regarded as comedies in Japan though some scenes may appear fairly grim and even grotesque at times.

Though Itakura may be relegated more to the background in this sequel, she is still a strongly portrayed character: She is a woman who is given much responsibility in a male-dominated culture. Yet, it is hard to determine whether Itakura is portrayed ideally or idealistically. She believes in what she is doing, but her society rarely seems to support or respect her (she is often verbally and physically abused by the people whom she is investigating). The men with whom she works are proud that they can go for days working on a case without going home. As a single (divorced) mother, however, Itakura does not have the same mindless luxury. One scene in *A Taxing Woman* touchingly shows her on the telephone telling her five-year-old how to microwave his dinner. In *A Taxing Woman's Return*, however, her son is never mentioned. It is almost as if he has been sacrificed to her career and is perhaps a touch of the realism of a working woman's situation in Japan: no husband, no children. The vulnerability of Itakura's character revealed in *A Taxing Woman* seems to have been completely replaced by her inexhaustible tenaciousness, until she has more in common with her equally bulldoglike partner Mishima than with any of the other female characters in the film.

Miyamoto plays Itakura flawlessly, and Itami shows a certain affinity for his leading lady; her presence is strongly felt even when she does not appear in several consecutive scenes. This affinity is perhaps not surprising as Miyamoto is Itami's wife and has appeared in some of his other films, including *Tampopo* (1986), a send-up of the spaghetti Western genre involving a female noodlemaker.

Japan is a country that has undergone extensive change since World War II, change that consists in part of Westernization of its culture. Many Western practices have been adopted and, in some cases, subverted. Japan has become a microcosm of some of the worst aspects of Western capitalism—a society of haves and have-nots. Real estate has been fraudulently overvalued, and a "speculative funnel cloud," as one economist has said, has developed at the center of the Japanese economy. Japan is nowhere near to being the conquering economic superpower that its reputation touts. As the film critic Vincent Canby noted, this film "has the manner of comedy, but the message is bleak": *A Taxing Woman's Return* is a not-so-mute testimony to the economic dark side of Japan.

Jo-Ellen Lipman Boon

Reviews
Boston Globe. July 21, 1989, p. 23.
Chicago Tribune. September 29, 1989, VII, p. 35.
The Christian Science Monitor. July 14, 1989, p. 11.
Houston Post. November 10, 1989, p. E6.
Los Angeles Times. July 20, 1989, VI, p. 1.
The New Republic. CCI, August 7, 1989, p. 26.
The New York Times. June 28, 1989, p. C17.
San Francisco Chronicle. July 26, 1989, p. E1.
Variety. CCCXXXII, August 31, 1988, p. 39.
The Washington Post. November 15, 1989, p. B13.

TRIUMPH OF THE SPIRIT

Production: Arnold Kopelson and Shimon Arama; released by Nova International Films
Direction: Robert M. Young
Screenplay: Andrzej Krakowski and Laurence Heath; based on a story by Shimon Arama and Zion Haen
Cinematography: Curtis Clark
Editing: Arthur Coburn
Production design: Jerzy Maslowska
Art direction: Krystyna Maslowska
Set decoration: Izabela Paprocka
Costume design: Hilary Rosenfeld
Choreography: Teddy Atlas
Sound: Eli Yarkoni
Music: Cliff Eidelman
MPAA rating: R
Running time: 120 minutes

Principal characters:

Salamo Arouch	Willem Dafoe
Gypsy	Edward James Olmos
Papa	Robert Loggia
Allegra	Wendy Gazelle
Elena	Kelly Wolf
Avram	Costas Mandylor
Jacko	Kario Salem
Janusch	Edward Zentara
Major Rauscher	Hartmut Becker

The most moving sequence of *Triumph of the Spirit* occurs at its very close. As the final credits roll, the audience sees a flashback that encapsulates all the precious life and joy that has just been crushed and lost in the concentration camps: Jacko (Kario Salem), Avram (Costas Mandylor), and Papa (Robert Loggia) join Salamo Arouch (Willem Dafoe) in a high-spirited, high-kicking Greek dance, applauded by the women of the family. At no other point in this dignified but dull film does the audience feel a comparable sense of loss.

A documentary style is established by the opening titles: plain letters on a plain black screen. Next, a close-up of the battered face of Salamo, and his retrospective voice-over narration (pitched in a distant monotone) establish the genre of the testament and the witnessing, and also clue the audience in at once to the fact that he will survive what is to come. Greece has been occupied by the Nazis. A few scenes from Salamo's life in the ghetto are shown. He works on the docks, shoulder to shoulder with his burly stevedore father; he wins a fight (a scene tinted with 1930's sepia); and he evades curfew by meeting his beloved, Allegra (Wendy Gazelle). The same night, the order goes out that the Jews are to be transported the following morning.

Allegra and her sister Elena (Kelly Wolf) are bundled onto the same train out. The family's hope in life survives a journey packed into cattle trucks, outlives the first sight of the camp (its furnaces glowing in the distance), and even surmounts the brutal separation of men from women and strong from weak. Every small step of the "admissions" process is shown, and order after order is barked out in German, untranslated, alien.

In the men's barracks, Salamo meets the brutal capo. "He uses people like punching bags," warns his gypsy sidekick (Edward James Olmos). To grotesquely cheerful Bavarian marching music, provided by the camp orchestra, the prisoners go to work. The women pull railway trucks through sludge. The men build pipelines. Stacked in bunks like goods in pallets, Salamo and his brother sleep snuggled for comfort against their strong father: He holds their hands for comfort. Salamo is too bold for the punchy capo, the camp boxing champion, to delay picking on him long. When the capo strikes Salamo, however, he finds, to his surprise, that he has a real fight on his hands, and he loses. Everyone expects Salamo will be taken away, but he is not. Instead, the capo is shot where he lies, in the dirt; his usefulness is over, and Salamo's is about to begin.

The next morning, the men take out the bodies of the prisoners who died overnight. Meanwhile, humanity starts to break down in the women's barracks. Starving, Elena begs to lick her sister's bowl. Rebuffed, she wails that she is pregnant. Two senior officers call for Salamo and ask if he is fit to fight. They gamble heavily on the bouts and do not like to lose. Neither does Salamo. He tells them that he is still strong and that he will win for them. This is his introduction to the gladiatorial combat of camp boxing matches. When he asks how many rounds there will be, he is told to fight until he can no longer get up. Salamo knocks his opponent out three times in a row, efficiently. Allegra offers to trade a ration or two with the female capo, in return for an abortion for her sister. Salamo's brother, Avram, is marched off to a new task: He is to scrub down the gas chamber and feed the flames with bodies, or be himself consumed. Avram refuses and is shot. Word trickles back to the barracks: The prisoners salute Avram, but his father's wordless grief, filmed in embarrassing close-up, is a terrible spectacle. Salamo cradles him. He knows he must be stronger now. Another boxing opponent is ruthlessly dispatched. After the fight, Salamo draws closer to the gypsy. He sees the motive for his cruel will to survive—a wife and child, kept in a hut beyond the electric fence.

In the women's barracks, Elena's clogs are stolen. Allegra has a fistfight with a skeletal prisoner to get them back: Elena will not survive without them. Elena refuses an abortion, and Allegra starts to share her food. Salamo, meanwhile, is assigned to better work, in the steel mill, where he meets up with his best friend Jacko, now a resistance fighter. His father, however, is weakening and fails the periodic strength test. Salamo turns to the gypsy for help, but there is no one to take his father's place on the condemned list. Next, in slow-motion montage, Salamo, the family's one survivor, is shown winning bout after bout and turning to meet the triumphant look of his Schützstaffeln (SS) "master."

Elena begs extra food, unashamedly. The women have had enough and examine her brutally to find that she is not pregnant and that she lied. Allegra is stunned, but, as compensation, she gets her first glimpse of Salamo in the camp. Jacko enlists Salamo's help in the resistance: They have hidden explosives in the crematorium. Jacko, however, is doomed when an informer betrays him, and he is taken away. The Russians are advancing; all able-bodied prisoners are to be shipped to Germany; and camp order starts to deteriorate.

In these last days of the camp, Salamo, like his brother before him, is ordered to the furnaces to shovel bodies. This time, however, there is a fight—resistance members turn on the guards and capos, and the furnace explodes. Salamo survives, only to undergo tortuous interrogation. While he is in his cell, the door suddenly opens to reveal the gypsy, who proclaims that the war is over and that Auschwitz has been liberated.

Three films about the Holocaust were released, surprisingly, during the Christmas holiday season of 1989; of these, the most distinguished, *Enemies, A Love Story* (reviewed in this volume), was based on a novel by Isaac Bashevis Singer. Two of these films, Constantin Costa-Gavras' *Music Box* and *Triumph of the Spirit*, were based, with less success, on real-life stories. *Triumph of the Spirit* was "inspired" by the story of Salamo Arouch (adviser to and producer of the film), 1936 Balkans middleweight champion, who in real life fought more than two hundred bouts for the entertainment of the SS officers of Auschwitz.

Triumph of the Spirit, however, never surmounts two problems, the first of which it creates for itself by tampering with its "inspiration." In real life, Arouch had no Allegra. The intrusion into his story of a death-camp romance cooked up for the benefit of facile emotionalism, easy audience "identification," and "uplift" of the spirits strikes innumerable false notes, splits the film's focus and power, and produces underrealized, unfelt, and underwritten scenes concerning Allegra's parallel experiences in the camp. To make matters worse, this "uplift" is underscored by loudly intrusive romantic-ethnic-operatic music. This problem is all the more serious since it is only in Allegra's scenes that we ever touch directly on the central issues of how far a human being is justified in going to save himself, of when survival becomes betrayal, and of the limits of humanity. Such displacement seems unwarranted. In the main plot, the gypsy-capo's betrayals and loyalties are merely presented, never questioned (his role too seems nebulous, unfinished), and even Salamo's descent into the hell of the ovens is likewise fudged, the call to rebellion eliminating the necessity of facing the issue; the focus is not on any aspect of the mental struggle and spiritual compromise involved in his determined defeat of "opponent" after "opponent" (while the real "opponents" booze, bet, laugh, and applaud) but on the physical details of his meaningless "victories" in the ring.

The film's second problem is the far broader issue of whether it is possible to make feature films about the Holocaust at all. One of the horrors of the death camps was their very mundanity—the routine efficiency, the "cleanliness," the daily round of forced labor and death, but to present horror in the guise of routine fiction almost results here in making horror itself mundane. Director Robert M. Young is clearly aware of this problem. Thus he suggests the actual deaths only elliptically: The cannisters of poison crystals are opened with a tin-opener, while down in the "shower-room" the naked prisoners are promised a hot shower, like tired travelers finally arrived at a Spartan holiday camp. Overall, however, dignified but bland writing and direction and particularly uninspired cinematography leave the film without dramatic tension and fail to exploit the film's extraordinary location or to convey any sense of the experience of death in the camps. Alain Resnais's 1956 documentary, *Nuit et brouillard* (*Night and Fog*), also filmed in Auschwitz, remains perhaps the most powerfully moving filmic statement that will ever be made about the Holocaust precisely because its style renders history as experience and sensation. Only at one point do Young and cinematographer Curtis Clark attempt anything similar, when Salamo is dragged feet-first downstairs to a cell by a guard, and (from the guard's point-of-view) the viewer sees Salamo's head thumping on every step.

The film has other problems too. Most crucial is the presentation of a Jewish victim as an active hero of his story. The film makes mention of the 1936 Olympics, and the film's title is a clear allusion to Leni Riefenstahl's 1935 classic lyrical documentary celebration of Aryan prowess at the Games, *Triumph des Willens* (*Triumph of the Will*): *Triumph of the Spirit* gives the audience instead the Jew as consummate athlete and winner (Arouch was nicknamed "the ballerina," and in Dafoe's portrayal does indeed dance as lightly and dangerously as Muhammad Ali). So straightforward a substitution does not work. Young also taps, to confusing effect, into a cinematic tradition of the boxer as exploited proletarian hero, a theme most powerful in the days of radical playwright-screenwriter Clifford Odets and *Golden Boy* (1939) but still capable of producing such classics as *Raging Bull* (1980) and such block-busters as *Rocky* (1976). A cruel critic might be tempted to dub *Triumph of the Spirit* "Rocky in Auschwitz."

In the final analysis, *Triumph of the Spirit* survives criticism: It should be much worse a film than it is. It is redeemed by dedicated acting. Dafoe, looking gaunt and exhausted, adds another distinguished (even harrowing) portrait to his gallery of compromised saints (*Platoon*, 1986, *The Last Temptation of Christ*, 1988); Robert Loggia as Papa does not need even the few lines of dialogue he is granted to convey a near-elemental sense of the archetypal fatherhood; the whole cast visibly fell under the grotesque spell of Auschwitz itself during their four months of location shooting there (many extras were themselves Auschwitz survivors), and their emotion communicates itself, however haphazardly, to the audience.

Joss Lutz Marsh

Reviews

Chicago Tribune. February 2, 1990, VII, p. 9.
The Christian Science Monitor. January 5, 1990, p. 10.
Commonweal. CXVII, January 12, 1990, p. 16.
Los Angeles Times. December 8, 1989, VI, p. 6.
The New Republic. CCI, December 25, 1989, p. 26.
The New York Times. December 8, 1989, p. C10.
Time. CXXXV, January 8, 1990, p. 76.
Variety. CCCXXXVII, December 6, 1989, p. 34.
The Washington Post. February 2, 1990, p. C7.

TRUE BELIEVER

Production: Walter F. Parkes and Lawrence Lasker; released by Columbia Pictures
Direction: Joseph Ruben
Screenplay: Wesley Strick
Cinematography: John W. Lindley
Editing: George Bowers
Production design: Lawrence Miller
Art direction: Jim Pohl
Set decoration: Jim Poynter
Set design: William Beck
Special effects: John McLeod
Makeup: Deborah Figuly
Costume design: Erica Edell Phillips
Sound: Michael Evje
Music: Brad Fiedel
MPAA rating: R
Running time: 103 minutes

> *Principal characters:*
> Eddie Dodd . . . . James Woods
> Roger Baron . . . . Robert Downey, Jr.
> Kitty Greer . . . . Margaret Colin
> Shu Kai Kim . . . . Yuji Okumoto
> Robert Reynard . . . . Kurtwood Smith
> Cecil Skell . . . . Tom Bower
> Art Esparza . . . . Miguel Fernandes
> Vincent Dennehy . . . . Charles Hallahan
> Maraquilla Esparza . . . . Sully Diaz
> Chucky Loeder . . . . John Snyder
> Sklaroff . . . . Graham Beckel
> Montell . . . . Tony Haney

True Believer sets 1960's altruism against 1980's cynicism in the context of a taut courtroom thriller. By cradling its messages within a gritty, fast-breaking, generally plausible mystery, the film expresses its nostalgia for more socially committed times better than most that try to exalt hippie values while taking to task yuppie ones. On the heels of his critical breakthrough film *The Stepfather* (1987), director Joseph Ruben expands his pathological net from one man's insane dream of perfect family life to a city law enforcement system's willingness to compromise justice in the name of order. Yet, along with its muckrakingly gleeful agenda of indictment, *True Believer* is also very much about expiation and redemption, most obviously in the case of main character Eddie Dodd (James Woods) and also for several secondary characters.

Based on real-life defense attorney J. Tony Serra, Dodd was a headline-making civil rights lawyer twenty years ago. These days, however, his living comes from defending smug, mid-level Manhattan drug dealers. Serra's only attachments to his past seem to be fondnesses for marijuana and Fourth Amendment rationalizations, and a long, shaggy ponytail.

The hair, in fact, causes Dodd's idealistic new assistant Roger Baron (Robert Downey, Jr.), to mistake Dodd for one of his clients at their first meeting. That is not the only surprise that earnest, fresh-out-of-law-school Baron has in store; though Dodd's cramped, Greenwich Village office is decorated with clips of the attorney's past crusading exploits, he is far from the hero about whom Baron read in school. When an elderly Korean woman begs Dodd to take the case of her incarcerated son, who has just killed a neo-Nazi in a prison knife fight, Dodd declines, to Baron's vocal chagrin.

The following day, Dodd has a change of heart. He and Baron interview Shu Kai Kim (Yuji Okumoto) at Sing Sing. Kim was convicted eight years earlier of shooting Jimmy Chin on a Chinatown street, an initiation rite for one of the neighborhood gangs. Though reticent, Kim strikes Dodd as having been railroaded for the original crime. Deciding that the best way to get the prison murder charge thrown out as self-defense is to acquit Kim of the Chinatown slaying, Dodd sets about reopening the case.

Although Kim's only eyewitness is Cecil Skell (Tom Bower), a schizophrenic who is also sure that the phone company killed President John F. Kennedy, Dodd gets a judge to order a retrial on Skell's testimony that it was not an Asian whom he saw shoot Chin. Soon after, Dodd is summoned to lunch by District Attorney Robert Reynard (Kurtwood Smith), who rode the publicity of a spectacular breakup of a Colombian narcotics ring into office around the time of the Chinatown killing and seems inordinately committed to keeping Kim in jail. Reynard threatens the rusty Dodd with a losing battle if he does not plea-bargain the case away. Dodd refuses.

Dodd is beaten outside his office/apartment by Chucky Loeder (John Snyder), who claims to be with the Aryan Army. Checking his story with some real Nazis, Dodd and Baron learn that Loeder was expelled from the movement for using drugs. Dodd's private investigator, Kitty Greer (Margaret Colin), tries to find Loeder through the vague clues that the neo-Nazis provide.

Meanwhile, Reynard is demolishing Dodd's case in court. The murder weapon was found in Kim's apartment, another (saner) eyewitness identifies Kim as the killer, and one of the three arresting officers, Vincent Dennehy (Charles Hallahan), testifies from a wheelchair, too feeble for Dodd to cross-examine effectively. Smelling racism and conspiracy, Dodd becomes only more determined to win. He stops smoking marijuana and seems to have regained his old radical fire.

Still, Dodd's only route to victory passes through what Loeder knows. Greer finally traces Loeder to a plumbing supply warehouse on Long Island. Dodd chases Loeder through the back shop, but Loeder escapes. The company's owner, Art

Esparza (Miguel Fernandes), explains to Dodd and Baron that all of his employees, like himself, are former convicts and that neither of them will likely see the spooked Loeder again. Dodd and Baron, however, subsequently trace Loeder to a welfare hotel room, but he is dead of a drug overdose by the time they get there.

His key witness' convenient death, coupled with further damaging testimony against Kim, nearly destroys Dodd's spirit. Baron, however, notices Esparza's wife (Sully Diaz) in the courtroom gallery one day, follows her, and makes her confess that she had had an affair with Jimmy Chin. Dodd and Baron check Esparza's arrest records and find a high number of cases that, suspiciously, never came to trial. Further, they discover an eight-year-old police record photograph of Esparza before he lost his hair and shaved his beard—he is almost a dead ringer for Shu Kai Kim. Crazy Skell was right.

Dodd breaks into the infirm Dennehy's bedroom. Dennehy confesses that Esparza, who was the key informer for Reynard's big Columbian narcotics ring breakup, shot Chin in a fit of jealousy and that Reynard ordered Dennehy and his partners to attribute the crime to someone else—Kim. As Dodd tries to take Dennehy to a hospital and then to the courtroom, he and Dennehy are attacked by Esparza and Dennehy's former partners, Sklaroff (Graham Beckel) and Montell (Tony Haney). Dennehy insists on airing his guilt, and Dodd refuses to promise not to enter the new information into evidence. Forty years of Kim's life are at stake, even though the decision may cost Dodd his.

Esparza orders Sklaroff and Montell to kill Dodd and Dennehy, telling them "the man" will take care of it. Sklaroff shoots Esparza instead, muttering that they should have done that eight years ago. Montell is not so resigned; he raises his gun at Dodd as the lawyer walks away, commanding him to stop. Yet Dodd arrives safely back in the courtroom, where he puts a surprised Reynard on the witness stand. As the hardnosed district attorney sees his cover-up unraveling, he sternly avers that protecting his big narcotics ring breakup was worth sending an innocent man to jail. He argues that his actions served a larger good and that he would do it again. Kim is acquitted. Dodd enthusiastically explains to young Baron that this only proves how important it is for them to defend the indefensible.

Dodd is a shrewder and more self-controlled spiritual cousin to Woods's Oscar-nominated portrayal of Richard Boyle, the dissolute, leftist journalist in Oliver Stone's *Salvador* (1986). A man whose countercultural idealism has been eroded by social evolution and his own pragmatic maturation, Dodd has been waging a losing battle against being absorbed by establishment corruption for years. The heroic key to the character, however, is that he has, at least, been fighting the corruption. He could probably have found more worthwhile outlets for his legal talents, yet the very disreputability associated with defending unsavory, obviously guilty cocaine dealers is, like his unfashionable ponytail, a surefire way of expressing contempt for the system.

Dodd has been hiding behind his own recreational drug use. The film has a highly complex (and very 1960's) association frame between antidrug sentiment and corruption. Marijuana smoking represents Dodd's flaws (and, by extension, the Achilles heel of the entire counterculture movement). Yet Reynard's willingness to trample on the Constitution—even to let an ally get away with murder—in the name of cleaning up a narcotics ring is clearly portrayed as the worse evil. Some may have dismissed this premise as the paranoid conspiracy delusions of aging hippies when the film was released in February; by the time the U.S. Army was sent into Panama to catch drug dealers the following December, however, *True Believer* was starting to look discomfitingly prophetic.

Ruben and screenwriter Wesley Strick have great fun looking at the 1980's social landscape through paisley-colored glasses. Few contemporary thrillers have generated so much suspenseful, pulpy energy out of such unpopular takes on narcotics law enforcement, officially sanctioned racism, and self-justifying Fascism. The filmmakers even manage the trick of turning their white supremacist subplot into a source of comic relief without ever diminishing its fearsome potential.

Ruben's swift, no-nonsense pacing provides room for maximum exposition and a wide range of social commentary without ever bogging down the narrative or, more importantly, becoming tediously pedantic. Conversant with his expressionist shadow tricks, Ruben rarely lets them call undue attention to themselves. *True Believer* is the work of a smart, committed cineast and social commentator who also has a soft spot for fast and amusing entertainment values.

Ruben seems to have found his perfect mouthpiece in Woods. Although Downey never missteps as the callow but quick-learning assistant and the character actors all do their jobs effectively, it is Woods who holds center stage. He always does, but this time he does it without any of the psychotic or dysfunctional traits that have propped up most of his major roles. Free from addictions and mental disorders, Woods gives one of his most humane performances as an intelligent man cursed with a profound sense of disappointment and blessed with an insightful sense of humor. The way Woods plays him, the audience wants to see Dodd redeemed as much as it wants to see Kim vindicated. Dodd deserves it, if only for vaguely remembering his ideals through times when many have found doing such a thing to be very inconvenient.

Bob Strauss

Reviews

American Film: Magazine of the Film and Television Arts. XIV, January, 1989, p. 13.
Chicago Tribune. February 17, 1989, VII, p. 24.
The Christian Science Monitor. March 15, 1989, p. 10.
Los Angeles Times. February 17, 1989, VI, p. 6.
The New York Times. February 17, 1989, p. C10.
The New Yorker. LXV, February 20, 1989, p. 95.
Time. CXXXII, February 20, 1989, p. 94.
Variety. CCCXXXIV, February 8, 1989, p. 18.

TRUE LOVE

Production: Richard Guay and Shelley Houis for Forward Films; released by United
    Artists
Direction: Nancy Savoca
Screenplay: Nancy Savoca and Richard Guay
Cinematography: Lisa Rinzler
Editing: John Tintori
Production design: Lester W. Cohen
Art direction: Pamela Woodbridge
Set decoration: Jessica Lanier
Makeup: Chris Bingham
Costume design: Deborah Anderko
Sound: Mathew Price
Music: Jeffrey Kimball
MPAA rating: R
Running time: 100 minutes

Principal characters:

Donna	Annabella Sciorra
Michael	Ron Eldard
Grace	Aida Turturro
Dom	Roger Rignack
J. C.	Star Jasper
Brian	Michael J. Wolfe
Yvonne	Kelly Cinnante
Kevin	Rick Shapiro
Fran	Suzanne Costallos
Angelo	Vinny Pastore
Trudy	Mary Portser
Stripper	Al Juliano

Italian-American directors have been few and far between, and their films un-
abashedly male. The latter, at least, changes with Nancy Savoca's directorial debut.
True Love features no tormented, grandiose mythmakers, no Mafia stereotypes, no
urban crazies; rather, it examines the effects of cultural straitjackets on the lives of
its young, infinitely naïve protagonists. The result, a far cry from the saccharine
romanticism of *Moonstruck* (1987), is a wry, feminist view of marriage, Italian style.

The film opens with a videotaped home movie of the engagement party for
Donna (Annabella Sciorra) and Michael (Ron Eldard). The color videotape is
spontaneous, chaotic, marred by stripes, and played both forward and backward.
Donna and Michael have been engaged for about two years and are to be married
shortly. The film proper begins in a delicatessen, where Michael banters with his

customers about his upcoming wedding. One old man warns him that Donna, who has just made a brief appearance to tell him that they are baby-sitting that night, will "blow up" after she has her first child.

As Donna chats about apartment prices in a pizza place with her taxi-driver friend J. C. (Star Jasper), who plans to flee her alcoholic parents with her twelve-year-old sister, Michael's friends, Brian (Michael J. Wolfe) and Kevin (Rick Shapiro) appear outside in their car. Brian is interested in J. C., and Kevin warns him that she is "weird" but urges him to try to pick her up anyway. She agrees to go view a possible apartment with him after work that night.

Fooling around later that afternoon in Michael's home kitchen, Donna and Michael fill out a popular magazine's questionnaire on marital compatibility. Michael's idea of a night out is not a candlelit dinner or an evening at the theater or a trip to a disco but a night watching reruns of *The Honeymooners* at the bar that his friend Dom (Roger Rignack) owns. Both, however, agree on their dream house: a two-family in the Bronx. Later that night, Donna and Michael baby-sit for Michael's niece and nephew. First, they play Monopoly, and Donna tries to bargain for a real-life concession: She wants Michael to come back and take her out after his upcoming bachelor party. He refuses, and later, as they begin making love on the couch, they are interrupted by Dom and Kevin, who come and lure Michael out.

Undeterred by their nascent doubts about the whole idea, Donna and Michael begin the endless round of wedding errands. They visit a caterer to pick the room and the menu: ribs, baby peas, and mashed potatoes. The caterer suggests that they have the mashed potatoes died pastel blue to match some of the wedding colors. Michael balks, refusing to eat blue food. Later they bicker again, this time about the colors the men are to wear. Donna wants them in gray tuxedos with pastel shirts; Michael insists on black tuxedos with white shirts. Finally they pick out the rings. The salesman tries to sell them a trio of bride's rings: one for everyday, one for weekends, and one for very special occasions. They settle for a simpler ring, and Michael is reluctantly persuaded to wear a ring himself.

They continue to quibble over the bachelor party, and finally Donna extorts a reluctant promise of a date from Michael. The night arrives, and after viewing some boring pornographic films at his uncle Benny's home, Michael and his friends go to Dom's bar for the rest of the evening. Michael becomes drunk, dances a wild dance with Trudy (Mary Portser) after her current boyfriend has drifted home, and carouses all night with his friends.

Meanwhile, Donna, spending the evening with her sister Yvonne (Kelly Cinnante) and friends J. C. and Grace (Aida Turturro), has just received the keys to her apartment. She tries to call Michael after it gets late, but, when she figures out that he has stood her up, her friends suggest that they all go to a nightclub and forget about him. They go to watch a male stripper (Al Juliano) and, once there, join the other women in raucously stuffing money into his G-string. He entices Donna into dancing briefly with him on the stage, but she is too shy and returns to her seat.

The next morning, Donna tries to call Michael, who has a terrible hangover and

keeps excusing himself to vomit. Michael is feeling trapped, and Donna is beginning to sense his lack of responsibility. Michael talks to his friend Dom, who tries
to reassure him that marriage is alright. Donna speaks to her mother, Fran (Suzanne
Costallos), who has bought her, as a surprise gift, a sexy negligee. Later, when
Donna asks her mother why she eloped, Fran confesses that she was pregnant.
Savoca paints a loving bond between Donna and her mother, a worn, plain, but
basically sensuous woman who sways to sexy music while she cleans the sink and
who is intrigued by Donna's suggestion that she go see the stripper.

The night before the wedding, both bride and groom are spending time with their
friends. Around midnight, when her friends are exhorting her to leave so as not to
see Michael on her wedding day and thus bring bad luck, Donna takes Michael
aside and, whipping out a knife, cuts their fingers and performs a "blood-wedding."

In the limousine on the way to the wedding, Donna's father, Angelo (Vinny
Pastore), assures her that she does not have to go through with it. She does,
however, and at the reception everything seems to be going smoothly. Michael,
however, suggests to his horrified friends that they go out for a few drinks after the
reception, and Kevin persuades them to agree. When Michael breaks the news to
Donna, she, furious, bolts for the women's rest room, followed by Grace, J. C., and
Yvonne. In the film's most amusing yet saddest scene, she sits in one of the stalls
on the toilet seat in tears as they try to reassure her. Michael comes into the
women's restroom, Donna slams the stall door shut, and the two argue. She tells
him that she does not want this kind of life, but he pulls her gently back out. In the
last scene, they are having their wedding pictures taken, but Donna cannot seem to
maintain a smile long enough for the photographer to snap. The film's final credits
sport another video. This one is in cool, clear black and white. The camera advances relentlessly from one relative to another as each speaks directly into the
camera, addressing Michael and Donna. One ill-favored older woman wishes them
as much happiness as she has had. Michael advises himself "Don't do it!"

One of *True Love*'s strengths is the director's love for her characters. Whether
they are picking the correct shade of blue for the mashed potatoes or selecting
small, gold Christ headpins for the ushers' presents, there is never a hint of conde-
scension, perhaps because Savoca herself grew up in the Bronx, where she still lives
with her husband, cowriter and producer Richard Guay, and their two children, one
of whom was about to be delivered when she received the news that her film had
won the Grand Prize at the 1989 United States Film Festival in Utah. Yet the actors,
many of whom are nonprofessionals, have to get much of the credit.

Savoca's style is sympathetic. Most of the camera work is fairly flat; characters
are never filmed either in long shot or in extreme close-up. The film has a bois-
terous, playful tone, sustained partly by its jaunty rhythms, which are often synchronized with the catchy songs, all of which originate from sources within the
film. During the wild bachelor party, Savoca films the drunken Michael from the
point of view of the jukebox as he picks out Chuck Berry's "Hucklebuck" for his
bawdy dance with Trudy. When he and the boys troop to an automatic teller

machine to replenish their money, Savoca shoots again from the machine's point of view, and this time the camera staggers along with them.

Savoca constructs her settings and compositions with great attention to detail. The physical space in which the characters move is small, cluttered, gaudy, and almost medieval in its lack of privacy. Family members wander in and out of the frame as if there were no room dividers. People seem almost too big for the sets, mostly small, tacky working-class interiors. The garish bathroom to which Donna flees in the last scenes of the film is a classic: purple ceramic lavatory basins topped by matching vases of artificial flowers flanked by fake Grecian columns complete with little gilt cupids. In this world, the toilet stall is the only private space.

Though the story is told in parallel montage, alternating vignettes of Michael and his friends with Donna and hers, and though Donna's demand for a post-bachelor-party date is unreasonable, clearly the film's sympathies are more with Donna. Michael's insensitivity is serious. By abandoning their lovemaking on the couch to go out with his friends and by himself suggesting a few drinks with them on his wedding night, he signals that life with him is going to be one long series of interrupted experiences. Yet it is he who leads her back to the wedding reception after she has said, "I don't want to live like this." Clearly he is the one who will profit most from the marriage, and he knows it.

Earlier in the film, expressing her misgivings to J. C., Donna said that if she did not go through with the wedding, she could not live in the neighborhood any-more—she would have to move upstate and live on her own. The marriage that delivers her from this fate is an even lonelier situation.

Joan Esposito

Reviews
Boston Globe. September 14, 1989, p. 82.
Chicago Tribune. September 15, 1989, VII, p. 38.
The Christian Science Monitor. LXXXI, October 13, 1989, p. 10.
Houston Post. November 22, 1989, p. D4.
Los Angeles Times. November 10, 1989, VI, p. 10.
The New York Times. CXXXIX, October 20, 1989, p. C10.
Rolling Stone. September 21, 1989, p. 48.
Times-Picayune. December 8, 1989, p. LAG27.
Variety. CCCXXXIV, February 15, 1989, p. 29.
The Washington Post. September 15, 1989, p. C7.

UNCLE BUCK

Production: John Hughes and Tom Jacobson; released by Universal
Direction: John Hughes
Screenplay: John Hughes
Cinematography: Ralf Bode
Editing: Lou Lombardo, Tony Lombardo, and Peck Prior
Production design: John W. Corso
Set decoration: Dan May
Special effects: Dan Cangemi
Makeup: Ben Nye, Jr., and Jamie Weiss
Costume design: Marilyn Vance-Straker
Music: Ira Newborn
MPAA rating: PG
Running time: 100 minutes

> *Principal characters:*
> Uncle Buck............................ John Candy
> Tia Russell .... Jean Kelly
> Maizy Russell .... Gaby Hoffman
> Miles Russell .... Macaulay Culkin
> Chanice Kobolowski .... Amy Madigan
> Cindy Russell .... Elaine Bromka
> Bob Russell .... Garrett M. Brown
> Marcie Dahlgren-Frost .... Laurie Metcalf
> Bug................................ Jay Underwood
> Rog................................ Brian Tarantina
> Pooter-the-Clown........................ Mike Starr
> Mrs. Hogarth.................... Suzanne Shepherd

Early in the 1980's, director John Hughes built a sizable reputation as a maker of teenage melodramas (such as 1985's *The Breakfast Club*) and tales about contemporary young love (*She's Having a Baby*, 1988). Yet films such as these were also criticized by adult audiences for their bow to unbelievability and their often formulated melodrama. More recently, Hughes found success when he teamed comedians Steve Martin and John Candy and stretched his humor to accommodate more sophisticated scripts if not more searching attempts to touch upon adult humor and compassion (witness 1987's successful *Trains, Planes, and Automobiles*). Not surprisingly to some audiences, Hughes's filmic meeting of minds with John Candy, especially, has proven to be a stroke of luck if not brilliance. In Candy, the director seems to have touched upon a character actor with the uncanny combination of adulthood and childlike sensibilities that match Hughes's own vision of his place in the world. Thus the news of *Uncle Buck*'s arrival held more than a passing interest for many American filmgoers.

Uncle Buck plays heavily with the sympathetic support system that Candy is able to inject into the most unlikely of characters he tackles. Coupling a brand of sympathetic humanism with that of his unique swerve of bumbling bravado, Candy surfaces always with a wash of good-heartedness that bridges the age gap in his wide-reaching audience. He is, simply put, a comedian for all ages. With a veneer of seeming ineptitude, he propels quickly into the kind of emotional sincerity and forthrightness that works so well, not only in Hughes's cinematic landscapes but also in our contemporary need for believability and unflinching moral certitude. Candy projects a leap many wish to take: the ability to be vulnerable and decent, free-wheeling yet endearing, without forfeiting any one of these qualities to the others.

Uncle Buck provides Candy with an arena into which to project the complexity of his character as an actor. He is given support from Hughes to achieve this complexity simply because Hughes knows how to take chances as a filmmaker: He is faithful to his often outrageous sense of humor. With this combination of actor and director, the film is lifted far above its native potential. Playing upon the audience's memory of the *Mr. Belvedere* films of the 1940's and 1950's, of that stern housekeeper and house mender Clifton Webb, *Uncle Buck* is a contemporary reworking of the familiar housekeeper-transforms-family theme. Yet this time the housekeeper is a bumbling do-gooder, and the family is kept under lock and key of director Hughes's unflinching sense of the outrageous.

The film's opening sequence exhibits its use of dramatic convention, signaling Hughes's crafty cinematic techniques and his self-consciousness as a director. The protagonists are identified quickly and add up to a quirky family unit. As the credits roll, three children, one by one, return from school to an upper-middle-class home somewhere in suburban Chicago. First Tia Russell (Jean Kelly), a beautiful fifteen-year-old girl who obviously has a chip on her shoulder, walks up to the house as if carrying a heavy weight on her mind. Next her younger sister, Maizy Russell (Gaby Hoffman), having just emerged from a school bus, is arriving home from her elementary school. Third and last comes their brother, Miles Russell (Macaulay Culkin), also an elementary school student, who runs into the house obviously to the chagrin of his elder sister, Tia, now in charge of her young siblings until the Russell parents arrive. As if characters in a stage play, the children take their places within the scene and set up the fundamental conflicts of the story: Tia is unhappy that her parents have recently transplanted the family from their home in Indianapolis to this new suburbia; she is equally chagrined at the prospect of having to care for her younger siblings.

The film soon flashes to another setup: the Russell family at dinner, silently chewing their take-out Chinese dinner (the boxes are lined up on the dining room table) and making awkward attempts to strike up a conversation. Their mother figure, as Tia has referred to her mother, Cindy Russell (Elaine Bromka), is confronted by hostile glances from her teenage daughter, who is eager to criticize her mother at the slightest turn. This is one family teetering on the brink of emotional disaster: Anger and frustration are contained beneath the surface and are about to erupt in the most violent of ways.

Later that night, around three in the morning, the Russell parents are awakened by a phone call: Cindy Russell's father has just had a heart attack. Having to leave their children to visit Mrs. Russell's father, Cindy and Bob Russell (Garrett M. Brown) are at a loss about whom to leave in charge of their children. All possibilities prove unavailable, and, as an emergency tactic, they have no choice but to call on Bob's brother, Buck (John Candy).

Enter Uncle Buck, an out-of-work outside chance. Buck does not want responsibility. The thought of him caring for three children seems almost to defy believability. He is the one relative in the family who is a complete embarrassment, a forty-year-old adolescent who can hardly, it seems, take care of himself. Clearly, in director Hughes's scheme of things, Uncle Buck, the ultimate hedonist, is the signifier for those very contained emotions within the Russell family that are about to explode and disrupt the orderliness of their lives. Buck is chaos incarnate: He has been avoiding not only work but also the marriage plans of his girlfriend of eight years, Chanice Kobolowski (Amy Madigan). When he receives the phone call from his brother asking him to take care of the three children, Buck is quick to oblige. Having just run out of excuses not to work, having promised Chanice that he would show up at her tire company the next morning to begin an unexciting career (he would rather spend an occasional evening at the racetrack to make his living), Buck consents to be the Russell live-in for several days. Yet much of his enthusiasm also comes from his desire to reenter the family that banished him. The idea of spending time with his nieces and nephew makes a direct emotional signal to his heart. His character is, more than anything else, a creature of the heart.

Heart is where Hughes hits his mark as a director. Behind every gag, behind every grimace, lies a big-hearted laugh, a wish to grab in his audience that landscape where the heart lives. The Russell kitchen, where lies the seat of this comedy, comes full of appliances and dishware, set up so that Uncle Buck can invent his comic discourse with them. He bumbles with the dishwasher, he dries clothes in the microwave, and he makes culinary concoctions from the most unlikely of ingredients from the refrigerator. Uncle Buck makes every environment his home, and Hughes accommodates him with as many sight gags as possible. These gags work, not because they are familiar to us but because they are written and performed with the generosity of heart that is inherent in Buck's character.

The generosity of Buck's spirit, however, is played out within the narrative of the film as much as in its physical comedy. Buck's ability to take charge of the Russell children generates from his relationship with his troubled niece, Tia. She, unlike her younger siblings, refuses to take to Buck; moreover, the central tension and denouement of the film evolve from her initial refusal of Buck's affection for her and her ultimate acceptance of him at the film's conclusion. Refusing to acknowledge Buck as a possible source of parental caring, she does all she can to strike up an antagonism. She disobeys his orders and leaves the house to be with a boyfriend who abuses her emotionally. Yet Buck cares enough for Tia to allow her to make these mistakes. At the end of the narrative, however, Tia makes her big mistake. She goes to a party with her boyfriend and is betrayed by him: He ends up with another girl. Buck goes to find Tia, and, discovering that she has been betrayed, punishes the boyfriend by grabbing him and locking him in the trunk of his car. The scene is played for laughs, yet in the end it is not the gag that works but rather the believable affection that Buck has for Tia. At this moment, Tia realizes that Buck is indeed her best friend, even the caring mother whom she so desperately longs to know. It is the denouement that allows the audience to cheer for Buck and to experience what it always knew about him: Beneath his bumbling surface and his stumbling antics, his basic goodness needs its chance to emerge. Buck proves to be the spirit and the force that unites Tia with her mother in the film's final sequences.

The film ends as a lopsided, off-kilter fairy tale. The children's parents return and find their house to be in the midst of an emotional recovery. Buck has become the catalyst that holds the family together. Yet the quality of fairy tale in this film does not overwhelm it. Rather, Hughes allows Buck's character to remain bumbling and uneven. An emotional rescue he may be, yet Buck keeps his edge and retains the possibility of being always that childlike man whose big heart gets him into trouble as much as it pulls him through the most desperate (and the most hilarious) of situations.

As an actor who is at his best with children, Candy is the strength of the film. Still, it is Hughes's natural feel for children's emotional landscapes that allows Candy to work in his natural habitat. Infused with the wonders of childhood and teenage imaginings, not to mention a procession of intelligent and humorous sight gags, *Uncle Buck* is a smart and clever cinematic adventure. It is faithful to its intention: to play off the talents of Candy and to give him a vehicle wherein his complex psychology as both a comedian and a serious actor take free reign. Candy is Mr. Belvedere without the fussiness of Clifton Webb. He takes risks, and he wins in the end. In this way he is our wish-fulfillment for a comedic hero of the 1980's.

Marilyn Moss

Reviews
American Spectator. XXII, November, 1989, p. 39.
Chicago Tribune. August 16, 1989, V, p. 1.
The Christian Science Monitor. September 8, 1989, p. 10.
The Hollywood Reporter. August 16, 1989, p. 4.
Los Angeles Times. August 16, 1989, VI, p. 8.
The New York Times. August 16, 1989, p. C13.
Newsweek. CXIV, September 4, 1989, p. 68.
Rolling Stone. September 7, 1989, p. 32.
Variety. CCCXXXVI, August 16, 1989, p. 20.
The Washington Post. August 16, 1989, p. D1.

VALMONT

Origin: France and Great Britain
Released: 1989
Released in U.S.: 1989
Production: Raul Rassam and Michael Hausman for Claude Berri and Renn
   Productions; released by Orion Pictures
Direction: Miloš Forman
Screenplay: Jean-Claude Carrière; adapted from the novel *Les Liaisons*
   dangereuses, by Choderlos de Laclos
Cinematography: Miroslav Ondricek
Editing: Alan Heim and Nena Danovic
Production design: Pierre Guffroy
Art direction: Albert Rajau, Loula Morin, and Martina Skala
Special effects: Garth Inns and Michel Norman
Makeup: Jean-Pierre Eychenne and Paul Lemarinal
Costume design: Theodor Pistek
Choreography: Ann Jacoby
Sound: Chris Newman
Music: Christopher Palmer
MPAA rating: R
Running time: 137 minutes

   Principal characters:
   Valmont............................... Colin Firth
   Merteuil............................ Annette Bening
   Tourvel .... Meg Tilly
   Cécile .... Fairuza Balk
   Madame de Volanges .... Sian Phillips
   Gercourt .... Jeffrey Jones
   Danceny .... Henry Thomas
   Madame de Rosemonde .... Fabia Drake

   Miloš Forman's *Valmont,* with a screenplay by Jean-Claude Carrière, is the
fourth treatment of Choderlos de Laclos' 1782 novel, *Les Liaisons dangereuses,* to
make its appearance in the last two years. Christopher Hampton's 1987 play *Dangerous Liaisons* become Stephen Frears's 1988 film of the same name; Roger
Vadim's 1959 film *Les Liaisons Dangereuses, 1960,* a modernization of Laclos, was
revived following the success of the Frears treatment. Particularly given both the
critical and commercial success of *Dangerous Liaisons,* and the magnitude of its
cast, comparisons between Frears's film and *Valmont* are—as borne out by the
press—inevitable.
   While Forman's film shifts not only the focus of its action and its morality but

also several plot elements, the basic story remains the same. *Valmont* opens with the Marquise de Merteuil (Annette Bening), a worldly young widow, accompanying her cousin Madame de Volanges (Sian Phillips) to the convent to retrieve Volanges's fifteen-year-old daughter, Cécile (Fairuza Balk). The girl has been promised in marriage to a mysterious aristocrat, who has sought to ensure her purity by paying for her convent education. Volanges expresses her hope that Merteuil will take Cécile under her wing before the marriage and teach her to be "as innocent as she is—as wise as you are." The mischievous Merteuil enjoys the irony, and she quickly wins Cécile's clumsy affection. Yet at Cécile's presentation to society, Merteuil discovers that it is her own lover, Gercourt (Jeffrey Jones), who is to be Cécile's husband. As revenge, she decides to arrange Cécile's premarital loss of virginity—a move that will render Gercourt, who had so carefully protected his future bride's virtue, the laughingstock of society.

To perform this despoiling, she chooses her former lover, the Vicomte de Valmont (Colin Firth), whose whole life is a game of sexual conquests and subsequent betrayals. Yet Valmont, whom she finds in the country at the estate of his aunt, Madame de Rosemonde (Fabia Drake), is instead intent upon seducing the virtuous Madame de Tourvel (Meg Tilly). Irritated, Merteuil bets him that he cannot win Tourvel. If she proves right, Valmont must enter a monastery, but, if she loses, she herself will become his prize. Fortunately for Merteuil's goal, Cécile has fallen in love with her seventeen-year-old music teacher, the Chevalier Danceny (Henry Thomas). Merteuil helps the girl respond to Danceny's love letters and sets up a meeting for the two in a private boudoir, which ends unconsummated when the enraged Volanges discovers that her daughter is missing. After this failure, Merteuil persuades Volanges to take Cécile to Madame de Rosemonde's estate. It is there, finally, that Valmont disinterestedly seduces the girl while helping her compose a letter to Danceny.

It is during this visit, as well, that Valmont breaks down Tourvel's resistance to the point that she flees for Paris. Following her, he seduces and then abandons her. Triumphant, he goes to Merteuil to collect his prize, but she laughs and says that the stakes were unreal. Enraged, Valmont declares war upon her. Now that Merteuil has ensured Cécile's impurity, she is eager to see her married and Gercourt shamed. Valmont, however, in his fury, wishes to deny her that triumph by convincing Cécile to marry Danceny. He acts as their go-between and turns Danceny against Merteuil by telling him that Merteuil is trying to ensure Cécile's marriage to Gercourt.

In the meantime, Tourvel, nearly mad after Valmont's betrayal, has taken to shadowing him. Finally, Valmont takes her in, but the next morning it is she who disappears. Seized with some ambiguous emotion, Valmont goes after her only to find that her husband has returned from his business journey; the affair is plainly at an end. The same emotion sends him to Merteuil, who weeps and tells him she still loves him, and then laughs and throws open her bedroom door to reveal Danceny in bed. Danceny, whom Merteuil has now turned against Valmont by telling him of Cécile's seduction, challenges Valmont to a duel.

Valmont, who spends the night before the duel drinking, is killed by Danceny. Cécile marries Gercourt while carrying Valmont's child, much to the delight of Madame de Rosemonde, who grieves for her nephew. The film ends with a stony Merteuil, still shaken from Valmont's funeral, watching as Danceny flirts with a group of girls at Cécile's wedding and Tourvel places flowers on Valmont's grave before being handed into a carriage by her silent husband.

Because Forman and Carrière handle the characters so differently from those in Frears's film, *Valmont* has a moral ambiguity when compared to the sharp closure of *Dangerous Liaisons*. Several critics noted the film's lack of punishment: In the novel and Frears's treatment, for example, Tourvel dies. Similarly, Frears's Valmont and Merteuil (played, respectively, by John Malkovich and Glenn Close) go through moral epiphanies at the end, each mourning the havoc he or she has wrought. Forman, however, has never been satisfied with simple fables. The complexity with which he treats his characters (often noted as his "humanity") has become a trademark, visible in some of the most critically and commercially successful films of the last two decades, including Oscar-winners *One Flew over the Cuckoo's Nest* (1975) and *Amadeus* (1984). Similarly, Carrière is most noted in the United States for his sophisticated adaptation (with Philip Kaufman) of Milan Kundera's *The Unbearable Lightness of Being* (1988).

Part of the complexity of *Valmont* stems from Forman's casting. In order to emphasize youthful ignorance over adult cold calculation, Forman chose a much younger cast than did Frears, one more in line with the ages of Laclos' characters. In a trademark move, his cast was composed of little-known actors. While superstar Glenn Close plays *Dangerous Liaisons* replete with breast beating and an intricate sexual strategy, Bening's Merteuil reacts as much as she acts, permitting the events around her to unfold with a frightening inevitability. Similarly, Firth's Valmont is a subtle mix of self-delusion, studied callousness, and youthful indifference, far from the near villain that Malkovich portrays. Although Michelle Pfieffer gave the stand-out performance in *Dangerous Liaisons* as Tourvel, Tilly's interpretation of a naïf is ultimately more believable and contextual than Pfieffer's hyper-religious leap into sin. Also notable is the work of Balk as Cécile and Thomas (who earned fame as little Eliot in Steven Spielberg's 1982 blockbuster, *E. T.: The Extra-Terrestrial*) as Danceny. Both bring to their characters an innocent passion and vulnerability lacking in the peasant sensuality of Uma Thurman's Cécile and the affectlessness of Keanu Reeves's Danceny in *Dangerous Liaisons*.

As proven by his previous films, especially such period pieces as *Amadeus* and *Ragtime* (1981), Forman is a master of *mise en scène*: His meticulous production values meld with the performances to give *Valmont* a notable realism. Because most of the film is composed of long shots in deep focus, each frame is an opportunity for exquisite detail. In one scene, for example, Gercourt fences, while in the background riders practice impeccable dressage. Another scene, plainly included as a visual study, follows Tourvel to market and focuses less on her than on the goods and merchants. Although many critics dismissed such techniques as digressive, they prove a rich context that renders *Dangerous Liaisons*, shot primarily indoors and in close-up (perhaps because of Frears's beginnings in television), comparatively static.

The most interesting thing about *Valmont*, however, has to do with why, in the late twentieth century, it should be brought to life and join three other treatments of an obscure, epistolary eighteenth century French novel. Although few critics asked this question, the ones that did answered it with one word: AIDS. If liaisons in the 1980's are dangerous, however, *Valmont* offers a very different subtext from the more popular *Dangerous Liaisons*. While the latter gleefully ends with its willful protagonists as their own hapless victims, the ambiguity of *Valmont* emplaces a tiny flash of hope with Cécile's pregnancy, Danceny's laughter, the tenderness of Madame de Tourvel's gesture, and even Merteuil's stoicism. Whether the revival of Laclos' story was a response to the sexual paranoia of the decade, Forman's complex handling of Carrière's screenplay confirms his status as, among other things, a director with "humanity."

Gabrielle J. Forman

Reviews
Commonweal. CXVI, December 1, 1989, p. 670.
Life. XII, Spring 1989, p. 70.
The New Republic. CCI, December 11, 1989, p. 24.
The New Yorker. LXV, November 27, 1989, p. 105.
San Francisco Chronicle. December 22, 1989, V, p. 1.
Variety. November 15, 1989, p. 20.
The Village Voice. November 21, 1989, p. 92.

THE WAR OF THE ROSES

Production: James L. Brooks and Arnon Milchan; released by Twentieth Century-
   Fox
Direction: Danny DeVito
Screenplay: Michael Leeson; based on the novel by Warren Adler
Cinematography: Stephen H. Burum
Editing: Lynzee Klingman
Production design: Ida Random
Art direction: Mark Mansbridge
Set decoration: Anne McCulley
Set design: Stan Tropp, Mark Fabus, and Perry Gray
Special effects: John Frazier
Makeup: Stephen Abrums
Costume design: Gloria Gresham
Sound: Jeff Wexler
Music: David Newman
MPAA rating: R
Running time: 116 minutes

> *Principal characters:*
> Oliver Rose .... Michael Douglas
> Barbara Rose....................... Kathleen Turner
> Gavin D'Amato .... Danny DeVito
> Susan........................ Marianne Sägebrecht

The War of the Roses is a dark and mischievous comedy that depicts a promising marriage that starts with much hope but soon spirals into homicidal conflict. With his cinematic interpretation of Warren Adler's novel, actor-director Danny DeVito finally discovers the perfect vehicle for his impish and cynical wit. The credits provide an early clue to where DeVito and screenwriter Michael Leeson will take the audience. As the camera tracks languidly over what appears to be white satin sheets, David Newman's score suggests sophisticated romance. Then the camera pulls away: What the audience is really seeing is a handkerchief with which De-Vito—playing the role of lawyer Gavin D'Amato—proceeds to blow his nose. Already there is the forewarning that little in this film will be sacred, predictable, or sweet-tempered.

Ensconced in his lush office, with a view of a strangely artificial-looking Washington, D.C., D'Amato begins to narrate his tale of Barbara and Oliver Rose to a man who has come for divorce advice. D'Amato's omniscient flashback descriptions—often visually presented with high- or low-angled shots—will serve as an important narrative conceit. The plot jumps often from past to present, with D'Amato's office view regularly reflecting the tone of the Roses' relationship. (In succession the windowed panorama goes from storm to fiery sunset to icy snow.) DeVito's waggish intentions extend to his casting: The Roses are played by Michael Douglas and Kathleen Turner, the romantic if slightly competitive couple in *Romancing the Stone* (1984) and *The Jewel of the Nile* (1985). *The War of the Roses* will hardly deliver the genial farce that these films have conditioned audiences to expect from these two stars.

Oliver (Douglas), a lawyer, and Barbara (Turner) meet in an auction tent on Nantucket Island. The two bid against each other for a sixteenth century Chinese ivory figure of a nude woman. It is an interesting bit of propsmanship: Chinese doctors were not allowed to examine directly their female patients; these figurines served as anatomy charts in porcelain. Oliver's understanding of women in general and of Barbara in particular will turn out to be as simplistic, superficial, and detached as that of ancient Chinese doctors must have been.

Barbara and Oliver soon bed and wed. They at first have an idyllic relationship: two children, a cozy home, and, at Christmastime, an exchange of extravagant gifts. Their personalities, though, begin to change: She is transforming herself into the cultured spouse that he wants, and he is becoming an ambitious but distracted provider. The seeds of discontent begin to germinate. He cuts off her rambling dinnertime anecdote and improves on it. She rejects him in bed. Yet their disagreements still seem minor.

The film's second act will change that. Barbara inadvertently walks in on a funeral reception in a fine old house. Taken as a friend of the deceased, she quickly plays the role and offers to buy the dead woman's home. This house will become the pivot point of the Roses' battle, a sterile showcase for each character's obsessions. Barbara's pent-up and hostile ambitions are becoming overt. She sets up her own catering service, buys a $25,000 truck, hires a German housekeeper (Marianne Sägebrecht, a brilliant actress in an underdeveloped role), and amasses an overwhelming collection of shoes, porcelains, and crystalware. In turn, Oliver attends to only his legal practice and a desire for showy one-upmanship.

DeVito gives clever visual correlatives for the Roses' increasingly hostile conflict. In one scene, Barbara and Oliver eat at opposite ends of a too-long table, a scene that conjures a similar moment in *Citizen Kane* (1941). In another, Oliver looks at himself in the mirror: The magnified image shown reflects his ballooning ego. The song "Only You" plays on the television while Barbara uses her fingers to plug up the nose of a snoring Oliver. In a recurring bit of obvious symbolism, Barbara taunts Oliver's simpleminded but faithful dog, while Oliver throws Barbara's cat around as if it were one more bit of domestic bric-a-brac.

To this point the Roses' conflict has remained a minor series of skirmishes. This will soon change. Oliver, wishing to go to bed with Barbara, gets slapped in the face. He believes that she is being frisky; she shows him that is not the case by getting him in a wrestlelike leg lock and virtually squeezing the life out of him. (Already established is that Barbara was an athlete-gymnast). The next day, over a business luncheon, Oliver has what appears to be a heart attack. (It proves to be a minor muscle pull.) Barbara, however, does not even bother to show up at the hospital. Later Oliver asks why. Her explanation is that she drove to the hospital but pulled off the road, frightened. Offhandedly, she tells him, "I got scared because I felt happy." To the myopic and self-absorbed Oliver, her pronouncement comes out of left field, as do Barbara's next words: "I want a divorce."

The third act brings DeVito's tale to full fury. Barbara's settlement request seems fair: She forgoes alimony and a percentage of Oliver's business in exchange for the house. Yet too much of Oliver's ego resides in that house. He refuses. D'Amato— who now legally represents Oliver—unearths an arcane law that will permit Oliver to remain in the house, even while his wife continues to live there.

Like two animals fighting for turf, Oliver and Barbara perpetrate an escalating series of outrages against each other. He saws off the heels of all of her shoes, embarrasses her at a dinner for her clients, wrecks her designer kitchen stove, and boards her into the house with him. She, in turn, runs her truck over his car (with him in it, just escaping injury), locks him into a hellishly hot sauna, and, in an ultimate bit of sadistic one-upmanship, serves him a pâté that she implies is all that remains of his dog. (A cutaway to the dog, still alive, seems suspiciously like an afterthought concession to good taste.) DeVito reinforces these alarming sequences with shadowy lighting, brooding music, lopsided camera angles, and several visual allusions to Alfred Hitchcock's Psycho (1960) and Vertigo (1958).

With their war reaching medieval ferocity—indeed the film's title alludes to the British internecine war of the same name—the Roses find themselves hanging from their home's chandelier. For a moment there is hope that the arriving D'Amato and the Rose's housekeeper will save them. Yet the Roses and their chandelier crash to the terrazzo floor. Oliver stirs and places his hand on Barbara's shoulder. She moves too. DeVito, however, is uncompromising. Barbara brushes Oliver's hand away. They then both die.

The War of the Roses walks a tightrope of taste but rarely loses its balance, thanks to the filmmakers' careful use of sets, lighting, music, acting, and, especially, a tightly wound script and outrageously comedic narrative structure. The film brims with memorable lines: "If love is blind, marriage is like having a stroke;" "A civilized divorce is a contradiction in terms"; "What do you call five hundred lawyers at the bottom of the ocean? An excellent start." The use of foreshadowing, especially, layers this comedy with a sense of doom. Oliver and Barbara first talk while walking through a Nantucket graveyard; Barbara obtains the house during a wake; a patient next to Oliver in the hospital matter-of-factly announces that his wife has stabbed him with a nail file; and the first glimpse of the house tracks down from the deadly chandelier.

The War of the Roses does perhaps have a problem of plausibility. Why did the Roses' case not become known to D'Amato's client, the audience's surrogate in the film? (D'Amato says he kept it out of the press, but that seems hard to believe.) Why are the views outside D'Amato's office such obviously artificial backdrops? How can Barbara escape Oliver by cartwheeling down a staircase? (Even a gymnast would find that impossible.) Finally, how can D'Amato know so many details about the couple's slaughterhouse escapades, especially those that take place in the hours before their death?

One possible solution is to eschew a literal approach to the film. *The War of the Roses* thus becomes a cartoon battle, with flights of whimsy and escapes from sure injury that have their eschatology in Punch and Judy shows and Warner Bros. animation shorts. Another approach is more intriguing. Is this simply a fable concocted by D'Amato for the benefit of his mute client (and, by extension, for the audience)? D'Amato's omniscience seems out of kilter with the film's carefully crafted internal logic. The film's several patently phony sets could be a hint that deliberate artificiality extends beyond staging to storytelling. It is certain that D'Amato's goal is to dissuade his client from divorce, for he plainly states at the end: "You can get up and go home and try to find one shred of what you once loved about the sweetheart of your youth." The client leaves, and D'Amato smiles and then calls his own wife, saying, "I'm coming home. Love You."

The notion of a divorce lawyer who deflects a client from divorce by concocting a fable about a prince who becomes a toad and a princess who becomes a witch is difficult to accept. There is no doubt that D'Amato, the puppeteer of this Punch and Judy morality tale, is a spokesman for the director DeVito. (Indeed, at one point Oliver calls D'Amato DeVito, an actor's slip that was left in.) One thing seems certain: The director is saying that marriages should be at least as precious and protected as crystal and, perhaps allegorically, that conflicts—at any level—can escalate into barbaric and lethal insanity.

Marc Mancini

Reviews

American Film: Magazine of the Film and Television Arts. XIV, September, 1989, p. 42.
Chicago Tribune. December 8, 1989, VII, p. 44.
The Christian Science Monitor. December 22, 1989, p. 10.
Commonweal. CXVII, January 26, 1990, p. 54.
Los Angeles Times. December 8, 1989, VI, p. 1.
The Nation. CCL, January 1, 1990, p. 31.
The New York Times. December 8, 1989, p. C16.
Newsweek. CXIV, December 11, 1989, p. 88.
Time. CXXXIV, December 11, 1989, p. 93.
Variety. CCCXXXVII, December 6, 1989, p. 32.

WE'RE NO ANGELS

Production: Art Linson; released by Paramount Pictures
Direction: Neil Jordan
Screenplay: David Mamet
Cinematography: Philippe Rousselot
Editing: Mick Audsley and Joke Van Wijk
Production design: Wolf Kroeger
Art direction: Richard Harrison
Set decoration: David Birdsall and Peter Lando
Special effects: William H. Orr
Costume design: Theoni V. Aldredge
Sound: Kant Pan
Music: George Fenton
MPAA rating: PG-13
Running time: 108 minutes

Principal characters:
Ned	Robert De Niro
Jim	Sean Penn
Molly	Demi Moore
Father Levesque	Hoyt Axton
Deputy	Bruno Kirby
Warden	Ray McAnally
Bobby	James Russo
Translator	Wallace Shawn
Young Monk	John C. Reilly
Bishop Nogulich	Ken Buhay

On the surface, *We're No Angels* has all the ingredients for success in terms of its talented actors, director, screenwriter, cinematographer, and production designer. Robert De Niro and Sean Penn, the most talented "volatile" actors of their respective generations, appear on the screen together for the first time. Director Neil Jordan, who cowrote and directed the acclaimed drama *Mona Lisa* (1986), teams up with playwright David Mamet to examine once more the underworld of convicts and con men.

The film's major flaw stems from its uneasy mix of the light humor of the original 1955 film with Humphrey Bogart, upon which *We're No Angels* claims to be "loosely based," and Mamet's trademark dark moral explorations, such as *House of Games* (1987), which Mamet wrote and directed. Ned (Robert De Niro) and Jim (Sean Penn) are two small-time convicts, whose limited intelligence leaves little for Mamet to explore. The humor, then, remains situational throughout the film, and the basic premise—that Ned and Jim can pass as renowned theologians—collapses the moment Jim opens his mouth.

Yet, while the film fails on a narrative level, its camerawork and location sets are exquisite. French-born cinematographer Philippe Rousselot—who worked under Nestor Almendros before filming such visually striking films as *Diva* (1982), *Hope and Glory* (1987), and *Dangerous Liaisons* (1988)—captures the harsh winter beauty of the Stave Lake Falls region in British Columbia, Canada. He works generally well within the enormous Britania Mines that are used for the prison scenes and in the shanty town and monastery that production designer Wolf Kroeger built from the ground up.

Like the original film, *We're No Angels* involves three escaped convicts who find refuge in an unlikely environment: a French family in the former film and a bordertown monastery in the latter. *We're No Angels* begins in a Depression-era prison mine, with Jim and Ned as two simple and mild prisoners who are forced to witness the execution of Bobby (James Russo), a hardcore murderer. Within moments, however, Bobby initiates a maniacal and breakneck escape, forcing Jim and Ned to join him as he leaps into the snow-covered wilderness.

Jim and Ned, who are chained together, become separated from Bobby and must hobble toward the Canadian border. Outside a New England bordertown, Jim notices a sign with an inscription from the Bible: "Do not neglect to show hospitality to strangers: for thereby some have entertained angels unawares" (Heb. 13:1). When an old woman drives up and questions the two men, Jim repeats the line. She assumes that Jim and Ned are the renowned theologians expected at the local monastery to inspect the shrine of the weeping Virgin, which the theologians have written about but never seen.

Since the town and monastery are next to the bridge that crosses the river into Canada, Jim and Ned decide to pose as the theologians until a safe enough opportunity arises for the timid fugitives to cross. The remainder of the film consists of the futile attempts of Jim and Ned to escape into Canada before the monks discover their disguise. In the meantime, the prison warden (Ray McAnally) arrives and begins to search the town, whereupon he captures Bobby disguised as a woman. When Bobby recognizes Jim and Ned, he threatens to expose them unless they include him in their plans to cross the bridge with the annual procession that carries the shrine to a neighboring monastery.

By this point, neither Jim nor Ned have "reformed," although Jim finds a companionate simpleness in the monastery, while Ned falls for a local unwed mother, Molly (Demi Moore), who makes ends meet through prostitution. Rather than elevate Jim and Ned, the film exposes the townspeople themselves as moral hypocrites. Father Levesque (Hoyt Axton) admits to Ned that the shrine's weeping is caused by a leak in the roof. The local deputy (Bruno Kirby), who is married, sleeps with Molly but insists that she is the evil one.

Neither Penn nor De Niro, however, are able to make credible their roles as naïve "angels" who rectify the town's evils. Penn's cryptic lines are more appropriate to his earlier film *Fast Times at Ridgemont High* (1982), and his big speech, which tries to mimic the populist speeches of Frank Capra films, comes across as flat rather than as humorous or insightful. De Niro, on the other hand, mumbles and mugs his way through the entire film, with only occasional flashes of emotion. Thus, neither actor develops a coherent character.

In the end, it is an instinctual act that proves the inner goodness of Jim and Ned. In order to qualify for the procession, Ned convinces Molly to let him take her mute daughter. Bobby, who is hidden under the shrine, is discovered midway across the bridge. When he threatens to shoot the girl, Jim grabs the gun and struggles with him. Meanwhile, the shrine comes loose and falls over, knocking the girl into the river. Ned, who cannot swim, nevertheless jumps in after her. He grabs the girl and is swept over the waterfall along with the shrine. Trapped underwater, Ned reaches out to the shrine, grabs the Virgin's hand, and is pulled to the surface when the wooden shrine begins to rise.

The traumatic experience cures the mute girl, whose first word about Jim and Ned, "convicts," is misunderstood as "converts." The monks are therefore quick to forgive the two false theologians, and the warden decides to look elsewhere for the fugitives. Jim returns to the monastery to live, while Ned strolls across the bridge with Molly at his side.

Despite his heroic rescue effort, Ned remains an opportunist at heart, as does Jim, whose motivations are more corporeal than spiritual. Likewise, the characters' opportunism is reflected in the making of the film. *We're No Angels* represents a calculation on the part of De Niro to enter into film production, with his new production company, Tribeca Films. The decision to team up with Penn partakes of the same May-December "mergers," usually with Tom Cruise, that have revived the careers of other middle-aged male leads. Since De Niro's effort to become involved in all phases of film production depends upon his screen presence, he is slated to star in no less than six films to be shot in 1990.

We're No Angels, however, presents itself as a film with a message. The narrative is set in 1935, because, as director Jordan claims, "by not being contemporary, the story could become more of a fable." Oddly enough, however, Jordan never links the authentic Depression-era setting—with its poverty and moral hypocrisy—to an explicit moral investigation or lesson, even a sardonic one in the manner of Mamet. Thus, if the film is a fable for the 1990's, its implicit lesson seems to be that no moral higher ground exists and that the best one can hope for is to be comfortable, do the right thing in a pinch, and make people laugh. As a lesson, the film might have succeeded had it been able to live up to the last criterion.

Chon Noriega

Reviews
Chicago Tribune. December 15, 1989, VII, p. 30.
The Christian Science Monitor. January 19, 1990, p. 10.

Los Angeles Times. December 15, 1989, VI, p. 12.
The Nation. CCL, January 1, 1990, p. 31.
National Review. XLII, January 22, 1990, p. 56.
The New York Times. December 15, 1989, p. C20.
Newsweek. CXIV, December 25, 1989, p. 74.
Variety. CCCXXXVII, December 13, 1989, p. 5.
The Village Voice. December 26, 1989, p. 102.
The Wall Street Journal. December 28, 1989, p. A7.
The Washington Post. December 15, 1989, p. D7.

WHEN HARRY MET SALLY

Production: Rob Reiner and Andrew Scheinman for Castle Rock Entertainment; released by Columbia Pictures
Direction: Rob Reiner
Screenplay: Nora Ephron
Cinematography: Barry Sonnenfeld
Editing: Robert Leighton
Production design: Jane Musky
Art direction: Harold Thrasher
Set decoration: George R. Nelson and Sabrina Wright-Basile
Makeup: Stephen Abrums, Joseph A. Campayno, Kenneth Chase, and Peter Montagna
Costume design: Gloria Gresham
Sound: Robert Eber
Music: Marc Shaiman
MPAA rating: R
Running time: 95 minutes

Principal characters:
Harry Burns .... Billy Crystal
Sally Albright .... Meg Ryan
Marie .... Carrie Fisher
Jess .... Bruno Kirby
Joe .... Steven Ford
Alice .... Lisa Jane Persky

When Harry Met Sally is a more personalized Woody Allen than Rob Reiner romantic comedy even though it is the latter's fifth directorial picture. After retiring from his role as Meathead Mike Stivic in television's *All in the Family*, Reiner began directing genre films. First came his satiric *This Is Spinal Tap* (1985), then the sensitive teen films *The Sure Thing* (1985) and *Stand by Me* (1986), and finally the popular fairy tale, *The Princess Bride* (1987). Ironically, each of these very different films seemed more characteristic of Rob Reiner than the one he claims as his most personal, *When Harry Met Sally*.

The idea for *When Harry Met Sally* evolved in the mid-1980's following Reiner's marital breakup with comedian/director Penny Marshall. He shared his thoughts with producer/partner Andrew Scheinman and writer Nora Ephron (another divorcée). Ephron then compiled all three of their romances into the screenplay of *When Harry Met Sally*.

The plot of the film focuses on the budding relationship of Harry Burns (Billy Crystal) and Sally Albright (Meg Ryan). The two meet following their college graduation when Sally drives Harry, her best friend's boyfriend, to New York from their school in Chicago. They instantly dislike each other. Harry is cynical, sexist, obsessed with sex and death, and argumentative. He is also a slob. Neglecting to roll down the window while eating grapes, he spits the seeds all over the glass with no apology whatsoever. Sally is the quintessential blonde Wonder Bread girl; sweet, doughy, all smiles, but very rigid and uptight. She would like to have Harry as a friend in New York since neither one knows a soul there. Harry makes it quite clear, though, that men and women cannot be merely friends, because sex will always interfere. Then, he proceeds to make a pass at her. Horrified and indignant, Sally agrees that the two cannot be friends.

Five years later, Harry and Sally run into each other again. Her hair is looser now, as are her personality and morals. Harry is not quite as boorish as when they last met. He has donned a suit and tie and has become a political consultant. Harry is about to be wed, and Sally is in love with Joe (Steven Ford), an acquaintance of Harry. They part again.

Another five years slip by, and both of their relationships have cracked or dissolved. Feeling rejected and alone, they decide they can give friendship a try. An extremely close one blossoms over time amid walks in the park and late-night phone marathons. They help each other through the hard times and finally decide to help each other become involved again. She introduces him to her best friend, Marie (Carrie Fisher), a woman who totes around an index of available men, and he sets her up with his best buddy, Jess (Bruno Kirby). Unfortunately, the best friends find they can do much better without Harry and Sally and escape in a cab, leaving the two matchmakers on the street alone. There is no regret, since neither Harry nor Sally cared much for their prearranged date.

Harder times are just around the corner when Harry runs into his former wife with her new boyfriend. He begins to brood and finds it very difficult to congratulate Marie and Jess on their new relationship. Then, when Sally hears that her former lover is going to be wed, the feeling of relationship finality grips her. In his attempts to calm a hysterical woman, Harry somehow manages to wind up in bed with Sally. Their surprise and horror over the incident is greeted by their best friends with relief and joy. Trauma takes root though. Harry has had only one relationship, and that failed miserably. Everything else had been one-night stands, from which he always took his leave immediately following orgasm. When Sally sees that she is being treated like all of his other women, she dissolves their friendship.

Thus begins Harry's change of heart and frustrated attempts to reunite with Sally. Finally, on New Year's Eve, he makes a melodramatic race through Manhattan in the rain to appear at the formal party drenched and dressed in jeans, looking for Sally. Sally, who has just ditched her dreary date, listens to Harry's proclamation of undying love for her. She accepts it, and they live happily ever after.

Although *When Harry Met Sally* may have incorporated the romantic histories of Reiner and his friends in a lightweight situation comedy, the film's façade is fervently that of Woody Allen. There is Manhattan in June, the romantic George Gershwin tunes, the black-and-white titles. Harry Burns, a better-looking Woody

Allen, is still obsessed with sex and death. Direct camera interviews are performed as they were in Woody Allen's *Annie Hall* (1977). The *Casablanca* (1942) obsession that is shared with Harry and Sally echoes the obsession in *Play It Again, Sam* (1972). Even the year that Harry and Sally meet, 1977, is the year that *Annie Hall* was made. (Also of note is the Annie Hall style of clothes and hats that Sally wears.) The title song in the film, "It Had to Be You," was even sung by Keaton in *Annie Hall*.

The humor differs from that of a true Woody Allen film. In *When Harry Met Sally*, neuroses is sacrificed for the saccharine-sweet; clever has triumphed over credible. It seems that every time that sex is a subject to be discussed by Sally, it is done in a crowded restaurant. This may be situationally amusing, but it is not the kind of public place in which someone who acts as though "sex" were a dirty word would enjoy discussing the subject. The first time the two meet, Harry tells her as they are entering a diner that she has never had good sex. Infuriated, she blurts out in the quiet café that she has had plenty of good sex. Although it is humorous how everyone stops eating to listen, this display is completely out of character for someone who consistently sounds like an uptight virgin. Ten years later, even though she has somewhat loosened up, it is not believable that Sally Albright would fake a screaming orgasm in a crowded restaurant, continuing it so loudly and for so long.

Although Crystal and Ryan are Allen and Keaton on the surface, they seem to lack the neurotic depth of the other characters. Allen and Crystal both portray angry, hostile men underneath, but this rage, when emanating from a mealy-mouthed weakling such as Allen's persona, is humorous as well as thought-provoking. With Crystal's Harry, the anger is more brutal, and this brutality makes it more difficult to believe his unnatural turnaround into a wonderfully amorous suitor at the film's end. He has completely lost the edge that was such an integral part of his character. Furthermore, when watching Diane Keaton's Annie, the viewer has the feeling of seeing a truly neurotic creature at work. Watching Meg Ryan's Sally in her most emotional scene—crying over the planned marriage of her former lover with another woman—is like watching the frenetic and forced weeping of Mary Tyler Moore in one of her sitcoms.

When Harry Met Sally is much easier to watch than a Woody Allen film. It is pure entertainment, like an easy evening of television comedy. A Woody Allen film leaves one unsettled. There is a complexity and wrestling with life that surges beneath the surface and defies complacency. *When Harry Met Sally* will reach a far wider audience precisely because television reaches a wider audience than film. It is a night in front of the television, a formula picture with fun, entertaining situation-comedy characterizations. It is two hours of relaxed humor that may leave viewers reveling in the story or may leave them longing for the same type of fairy-tale romance.

Steven C. Kowall

Reviews

American Film: Magazine of the Film and Television Arts. XIV, July, 1989, p. 28.
Chicago Tribune. July 12, 1989, V, p. 1.
Films in Review. XL, October, 1989, p. 484.
Los Angeles Times. July 16, 1989, VI, p. 1.
Maclean's. CII, July 24, 1989, p. 51.
The New Republic. CCI, August 21, 1989, p. 26.
The New York Times. July 9, 1989, p. 22.
The New Yorker. LXV, August 7, 1989, p. 74.
Newsweek. CXIV, July 17, 1989, p. 52.
Time. CXXXIV, July 31, 1989, p. 65.
Variety. CCCXXXV, July 12, 1989, p. 24.
The Village Voice. July 18, 1989, p. 68.

WIRED

Production: Edward S. Feldman and Charles R. Meeker for F/M Entertainment and
   Lion Screen Entertainment; released by Taurus Entertainment
Direction: Larry Peerce
Screenplay: Earl Mac Rauch; based on the book by Bob Woodward
Cinematography: Tony Imi
Editing: Eric Sears
Production design: Brian Eatwell
Costume design: Shari Feldman
Sound: Robert Wald
Music: Basil Poledouris
MPAA rating: R
Running time: 110 minutes

> *Principal characters:*
> John Belushi .... Michael Chiklis
> Angel Velasquez .... Ray Sharkey
> Bob Woodward .... J. T. Walsh
> Judy Belushi....................... Lucinda Jenney
> Dan Aykroyd .... Gary Groomes
> Cathy Smith .... Patti D'Arbanville

Perhaps the most haunting sequence in Larry Peerce's *Wired* occurs toward the
end of the film, on the last evening of actor John Belushi's life. The setting is the
rented cottage in which Belushi (Michael Chiklis) is about to die. Belushi is joined
by the cowriter working with him on the draft of a new screenplay and by Cathy
Smith (Patti D'Arbanville), who is present for the final fling that culminates in
Belushi's death. The cowriter is given a pseudonym, though stories surrounding
Belushi's death (and journalist Bob Woodward's treatment of it in the book *Wired*)
identified him as a staffer and occasional performer on *Saturday Night Live*, which
helped make Belushi a national sensation.

Belushi, Smith, and the comic are not alone. The cottage is quite full. Belushi
stumbles into the living room, glazed and craving, and orders almost everyone out
as he prepares for the final fix. The room is in darkness, and the audience sees
shapes or an occasional cigarette end. Faces are not shown, and there is no clue as
to who these people might be. The questions persist, however, especially in the light
of the rumors and investigations following Belushi's death and Woodward's book,
about who shared the closing hours of Belushi's life. Who supplied the drugs, or
helped to consume them, or stood eager to capitalize on Belushi's comic energy?
Who ultimately was at fault?

Part of the intrigue in watching this film is in pursuing these questions, especially the last one, and in guessing at the identity of Belushi's colleagues. Peerce gives few of them recognizable names, even if they had been identified in the book. The director who accosts Belushi on a film set, whose name would be instantly recognized, is hidden. The agent who continues to represent Belushi in the last days despite his shock at Belushi's degeneration is also disguised. Nobody from the *Saturday Night Live* cast or crew is named. Smith, Belushi's wife, Judy (Lucinda Jenney), and Dan Aykroyd (Gary Groomes) appear, but none fares badly. Identity guessing is futile, however, because, in Peerce's vision, no number of celebrities, however involved with Belushi, can really help to attribute responsibility for what finally happened in that hotel.

Instead, the film holds Belushi uncomfortably on the hook, making him accountable for his own destruction and doing so with little of the moralizing or head-wagging that greeted some of the critical and popular response to *Wired*, the book. Peerce's fidelity to this vision of chemical dependency makes for a harrowing cautionary tale, a kind of cross between Everyman and *The Rake's Progress*. At this level, the film is successful, and the fact that it treats a recently deceased famous person lends it urgency and pertinence. With cinematographer Tony Imi and production designer Brian Eatwell, Peerce contrives a stylish and at times visually compelling document—a journey into the reaches of hell. Michael Chiklis is effective enough as Belushi to make that journey comic, at least in part. The result, however, is a picture of the performer that is itself hellish and ultimately unpalatable.

Had the film kept its sights there, it would have remained ambitious (though probably still hellish and unpalatable). Yet Peerce tries to do much more, to factor Woodward into the story as a character in a drama in which, in real life, he had no part. In fact, Peerce seems almost as interested in Woodward as he is in Belushi. This gives the biography a dual focus. Yet Belushi's story so overwhelms Woodward that the focus is always a bit off. In the end, partly because of just how good Chiklis is in his role, Woodward seems overpowered.

Peerce tells the Belushi story through a peculiar narrative structure that relies on extensive (if not frenetic) cross-cutting and asks the audience to accept narratives moving in two temporal directions until, strangely, they converge at Belushi's deathbed. The film begins with the death. Belushi is first seen in the morgue as he unzips himself from a body bag, shrouds himself in whatever he can find, and (in a manner reminiscent of Bluto in *Animal House*, 1978) makes his escape from the morgue, grabbing a curbside cab driven by Angel Velasquez (Ray Sharkey). Belushi gradually learns that he is dead, as is his driver. The rest of the film (or at least that part of the film that centers on Belushi's spirit) consists of Angel's guiding Belushi on a quick tour of his personal and professional life, through which Belushi comes to realize that he is, in fact, dead, that his lifestyle killed him, and that no deals are now possible.

Angel, the audience learns, ended his time on earth through similar chemical habits. He presents Belushi with a guided tour of his life and rubs the comic's nose substantially in his history. The life story is not very appealing, though it had promise. The early days seem particularly bright. John dates Judy, whom he later marries; John, Judy, and Dan share a small apartment in the early days of their comic training and experience, before cracking the big-time on *Saturday Night Live*. Yet even then there is trouble: John uses too much cocaine and drinks and eats too much. People notice his substance abuse at times (both Judy and Dan try to talk to him about it); it interferes with work (a director hits him for being incapacitated on the set); and it has warped his interpersonal attitudes, revealing animosities, antagonisms, and rages that seem equally composed of appetite and denial. Yet nobody can do much about it, and few seem very eager to try. The film suggests that, apart from Judy, Dan was the closest person to Belushi. As played by Gary Groomes, Dan Aykroyd is well-meaning, fiercely loyal, and talented, but very limited. His devotion in the face of Belushi's degeneration seems almost bovine in his ability to ignore reality.

The film has lighter moments that seem bizarre in contrast. Belushi is shown (and the Belushi character sees himself) in the contexts in which he faced 1970's America. He watches a screening of *Animal House*, laughs, and remarks that he was good. He is right. He was good, but the past tense is the critical part of his remark. In retrospect, the sequence is not really very amusing. Bluto goes wild in the college cafeteria, loading his plate (and himself) with everything he can find. What Belushi (the spirit) does not recognize (as Angel and the audience do) is that Bluto is not even a parody of the real Belushi. Bluto will walk away from this orgy of excess. Belushi will not.

As Belushi reviews his life, Bob Woodward (J. T. Walsh) accepts Judy's request to write her husband's biography, to show the world the real John. Woodward's quest is faintly reminiscent of *Citizen Kane* (1941), in which Kane's life unfolds through episodic flashbacks narrated in interviews by several of the people who knew him best. Woodward, however, is famous. He would draw attention even had director Peerce not devoted much of the story to him. Woodward is doing more than attempting to understand Belushi. He is on a personal quest as well.

Belushi and Woodward seem worlds apart. Woodward appears straight-laced, conventional, and perhaps naïve. He pales beside the enormous energy, spontaneity, and sheer lunacy of the John Belushi seen on television or in film. Yet the film suggests that each of these men is the shadow side of the other. Both came from Wheaton, Illinois, the clean-cut Chicago bedroom community that is perhaps best known as the home of one of the nation's most steadfastly conservative evangelical Christian colleges. Woodward knew Belushi's turf, because it was his own. His job in the film becomes personal, a journey into an underworld whose entrance may have been his own hometown.

Unfortunately, the story slights Woodward. Belushi's character (and Chiklis' performance) so fill the screen that they eclipse Walsh, whose Woodward shows much dogged determination but little of the fire that occupied and ultimately consumed his subject. The culmination of Woodward's quest is the cottage itself, which

Woodward enters and examines after he has interviewed everyone he can. He is trying to understand what separated the two men.

Woodward joins Belushi as the last fix takes over, speaking with him as the comic dies. This final twist explicates the parallel that Peerce hopes to make but does so at the cost of credibility and coherence. It is finally uncertain whether Woodward learns anything about Belushi or even about himself. An audience probably finds itself in the same position: Belushi's demise is dramatic, harrowing, and a waste of a talent that might, over the decades, have become one of Hollywood's greats. Yet *Wired* leaves the audience chiefly with a bad feeling, a sense of a project wildly scattered among too many sequences, too many parallels, and too much intention.

John Hollwitz

Reviews

Chicago Tribune. August 25, 1989, VII, p. 37.
The Christian Science Monitor. August 29, 1989, p. 10.
Los Angeles Times. August 25, 1989, VI, p. 1.
Maclean's. CII, August 28, 1989, p. 52.
New Statesman and Society. II, October 13, 1989, p. 45.
The New York Times. August 25, 1989, p. C14.
Newsweek. CXIV, September 4, 1989, p. 68.
Rolling Stone. September 7, 1989, p. 32.
Time. CXXXIV, August 28, 1989, p. 64.
Variety. CCCXXXVI, August 9, 1989, p. 20.

388

MORE FILMS OF 1989

Abbreviations: *Pro.* = Production *Dir.* = Direction *Scr.* = Screenplay *Cine.* = Cinematography *Ed.* = Editing *P.d.* = Production design *A.d.* = Art direction *S.d.* = Set decoration *Mu.* = Music *R.t.* = Running time *MPAA* = MPAA rating

---

THE ADVENTURES OF MILO AND OTIS (Japan, 1989)

Pro. Masaru Kakutani and Satoru Ogata; Columbia Pictures *Dir.* Masanori Hata *Scr.* Mark Saltzman; based on an original story by Masanori Hata *Cine.* Hideo Fujii and Shinji Tomita *Ed.* Chizuko Osada *A.d.* Takeharu Sakaguchi *Mu.* Michael Boddicker *R.t.* 76 min. *MPAA* G. *Narration:* Dudley Moore.

In an all-animal story, a cat named Milo and a dog named Otis leave the farm on which they live for a journey that involves them in a series of adventures with other animals and sometimes malevolent natural forces. Eventually, they return home and begin to raise families. Director Masanori Hata is a zoologist who filmed this work on his island menagerie.

AFTER MIDNIGHT

Pro. Ken Wheat, Jim Wheat, Richard Arlook, and Peter Greene for High Bar Pictures; Metro-Goldwyn-Mayer/United Artists *Dir.* Ken Wheat and Jim Wheat *Scr.* Ken Wheat and Jim Wheat *Cine.* Phedon Papamichael *Ed.* Phillip Linson and Quinnie Martin, Jr. *P.d.* Paul Chadwick *A.d.* Chris Henry *Mu.* Marc Donahue *R.t.* 90 min. *MPAA* R. *Cast:* Jillian McWhirter, Pamela Segall, Ramy Zade, Nadine Van Der Velde, Marc McClure, Marg Helgenberger, Billy Ray Sharkey.

A group of college coeds meet at the home of an unorthodox psychology professor (Ramy Zade) to exchange stories of fear, while a threat of horrible violence hangs over them.

ALL'S FAIR

Pro. Jon Gordon; Moviestore Entertainment *Dir.* Rocky Lang *Scr.* Randee Russel, John Finegan, Tom Rondinella, and William Pace; based on a story by Finegan and Watt Tyler *Cine.* Peter Lyons Collister *Ed.* Maryann Brandon *Mu.* Bill Myers *R.t.* 89 min. *MPAA* PG-13. *Cast:* George Segal, Sally Kellerman, Robert Carradine, Jennifer Edwards, Jane Kaczmarek, John Kapelos, Lou Ferrigno.

There is a battle of the sexes when frustrated wives and female coworkers try to beat their husbands and bosses at their own game. Businessmen Colonel (George Segal) and Mark (Robert Carradine) enjoy playing weekend war games where they shoot each other with paint pellets instead of bullets. Their wives and female coworkers jump into the fray enlisting muscular Klaus (Lou Ferrigno) to help them win the battle.

AMANDA

Pro. Jeff Meyer and Gail Kappler Rosella *Dir.* Jeff Meyer and Gail Kappler Rosella *Scr.* Jeff Meyer and Gail Kappler Rosella *Cine.* Mark Shapiro *Ed.* Jeff Meyer and Gail Kappler Rosella *R.t.* 120 min. *Cast:* Jeff Meyer, Gail Kappler Rosella, William Mitchell, Ann Bowden, Claire Janell, Drew Forsythe, Vern Taylor.

An aspiring and struggling photographer dedicates himself to his art. He meets a young, wealthy woman, who solves his financial problems and uses her contacts to help him achieve success. This proves to be a dream, but he later meets Amanda, the girl in his dream.

AMERICAN NINJA III: BLOOD HUNT

Pro. Harry Alan Towers; Cannon Films *Dir.* Cedric Sundstrom *Scr.* Cedric Sundstrom

Cine. George Bartels *Ed.* Michael J. Duthie *Mu.* George S. Clinton *P.d.* Ruth Strimling *R.t.* 90 min. *MPAA* R. *Cast:* David Bradley, Steve James, Marjoe Gortner, Michele Chan, Yehuda Efroni, Calvin Jung, Adrienne Pearce, Evan J. Klisser, Grant Preston.

David Bradley replaces Michael Dudikoff as the hero of the Ninja series in this third installment. A group of martial arts combatants gather on a tropical island for a tournament where Cobra (Marjoe Gortner) has perfected a deadly virus he wants to try out on Sean (David Bradley).

AMERICAN STORIES (*Histoires d'Amerique*. France and Belgium, 1989)

Pro. Mallia Films *Dir.* Chantal Akerman *Scr.* Chantal Akerman *Cine.* Luc Ben Hamou *Ed.* Patrick Mimouni *Mu.* Sonia Wieder Atherton *P.d.* Marilyn Watelet *R.t.* 99 min. *Cast:* Mark Amitin, Eszter Balint, Stefan Balint, Kirk Baltz, George Bartenieff, Bill Bastiani, Isha Manna Beck, Jacob Becker, Max Brandt, Maurice Brenner, David Buntzman, Marilyn Chris, Sharon Diskin, Carl Don, Pierre Epstein, Michael Grodenchik, Ben Hammer, Dean Jackson, Robert Katims, Mordecai Lawner, Boris Leskin, Elliott Levine, Justine Lochtman, Judith Malina, Jerry Matz, Charles Mayer, Roy Nathanson, Bruce Nozik, Deborah Offner, Irina Pasmur, Herschel Rosen, Joan Rosenfels, Herbert Rubens, Claudia Silver, Arthur Tracy, Victor Talmadge.

Filmed by Belgian director Chantal Akerman, *American Stories* is a series of anecdotes, tragic, comic, and slice-of-life, that find inspiration in the Jewish-American experience. Performed by New York Jewish actors, the stories all have contemporary settings although they are based on almost a century of Jewish culture and folklore.

ANIMAL BEHAVIOR

Pro. Kjehl Rasmussen; Millimeter Films *Dir.* H. Anne Riley *Scr.* Susan Rice *Cine.* David Spellvin *Ed.* Joseph Weintraub *Mu.* Cliff Eidelman *P.d.* Jeannine Claudia Oppewall *A.d.* David Brisbin *S.d.* Lisa Fischer *R.t.* 90 min. *MPAA* PG. *Cast:* Karen Allen, Armand Assante, Holly Hunter, Josh Mostel, Richard Libertini, Alexa Kenin, Jon Mathews, Nan Martin, Crystal Buda.

At a Southwestern college, Mark (Armand Assante), a music teacher and composer, romantically pursues Alex (Karen Allen), an animal behavior researcher who lives in a trailer with a chimpanzee.

ASTONISHED

Pro. Sydney Kahn and Herman Kahn; Dream Bird Productions *Dir.* Jeff Kahn *Scr.* Jeff Kahn *Cine.* Peter Fernberger and Robert Draper *Ed.* Peter Friedman and Bill Daughton *Mu.* Michael Urbaniak *A.d.* Chris Barreca *R.t.* 103 min. *Cast:* Liliana Komorowski, Ken Ryan, Rock Dutton, Theresa Merritt, Fred Neuman, Tommy Hollis.

A young woman, Sonia (Liliana Komorowski), who cannot pay her rent, is propositioned by her landlord, who is also a brutal pimp. After seeing him beat up another girl, Sonia murders the man. She ends up in Brazil with the detective who investigates the case.

BABAR: THE MOVIE

Pro. Patrick Loubert, Michael Hirsh, and Clive A. Smith; New Line Cinema *Dir.* Alan Bunce *Scr.* Peter Sauder, J. D. Smith, John De Klein, Raymond Jeffelice, and Alan Bunce; based on a story by Peter Sauder, Patrick Loubert, and Michael Hirsh and characters created by Jean de Brunhoff and Laurent de Brunhoff *Ed.* Evan Landis *Mu.* Milan Kymlicka *P.d.* Ted Bastien *A.d.* Clive Powsey and Carol Bradbury *R.t.* 70 min. *MPAA* G. *Voices:* Gordon Pinsent, Gavin Magrath, Elizabeth Hanna, Sarah Polley, Chris Wiggins, Stephen Ouimette, John Stocker, Charles Kerr.

Based on the classic storybook characters, this animated feature tells the story of a youthful Babar (voice of Gavin Magrath) saving Elephantland from villainous rhinos and aiding his sweetheart Celeste (voice of Sarah Polley), whose mother has been abducted. Primarily for children, the action-filled tale is enhanced by a number of songs.

BAD BLOOD

Pro. Chuck Vincent; Platinum Pictures *Dir.* Chuck Vincent *Scr.* Craig Horrall *Cine.* Larry Revene *Ed.* James Davalos *Mu.* Joey Mennonna *A.d.* Hilary Wright *R.t.* 103 min. *MPAA* R. *Cast:* Georgina Spelvin, Gregory Patrick, Troy Donahue, Carolyn Van Bellinghen, Linda Blair, Harvey Siegel, Scott Baker, Christina Veronica, Daniel Chapman, Jane Hamilton.

The reunion of Arlene Billings (Georgina Spelvin) and her long-lost adult son Ted Barnes (Gregory Patrick) sets into motion a Gothic melodrama in a contemporary setting. When Ted's wife Evie (Linda Blair) dies violently, incestuous undercurrents rise to the surface. Billed under the pseudonym "Ruth Raymond," Georgina Spelvin—famed for her accomplished acting in the pornographic *The Devil in Miss Jones*—enjoys a tour-de-force role as Arlene.

BERT RIGBY, YOU'RE A FOOL

Pro. George Shapiro; Warner Bros. *Dir.* Carl Reiner *Scr.* Carl Reiner *Cine.* Jan de Bont *Ed.* Bud Molin *Mu.* Ralph Burns *P.d.* Terence Marsh *A.d.* Dianne Wager *S.d.* John Franco, Jr. *R.t.* 94 min. *MPAA* R. *Cast:* Robert Lindsay, Cathryn Bradshaw, Robbie Coltrane, Anne Bancroft, Corbin Bernsen, Jackie Gayle, Liberty Mounten.

Dazzled by show business, an out-of-work coal miner enters a talent contest in his native English town, where his act becomes inadvertently comic. He winds up in California where his misadventures make up most of this gentle satire.

BEST OF THE BEST

Pro. Phillip Rhee and Peter E. Strauss; Taurus Entertainment in association with Kuys Entertainment Group *Dir.* Bob Radler *Scr.* Paul Levine; based on a story by Phillip Rhee and Paul Levine *Cine.* Doug Ryan *Ed.* William Hoy *Mu.* Paul Gilman *P.d.* Kim Rees *A.d.* Maxine Shepard *R.t.* 95 min. *MPAA* PG-13. *Cast:* Eric Roberts, James Earl Jones, Sally Kirkland, Phillip Rhee, Christopher Penn, John Dye, David Agresta, Tom Everett, Louise Fletcher, John P. Ryan, Edan Gross, Simon Rhee, Ahmad Rashad, Master Hee Il Cho, James Lew, Ken Nagayama, Ho Sik Pak, Dae Kyu Chang, Samantha Scully, Adrianne Sachs, Kane Jodder.

Tommy (Phillip Rhee), a member of the U.S. martial arts team, seeks revenge against the Korean (Simon Rhee) who killed his brother in a match; in their own climactic match, however, finer impulses prevail.

BEVERLY HILLS BRATS

Pro. Terry Moore and Jerry Rivers; Taurus Entertainment *Dir.* Dimitri Sotirakis *Scr.* Linda Silverthorn; based on a story by Terry Moore and Jerry Rivers *Cine.* Harry Mathias *Ed.* Jerry Frizell *Mu.* Barry Goldberg *P.d.* George Costello *A.d.* Jay Burkhardt *S.d.* Marla Caso *R.t.* 91 min. *MPAA* PG-13. *Cast:* Burt Young, Martin Sheen, Terry Moore, Peter Billingsley, Ramon Sheen, Cathy Podewell.

Scooter (Peter Billingsley)—the son of affluent Jeffrey (Martin Sheen) and Veronica Miller (Terry Moore)—fakes his own kidnapping to get attention, involving a small-time hoodlum, Clive (Burt Young), in the scheme. Conceived and played broadly, the comedy marks the return to the screen after a long absence of co-producer Terry Moore, a notable ingenue of the 1950's.

BIG MAN ON CAMPUS

Pro. Arnon Milchan; Vestron Entertainment *Dir.* Jeremy Kagan *Scr.* Allan Katz *Cine.*

Bojan Bazelli *Ed.* Howard Smith *Mu.* Joseph Vitarelli *A.d.* Michael Day *S.d.* Lauri Gaffin *R.t.* 105 min. *MPAA* PG-13. *Cast:* Allan Katz, Corey Parker, Cindy Williams, Melora Hardin, Tom Skerritt, Jessica Harper, Gerrit Graham, John Finnegan.

An uneasy attempt to mingle comedy and sentiment marks the contemporary story of a collegiate "Hunchback of Notre Dame" named Bob (Allan Katz), who becomes involved with blonde beauty Cathy (Melora Hardin) and her boyfriend Alex (Corey Parker). All involved gain some maturity and understanding by the fadeout.

THE BIG PICTURE

Pro. Michael Varhol for Aspen Film Society; Columbia Pictures *Dir.* Christopher Guest *Scr.* Michael Varhol, Christopher Guest, and Michael McKean; based on a story by Varhol and Guest *Cine.* Jeff Jur *Ed.* Marty Nicholson *Mu.* David Nichtern *P.d.* Joseph Garrity *A.d.* Patrick Tagliaferro *S.d.* Jerie Kelter *R.t.* 99 min. *Cast:* Kevin Bacon, Emily Longstreth, J. T. Walsh, Jennifer Jason Leigh, Martin Short, Michael McKean, Kim Miyori, Teri Hatcher, Dan Schneider, Jason Gould, Tracy Brooks Swope, Don Franklin, Fran Drescher, Eddie Albert, June Lockhart, Stephen Collins, Roddy McDowall, John Cleese, Elliot Gould.

This film is a good-natured satire on the values and mores of present-day Hollywood. The story follows the rise and fall and rise again of a wunderkind director (Kevin Bacon) as he finds his way to an upbeat ending.

BLOODFIST

Pro. Roger Corman for Concorde/New Horizons; Concorde Pictures *Dir.* Terence H. Winkless *Scr.* Robert King *Cine.* Ricardo Jacques Gale *Ed.* Karen Horn *Mu.* Sasha Matson *R.t.* 85 min. *MPAA* R. *Cast:* Don Wilson, Joe Marie Avellana, Michael Shaner, Riley Bowman, Rob Kaman, Billy Blanks, Kris Aguilar, Vic Diaz.

A kickboxer named Jake—played by Don (The Dragon) Wilson—seeks revenge on the killer of his brother in this straightforward action film which, like the recent *Kickboxer*, is intended to appeal to fans of the sport rather than to general audiences.

BLOODHOUNDS OF BROADWAY

Pro. Howard Brookner for American Playhouse; Vestron Pictures *Dir.* Howard Brookner *Scr.* Brookner and Colman DeKay; based on short stories by Damon Runyon *Cine.* Elliot Davis *Ed.* Camilla Toniolo *Mu.* Jonathan Sheffner *R.t.* 101 min. *Cast:* Julie Hagerty, Randy Quaid, Madonna, Esai Morales, Ethan Phillips, Matt Dillon, Jennifer Grey, Josef Sommer, Anita Morris, Rutger Hauer.

Set on New Year's Eve during Prohibition, this film depicts gangsters, Broadway showgirls, and high society celebrating together at a party given by Harriet Mackyle (Julie Hagerty).

BREAKING IN

Pro. Harry Gittes for Act III Productions; Samuel Goldwyn Company *Dir.* Bill Forsyth *Scr.* John Sayles *Cine.* Michael Coulter *Ed.* Michael Ellis *Mu.* Michael Gibbs *P.d.* Adrienne Atkinson and John Willett *R.t.* 91 min. *Cast:* Burt Reynolds, Casey Siemaszko, Sheila Kelley, Lorraine Toussant, Albert Salmi, Harry Carey.

Two petty criminals, the aging Ernie Mullins (Burt Reynolds) and the young Mike Lefebb (Casey Siemaszko), become partners then go their separate ways, yet they remain involved with each other in an unexpected way. Not a crime thriller, this is an offbeat character study, as one would expect from gifted Scottish director Bill Forsyth (*Housekeeping*, 1987) and screenwriter John Sayles (*Eight Men Out*, 1988).

BUYING TIME

Pro. Richard Gabourie; Metro-Goldwyn-Mayer/United Artists *Dir.* Mitchell Gabourie *Scr.*

Mitchell Gabourie and Richard Gabourie   *Cine.* Manfred Guthe   *Ed.* Michael Todd   *Mu.* David Krystal   *A.d.* Bill Fleming   *R.t.* 97 min.   *MPAA* R.   *Cast:* Jeff Schultz, Page Fletcher, Laura Cruickshank, Leslie Toth, Dean Stockwell.

Jabber (Jeff Schultz), a youthful car wash employee, helps a friend, Reno (Leslie Toth), pull a robbery to square accounts with an unsavory bookie. As a result, he is blackmailed by a couple of cops, principally the ambiguous Detective Novak (Dean Stockwell), into helping them catch the killers of a small-time drug pusher.

CAGE

Pro. Lang Elliott for Lang Elliott Entertainment; New Century/Vista   *Dir.* Lang Elliott   *Scr.* Hugh Kelley   *Cine.* Jacques Haitkin   *Ed.* Mark S. Westmore   *Mu.* Michael Wetherwax   *P.d.* Joseph M. Altadona   *R.t.* 101 min.   *MPAA* R.   *Cast:* Lou Ferrigno, Reb Brown, Michael Dante, Mike Moroff, Marilyn Tokuda, Al Leong, James Shigeta, Branscombe Richmond, Tiger Chung Lee, Al Ruscio, Daniel Martine, Rion Hunter, Dana Lee, Maggie Mae Miller.

Longtime friends Billy (Lou Ferrigno) and Scott (Reb Brown) are introduced to the barbaric world of cage fighting when gamblers kidnap the hulking but innocent Billy and take him to Chinatown to fight.

CAMERON'S CLOSET

Pro. Luigi Cingolani for Smart Egg Pictures; SVS Films   *Dir.* Armand Mastroianni   *Scr.* Gary Brandner; based on his novel   *Cine.* Russell Carpenter   *Mu.* Harry Manfredini   *R.t.* 86 min.   *MPAA* R.   *Cast:* Cotter Smith, Mel Harris, Scott Curtis, Chuck McCann, Leigh McCloskey, Kim Lankford, Gary Hudson, Tab Hunter.

A father's psychokinetic experiments on his young son cause an ancient Mayan demon to appear in the boy's closet. A police detective investigating killings committed by the monster achieves a psychic link with the boy.

CATCH ME IF YOU CAN

Pro. Jonathan D. Krane and Don Schain; MCEG   *Dir.* Stephen Sommers   *Scr.* Stephen Sommers   *Cine.* Ronn Schmidt   *Ed.* Bob Ducsay   *Mu.* Tangerine Dream   *A.d.* Stuart Blatt   *R.t.* 105 min.   *MPAA* PG.   *Cast:* Matt Lattanzi, Loryn Locklin, Grant Heslov, Billy Morrissette, Geoffrey Lewis, M. Emmet Walsh.

Dylan (Matt Lattanzi), a drag racer, and Melissa (Loryn Locklin), class president of her high school, save the financially depressed school from closure by betting on Dylan's races. The simple premise and its development are geared to younger audiences.

CHANCES ARE

Pro. Mike Lobell; Tri-Star Pictures   *Dir.* Emile Ardolino   *Scr.* Perry Howze and Randy Howze   *Cine.* William A. Fraker   *Ed.* Harry Keramidas   *Mu.* Maurice Jarre   *P.d.* Dennis Washington   *R.t.* 108 min.   *MPAA* PG.   *Cast:* Cybill Shepherd, Robert Downey, Jr., Ryan O'Neal, Mary Stuart Masterson, Christopher McDonald, Josef Sommer, Joe Grifasi, Susan Ruttan, Fran Ryan, James Noble.

A dead man (Robert Downey, Jr.) escapes heaven to return to Earth and Corinne (Cybill Shepherd), the love he left behind. When he returns it is twenty-three years later and Downey is now the age of Corinne's attractive grown-up daughter (Mary Stuart Masterson).

CHECKING OUT

Pro. Ben Myron for Handmade Films; Warner Bros.   *Dir.* David Leland   *Scr.* Joe Eszterhas   *Cine.* Ian Wilson   *Ed.* Lee Percy   *Mu.* Carter Burwell   *P.d.* Barbara Ling   *R.t.* 93 min.   *MPAA* R.   *Cast:* Jeff Daniels, Melanie Mayron, Michael Tucker, Kathleen York, Allan Havey, Ann Magnuson, Jo Harvey Allen, Felton Perry, Ian Wolfe, John Durbin.

When his best friend dies of a heart attack, Ray Macklin (Jeff Daniels) becomes convinced that he will suffer the same fate. He attempts to deal with his hypochondria through a series of gags, bad jokes, and misadventures, jeopardizing both his home and work life in the process.

CHEETAH

Pro. Robert Halmi, Sr., for Walt Disney Pictures; Buena Vista *Dir.* Jeff Blyth *Scr.* Erik Tarloff, John Cotter, and Griff Du Rhone; from a story by Cotter, based on the book *The Cheetahs* by Alan Caillou *Cine.* Tom Burstyn *Ed.* Eric Albertson *Mu.* Bruce Rowland *P.d.* Jane Cavedon *R.t.* 84 min. *MPAA* G. *Cast:* Keith Coogan, Lucy Deakins, Collin Môthupi, Timothy Landfield, Breon Gorman, Ka Vundla, Lydia Kigada, Kuldeep Bhakoo, Paul On-songo, Anthony Baird.

Ted (Keith Coogan) and Susan (Lucy Deakins), two American children on a temporary stay in Kenya while their father (Timothy Landfield) completes a job there, befriend a native, Morogo (Collin Môthupi), and an orphaned baby cheetah. When the cheetah is kidnapped, the children set off to rescue it even though ultimate separation is inevitable. In spirit, the film is a return to the Disney studios' earliest live-action shorts and features.

CHOCOLAT (France, 1989)

Pro. Cinemanuel, Marin Karmitz-MK 2 Productions, Cerito Films, Wim Wenders Produktion, La S.E.P.T., Caroline Productions, Le F.O.D.I.C., and TFI Films; Orion Classics *Dir.* Claire Denis *Scr.* Claire Denis and Jean-Pol Fargeau *Cine.* Robert Alazraki *Ed.* Claude Merlin *Mu.* Abdullah Ibrahim *A.d.* Thierry Flamand *R.t.* 105 min. *MPAA* PG-13. *Cast:* Isaach de Bankolé, Giulia Boschi, François Cluzet, Cécile Ducasse, Jean-Claude Adelin, Kenneth Cranham, Mireille Perrier, Jacques Denis.

When France Dalens (Mireille Perrier) returns to Africa in the 1980's, she remembers her childhood there (young France is played by Cécile Ducasse)—a time when the disturbing realities of colonialism and racial injustice were still a part of everyday life. Her friendship with a black houseboy, Protée (Isaach de Bankolé), is the principal thread of the domestic story and the relationship which has the greatest influence on her maturity. Writer-director Claire Denis derived the fictional story from her own childhood experiences.

A CHORUS OF DISAPPROVAL

Pro. Michael Winner for South Gate Entertainment Productions; South Gate Entertainment *Dir.* Michael Winner *Scr.* Michael Winner and Alan Ayckbourn; based on Ayckbourn's play *Cine.* Alan Jones *Ed.* Chris Barnes *Mu.* John DuPrez *R.t.* 100 min. *Cast:* Jeremy Irons, Anthony Hopkins, Prunella Scales.

Guy Jones (Jeremy Irons), an introverted widower, moves to a small seaside town in Northern England, where he joins a drama group and innocently begins to affect the lives of others, especially his director Dafydd Llewellyn (Anthony Hopkins) and Llewellyn's wife Hannah (Prunella Scales).

COLD COMFORT

Pro. Ilana Frank and Ray Sager; Norstar Entertainment *Dir.* Vic Sarin *Scr.* Richard Beattie and L. Elliott Simms *Cine.* Vic Sarin *Ed.* Nick Rotundo *Mu.* Jeff Danna and Mychael Danna *A.d.* Jo-Ann Chorney *R.t.* 90 min. *Cast:* Maury Chaykin, Margaret Langrick, Paul Gross.

In this low-budget psychological thriller, a mentally deranged father, Floyd (Maury Chaykin), obsessed with his daughter Dolores (Margaret Langrick), kidnaps a traveler, Stephen (Paul Gross), with the intention of presenting him as a sexual object for Dolores.

COLD FEET

Pro. Cassian Elwes for Avenue Pictures; Avenue Pictures *Dir.* Robert Dornhelm *Scr.* Tom

McGuane and Jim Harrison *Cine.* Bryan Douggan *Ed.* David Rawlins and Debra McDermott *Mu.* Tom Bahler *P.d.* Bernt Capra *A.d.* Cory Kaplan *R.t.* 91 min. *MPAA* R. *Cast:* Keith Carradine, Sally Kirkland, Tom Waits, Bill Pullman, Rip Torn, Kathleen York, Macon McCalman, Bob Mendelsohn, Vincent Schiavelli, Amber Bauer, Tom McGuane, Jeff Bridges.

A hitman named Kenny (Tom Waits) and two reluctant partners-in-crime, Maureen (Sally Kirkland) and Monte (Keith Carradine), drive north to Montana, in an unusual narrative. Coauthor McGuane at times evokes his well-regarded *Rancho Deluxe* (1975), though this is a darker story.

COOKIE

Pro. Laurence Mark for Lorimar Film Entertainment; Warner Bros. *Dir.* Susan Seidelman *Scr.* Nora Ephron and Alice Arlen *Cine.* Oliver Stapleton *Ed.* Andrew Mondshein *Mu.* Thomas Newman *P.d.* Michael Haller *A.d.* Bill Groom *S.d.* Leslie Bloom *R.t.* 93 min. *MPAA* R. *Cast:* Peter Falk, Dianne Wiest, Emily Lloyd, Michael V. Gazzo, Brenda Vaccaro, Adrian Pasdar, Lionel Stander, Jerry Lewis, Bob Gunton, Ben Rayson, Ricki Lake, Joe Mantello.

When a mobster, Dino (Peter Falk), is paroled after thirteen years in prison, he finds himself uneasy in a new relationship with the daughter, Cookie (Emily Lloyd), he barely knows. While the script follows Dino's efforts to obtain revenge against an associate, Carmine (Michael V. Gazzo), and Cookie's gradual assimilation into his way of life, director Seidelman gives much attention to the garish milieu and offbeat characters, such as Dino's mistress Lenore (Dianne Wiest).

COUSINS

Pro. William Allyn; Paramount Pictures *Dir.* Joel Schumacher *Scr.* Stephen Metcalfe; based on the 1975 film *Cousin, Cousine*, directed and written by Jean-Charles Tacchella *Cine.* Ralf Bode *Ed.* Robert Brown *Mu.* Angelo Badalamenti *P.d.* Mark Freeborn *S.d.* Linda Vipond *R.t.* 110 min. *MPAA* PG-13. *Cast:* Ted Danson, Isabella Rossellini, Sean Young, William Petersen, Lloyd Bridges, Norma Aleandro, Keith Coogan, Gina de Angelis.

Larry (Ted Danson) becomes related to beautiful Maria (Isabella Rossellini) when his uncle (Lloyd Bridges) marries her mother (Norma Aleandro). At the wedding their respective spouses run off for a tryst, throwing Larry and Maria together in a friendship of commiseration and support. This friendship turns into love and they embark on a bitter-sweet affair. An American remake of the French hit *Cousin, Cousine*, this film marks Danson's first outing as a cinematic leading man.

CRACK HOUSE

Pro. Jim Silverman for Silverman Entertainment; Cannon Pictures *Dir.* Michael Fischa *Scr.* Blake Schaefer; based on a story by Jack Silverman *Cine.* Arledge Armenaki *Ed.* Claudia Finkle *Mu.* Michael Piccirillo *P.d.* Keith Barrett *R.t.* 90 min. *MPAA* R. *Cast:* Jim Brown, Anthony Geary, Richard Roundtree, Cheryl Kay, Gregg Gomez Thomsen, Angel Tompkins, Clyde R. Jones, Albert Michel, Jr., Heidi Thomas, Kenneth Edwards, Joey Green.

Melissa (Cheryl Kay) and Rick (Gregg Gomez Thomsen) are a young couple trying to transcend the bad influences of their poor neighborhood. When Rick, who is an ex-gang member, gets in trouble as the result of a friend's death, Melissa is taken advantage of by drug dealers and Rick must rescue her from the evil drug kingpin Steadman (Jim Brown).

CRIMINAL LAW

Pro. Robert MacLean and Hilary Heath for Hemdale; Hemdale *Dir.* Martin Campbell *Scr.* Mark Kasdan *Cine.* Philip Meheux *Ed.* Christopher Wimble *Mu.* Jerry Goldsmith *P.d.*

Curtis Schnell *R.t.* 112 min. *MPAA* R. *Cast:* Gary Oldman, Kevin Bacon, Karen Young, Joe Don Baker, Tess Harper, Ron Lea, Karen Wooldridge.

Ben Chase (Gary Oldman), a Boston defense attorney, is successful in obtaining an acquittal for Martin Thiel (Kevin Bacon), accused of rape and murder. Later developments convince Chase that Thiel is guilty. Horrified, Chase steps outside his role as lawyer to entrap the psychotic killer. Placing complex questions about lawyer ethics into a thriller framework, the film attempts to generate some disturbing reactions to the principal characters and the hypothetical situation.

CYBORG

Pro. Menahem Golan and Yoram Globus; Cannon Entertainment *Dir.* Albert Pyun *Scr.* Kitty Chalmers *Cine.* Philip Alan Waters *Ed.* Rozanne Zingale and Scott Stevenson *Mu.* Kevin Bassinson *P.d.* Douglas Leonard *S.d.* Yvonne Hegney *R.t.* 85 min. *MPAA* R. *Cast:* Jean-Claude Van Damme, Deborah Richter, Vincent Klyn, Alex Daniels, Dayle Haddon, Blaise Loong, Rolf Muller, Haley Peterson, Terrie Batson.

Set in a futuristic, bleak and trashy landscape, this film is basically a series of martial arts fights. The karate-kicking hero searches for the cure to a nasty plague, while also searching for the even nastier villain who brutally murdered his family.

DANCE OF THE DAMNED

Pro. Andy Ruben; Concorde Pictures *Dir.* Katt Shea Ruben *Scr.* Andy Ruben and Katt Shea Ruben *Cine.* Phedon Papamichael *Ed.* Carole Kravetz *Mu.* Gary Stockdale *P.d.* Stephen Greenberg *R.t.* 83 min. *MPAA* R. *Cast:* Starr Andreeff, Cyril O'Reilly, Deborah Ann Nassar, Maria Ford, Athen Worthy, Tom Ruben.

In despair over a court order barring her from contact with her son, a stripper (Starr Andreef) becomes involved with a handsome vampire (Cyril O'Reilly), who promises to kill her after a one-night stand.

DEAD BANG

Pro. Steve Roth for Lorimar Film Entertainment; Warner Bros. *Dir.* John Frankenheimer *Scr.* Robert Foster *Cine.* Gerry Fisher *Ed.* Robert F. Shugrue *Mu.* Gary Chang *P.d.* Ken Adam *A.d.* Richard Hudolin and Alan Manzer *S.d.* Art Parker *R.t.* 105 min. *MPAA* R. *Cast:* Don Johnson, Penelope Ann Miller, William Forsythe, Bob Balaban, Frank Military, Tate Donovan, Tim Reid.

A down-and-out Los Angeles cop, Jerry Beck (Don Johnson), gets involved in a big case when a fellow police officer is killed by white supremacists. Chasing the neo-Nazis to Oklahoma, he joins forces with the local, predominantly black police force, and the film ends with a shoot-out.

DEAD CALM (Australia, 1989)

Pro. Terry Hayes, Doug Mitchell, and George Miller; Warner Bros. *Dir.* Phillip Noyce *Scr.* Terry Hayes; based on the novel by Charles Williams *Cine.* Dean Semler *Ed.* Richard Francis-Bruce *Mu.* Graeme Revill *P.d.* Graham (Grace) Walker *R.t.* 96 min. *MPAA* R. *Cast:* Sam Neill, Nicole Kidman, Billy Zane.

As a young married couple begins a cruise aboard their private yacht to recover from the death of their infant son, they are confronted with a man who claims that all the passengers aboard his yacht died from food poisoning. While the disbelieving husband investigates, the strange man, in reality a deranged killer, overcomes the woman and seizes control of the yacht.

DEALERS (Great Britain, 1989)

Pro. William P. Cartlidge for Euston Films; Rank Organization *Dir.* Colin Bucksey *Scr.*

Andrew MacLear *Cine.* Peter Sinclair *Ed.* Jon Costelloe *Mu.* Richard Hartley *P.d.* Peter J. Hampton *R.t.* 89 min. *Cast:* Paul McGann, Rebecca DeMornay, Derrick O'Connor, John Castle, Paul Guilfoyle, Rosalind Bennett, Adrian Dunbar, Nicholas Hewetson, Sara Sugarman.

Daniel Pascoe (Paul McGann), an ambitious young man in the banking business, finds himself in competition with a beautiful young woman, Anna Schuman (Rebecca DeMornay), and romances her. The relationship develops against a background of mordant observations of contemporary obsessions with money.

DEEPSTAR SIX

Pro. Sean S. Cunningham and Patrick Markey; Tri-Star Pictures *Dir.* Sean S. Cunningham *Scr.* Lewis Abernathy and Geof Miller; based on a story by Abernathy *Cine.* Mac Ahlberg *Ed.* David Handman *Mu.* Harry Manfredini *P.d.* John Reinhart *A.d.* Larry E. Fulton and Don Diers *S.d.* Christina Volz *R.t.* 100 min. *MPAA* R. *Cast:* Taurean Blacque, Nancy Everhard, Greg Evigan, Miguel Ferrer, Nia Peeples, Matt McCoy, Cindy Pickett, Marius Weyers.

While trying to create a level launch site on the ocean floor for Navy missiles, the crew of a submarine disturbs a creature that has been dwelling there for eons. The creature attacks the crew and kills them one by one. Unless the remaining crew can get away, their craft will explode.

DISORGANIZED CRIME

Pro. Lynn Bigelow for Touchstone Pictures in association with Silver Screen Partners IV; Buena Vista *Dir.* Jim Kouf *Scr.* Jim Kouf *Cine.* Ron Garcia *Ed.* Frank Morriss and Dallas Puett *Mu.* David Newman *P.d.* Waldemar Kalinowski *A.d.* David Lubin *S.d.* Florence Fellman *R.t.* 101 min. *MPAA* R. *Cast:* Hoyt Axton, Corbin Bernsen, Ruben Blades, Fred Gwynne, Ed O'Neill, Lou Diamond Phillips, Daniel Roebuck, William Russ.

Four criminals wait for their escaped convict friend Frank Salazar (Corbin Bernsen) to appear in a Montana town where they have planned a bank robbery. While waiting, the four men get into trouble with the law. Meanwhile, Salazar and the police pursuing him become lost in the wilderness.

THE DISTRIBUTION OF LEAD

Pro. Charles Libin; Zeno Films *Dir.* Charles Libin *Scr.* Charles Libin *Cine.* Paul A. Cameron *Ed.* Charles Libin *Mu.* John Zorn *A.d.* Donna Vega *R.t.* 77 min. *Cast:* Katherine Rose, Ely Rowe, Chasen Ebrahimian, Derek Lynch, Corey Shaff, Pouran Esrafily, Ellen Berkenblit, Mindel Goldstein, Paul Libin.

Led by hardbitten Paula (Pouran Esrafily), a group of young business types hides out in a Manhattan apartment after an abortive corporate takeover attempt that resulted in murder. More violence follows as this intense low-budget work attempts to deal with various aspects of modern society.

DREAM A LITTLE DREAM

Pro. D. E. Eisenberg and Marc Rocco; Vestron Pictures *Dir.* Marc Rocco *Scr.* Daniel Jay Franklin, Marc Rocco, and D. E. Eisenberg *Cine.* King Baggot *Ed.* Russell Livingstone *Mu.* John William Dexter *P.d.* Matthew Jacobs *R.t.* 99 min. *MPAA* PG-13. *Cast:* Corey Feldman, Corey Haim, Meredith Salenger, Jason Robards, Piper Laurie, Harry Dean Stanton, William McNamara.

Two teenagers, Bobby (Corey Feldman) and Lainie (Meredith Salenger) collide in a bicycle accident; while unconscious, they take on the personalities of an older couple (Jason Robards and Piper Laurie).

THE DREAM TEAM

Pro. Christopher W. Knight for Imagine Entertainment; Universal *Dir.* Howard Zieff *Scr.* Jon Connolly and David Loucka *Cine.* Adam Holender *Ed.* C. Timothy O'Meara *Mu.* David McHugh *P.d.* Todd Hallowell *A.d.* Christopher Nowak and Greg Keen *S.d.* John Alan Hicks, Mike Harris, Robert James, Jaro Dick, Elena Kenney, and Dan Conley *R.t.* 113 min. *MPAA* PG-13. *Cast:* Michael Keaton, Christopher Lloyd, Peter Boyle, Stephen Furst, Dennis Boutsikaris, Lorraine Bracco, Milo O'Shea, Philip Bosco, James Remar, Jack Gilpin, Macintyre Dixon, Michel Lembeck.

Four psychiatric patients leave the hospital to attend a Yankees game with their freethinking therapist and are soon left to confront the outside world alone when the doctor becomes the target of murderers. The four soon learn to cope on the streets of New York City in a comical, high-spirited adventure.

EARTH GIRLS ARE EASY

Pro. Tony Garnett; Vestron Pictures *Dir.* Julien Temple *Scr.* Julie Brown, Charlie Coffey, and Terrence E. McNally *Cine.* Oliver Stapleton *Ed.* Richard Halsey *Mu.* Nile Rodgers *P.d.* Dennis Gassner *R.t.* 100 min. *MPAA* PG. *Cast:* Geena Davis, Jeff Goldblum, Jim Carrey, Damon Wayans, Julie Brown, Michael McKean, Charles Rocket, Larry Linville, Rick Overton.

When three aliens from Jhazzala, Mac (Jeff Goldblum), Wiploc (Jim Carrey), and Zeebo (Damon Wayans), crash in the swimming pool of an amiable manicurist, Valerie (Geena Davis), comic and romantic complications ensue, involving Valerie's boss, Candy (Julie Brown), and Valerie's boyfriend, Ted (Charles Rocket). Partly a satire on contemporary suburban life, the film also reflects director Julien Temple's background in music videos and affection for Hollywood musicals.

ECHOES OF PARADISE

Pro. Jane Scott; Quartet Films Inc. *Dir.* Phillip Noyce *Scr.* Jan Sharp *Cine.* Peter James *Ed.* Frans Vandenburg *Mu.* Bill Motzig *P.d.* Clarissa Patterson *R.t.* 106 min. *MPAA* R. *Cast:* Wendy Hughes, John Lone, Rod Mullinar, Peta Toppano, Steven Jacobs, Gillian Jones.

A housewife (Wendy Hughes), fed up with her adulterous husband, travels from her Australian home to Thailand, where she meets an attractive Balinese dancer (John Lone). The woman embarks on a romantic relationship with the dancer and learns a lot about herself along the way.

EDDIE AND THE CRUISERS II: EDDIE LIVES (Canada, 1989)

Pro. Stephane Reichel for Les Prods. Alliance; Scotti Bros. Pictures in association with Aurora Film Partners *Dir.* Jean-Claude Lord *Scr.* Charles Zev Cohen and Rick Doehring; based on characters created by P. F. Kluge *Cine.* Rene Verzier *Ed.* Jean-Guy Montpetite *Mu.* Marty Simon and Leon Aronson *A.d.* Dominic Ricard *S.d.* Gilles Aird *R.t.* 103 min. *MPAA* PG-13. *Cast:* Michael Pare, Marina Orsini, Bernie Coulson, Matthew Laurance, Michael Rhoades, Anthony Sherwood, Mark Holmes, David Matheson, Paul Markle, Kate Lynch, Harvey Atkin, Vlasta Vrana, Larry King, Bo Diddley, Martha Quinn, Merrill Shindler, Sunny Joe White, Michael (Tunes) Antunes.

Drop-out rock-and-roll superstar Eddie Wilson (Michael Pare), long presumed dead though the body was never found, has been living under a new identity as a Montreal construction worker. In this sequel, he returns to music and reveals his true identity during a climactic concert. John Cafferty's songs are a central focus of the drama.

EDGE OF SANITY (Great Britain and Hungary, 1989)

Pro. Edward Simons and Harry Alan Towers; Millimeter Films *Dir.* Gerard Kikoine *Scr.*

J. P. Felix and Ron Raley; based on *The Strange Case of Dr. Jekyll and Mr. Hyde*, by Robert Louis Stevenson   *Cine.* Tony Spratling   *Ed.* Malcolm Cooke   *Mu.* Frederic Talgorn   *P.d.* Jean Charles Dedieu   *A.d.* Fred Carter and Tivadar Bertalan   *R.t.* 90 min.   *MPAA* R.   *Cast:* Anthony Perkins, Glynis Barber, Sarah Maur-Thorp, David Lodge, Ben Cole, Ray Jewers, Jill Melford, Lisa Davis, Noel Coleman.

In this reworking of the Jekyll and Hyde tale, Mr. Hyde's rampages are caused by Dr. Jekyll's abuse of cocaine—abuse made easier by his pet monkey's accidental invention of freebasing. This Mr. Hyde also turns out to be Jack the Ripper.

ERIK THE VIKING (Great Britain, 1989)

Pro. John Goldstone for John Goldstone/Prominent Features in association with Svensk Filmindustri; Orion Pictures   *Dir.* Terry Jones   *Scr.* Terry Jones   *Cine.* Ian Wilson   *Ed.* George Akers   *Mu.* Neil Innes   *P.d.* John Beard   *A.d.* Gavin Bocquet and Roger Cain   *R.t.* 103 min.   *MPAA* PG-13.   *Cast:* Tim Robbins, Gary Cady, Mickey Rooney, Eartha Kitt, Terry Jones, Imogen Stubbs, John Cleese, Anthony Sher, John Gordon Sinclair, Samantha Bond, Tim McInnerny, Richard Ridings, Freddie Jones, Charles McKeown, Danny Schiller, Tsutomu Sekine.

Director Terry Jones, who helmed several satires of historical costume dramas for the Monty Python group, returns to that genre with the story of Erik (Tim Robbins), a Viking warrior who idealistically wants to end the age of rape and pillage, and who makes an eventful journey to accomplish his goal.

ESCAPE FROM SAFEHAVEN

Pro. Steven Mackler for Avalon; SVS Films   *Dir.* Brian Thomas Jones and James McCalmont   *Scr.* Brian Thomas Jones and James McCalmont; based on a story by Mark Bishop and Ethan Reiff   *Cine.* James McCalmont   *Ed.* Brian O'Hara   *Mu.* Taj   *P.d.* Mikhail Fishgoyt   *R.t.* 85 min.   *MPAA* R.   *Cast:* Rick Gianasi, John Wittenbauer, Roy MacArthur, William Beckwith, Sammi Gavich, Mollie O'Mara, Marcus Powell, Jessica Dublin, Sharon Shahinian, Damon Clarke, Tere Malson, Rick Siler.

Set in the future after some unknown global disaster and filmed in gutted sections of the Bronx, *Escape from Safehaven* follows the rebellion of the oppressed residents of Safehaven 186 against the gang members who rule the community.

THE EVERLASTING SECRET FAMILY (Australia, 1989)

Pro. Michael Thornhill for Anthony I Ginnane; International Film Exchange   *Dir.* Michael Thornhill   *Scr.* Frank Moorhouse; based on his collection of short stories *The Everlasting Secret Family and Other Secrets*   *Cine.* Julian Penney   *Ed.* Pam Barnetta   *A.d.* Peta Lawson   *R.t.* 93 min.   *Cast:* Arthur Dignam, Mark Lee, Heather Mitchell, John Meillon, Dennis Miller, Paul Goddard.

A member of a secret homosexual society, a Senator (Arthur Dignam) recruits a boy (Mark Lee) out of a private school to become his lover. The young man becomes adept at manipulating people in his quest for eternal youth, which he believes is the source of his control over others.

FAKEBOOK

Pro. Ralph Toporoff; Vested Interests/Fakebook   *Dir.* Ralph Toporoff   *Scr.* Gilbert Girion; based on a story by Ralph Toporoff and Girion   *Cine.* Joey Forsyte   *Ed.* Jack Haigis   *Mu.* Larry Schanker   *P.d.* Charles Lagola   *A.d.* Katharine Fredericks   *R.t.* 96 min.   *Cast:* Peter MacNicol, Carl Capotorto, Tim Guiness, Bill Christopher-Myers, Jonathan Walker, Charlotte d'Amboise, Louis Guss, Zohra Lampert, Margaret Devine, Trini Alvarado.

In the early 1960's, Jack Solow (Peter MacNicol) tries to launch a jazz band while romancing a dancer, Benita (Charlotte d'Amboise). After a dispiriting year of one dull job after another, Jack and his four fellow musicians give up the band.

FAR FROM HOME

Pro. Donald P. Borchers for Lightning Pictures; Vestron Pictures *Dir.* Meiert Avis *Scr.* Tommy Lee Wallace; based on a story by Ted Gershuny *Cine.* Paul Elliott *Ed.* Marc Grossman *Mu.* Jonathan Elias *P.d.* Victoria Paul *R.t.* 86 min. *MPAA* R. *Cast:* Matt Frewer, Drew Barrymore, Richard Masur, Karen Austin, Susan Tyrrell, Anthony Rapp, Jennifer Tilly, Andras Jones, Dick Miler, Connie Sawyer, Stephanie Walski, Teri Weigel.

A mad killer terrorizes Banco, Nevada, residents as well as vacationer Charlie Cross (Matt Frewer) and his attractive daughter Joleen (Drew Barrymore). Director Avis' first film uses familiar character types and plot elements, while serving to initiate child-star Barrymore into adult roles.

FAREWELL TO THE KING

Pro. Albert S. Ruddy and Andre Morgan for Vestron Entertainment; Ariane Distribution and Orion Pictures *Dir.* John Milius *Scr.* John Milius; based on a novel by Pierre Schoendoerffer *Cine.* Dean Semler *Ed.* C. Timothy O'Meara and Anne V. Coates *Mu.* Basil Poledouris *A.d.* Bernard Hides and Gil Parrondo *R.t.* 117 min. *MPAA* PG-13. *Cast:* Nick Nolte, Nigel Havers, James Fox, Marilyn Tokuda, Frank MacRae, Aki Aleong, William Wise, Gerry Lopez, Marius Weyers, Elan Oberon, Choy Chan Wing.

A former sergeant (Nick Nolte) who went AWOL after General Douglas MacArthur's defeat at Corregidor has become the leader of a tribe of Borneo jungle natives. Wanting no part of the approaching conflict between the Allies and the Japanese, he finally fights the Japanese after they have killed his family.

FAST FOOD

Pro. Stan Wakefield and Michael A. Simpson for Double Helix Films; Fries Entertainment *Dir.* Michael A. Simpson *Scr.* Clark Brandon and Lanny Horn; based on a story by Scott B. Sowers and Jim Basile *Cine.* Bill Mills *Ed.* John D. Allen *Mu.* Iris Gillon *A.d.* Shad Leach *S.d.* Julie Malm *R.t.* 92 min. *MPAA* PG-13. *Cast:* Clark Brandon, Randal Patrick, Tracy Griffith, Michael J. Pollard, Lanny Horn, Jim Varney, Blake Clark, Traci Lords, Pamela Springsteen, Randi Layne, Kevin McCarthy.

Auggie (Clark Brandon) and Drew (Randal Patrick), two youthful con men recently expelled from college, come to the aid of an attractive gas-station owner, Samantha (Tracy Griffith), whose property is on the verge of being taken over by a fast food entrepreneur, "Wrangler Bob" Bundy (Jim Varney). Creating their own successful hamburger laced with an aphrodisiac, the two heroes redeem themselves by the fadeout of this good-natured comedy.

FAT MAN AND LITTLE BOY

Pro. Tony Garnett for Lightmotive; Paramount Pictures *Dir.* Roland Joffe *Scr.* Bruce Robinson and Roland Joffe; based on a story by Robinson *Cine.* Vilmos Zsigmond *Ed.* Francoise Bonnot *Mu.* Ennio Morricone *P.d.* Gregg Fonseca *A.d.* Peter Landsdown Smith and Larry E. Fulton *S.d.* Dorree Cooper *R.t.* 126 min. *MPAA* PG-13. *Cast:* Paul Newman, Dwight Schultz, Bonnie Bedelia, John Cusack, Laura Dern, Ron Frazier, John C. McGinley, Nathasha Richardson, Ron Vawter.

The development of the atomic bomb during World War II in what was known as the Manhattan Project is traced through a story which contrasts the personalities of two participants—J. Robert Oppenheimer (Dwight Schultz), the scientist picked to lead the team which builds the bomb, and General Groves (Paul Newman), the military man who pushes the project forward.

FEAR, ANXIETY AND DEPRESSION

Pro. Stanley Wlodowski, Steve Golin, and Joni Sighvatsson for Propaganda Films; Samuel Goldwyn Co. *Dir.* Todd Solondz *Scr.* Todd Solondz *Cine.* Stefan Czapsky *Ed.* Peter Austin, Emily Paine, and Barry Rubinow *Mu.* Karyn Rachtman, Joe Romano, and Moogy Klingman *P.d.* Marek Dobrowolski *A.d.* Susan Block *R.t.* 85 min. *Cast:* Todd Solondz, Max Cantor, Alexandra Gersten, Jane Hamper, Stanley Tucci.

Ira (Todd Solondz), a youthful playwright, is pursued by a grasping young woman, Janice (Alexandra Gersten), in this comedy which attempts to follow in the tradition of Woody Allen.

FISTFIGHTER

Pro. Carlos Vasallo for Izaro Films, Eagle Film, and Esme Productions; Taurus Entertainment *Dir.* Frank Zuniga *Scr.* Max Bloom; based on a story by Carlos Vasallo *Cine.* Hans Burman *Ed.* Drake Silliman *Mu.* Emiliano Redondo *S.d.* Francisco Magallon and Seth Santacruz *R.t.* 100 min. *MPAA* R. *Cast:* George Rivero, Edward Albert, Mike Connors, Brenda Bakke, Matthias Hues, Simon Andreu.

C. J. Thunderbird (George Rivero), a bare knuckles street fighter, journeys to a corrupt South American country to avenge a friend, and joins with a peg-legged ex-fighter named Punchy (Edward Albert) to bring down the local criminals who are causing both men trouble. Shot in both Spanish and English versions, the action drama relies on some knowing actors to bring dimension to the characters while emphasizing the violence of its many fights.

THE FLY II

Pro. Steven-Charles Jaffe for Brooksfilms; Twentieth Century-Fox *Dir.* Chris Walas *Scr.* Mick Garris, Jim Wheat, Ken Wheat, and Frank Darabont; based on a story by Mick Garris and characters created by George Langelaan *Cine.* Robin Vidgeon *Ed.* Sean Barton *Mu.* Christopher Young *P.d.* Michael S. Bolton *A.d.* Sandy Cochrane *S.d.* Rose Mari McSherry *R.t.* 105 min. *MPAA* R. *Cast:* Eric Stoltz, Daphne Zuniga, Lee Richardson, John Getz, Frank Turner, Ann Marie Lee, Gary Chalk, Saffron Henderson, Harley Cross, Matthew Moore.

The Fly II is a sequel to *The Fly,* the 1986 hit remake of the 1958 science fiction classic of the same name. Eric Stoltz plays Martin Brundle, the son of the mutated scientist of the 1986 film, and he has genetically inherited his father's problem. This gory sequel pits the transformed but humane Brundle against a human but beastly evil scientist who had worked with his father.

FOOD OF THE GODS II

Pro. David Mitchell and Damian Lee for Carolco Pictures; Concorde-Centaur Films *Dir.* Damian Lee *Scr.* Richard Bennett and E. Kim Brewster *Cine.* Curtis Petersen *Mu.* Parsons/Haines *R.t.* 91 min. *MPAA* R. *Cast:* Paul Coufos, Lisa Schrage, Colin Fox, Frank Moore, Real Andrews, Jackie Burroughs, Stuart Hughes.

Protestors against animal research in the film's opening scenes should consider the rest of the narrative poetic justice as giant rats—grown to monstrous size because of an experimental growth serum—terrorize campus residents. This loose remake of the 1976 film relies on crudely realized effects.

FREE AND EASY (Japan, 1989)

Pro. Shochiku Presentation *Dir.* Tomio Kuriyama *Scr.* Yoji Yamada and Akira Momoi; based on a comic book series by Juzo Yamazaki and Kenichi Kitami *Cine.* Kosuke Yasuda *A.d.* Shigemori Shigeta *R.t.* 93 min. *Cast:* Toshiyuki Nishida, Eri Ishida, Rentaro Mikuni, Yatsuko Tanami, Kei Tani.

This film shows the friendship that develops between a recently transferred construction-company clerk and his new employer as they undertake a fishing trip at the clerk's suggestion. This relationship, seemingly unlikely in the Japanese corporate world, is possible because the employee is unaware of his boss's identity, kept secret by the boss in order to maintain the friendship. All is neatly resolved after the secret is discovered.

FRIDAY THE 13TH PART VIII: JASON TAKES MANHATTAN

Pro. Randolph Cheveldave for Horror Inc.; Paramount Pictures *Dir.* Rob Hedden *Scr.* Rob Hedden *Cine.* Bryan England *Ed.* Steve Mirkovich *Mu.* Fred Mollin *P.d.* David Fischer *S.d.* Linda Vipond *R.t.* 100 min. *MPAA* R. *Cast:* Jensen Daggett, Scott Reeves, Peter Mark Richman, Barbara Bingham, V. C. Dupree, Kane Hodder, Sharlene Martin, Martin Cummins, Timothy Burr Mirkovich, Amber Pawlick.

Jason (Kane Hodder), the hockey-masked killer from Camp Crystal Lake, joins a group of teenagers on a boat trip to New York so that the basic plot line of the first seven films in this series may be resurrected once again.

FUN DOWN THERE

Pro. Roger Stigliano for Angelina *Dir.* Roger Stigliano *Scr.* Roger Stigliano *Cine.* Peggy Ahwesh and Eric Saks *Ed.* Roger Stigliano and Keith Sanborn *Mu.* James Baker, Wayne Hammond *P.d.* Roger Stigliano *R.t.* 85 min. *Cast:* Michael Waite, Nicholas B. Nagourney, Martin Goldin, Jeanne Smith, Betty Waite, Harold Waite, Yvonne Fisher, Gretschen Somerville, Gary Onsum, Paul Saindon, Kenneth R. Clarke, Judy Joseph, Kayla Serotti, Caroline Paddock, Howard Roxs, Richard Hailey.

A coming-of-age gay love story about a young man (Michael Waite) from an upstate New York farm who goes to New York City. Once in Manhattan he discovers sex, love, and a whole new life-style with a healthy attitude that is mindful of AIDS and safe sex.

THE GAME

Pro. Curtis Brown for Curtis Films; Visual Perspectives *Dir.* Curtis Brown *Scr.* Julia Wilson and Curtis Brown; based on a story by Brown *Cine.* Paul Gibson *Ed.* Gloria Whittemore and Daniel Barrientos *Mu.* Julia Wilson *P.d.* Walter Jorgenson *R.t.* 116 min. *Cast:* Curtis Brown, Richard Lee Ross, Vaness Shaw, Billy Williams, Charles Timm, Michael Murphy, Dick Biel, Carolina Beaumont, Bruce Grossberg, Damon Clarke, Erick Shawn, Erick Coleman, Joanna Wahl, Rick Siler, Claire Waters, Jerome King.

Leon Hunter (Curtis Brown), an ambitious black man working for a public relations firm, becomes obsessive and amoral in his attempt to get a white candidate for mayor, Carl Rydell (Dick Biel), elected. Debuting filmmaker Brown attempts a complex look at race relations and the politics of power in his native New York.

GINGER ALE AFTERNOON

Pro. Susan Hillary Shapiro and Rafal Zielinski for NeoPictures *Dir.* Rafal Zielinski *Scr.* Gina Wendkos; based on her play *Cine.* Yuri Neyman *Ed.* Lorenzo De Stefano *Mu.* Willie Dixon *P.d.* Michael Helmy *A.d.* Vally Mestroni *R.t.* 94 min. *Cast:* Dana Andersen, John M. Jackson, Yeardly Smith.

Living in a trailer court, an unhappily married couple, Jesse (Dana Andersen) and Hank Mickers (John M. Jackson), spend most of their time quarreling while awaiting their baby's birth. Jesse discovers that Hank is having an affair with Bonnie (Yeardly Smith), but the Mickers reconcile in time for the blessed event.

GLEAMING THE CUBE

Pro. Lawrence Turman and David Foster; Twentieth Century-Fox *Dir.* Graeme Clifford *Scr.* Michael Tolin *Cine.* Reed Smoot *Ed.* John Wright *Mu.* Jay Ferguson *P.d.* John Muto *A.d.*

Dan Webster *S.d.* Susan Emshwiller *R.t.* 105 min. *MPAA* PG-13. *Cast:* Christian Slater, Steven Bauer, Le Tuan, Min Luong, Art Chudabala, Richard Herd.

An Orange County, California, kid (Christian Slater), who is a skateboarding enthusiast, determines to find out who killed his adopted Vietnamese brother (Art Chudabala).

GOD'S WILL

Pro. Julia Cameron; Power and Light Production *Dir.* Julia Cameron *Scr.* Julia Cameron *Cine.* William Nusbaum *Mu.* Christopher "Hambone" Cameron *R.t.* 100 min. *Cast:* Marge Kotlisky, Daniel Region, Laura Margolis, Domenica Cameron-Scorsese, Linda Edmond, Mitchell Canoff, Holly Fulger, Tim Hopper, Tony Lincoln, Nick Faust.

A show business couple die suddenly, and they find themselves in heaven arguing about their daughter's future. She is still alive and in the custody of the deceased couple's new spouses (Linda Edmond and Mitchell Canoff).

GROSS ANATOMY

Pro. Howard Rosenman and Debra Hill for Hill/Rosenman Productions; Touchstone Pictures in association with Silver Screen Partners IV *Dir.* Thom Eberhardt *Scr.* Ron Nyswander and Mark Spragg; based on a story by Mark Spragg, Howard Rosenman, Alan Jay Glueckman, and Stanley Isaacs *Cine.* Steve Yaconelli *Ed.* Bud Smith and Scott Smith *Mu.* David Newman *P.d.* William F. Matthews *A.d.* P. Michael Jonston *S.d.* Catherine Mann *R.t.* 113 min. *MPAA* PG-13. *Cast:* Matthew Modine, Daphne Zuniga, Christine Lahti, Todd Field, John Scott Clough, Alice Carter, Robert Desiderio, Zakes Mokae, J. C. Quinn, Rutanya Alda.

Five would-be doctors go through medical school. The focus is principally on selfish, flippant Joe Slovak (Matthew Modine), but his fellow students, including initially aloof Laurie (Daphne Zuniga), whom he successfully romances, also receive attention, as does an acerbic professor, Rachel Woodruff (Christine Lahti).

THE GUESTS OF HOTEL ASTORIA (Turkey, 1989)

Pro. Rafigh Pouya for Take 7; Melior Films *Dir.* Reza Alamehzadeh *Scr.* Reza Alamehzadeh *Cine.* Charles Burnett *Mu.* Esfandiar Monfaredzadeh *R.t.* 112 min. *Cast:* Shohreh Aghadashloo, Mohsen Marzban, Hooshang Touzi, Vida Ghahremany, Bahram Vatanparast, Vacheh Mangasarian, Soraya Mophid, Naser Rahmany Nejad, Kamran Nozad.

The lives of Iranian refugees fleeing the Khomeini regime are intertwined as they wind up in a hotel in Istanbul. Trouble and danger continue to plague them, though intimations of possible joy in the future are also part of the narrative. The ordeals suffered by the protagonists were based on writer-director Reza Alamehzadeh's own experiences and those of his friends.

HALLOWEEN V: THE REVENGE OF MICHAEL MYERS

Pro. Ramsey Thomas for Magnum Pictures; Galaxy International *Dir.* Dominique Othenin-Girard *Scr.* Michael Jacobs, Dominique Othenin-Girard, and Shem Bitterman *Cine.* Robert Draper *Ed.* Charles Tetoni *Mu.* Alan Howarth (Halloween theme by John Carpenter) *P.d.* Brenton Swift *S.d.* Steve Lee and Chava Danielson *R.t.* 96 min. *MPAA* R. *Cast:* Donald Pleasence, Danielle Harris, Wendy Kaplan, Ellie Cornell, Donald L. Shanks, Jeffrey Landman, Beau Starr, Betty Carvalho, Tamara Glynn.

The evil and insane—and seemingly unkillable—Michael Myers (Donald L. Shanks) once more returns to his small hometown in Illinois to terrorize and kill lustful teenagers, this time aided by his essentially innocent nine-year-old niece Jamie (Danielle Harris), whose mind is intermittently under his control. Inevitably, Dr. Loomis (Donald Pleasence) once more tries to stop Michael, the long-time object of his obsession.

HANUSSEN (Hungary and Germany, 1989)
Pro. Objektir Studio, CCC Filmkunst, 2DF, Hungarofilm and Mokep *Dir.* Istvan Szabo *Scr.* Istvan Szabo and Peter Dobai *Cine.* Lajos Koltai *R.t.* 117 min. *MPAA* R. *Cast:* Klaus Maria Brandauer, Erland Josephson, Karoly Eperjes, Ildiko Bansagi, Walter Schmidinger.

The film, which was nominated for Best Foreign-Language Film by the Academy of Motion Picture Arts and Sciences, tells the post-World War I story of Schneider (Klaus Maria Brandauer), a former vaudevillian, who teams up with a demobilized officer, Nowotny (Karoly Eperjes), in order to work as a stage hypnotist and seer. Schneider changes his name to Hanussen, and he becomes caught up in the Nazi rise to power.

HEART OF DIXIE
Pro. Steve Tisch; Orion Pictures *Dir.* Martin Davidson *Scr.* Tom McCown; based on the novel *Heartbreak Hotel*, by Anne Rivers Siddons *Cine.* Robert Elswit *Ed.* Bonnie Koehler *Mu.* Kenny Vance *P.d.* Glenda Ganis *A.d.* Sharon Seymour *R.t.* 95 min. *MPAA* PG. *Cast:* Ally Sheedy, Virginia Madsen, Phoebe Cates, Treat Williams, Don Michael Paul, Kyle Secor, Francesca Roberts, Peter Berg, Jenny Robertson, Lisa Zane, Ashley Gardner, Kurtwood Smith, Richard Bradford, Barbara Babcock.

In 1957 at a Southern university, Maggie (Ally Sheedy) initially shares the narrow, if intensely felt, interests and values of her sorority sisters. But a violent racial incident at a concert radicalizes her and she reports on it in the school newspaper, for which she is expelled. Civil rights share the focus with a caustic look at sorority rites in this evocation of a period of change.

HEART OF MIDNIGHT
Pro. Andrew Gaty; The Samuel Goldwyn Co. *Dir.* Matthew Chapman *Scr.* Matthew Chapman *Cine.* Ray Rivas *Ed.* Penelope Shaw *P.d.* Gene Rudolf *R.t.* 93 min. *MPAA* R. *Cast:* Jennifer Jason Leigh, Peter Coyote, Gale Mayron, Sam Schacht, Denise Dummont, Frank Stallone, Steve Buscemi.

This suspense melodrama stars Jennifer Jason Leigh as a young woman who inherits a rundown Charleston nightclub. Strange events occur, and it is not clear whether these things really happen or are the result of the young woman's emotional state.

HELL HIGH (also known as *Raging Fury*)
Pro. David Steinman and Douglas Grossman; Metro-Goldwyn-Mayer Enterprises *Dir.* Douglas Grossman *Scr.* Leo Evans and Douglas Grossman *Cine.* Steven Fierberg *Ed.* Claire Simpson-Crozier and Greg Sheldon *Mu.* Rich Macar and Christopher Hyans-Hart *A.d.* William Bilowit and Joan Brockschmidt *R.t.* 79 min. *MPAA* R. *Cast:* Christopher Stryker, Maureen Mooney, Christopher Cousins, Millie Prezioso, Jason Brill, Kathy Rossetter, J. R. Horne, Daniel Beer, Karen Russell, Webster Whinery.

A young girl witnesses a double murder in a nearby swamp. Later, as a high school biology teacher, she becomes the victim of her students, who attempt to rape her. Left for dead, she comes back for revenge.

HELLBENT (also known as *Rock n' Roll Meller*)
Pro. Louise Jaffe; Hellbent *Dir.* Richard Casey *Scr.* Richard Casey *Cine.* Jim Gillie *Ed.* Matthew Harrison and Richard Casey *Mu.* Greg Burk, Mark Wheaton, and Trotsky Icepick *A.d.* Fred Wasser and Richard Scully *R.t.* 87 min. *Cast:* Phil Ward, Lyn Levand, Cheryl Slean, David Marciano, James Orr, Phil Therrien, Paul Greenstein, Leigh Decio, Stanley Wells, Daniel W. Devorkin, Steve Devorkin.

Hellbent highlights the Los Angeles rock and roll scene, as Lemmy (Phil Ward) trades his soul to the owner of the Bar Sinister, Tanas (David Marciano), in exchange for a kickstart to his career. The expected change never seems to take place as Lemmy spends his time taking drugs and avoiding the bloodshed caused by Tanas' gang.

HER ALIBI

Pro. Keith Barish; Warner Bros.   *Dir.* Bruce Beresford   *Scr.* Charlie Peters   *Cine.* Freddie Francis   *Ed.* Anne Goursaud   *Mu.* Georges Delerue   *P.d.* Henry Bumstead   *A.d.* Steve Walker   *S.d.* James W. Payne   *R.t.* 94 min.   *MPAA* PG.   *Cast:* Tom Selleck, Paulina Porizkova, William Daniels, James Farentino, Hurd Hatfield, Ronald Guttman, Victor Argo, Patrick Wayne, Tess Harper.

A successful mystery writer (Tom Selleck) suffering from writer's block searches the courts looking for ideas and finds one in the form of a beautiful young woman (Paulina Porizkova) who is being arraigned for murder. Claiming that he was with her on the night of the murder, he becomes her alibi and is given custody of her. He takes her to his country house but begins to have doubts about her innocence.

HIT LIST

Pro. Paul Hertzberg; New Line Cinema   *Dir.* William Lustig   *Scr.* John Goff and Peter Brosnan   *Cine.* James Lemmo   *Ed.* David Kern   *Mu.* Gary Schyman   *A.d.* Pamela Marcotte   *S.d.* Michael Warga   *R.t.* 87 min.   *MPAA* R.   *Cast:* Jan-Michael Vincent, Leo Rossi, Lance Henriksen, Charles Napier, Rip Torn, Jere Burns, Ken Lerner, Harriet Hall, Junior Richard, Jack Andreozzi, Harold Sylvester.

A hit man (Lance Henriksen) for a mafioso (Rip Torn) goes to the wrong address and kidnaps the son of Jack Collins (Jan-Michael Vincent). Collins' quest to rescue his son makes up the bulk of this action-adventure tale.

THE HORROR SHOW

Pro. Sean S. Cunningham for United Artists Pictures; Metro-Goldwyn-Mayer/United Artists   *Dir.* James Isaac   *Scr.* Alan Smithee (Allyn Warner) and Leslie Bohem   *Cine.* Mac Ahlberg   *Ed.* Edward Anton   *Mu.* Harry Manfredini   *R.t.* 95 min.   *MPAA* R.   *Cast:* Lance Henriksen, Brion James, Rita Taggart, Dedee Pfeiffer, Aron Eisenberg, Thom Bray, Matt Clark, David Oliver, Terry Alexander, Lewis Arquette, Lawrence Tierney, Alvy Moore.

After maniacal killer Max Jenke (Brion James) is executed, his vengeful spirit causes problems for the detective, Lucas McCarthy (Lance Henriksen), who arrested him.

HOW I GOT INTO COLLEGE

Pro. Michael Shamberg for Twentieth Century-Fox; Twentieth Century-Fox   *Dir.* Savage Steve Holland   *Scr.* Terrel Seltzer   *Cine.* Robert Elswit   *Ed.* Sonya Sones Tramer and Kaja Fehr   *Mu.* Joseph Vitarelli   *P.d.* Ida Random   *A.d.* Richard Reynolds   *S.d.* Kathe Klopp   *R.t.* 89 min.   *MPAA* PG-13.   *Cast:* Anthony Edwards, Corey Parker, Lara Flynn Boyle, Finn Carter, Charles Rocket, Christopher Rydell, Brian-Doyle Murray, Tichina Arnold, Bill Raymond, Philip Baker Hall.

High school students, principally the uncharismatic but likeable Marlon (Corey Parker), struggle against SAT exams and college admissions boards, while engaging in now familiar classroom humor. The quirky personality evident in director Savage Steve Holland's previous films is again present in this modest effort.

HOW TO GET AHEAD IN ADVERTISING (Great Britain, 1989)

Pro. David Wimbury for Hand Made Films; Warner Bros.   *Dir.* Bruce Robinson   *Scr.* Bruce Robinson   *Cine.* Peter Hannan   *Ed.* Alan Strachan   *Mu.* David Dundas and Rick Wentworth   *P.d.* Michael Pickwoad   *A.d.* Henry Harris   *R.t.* 95 min.   *Cast:* Richard E. Grant, Rachel Ward, Richard Wilson, Jacqueline Tong, John Shrapnel, Susan Wooldridge, Mick Ford, Jacqueline Pearce, Roddy Maude-Roxby.

British advertising executive Bagley (Richard E. Grant) becomes so obsessed with a pimple-cream campaign on which he is working that a boil appears on his own neck. The boil grows, begins to talk, and takes on all of Bagley's unsavory personality traits as well as his appearance. In surgery, the boil persuades the doctors to remove Bagley, but the doctors leave a small part so that Bagley is now a boil on the boil.

A HUNGARIAN FAIRY TALE (Hungary, 1989)

Pro. MD Wax/Courier Films *Dir.* Gyula Gazdag *Scr.* Gyula Gazdag and Miklos Gyorffy *Cine.* Elemer Ragalyi *Ed.* Julia Sivo *Mu.* Istvan Martha *R.t.* 97 min. *Cast:* David Vermes, Maria Varga, Frantisek Husak.

After a man and woman conceive a child and then part forever, the woman learns that Hungarian law demands that she file a birth certificate with a fictitious name for the father. She uses the name of the civil servant supervising her case; the latter also prepares a secret certificate that will eventually inform the boy of the fictitious name. When the boy is suddenly orphaned, he goes in search of his father. This sweet-natured fantasy is imbued with a satirical tone toward Hungarian bureaucracy that is characteristic of director Gyula Gazdag.

I, MADMAN

Pro. Rafael Eisenman for Sarlvi/Diamant; Trans World Entertainment *Dir.* Tibor Takacs *Scr.* David Chaskin *Cine.* Bryan England *Ed.* Marcus Manton *Mu.* Michael Hoenig *P.d.* Ron Wilson and Matthew Jacobs *R.t.* 89 min. *MPAA* R. *Cast:* Jenny Wright, Clayton Rohner, Randall William Cook, Steven Memel, Stephanie Hodge, Bruce Wagner.

An acting student (Jenny Wright) who works in an antiquarian bookstore has trouble convincing Richard (Clayton Rohner), her boyfriend and also a police officer, that a series of grisly murders resulted from the nefarious plottings of novelist Malcolm Brand (Randall William Cook).

I WANT TO GO HOME (France, 1989)

Pro. Marin Karmitz for MK2 productions and Films A2/La SEPT; MK2 *Dir.* Alain Resnais *Scr.* Jules Feiffer *Cine.* Charlie Van Damme *Ed.* Albert Jurgenson *Mu.* John Kander *A.d.* Jacques Sauinier *R.t.* 105 min. *Cast:* Adolph Green, Gérard Depardieu, Linda Lavin, Laura Benson, Micheline Presle, Geraldine Chaplin, John Ashton, Caroline Sihol, Francois-Eric Gendron.

A cartoonist, Joey Wellman (Adolph Green), travels to France for an exhibition that includes his work. He is motivated by a desire to reconcile with his daughter Elise (Laura Benson), who is in love with a teacher (Gérard Depardieu) who ardently admires her father.

ICE HOUSE

Pro. Bo Brinkman for Cactus Films; Upfront Films *Dir.* Eagle Pennell *Scr.* Bo Brinkman; based on his play *Ice House Heat Waves* *Cine.* Brown Cooper *Ed.* John Murray *Mu.* Carmen Yates and Tony Fortuna *P.d.* Lynn Ruth Appel *R.t.* 77 min. *Cast:* Melissa Gilbert, Bo Brinkman, Andreas Manolikakis, Lynn Miller, Buddy Quaid, Nikki Letts.

Pake (Bo Brinkman), a drifter from Texas, spends a night in a Los Angeles hotel room trying to persuade former girlfriend Kay (Melissa Gilbert) to go home with him and start a new life. A play-to-film adaptation by Brinkman, the work is primarily a very intense study of character, though it is opened up with flashbacks.

IDENTITY CRISIS

Pro. Melvin Van Peebles; Block & Chip Productions *Dir.* Melvin Van Peebles *Scr.* Mario Van Peebles *Cine.* Jim Hinton *Ed.* Victor Kanefsky and Melvin Van Peebles *Mu.* E. Pearson *R.t.* 90 min. *Cast:* Mario Van Peebles, Ilan Mitchell-Smith, Shelly Burch, Richard

Fancy, Nicholas Kepros, Richard Clarke, Rick Aviles, Tab Thacker.

For this action comedy, the father and son team of director Melvin Van Peebles and writer-star Mario Van Peebles use an absurd story of a French fashion designer (Richard Fancy) being reincarnated in the youthful body of black rapper Chilly D. (Mario Van Peebles) after being murdered. The slain man, while alternating personalities, solves the mystery of the killing with the aid of his son Sebastian (Ilan Mitchell-Smith) while the filmmakers satirize all available targets.

AN INNOCENT MAN

Pro. Ted Field and Robert W. Cort for Touchstone Pictures; Buena Vista in association with Silver Screen Partners IV *Dir.* Peter Yates *Scr.* Larry Brothers *Cine.* William A. Fraker *Ed.* Stephen A. Rotter and William S. Scharf *Mu.* Howard Shore *P.d.* Stuart Wurtzel *A.d.* Frank Richwood *S.d.* Chris A. Butler *R.t.* 113 min. *MPAA* R. *Cast:* Tom Selleck, F. Murray Abraham, Laila Robins, David Rasche, Richard Young, Badja Djola, Todd Graff.

Framed for cocaine dealing and sent to prison, solid citizen Jimmie Rainwood (Tom Selleck) is brutalized by the experience but taught to survive by a hardened fellow convict, Virgil Cane (F. Murray Abraham). Upon his release, Rainwood seeks revenge against the two corrupt vice detectives (David Rasche, Richard Young) who set him up.

THE IRON TRIANGLE

Pro. Tony Scotti and Angela P. Schapiro for Eurobrothers in association with International Video Entertainment; Scotti Bros. Entertainment *Dir.* Eric Weston *Scr.* Eric Weston, John Bushelman, and Larry Hilbrand, narration written by Marshall Drazen *Cine.* Irv Goodnoff *Ed.* Roy Watts *Mu.* Michael Lloyd, John D'Andrea, and Nick Strimple *P.d.* Errol Kelly *R.t.* 91 min. *MPAA* R. *Cast:* Beau Bridges, Haing S. Ngor, Johnny Hallyday, Liem Whatley, James Ishida, Ping Wu, Iilana B'tiste.

This film takes place during the Vietnamese War but with a twist: a sympathetic perspective is given to the Viet Cong, and the South Vietnamese are shown as cold-blooded and political. A captured American soldier (Beau Bridges) is saved from death at the hands of an ambitious Viet Cong guerrilla by an idealistic Viet Cong soldier (Liem Whatley). As they make their way back to the Viet Cong camp, the two learn a wary camaraderie and respect for each other.

IT HAD TO BE YOU

Pro. Richard Abramson and Tom Yanez; Limelite Studios *Dir.* Renee Taylor and Joseph Bologna *Scr.* Renee Taylor and Joseph Bologna *Cine.* Bart Lau *Ed.* Tom Finan *Mu.* Charles Fox; lyrics, Hal David *P.d.* Steven Wolff *S.d.* Regina McLarney *R.t.* 105 min. *MPAA* R. *Cast:* Renee Taylor, Joseph Bologna, William Hickey, Eileen Brennan, Donna Dixon, Tony Randall, Gabriel Bologna.

Theda Blau (Renee Taylor), a bit player and frustrated playwright, schemes to connect with a director of television commercials, Vito Pignoli (Joseph Bologna), with an eye toward collaboration. Most of the film, adapted from Taylor and Bologna's own play, is given over to the self-revelations of the two characters.

THE JANUARY MAN

Pro. Norman Jewison and Ezra Swerdlow; MGM/UA *Dir.* Pat O'Connor *Scr.* John Patrick Shanley *Cine.* Jerzy Zielinski *Ed.* Lou Lombardo *Mu.* Marvin Hamlisch *P.d.* Philip Rosenberg *R.t.* 97 min. *MPAA* R. *Cast:* Kevin Kline, Susan Sarandon, Mary Elizabeth Mastrantonio, Harvey Keitel, Danny Aiello, Rod Steiger, Alan Rickman, Faye Grant, Ken Walsh, Jayne Haynes, Brian Tarantina, Bruce Macvittie, Bil Cobbs, Greg Walker, Tandy

Cronyn, Gerard Parkes, Errol Slue.

Nick Starkey (Kevin Kline) is a disgraced policeman who is recalled to duty to solve an unsolvable crime.

JOHNNY HANDSOME

Pro. Charles Roven for Carolco and Guber-Peters Co.; Tri-Star Pictures *Dir.* Walter Hill *Scr.* Ken Friedman; based on the book *The Three Worlds of Johnny Handsome*, by John Godey *Cine.* Matthew F. Leonetti *Ed.* Freeman Davis *Mu.* Ry Cooder *P.d.* Gene Rudolf *R.t.* 95 min. *MPAA* R. *Cast:* Mickey Rourke, Ellen Barkin, Elizabeth McGovern, Morgan Freeman, Forest Whitaker, Lance Henriksen, Scott Wilson.

A horribly disfigured hoodlum named Johnny (Mickey Rourke) finds his life dramatically changed after an abortive holdup in which he was set up by two accomplices. Transformed by plastic surgery while in prison, he falls in love with Donna (Elizabeth McGovern) a decent young woman, but is ultimately consumed by his thirst for revenge against Sunny (Ellen Barkin) and Rafe (Lance Henricksen), who killed his friend (Scott Wilson) and doublecrossed him. Action specialist Walter Hill confines most of the violence to the opening and closing sequences while attempting a moody character study.

THE KARATE KID III

Pro. Jerry Weintraub for Jerry Weintraub Productions; Columbia Pictures *Dir.* John G. Avildsen *Scr.* Robert Mark Kamen *Cine.* Stephen Yaconelli *Ed.* John Carter and John G. Avildsen *Mu.* Bill Conti *P.d.* William F. Matthews *A.d.* Chris Burian-Mohr *S.d.* Catherine Mann *R.t.* 111 min. *MPAA* PG. *Cast:* Ralph Macchio, Noriyuki "Pat" Morita, Robyn Lively, Thomas Ian Griffith, Martin L. Kove, Sean Kanan.

The eponymous hero (Ralph Macchio), still youthful and in some ways callow despite years of tutoring in this film's predecessors by wise and self-possessed Miyagi (Noriyuki "Pat" Morita), is tempted into action by some unusually nasty villains (Thomas Ian Griffith, Sean Kanan) set in motion by old nemesis Kreese (Martin L. Kove).

KICKBOXER

Pro. Mark DiSalle for Kings Road Entertainment; Pathe Entertainment *Dir.* Mark DiSalle and David Worth *Scr.* Glenn Bruce; based on a story by Mark DiSalle and Jean-Claude Van Damme *Cine.* Jon Kranhouse *Ed.* Wayne Wahram *Mu.* Paul Hartzop *P.d.* Shay Austin *R.t.* 105 min. *MPAA* R. *Cast:* Jean-Claude Van Damme, Dennis Alexio, Dennis Chan, Tong Po, Haskell Anderson, Rochelle Ashana.

In Thailand, Kurt Sloane (Jean-Claude Van Damme) avenges the crippling of his brother Eric (Dennis Alexio), a kickboxing champion, by besting a malevolent Thai fighter. The kickboxing action staged by the star is the film's *raison d'etre*.

KILL ME AGAIN

Pro. David W. Warfield, Sigurjon Sighvatsson, and Steve Golin for Propaganda Films; Polygram Pictures and Metro-Goldwyn-Mayer *Dir.* John Dahl *Scr.* John Dahl and David W. Warfield *Cine.* Jacques Steyn *Ed.* Frank Jimenez, Jonathan Shaw, and Jacques Steyn *Mu.* William Olvis *P.d.* Michelle Minch *R.t.* 94 min. *MPAA* R. *Cast:* Joanne Whalley-Kilmer, Val Kilmer, Michael Madsen, Pat Mulligan, Nick Dimitri, Bibi Besch, Jonathan Gries, Michael Sharrett.

After they rob some racketeers, Fay Forrester (Joanne Whalley-Kilmer) doublecrosses her boyfriend Vince Miller (Michael Madsen) and takes off on her own with the money. She hires a down-and-out detective, Jack Andrews (Val Kilmer), to fake her death but doublecrosses him, too. Echoes of *film noir* resonate in this modestly ambitious thriller as the story moves forward to a violent conclusion in the desert.

KINJITE: FORBIDDEN SUBJECTS

Pro. Pancho Kohner for Golan-Globus; Cannon Entertainment *Dir.* J. Lee Thompson *Scr.* Harold Nebenzal *Cine.* Gideon Porath *Ed.* Peter Lee Thompson and Mary E. Jochem *Mu.* Greg DeBelles *A.d.* W. Brooke Wheeler *S.d.* Margaret C. Fischer *R.t.* 97 min. *MPAA* R. *Cast:* Charles Bronson, Perry Lopez, Juan Fernandez, Peggy Lipton, James Pax, Sy Richardson, Marion Kodama Yue, Bill McKinney, Gerald Castillo, Nicole Eggert, Amy Hathaway, Kumiko Hayakawa, Michelle Wong, Alex Hyde-White, Richard Egan, Jr.

Lieutenant Crowe (Charles Bronson) is a vigilante cop assigned to find the kidnapped daughter (Kumiko Hayakawa) of a man (James Pax) who has molested Crowe's daughter (Amy Hathaway). Kinjite (pronounced Kin-ja-tay) means "forbidden subjects."

LET IT RIDE

Pro. David Giler; Paramount Pictures *Dir.* Joe Pytka *Scr.* Ernest Morton; based on the book *Good Vibes*, by Jay Cronley *Cine.* Curtis J. Wehr *Ed.* Dede Allen and Jim Miller *Mu.* Giorgio Moroder *P.d.* Wolf Kroeger *S.d.* William D. McLane *R.t.* 86 min. *MPAA* PG-13. *Cast:* Richard Dreyfuss, David Johansen, Teri Garr, Jennifer Tilly, Allen Garfield, Ed Walsh.

Jay Trotter (Richard Dreyfuss), a cab driver, gets a tip on a fixed horse race and parlays a bet on it into ever-greater winnings during a manic day at the track. In the meantime, he is neglecting the opportunity to reconcile with his wife Pam (Teri Garr). The atmosphere is raucous in this neo-Runyonesque fable by first-time feature director Pytka.

LEVIATHAN

Pro. Luigi De Laurentiis and Aurelio De Laurentiis for Gordon Company; Metro-Goldwyn-Mayer/United Artists *Dir.* George P. Cosmatos *Scr.* David Peoples and Jeb Stuart; based on a story by Peoples *Cine.* Alex Thomson *Ed.* Roberto Silvi and John F. Burnett *Mu.* Jerry Goldsmith *P.d.* Rob Cobb *A.d.* David Klassen and Franco Ceraolo *S.d.* Robert Gould and Bruno Cesari *R.t.* 98 min. *MPAA* R. *Cast:* Peter Weller, Richard Crenna, Amanda Stern, Daniel Stern, Ernie Hudson, Michael Carmine, Lisa Eilbacher, Hector Elizondo, Meg Foster.

About 16,000 feet beneath the Atlantic Ocean is a mining camp where a team of men and women work. During a delay caused by a hurricane, one crew member explores a Russian sunken ship called Leviathan. He dies and begins transforming into a grotesque eel-like creature. The rest of the crew suffer the same fate.

LIFE AND NOTHING BUT (*La Vie est rien d' autre*, France, 1989)

Pro. Frederic Bourboulon and Albert Precost for Hachette Premiere et Cie/Ab Films/Little Bear/Films A2; UGC *Dir.* Bertrand Tavernier *Scr.* Bertrand Tavernier and Jean Cosmos *Cine.* Bruno de Keyzer *Ed.* Armand Psenny *Mu.* Oswald d'Andrea *A.d.* Guy-Claude François *R.t.* 135 min. *Cast:* Philippe Noiret, Sabine Azema, Pascale Vignal, Maurice Barrier, Francois Perrot, Jean-Pol Dubois, Daniel Russo, Michel Duchaussoy.

Following World War I, a number of women, principally wealthy Irene de Courtil (Sabine Azema) and a young schoolteacher named Alice (Pascale Vignal), search the battlefields of Europe for missing husbands, lovers, and other men in their lives. Unexpectedly, love emerges between Irene and a hardened officer (Philippe Noiret) who has been assigned the bleak task of exhuming bodies.

LIFE IS CHEAP

Pro. Winnie Fredriksz for Far East Stars *Dir.* Wayne Wang *Scr.* Spencer Nakasako *Cine.* Amir Mokri *Ed.* Chris Sanderson and Sandy Nervig *Mu.* Mark Adler *A.d.* Collete Koo *R.t.* 90 min. *Cast:* Spencer Nakasako, Cora Miao, Victor Wong, John K. Chan, Chan Kim Wan, Cheng Kwan Min, Allen Fong, Cinda Hui, Lam Chung, Lo Wai, Gary Kong, Rocky

Ho, Lo Lieh, Bonnie Ngai, Wu Kin Man, Yu Chien, Mr. Kai-Bong Chau, Mrs. Kai-Bong Chau.

Scenarist Nakasako plays a "Man With No Name" who travels from San Francisco to Hong Kong to deliver an attache case to a "Big Boss" (Lo Wai) in director Wang's ambitious comedy that satirizes various film genres.

LISTEN TO ME

Pro. Marykay Powell; Weintraub Entertainment Group   *Dir.* Douglas Day Stewart   *Scr.* Douglas Day Stewart   *Cine.* Fred Koenekamp   *Ed.* Anne V. Coates   *Mu.* David Foster   *P.d.* Gregory Pickrell   *S.d.* Kim Samson   *R.t.* 107 min.   *MPAA* PG-13.   *Cast:* Kirk Cameron, Jami Gertz, Roy Scheider, Amanda Peterson, Tim Quill, George Wyner, Anthony Zerbe, Christopher Atkins, Quinn Cummings, Jason Gould.

United in their expertise as members of a college debating team, three students— Muldowney (Kirk Cameron), Tomanski (Jami Gertz), and McKellar (Tim Quill)—try to resolve conflicts about their futures while engaging in typical campus antics. A debate about the timely issue of abortion climaxes the unusual comedy-drama.

LITTLE MONSTERS

Pro. Jeffrey Mueller, Andrew Licht, and John A. Davis of Davis Entertainment Co., Licht/ Mueller Film Corp.; United Artists in association with Vestron Pictures   *Dir.* Richard Alan Greenberg   *Scr.* Terry Rossio and Ted Elliott   *Cine.* Dick Bush   *Ed.* Patrick McMahon   *Mu.* David Newman   *P.d.* Paul Peters   *R.t.* 100 min.   *MPAA* PG.   *Cast:* Fred Savage, Howie Mandel, Daniel Stern, Margaret Whitton, Rick Ducommun, Frank Whaley, Ben Savage, William Murray Weiss, Devin Ratray, Amber Barretto.

A boy, Brian (Fred Savage), is befriended by a monster, Maurice (Howie Mandel), who lives in an underground world, and follows the creature to that world for revels. But Maurice and his kind, who cannot bear the light of day, are not as benign as they first appear.

THE LITTLE THIEF (*La Petite Veleuse*, France, 1989)

Pro. Jean-Jose Richer; AMLF   *Dir.* Claude Miller   *Scr.* Claude Miller, Annie Miller, and Luc Beraud; based on an original scenario by François Truffaut and Claude de Givray   *Cine.* Dominique Chapuis   *Ed.* Albert Jurgenson   *Mu.* Alain Jomy   *A.d.* Jean-Pierre Kohut-Svelko   *R.t.* 105 min.   *Cast:* Charlotte Gainsbourg, Didier Bezace, Simone de la Brosse, Raoul Billery, Chantal Banlier, Nathalie Cardone, Clotilde de Bayser, Philippe Deplanche, Marion Grimault, Erick Deshores, Remy Kirch, Renee Faure, Claude Cuyonnet.

Charlotte Gainsbourg plays Janine Castang, a troubled teenager in the 1950's who steals and hangs out in film theaters. The film depicts her emotional and social growth.

LITTLE VERA (USSR, 1989)

Pro. Gorky Film Studios; International Film Exchange   *Dir.* Vasily Pichul   *Scr.* Maria Khmelik   *Cine.* Yefim Reznikov   *Ed.* Elena Zabolockaja   *Mu.* P. Drosvev   *A.d.* Vladimir Pasternak   *R.t.* 110 min.   *Cast:* Natalya Negoda, Andrei Sokolov, Ludmila Zaitzeva, Yuri Nazarov.

The harsh realities of urban Soviet life are delineated in this bleak character study of Vera (Natalya Negoda), a rebellious, frustrated teenager. Her affair with Sergei (Andrei Sokolov), a cynical and irresponsible youth, triggers a series of events which end in violence and affect her whole family.

LOCK UP

Pro. Lawrence Gordon and Charles Gordon for White Eagle and Carolco Pictures; Tri-Star Pictures   *Dir.* John Flynn   *Scr.* Richard Smith, Jeb Stuart, and Henry Rosenbaum   *Cine.* Donald E. Thorin   *Ed.* Michael N. Knue and Donald Brochu   *Mu.* Bill Conti   *P.d.* Bill

Kenney   *A.d.* William Ladd Skinner and Bill Groom   *S.d.* Jerry Adams and Tim Galvin   *R.t.* 105 min.   *MPAA* R.   *Cast:* Sylvester Stallone, Donald Sutherland, John Amos, Sonny Landham, Tom Sizemore, Frank McRae, Darlanne Fluegel.

Frank (Sylvester Stallone), an auto mechanic who was sent to prison unjustly, has made a dangerous enemy—sadistic Warden Drumgoole (Donald Sutherland). This hard-edged action drama focuses on the protagonist's efforts to survive his dangerous and demoralizing situation while keeping his humanity intact.

LODZ GHETTO

Pro. Alan Adelson; Jewish Heritage Project   *Dir.* Kathryn Taverna and Alan Adelson   *Scr.* Alan Adelson   *Cine.* Jozef Piwkowski and Eugene Squires   *Ed.* Kathryn Taverna   *Mu.* Wendy Blackstone   *R.t.* 103 min.   *Narration:* Jerzy Kosinski, Nicholas Kepros, David Warrilow, Barbara Rosenblat, Gregory Gordon, Theodore Bikel, Julie Cohen, Lynn Cohen, Jerry Matz, Frederick Newmann, Sam Tsousouvas, Eva Wellisz.

In telling the story of Poland's Lodz Ghetto during World War II—where 200,000 Jews suffered a marginal existence before being taken to Nazi concentration camps—this documentary uses old photographs, slides, and film as well as new footage and employs the talents of a number of actors to read from diaries and to re-create first-person accounts of the events.

THE LONG WEEKEND (also known as *O' Despair*)

Pro. Gregg Araki; Desperate Pictures   *Dir.* Gregg Araki   *Scr.* Gregg Araki   *Cine.* Gregg Araki   *Ed.* Gregg Araki   *Mu.* Steven Fields, Iron Curtain, Fred's Crashshop, Steve Burr, Dirt Tribe and Harepeace   *R.t.* 87 min.   *Cast:* Bretton Vail, Maureen Dondanville, Andrea Beane, Nicole Dillenberg, Marcus D'Amico, Lance Woods.

A sextet of youthful characters suffers through a depressing weekend in Los Angeles while trying to sort out personal problems and resolve relationships.

LORDS OF THE DEEP

Pro. Roger Corman; Concorde   *Dir.* Mary Ann Fisher   *Scr.* Howard Cohen and Daryl Haney   *Cine.* Austin McKinney   *Ed.* Nina Gilberti   *Mu.* Jim Berenholtz   *A.d.* Troy Myers   *S.d.* Ildiko Toth   *R.t.* 82 min.   *MPAA* PG-13.   *Cast:* Bradford Dillman, Priscilla Barnes, Melody Ryane, Daryl Haney, Eb Lottimer, Greg Sobeck, Richard Young, Steven Davies.

In the year 2020, a submarine crew commanded by Dobler (Bradford Dillman) encounters undersea aliens. The aliens, it turns out, are friendly—they have come from the future to warn humans to stop poisoning the Earth. Dobler deteriorates into psychosis as he finds himself losing control of the sub.

LOST ANGELS

Pro. Howard Rosenman and Thomas Baer; Orion Pictures   *Dir.* Hugh Hudson   *Scr.* Michael Weller   *Cine.* Juan Ruiz-Anchia   *Ed.* David Gladwell   *Mu.* Philippe Sarde   *P.d.* Assheton Gorton   *A.d.* Alex Tavoularis   *S.d.* Robert Kensinger   *R.t.* 116 min.   *MPAA* R.   *Cast:* Donald Sutherland, Adam Horovitz, Amy Locane, Don Blommfield, Celia Weston, Graham Beckel, Patricia Richardson, Ron Frazier, Joseph d'Angerio, William O'Leary, Leonard Porter Salazar.

Rebellious and misunderstood teenagers are thrown into a San Fernando Valley mental hospital when their parents are unable to cope with them. The focus is on brooding Tim Doolan (Adam Horovitz), who somehow manages to resolve his conflicting loyalties by the fadeout in still another attempt to update *Rebel Without a Cause*.

LOVERBOY

Pro. Gary Foster and Willie Hunt; Tri-Star Pictures   *Dir.* Joan Micklin Silver   *Scr.* Robin

Schiff, Tom Ropelewski, and Leslie Dixon; based on a story by Schiff *Cine.* John Hora *Ed.*
Rich Shaine *Mu.* Michel Colombier *P.d.* Dan Leigh *A.d.* Ann Champion *S.d.* Ethel
Robins Richards *R.t.* 98 min. *MPAA* PG-13. *Cast:* Patrick Dempsey, Kate Jackson, Robert
Ginty, Nancy Valen, Barbara Carrera, Charles Hunter Walsh, Kirstie Alley, Carrie Fisher,
Kim Miyori.

A pizza delivery boy, Randy Bodek (Patrick Dempsey), romances a number of women
during the summer but wins back his girlfriend, Jenny (Nancy Valen), before school begins
in the fall. This sex comedy attempts to revitalize familiar material by the offbeat casting of
Dempsey and the use of noted director Silver (*Crossing Delancey*).

THE LUCKIEST MAN IN THE WORLD

Pro. Norman I. Cohen; Second Effort Company *Dir.* Frank D. Gilroy *Scr.* Frank D. Gilroy
Cine. Jeri Sopanen *Ed.* John Gilroy *Mu.* Warren Vache and Jack Gale *P.d.* Nick Romanec
R.t. 82 min. *Cast:* Philip Bosco, Doris Belack, Joanne Camp, Matthew Gottlieb, Arthur
French, Stan Borges, J. D. Clarke, Moses Gunn.

Wealthy and mean, Sam Posner (Philip Bosco) decides to change his ways and be a nice
guy after he narrowly avoids death by missing a plane that crashes. The problem is that his
change of behavior knocks out of balance the lives of his family and friends, who are not as
willing to change their own ways and circumstances.

MANIFESTO

Pro. Menahem Golan and Yoram Globus; Cannon *Dir.* Dusan Makavejev *Scr.* Dusan
Makavejev; inspired by the story "A Night of Love," by Émile Zola *Cine.* Tomislav Pinter
Ed. Tony Lawson *Mu.* Nicola Piovani *P.d.* Veljko Despotovic *R.t.* 96 min. *Cast:* Camilla
Soeberg, Alfred Molina, Simon Callow, Lindsay Duncan, Eric Stoltz.

In an expansive satire of small-town mores and postrevolutionary self-deceptions, director-
writer Dusan Makavejev—acclaimed for his earlier films with similar or related themes—
imagines life as it might have been in the 1920's in a Hungarian village. The plot is set in
motion when Inspector Avanti (Alfred Molina), a policeman, sets out to seduce a liberated
village girl, Svetlana (Camilla Soeberg), and widens to include many different characters.

MASQUE OF THE RED DEATH

Pro. Roger Corman; Concorde Films *Dir.* Larry Brand *Scr.* Daryl Haney and Larry Brand
Cine. Edward Pie *Ed.* Stephen Mark *Mu.* Mark Governor *A.d.* Troy Myers *R.t.* 85 min.
MPAA R. *Cast:* Patrick Macnee, Adrian Paul, Clare Hoak, Jeff Osterhage, Tracy Reiner.

In medieval times, a plague rages across Europe while Prince Prospero (Adrian Paul)
insulates himself and fellow revelers within his castle. Inevitably, though, death cannot be
escaped. A very free adaptation of the Edgar Allan Poe story, the film is also a remake of a
1964 effort directed by Roger Corman, here the producer.

MEET THE HOLLOWHEADS

Pro. Joseph Grace and John Chavez for Linden Productions; Moviestore Entertainment *Dir.*
Tom Burman *Scr.* Tom Burman and Lisa Morton, with additional dialogue by Stanley
Mieses *Cine.* Marvin Rush *Ed.* Carl Kress *Mu.* Glenn Jordan *P.d.* Ed Eyth *R.t.* 86 min.
MPAA PG-13. *Cast:* John Glover, Nancy Mette, Richard Portnow, Matt Shakman, Juliette
Lewis, Lightfield Lewis, Joshua Miller, Anne Ramsey, Logan Ramsey, Chaz Conner, Shot-
gun Britton.

In a futuristic society, the eponymous family prepares dinner for the father's boss. Crude
and cruel humor dominate this low-budget attempt at offbeat comedy.

MIDNIGHT

Pro. Norman Thaddeus Vane and Gloria J. Morrison for SVS and Midnight Films, in association with Kuys Entertainment Group and Gomillion Studios; SVS Films *Dir.* Norman Thaddeus Vane *Scr.* Norman Thaddeus Vane *Cine.* David Golia *Ed.* Sam Adelman *Mu.* Michael Wetherwax *A.d.* Mark Simon *R.t.* 84 min. *MPAA* R. *Cast:* Lynn Redgrave, Tony Curtis, Steve Parrish, Rita Gam, Gustav Vintas, Karen Witter, Frank Gorshin, Robert Miano, Wolfman Jack, Barry Diamond, Gloria Morrison, Robert Axelrod, Tom (Tiny) Lister, Jr.

A television-horror hostess, Midnight (Lynn Redgrave), becomes involved with a young aspiring actor, Mickey Modine (Steve Parrish), at the same time that people with whom she is associated begin to be murdered. The low-budget film imitates *Sunset Boulevard* with apparent satirical intent.

THE MIGHTY QUINN

Pro. Sandy Lieberson, Marion Hunt, and Ed Elbert; MGM/UA *Dir.* Carl Schenkel *Scr.* Hampton Fancher; based on the novel *Finding Maubee*, by A. H. Z. Carr *Cine.* Jacques Steyn *Ed.* John Jympson *Mu.* Anne Dudley *P.d.* Roger Murray-Leach *R.t.* 98 min. *MPAA* R. *Cast:* Denzel Washington, Robert Townsend, James Fox, Mimi Rogers, M. Emmet Walsh, Sheryl Lee Ralph, Art Evans, Esther Rolle, Norman Beaton, Alex Colon, Tyra Ferrell, Keye Luke, Carl Bradshae, Maria McDonald.

Detective Xavier Quinn (Denzel Washington) sets out to find a murderer and protect his boyhood friend (Robert Townsend), who is being framed for the killing.

MILK AND HONEY

Pro. Peter O'Brian; ABC Distribution Co. and Castle Hill *Dir.* Rebecca Yates and Glen Salzman *Scr.* Glen Salzman and Trevor Rhone *Cine.* Guy Dufaux *Ed.* Bruce Nyzink *Mu.* Micky Erbe and Maribeth Solomon *A.d.* François Séguin *R.t.* 94 min. *Cast:* Josette Simon, Lyman Ward, Djanet Sears, Fiona Reid, Leonie Forbes, Richard Mills, Errol Slue, Jane Dingle.

A young woman, Jo (Josette Simon), leaves Jamaica in search of a better life in Canada. There she endures considerable exploitation and much hardship while trying to make it possible for her son David (Richard Mills) to immigrate as well.

MILLENNIUM

Pro. Douglas Leiterman for Gladden Entertainment; Twentieth Century-Fox *Dir.* Michael Anderson *Scr.* John Varley; based on his short story "Air Raid" *Cine.* Rene Ohashi *Ed.* Ron Wisman *Mu.* Eric N. Robertson *P.d.* Gene Rudolf *A.d.* Charles Dunlop *R.t.* 108 min. *Cast:* Kris Kristofferson, Cheryl Ladd, Daniel J. Travanti, Robert Joy, Lloyd Bochner, Brent Carver.

After an air crash, Bill Smith (Kris Kristofferson), assigned to investigate the occurrence, discovers that airline employee Louise Baltimore (Cheryl Ladd) has come from a point in the future (one thousand years) at which the earth is nearing ecological exhaustion and the human race can no longer procreate. As both characters travel through time between present and future, they fall in love.

MINISTRY OF VENGEANCE

Pro. Brad Krevoy and Steve Stabler for Motion Picture Corporation of America; Concorde Pictures *Dir.* Peter Maris *Scr.* Brian D. Jeffries, Mervyn Emryys, and Ann Narus; based on a story by Randal Patrick *Cine.* Mark Harris *Ed.* Michael Haight *Mu.* Scott Roewe *P.d.* Stephen Greenberg *S.d.* Troy Myers *R.t.* 93 min. *MPAA* R. *Cast:* John Schneider, Ned Beatty, James Tolkan, Yaphet Kotto, George Kennedy, Apollonia, Robert Miano, Daniel Radell, Maria Richwine, Meg Register, Joey Peters.

David Miller (John Schneider), a former soldier turned minister, returns to violence in seeking revenge against the Arab terrorists who killed his wife and son. Aided by his former

Vietnam colonel (James Tolkan), Miller goes to Lebanon and succeeds in annihilating the master terrorist Ali Aboud (Robert Miano), who is, ironically, a CIA agent.

MIRACLE MILE

Pro. John Daly and Derek Gibson; Hemdale *Dir.* Steve de Jarnatt *Scr.* Steve de Jarnatt *Cine.* Theo van de Sande *Ed.* Stephen Semel and Kathie Weaver *Mu.* Tangerine Dream *P.d.* Christopher Horner *R.t.* 87 min. *MPAA* R. *Cast:* Anthony Edwards, Mare Winningham, Lou Hancock, Mykel T. Williamson, Kelly Minter, Kurt Fuller, Denise Crosby, Robert Doqui, O-Lan Jones.

Having just met the girl of his dreams, a young man answers a pay telephone only to hear that the missiles are on the way; nuclear war is imminent. He has one hour to escape from Los Angeles.

MISPLACED

Pro. Lisa Zwerling; Subway Films *Dir.* Louis Yansen *Scr.* Louis Yansen and Thomas DeWolfe *Cine.* Igor Sunara *Ed.* Michael Berenbaum *Mu.* Michael Urbaniak *P.d.* Beth Kuhn *R.t.* 95 min. *Cast:* John Cameron Mitchell, Viveca Lindfors, Elzbieta Czyzewska, Drew Snyder, Deirdre O'Connell.

A mother (Elzbieta Czyzewska) and son (John Cameron Mitchell) escape the 1981 Solidarity uprising in Warsaw to begin a new life in Washington, D.C. The two attempt to assimilate into American culture, the mother working her way up from custodian to announcer for Voice of America and the son confronting normal adolescent pressures with the added pressure of being an immigrant.

MUTANT ON THE BOUNTY

Pro. Robert Torrance and Martin Lopez for Canyon Films Inc.; Skouras Pictures *Dir.* Robert Torrance *Scr.* Martin Lopez; based on a story by Lopez and Robert Torrance *Cine.* Randolph Sellars *Ed.* Craig A. Colton *Mu.* Tim Torrance *P.d.* Clark Hunter *A.d.* Hilja Keading *R.t.* 94 min. *MPAA* PG-13. *Cast:* John Roarke, Deborah Benson, John Furey, Victoria Catlin, John Fleck, Kyle T. Heffner, Scott Williamson, John Durbin, Pepper Martin.

In this science-fiction parody, the title character, Max (Kyle T. Heffner), is a saxophone player who becomes a mutant while in some strange limbo, then winds up aboard a spaceship with an assortment of characters typical of the genre.

MY MOM'S A WEREWOLF

Pro. Steven J. Wolfe for Hairy Productions; Crown International Pictures *Dir.* Michael Fischa *Scr.* Mark Pirro *Cine.* Bryan England *Ed.* Claudia Finkle *Mu.* Barry Fasman and Dana Walden *R.t.* 84 min. *MPAA* PG. *Cast:* Susan Blakely, John Saxon, Katrina Caspary, John Schuck, Ruth Buzzi, Marcia Wallace, Marilyn McCoo.

A suburban housewife (Susan Blakely) becomes a werewolf but is saved by her daughter (Katrina Caspary) before the transformation is complete. The premise, tragic in the classic films and legends which established the figure of the werewolf, is here played for comedy in a contemporary American setting.

NATIONAL LAMPOON'S CHRISTMAS VACATION

Pro. John Hughes and Tom Jacobson for Hughes Entertainment; Warner Bros. *Dir.* Jeremiah S. Chechik *Scr.* John Hughes *Cine.* Thomas Ackerman *Ed.* Jerry Greenberg *Mu.* Angelo Badalamenti *P.d.* Stephen Marsh *A.d.* Beala B. Neel *S.d.* Lisa Fischer *R.t.* 97 min. *MPAA* PG-13. *Cast:* Chevy Chase, Beverly D'Angelo, Randy Quaid, Diane Ladd, John Randolph, E. G. Marshall, Doris Roberts, Julia Louis-Dreyfus, Mae Questel, William Hickey, Brian Doyle-Murray, Juliette Lewis, Johnny Galecki, Nicholas Guest, Miriam Flynn, Ellen Hamilton Latzen.

In this third film in a comic series focusing on the hapless all-American Griswold family, father Clark (Chevy Chase) promises his wife Ellen (Beverly D'Angelo) and children Rusty (Johnny Galecki) and Audrey (Juliette Lewis) an old-fashioned Christmas, complete with 25,000 Christmas lights and almost as many relatives.

NEW YEAR'S DAY

Pro. Judith Wolinsky; International Rainbow Pictures *Dir.* Henry Jaglom *Scr.* Henry Jaglom *Cine.* Joey Forsyte *R.t.* 89 min. *Cast:* Maggie Jakobson, Gwen Welles, Melanie Winter, Henry Jaglom, David Duchovny, Milos Forman, Michael Emil, Donna Germain, Tracy Reiner, Harvey Miller, Irene Moore, James DePreist.

Flying back to New York, a depressed Drew (Henry Jaglom) finds that the three women who are leasing his apartment—Lucy (Maggie Jakobson), Annie (Gwen Welles), and Winona (Melanie Winter)—have not yet moved out, so he joins them in a "last day" party and becomes involved in their lives.

NEXT OF KIN

Pro. Les Alexander and Don Enright for Lorimar Film Entertainment presentation of a Barry and Enright Production; Warner Bros. *Dir.* John Irvin *Scr.* Michael Jenning *Cine.* Steven Poster *Ed.* Peter Honess *Mu.* Jack Nitzsche *P.d.* Jack T. Collis *S.d.* Jim Duffy *R.t.* 108 min. *MPAA* R. *Cast:* Patrick Swayze, Liam Neeson, Adam Baldwin, Helen Hunt, Andreas Katsulas, Bill Paxton, Ben Stiller, Michael J. Pollard, Ted Levine, Del Close, Valentino Cimo, Paul Greco, Vincent Guastaferro, Paul Herman.

Truman Gates (Patrick Swayze), a Chicago police detective, sets out to avenge the killing of his younger brother Gerald (Bill Paxton) by gangsters; he intends to function within the law but does not count on the more primitive intentions of his older brother Briar (Liam Neeson) from the hills of Kentucky.

NIGHT GAME

Pro. George Litto for Epic; Trans World Entertainment *Dir.* Peter Masterson *Scr.* Spencer Eastman and Anthony Palmer; based on a story by Eastman *Cine.* Fred Murphy *Ed.* Robert Barrere *Mu.* Pino Donaggio *P.d.* Neil Spisak *R.t.* 95 min. *MPAA* R. *Cast:* Roy Scheider, Karen Young, Richard Bradford, Paul Gleason, Carlin Glynn.

The actions of a serial killer are strangely linked to Houston Astro baseball wins. A police detective, Seaver (Roy Scheider) investigates and solves the mystery, but not before his girlfriend Roxy (Karen Young) finds herself in jeopardy in this thriller of modest ambition.

NIGHT VISITOR

Pro. Alain Silver for Premiere Pictures; Metro-Goldwyn-Mayer/United Artists *Dir.* Rupert Hitzig *Scr.* Randal Viscovich *Cine.* Peter Jensen *Ed.* Glenn Erickson *Mu.* Parmer Fuller *P.d.* Jon Rothschild *R.t.* 93 min. *MPAA* R. *Cast:* Elliot Gould, Richard Roundtree, Allen Garfield, Michael J. Pollard, Derek Rydall.

Billy Colton (Derek Rydall), a high school boy, witnesses a murder but cannot persuade the police to believe his story. As a result, he is imperiled by devil worshippers until justice finally triumphs in this straightforward thriller.

A NIGHTMARE ON ELM STREET V: THE DREAM CHILD

Pro. Robert Shaye and Rupert Harvey for New Line/Heron Communications/Smart Egg Pictures; New Line Cinema *Dir.* Stephen Hopkins *Scr.* Leslie Bohem; based on a story by Bohem, John Skip, and Craig Spector and characters created by Wes Craven *Cine.* Peter Levy *Ed.* Chuck Weiss and Brent Schoenfeld *Mu.* Jay Ferguson *P.d.* C. J. Strawn *A.d.* Tim Gray *S.d.* John Jockinsen *R.t.* 89 min. *MPAA* R. *Cast:* Robert Englund, Lisa Wilcox, Danny Hassel, Kelly Minter, Erika Anderson, Whitby Hertford, Nick Mele, Beatrice

Boepple, Joe Seely, Valorie Armstrong, Burr DeBenning, Pat Surges, Clarence Felder.

Dream monster Freddy Krueger (Robert Englund) lives on in the nighmares of Alice (Lisa Wilcox), the character who vanquished him in part 4, as he struggles for the soul of her child, personified by ten-year-old dream figure Jacob (Whitby Hertford).

976-EVIL
Pro. Lisa M. Hansen for CineTel Films; New Line Cinema *Dir.* Robert Englund *Scr.* Rhet Topham and Brian Helgeland *Cine.* Paul Elliott *Ed.* Stephen Myers *Mu.* Thomas Chase and Steve Rucker *A.d.* David Brian Miller *S.d.* Nancy Booth *R.t.* 100 min. *MPAA* R. *Cast:* Stephen Geoffreys, Sandy Dennis, Patrick O'Bryan, Jim Metzler, Maria Rubell, Lezlie Deane, Jim Thiebaud, Gunther Jensen, Darren Burrows, Robert Piccardo.

Teenage cousins Hoax (Stephen Geoffreys) and Spike (Patrick O'Bryan) continually call a 976 "Horrorscope" for fun until they realize that it is, in fact, evil. Hoax decides to use it to take revenge on the kids at school who taunt him and his mother, who is a religious zealot. Fish fall from the sky into his mother's backyard, and Hoax grows large hands and feet with sharp talons with which he begins clawing to death everyone who has ever crossed him.

NO HOLDS BARRED
Pro. Michael Rachmil for Shane Productions; New Line Cinema *Dir.* Thomas J. Wright *Scr.* Dennis Hackin *Cine.* Frank Beascoechea *Ed.* Tom Pryor *Mu.* Jim Johnston *P.d.* James Shanahan *S.d.* Lynn Wolverton *R.t.* 91 min. *MPAA* PG-13. *Cast:* Hulk Hogan, Kurt Fuller, Joan Severance, Tom (Tiny) Lister, Jr., Mark Pellegrino, Bill Henderson, Charles Levin, David Palmer, (The Lariat) Hansen, Armelia McQueen, Jesse (The Body) Ventura, Gene Okerlund, Howard Finkel.

Wrestling champion Hulk Hogan plays a thinly fictionalized version of himself in a story in which he bests some criminals and saves a girlfriend (Joan Severance) while engaging in a number of wrestling matches. The production is clearly aimed primarily at devotees of wrestling action.

NO RETREAT, NO SURRENDER II
Pro. Roy Horan for Seasonal Films; Shapiro Glickenhaus Entertainment *Dir.* Corey Yuen *Scr.* Roy Horan, Keith W. Strandberg, and Maria Elene Cellino *Cine.* Nicholas Von Sternberg and Ma Kam Cheung *Ed.* Allen Poon and Kevin Sewelson *Mu.* David Spear *R.t.* 92 min. *MPAA* R. *Cast:* Loren Avedon, Max Thayer, Cynthia Rothrock, Matthias Hues.

While searching for his kidnapped girlfriend, the hero of this story (Loren Avedon) uncovers a Soviet plot to take over the nations of Southeast Asia. The action involves martial arts fighting.

OFFICE PARTY
Pro. George Flak; SC Entertainment *Dir.* George Mihalka *Scr.* Stephen Zoller and Michael A. Gilbert; based on Gilbert's novel *Cine.* Ludek Bogner *Ed.* Stan Cole *Mu.* Billy Bryans *R.t.* 95 min. *Cast:* David Warner, Michael Ironside, Kate Vernon, Jayne Eastwood, Will Lyman, Graeme Campbell.

Eugene (David Warner), an employee at a hydroelectric plant, brings a machine gun to work and, for no apparent reason, orders his boss, the office manager, and the secretary to handcuff themselves to their chairs. The plant is surrounded by police sharpshooters, while the hostages try to persuade Eugene to surrender.

OUT COLD
Pro. George C. Braustein and Ron Hamady; Hemdale Film Corp. *Dir.* Malcolm Mowbray *Scr.* Howard Glasser and George Malko; based on a story by Glasser *Cine.* Tony Pierce-Roberts *Ed.* Dennis M. Hill *Mu.* Michel Colombier *P.d.* Linda Pearl *A.d.* Lisa Fischer

R.t. 91 min. *MPAA* R. *Cast:* John Lithgow, Teri Garr, Randy Quaid, Bruce McGill, Lisa Blount, Alan Blumenfeld, Morgan Paull, Barbara Rhoades, Tom Blyrd, Frederick Coffin, Fran Ryan.

John Lithgow, Terri Garr and Randy Quaid star in this suspense comedy about intrigue, butchers, murder and how to dispose of a murder victim locked in a freezer.

OUT OF THE DARK

Pro. Zane W. Levitt for Zel Films; CineTel Films *Dir.* Michael Schroeder *Scr.* J. Greg DeFelice and Zane W. Levitt *Cine.* Julio Macat *Ed.* Marl Manos *Mu.* Paul F. Antonelli and David Wheatley *P.d.* Robert Schulenberg *R.t.* 90 min. *MPAA* R. *Cast:* Cameron Dye, Karen Black, Bud Cort, Lynn Danielson, Starr Andreeff, Divine, Paul Bartel, Geoffrey Lewis, Tracey Walter, Tab Hunter, Zane W. Levitt, J. Greg DeFelice.

A killer clown is strangling and slashing the staff of a phone sex service, and the principal suspect, a freelance photographer named Kevin (Cameron Dye), attempts to find the real culprit.

THE PACKAGE

Pro. Beverly J. Camhe and Tobie Haggerty; Orion Pictures *Dir.* Andrew Davis *Scr.* John Bishop *Cine.* Frank Tidy *Ed.* Don Zimmerman and Billy Weber *Mu.* James Newton Howard *P.d.* Michael Levesque *R.t.* 108 min. *MPAA* R. *Cast:* Gene Hackman, Joanna Cassidy, Tommy Lee Jones, John Heard, Dennis Franz.

When career soldier Johnny Gallagher (Gene Hackman) gets too close to a Soviet-American military conspiracy to prevent those countries from reaching a peace accord, he is diverted by a phony mission involving a professional assassin named Boyette (Tommy Lee Jones) posing as a military prisoner. Gallagher is framed for murder before exposing the conspiracy in a thriller that moves from Berlin to Chicago with much action along the way.

PARENTS

Pro. Bonnie Palef in association with Great American Films Limited Partnership; Vestron Entertainment *Dir.* Bob Balaban *Scr.* Christopher Hawthorne *Cine.* Ernest Day and Robin Vidgeon *Ed.* Bill Pankow *Mu.* Jonathan Elias *A.d.* Andris Hausmanis *S.d.* Michael Harris *R.t.* 82 min. *MPAA* R. *Cast:* Randy Quaid, Mary Beth Hurt, Sandy Dennis, Bryan Madorsky, Juno Mills-Cockell, Kathryn Grody, Deborah Rush, Graham Jarvis.

This black comedy is a satire on middle-class values, using cannibalism as its metaphor for the hidden horrors and perversities that lie behind the polished formica and chrome exteriors of the characters' lives.

PENN AND TELLER GET KILLED

Pro. Arthur Penn for Lorimar Film Entertainment; Warner Bros. *Dir.* Arthur Penn *Scr.* Penn Jillette and Teller *Cine.* Jan Weincke *Ed.* Jeffrey Wolf *Mu.* Paul Chihara *P.d.* John Arnone *R.t.* 89 min. *MPAA* R. *Cast:* Penn Jillette, Teller, Caitlin Clarke, David Patrick Kelly, Leonardo Cimino, Christopher Durang, Alan North, Jon Cryer.

In a story in which comedians Penn and Teller play themselves, the duo's speculations about being stalked by a killer set in motion a series of pranks. The teams' specialized brand of humor is geared toward a kind of audience that enjoys offbeat and macabre entertainment.

THE PERFECT MODEL

Pro. Darryl Roberts; Chicago Cinema Entertainment *Dir.* Darryl Roberts *Scr.* Darryl Roberts and McDade Ivory Ocean *Cine.* Sheldon Lane *Ed.* Tom Miller *Mu.* Joe Thomas and Steve Grissette *P.d.* Phillipe Roberts *A.d.* Simmie Williams *S.d.* Phillipe Roberts *R.t.* 89 min. *MPAA* R. *Cast:* Stoney Jackson, Anthony Norman McKay, Liza Cruzet, Tatiana Tumbtzen, Catero Colbert, Reggie Theus, Darryl Roberts.

In this Hollywood romance, a pageant promoter (Stoney Jackson) tries to turn a ghetto girl (Liza Cruzet) into a classy model, but the plan fails. Another variation on the Cinderella story, with a fine original musical score.

PERSONAL CHOICE

Pro. Joseph Perez for Five Star Entertainment Productions; Moviestore Entertainment *Dir.* David Saperstein *Scr.* David Saperstein *Cine.* John Bartley *Ed.* Patrick McMahon *Mu.* Goeff Levin and Chris Smart *P.d.* John Jay Moore *A.d.* Douglas Higgins *R.t.* 88 min. *MPAA* PG. *Cast:* Martin Sheen, Christian Slater, Robert Foxworth, Sharon Stone, Olivia d'Abo, F. Murray Abraham, Don Davis.

Infected by radiation poisoning during a moon walk, bitter former astronaut Paul Andrews (Martin Sheen) forms a relationship with a teenager, Eric (Christian Slater), who idolizes him. Conflict with the boy's father, NASA scientist Richard Michaels (Robert Foxworth), is one of several elements meant to project drama into what is essentially a message picture about man's wisdom in facing the future, both on Earth and in space.

THE PHANTOM OF THE OPERA

Pro. Harry Alan Towers for Menahem Golan; 21st Century Film Corporation *Dir.* Dwight H. Little *Scr.* Duke Sandefur; based on a screenplay by Gerry O'Hara *Cine.* Elemer Ragalyi *Ed.* Charles Bornstein *Mu.* Misha Segal *A.d.* Tivadar Bertalan *R.t.* 90 min. *MPAA* R. *Cast:* Robert Englund, Jill Schoelen, Alex Hyde-White, Bill Nighy, Stephanie Lawrence, Terence Harvey, Nathan Lewis, Molly Shannon, Emma Rawson.

In this version of *The Phantom of the Opera*, a contemporary woman, Christine (Jill Schoelen), time travels to London at the turn of the century. The demented composer Erik, the Phantom (Robert Englund), is a homicidal maniac in the tradition of Englund's Freddy from the *A Nightmare on Elm Street* series.

PHYSICAL EVIDENCE

Pro. Martin Ransohoff; Columbia Pictures *Dir.* Michael Crichton *Scr.* Bill Phillips; based on a story by Steve Ransohoff and Phillips *Cine.* John A. Alonzo *Ed.* Glenn Farr *Mu.* Henry Mancini *P.d.* Dan Yarhi *A.d.* Dennis Davenport *S.d.* Jacques Bradette *R.t.* 99 min. *MPAA* R. *Cast:* Burt Reynolds, Theresa Russell, Ned Beatty, Kay Lenz, Ted McGinley, Tom O'Brien, Kenneth Welsh, Ray Baker, Ken James, Michael P. Moran, Angelo Rizacos, Lamar Jackson, Paul Hubbard, Larry Reynolds, Peter MacNeil, Laurie Paton, Don Granbery.

This courtroom/crime story revolves around the relationship between a defense attorney (Theresa Russell) and her client (Burt Reynolds). He is accused of murder, and her growing emotional involvement with him could put her life in danger if he is guilty.

PINK CADILLAC

Pro. David Valdes for Malpaso; Warner Bros. *Dir.* Buddy Van Horn *Scr.* John Eskow *Cine.* Jack N. Green *Ed.* Joel Cox *Mu.* Steve Dorff *P.d.* Edward C. Carfagno *S.d.* Thomas L. Roysden *R.t.* 122 min. *MPAA* PG-13. *Cast:* Clint Eastwood, Bernadette Peters, Timothy Carhart, John Dennis Johnston, Michael Des Barres, Geoffrey Lewis.

A young mother (Bernadette Peters) and her baby run off in a pink cadillac. She is jumping bail and leaving her ex-con husband. Soon fugitive-hunter Tommy Nowak (Clint Eastwood) is chasing, catching, and loving her.

POLICE ACADEMY VI: CITY UNDER SIEGE

Pro. Paul Maslansky; Warner Bros. *Dir.* Peter Bonerz *Scr.* Stephen J. Curwick; based on characters created by Neal Israel and Pat Proft *Cine.* Charles Rosher, Jr. *Ed.* Hubert de la Bouillerie *Mu.* Robert Folk *P.d.* Tho E. Azzari *R.t.* 83 min. *MPAA* PG. *Cast:* Bubba Smith, David Graf, Michael Winslow, Leslie Easterbrook, Marion Ramsey, Lance Kinsey,

Matt McCoy, Bruce Mahler, G. W. Bailey, George Gaynes, Kenneth Mars, Gerrit Graham, George R. Robertson.

Another in the popular series, this comic film features Lassard and his team in an attempt to stop a wave of robberies.

PRANCER

Pro. Raffaella De Laurentiis for Nelson Entertainment in association with Cineplex Odeon Films; Orion Pictures   *Dir.* John Hancock   *Scr.* Greg Taylor   *Cine.* Misha Suslov   *Ed.* Dennis O'Connor   *Mu.* Maurice Jarre   *P.d.* Chester Kaczenski   *A.d.* Marc Dabe   *S.d.* Judi Sandin   *R.t.* 103 min.   *MPAA* G.   *Cast:* Sam Elliott, Rebecca Harrell, Cloris Leachman, Rutanya Alda, John Joseph Duda, Abe Vigoda, Michael Constantine, Ariana Richards, Frank Welker.

Eight-year-old Jessica (Rebecca Harrell) maintains an optimistic attitude despite a hard life on the farm with her widower father (Sam Elliott) and her brother (John Joseph Duda). When she finds a wounded reindeer one winter, she believes it is the legendary Prancer and vows to make it well and help it find its way home. Faith and fantasy thus soften the hard edges of reality in the tradition of Christmas stories.

PURGATORY

Pro. Ami Artzi in association with International Media Exchange, Filmco, and Kingsway Communications; New Star Entertainment   *Dir.* Ami Artzi   *Scr.* Felix Kroll and Paul Aratow   *Cine.* Tom Fraser   *Ed.* Ettie Feldman   *Mu.* Julian Laxton   *P.d.* Robert van der Coolwijk   *S.d.* Eva Strack   *R.t.* 93 min.   *MPAA* R.   *Cast:* Tanya Roberts, Julie Pop, Hal Orlandini, Rufus Swart, Adrienne Pearce, Marie Human, David Sherwood, Clare Marshall, Hugh Rouse, John Newland.

Purgatory is the name of a hellish prison in a fictional African nation into which two Peace Corps workers (Tanya Roberts and Julie Pop) are thrown on trumped-up drug charges.

RACE FOR GLORY

Pro. Jon Gordon and Daniel A. Sherkow for BPS Productions; New Century/Vista   *Dir.* Rocky Lang   *Scr.* Scott Swanton; based on a story by Rocky Lang   *Cine.* Jack N. Green   *Ed.* Maryann Brandon   *Mu.* Jay Ferguson   *P.d.* Cynthia Kay Charette   *A.d.* Kurt Gauger and J. M. Hugon   *S.d.* Donna Casey and Annie Seneghal   *R.t.* 96 min.   *MPAA* R.   *Cast:* Alex McArthur, Peter Berg, Pamela Ludwig, Ray Wise, Oliver Stritzel, Brut Kwouk, Jerome Dempsey, Lane Smith.

Two friends, motorcycle racer Cody (Alex McArthur) and his mechanic Chris (Peter Berg), dream of glory on the international racing circuit but have a quarrel in which Cody also loses his girlfriend Jenny (Pamela Ludwig). After having been used by his backers in Europe with tragic results, a disillusioned Cody returns home, where a reunion assures that the narrative will result in a victory in the big race.

THE RACHEL PAPERS (Great Britain, 1989)

Pro. Andrew S. Karsch for Initial Productions and Longfellow Pictures; United Artists   *Dir.* Damian Harris   *Scr.* Damian Harris; based on the novel by Martin Amis   *Cine.* Alex Thomson   *Ed.* David Martin   *Mu.* Chaz Jankel   *P.d.* Andrew McAlpine   *R.t.* 95 min. *MPAA* R.   *Cast:* Dexter Fletcher, Ione Skye, Jonathan Pryce, James Spader, Bill Patterson, Lesley Sharp, Michael Gambon.

Home computers play a role in the torrid but short-lived affair between wealthy, youthful Charles Highway (Dexter Fletcher) and beautiful Rachel Noyce (Ione Skye).

RED SCORPION

Pro. Jack Abramoff; Shapiro Glickenhaus Entertainment   *Dir.* Joseph Zito   *Scr.* Arne Olsen;

based on a story by Robert Abramoff, Jack Abramoff, and Olsen *Cine.* Joao Fernandes *Ed.*
Daniel Loewenthal *Mu.* Jay Chattaway *P.d.* Ladislav Wilheim *R.t.* 102 min. *MPAA* R.
Cast: Dolph Lundgren, M. Emmet Walsh, Al White, T. P. McKenna, Carmen Argenziano,
Alex Colon, Brion James, Regopstaan.

A Russian special services officer, Lieutenant Nikolai (Dolph Lundgren), leads African
rebels into successful battle against Russian and Cuban forces.

RELENTLESS

Pro. Howard Smith for CineTel Films; New Line Cinema *Dir.* William Lustig *Scr.*
Jack T. D. Robinson (Phil Alden Robinson) *Cine.* James Lemmo *Ed.* David Kern *Mu.* Jay
Chattaway *P.d.* Gene Abel *S.d.* Ann Job *R.t.* 92 min. *Cast:* Judd Nelson, Robert Loggia,
Leo Rossi, Meg Foster, Patrick O'Bryan, Mindy Seeger, Ron Taylor, Beau Starr, Angel
Tompkins, Harriet Hall, Ken Lerner, Frank Pesce, George (Buck) Flower, Armand
Mastroianni.

Dedicated policeman Sam Dietz (Leo Rossi) determines to do whatever it takes to find a
psychotic killer (Judd Nelson).

RENEGADES

Pro. David Madden for Morgan Creek Productions and Interscope Communications; Uni-
versal Pictures *Dir.* Jack Sholder *Scr.* David Rich *Cine.* Philip Meheux *Ed.* Caroline
Biggerstaff *Mu.* Michael Kamen *P.d.* Carol Spier *A.d.* James McAteer *R.t.* 106 min.
MPAA R. *Cast:* Kiefer Sutherland, Lou Diamond Phillips, Jami Gertz, Rob Knepper, Bill
Smitrovich, Floyd Westerman.

A Philadelphia cop (Kiefer Sutherland) on an undercover mission to unearth corruption in
the department becomes involved in a robbery. During the crime, the gang boss Marino (Rob
Knepper) steals a Native American lance.

THE RETURN OF THE MUSKETEERS (Great Britain, France, and Spain, 1989)

Pro. Michelle De Broca and Pierre Spengler for Timothy Burill Productions/Filmdebroc-Cine
5/Iberoamericana Films; Universal Pictures *Dir.* Richard Lester *Scr.* George MacDonald
Fraser; based on the novel *Twenty Years After*, by Alexander Dumas *Cine.* Bernard Lutic *Ed.*
John Victor Smith *Mu.* Jean-Claude Petit *P.d.* Gil Arrondo *Cast:* Michael York, Oliver
Reed, Frank Finlay, C. Thomas Howell, Kim Cattrall, Richard Chamberlain, Philippe Noiret,
Roy Kinnear, Geraldine Chaplin, Christopher Lee, Eusebio Lazaro, Jean-Pierre Cassel, David
Birkin, Alan Howard.

Alexandre Dumas' novel *Twenty Years After*, which reunited his famous four musketeers
(D'Artagnan, Athos, Porthos, and Aramis) in another swashbuckling adventure, is adapted to
the screen by director Richard Lester with most of the cast members reprising their earlier
roles.

THE RETURN OF THE SWAMP THING

Pro. Ben Melniker and Michael Uslan; Lightyear Entertainment *Dir.* Jim Wynorski *Scr.*
Derek Spencer and Grant Morris; based on the D. C. Comics character *Cine.* Zoran
Hochstatter *Ed.* Leslie Rosenthal *Mu.* Chuck Cirino *P.d.* Robb Wilson King *S.d.* Frank
Galline *R.t.* 88 min. *MPAA* PG-13. *Cast:* Louis Jourdan, Heather Locklear, Sarah Doug-
las, Dick Durock, Ace Mask, Joey Sagal.

A young woman, Abby Arcane (Heather Locklear), arrives at a remote Florida mansion
to confront her evil stepfather, Dr. Anton Arcane (Louis Jourdan), about her mother's
mysterious death. While there, the beautiful, young vegetarian falls in love with a plant (Dick
Durock). This spoof is the second attempt to bring the eponymous D. C. Comics character to
cinematic life.

RIDING THE EDGE

Pro. Wolf Schmidt for Kodiak Films; Trans World Entertainment   *Dir.* James Fargo   *Scr.* Ronald A. Suppa   *Cine.* Bernard Salzmann   *Ed.* James Ruxin   *Mu.* Michael Gibbs   *P.d.* James Shanahan   *R.t.* 95 min.   *MPAA* R.   *Cast:* Raphael Sbarge, Catherine Mary Stewart, Peter Haskell, Lyman Ward, Asher Sarfati, Benny Bruchim, Michael Sarne, Nili Zomer, James Fargo, Brooke Bundy.

An American youth acts as a courier to rescue his kidnapped father in the Mideast. A motocross enthusiast, the boy rides through the desert on his mission, getting assistance along the way from a female United States agent and a young African prince.

RIVER OF DEATH

Pro. Harry Alan Towers and Avi Lerner; Cannon Releasing   *Dir.* Steve Carver   *Scr.* Andrew Deutsch and Edward Simpson; based on the novel by Alistair MacLean   *Cine.* Avi Karpick   *Ed.* Ken Bornstein   *Mu.* Sasha Matson   *A.d.* John Rosewarne   *R.t.* 103 min.   *MPAA* R.   *Cast:* Michael Dudikoff, Robert Vaughn, Donald Pleasence, Herbert Lom, L. Q. Jones, Sarah Maur Thorp, Cynthia Erland, Foziah Davidson.

Led by adventurer John Hamilton (Michael Dudikoff), a group of diverse characters travel up the Amazon river in search of an ex-Nazi doctor, Wolfgang Manteuffel (Robert Vaughn), who is continuing his evil experiments in the jungle depths.

RIVERBEND

Pro. Sam Vance for Vandale Productions; Intercontinental   *Dir.* Sam Firstenberg   *Scr.* Sam Vance   *Cine.* Ken Lamkin   *Ed.* Marcus Manton   *Mu.* Paul Loomis   *A.d.* Jack Marty   *R.t.* 100 min.   *Cast:* Steve James, Margaret Avery, Tony Frank, Julius Tennon, Alex Morris, Vanessa Tate, T. J. Kennedy, Linwood Walker, Norm Colvin, Keith Kirk, John Norman, Al Evans.

In Georgia in 1966, three black soldiers eluding a court martial for failing to follow orders in Vietnam come to the aid of black townfolk being persecuted by an evil white sheriff (Tony Frank). Led by Major Quinton (Steve James), the three heroes help set things right in an action fantasy which seeks to treat race relations of the period in a meaningful way.

ROAD HOUSE

Pro. Joel Silver for Silver Pictures; United Artists   *Dir.* Rowdy Herrington   *Scr.* David Lee Henry and Hilary Jenkin; based on a story by Henry   *Cine.* Dean Cundey   *Ed.* Frank Urioste and John Link   *Mu.* Michael Kamen   *S.d.* Phil M. Leonard   *R.t.* 114 min.   *MPAA* R.   *Cast:* Patrick Swayze, Kelly Lynch, Sam Elliott, Ben Gazzara, Marshall Teague, Julie Michaels, Red West, Sunshine Parker, Jeff Healey, Kevin Tighe.

A tough loner named Dalton (Patrick Swayze) is hired as a bouncer in a bar and winds up cleaning up a whole town while romancing a local doctor named Doc (Kelly Lynch). This film is not a remake of the 1948 Fox release *Road House*.

ROMERO

Pro. Ellwood E. Kieser for Paulist Pictures; Four Seasons   *Dir.* John Duigan   *Scr.* John Sacret Young   *Cine.* Geoff Burton   *Ed.* Frans Vandenburg   *Mu.* Gabriel Jared   *P.d.* Roger Ford   *S.d.* Olivia Bond   *R.t.* 94 min.   *Cast:* Raul Julia, Richard Jordan, Ana Alicia, Tony Plana, Harold Gould.

Father Oscar Romero (Raul Julia), a Catholic priest, is transformed into a forceful, committed leader of the people in politically troubled El Salvador before being assassinated in 1980. The biography of Romero, who rose from anonymity to become an archbishop, seeks to engage emotions and raise consciousness about the social and political struggles of the Salvadoran people while providing a textured portrait of the central figure.

ROOFTOPS

Pro. Howard W. Koch, Jr.; New Visions Pictures *Dir.* Robert Wise *Scr.* Terence Brennan; based on a story by Allan Goldstein and Tony Mark *Cine.* Theo Van de Sande *Ed.* William Reynolds *Mu.* David A. Stewart and Michael Kamen *P.d.* Jeannine Claudia Oppewall *A.d.* John Wright Stevens *S.d.* Gretchen Rau *R.t.* 95 min. *MPAA* R. *Cast:* Jason Gedrick, Troy Beyer, Eddie Velez, Alexis Cruz, Tisha Campbell, Allen Payne.

A group of ghetto youth live a makeshift existence on the roofs of abandoned tenements in Manhattan. Rivalry with a drug-dealing gang erupts, and the beautiful Elena (Troy Beyer) is forced to choose between loyalty to her cousin Lobo (Eddie Velez) and her attraction to T (Jason Gedrick), an expert in the Brazilian martial arts-dance known as capoeira.

THE ROSE GARDEN

Pro. Artur Brauner for CCC Filmkunst (Berlin) in association with Cannon Film, ZDF (Mainz), ORF (Vienna); Pathe International *Dir.* Fons Rademakers *Scr.* Paul Henugge *Cine.* Gernot Roll *Ed.* Kees Lindhorst *Mu.* Egisto Macchi *P.d.* Jan Schluback *R.t.* 112 min. *Cast:* Liv Ullmann, Maximilian Schell, Peter Fonda, Jan Nicklas, Katarina Lena Muller, Kurt Hubner, Hanns Zischler, Gila Almagor, Mareike Carriere, George Marischka, Nicolaus Sombart, Ozay Fecht, Achim Ruppel, Friedhelm Lehmann.

Based on a true World War II incident involving the hanging of twenty Jewish children by an SS officer, this courtroom drama involves a fictional escapee from the incident, Aaron Reichenbacher (Maximilian Schell), and his defense attorney, Gabriele Freund (Liv Ullmann), who discovers the truth of the old man's attack on the still unpunished SS officer.

RUDE AWAKENING

Pro. Aaron Russo for Aaron Russo Entertainment; Orion Pictures *Dir.* Aaron Russo and David Greenwalt *Scr.* Neil Levy and Richard LaGravenese; based on a story by Levy *Cine.* Tom Sigel *Ed.* Paul Rothchild *Mu.* Jonathan Elias *P.d.* Mel Bourne *S.d.* Carol Nast *R.t.* 100 min. *MPAA* R. *Cast:* Cheech Marin, Eric Roberts, Julie Hagerty, Robert Carradine, Buck Henry, Louise Lasser, Cindy Williams, Andrea Martin, Cliff De Young, Aaron Russo, Timothy Leary, Jerry Rubin, Bobby Seale, David Peel, Greg Rex, Dion Anderson, Peter Boyden, Nicholas Wyman, Michael Luciano, Ed Fry, Timothy L. Halpern, Davidson Thomson, Kevin Dornan, Denna Levy.

The 1960's collide with the 1980's as two unreconstructed hippies, Hesus (Cheech Marin) and Fred (Eric Roberts), return to New York and are pursued by a crazed CIA agent (Cliff De Young).

SAVAGE BEACH

Pro. Arlene Sidaris; Malibu Bay Films *Dir.* Andy Sidaris *Scr.* Andy Sidaris *Cine.* Howard Wexler *Ed.* Michael Haight *Mu.* Gary Stockdale *P.d.* Jimmy Hadder *R.t.* 95 min. *MPAA* R. *Cast:* Dona Speir, Hope Marie Carlton, John Aprea, Bruce Penhall, Rodrigo Obregon, Michael Mikasa, Michael Shaner, Teri Weigel, Dann Seki, Al Leong, Eric Chen, Paul Cody, Lisa London, Patty Duffek.

Female adventurers Donna (Dona Speir) and Taryn (Hope Marie Carlton), government drug enforcement agents who moonlight as air cargo haulers, become involved with a conflict over a horde of gold after they crash-land on a remote island. The action is mostly light in this third followup to *Malibu Express*, which introduced the leads.

SEASON OF FEAR

Pro. Scott J. Mulvaney for Filmstar; Metro-Goldwyn-Mayer/United Artists *Dir.* Doug Campbell *Scr.* Doug Campbell; based on a story by Campbell and Scott J. Mulvaney *Cine.*

Chuy Elizondo *Ed.* Dan Selakovich *Mu.* David Wolinski *P.d.* Phillip Michael Brandes *R.t.* 89 min. *MPAA* R. *Cast:* Michael Bowen, Ray Wise, Clancy Brown, Clara Wren, Michael J. Pollard.

Mick Drummond (Michael Bowen), though long estranged from his father Fred (Ray Wise), responds to a letter from the older man and winds up involved in an affair with his stepmother Sara (Clara Wren) that leads to murder.

SECOND SIGHT

Pro. Mark Tarloy for Lorimar Film Entertainment and Ursus Film; Warner Bros. *Dir.* Joel Zwick *Scr.* Tom Schulman and Patricia Resnick *Cine.* Dana Christiaansen *Ed.* David Ray *Mu.* John Morris *P.d.* James L. Schoppe *A.d.* Paul W. Gorfine *S.d.* Bryan Thetford *R.t.* 84 min. *MPAA* PG. *Cast:* John Larroquette, Bronson Pinchot, Bess Armstrong, Stuart Pankin, John Schuck, James Tolkan, William Prince, Michael Lombard, Christine Estabrook, Marisol Massey.

Three detectives, Wills (John Larroquette), Preston (Stuart Pankin), and Bobby McGee (Bronson Pinchot), attempt to establish their agency's reputation based on Bobby's psychic abilities.

SEE YOU IN THE MORNING

Pro. Alan J. Pakula for Lorimar; Warner Bros. *Dir.* Alan J. Pakula *Scr.* Alan J. Pakula *Cine.* Donald McAlpine *Ed.* Evan Lottman *Mu.* Michael Small *P.d.* George Jenkins *A.d.* Robert Guerra *R.t.* 119 min. *MPAA* PG-13. *Cast:* Jeff Bridges, Alice Krige, Farrah Fawcett, Drew Barrymore, Lukas Haas, David Dukes, Frances Sternhagen, Heather Lilly.

Jeff Bridges plays Larry Livingston, a Manhattan psychiatrist who is torn by his feelings of responsibility to his second marriage and to his kids from his first marriage.

SEVERANCE

Pro. Ann Bohrer and David Max Steinberg; Fox/Lorber Films *Dir.* David Max Steinberg *Scr.* David Max Steinberg and Cynthia Hochman *Cine.* David Max Steinberg *Ed.* David Max Steinberg, Thomas R. Rodinella, and Cecilia Zanuso *Mu.* Daniel May *R.t.* 105 min. *Cast:* Lou Liotta, Lisa Nicole Wolpe, Linda Christian-Jones, Carl Pistilli, Sandra Soehngen, Martin Haber, Lou Bonaki.

A former Air Force officer, Ray (Lou Liotta), has turned into an alcoholic bum after a car accident in which his wife was killed. Eventually Ray reconciles with his estranged daughter, who was a child when the accident occurred, and has been supporting herself by working in a sleazy bar.

SEXBOMB

Pro. Rick Eye; Phillips & Mora Entertainment/Film Barns Productions *Dir.* Jeff Broadstreet *Scr.* Robert Benson *Cine.* Dale Larson *Ed.* Todd Felker *Mu.* Leonard Marcel *A.d.* Liz Simakis *R.t.* 89 min. *Cast:* Robert Quarry, Linnea, Stuart Benton, Delia Sheppard, Stephen Liska, Kathryn Stanleigh, Spice Williams.

A crass producer of low-grade films, King Faraday (Robert Quarry), is murdered by a bitter would-be screenwriter, Lou Lurrod (Stuart Benton), at the urging of King's bored wife Candy (Delia Sheppard).

SHE'S OUT OF CONTROL

Pro. Stephen Deutsch; Columbia Pictures *Dir.* Stan Dragoti *Scr.* Seth Winston and Michael J. Nathanson *Cine.* Donald Peterman *Ed.* Dov Hoenig *Mu.* Alan Silvestri *P.d.* David L. Snyder *A.d.* Joe Wood *S.d.* Bruce Gibeson *R.t.* 95 min. *MPAA* PG. *Cast:* Tony Danza, Catherine Hicks, Wallace Shawn, Dick O'Neill, Ami Dolenz, Laura Mooney, Derek McGrath, Dana Ashbrook, Matthew L. Perry.

General manager of a Los Angeles rock radio station, Doug Simpson (Tony Danza) is bewildered when his girlfriend, Janet (Catherine Hicks), turns his studious daughter (Ami Dolenz) into a wild teenager. The father seeks advice from an offbeat psychiatrist (Wallace Shawn), and the daughter is besieged by young men.

SHIRLEY VALENTINE

Pro. Lewis Gilbert for Paramount Pictures; Paramount Pictures *Dir.* Lewis Gilbert *Scr.* Willy Russell; based on his play *The Wit and Wisdom of Shirley Valentine Cine.* Alan Hume *Ed.* Lesley Walker *Mu.* George Hadjinassios and Willy Russell *P.d.* John Stoll *R.t.* 108 min. *MPAA* R. *Cast:* Pauline Collins, Tom Conti, Alison Steadman, Julia McKenzie, Joanna Lumley, Bernard Hill, Sylvia Sims, Gillian Kearney, Catherine Duncan.

Shirley Valentine (Pauline Collins), a middle-aged Liverpool housewife with a streak of rebelliousness, muses about events in her life while they are being dramatically enacted. Based on a one-woman play, this cinematic adaptation opens up the monologue while keeping Shirley's distinctive point of view as principal focus.

SHOCKER

Pro. Marianne Maddalena and Barin Kumar for Alive Films; Universal *Dir.* Wes Craven *Scr.* Wes Craven *Cine.* Jacques Haitkin *Ed.* Andy Blumenthal *Mu.* William Goldstein *P.d.* Cynthia Kay Charette *A.d.* Randy Moore *S.d.* Naomi Shohan *R.t.* 110 min. *MPAA* R. *Cast:* Michael Murphy, Peter Berg, Mitch Pileggi, Cami Cooper, Richard Brooks, Theodore Raimi, John Tesh.

Executed murderer Horace Pinker (Mitch Pileggi) lives on as a spirit inhabiting numerous others by means of the television airwaves while seeking revenge on the young man who aided in his capture.

SIGNS OF LIFE

Pro. Marcus Viscidi and Andrew Reichman for American Playhouse Theatrical Film; Avenue Pictures *Dir.* John David Coles *Scr.* Mark Malone *Cine.* Elliot Davis *Ed.* William Anderson and Angelo Corrao *Mu.* Howard Shore *P.d.* Howard Cummings *A.d.* Beth Rubino *S.d.* Jeanette Scott *R.t.* 91 min. *MPAA* PG-13. *Cast:* Arthur Kennedy, Kevin J. O'Connor, Vincent Philip D'Onofrio, Michael Lewis, Beau Bridges, Kate Reid, Mary Louise Parker, Georgia Engel, Kathy Bates.

Residents of a small, coastal town in Maine face a crisis as the wooden fishing-boat factory on which the town depends closes.

SILENT NIGHT, DEADLY NIGHT III: BETTER WATCH OUT!

Pro. Arthur H. Gorson; Quiet Films *Dir.* Monte Hellman *Scr.* Carlos Lazlo, Monte Hellman, and Richard N. Gladstein; based on a story by Lazlo *Cine.* Joseph M. Civit *Ed.* Ed Rothkowitz *Mu.* Steven Soles *P.d.* Philip Thomas *A.d.* Laurie Post *R.t.* 91 min. *MPAA* R. *Cast:* Richard Beymer, Bill Moseley, Samantha Scully, Eric Da Re, Laura Herring, Elizabeth Hoffman, Robert Culp, Isabel Cooley, Leonard Mann, Carlos Palomino.

The "Santa Claus" killer, Ricky (Bill Moseley), of two earlier horror films is roused from a coma and kills again, destroying even the scientist (Richard Beymer) who had been experimenting with resurrection of his inner being.

A SINFUL LIFE

Pro. Daniel Raskov; New Line Cinema *Dir.* William Schreiner *Scr.* Melanie Graham; based on her play *Just Like the Pom Pom Girls Cine.* Jonathan West *Ed.* Jeffrey Reiner *Mu.* Todd Hayden *P.d.* Robert Zentis *R.t.* 90 min. *MPAA* R. *Cast:* Anita Morris, Rick Overton, Dennis Christopher, Blair Tefkin, Mark Rolston, Cynthia Szigeti.

An alcoholic, unfit mother is given a short period of time in which to straighten up, or her daughter will be taken away by the authorities. The film centers on the mother's attempt to become respectable by marrying, cleaning her apartment, and remembering her daughter's birthday.

SING

Pro. Craig Zadan for Storyline Productions; Tri-Star Pictures *Dir.* Richard Baskin *Scr.* Dean Pitchford *Cine.* Peter Sova *Ed.* Bud Smith, Jere Huggins, and Scott Smith *Mu.* Jay Gruska *P.d.* Carol Spier *A.d.* James McAteer *S.d.* Michael Harris *R.t.* 97 min. *MPAA* PG-13. *Cast:* Lorraine Bracco, Peter Dobson, Jessica Steen, Louise Lasser, George DiCenzo, Patti LaBelle, Susan Peretz, Laurnea Wilkerson, Rachel Sweet.

The students of a Brooklyn high school which is threatened with closing by the authorities mount a musical talent show. The stock plot includes a romance between a street hood (Peter Dobson) who has a talent for dance and pristine Hannah (Jessica Steen).

SKIN DEEP

Pro. Tony Adams for Morgan Creek Productions; Twentieth Century-Fox *Dir.* Blake Edwards *Scr.* Blake Edwards *Cine.* Isidore Mankofsky *Ed.* Robert Pergament *P.d.* Rodger Maus *S.d.* Marvin March *R.t.* 101 min. *MPAA* R. *Cast:* John Ritter, Vincent Gardenia, Alyson Reed, Joel Brooks, Julianne Phillips, Raye Hollit, Michael Kidd, Chelsea Field.

Blake Edwards directs John Ritter as Zach, a successful, Pulitzer Prize-winning author trapped in a life of excess in the playground of Los Angeles. Zach indulges in his penchant for womanizing and excessive drinking and then turns to the psychiatrist to overcome the remorse his habits cause him.

SLAVES OF NEW YORK

Pro. Ismail Merchant and Gary Hendler; Tri-Star Pictures *Dir.* James Ivory *Scr.* Tama Janowitz; based on her stories *Cine.* Tony Pierce-Roberts *Ed.* Katherine Wenning *Mu.* Richard Robbins *P.d.* David Gropman *A.d.* Karen Schultz *R.t.* 121 min. *MPAA* R. *Cast:* Bernadette Peters, Adam Coleman Howard, Nick Corri, Madeleine Potter, Charles Mc-Caughan, Chris Sarandon, Mary Beth Hurt, Mercedes Ruehl, John Harkins, Anna Katarina, Bruce Peter Young, Michael Schoeffing, Steve Buscemi, Christine Dunford, Betty Comden, Tammy Grimes, Tama Janowitz, Joe Leeway, Michael Butler, Johann Carlo, Philip Lenkowsky, Harsh Nayyar, Stanley Tucci, Louis Guss, Maura Moynihan, Kim Larese, Ken Kensei, Kevin John Gee, Rick Hara, Francine Hunter.

Eleanor (Bernadette Peters), a hat designer with low self-esteem, is struggling to get her life together. Her boyfriend manipulates her vulnerability, her best friend sleeps with Eleanor's boyfriend, and a crazy artist wants her to pose in the nude for him. All of this takes place in the downtown Manhattan art scene.

SONS

Pro. Mark Toberoff; Pacific Pictures *Dir.* Alexandre Rockwell *Scr.* Alexandre Rockwell and Brandon Cole *Cine.* Stefan Czapsky *Ed.* Jan Freund *Mu.* Mader *A.d.* Virginia Fields *R.t.* 88 min. *Cast:* William Forsythe, D. B. Sweeney, Robert Miranda, Samuel Fuller, Stephane Audran, Judith Godreche, William Hickey, Bernard Fresson, Jennifer Beals, Shirley Stoller.

Three half-brothers—Mikey (William Forsythe), Ritchie (D. B. Sweeney), and Fred (Robert Miranda)—put aside temperamental differences to pool their resources in a united effort to find the lost love, Florence (Stephane Audran), of their paralyzed father (Samuel Fuller).

SPEED ZONE

Pro. Murray Shostak for Entcorp Communications; Orion Pictures *Dir.* Jim Drake *Scr.* Michael Short *Cine.* François Protat and Robert Saad *Ed.* Mike Economou *Mu.* David

Wheatley *P.d.* Richard Hudolin *S.d.* Gilles Aird and Patti Hall *R.t.* 95 min. *MPAA* PG. *Cast:* John Candy, Donna Dixon, Matt Frewer, Joe Flaherty, Tim Matheson, Mimi Kuzyk, Melody Anderson, Shari Belafonte, Peter Boyle, Dick Smothers, Tom Smothers, John Schneider, Jamie Farr, Lee Van Cleef, Eugene Levy, Michael Spinks, Brooke Shields, Carl Lewis.

A bizarre group of characters unexpectedly become competitors in an illicit cross-country road race. The mixture of car crashes and laughs is derived from previous films which have not enjoyed a good critical reputation.

SPICES (India, 1989)

Pro. National Film Development Corporation; Upfront Films in association with Cinema Four *Dir.* Ketan Mehta *Scr.* Shafi Hakim and Ketan Mehta; based on a story by Chunilal Madia *Cine.* Jahangir Choudhury *Ed.* Sanjiv Shah *Mu.* Rajat Dholakia *R.t.* 98 min. *Cast:* Naseeruddin Shah, Smita Patil, Om Puri, Suresh Oberoi, Raj Babbar, Raghu Nath, Deepti Naval.

In a small village in India in the 1940's, Sonbai (Smita Patil), whose husband has gone to work in the city, rebels against the demands of a feudal overlord and takes refuge in the spice factory where she works. She is protected by an elderly watchman, Abu Mian (Om Puri), until his death sets in motion a melodramatic climax which underscores the feminism and social protest that animate the story.

STEPFATHER II

Pro. William Burr and Darin Scott for ITC Entertainment Group; Millimeter Films *Dir.* Jeff Burr *Scr.* John Auerbach; based on characters created by Carolyn Lefcourt, Brian Garfield, and Donald E. Westlake *Cine.* Jack Laskus *Ed.* Pasquale A. Buba *Mu.* Jim Manzie *P.d.* Byrnadette Di Santo *A.d.* Aram Allen *S.d.* Johanna Butler *R.t.* 86 min. *MPAA* R. *Cast:* Terry O'Quinn, Meg Foster, Caroline Williams, Jonathan Brandis, Henry Brown, Mitchell Laurance, Leon Martell, Renata Scott, John O'Leary, Eric Brown.

Despite what seemed certain death in this film's critically lauded predecessor *The Step-father*, the protagonist (Terry O'Quinn, reprising the role he created) emerges from an asylum to seek the perfect middle-class American life and family. He is disappointed in what he finds, however, and is thus provoked into further violence.

STREET STORY

Pro. Joseph B. Vasquez; Films Around the World *Dir.* Joseph B. Vasquez *Scr.* Joseph B. Vasquez *Ed.* Joseph B. Vasquez *Mu.* Edward W. Burrows *R.t.* 90 min. *Cast:* Angelo Lopez, Cookie, Lydia Ramirez, Melvin Muza, Soraya Andrade, Zerocks, Rena Zentner, Edward W. Burrows.

This is a tragic story about Junior (Angelo Lopez) and Joey (Cookie), two brothers in the New York slums, whose father, a barber, pays protection money to the mafia. When Joey's girlfriend is murdered, he goes on a shooting rampage.

STRIPPED TO KILL II

Pro. Andy Ruben; Concorde *Dir.* Katt Shea Ruben *Scr.* Katt Shea Ruben *Cine.* Phedon Papamichael *Ed.* Stephen Mark *Mu.* Gary Stockdale *P.d.* Virginia Lee *A.d.* Greg Maher *S.d.* John Shapiro *R.t.* 82 min. *MPAA* R. *Cast:* Maria Ford, Eb Lottimer, Karen Mayo Chandler, Birke Tan, Marjean Holden, Debra Lamb, Lisa Glaser, Tom Ruben, Virginia Peters.

A low-budget suspense film, this sequel features a stripper who starts having nightmares that she is murdering her fellow dancers. When the dancers are murdered, Sergeant Decker (Eb Lottimer) tries to prove her innocence by finding the real killer.

THE SUITORS

Pro. Ghasem Ebrahimian and Coleen Higgins for First Run Features; First Run Features *Dir.* Ghasem Ebrahimian *Scr.* Ghasem Ebrahimian *Cine.* Manfred Reiff *Ed.* Amir Naderi and Ghasem Ebrahimian *Mu.* Nicholas Kean, F. Shahbazian, and A. Vaseghi *R.t.* 106 min. *Cast:* Pouran, Ali Azizian, Shahab Navab, Assurbanipal Babila, Bahman Maghsoudlou, Manuchehr Harsini, Bahman Soltani, Mariyam Touzi.

To celebrate their friend's marriage, a group of Iranian friends in New York travel upstate and steal a sheep. Later they slaughter the sheep in a bathtub in Manhattan. Blood drips through the ceiling, and the men are mistaken for terrorists. The new husband is shot, and his friends begin courting his widow.

SUNDAY'S CHILD

Pro. Nour Film *Dir.* Marianne Rosenbaum *Scr.* Marianne Rosenbaum; based on a book by Gudrun Mebs *Cine.* Alexander Opp *Ed.* Helga Endler *Mu.* Konstantin Wecker *R.t.* 89 min. *Cast:* Gudrun Mebs, Nurith-Hayat Samaan, Hans Peter Korff, Mirjam Niemeier, Wenzel Heubeck, Timm Schnabbe, Udo Weinberger, Johannes Wilbrink, Dietrich von Watzdorf, Luca Lombardi.

Anna (Gudrun Mebs), a writer, becomes a "Sunday mother" to Barbara (Nurith-Hayat Samaan), an orphan. Eventually they become close, and when Anna tries to adopt Barbara, the bureaucracy makes their legal union nearly impossible.

TANGO BAR

Pro. Roberto Gandara and Juan Carlos Codazzi for Zaga Films/Beco Films; Manley Productions *Dir.* Marcos Zurinaga *Scr.* Jose Pablo Feinman, Juan Carlos Codazzi, and Marcos Zurinaga *Cine.* Marcos Zurinaga *Ed.* Pablo Mari *Mu.* Atilio Stampone *P.d.* Maria Julia Bertotto *R.t.* 90 min. *Cast:* Raul Julia, Valeria Lynch, Ruben Juárez.

The film describes the evolution of the tango and its important role in the culture of Argentina. Raul Julia plays the owner of the Tango Bar and reminisces about the days when he and his partner (Ruben Juárez) produced an act about the history of the tango.

TEEN WITCH

Pro. Alana Lambros and Rafael Eisenman; Trans World Entertainment *Dir.* Dorian Walker *Scr.* Vernon Zimmerman and Robin Menken *Cine.* Marc Reshovsky *Ed.* Natan Zahavi *Mu.* Richard Elliot *P.d.* Stephen Rice *A.d.* Dana Torrey *S.d.* Anna Rita Raineri *R.t.* 105 min. *MPAA* PG-13. *Cast:* Robyn Lively, Dan Gauthier, Joshua Miller, Caren Kaye, Dick Sargent, Lisa Fuller, Mandy Ingber, Zelda Rubinstein, Noah Blake, Tina Marie Caspary, Megan Gallivan, Alssari Al-Shehail, Shelly Berman.

When fifteen-year-old Louise (Robyn Lively) discovers her magical powers via a fortune teller, she begins to imagine how she will exercise those powers, which she has been told will materialize on her sixteenth birthday. She soon finds that the result of her magic is more than she can handle.

THE TERROR WITHIN

Pro. Roger Corman; Concorde Pictures *Dir.* Thierry Notz *Scr.* Thomas M. Cleaver *Cine.* Ronn Schmidt *Ed.* Brent Schoenfeld *Mu.* Rick Conrad *P.d.* Kathleen B. Cooper *R.t.* 86 min. *MPAA* R. *Cast:* George Kennedy, Andrew Stevens, Starr Andreeff, Terri Treas, John LaFayette, Tommy Hinchley, Yvonne Saa, Roren Summer.

After most of the human race is destroyed by a bacteriological plague, a small group of scientists fights mutant creatures.

THREE FUGITIVES

Pro. Lauren Shuler-Donner for Silver Screen Partners IV; Touchstone Pictures *Dir.* Frances

Veber *Scr.* Frances Veber *Cine.* Haskell Wexler *Ed.* Bruce Green *Mu.* David McHugh *P.d.*
Rick Carter *A.d.* Margie Stone McShirley *S.d.* Richard C. Goddard *R.t.* 93 min. *MPAA*
PG-13. *Cast:* Nick Nolte, Martin Short, Sarah Rowland Doroff, James Earl Jones, Alan
Ruck, Kenneth McMillan.

An ex-convict (Nick Nolte) enters a bank to make an honest transaction and is taken
hostage by an inept robber (Martin Short) who desperately needs the money to help his
emotionally withdrawn daughter (Sarah Rowland Doroff). The police think that the hostage
is in on the heist, so all three become fugitives trying to leave the country.

TO DIE FOR

Pro. Barin Kumar; Entertainment/Lee Caplin *Dir.* Deren Sarafian *Scr.* Leslie King *Cine.*
David Boyd *Ed.* Michael D. Conner *Mu.* Laura Perlman *A.d.* Greg Oehler *R.t.* 90 min.
MPAA R. *Cast:* Brendan Hughes, Sydney Walsh, Amanda Wyss, Scott Jacoby, Micah Grant,
Duane Jones, Steve Bond, Remy O'Neill, Al Fann, Philip Granger, Julie Maddalena.

Despairing of finding passionate love, Kate Wooten (Sydney Walsh) is drawn to a vampire,
Vlad (Brendan Hughes), who returns her love. Complicating the dangerous romance is the
intended revenge on Vlad of another vampire, Tom (Steve Bond).

TORA-SAN GOES TO VIENNA (Japan, 1989)

Pro. Kiyoshi Shimazu and Kiyo Kurosu for Shochiku Company; Kino International *Dir.*
Yoji Yamada *Scr.* Yoji Yamada and Yoshitake Asama *Cine.* Tetsuo Takaba *Mu.* Naozumi
Yamamoto *A.d.* Mitsuo Degawa *R.t.* 110 min. *Cast:* Kiyoshi Atsumi, Chieko Baisho, Gin
Maeda, Massami Shimojo, Chishu Ryu, Akiro Emoto.

The lovable street vendor Tora-san (Kiyoshi Atsumi) befriends an exhausted businessman
(Akiro Emoto) and travels with him to Vienna. By the time Tora-san (the central character in
40 previous films) returns to Japan, he has once more helped others while suffering personal
heartbreak.

THE TOXIC AVENGER, PART II

Pro. Lloyd Kaufman and Michael Herz in association with Lorimar; Troma *Dir.* Lloyd
Kaufman and Michael Herz *Scr.* Gay Partington Terry; based on an original story by Lloyd
Kaufman *Cine.* James London *Ed.* Michael Schweitzer *Mu.* Barrie Guard *A.d.* Alexis
Grey *R.t.* 95 min. *MPAA* R. *Cast:* Ron Fazio, John Altamura, Phoebe Legere, Rick
Collins, Rikiya Yasouka, Tsutomu Sekine, Mayako Katsuragi, Shinoburyu, Lisa Gaye, Jessica
Dublin, Jack Cooper, Erika Schickel.

In this sequel to *The Toxic Avenger* (1986), superhero Toxic Avenger (Ron Fazio and John
Altamura) is beset by emotional problems. A trip to Japan to find his father, Big Mac (Rikiya
Yasouka), an underworld cocaine dealer, is the answer.

THE TOXIC AVENGER, PART III: THE LAST TEMPTATION OF TOXIE

Pro. Lloyd Kaufman and Michael Herz; Troma *Dir.* Lloyd Kaufman and Michael Herz *Scr.*
Gay Partington Terry and Lloyd Kaufman; based on a story by Kaufman *Cine.* James
London *Ed.* Joseph McGirr *Mu.* Christopher Demarco; based on music by Antonin Dvořák
A.d. Alexis Grey *R.t.* 89 min. *MPAA* R. *Cast:* Ron Fazio, John Altamura, Phoebe Legere,
Rick Collins, Lisa Gaye, Jessica Dublin.

In this third installment of the low-budget series that emphasizes gore as well as its
socially pertinent themes, "Toxie" takes on a monolithic corporation named Apocalypse,
Inc., more evil than even he would imagine.

TROOP BEVERLY HILLS

Pro. Ava Ostern Fries for Fries Entertainment and Avanti; Weintraub Entertainment Group
Dir. Jeff Kanew *Scr.* Pamela Norris and Margaret Griece Oberman; based on a story by Ava

Ostern Fries *Cine.* Donald E. Thorin *Ed.* Mark Melnick *Mu.* Randy Edelman *P.d.* Robert F. Boyle *A.d.* Jack G. Taylor, Jr. *S.d.* Anne McCulley *R.t.* 105 min. *MPAA* PG. *Cast:* Shelley Long, Craig T. Nelson, Betty Thomas, Mary Gross, Stephanie Beacham, Audra Lindley, Edd Byrnes, Jenny Lewis, Tasha Scott, Ami Foster, Carla Gugino, Heather Hopper, Aquilina Soriano.

Phyllis Nefler (Shelley Long), a young Beverly Hills matron, becomes den mother to a flagging troop of Beverly Hills Wilderness Girls, awarding merit badges for "sushi appreciation" and otherwise casting a Beverly Hills patina on their activities, in this comedy that eventually extols the down-home virtues over the glitz of wealth.

TRUE BLOOD

Pro. Peter Maris for Maris Entertainment; Fries Entertainment *Dir.* Frank Kerr *Scr.* Frank Kerr *Cine.* Mark H. L. Morris *Ed.* Mac Haight *Mu.* Scott Roewe *R.t.* 97 min. *MPAA* R. *Cast:* Jeff Fahey, Chad Lowe, Sherilyn Fenn, James Tolkan, Billy Drago, Ken Foree.

Brothers Ray (Jeff Fahey) and Donny Trueblood (Chad Lowe) are separated for ten years after an incident in a gang rumble leads to Ray being set up as a cop killer. Violent and romantic developments which are characteristic of the urban crime genre help to resolve the drama.

TRUST ME

Pro. George Edwards for Bruce Feldman, Harry Clein, and David Weisman; Cinecom Pictures *Dir.* Bobby Houston *Scr.* Bobby Houston and Gary Rigdon *Cine.* Thomas Jewett *Ed.* Barry Zetlin *Mu.* Pray For Rain *S.d.* Richard Dearborn *R.t.* 104 min. *MPAA* R. *Cast:* Adam Ant, David Packer, Talia Balsam, William DeAcutis, Joyce Van Patten, Barbara Bain, Brooke Davida, Simon McQueen, Alma Beltran, Marilyn Tokuda, Barbara Perry, Virgil Frye, Morri Beers, Anna Cray Carduno.

James Calendar (Adam Ant), a British art dealer living in Los Angeles, believes that the work of a young painter, Sam Brown (David Packer), will be worth more if Brown is dead. So he attempts to see that Brown does die—violently or otherwise—in this contemporary comedy which features many real artists in addition to its own quirky characters.

TURNER AND HOOCH

Pro. Raymond Wagner for Touchstone Pictures in association with Silver Screen Partners IV; Buena Vista *Dir.* Roger Spottiswoode *Scr.* Dennis Shryack, Michael Blodgett, Daniel Petrie, Jr., Jim Cash, and Jack Epps, Jr.; based on a story by Dennis Shryack, Michael Blodgett, and Daniel Petrie, Jr. *Cine.* Adam Greenberg *Ed.* Garth Craven *Mu.* Charles Gross *P.d.* John DeCuir, Jr. *A.d.* Sig Tinglof *S.d.* Cloudia *R.t.* 100 min. *MPAA* PG. *Cast:* Tom Hanks, Mare Winningham, Craig T. Nelson, Reginald Vel Johnson, Scott Paulin, J. C. Quinn, John McIntire.

In order to solve a murder case, a fastidious police investigator, Scott Turner (Tom Hanks) must rely on a huge, messy dog named Hooch, of whom he eventually becomes fond.

UHF

Pro. Gene Kirkwood and John Hyde for Cinecorp; Orion Pictures *Dir.* Jay Levey *Scr.* Al Yankovic and Jay Levey *Cine.* David Lewis *Ed.* Dennis O'Connor *Mu.* John Du Prez *P.d.* Ward Preston *R.t.* 96 min. *MPAA* PG-13. *Cast:* Weird Al Yankovic, Victoria Jackson, Kevin McCarthy, Michael Richards, David Bowe, Stanley Brock, Anthony Geary, Trinidad Silva, Gedde Watanabe, Billy Barty, John Paragon, Fran Drescher, Sue Ane Langdon, David Proval, Grant James, Emo Philips, Jay Levey.

Weird Al Yankovic plays George Newman, who makes a success of a faltering television station, Channel 62, along the way providing a frame for numerous parody sequences.

VALENTINO RETURNS

Pro. Peter Hoffman and David Wisnievitz for Owl Productions; Vidmark Entertainment *Dir.* Peter Hoffman *Scr.* Leonard Gardner; based on his story "Christ Has Returned to Earth and Preaches Here Nightly" *Cine.* Jerzy Zielinski *Ed.* Denine Rowan *A.d.* Woody Romine *R.t.* 88 min. *MPAA* R. *Cast:* Barry Tubb, Frederic Forrest, Veronica Cartwright, Jenny Wright, David Parker, Seth Isler, Miguel Ferrer, Kit McDonough, Macon McCalman, Jenny Gago, Leonard Gardner, William Frankfather, Jerry Hardin.

In an American small town in the 1950's, Wayne Gibbs (Barry Tubb), an appealing teenager, romances a chicken farmer's daughter, Sylvia (Jenny Wright), while trying to keep his home life stable even though his father Sonny (Frederic Forrest) and mother Patricia (Veronica Cartwright) have a highly volatile relationship.

VAMPIRE'S KISS

Pro. Barbara Zitwer and Barry Shils; Hemdale *Dir.* Robert Bierman *Scr.* Joseph Minion *Cine.* Stefan Czapsky *Ed.* Angus Newton *Mu.* Colin Towns *P.d.* Christopher Nowak *R.t.* 96 min. *MPAA* R. *Cast:* Nicolas Cage, Maria Conchita Alonso, Jennifer Beals, Elizabeth Ashley, Kasi Lemmons, Bob Lujan, Jessica Lundy, John Walker.

A Manhattan literary agent, Peter Loew (Nicolas Cage), is convinced that he has become a vampire after becoming involved with a mysterious, passionate young woman, Rachel (Jennifer Beals).

WARLOCK

Pro. Steve Miner; New World Pictures *Dir.* Steve Miner *Scr.* David Twohy *Cine.* David Eggby *Ed.* David Finfer *P.d.* Roy Forge Smith *A.d.* Gary Steele *R.t.* 102 min. *Cast:* Richard E. Grant, Julian Sands, Lori Singer, Kevin O'Brien, Richard Kuse, Juli Burkhart, Chip Johnson, David Carpenter, Anna Levine.

Giles Redferne (Richard E. Grant) pursues a 17th century warlock (Julian Sands) through time with the aid of Kassandra (Lori Singer).

WARM SUMMER RAIN

Pro. Cassian Elwes and Lionel Wigram for Smoking Gun Productions; Cinema Corp. *Dir.* Joe Gayton *Scr.* Joe Gayton *Cine.* Fernando Arguelles *Ed.* Ed Rothkowitz and Robin Katz *Mu.* Roger Eno *P.d.* Richard Helo *A.d.* Patricia Ellis *R.t.* 82 min. *Cast:* Kelly Lynch, Barry Tubb, Ron Sloan.

Following a suicide attempt, Kate (Kelly Lynch) wakes up one morning next to Guy (Barry Tubb), a stranger, in an abandoned house in the desert.

WEEKEND AT BERNIE'S

Pro. Victor Drai for Gladden Entertainment Corp.; Twentieth Century-Fox *Dir.* Ted Kotcheff *Scr.* Robert Klane *Cine.* Francois Protat *Ed.* Joan E. Chapman *Mu.* Andy Summers *P.d.* Peter Jamison *A.d.* Michael Novotny and Dean Taucher *S.d.* Jerie Kelter and R. W. Carpenter *R.t.* 97 min. *MPAA* PG-13. *Cast:* Andrew McCarthy, Jonathan Silverman, Catherine Mary Stewart, Terry Kiser, Don Calfa, Catherine Parks, Eloise Broady, Gregory Salata, Louis Giambalvo, Ted Kotcheff.

When two young office workers, Larry Wilson (Andrew McCarthy) and Richard Parker (Jonathan Silverman), are invited by their boss Bernie (Terry Kiser) for a weekend at his beach house, they do not realize that Bernie has dangerous associates. Bernie's murder leads to a slapstick storyline on the black side as the two heroes attempt to hide his corpse.

WELCOME HOME

Pro. Martin Ransohoff; Columbia Pictures and Rank Organization *Dir.* Franklin J. Schaffner *Scr.* Maggie Kleinman *Cine.* Fred J. Koenekamp *Ed.* Bob Swink *Mu.* Henry Mancini *P.d.*

Dan Yarhi and Dennis Davenport *R.t.* 87 min. *Cast:* Kris Kristofferson, JoBeth Williams, Brian Keith, Sam Waterston, Trey Wilson, J. J. (John Marshall Jones, Jr.), Thomas Brown, Kieu Chinh (Nguyen), Lela Ivey, Jamie Jones, Jeremy Ratchford, Nora Grant, Bill Lynn.

Lieutenant Jake Robbins (Kris Kristofferson) is presumed dead after becoming a POW in Vietnam, though in reality he escaped to Cambodia and married Leang (Kieu Chinh), a Cambodian girl, who bore him two children. Seventeen years later, he goes home to Vermont and faces the many complications of his life.

WHEN THE WHALES CAME (Great Britain, 1989)

Pro. Simon Channing Williams for Golden Swan; Twentieth Century-Fox *Dir.* Clive Rees *Scr.* Michael Morpurgo; based on his novel *Why the Whales Came* *Cine.* Robert Paynter *Ed.* Andrew Boulton *Mu.* Christopher Gunning *P.d.* Bruce Grimes *R.t.* 99 min. *MPAA* PG. *Cast:* Paul Scofield, David Threlfall, Helen Mirren, David Suchet, Helen Pearce, Max Rennie, Jeremy Kemp, John Hallam, Barbara Ewing, Dexter Fletcher, Nicholas Jones, Joanna Bartholomew.

In 1914 on the British island of Bryher, two children, Daniel (Max Rennie) and Gracie (Helen Pearce), befriend the Birdman (Paul Scofield), a mysterious individual isolated from the community. When a whale is beached on the island, their trust and belief in the Birdman helps save the whale and possibly lift a curse from the island.

WHO'S HARRY CRUMB?

Pro. Arnon Milchan; Tri-Star Pictures *Dir.* Paul Flaherty *Scr.* Robert Conte and Peter Martin Wortmann *Cine.* Stephen M. Katz *Ed.* Danford B. Greene *Mu.* Michel Colombier *P.d.* Trevor Williams *A.d.* Stephen Geaghan *S.d.* Elizabeth Wilcox *R.t.* 98 min. *MPAA* PG-13. *Cast:* John Candy, Jeffrey Jones, Annie Potts, Tim Thomerson, Barry Corbin, Shawnee Smith, Valri Bromfield, Doug Steckler, Renee Coleman, Wesley Mann, Fiona Roeske.

John Candy stars as bungling detective Harry Crumb, who ineptly solves the kidnapping of a Beverly Hills heiress.

WICKED STEPMOTHER

Pro. Robert Littman; Metro-Goldwyn-Mayer/United Artists *Dir.* Larry Cohen *Scr.* Larry Cohen *Cine.* Bryan England *Ed.* David Kern *Mu.* Robert Folk *A.d.* Gene Abel *R.t.* 92 min. *MPAA* PG-13. *Cast:* Bette Davis, Barbara Carrera, Colleen Camp, David Rasche, Lionel Stander, Tom Bosley, Shawn Donahue, Richard Moll, Evelyn Keyes, Susie Garrett, Laurene Landon.

Bette Davis stars as the stepmother of the title in this supernatural comedy about witchcraft and detective work. Davis and director Larry Cohen had a well-publicized dispute that resulted in Davis' leaving the production halfway through the film. Her character is replaced by Barbara Carrera who plays Priscilla, her daughter.

WINTER PEOPLE

Pro. Robert H. Solo for Nelson Entertainment; Columbia Pictures *Dir.* Ted Kotcheff *Scr.* Carol Sobieski; based on the novel by John Ehle *Cine.* François Protat *Ed.* Thom Noble *Mu.* John Scott *P.d.* Ron Foreman *A.d.* Chas Butcher *S.d.* Leslie Morales *R.t.* 110 min. *MPAA* PG-13. *Cast:* Kurt Russell, Kelly McGillis, Lloyd Bridges, Mitchel Ryan, Amelia Burnette, Eileen Ryan, Lanny Flaherty, Don Michael Paul, David Dwyer, Jeffrey Meek.

A widower, Wayland Jackson (Kurt Russell), and his little daughter arrive at a remote cabin in the old North Carolina hills occupied by Collie Wright (Kelly McGillis) and her baby son. Jackson and Collie fall in love, and he proves himself to her three brothers and her father (Lloyd Bridges), who are feuding with the evil Campbell clan. When a Campbell is killed, the clan demands that one of the Wrights be sacrificed to avenge the loss.

THE WIZARD

Pro. David Chisholm and Ken Topolsky for Finnegan-Pinchuk; Universal   *Dir.* Todd Holland
Scr. David Chisholm   *Cine.* Robert Yeoman   *Ed.* Tom Finan   *Mu.* J. Peter Robinson   *P.d.*
Michael Mayer   *A.d.* Rob Sissman   *S.d.* Claire J. Bowin   *R.t.* 99 min.   *MPAA* PG.   *Cast:*
Fred Savage, Beau Bridges, Christian Slater, Jenny Lewis, Luke Edwards, Will Seltzer, Sam
McMurray, Wendy Phillips.

Precocious Corey Woods (Fred Savage) sneaks his mentally ill brother Jimmy (Luke
Edwards) out of an institution in hopes of cashing in on Jimmy's wizardry at video games.
Accompanied by runaway Haley (Jenny Lewis) and pursued by various adults, they head for a
video game tournament in Los Angeles.

WONDERLAND (Great Britain, 1989)

Pro. Steve Morrison; Vestron Pictures   *Dir.* Philip Saville   *Scr.* Frank Clarke   *Cine.* Dick
Pope   *Ed.* Richard Bedford   *Mu.* Hans Zimmer   *P.d.* David Brockhurst   *R.t.* 103 min.   *MPAA*
R.   *Cast:* Emile Charles, Tony Forsyth, Robert Stephens, Clare Higgins, Bruce Payne,
Robbie Coltrane, Carsten Norgaard.

Two gay youths growing up in Liverpool—introverted Eddie (Emile Charles) and worldly
Michael (Tony Forsyth)—witness a murder and, partly to escape the pursuing killer, go to
Brighton with a lascivious opera singer, Vincent (Robert Stephens).

WORTH WINNING

Pro. Gil Friesen and Dale Pollock for A&M Films; Twentieth Century-Fox   *Dir.* Will Mac-
kenzie   *Scr.* Josanne McGibbon and Sara Parriott; based on a novel by Dan Lewandowski
Cine. Adam Greenberg   *Ed.* Sidney Wolinsky   *Mu.* Patrick Williams   *P.d.* Lilly Kilvert *A.d.*
Jon Hutman   *S.d.* Linda Spheeris   *R.t.* 102 min.   *MPAA* PG-13.   *Cast:* Mark Harmon,
Madeleine Stowe, Lesley Ann Warren, Maria Holvoe, Mark Blum, Andrea Martin, Tony
Longo, Alan Blumenfeld, Devin Ratray, David Brenner.

Taylor (Mark Harmon), an attractive young television weatherman, is very successful with
women but fears commitment. His friends make a bet with him that he cannot persuade
three different women—Veronica (Madeleine Stowe), Eleanor (Lesley Ann Warren), and
Erin (Maria Holvoe)—to accept his marriage proposals within a three-month period, hoping
to instill in him a greater sense of responsibility in his relationships.

OBITUARIES

Reg Allen (1917-March 30, 1989). Allen was a set decorator who worked frequently with director Blake Edwards. He was nominated for an Academy Award for his work on Edwards' *Darling Lili* (1970). His additional film credits include *The Pink Panther* (1964), *The Party* (1968), *Lady Sings the Blues* (1972), and *The Parallax View* (1974).

May Allison (June 14, 1895-March 27, 1989). Allison was an actress in the silent era. She was often paired with actor Harold Lockwood, and the two were featured in a series of popular romantic films, including *The Masked Rider* (1916) and *The Promise* (1917). Her last film was *The Telephone Girl* (1927).

Harry Andrews (November 10, 1911-March 7, 1989). Andrews was a rugged British character actor who had a lengthy stage career prior to making his first film, *The Red Beret* (1952). Often cast as a military man, his additional films include *Moby Dick* (1956), *The Agony and the Ecstasy* (1965), and *Nicholas and Alexandra* (1971).

Jim Backus (February 25, 1913-July 3, 1989). Backus was an actor in film and television. Perhaps best known to contemporary audiences as a member of the cast of the popular television series *Gilligan's Island*, Backus also provided the voice of the nearsighted cartoon character Mister Magoo in such animated shorts as *When Magoo Flew* (1954) and *Mister Magoo's Puddle Jumper* (1956), both of which won Academy Awards. His most notable dramatic role was in *Rebel Without a Cause* (1955), in which he played James Dean's hapless father. His additional film credits include *Father Was a Fullback* (1949), *Pat and Mike* (1952), *It's a Mad, Mad, Mad, Mad World* (1963), and *Pete's Dragon* (1977).

Lucille Ball (August 6, 1911-April 26, 1989). Ball was a red-haired actress whose extensive film career was overshadowed by her enormous popularity as a television comedienne. *I Love Lucy*, in which she starred with her then-husband Desi Arnaz, originally ran from 1951 to 1957 and continues to be seen extensively in syndication; it is one of the most popular television series in the history of the medium.

Ball began her film career as a Goldwyn Girl, appearing in small roles in numerous films between 1933 and 1937. She was graduated to supporting roles and finally to comic leads with *The Affairs of Annabel* (1938) and *Annabel Takes a Tour* (1938), in which she was first seen as a redhead. Throughout the 1940's, she made dozens of films under contract to RKO, Metro-Goldwyn-Mayer, and Columbia, often appearing opposite such comic stars as the Marx Brothers, Red Skelton, and Bob Hope.

With the advent of her television success in the 1950's, Ball's film work was substantially reduced. She and Arnaz appeared in *The Long, Long Trailer* (1954) and *Forever Darling* (1956), and she was featured in *The Facts of Life* (1960) and *Yours, Mine and Ours* (1968) during the 1960's. Her last film, the musical *Mame* (1974), was a critical and financial failure, and thereafter she devoted her energies to television work. Her additional film credits include *Top Hat* (1935), *Stage Door* (1937), *Room Service* (1938), *Sorrowful Jones* (1949), *Miss Grant Takes Richmond* (1949), and *The Fuller Brush Girl* (1950).

Lynn Bari (December 18, 1913-November 20, 1989). Born Marjorie Schuyler Fisher, Bari was an actress who appeared in more than sixty films, usually in supporting roles in feature films and in lead roles in B-pictures. Indeed, she was known for a time as the "Queen of the B's" for her appearances in numerous low-budget pictures in the 1930's and 1940's. Her screen credits include *Mr. Moto's Gamble* (1938), *Charlie Chan in the City of Darkness* (1939), *Sun Valley Serenade* (1941), and *Orchestra Wives* (1942).

James Lee Barrett (November 19, 1929-October 15, 1989). Barrett was a screenwriter who specialized in action films and Westerns. His film credits include *The D.I.* (1957), *The Green Berets* (1968), and *Smokey and the Bandit* (1977).

Frances Bavier (1903-December 6, 1989). Bavier was an actress best known for her role as Aunt Bee in the popular television series *The Andy Griffith Show*. She also played character roles in a number of films, including *The Lady Says No* (1951), *The Day the Earth Stood Still* (1951), *Bend of the River* (1952), and *The Stooge* (1952).

John Beckman (1898-October 26, 1989). Beckman was a set designer and art director who worked on some of the most memorable films of Hollywood's golden age. As set designer, his screen credits include *The Maltese Falcon* (1941), *Casablanca* (1942), and *Mildred Pierce* (1945). As art director, his work includes *Monsieur Verdoux* (1947), *The Devil at Four O'Clock* (1961), and *Gypsy* (1962).

Irving Berlin (May 11, 1888-September 22, 1989). Born Israel Isidore Baline in Russia, Berlin was the Tin Pan Alley composer who wrote "God Bless America" and "White Christmas." He has been hailed as the most prolific and successful writer of popular songs of the twentieth century. Berlin immigrated to the United States with his parents in 1893, grew up on New York's Lower East Side, and published his first song at the age of seventeen. His first big hit, "Alexander's Ragtime Band," came in 1911, and by the time sound came to film, Berlin was already a legend in the music world. Al Jolson sang his "Blue Skies" in the first talking picture, *The Jazz Singer* (1927).

Although Berlin's primary focus was never film—he wrote scores for twenty-three Broadway plays and more than a thousand songs—his contributions to cinema were nevertheless significant. He wrote scores for eighteen films, and his songs were heard in countless more. Two of his screenplays—*Alexander's Ragtime Band* (1938), and *Holiday Inn* (1942), were nominated for Academy Awards, and he received nine additional nominations for Best Song, winning the Academy Award in this category for "White Christmas" in *Holiday Inn*.

Berlin's screen credits span fifty years and include *Top Hat* (1935), *Carefree* (1938), *Second Fiddle* (1939), *This Is the Army* (1943, in which Berlin appeared as a performer), *Blue Skies* (1946), *Easter Parade* (1948), *Annie Get Your Gun* (1950), *White Christmas* (1954), *There's No Business Like Show Business* (1954), and *Sayonara* (1957).

Amanda Blake (February 20, 1929-August 16, 1989). Born Beverly Louise Neill, Blake was best known for her role as Miss Kitty in the popular television series *Gunsmoke*. She appeared in several films, usually in supporting roles, prior to her television career, including *Stars in My Crown* (1950), *Lili* (1953), *A Star Is Born* (1954), and *High Society* (1955).

Mel Blanc (May 30, 1908-May 19, 1989). Blanc was an actor who provided the voices for some of the most famous animated cartoon characters in film history. He began working for Warner Bros. in 1938 and is first heard as the voice of Porky Pig in *Porky's Hare Hunt* (1938). He later helped the studio develop their animated "star," providing the Bronx accent for the character he named Bugs Bunny after persuading Warner Bros. to drop the "Happy Rabbit" name they had picked out. Blanc worked on an estimated 850 cartoon shorts, providing an estimated 400 different characters with voices. Among his most memorable vocal characterizations were Daffy Duck, Tweety Pie, Sylvester, Yosemite Sam, and Speedy Gonzalez.

Blanc worked for other studios as well, providing the voice for the 1940's Woody Woodpecker and for Barney Rubble in the television series *The Flintstones* in the 1960's. He appeared occasionally in live-action films, usually in cameo roles; these included *Neptune's Daughter* (1949) and *Kiss Me, Stupid* (1964). His full-length feature animated credits include *Hey There, It's Yogi Bear* (1964), and *The Man Called Flintstone* (1966).

Bernard Blier (January 11, 1916-March 29, 1989). Born in Argentina of French parents, Blier was an actor who appeared in more than 150 films, most of which were French or Italian productions. Bald and portly, he was featured in character roles in such films as *Hôtel du Nord* (1938), *Quai des orfèvres* (1947), *Dédée d'Anvers* (1948; Dédée), and *The Tall Blond Man with One Black Shoe* (1972).

John Bright (1908-September 14, 1989). Bright was a politically conscious screenwriter who, along with his frequent collaborator Kubec Glasmon, was one of the founders of the Screen Writers Guild. Accused of being a Communist, he was blacklisted in the 1950's. His screenwriting credits include *The Public Enemy* (1931), *Blonde Crazy* (1931), *The Crowd Roars* (1932), *I Walk Alone* (1948), and *The Brave Bulls* (1951).

Donald Brittain (1928-July 21, 1989). Born in Canada, Brittain was an award-winning documentary filmmaker. His *Volcano: An Inquiry into the Life and Death of Malcolm Lowry* (1976) won an Academy Award.

Jack Buetel (September 5, 1917-June 27, 1989). Born Jack Beutel, Buetel was an actor who changed the spelling of his last name at the behest of Howard Hughes, who featured him as Billy the Kid in *The Outlaw* (released briefly in 1941 and 1943, but not distributed generally until 1950 because of censorship problems involving costar Jane Russell). The controversy surrounding the film proved harmful to Buetel's career; he appeared in only a few additional films, most of which were B Westerns. His screen credits include *Rose of the Cimarron* (1952), and *Mustang* (1959).

Vittorio Caprioli (1921-October 2, 1989). Caprioli was an Italian actor and director active in film work since 1950. He appeared in Federico Fellini's *Variety Lights* (1950), and Roberto Rossellini's *General Della Rovere* (1960). His first work as a director was *Lions in the Sun* (1961), and he also directed *Paris, My Love* (1962) and *The Splendors and Miseries of Madame Royale* (1969). His additional acting credits include *Zazie dans le Métro* (1960) and *The Tragedy of a Ridiculous Man* (1981).

John Cassavetes (December 9, 1929-February 3, 1989). Cassavetes was an actor, screenwriter, and director who was nominated for Academy Awards in each of these categories. As an actor, he was known for his intensity and a preference for improvisation. He took work in television to finance his filmmaking debut, *Shadows* (1960). This story of an interracial love affair won the Critics Award at the Venice Film Festival and led to his being hired by two major studios to direct films for them. Neither of these projects met with critical or commercial success.

Blaming studio interference for his problems, Cassavetes became one of the pioneering independent filmmakers of the 1960's, raising money for the production and distribution of his own films. He used such techniques as a hand-held camera and relied heavily on improvisation from his cast, which often featured his wife, Gena Rowlands, and his friend, Peter Falk. These films often lacked polish, but they had an immediacy that attracted critics and audiences. *Faces* (1968) earned for Cassavetes an Academy Award nomination for his screenplay; *A Woman Under the Influence* (1974) won for him a nomination for his direction; and Rowlands was nominated for the Best Actress award for her work in *Gloria* (1980). Cassavetes himself was nominated for an Academy Award as Best Supporting Actor for his role as a psychotic soldier in *The Dirty Dozen* (1967).

Cassavetes' additional acting credits include *The Killers* (1964), *Devil's Angels* (1967), *Rosemary's Baby* (1968), and *Mikey and Nicky* (1976). As director and writer, his credits include *Too Late Blues* (1962), *Husbands* (1970), *Minnie and Moskowitz* (1971), *The Killing of a Chinese Bookie* (1976), and *Big Trouble* (1985).

Graham Chapman (1941-October 4, 1989). Chapman was a British writer and actor who is best known as a member of the Monty Python satirical group. He helped write and also acted in the troupe's *Monty Python and the Holy Grail* (1974), *Monty Python's Life of Brian* (1979), and *Monty Python's The Meaning of Life* (1983).

Mario Chiari (July 14, 1909-April 9, 1989). Chiari was an art director who worked with many of the most important European directors of the postwar era. His films include Vittorio De Sica's *Miracle in Milan* (1951), for which he designed the costumes; Jean Renoir's *The Golden Coach* (1952); Federico Fellini's *I Vitelloni* (1953); and Luchino Visconti's *White Nights* (1957). He also worked on John Huston's *The Bible* (1966) and on *Doctor Dolittle* (1967).

William Ching (1914-July 1, 1989). Ching was a character actor who appeared in numerous films in the 1940's and 1950's. He is best remembered as Spencer Tracy's rival for Katharine Hepburn in *Pat and Mike* (1952). His additional screen credits include *D.O.A.* (1949), *Oh, Susannah* (1951), *Scared Stiff* (1953), and *Give the Girl a Break* (1953).

T. E. B. Clarke (June 7, 1907-February 11, 1989). Clarke was a British screenwriter who specialized in comedy, winning an Academy Award for his work on *The Lavender Hill Mob* (1952) and earning nominations for two other films: *Passport to Pimlico* (1949) and *Sons and Lovers* (1960). His additional film credits include *Hue and Cry* (1947) and *A Man Could Get Killed* (1966).

George Coulouris (October 1, 1903-April 24, 1989). Coulouris was a British actor who specialized in character roles. An original member of Orson Welles' Mercury Theatre, his screen credits spanned five decades and included such films as *Citizen Kane* (1941), *For Whom the Bell Tolls* (1943), *An Outcast of the Islands* (1951), *Arabesque* (1966), and *Murder on the Orient Express* (1974).

James Crabe (1931-May 2, 1989). Crabe was a cinematographer who photographed numerous films since the early 1970's. He was nominated for an Academy Award for his work on *The Formula* (1980). His additional film credits include *Rocky* (1976), *The China Syndrome* (1979), *The Karate Kid* (1984), and *The Karate Kid Part II* (1986).

Jack Cummings (1900-April 28, 1989). Cummings was a producer who started at the bottom as an office boy at Metro-Goldwyn-Mayer and went on to produce some of the studio's most memorable musicals, including *Kiss Me Kate* (1953) and *Seven Brides for Seven Brothers* (1954). His additional films include *I Dood It* (1943), *Teahouse of the August Moon* (1956), *Can Can* (1960), and *Viva Las Vegas* (1964).

Morton Da Costa (March 7, 1914-January 29, 1989). Born Morton Tecosky, Da Costa was a Broadway actor and director whose film career was relatively limited. He directed the film versions of two of his biggest stage hits—*Auntie Mame* (1958), which was nominated for six Academy Awards, including Best Picture, and *The Music Man* (1962), which he also produced. He was involved with one other film, producing and directing *Island of Love* (1963), before returning to the stage exclusively.

Salvador Dalí (March 11, 1904-January 23, 1989). Dalí was a Spanish surrealist painter who worked with film early in his career, collaborating with Luis Buñuel on *Un Chien Andalou* (1928) and *L'Âge d'or* (1930). He also worked with Alfred Hitchcock on *Spellbound* (1945).

Ian Dalrymple (August 26, 1903-April 28, 1989). Born in South Africa, Dalrymple was a screenwriter, producer, and director who began his career in the documentary field; his *London Can Take It* (1940) and *Listen to Britain* (1941) were morale builders during World War II. His feature film credits include *Pygmalion* (1938, as screenwriter), *Old Bill and Son*

(1939, as director and screenwriter), *The Heart of the Matter* (1952, as producer and screenwriter), and *The Admirable Crichton* (1957, as producer).

Bette Davis (April 5, 1908-October 6, 1989). Born Ruth Elizabeth Davis, Davis was an actress of great stature in American cinema. Famous for her battles with her studios for scripts that would showcase her talents properly, she is remembered both for her suffering roles in romantic melodramas and for her portrayals of fiercely independent women. Her acting career lasted nearly six decades.

Davis' career began at Warner Bros., and she gradually earned critical raves for her performances in generally mediocre films. She had good roles in *Of Human Bondage* (1934), *Dangerous* (1935, for which she won her first Academy Award), and *The Petrified Forest* (1936), but these films were interspersed with others that did nothing to enhance her career. She threatened to break her contract, and, although she lost the ensuing court case, Warner Bros. soon began to placate their unhappy star. Her performance in *Jezebel* (1938) earned for her another Academy Award, and by 1940 she was Hollywood's most popular female box-office attraction.

She left Warner Bros. in 1949, but trouble with inferior films continued to dog her. *All About Eve* (1950) and *The Virgin Queen* (1955) were her only noteworthy film roles in the 1950's. Her career was revived in the next decade by two unlikely horror films. The first was *What Ever Happened to Baby Jane?* (1962) a black comedy in which Davis played a long-forgotten child star who torments costar Joan Crawford. The second was *Hush. . . . Hush, Sweet Charlotte* (1965), a similar film in which Davis is tormented by Olivia De Havilland. Her last film of note was *The Whales of August* (1987), in which she starred opposite Lillian Gish.

During her long and productive career, Davis was nominated for ten Academy Awards, winning two. She is also credited with nicknaming the award statuette "Oscar," supposedly for its resemblance to her then-husband, Ham Oscar Nelson. She wrote three volumes of autobiography, *The Lonely Life* (1962), *Mother Goddam* (1974), and *This 'n That* (1987).

Emile de Antonio (1920-December 15, 1989). De Antonio was a documentary filmmaker whose radical political views were reflected in his work. One of his best-known films is *Point of Order!* (1964), which was assembled from footage of the 1954 Congressional investigation of Senator Joseph McCarthy. His film *Underground* (1977), which he made with Haskell Wexler and Mary Lampson, chronicled the activities of the fugitive Weather Underground, and de Antonio defied an attempt by the Federal Bureau of Investigation (FBI) to subpoena his raw footage for use in their legal case against the group. De Antonio's additional films include *Rush to Judgment* (1967), *In the Year of the Pig* (1969), and *Milhouse: A White Comedy* (1971).

Mark Dignam (1909-September 29, 1989). Dignam was a British character actor who had a sixty-year career on stage and in film. His screen credits include *The Prisoner* (1955), *Sink the Bismarck!* (1960), and *Hamlet* (1969).

Sammy Fain (June 17, 1902-December 6, 1989). Born Samuel Feinberg, Fain was a songwriter who composed many popular tunes during the 1920's Tin Pan Alley era. He moved to Hollywood in the 1930's, where he wrote songs for numerous films, including the Academy Award-winning "Secret Love" for *Calamity Jane* (1953) and the title song for *Love Is a Many-Splendored Thing* (1955). He was nominated for the Academy Award eight more times, for songs from the films *Vogues of 1938* (1937), *April Love* (1957), *A Certain Smile* (1958), *Marjorie Morningstar* (1958), *Tender Is the Night* (1962), *The Stepmother* (1972), *Half a House* (1976), and *The Rescuers* (1977).

Evelyn Finley (1915-April 7, 1989). Finley was an actress who was featured in numerous B Westerns in the 1940's. After that genre lost its popularity in the 1950's, she worked for two more decades as a stuntwoman and double for such stars as Elizabeth Taylor, Donna Reed, and Kim Novak. Her acting credits include *Arizona Frontier* (1940), *Cowboy Commandos* (1943), *Ghost Guns* (1945), and *Sheriff of Medicine Bend* (1948).

William H. Forrest (1902-January 26, 1989). Forrest was a character actor who appeared in scores of films from the 1940's through the 1960's. His acting credits include *Meet John Doe* (1941), *Laura* (1944), *Miracle on 34th Street* (1947), *Fort Apache* (1948), *Love Me Tender* (1956), and *One-Eyed Jacks* (1961).

Milton Frome (1910-March 21, 1989). Frome was an actor and comic who specialized in "straight man" roles. He appeared in more than fifty films, including *Pardners* (1956), *The Delicate Delinquent* (1957), *Bye Bye Birdie* (1963), and *The Nutty Professor* (1963).

Alan Gifford (1910-March 20, 1989). Born John Lennox, Gifford was an American actor who spent most of his career in England. His film credits include *A King in New York* (1957), *The Road to Hong Kong* (1962), *The Countess from Hong Kong* (1967), and *Ragtime* (1981).

Johnny Green (October 10, 1908-May 15, 1989). Green was a composer, conductor, and musical director who is best known for his work at Metro-Goldwyn-Mayer (MGM) in the 1940's. He won five Academy Awards over his long career; four of them were for his work on the scores of *Easter Parade* (1948), *An American in Paris* (1951), *West Side Story* (1961), and *Oliver!* (1968), and the fifth for producing *The Merry Wives of Windsor Overture* (1953), an MGM short subject. His additional films include *Fiesta* (1947), *The Great Caruso* (1951), *High Society* (1956), *Meet Me in Las Vegas* (1956), *Raintree County* (1956), *Pepe* (1960), *Bye Bye Birdie* (1963), and *They Shoot Horses Don't They?* (1969), all of which earned for him Academy Award nominations for their scores.

Chris Greenham (1923-January 21, 1989). Born Vivian Greenham, Greenham was a British sound editor who won an Academy Award for his work on *The Guns of Navarone* (1961). His additional screen credits include *Expresso Bongo* (1960), *This Sporting Life* (1963), *Casino Royale* (1967), *The Lion in Winter* (1968), and *Superman* (1978).

Madeline Hurlock (1905-April 4, 1989). Hurlock was an actress in the silent era. She was one of Mack Sennett's Bathing Beauties, and comedy was her forte. She starred opposite such silent comedy luminaries as Ben Turpin and Harry Langdon. Her screen credits include *The Halfback of Notre Dame* (1924), *The Wild Goose Chase* (1925), and *Love in a Police Station* (1927).

Charles Lampkin (1912-April 17, 1989). Lampkin was a black character actor who played a variety of roles in films from the 1950's through the 1980's. His screen credits include *Five* (1951), *Toys in the Attic* (1963), *The Thomas Crown Affair* (1968), *The Great White Hope* (1970), *S.O.B.* (1981), and *Cocoon* (1985).

Joseph LaShelle (1905-August 20, 1989). LaShelle was a cinematographer whose expertise extended to both black-and-white and color film. He often worked with directors John Ford and Billy Wilder. LaShelle won an Academy Award for *Laura* (1944) and was nominated eight more times for the following films: *Come to the Stable* (1949), *My Cousin Rachel* (1952), *Marty* (1955), *Career* (1959), *The Apartment* (1960), *How the West Was Won* (1963), *Irma La Douce* (1963), and *The Fortune Cookie* (1966).

Reginald LeBorg (December 11, 1902-March 25, 1989). Born in Austria, LeBorg was a director who specialized in adventure and horror films. He began directing at Metro-Goldwyn-Mayer, where the short subject *Heavenly Music* (1943), for which he wrote the script, won an Academy Award. By the mid-1940's, he was a prolific director of B-pictures such as *The Mummy's Ghost* (1944), *Joe Palooka—Champ* (1946), *Port Said* (1948), *G.I. Jane* (1951), and *Voodoo Island* (1957).

Billy Lee (1929-November 17, 1989). Born Billy Lee Schlensker, Lee was a child actor who was featured in several films in the 1930's and 1940's. He is best known for his role in the original version of *The Biscuit Eater* (1940). His additional film credits include *Sons of the Legion* (1937), *Cocoanut Grove* (1938), *Boy Trouble* (1939), *Reg'lar Fellers* (1941), and *War Dogs* (1943).

Sergio Leone (January 23, 1929-April 30, 1989). Leone was an Italian director who made Clint Eastwood into an international star in the so-called spaghetti Westerns of the 1960's. Leone was the son of a director and an actress; as a teenager he began an apprenticeship with a series of Italian and American filmmakers on location in Italy. He made his official directorial debut with *The Colossus of Rhodes* (1961).

In 1964, Leone cast an obscure American television actor named Clint Eastwood in a remake of Akiro Kurosawa's *Yojimbo* (1961) set in the American West. *A Fistful of Dollars* (1964) was an international hit. Even more successful were two sequels, *For a Few Dollars More* (1965) and *The Good, the Bad and the Ugly* (1966), both of which featured much violence. Leone's next film, *Once Upon a Time in the West* (1968), reversed that trend and proved a commercial failure in America.

None of Leone's later films made any impact on American audiences, except for the controversial *Once Upon a Time in America*, which starred Robert De Niro and was shortened drastically from 227 minutes to 139 minutes for its American release. Leone's additional film credits include *Duck You Sucker* (1972); he produced *My Name is Nobody* (1973), *The Genius* (1975), and *Fun is Beautiful* (1979).

Edward LeVeque (1896-January 28, 1989). Born in Mexico, LeVeque was an actor during the silent era. He specialized in comedy and was the last surviving Keystone Kop, having appeared in numerous Mack Sennett comedy shorts. His film credits include *Intolerance* (1916), *The Four Horsemen of the Apocalypse* (1924), and *The Black Pirate* (1926).

Nathaniel Levine (1899-August 6, 1989). Levine was president of two film studios, Mascot and Republic, in the 1930's and 1940's. His penchant for producing multipart matinee programmers earned for him the title "King of the Serials." These included *King of the Congo* (1929), *The Galloping Ghost* (1931), and *The Lost Jungle* (1934). He also made feature films and is credited with starting the "Singing Cowboy" phenomenon with *In Old Santa Fe* (1934), the first of many films that Gene Autry made for Levine.

Beatrice Lillie (May 29, 1894-January 20, 1989). Born in Canada, Lillie was a popular stage and cabaret star in the United States and England, specializing in comedy. She appeared in a handful of films through the course of her career, including *Exit Smiling* (1926), *Dr. Rhythm* (1938), *Around the World in 80 Days* (1956), and *Thoroughly Modern Millie* (1967).

John Loder (January 3, 1898-December, 1989). Born John Lowe, Loder was a British actor who starred in numerous films of the 1930's and 1940's. Married for a time to actress Hedy Lamarr, he was featured with her in *Dishonored Lady* (1947). His additional film credits include *Lorna Doone* (1935), *King Solomon's Mines* (1937), *How Green Was My Valley* (1941), and *Now, Voyager* (1942).

Arthur Lonergan (1905-January 23, 1989). Lonergan was a production designer whose work earned for him an Academy Award nomination for *The Oscar* (1966). His additional film credits include *The Tender Trap* (1955), *Forbidden Planet* (1956), *Yours, Mine and Ours* (1968), *Che!* (1969), and *MH* (1970).

Warren Low (1906-July 27, 1989). Low was a film editor whose work earned for him four Academy Award nominations for *The Letter* (1940), *Come Back, Little Sheba* (1952), *The Rose Tattoo* (1955), and *Gunfight at the O.K. Corral* (1957). His career spanned the years 1936-1971, and his film credits include *The Life of Émile Zola* (1937), *Now, Voyager* (1942), *King Creole* (1958), *G.I. Blues* (1960), *Will Penny* (1968), and *True Grit* (1969).

Gordon K. McCallum (1919-September 10, 1989). McCallum was a sound engineer who worked on more than three hundred films, winning an Academy Award for his work on *Fiddler on the Roof* (1971). He was previously nominated for *Ryan's Daughter* (1970). His additional film credits include *Great Expectations* (1946), *Day of the Jackal* (1973), *The Man Who Would Be King* (1975), and *Superman* (1978).

Marion Mack (1905-May 1, 1989). Born Joey Marion McCreery, Mack was an actress in the silent era. Her best-known role was that of Buster Keaton's girlfriend in *The General* (1927). Her additional film credits include *Mary of the Movies* (1922), *One of the Bravest* (1925), *Alice in Movieland* (1926), and *Carnival Girl* (1926).

Kenneth McMillan (1933-January 8, 1989). McMillan was a character actor whose career blossomed as he reached middle age. Perhaps best known for his portrayal of the fire chief in *Ragtime* (1981), he specialized in tough, burly roles in films such as *The Taking of Pelham One Two Three* (1974), *The Stepford Wives* (1975), *Carny* (1980), *The Pope of Greenwich Village* (1984), and *Dune* (1984).

Jock Mahoney (February 7, 1919-December 14, 1989). Born Jacques O'Mahoney, Mahoney was an actor in television and films who specialized in action films. He is best remembered as the thirteenth actor to portray Tarzan, having played a villain in *Tarzan the Magnificent* (1960) and moving up to the title role in *Tarzan Goes to India* (1962) and *Tarzan's Three Challenges* (1963). His additional film credits include *I've Lived Before* (1956), *Slim Carter* (1957), and *The Glory Stompers* (1967).

Gina Manès (April 7, 1895-September 6, 1989). Manès was a French actress whose career spanned nearly fifty years. She is best remembered for her portrayal of Josephine in Abel Gance's *Napoleon* (1927). Her additional screen credits include *L'Homme sans visage* (1919), *Thérèse Raquin* (1928), *Mayerling* (1936), and *Pas de panique* (1965).

Silvano Mangano (April 21, 1930-December 16, 1989). Mangano was one of the leading Italian actresses of the postwar era. Her first starring role was in *Bitter Rice* (1949), and she married the film's producer, Dino De Laurentiis, that same year. She appeared in dozens of films over the next four decades, including *Anna* (1951), *Ulysses* (1954), *Teorema* (1968), and *Death in Venice* (1971).

Yusaku Matsuda (1949-November 6, 1989). Matsuda was a Japanese actor best known for his portrayal of tough, often criminal characters. He won the Japanese equivalent of the Academy Award for his role in *Kazoku geimu* (1983), and was featured opposite Michael Douglas as a gang assassin in *Black Rain* (1989). His additional film credits include *Okami no monsho* (1973) and *Ningen no shomei* (1977).

Ernie Morrison (1913-July 24, 1989). Morrison was a black actor who was graduated from children's roles in the silent era to adult roles in the 1940's. He starred for Hal Roach in the "Sunshine Sammy" short comedies in 1921 and 1922, and this role led to the creation of the hugely successful Our Gang comedies, which were centered around Morrison in twenty-eight films made between 1922 and 1924. Morrison spent the next sixteen years in vaudeville, returning to the screen in the 1940's as one of the East Side Kids in films such as *Pride of the Bowery* (1940), *Spooks Run Wild* (1941), and *Let's Get Tough* (1942).

Arnold Moss (January 28, 1910-December 15, 1989). Moss was a character actor who specialized in playing villains on stage and in films. His screen credits include *Reign of Terror* (1949), *My Favorite Spy* (1951), *Viva Zapata!* (1952), and *Gambit* (1966).

Lionel Newman (1915-February 3, 1989). Newman was a composer and conductor who worked on more than 250 films during a four-decade career at Twentieth Century-Fox. He was nominated for eleven Academy Awards, winning the award for his work on *Hello, Dolly!* (1969). His additional screen credits include *The Cowboy and the Lady* (1938), *I'll Get By* (1950), *There's No Business Like Show Business* (1954), *Love Me Tender* (1956), *Let's Make Love* (1960), and *Doctor Dolittle* (1967).

Laurence Olivier (May 22, 1907-July 11, 1989). Olivier was a British actor who will be remembered as one of the preeminent stage and screen actors of the twentieth century. He made his stage debut in England at the age of fifteen, and seven years later he was performing on Broadway. His film work began shortly thereafter, with *The Temporary Widow* (1930) in England and *The Yellow Ticket* (1931) in the United States.

It was not until his role as Heathcliff in *Wuthering Heights* (1939) that Olivier became a star; this performance earned for him the first of his eleven Academy Award nominations. A second came a year later, for Alfred Hitchcock's *Rebecca* (1940).

Olivier's best-known films, however, are probably his cinematic adaptations of the works of William Shakespeare. He produced, directed, and starred in *Henry V* (1944), a wartime morale booster for Great Britain that earned for Olivier a special Academy Award for his achievement in bringing the play to the screen. *Hamlet* (1948), for which he also functioned as producer, director, and star, won five Academy Awards, including Best Picture and Best Actor for Olivier. He was nominated for Best Actor awards for *Richard III* (1956) and *Othello* (1965).

Olivier continued to split his time between film, stage, and later in his career, television. His film work continued to be outstanding even as his roles changed to fit those of an older actor. He received Academy Award nominations as Best Actor for his work in *The Entertainer* (1959), *Sleuth* (1972), and *The Boys from Brazil* (1978); his smaller role in *Marathon Man* (1976) earned for him a Best Supporting Actor nomination.

Olivier was knighted in 1947 and given the title of baron in 1970. He was married to actress Vivien Leigh from 1940 to 1960. He wrote two books: *Confessions of an Actor* (1982) and *On Acting* (1986). In 1976, Olivier was given an honorary Academy Award "for the full body of his work, for the unique achievements of his entire career, and his lifetime of contributions to the art of film." His additional screen credits include *Pride and Prejudice* (1940), *That Hamilton Woman* (1941), *The Prince and the Showgirl* (1957), *Khartoum* (1966), *The Three Sisters* (1970), and *The Seven-Per-cent Solution* (1976).

Muriel Ostriche (1897-May 3, 1989). Ostriche was an actress who was one of the most popular stars of the early silent film era. She made nearly two hundred films, including *A Tale of the Wilderness* (1913), *A Telephone Strategy* (1914), *A Circus Romance* (1916), and *Tinsel* (1918).

Gerd Oswald (June 9, 1916-May 22, 1989). The son of German producer/director Richard Oswald, Oswald was a director who immigrated to the United States with his family in 1938. He worked for several studios in a variety of increasingly responsible capacities before directing his first picture, *A Kiss Before Dying* (1956). Although most of his films were B-pictures, he was known for the high quality and attention to detail he brought to these films. His screen credits include *Valerie* (1957), *Screaming Mimi* (1958), *80 Steps to Jonah* (1969), and *Bunny O'Hare* (1971).

John Payne (May 23, 1912-December 6, 1989). Payne was an actor who starred in a number of films in the 1940's and 1950's. Early in his career, he was featured in musicals such as *Garden of the Moon* (1938), *Tin Pan Alley* (1940), and *Sun Valley Serenade* (1941). By the latter part of the decade, the handsome leading man opted for action films, including such Westerns as *El Paso* (1949), *Silver Lode* (1954), and *Tennessee's Partner* (1955). His additional film credits include *Hello Frisco Hello* (1943) and *Miracle on 34th Street* (1947).

Aileen Pringle (July 23, 1895-December 16, 1989). Born Aileen Bisbee, Pringle was an actress who starred in films of the silent and early sound eras. She specialized in playing provocative screen sirens in such films as *Souls for Sale* (1923), *Three Weeks* (1924), *His Hour* (1924), *Body and Soul* (1927), and *Puttin' on the Ritz* (1930).

Anthony Quayle (September 7, 1913-October 20, 1989). Quayle was a British actor who was knighted in 1984 for his contributions to the stage and screen. He played both lead and supporting roles, earning an Academy Award nomination as Best Supporting Actor for his portrayal of Cardinal Wolsey in *Anne of the Thousand Days* (1969). Active in film for four decades, his additional screen credits include *Hamlet* (1948), *The Wrong Man* (1957), *The Guns of Navarone* (1961), and *Lawrence of Arabia* (1962).

Richard Quine (November 12, 1920-June 10, 1989). Quine was a child actor who was graduated to directing films as an adult. His juvenile acting roles included *Jane Eyre* (1934), *A Dog of Flanders* (1935), and *My Sister Eileen* (1942). By the mid-1950's, he was directing films for Columbia, frequently using scripts provided by Blake Edwards, such as his musical remake of *My Sister Eileen* (1955) and *Operation Mad Ball* (1957). Both films starred Jack Lemmon, who was also featured in several other Quine pictures. Quine's career declined abruptly with the release of *Oh Dad, Poor Dad, Mama's Hung You in the Closet and I'm Feelin' So Sad* (1967). His additional directing credits include *Bell, Book and Candle* (1958), *The World of Suzie Wong* (1960), and *How to Murder Your Wife* (1965).

Gilda Radner (June 28, 1946-May 20, 1989). Radner was a comedian and actress best known for her work on the satirical television show *Saturday Night Live* in the 1970's. She appeared in several films, two of which—*The Woman in Red* (1984) and *Haunted Honeymoon* (1986)—were written and directed by her husband and co-star, Gene Wilder. Radner's additional film credits include *First Family* (1980), *Hanky Panky* (1982), and *Movers and Shakers* (1985).

Marguerite Roberts (1904-February 17, 1989). Roberts was a screenwriter for Metro-Goldwyn-Mayer in the 1940's. Her career was disrupted in 1951 after her refusal to testify before a Congressional committee investigating communism in the film industry, but she began working again in 1960. Her screenwriting credits include *Hollywood Boulevard* (1936), *Ziegfeld Girl* (1941), *Honky Tonk* (1941), *Dragon Seed* (1944), *Five Card Stud* (1968), and *True Grit* (1969).

Brunello Rondi (1924-November 7, 1989). Rondi was an Italian screenwriter and director best known for his association with directors Federico Fellini and Roberto Rossellini. For Fellini, he coauthored *La Dolce vita* (1960), *8½* (1963), and *Juliet of the Spirits* (1965); for Rossellini, he wrote *One Night in Rome* (1960) and *Arabella* (1969). He also directed *A Violent Life* (1962). His other film credits include *Check to the Queen* (1969), *Fellini Satyricon* (1970), and *City of Women* (1981).

Angelo Ross (1910-September 23, 1989). Ross was a film editor who earned an Academy Award nomination for his work on *Smokey and the Bandit* (1977). His additional film credits include *Walk East on Beacon* (1952), *I Never Sang for My Father* (1969), *The Cross and the Switchblade* (1972), and *The Victims* (1989).

Rebecca Schaeffer (1968-July 18, 1989). Schaeffer was an actress best known for her role in the television series *My Sister Sam*. Her film credits include *Radio Days* (1987) and *Scenes from the Class Struggle in Beverly Hills* (1989).

Franklin J. Schaffner (May 30, 1920-July 2, 1989). Schaffner was a director who won several Emmy Awards for his television work before moving to film in the early 1960's. He won an Academy Award for his direction of *Patton* (1970). His additional film credits include *The Stripper* (1963), *Planet of the Apes* (1968), *Papillon* (1973), and *The Boys from Brazil* (1978).

Walter Scott (1906-February 2, 1989). Scott was a set decorator who earned twenty-one Academy Award nominations for his work. He won the award six times, for *The Robe* (1953), *The King and I* (1956), *The Diary of Anne Frank* (1959), *Cleopatra* (1963), *Fantastic Voyage* (1966) and *Hello, Dolly!* (1969). His additional film credits include *All About Eve* (1950), *Daddy Long Legs* (1955), *The Sound of Music* (1965), and *Doctor Dolittle* (1967).

Massimo Serato (1917-December 22, 1989). Born Giuseppe Segato, Serato was an Italian actor who was a leading man in many Italian films of the 1940's. Later in his career, he took supporting roles in films produced throughout Europe and the United States. His screen credits include *Piccolo Mondo antico* (1941), *Sins of the Borgias* (1953), *El Cid* (1961), *55 Days at Peking* (1963), and *The Tenth Victim* (1965).

Joe Spinell (1937-January 13, 1989). Born Joseph Spagnuolo, Spinell was a character actor who specialized in playing tough guy and gangster roles. He appeared in *The Godfather* (1972), *The Godfather, Part II* (1974), *Rocky* (1976), *Taxi Driver* (1976), *Rocky II* (1979), and *Married to the Mob* (1989).

Jack Starrett (November 2, 1936-March 27, 1989). Starrett was an actor and director who specialized in low-budget action films, many of which involved motorcycles. He appeared in *Born Losers* (1967) and *Hell's Angels on Wheels* (1967), and directed *The Losers* (1970), *Cleopatra Jones* (1973), and *Final Chapter—Walking Tall* (1977).

Mary Treen (1907-July 20, 1989). Treen was an actress who appeared in dozens of films, often in supporting or comic relief roles, from the 1930's through the 1960's. Her acting credits include *Traveling Saleslady* (1935), *Kitty Foyle* (1940), *It's a Wonderful Life* (1946), *The Sad Sack* (1957), and *Paradise, Hawaiian Style* (1966).

Harry Tugend (February 17, 1898-September 11, 1989). Tugend was a screenwriter and producer who specialized in comedy. He wrote four Shirley Temple vehicles, including *The Poor Little Rich Girl* (1936), and three films for Bob Hope, including *Caught in the Draft* (1941). His other writing credits include *The Littlest Rebel* (1935), *Star Spangled Rhythm* (1942), and *Pocketful of Miracles* (1961). He produced *Cross My Heart* (1947), *Golden Earrings* (1947), *Road to Bali* (1953), and *Public Pigeon No. 1* (1957).

Lee Van Cleef (January 9, 1925-December 14, 1989). Van Cleef was an actor who specialized in playing sadistic villains. Best known for his roles in the "spaghetti Westerns" of the mid-1960's, Van Cleef appeared opposite Clint Eastwood in Sergio Leone's *For a Few Dollars More* (1965) and *The Good, the Bad, and the Ugly* (1966), which made him famous. His additional acting credits include supporting roles in *High Noon* (1952) and *The Man Who Shot Liberty Valence* (1962), and featured roles in *The Magnificent Seven Ride* (1972), *Killers* (1977), and *Escape from New York* (1981).

Charles Vanel (August 21, 1892-April 15, 1989). Vanel was a French character actor whose career spanned seven decades. Typically cast in dramatic roles, his screen credits include *Jim Crow* (1912), *Waterloo* (1928), *Les Miserables* (1933), *The Wages of Fear* (1952), *To Catch a Thief* (1955), and *Three Brothers* (1980).

Robert Webber (October 14, 1924-May 17, 1989). Webber was an actor who specialized in playing dapper but hypocritical villains. His film credits include *Twelve Angry Men* (1957), *The Stripper* (1963), *The Dirty Dozen* (1967), *Revenge of the Pink Panther* (1978), *10* (1979), and *S.O.B.* (1981).

Chrissie White (May 23, 1894-August 18, 1989). Born Ada White, White was a British actress. She was a teenage star of comedy shorts in the silent era and a romantic leading lady in the early sound era. She married her costar, Henry Edwards, who also directed her in numerous films. Her screen credits include *For the Little Lady's Sake* (1908), *Tilly the Tomboy Goes Boating* (1910), *The Mermaid* (1912), *Lilly of the Alley* (1923), and *Call of the Sea* (1930).

Cornel Wilde (October 13, 1915-October 15, 1989). Wilde was an actor and director. Initially cast in the role of the heavy, he found his first success as a romantic lead in B-pictures for Twentieth Century-Fox. On loan to Columbia, he was cast as Frédéric Chopin in *A Song to Remember* (1945), and his performance earned for him an Academy Award nomination. He played leads in feature films for a few years, specializing in swashbuckling roles. In 1955, he formed his own production company, and he produced, directed, and acted in several films, often featuring his wife, actress Jean Wallace. Wilde's acting credits include *The Bandit of Sherwood Forest* (1946), *Forever Amber* (1947), *At Sword's Point* (1952), and *Beyond Mombasa* (1957). As producer, director, and actor, he made *Maracaibo* (1958), *Lancelot and Guinevere* (1963), and *The 5th Musketeer* (1979).

Guy Williams (1923-May 6, 1989). Born Armand Catalano, Williams was an actor best known for his roles as the Mexican swordsman Zorro in the television series and the film *The Sign of Zorro* (1961). His additional film credits include *Take Me to Town* (1953), *Seven Angry Men* (1955), and *Sincerely Yours* (1955).

Roland Winters (November 22, 1904-October 22, 1989). Winters was an actor best known for his portrayal of the Chinese detective Charlie Chan. As the successor to Warner Oland and Sidney Toler, he made six of these films. He played character roles in scores of other films. His screen credits include *The Chinese Ring* (1947), *The Feathered Serpent* (1949), *So Big* (1953), and *Blue Hawaii* (1961).

Iris Wong (1921-September 2, 1989). Wong was a Chinese American actress who was one of the first women of her race to appear in feature roles in American films. Her screen credits include *The Good Earth* (1937), *Too Hot to Handle* (1938), and *China* (1943).

Al Woodbury (1909-May 26, 1989). Woodbury was a conductor and composer who was nominated for an Academy Award for his work on *They Shoot Horses Don't They?* (1969). His additional film credits include *Platinum Blonde* (1931), *Gigi* (1958), *Bye Bye Birdie* (1963), *My Fair Lady* (1964), *Star Wars* (1977), and *Out of Africa* (1985).

Joan Woodbury (December 17, 1915-February 22, 1989). Woodbury was an actress who specialized in playing tough, sexy women in low-budget action films of the 1940's. She played the title role in the thirteen-part serial *Brenda Starr—Reporter* (1945). Her additional acting credits include *Anthony Adverse* (1935), *Charlie Chan on Broadway* (1937), *King of the Zombies* (1941), *Confessions of Boston Blackie* (1941), and *The Whistler* (1944).

Cesare Zavattini (September 29, 1902-October 13, 1989). An important figure in the Italian neorealist movement, Zavattini was both a screenwriter and a film theorist. He wrote twenty-three films for Vittorio De Sica, including *Shoeshine* (1946), *Bicycle Thief* (1948), and *The Garden of the Finzi-Continis* (1971), all of which won Academy Awards. He wrote the screenplay for Réné Clément's *The Walls of Malapaga* (1949), which also won an Academy Award. His additional film credits include *Two Women* (1960), *Yesterday, Today and Tomorrow* (1963), and *Women Times Seven* (1967).

LIST OF AWARDS

Academy Awards
Best Picture: Driving Miss Daisy
Direction: Oliver Stone (*Born on the Fourth of July*)
Actor: Daniel Day-Lewis (*My Left Foot*)
Actress: Jessica Tandy (*Driving Miss Daisy*)
Supporting Actor: Denzel Washington (*Glory*)
Supporting Actress: Brenda Fricker (*My Left Foot*)
Original Screenplay: Tom Schulman (*Dead Poets Society*)
Adapted Screenplay: Alfred Uhry (*Driving Miss Daisy*)
Cinematography: Freddie Francis (*Glory*)
Editing: David Brenner and Joe Hutshing (*Born on the Fourth of July*)
Art Direction: Anton Furst and Peter Young (*Batman*)
Visual Effects: John Bruno, Dennis Muren, Hoyt Yeatman, and Dennis Skotak (*The Abyss*)
Sound Effects Editing: Ben Burtt and Richard Hymns (*Indiana Jones and the Last Crusade*)
Sound: Donald Mitchell, Elliot Tyson, Russell Williams, and Gregg Rudloff (*Glory*)
Makeup: Manlio Rochetti (*Driving Miss Daisy*)
Costume Design: Phyllis Dalton (*Henry V*)
Original Score: Alan Menken (*The Little Mermaid*)
Original Song: "Under the Sea" (*The Little Mermaid*: music and lyrics, Alan Menken and Howard Ashman)
Foreign-Language Film: Cinema Paradiso (Italy)
Short Film, Animated: Balance (Christoph Lauenstein and Wolfgang Lauenstein)
Short Film, Live Action: Work Experience (James Hendrie)
Documentary, Feature: Common Threads: Stories from the Quilt (Robert Epstein and Bill Couturie)
Documentary, Short Subject: The Johnstown Flood (Charles Guggenheim)

Directors Guild of America Award
Director: Oliver Stone (*Born on the Fourth of July*)

Writers Guild Awards
Original Screenplay: Woody Allen (*Crimes and Misdemeanors*)
Adapted Screenplay: Alfred Uhry (*Driving Miss Daisy*)

New York Film Critics Awards
Best Picture: My Left Foot
Direction: Paul Mazursky (*Enemies, A Love Story*)
Actor: Daniel Day-Lewis (*My Left Foot*)
Actress: Michelle Pfeiffer (*The Fabulous Baker Boys*)

Supporting Actor: Alan Alda (*Crimes and Misdemeanors*)
Supporting Actress: Lena Olin (*Enemies, A Love Story*)
Screenplay: Gus Van Sant and Daniel Yost (*Drugstore Cowboy*)
Cinematography: Ernest Dickerson (*Do the Right Thing*)
Foreign-Language Film: Story of Women (France)

Los Angeles Film Critics Awards
Best Picture: Do the Right Thing
Direction: Spike Lee (*Do the Right Thing*)
Actor: Daniel Day-Lewis (*My Left Foot*)
Actress: Andie MacDowell (*sex, lies and videotape*) and Michelle Pfeiffer (*The Fabulous Baker Boys*), tie
Supporting Actor: Danny Aiello (*Do the Right Thing*)
Supporting Actress: Brenda Fricker (*My Left Foot*)
Screenplay: Gus Van Sant and Daniel Yost (*Drugstore Cowboy*)
Cinematography: Michael Ballhaus (*The Fabulous Baker Boys*)
Original Score: Bill Lee (*Do the Right Thing*)
Foreign-Language Film: Distant Voices, Still Lives (England) and *Story of Women* (France), tie

National Society of Film Critics Awards
Best Picture: Drugstore Cowboy
Direction: Gus Van Sant (*Drugstore Cowboy*)
Actor: Daniel Day-Lewis (*My Left Foot*)
Actress: Michelle Pfeiffer (*The Fabulous Baker Boys*)
Supporting Actor: Beau Bridges (*The Fabulous Baker Boys*)
Supporting Actress: Anjelica Huston (*Enemies, A Love Story*)
Screenplay: Gus Van Sant and Daniel Yost (*Drugstore Cowboy*)
Cinematography: Michael Ballhaus (*The Fabulous Baker Boys*)
Documentary: Roger and Me (Michael Moore)

National Board of Review Awards
Best English-Language Film: Driving Miss Daisy
Direction: Kenneth Branagh (*Henry V*)
Actor: Morgan Freeman (*Driving Miss Daisy*)
Actress: Michelle Pfeiffer (*The Fabulous Baker Boys*)
Supporting Actor: Alan Alda (*Crimes and Misdemeanors*)
Supporting Actress: Mary Stuart Masterson (*Immediate Family*)
Foreign-Language Film: Story of Women (France)
Documentary: Roger and Me (Michael Moore)
The D. W. Griffith Career Achievement Award: Richard Widmark

Golden Globe Awards
Best Picture, Drama: Born on the Fourth of July
Best Picture, Comedy or Musical: Driving Miss Daisy
Direction: Oliver Stone (*Born on the Fourth of July*)
Actor, Drama: Tom Cruise (*Born on the Fourth of July*)
Actress, Drama: Michelle Pfeiffer (*The Fabulous Baker Boys*)
Actor, Comedy or Musical: Morgan Freeman (*Driving Miss Daisy*)
Actress, Comedy or Musical: Jessica Tandy (*Driving Miss Daisy*)
Supporting Actor: Denzel Washington (*Glory*)
Supporting Actress: Julia Roberts (*Steel Magnolias*)
Screenplay: Oliver Stone and Ron Kovic (*Born on the Fourth of July*)
Original Score: Alan Menken (*The Little Mermaid*)
Original Song: "Under the Sea" (*The Little Mermaid*: music and lyrics, Alan Menken and Howard Ashman)
Foreign-Language Film: Cinema Paradiso (Italy)

Golden Palm Awards (Forty-second Cannes International Film Festival)
Gold Palm: sex, lies and videotape (Steven Soderbergh)
Grand Special Jury Award: Cinema Paradiso (Giuseppe Tornatoro) and *Too Beautiful for You* (Bertrand Blier), tie
Actor: James Spader (*sex, lies and videotape*)
Actress: Meryl Streep (*A Cry in the Dark*)
Direction: Emir Kusturica (*Time of the Gypsies*)
Jury Prize: Jesus of Montreal (Roger Frappier and Pierre Gendron)
Artistic Contribution: Jim Jarmusch (direction, *Mystery Train*)

British Academy Awards
Best Picture: Dead Poets Society
Direction: Kenneth Branagh (*Henry V*)
Actor: Daniel Day-Lewis (*My Left Foot*)
Actress: Pauline Collins (*Shirley Valentine*)
Supporting Actor: Ray McAnally (*My Left Foot*)
Supporting Actress: Michelle Pfeiffer (*The Fabulous Baker Boys*)
Original Screenplay: Nora Ephron (*When Harry Met Sally*)
Adapted Screenplay: Christopher Hampton (*Dangerous Liaisons*)
Original Score: Maurice Jarre (*Dead Poets Society*)
Best Foreign-Language Film: Life and Nothing But (France)
The Michael Balcon Award: Dame Peggy Ashcroft

MAGILL'S
CINEMA
ANNUAL

TITLE INDEX

Abyss, The   19
Adventures of Baron Munchausen, The   23
Adventures of Milo and Otis, The   388
Affaire de Femmes, Une. *See* Story of Women.
After Midnight   388
All Dogs Go to Heaven   27
All's Fair   388
Always   32
Amanda   388
American Ninja III   388
American Stories   389
Animal Behavior   389
Astonished   389

Babar   389
Back to the Future Part II   36
Bad Blood   390
Batman   40
Bear, The [1988]   44
Bert Rigby, You're a Fool   390
Best of the Best   390
Beverly Hills Brats   390
Big Man on Campus   390
Big Picture, The   391
Bill and Ted's Excellent Adventure   48
Black Rain   52
Blaze   56
Bloodfist   391
Bloodhounds of Broadway   391
Born on the Fourth of July   60
Breaking In   391
'Burbs, The   65
Buying Time   391

Cage   392
Cameron's Closet   392
Camille Claudel [1988]   68
Casualties of War   71
Catch Me If You Can   392
Chances Are   392
Checking Out   392
Cheetah   393
Chocolat   393
Chorus of Disapproval, A   393
Cinema Paradiso   74
Cold Comfort   393
Cold Feet   393
Communion   78
Cookie   394
Cousins   394
Crack House   394
Crimes and Misdemeanors   82
Criminal Law   394
Cyborg   395

Dad   86
Dance of the Damned   395
Dead Bang   395
Dead Calm   395
Dead Poets Society   90
Dealers   395
Deepstar Six   396
Disorganized Crime   396
Distribution of Lead, The   396

Do the Right Thing   94
Dream a Little Dream   396
Dream Team, The   397
Driving Miss Daisy   99
Drugstore Cowboy   103
Dry White Season, A   107
Duel in the Sun [1946]   2

Earth Girls Are Easy   397
Eat a Bowl of Tea   111
Echoes of Paradise   397
Eddie and the Cruisers II   397
Edge of Sanity   397
Eighty-Four Charlie MoPic   115
Enemies, A Love Story   119
Erik the Viking   398
Escape from Safehaven   398
Everlasting Secret Family, The   398

Fabulous Baker Boys, The   123
Fakebook   398
Family Business   127
Far from Home   399
Farewell to the King   399
Fast Food   399
Fat Man and Little Boy   399
Fear, Anxiety and Depression   400
Field of Dreams   131
Fistfighter   400
Fletch Lives   135
Fly II, The   400
Food of the Gods II   400
For Queen and Country [1988]   139
Four Adventures of Reinette and Mirabelle [1986]   143
Free and Easy   400
Friday the 13th Part VIII   401
Fun Down There   401

Game, The   401
Gentlemen's Agreement [1947]   2
Getting It Right   147
Ghostbusters II   151
Ginger Ale Afternoon   401
Gleaming the Cube   401
Glory   155
God's Will   402
Great Balls of Fire!   160
Gross Anatomy   402
Guests of Hotel Astoria, The   402
Gunfighter, The [1950]   3

Halloween V   402
Hanussen   403
Harlem Nights   164
Heart of Dixie   403
Heart of Midnight   403
Heathers   168
Hell High   403
Hellbent   403
Henry V   173
Her Alibi   404
High Hopes [1988]   177
Histoires d'amerique. *See* American Stories.
Hit List   404
Honey, I Shrunk the Kids   181
Horror Show, The   404

How I Got into College   404
How to Get Ahead in Advertising   404
Hungarian Fairy Tale, A   405

I, Madman   405
I Want to Go Home   405
Ice House   405
Identity Crisis   405
Immediate Family   185
In Country   189
Indiana Jones and the Last Crusade   193
Innocent Man, An   406
Iron Triangle, The   406
It Had to Be You   406

Jacknife   197
January Man, The   406
Jesus of Montreal   201
Johnny Handsome   407

Karate Kid III, The   407
Keys of the Kingdom, The [1944]   1
Kickboxer   407
Kill Me Again   407
Kinjite   408
K-9   205

Lean on Me   209
Lectrice, La [1988]   213
Let It Ride   408
Lethal Weapon II   217
Leviathan   408
Licence to Kill   221
Life and Nothing But   408
Life Is Cheap   408
Life Lessons. *See* New York Stories.
Life Without Zoe. *See* New York Stories.
Listen to Me   409
Little Mermaid, The   225
Little Monsters   409
Little Thief, The   409
Little Vera   409
Lock Up   409
Lodz Ghetto   410
Long Weekend, The   410
Look Who's Talking   229
Lords of the Deep   410
Lost Angels   410
Loverboy   410
Luckiest Man in the World, The   411

Major League   233
Manifesto   411
Masque of the Red Death   411
Meet the Hollowheads   411
Midnight   411
Mighty Quinn, The   412
Milk and Honey   412
Millennium   412
Ministry of Vengeance   412
Miracle Mile   413
Misplaced   413
Miss Firecracker   237
Music Box   241

451

Mutant on the Bounty   413
My Left Foot   245
My Mom's a Werewolf   413
Mystery Train   249

National Lampoon's Christmas
   Vacation   413
Navigator, The [1988]   253
New Year's Day   414
New York Stories   257
Next of Kin   414
Night Game   414
Night Visitor   414
Nightmare on Elm Street V   414
976-EVIL   415
No Holds Barred   415
No Retreat, No Surrender II   415

O' Despair. See Long Weekend, The.
Oedipus Wrecks. See New York
   Stories.
Office Party   415
Old Gringo   262
Out Cold   415
Out of the Dark   416

Package, The   416
Parenthood   267
Parents   416
Penn and Teller Get Killed   416
Perfect Model, The   416
Personal Choice   417
Pet Sematary   271
Petite Veleuse, La. See Little Thief,
   The.
Phantom of the Opera, The   417
Physical Evidence   417
Pink Cadillac   417
Police Academy VI   417
Prancer   418
Purgatory   418

Quatre Aventures de Reinette et
   Mirabelle. See Four Adventures of
   Reinette and Mirabelle.
Queen of Hearts   275

Race for Glory   418
Rachel Papers, The   418
Raging Fury. See Hell High.
Rainbow, The   279
Red Scorpion   418
Relentless   419

Renegades   419
Return of the Swamp Thing,
   The   419
Return of the Musketeers, The   419
Riding the Edge   420
River of Death   420
Riverbend   420
Road House   420
Rock n' Roll Meller. See Hellbent.
Roger and Me   283
Roman Holiday [1953]   3
Romero   420
Rooftops   421
Rose Garden, The   421
Rude Awakening   421

Savage Beach   421
Say Anything   287
Scandal   291
Scenes from the Class Struggle in
   Beverly Hills   295
Sea of Love   299
Season of Fear   421
Second Sight   422
See No Evil, Hear No Evil   302
See You in the Morning   422
Severance   422
sex, lies and videotape   306
Sexbomb   422
She-Devil   310
She's Out of Control   422
Shirley Valentine   423
Shocker   423
Sidewalk Stories   315
Signs of Life   423
Silent Night, Deadly Night III   423
Sinful Life, A   423
Sing   424
Skin Deep   424
Slaves of New York   424
Sons   424
Speed Zone   424
Spellbound [1945]   1-2
Spices   425
Star Trek V   319
Staying Together   323
Steel Magnolias   328
Stepfather II   425
Story of Women [1988]   332
Street Story   425
Stripped to Kill II   425
Suitors, The   426
Sunday's Child   426

Talvisota   336
Tango and Cash   340
Tango Bar   426
Tap   344
Taxing Woman's Return, A
   [1988]   348
Teen Witch   426
Terror Within, The   426
Three Fugitives   426
To Die For   427
To Kill a Mockingbird [1962]   3-4
Tora-San Goes to Vienna   427
Toxic Avenger, Part II, The   427
Toxic Avenger, Part III, The   427
Triumph of the Spirit   351
Troop Beverly Hills   427
True Believer   356
True Blood   428
True Love   360
Trust Me   428
Turner and Hooch   428
Twelve O'Clock High [1949]   2-3

UHF   428
Uncle Buck   364

Valentino Returns   429
Valmont   368
Vampire's Kiss   429
Vie est rien d'autre, La. See Life and
   Nothing But.

War of the Roses, The   372
Warlock   429
Warm Summer Rain   429
Weekend at Bernie's   429
Welcome Home   429
We're No Angels   376
When Harry Met Sally   380
When the Whales Came   430
Who's Harry Crumb?   430
Wicked Stepmother   430
Winter People   430
Winter War, The. See Talvisota.
Wired   384
Wizard, The   430
Wonderland   431
Worth Winning   431

Yearling, The [1946]   2

DIRECTOR INDEX

ADELSON, ALAN
Lodz Ghetto 410

AKERMAN, CHANTAL
American Stories 389

ALAMEHZADEH, REZA
Guests of Hotel Astoria,
The 402

ALLEN, WOODY
Crimes and Misdemeanors 82
New York Stories 257

AMIEL, JON
Queen of Hearts 275

ANDERSON, MICHAEL
Millennium 412

ANNAUD, JEAN-JACQUES
Bear, The [1988] 44

ARAKI, GREGG
Long Weekend, The 410

ARCAND, DENYS
Jesus of Montreal 201

ARDOLINO, EMILE
Chances Are 392

ARTZI, AMI
Purgatory 418

AVILDSEN, JOHN G.
Karate Kid III, The 407
Lean on Me 209

AVIS, MEIERT
Far from Home 399

BALABAN, BOB
Parents 416

BARTEL, PAUL
Scenes from the Class Struggle
in Beverly Hills 295

BASKIN, RICHARD
Sing 424

BECKER, HAROLD
Sea of Love 299

BERESFORD, BRUCE
Driving Miss Daisy 99
Her Alibi 404

BIERMAN, ROBERT
Vampire's Kiss 429

BLUTH, DON
All Dogs Go to Heaven 27

BLYTH, JEFF
Cheetah 393

BOLOGNA, JOSEPH
It Had to Be You 406

BONERZ, PETER
Police Academy VI 417

BRANAGH, KENNETH
Henry V 173

BRAND, LARRY
Masque of the Red Death 411

BRITTAIN, DONALD
Obituaries 435

BROADSTREET, JEFF
Sexbomb 422

BROOKNER, HOWARD
Bloodhounds of Broadway 391

BROWN, CURTIS
Game, The 401

BUCKSEY, COLIN
Dealers 395

BUNCE, ALAN
Babar 389

BURMAN, TOM
Meet the Hollowheads 411

BURR, JEFF
Stepfather II 425

BURTON, TIM
Batman 40

CAMERON, JAMES
Abyss, The 19

CAMERON, JULIA
God's Will 402

CAMPBELL, DOUG
Season of Fear 421

CAMPBELL, MARTIN
Criminal Law 394

CAPRIOLI, VITTORIO
Obituaries 435

CARVER, STEVE
River of Death 420

CASEY, RICHARD
Hellbent 403

CASSAVETES, JOHN
Obituaries 435

CASTLE, NICK
Tap 344

CATON-JONES, MICHAEL
Scandal 291

CHABROL, CLAUDE
Story of Women [1988] 332

CHAPMAN, MATTHEW
Heart of Midnight 403

CHECHIK, JEREMIAH S.
National Lampoon's Christmas
Vacation 413

CLEMENTS, RON
Little Mermaid, The 225

CLIFFORD, GRAEME
Gleaming the Cube 401

COHEN, LARRY
Wicked Stepmother 430

COLES, JOHN DAVID
Signs of Life 423

COPPOLA, FRANCIS
New York Stories 257

COSMATOS, GEORGE P.
Leviathan 408

COSTA-GAVRAS, CONSTANTIN
Music Box 241

CRAVEN, WES
Shocker 423

CRICHTON, MICHAEL
Physical Evidence 417

CROWE, CAMERON
Say Anything 287

CUNNINGHAM, SEAN S.
Deepstar Six 396

DA COSTA, MORTON
Obituaries 436

DAHL, JOHN
Kill Me Again 407

DALI, SALVADOR
Obituaries 436

DALRYMPLE, IAN
Obituaries 437

DANIEL, ROD
K-9 205

DANTE, JOE
'Burbs, The 65

DAVIDSON, MARTIN
Heart of Dixie 403

DAVIS, ANDREW
Package, The 416

DE ANTONIO, EMILE
Obituaries 437

DENIS, CLAIRE
Chocolat 393

DEPALMA, BRIAN
Casualties of War 71

DEVILLE, MICHEL
Lectrice, La [1988] 213

DEVITO, DANNY
War of the Roses, The 372

DISALLE, MARK
Kickboxer 407

DONNER, RICHARD
Lethal Weapon II 217

DORNHELM, ROBERT
Cold Feet 393

DRAGOTI, STAN
She's Out of Control 422

DRAKE, JIM
Speed Zone 424

DUIGAN, JOHN
Romero 420

DUNCAN, PATRICK
Eighty-Four Charlie MoPic 115

EBERHARDT, THOM
Gross Anatomy 402

EBRAHIMIAN, GHASEM
Suitors, The 426

EDWARDS, BLAKE
Skin Deep 424

ELLIOTT, LANG
Cage 392

ENGLUND, ROBERT
976-EVIL 415

FARGO, JAMES
Riding the Edge 420

FIRSTENBERG, SAM
Riverbend 420

453

FISCHA, MICHAEL
Crack House   394
My Mom's a Werewolf   413
FISHER, MARY ANN
Lords of the Deep   410
FLAHERTY, PAUL
Who's Harry Crumb?   430
FLYNN, JOHN
Lock Up   409
FORMAN, MILOS
Valmont   368
FORSYTH, BILL
Breaking In   391
FRANKENHEIMER, JOHN
Dead Bang   395

GABOURIE, MITCHELL
Buying Time   391
GAYTON, JOE
Warm Summer Rain   429
GAZDAG, GYULA
Hungarian Fairy Tale, A   405
GILBERT, LEWIS
Shirley Valentine   423
GILLIAM, TERRY
Adventures of Baron Munchausen,
The   23
GILROY, FRANK D.
Luckiest Man in the World,
The   411
GLEN, JOHN
Licence to Kill   221
GOLDBERG, GARY DAVID
Dad   86
GRANT, LEE
Staying Together   323
GREENBERG, RICHARD ALAN
Little Monsters   409
GREENWALT, DAVID
Rude Awakening   421
GROSSMAN, DOUGLAS
Hell High   403
GUEST, CHRISTOPHER
Big Picture, The   391

HANCOCK, JOHN
Prancer   418
HARRIS, DAMIAN
Rachel Papers, The   418
HECKERLING, AMY
Look Who's Talking   229
HEDDEN, ROB
Friday the 13th Part VIII   401
HELLMAN, MONTE
Silent Night, Deadly
Night III   423
HEREK, STEPHEN
Bill and Ted's Excellent
Adventure   48
HERRINGTON, ROWDY
Road House   420
HERZ, MICHAEL
Toxic Avenger, Part II, The   427
Toxic Avenger, Part III, The   427
HILL, WALTER
Johnny Handsome   407

HILLER, ARTHUR
See No Evil, Hear No Evil   302
HITZIG, RUPERT
Night Visitor   414
HOFFMAN, PETER
Valentino Returns   429
HOLLAND, SAVAGE STEVE
How I Got into College   404
HOLLAND, TODD
Wizard, The   430
HOPKINS, STEPHEN
Nightmare on Elm Street V   414
HOUSTON, BOBBY
Trust Me   428
HOWARD, RON
Parenthood   267
HUDSON, HUGH
Lost Angels   410
HUGHES, JOHN
Uncle Buck   364

IRVIN, JOHN
Next of Kin   414
ISAAC, JAMES
Horrow Show, The   404
ITAMI, JUZO
Taxing Woman's Return, A
[1988]   348
IVORY, JAMES
Slaves of New York   424

JAGLOM, HENRY
New Year's Day   414
JARMUSCH, JIM
Mystery Train   249
JARNATT, STEVE DE
Miracle Mile   413
JEWISON, NORMAN
In Country   189
JOFFE, ROLAND
Fat Man and Little Boy   399
JOHNSTON, JOE
Honey, I Shrunk the Kids   181
JONES, BRIAN THOMAS
Escape from Safehaven   398
JONES, DAVID
Jacknife   197
JONES, TERRY
Erik the Viking   398
JORDAN, NEIL
We're No Angels   376

KAGAN, JEREMY
Big Man on Campus   390
KAHN, JEFF
Astonished   389
KANEW, JEFF
Troop Beverly Hills   427
KAPLAN, JONATHAN
Immediate Family   185
KAUFMAN, LLOYD
Toxic Avenger, Part II, The   427
Toxic Avenger, Part III, The   427
KERR, FRANK
True Blood   428

KIKOINE, GERARD
Edge of Sanity   397
KLEISER, RANDAL
Getting It Right   147
KLOVES, STEVE
Fabulous Baker Boys, The   123
KONCHALOVSKY, ANDREI
Tango and Cash   340
KOTCHEFF, TED
Weekend at Bernie's   429
Winter People   430
KOUF, JIM
Disorganized Crime   396
KURIYAMA, TOMIO
Free and Easy   400

LAMBERT, MARY
Pet Sematary   271
LANE, CHARLES
Sidewalk Stories   315
LANG, ROCKY
All's Fair   388
Race for Glory   418
LEBORG, REGINALD
Obituaries   439
LEE, DAMIAN
Food of the Gods II   400
LEE, SPIKE
Do the Right Thing   94
LEHMANN, MICHAEL
Heathers   168
LEIGH, MIKE
High Hopes [1988]   177
LELAND, DAVID
Checking Out   392
LEONE, SERGIO
Obituaries   439
LESTER, RICHARD
Return of the Musketeers,
The   419
LEVEY, JAY
UHF   428
LIBIN, CHARLES
Distribution of Lead, The   396
LITTLE, DWIGHT H.
Phantom of the Opera, The   417
LORD, JEAN-CLAUDE
Eddie and the Cruisers II   397
LUMET, SIDNEY
Family Business   127
LUSTIG, WILLIAM
Hit List   404
Relentless   419

MCBRIDE, JIM
Great Balls of Fire!   160
MCCALMONT, JAMES
Escape from Safehaven   398
MACKENZIE, WILL
Worth Winning   431
MAKAVEJEV, DUSAN
Manifesto   411
MARIS, PETER
Ministry of Vengeance   412

MASANORI HATA
  Adventures of Milo and Otis,
    The 388
MASTERSON, PETER
  Night Game 414
MASTROIANNI, ARMAND
  Cameron's Closet 392
MAZURSKY, PAUL
  Enemies, A Love Story 119
MEHTA, KETAN
  Spices 425
MEYER, JEFF
  Amanda 388
MIHALKA, GEORGE
  Office Party 415
MILIUS, JOHN
  Farewell to the King 399
MILLER, CLAUDE
  Little Thief, The 409
MINER, STEVE
  Warlock 429
MOORE, MICHAEL
  Roger and Me 283
MORA, PHILIPPE
  Communion 78
MOWBRAY, MALCOLM
  Out Cold 415
MURPHY, EDDIE
  Harlem Nights 164
MUSKER, JOHN
  Little Mermaid, The 225

NOTZ, THIERRY
  Terror Within, The 426
NOYCE, PHILLIP
  Dead Calm 395
  Echoes of Paradise 397
NUYTTEN, BRUNO
  Camille Claudel [1988] 68

O'CONNOR, PAT
  January Man, The 406
OSWALD, GERD
  Obituaries 442
OTHENIN-GIRARD, DOMINIQUE
  Halloween V 402

PAKULA, ALAN J.
  See You in the Morning 422
PALCY, EUZHAN
  Dry White Season, A 107
PARIKKA, PEKKA
  Talvisota 336
PEERCE, LARRY
  Wired 384
PENN, ARTHUR
  Penn and Teller Get Killed 416
PENNELL, EAGLE
  Ice House 405
PICHUL, VASILY
  Little Vera 409
PUENZO, LUIS
  Old Gringo 262
PYTKA, JOE
  Let It Ride 408

PYUN, ALBERT
  Cyborg 395

QUINE, RICHARD
  Obituaries 442

RADEMAKERS, FONS
  Rose Garden, The 421
RADLER, BOB
  Best of the Best 390
REES, CLIVE
  When the Whales Came 430
REINER, CARL
  Bert Rigby, You're a Fool 390
REINER, ROB
  When Harry Met Sally 380
REITMAN, IVAN
  Ghostbusters II 151
RESNAIS, ALAIN
  I Want to Go Home 405
RILEY, H. ANNE
  Animal Behavior 389
RITCHIE, MICHAEL
  Fletch Lives 135
ROBERTS, DARRYL
  Perfect Model, The 416
ROBINSON, BRUCE
  How to Get Ahead in
    Advertising 404
ROBINSON, PHIL ALDEN
  Field of Dreams 131
ROCCO, MARC
  Dream a Little Dream 396
ROCKWELL, ALEXANDRE
  Sons 424
ROHMER, ERIC
  Four Adventures of Reinette and
    Mirabelle [1986] 143
RONDI, BRUNELLO
  Obituaries 443
ROSELLA, GAIL KAPPLER
  Amanda 388
ROSENBAUM, MARIANNE
  Sunday's Child 426
ROSS, HERBERT
  Steel Magnolias 328
RUBEN, JOSEPH
  True Believer 356
RUBEN, KATT SHEA
  Dance of the Damned 395
  Stripped to Kill II 425
RUSSELL, KEN
  Rainbow, The 279
RUSSO, AARON
  Rude Awakening 421

SALZMAN, GLEN
  Milk and Honey 412
SAPERSTEIN, DAVID
  Personal Choice 417
SARAFIAN, DEREN
  To Die For 427
SARIN, VIC
  Cold Comfort 393
SAVILLE, PHILIP
  Wonderland 431

SAVOCA, NANCY
  True Love 360
SCHAFFNER, FRANKLIN J.
  Obituaries 443
  Welcome Home 429
SCHENKEL, CARL
  Mighty Quinn, The 412
SCHLAMME, THOMAS
  Miss Firecracker 237
SCHREINER, WILLIAM
  Sinful Life, A 423
SCHROEDER, MICHAEL
  Out of the Dark 416
SCHUMACHER, JOEL
  Cousins 394
SCORCESE, MARTIN
  New York Stories 257
SCOTT, RIDLEY
  Black Rain 52
SEIDELMAN, SUSAN
  Cookie 394
  She-Devil 310
SHATNER, WILLIAM
  Star Trek V 319
SHELTON, RON
  Blaze 56
SHERIDAN, JIM
  My Left Foot 245
SHOLDER, JACK
  Renegades 419
SIDARIS, ANDY
  Savage Beach 421
SILVER, JOAN MICKLIN
  Loverboy 410
SIMPSON, MICHAEL A.
  Fast Food 399
SODERBERGH, STEVEN
  sex, lies and videotape 306
SOLONDZ, TODD
  Fear, Anxiety and
    Depression 400
SOMMERS, STEPHEN
  Catch Me If You Can 392
SOTIRAKIS, DIMITRI
  Beverly Hills Brats 390
SPIELBERG, STEVEN
  Always 32
  Indiana Jones and the Last
    Crusade 193
SPOTTISWOODE, ROGER
  Turner and Hooch 428
STARRETT, JACK
  Obituaries 443
STEINBERG, DAVID MAX
  Severance 422
STELLMAN, MARTIN
  For Queen and Country
    [1988] 139
STEWART, DOUGLAS DAY
  Listen to Me 409
STIGLIANO, ROGER
  Fun Down There 401
STONE, OLIVER
  Born on the Fourth of July 60

SUNDSTROM, CEDRIC
  American Ninja III   388
SZABO, ISTVAN
  Hanussen   403

TAKACS, TIBOR
  I, Madman   405
TAVERNA, KATHRYN
  Lodz Ghetto   410
TAVERNIER, BERTRAND
  Life and Nothing But   408
TAYLOR, RENEE
  It Had to Be You   406
TEMPLE, JULIEN
  Earth Girls Are Easy   397
THOMPSON, J. LEE
  Kinjite   408
THORNHILL, MICHAEL
  Everlasting Secret Family,
  The   398
TOPOROFF, RALPH
  Fakebook   398
TORNATORE, GIUSEPPE
  Cinema Paradiso   74
TORRANCE, ROBERT
  Mutant on the Bounty   413

VANE, NORMAN THADDEUS
  Midnight   411
VAN HORN, BUDDY
  Pink Cadillac   417
VAN PEEBLES, MELVIN
  Identity Crisis   405
VAN SANT, GUS, JR.
  Drugstore Cowboy   103

VASQUEZ, JOSEPH B.
  Street Story   425
VEBER, FRANCES
  Three Fugitives   426
VINCENT, CHUCK
  Bad Blood   390

WALAS, CHRIS
  Fly II, The   400
WALKER, DORIAN
  Teen Witch   426
WANG, WAYNE
  Eat a Bowl of Tea   111
  Life Is Cheap   408
WARD, DAVID
  Major League   233
WARD, VINCENT
  Navigator, The [1988]   253
WEIR, PETER
  Dead Poets Society   90
WESTON, ERIC
  Iron Triangle, The   406
WHEAT, JIM
  After Midnight   388
WHEAT, KEN
  After Midnight   388
WILDE, CORNEL
  Obituaries   444
WINKLESS, TERENCE H.
  Bloodfist   391
WINNER, MICHAEL
  Chorus of Disapproval, A   393
WISE, ROBERT
  Rooftops   421
WORTH, DAVID
  Kickboxer   407

WRIGHT, THOMAS J.
  No Holds Barred   415
WYNORSKI, JIM
  Return of the Swamp Thing,
  The   419

YAMADA, YOJI
  Tora-San Goes to Vienna   427
YANSEN, LOUIS
  Misplaced   413
YATES, PETER
  Innocent Man, An   406
YATES, REBECCA
  Milk and Honey   412
YOUNG, ROBERT M.
  Triumph of the Spirit   351
YUEN, COREY
  No Retreat, No Surrender II   415

ZEMECKIS, ROBERT
  Back to the Future Part II   36
ZIEFF, HOWARD
  Dream Team, The   397
ZIELINSKI, RAFAL
  Ginger Ale Afternoon   401
ZITO, JOSEPH
  Red Scorpion   418
ZUNIGA, FRANK
  Fistfighter   400
ZURINAGA, MARCOS
  Tango Bar   426
ZWICK, EDWARD
  Glory   155
ZWICK, JOEL
  Second Sight   422

SCREENWRITER INDEX

ABERNATHY, LEWIS
Deepstar Six 396
ADELSON, ALAN
Lodz Ghetto 410
AKERMAN, CHANTAL
American Stories 389
ALAMEHZADEH, REZA
Guests of Hotel Astoria,
The 402
ALLEN, WOODY
Crimes and Misdemeanors 82
New York Stories 257
ARAKI, GREGG
Long Weekend, The 410
ARATOW, PAUL
Purgatory 418
ARCAND, DENYS
Jesus of Montreal 201
ARLEN, ALICE
Cookie 394
ASAMA, YOSHITAKE
Tora-San Goes to Vienna 427
AUERBACH, JOHN
Stepfather II 425
AYCKBOURN, ALAN
Chorus of Disapproval, A 393
AYKROYD, DAN
Ghostbusters II 151

BARAN, JACK
Great Balls of Fire! 160
BARRET, EARL
See No Evil, Hear No Evil 302
BARRETT, JAMES LEE
Obituaries 434
BEATTIE, RICHARD
Cold Comfort 393
BELSON, JERRY
Always 32
BENEDEK, BARBARA
Immediate Family 185
BENNETT, RICHARD
Food of the Gods II 400
BENSON, ROBERT
Sexbomb 422
BERAUD, LUC
Little Thief, The 409
BISHOP, JOHN
Package, The 416
BITTERMAN, SHEM
Halloween V 402
BLODGETT, MICHAEL
Turner and Hooch 428
BLOOM, MAX
Fistfighter 400
BOAM, JEFFREY
Indiana Jones and the Last
Crusade 193
Lethal Weapon II 217

BOHEM, LESLIE
Horrow Show, The 404
Nightmare on Elm Street V 414
BOLOGNA, JOSEPH
It Had to Be You 406
BOLOTIN, CRAIG
Black Rain 52
BORTNIK, AIDA
Old Gringo 262
BRACH, GERARD
Bear, The [1988] 44
BRANAGH, KENNETH
Henry V 173
BRAND, LARRY
Masque of the Red Death 411
BRANDNER, GARY
Cameron's Closet 392
BRANDON, CLARK
Fast Food 399
BRENNAN, TERENCE
Rooftops 421
BREWSTER, E. KIM
Food of the Gods II 400
BRIGHT, JOHN
Obituaries 435
BRINKMAN, BO
Ice House 405
BROOKNER, HOWARD
Bloodhounds of Broadway 391
BROSNAN, PETER
Hit List 404
BROTHERS, LARRY
Innocent Man, An 406
BROWN, CURTIS
Game, The 401
BROWN, JULIE
Earth Girls Are Easy 397
BRUCE, GLENN
Kickboxer 407
BUNCE, ALAN
Babar 389
BURMAN, TOM
Meet the Hollowheads 411
BURNS, MARK R.
She-Devil 310
BUSHELMAN, JOHN
Iron Triangle, The 406

CAMERON, JAMES
Abyss, The 19
CAMERON, JULIA
God's Will 402
CAMPBELL, DOUG
Season of Fear 421
CAPETANOS, LEON
Fletch Lives 135
CARRIERE, JEAN-CLAUDE
Valmont 368
CASEY, RICHARD
Hellbent 403

CASH, JIM
Turner and Hooch 428
CASSAVETES, JOHN
Obituaries 435
CASTLE, NICK
Tap 344
CELLINO, MARIA ELENE
No Retreat, No Surrender II 415
CHABROL, CLAUDE
Story of Women [1988] 332
CHALMERS, KITTY
Cyborg 395
CHAPMAN, GRAHAM
Obituaries 436
CHAPMAN, MATTHEW
Heart of Midnight 403
CHAPPLE, GEOFF
Navigator, The [1988] 253
CHASKIN, DAVID
I, Madman 405
CHISHOLM, DAVID
Wizard, The 430
CIDRE, CYNTHIA
In Country 189
CLARKE, FRANK
Wonderland 431
CLARKE, T. E. B.
Obituaries 436
CLEAVER, THOMAS M.
Terror Within, The 426
CLEMENTS, RON
Little Mermaid, The 225
CODAZZI, JUAN CARLOS
Tango Bar 426
COFFEY, CHARLIE
Earth Girls Are Easy 397
COHEN, CHARLES ZEV
Eddie and the Cruisers II 397
COHEN, HOWARD
Lords of the Deep 410
COHEN, LARRY
Wicked Stepmother 430
COLE, BRANDON
Sons 424
CONNAUGHTON, SHANE
My Left Foot 245
CONNOLLY, JON
Dream Team, The 397
CONTE, ROBERT
Who's Harry Crumb? 430
COPPOLA, FRANCIS
New York Stories 257
COPPOLA, SOFIA
New York Stories 257
COSMOS, JEAN
Life and Nothing But 408
COTTER, JOHN
Cheetah 393
CRAVEN, WES
Shocker 423

CROWE, CAMERON
Say Anything   287
CURWICK, STEPHEN J.
Police Academy VI   417

DAHL, JOHN
Kill Me Again   407
DALRYMPLE, IAN
Obituaries   437
DARABONT, FRANK
Fly II, The   400
DEFELICE, J. GREG
Out of the Dark   416
DEKAY, COLMAN
Bloodhounds of Broadway   391
DE KLEIN, JOHN
Babar   389
DENIS, CLAIRE
Chocolat   393
DEUTSCH, ANDREW
River of Death   420
DEVILLE, MICHEL
Lectrice, La [1988]   213
DEVILLE, ROSALINDE
Lectrice, La [1988]   213
DEWOLFE, THOMAS
Misplaced   413
DIXON, LESLIE
Loverboy   410
DOBAI, PETER
Hanussen   403
DOEHRING, RICK
Eddie and the Cruisers II   397
DUNCAN, PATRICK
Eighty-Four Charlie MoPic   115
DU RHONE, GRIFF
Cheetah   393

EASTMAN, SPENCER
Night Game   414
EBRAHIMIAN, GHASEM
Suitors, The   426
EDWARDS, BLAKE
Skin Deep   424
EISENBERG, D. E.
Dream a Little Dream   396
ELLIOTT, TED
Little Monsters   409
EMRYYS, MERVYN
Ministry of Vengeance   412
EPHRON, NORA
Cookie   394
When Harry Met Sally   380
EPPS, JACK, JR.
Turner and Hooch   428
ESKOW, JOHN
Pink Cadillac   417
ESZTERHAS, JOE
Checking Out   392
Music Box   241
EVANS, LEO
Hell High   403

FANCHER, HAMPTON
Mighty Quinn, The   412

FARGEAU, JEAN-POL
Chocolat   393
FEIFFER, JULES
I Want to Go Home   405
FEINMAN, JOSE PABLO
Tango Bar   426
FELDMAN, RANDY
Tango and Cash   340
FELIX, J. P.
Edge of Sanity   397
FINEGAN, JOHN
All's Fair   388
FOSTER, ROBERT
Dead Bang   395
FRANKLIN, DANIEL JAY
Dream a Little Dream   396
FRASER, GEORGE
MACDONALD
Return of the Musketeers,
The   419
FRIEDMAN, KEN
Johnny Handsome   407

GABOURIE, MITCHELL
Buying Time   391
GABOURIE, RICHARD
Buying Time   391
GALE, BOB
Back to the Future Part II   36
GANZ, LOWELL
Parenthood   267
GARDNER, LEONARD
Valentino Returns   429
GARRIS, MICK
Fly II, The   400
GAYTON, JOE
Warm Summer Rain   429
GAZDAG, GYULA
Hungarian Fairy Tale, A   405
GILBERT, MICHAEL A.
Office Party   415
GILLIAM, TERRY
Adventures of Baron Munchausen,
The   23
GILROY, FRANK D.
Luckiest Man in the World,
The   411
GIRION, GILBERT
Fakebook   398
GLADSTEIN, RICHARD N.
Silent Night, Deadly
Night III   423
GLASSER, HOWARD
Out Cold   415
GOFF, JOHN
Hit List   404
GOLDBERG, GARY DAVID
Dad   86
GOLDIN, MARILYN
Camille Claudel [1988]   68
GRAHAM, MELANIE
Sinful Life, A   423
GRISONI, TONY
Queen of Hearts   275
GROSSMAN, DOUGLAS
Hell High   403

GUAY, RICHARD
True Love   360
GUEST, CHRISTOPHER
Big Picture, The   391
GYORFFY, MIKLOS
Hungarian Fairy Tale, A   405

HACKIN, DENNIS
No Holds Barred   415
HAKIM, SHAFI
Spices   425
HAMM, SAM
Batman   40
HANEY, DARYL
Lords of the Deep   410
Masque of the Red Death   411
HARLING, ROBERT
Steel Magnolias   328
HARRIS, DAMIAN
Rachel Papers, The   418
HARRISON, JIM
Cold Feet   393
HAWTHORNE, CHRISTOPHER
Parents   416
HAYES, TERRY
Dead Calm   395
HEATH, LAURENCE
Triumph of the Spirit   351
HECKERLING, AMY
Look Who's Talking   229
HEDDEN, ROB
Friday the 13th Part VIII   401
HELGELAND, BRIAN
976-EVIL   415
HELLMAN, MONTE
Silent Night, Deadly
Night III   423
HENLEY, BETH
Miss Firecracker   237
HENRY, DAVID LEE
Road House   420
HENUGGE, PAUL
Rose Garden, The   421
HILBRAND, LARRY
Iron Triangle, The   406
HOCHMAN, CYNTHIA
Severance   422
HORAN, ROY
No Retreat, No Surrender II   415
HORN, LANNY
Fast Food   399
HORRALL, CRAIG
Bad Blood   390
HOUSTON, BOBBY
Trust Me   428
HOWARD, ELIZABETH JANE
Getting It Right   147
HOWZE, PERRY
Chances Are   392
HOWZE, RANDY
Chances Are   392
HUGHES, JOHN
National Lampoon's Christmas
Vacation   413
Uncle Buck   364

SCREENWRITER INDEX

ITAMI, JUZO
  Taxing Woman's Return, A
    [1988]   348

JACOBS, MICHAEL
  Halloween V   402
JAGLOM, HENRY
  New Year's Day   414
JANOWITZ, TAMA
  Slaves of New York   424
JARMUSCH, JIM
  Mystery Train   249
JARNATT, STEVE DE
  Miracle Mile   413
JARRE, KEVIN
  Glory   155
JEFFELICE, RAYMOND
  Babar   389
JEFFRIES, BRIAN D.
  Ministry of Vengeance   412
JENKIN, HILARY
  Road House   420
JENNING, MICHAEL
  Next of Kin   414
JILLETTE, PENN
  Penn and Teller Get Killed   416
JOFFE, ROLAND
  Fat Man and Little Boy   399
JONES, BRIAN THOMAS
  Escape from Safehaven   398
JONES, TERRY
  Erik the Viking   398

KAHN, JEFF
  Astonished   389
KAMEN, ROBERT MARK
  Karate Kid III, The   407
KASDAN, MARK
  Criminal Law   394
KATZ, ALLAN
  Big Man on Campus   390
KAUFMAN, LLOYD
  Toxic Avenger, Part III, The   427
KELLEY, HUGH
  Cage   392
KERR, FRANK
  True Blood   428
KHMELIK, MARIA
  Little Vera   409
KING, LESLIE
  To Die For   427
KING, ROBERT
  Bloodfist   391
KING, STEPHEN
  Pet Sematary   271
KLANE, ROBERT
  Weekend at Bernie's   429
KLEINMAN, MAGGIE
  Welcome Home   429
KLOVES, STEVE
  Fabulous Baker Boys, The   123
KOUF, JIM
  Disorganized Crime   396
KOVIC, RON
  Born on the Fourth of July   60

KRAKOWSKI, ANDRZEJ
  Triumph of the Spirit   351
KROLL, FELIX
  Purgatory   418
KURTZMAN, ANDREW
  See No Evil, Hear No Evil   302

LAGRAVENESE, RICHARD
  Rude Awakening   421
LANE, CHARLES
  Sidewalk Stories   315
LAZLO, CARLOS
  Silent Night, Deadly
    Night III   423
LEE, SPIKE
  Do the Right Thing   94
LEESON, MICHAEL
  War of the Roses, The   372
LEIGH, MIKE
  High Hopes [1988]   177
LEVEY, JAY
  UHF   428
LEVINE, PAUL
  Best of the Best   390
LEVITT, ZANE W.
  Out of the Dark   416
LEVY, NEIL
  Rude Awakening   421
LEWIS, WARREN
  Black Rain   52
LIBIN, CHARLES
  Distribution of Lead, The   396
LOPEZ, MARTIN
  Mutant on the Bounty   413
LOUCKA, DAVID
  Dream Team, The   397
LOUGHERY, DAVID
  Star Trek V   319
LYONS, KELY
  Navigator, The [1988]   253

MCBRIDE, JIM
  Great Balls of Fire!   160
MCCALMONT, JAMES
  Escape from Safehaven   398
MCCOWN, TOM
  Heart of Dixie   403
MCGIBBON, JOSANNE
  Worth Winning   431
MCGUANE, TOM
  Cold Feet   393
MCKEAN, MICHAEL
  Big Picture, The   391
MCKEOWN, CHARLES
  Adventures of Baron Munchausen,
    The   23
MACLEAR, ANDREW
  Dealers   395
MCNALLY, TERRENCE E.
  Earth Girls Are Easy   397
MAIBAUM, RICHARD
  Licence to Kill   221
MAKAVEJEV, DUSAN
  Manifesto   411

MALKO, GEORGE
  Out Cold   415
MALONE, MARK
  Signs of Life   423
MAMET, DAVID
  We're No Angels   376
MANDEL, BABALOO
  Parenthood   267
MATHESON, CHRIS
  Bill and Ted's Excellent
    Adventure   48
MAZURSKY, PAUL
  Enemies, A Love Story   119
MEHTA, KETAN
  Spices   425
MENKEN, ROBIN
  Teen Witch   426
MERRICK, MONTE
  Staying Together   323
METCALFE, STEPHEN
  Cousins   394
  Jacknife   197
MEYER, JEFF
  Amanda   388
MIESES, STANLEY
  Meet the Hollowheads   411
MILIUS, JOHN
  Farewell to the King   399
MILLER, ANNIE
  Little Thief, The   409
MILLER, CLAUDE
  Little Thief, The   409
MILLER, GEOF
  Deepstar Six   396
MINION, JOSEPH
  Vampire's Kiss   429
MOMOI, AKIRA
  Free and Easy   400
MOORE, MICHAEL
  Roger and Me   283
MOORHOUSE, FRANK
  Everlasting Secret Family,
    The   398
MORPURGO, MICHAEL
  When the Whales Came   430
MORRIS, GRANT
  Return of the Swamp Thing,
    The   419
MORTON, ERNEST
  Let It Ride   408
MORTON, LISA
  Meet the Hollowheads   411
MURPHY, EDDIE
  Harlem Nights   164
MUSKER, JOHN
  Little Mermaid, The   225
MYERS, SCOTT
  K-9   205

NAHA, ED
  Honey, I Shrunk the Kids   181
NAKASAKO, SPENCER
  Life Is Cheap   408
NARUS, ANN
  Ministry of Vengeance   412

NATHANSON, MICHAEL J.
  She's Out of Control   422
NEBENZAL, HAROLD
  Kinjite   408
NORRIS, PAMELA
  Troop Beverly Hills   427
NUYTTEN, BRUNO
  Camille Claudel [1988]   68
NYSWANDER, RON
  Gross Anatomy   402

OBERMAN, MARGARET GRIECE
  Troop Beverly Hills   427
OCEAN, MCDADE IVORY
  Perfect Model, The   416
O'HAGAN, COLO TAVERNIER
  Story of Women [1988]   332
OLSEN, ARNE
  Red Scorpion   418
OLSEN, DANA
  'Burbs, The   65
OTHENIN-GIRARD, DOMINIQUE
  Halloween V   402

PACE, WILLIAM
  All's Fair   388
PAKULA, ALAN J.
  See You in the Morning   422
PALCY, EUZHAN
  Dry White Season, A   107
PALMER, ANTHONY
  Night Game   414
PARIKKA, PEKKA
  Talvisota   336
PARRIOTT, SARA
  Worth Winning   431
PATRICK, VINCENT
  Family Business   127
PENN. See JILLETTE, PENN
PEOPLES, DAVID
  Leviathan   408
PETERS, CHARLIE
  Her Alibi   404
PETRIE, DANIEL, JR.
  Turner and Hooch   428
PHILLIPS, BILL
  Physical Evidence   417
PIERSON, FRANK
  In Country   189
PIRRO, MARK
  My Mom's a Werewolf   413
PITCHFORD, DEAN
  Sing   424
PRICE, RICHARD
  New York Stories   257
  Sea of Love   299
PUENZO, LUIS
  Old Gringo   262

RABE, DAVID
  Casualties of War   71
RALEY, RON
  Edge of Sanity   397
RAMIS, HAROLD
  Ghostbusters II   151

RASCOE, JUDITH
  Eat a Bowl of Tea   111
RAUCH, EARL MAC
  Wired   384
REINER, CARL
  Bert Rigby, You're a Fool   390
RESNICK, PATRICIA
  Second Sight   422
RHONE, TREVOR
  Milk and Honey   412
RICE, SUSAN
  Animal Behavior   389
RICH, DAVID
  Renegades   419
RIGDON, GARY
  Trust Me   428
ROBERTS, DARRYL
  Perfect Model, The   416
ROBERTS, MARGUERITE
  Obituaries   442
ROBINSON, BRUCE
  Fat Man and Little Boy   399
  How to Get Ahead in
    Advertising   404
ROBINSON, JACK T. D.
  Relentless   419
ROBINSON, PHIL ALDEN. See
    also ROBINSON, JACK T. D.
  Field of Dreams   131
ROCCO, MARC
  Dream a Little Dream   396
ROCKWELL, ALEXANDRE
  Sons   424
ROHMER, ERIC
  Four Adventures of Reinette and
    Mirabelle [1986]   143
RONDI, BRUNELLO
  Obituaries   443
RONDINELLA, TOM
  All's Fair   388
ROPELEWSKI, TOM
  Loverboy   410
ROSELLA, GAIL KAPPLER
  Amanda   388
ROSENBAUM, HENRY
  Lock Up   409
ROSENBAUM, MARIANNE
  Sunday's Child   426
ROSSIO, TERRY
  Little Monsters   409
RUBEN, ANDY
  Dance of the Damned   395
RUBEN, KATT SHEA
  Dance of the Damned   395
  Stripped to Kill II   425
RUSSEL, RANDEE
  All's Fair   388
RUSSELL, KEN
  Rainbow, The   279
RUSSELL, VIVIAN
  Rainbow, The   279
RUSSELL, WILLY
  Shirley Valentine   423

SALTZMAN, MARK
  Adventures of Milo and Otis,
    The   388
SALZMAN, GLEN
  Milk and Honey   412
SANDEFUR, DUKE
  Phantom of the Opera, The   417
SAPERSTEIN, DAVID
  Personal Choice   417
SAUDER, PETER
  Babar   389
SAVOCA, NANCY
  True Love   360
SAYLES, JOHN
  Breaking In   391
SCHAEFER, BLAKE
  Crack House   394
SCHIFF, ROBIN
  Loverboy   410
SCHIFFER, MICHAEL
  Lean on Me   209
SCHULMAN, TOM
  Dead Poets Society   90
  Honey, I Shrunk the Kids   181
  Second Sight   422
SELTZER, TERREL
  How I Got into College   404
SHANLEY, JOHN PATRICK
  January Man, The   406
SHARP, JAN
  Echoes of Paradise   397
SHELTON, RON
  Blaze   56
SHERIDAN, JIM
  My Left Foot   245
SHORT, MICHAEL
  Speed Zone   424
SHRYACK, DENNIS
  Turner and Hooch   428
SIDARIS, ANDY
  Savage Beach   421
SIEGEL, STEVEN
  K-9   205
SILVERTHORN, LINDA
  Beverly Hills Brats   390
SIMMS, L. ELLIOTT
  Cold Comfort   393
SIMON, ROGER L.
  Enemies, A Love Story   119
SIMPSON, EDWARD
  River of Death   420
SKAAREN, WARREN
  Batman   40
SMITH, J. D.
  Babar   389
SMITH, RICHARD
  Lock Up   409
SMITHEE, ALAN
  Horrow Show, The   404
SOBIESKI, CAROL
  Winter People   430
SODERBERGH, STEVEN
  sex, lies and videotape   306

SOLOMON, ED
Bill and Ted's Excellent
Adventure 48
SOLONDZ, TODD
Fear, Anxiety and
Depression 400
SOMMERS, STEPHEN
Catch Me If You Can 392
SPENCERN, DEREK
Return of the Swamp Thing,
The 419
SPRAGG, MARK
Gross Anatomy 402
STEINBERG, DAVID MAX
Severance 422
STELLMAN, MARTIN
For Queen and Country
[1988] 139
STEWART, DOUGLAS DAY
Listen to Me 409
STIGLIANO, ROGER
Fun Down There 401
STONE, OLIVER
Born on the Fourth of July 60
STRANDBERG, KEITH W.
No Retreat, No Surrender II 415
STRICK, WESLEY
True Believer 356
STRIEBER, WHITLEY
Communion 78
STRUGATZ, BARRY
She-Devil 310
STUART, JEB
Leviathan 408
Lock Up 409
SULTAN, ARNE
See No Evil, Hear No Evil 302
SUNDSTROM, CEDRIC
American Ninja III 388
SUPPA, RONALD A.
Riding the Edge 420
SWANTON, SCOTT
Race for Glory 418
SZABO, ISTVAN
Hanussen 403

TARLOFF, ERIK
Cheetah 393
TAVERNIER, BERTRAND
Life and Nothing But 408
TAYLOR, GREG
Prancer 418
TAYLOR, RENEE
It Had to Be You 406
TELLER
Penn and Teller Get Killed 416

TERRY, GAY PARTINGTON
Toxic Avenger, Part II, The 427
Toxic Avenger, Part III, The 427
THOMAS, DIANE
Always 32
THOMAS, MICHAEL
Scandal 291
TOLIN, MICHAEL
Gleaming the Cube 401
TOPHAM, RHET
976-EVIL 415
TORNATORE, GIUSEPPE
Cinema Paradiso 74
TUGEND, HARRY
Obituaries 443
TUURI, ANTTI
Talvisota 336
TWOHY, DAVID
Warlock 429

UHRY, ALFRED
Driving Miss Daisy 99

VANCE, SAM
Riverbend 420
VANE, NORMAN THADDEUS
Midnight 411
VAN PEEBLES, MARIO
Identity Crisis 405
VAN SANT, GUS, JR.
Drugstore Cowboy 103
VARHOL, MICHAEL
Big Picture, The 391
VARLEY, JOHN
Millennium 412
VASQUEZ, JOSEPH B.
Street Story 425
VEBER, FRANCES
Three Fugitives 426
VISCOVICH, RANDAL
Night Visitor 414

WAGNER, BRUCE
Scenes from the Class Struggle
in Beverly Hills 295
WALD, ELIOT
See No Evil, Hear No Evil 302
WALLACE, TOMMY LEE
Far from Home 399
WARD, DAVID
Major League 233
WARD, VINCENT
Navigator, The [1988] 253
WARFIELD, DAVID W.
Kill Me Again 407
WARNER, ALLYN. See SMITHEE,
ALAN

WATERS, DANIEL
Heathers 168
WEISS, DAVID
All Dogs Go to Heaven 27
WELLAND, COLIN
Dry White Season, A 107
WELLER, MICHAEL
Lost Angels 410
WENDKOS, GINA
Ginger Ale Afternoon 401
WESTON, ERIC
Iron Triangle, The 406
WHEAT, JIM
After Midnight 388
Fly II, The 400
WHEAT, KEN
After Midnight 388
Fly II, The 400
WILDER, GENE
See No Evil, Hear No Evil 302
WILSON, JULIA
Game, The 401
WILSON, MICHAEL G.
Licence to Kill 221
WINNER, MICHAEL
Chorus of Disapproval, A 393
WINSTON, SETH
She's Out of Control 422
WORRELL, TRIX
For Queen and Country
[1988] 139
WORTMANN, PETER MARTIN
Who's Harry Crumb? 430

YAMADA, YOJI
Free and Easy 400
Tora-San Goes to Vienna 427
YANKOVIC, AL
UHF 428
YANSEN, LOUIS
Misplaced 413
YOST, DANIEL
Drugstore Cowboy 103
YOUNG, JOHN SACRET
Romero 420

ZAVATTINI, CESARE
Obituaries 445
ZEMECKIS, ROBERT
Back to the Future Part II 36
ZIMMERMAN, VERNON
Teen Witch 426
ZOLLER, STEPHEN
Office Party 415
ZURINAGA, MARCOS
Tango Bar 426

CINEMATOGRAPHER INDEX

ACKERMAN, THOMAS
National Lampoon's Christmas
Vacation 413
AHLBERG, MAC
Deepstar Six 396
Horrow Show, The 404
AHWESH, PEGGY
Fun Down There 401
ALAZRAKI, ROBERT
Chocolat 393
ALBERT, ARTHUR
Miss Firecracker 237
ALMENDROS, NESTOR
New York Stories 257
ALONZO, JOHN A.
Physical Evidence 417
Steel Magnolias 328
ARAKI, GREGG
Long Weekend, The 410
ARGUELLES, FERNANDO
Warm Summer Rain 429
ARMENAKI, ARLEDGE
Crack House 394

BAGGOT, KING
Dream a Little Dream 396
BALLHAUS, MICHAEL
Fabulous Baker Boys, The 123
BARTELS, GEORGE
American Ninja III 388
BARTKOWIAK, ANDRZEJ
Family Business 127
BARTLEY, JOHN
Personal Choice 417
BAZELLI, BOJAN
Big Man on Campus 390
BEASCOECHEA, FRANK
No Holds Barred 415
BEATO, AFFONSO
Great Balls of Fire! 160
BEAVER, CHRISTOPHER
Roger and Me 283
BLOSSIER, PATRICK
Music Box 241
BODE, RALF
Cousins 394
Uncle Buck 364
BOGNER, LUDEK
Office Party 415
BONT, JAN DE
Bert Rigby, You're a Fool 390
BOYD, DAVID
To Die For 427
BOYD, RUSSELL
In Country 189
BURMAN, HANS
Fistfighter 400
BURNETT, CHARLES
Guests of Hotel Astoria,
The 402

BURSTYN, TOM
Cheetah 393
BURTON, GEOFF
Romero 420
BURUM, STEPHEN H.
Casualties of War 71
War of the Roses, The 372
BUSH, DICK
Little Monsters 409
Staying Together 323

CAMERON, PAUL A.
Distribution of Lead, The 396
CARPENTER, RUSSELL
Cameron's Closet 392
CASO, ALAN
Eighty-Four Charlie MoPic 115
CHAPMAN, MICHAEL
Ghostbusters II 151
CHAPUIS, DOMINIQUE
Little Thief, The 409
CHEUNG, MA KAM
No Retreat, No Surrender II 415
CHOUDHURY, JAHANGIR
Spices 425
CHRISTIAANSEN, DANA
Second Sight 422
CIVIT, JOSEPH M.
Silent Night, Deadly
Night III 423
CLARK, CURTIS
Triumph of the Spirit 351
COLLISTER, PETER LYONS
All's Fair 388
CONROY, JACK
My Left Foot 245
COOPER, BROWN
Ice House 405
COULTER, MICHAEL
Breaking In 391
CRABE, JAMES
Obituaries 436
CUNDEY, DEAN
Back to the Future Part II 36
Road House 420
CUNNINGHAM, GLENN
Dry White Season, A 107
CZAPSKY, STEFAN
Fear, Anxiety and
Depression 400
Sons 424
Vampire's Kiss 429

DAVIS, ELLIOT
Bloodhounds of Broadway 391
Signs of Life 423
DAY, ERNEST
Parents 416
DEBONT, JAN
Black Rain 52
DICKERSON, ERNEST
Do the Right Thing 94

DILL, BILL
Sidewalk Stories 315
DOUGGAN, BRYAN
Cold Feet 393
DRAPER, ROBERT
Astonished 389
Halloween V 402
DUFAUX, GUY
Jesus of Montreal 201
Milk and Honey 412

EGGBY, DAVID
Warlock 429
ELIZONDO, CHUY
Season of Fear 421
ELLIOTT, PAUL
Far from Home 399
976-EVIL 415
ELSWIT, ROBERT
Heart of Dixie 403
How I Got into College 404
ENGLAND, BRYAN
Friday the 13th Part VIII 401
I, Madman 405
My Mom's a Werewolf 413
Wicked Stepmother 430

FERNANDES, JOAO
Red Scorpion 418
FERNBERGER, PETER
Astonished 389
FIERBERG, STEVEN
Hell High 403
Scenes from the Class Struggle
in Beverly Hills 295
FISHER, GERRY
Dead Bang 395
FORSYTE, JOEY
Fakebook 398
New Year's Day 414
FRAKER, WILLIAM A.
Chances Are 392
Innocent Man, An 406
FRANCIS, FREDDIE
Glory 155
Her Alibi 404
FRASER, TOM
Purgatory 418
FUJII, HIDEO
Adventures of Milo and Otis,
The 388

GALE, RICARDO JACQUES
Bloodfist 391
GARCIA, RON
Disorganized Crime 396
GIBSON, PAUL
Game, The 401
GILLIE, JIM
Hellbent 403
GIURATO, BLASCO
Cinema Paradiso 74

CINEMATOGRAPHER INDEX

GLENN, PIERRE-WILLIAM
Dry White Season, A 107
GOLDBLATT, STEPHEN
Lethal Weapon II 217
GOLIA, DAVID
Midnight 411
GOODNOFF, IRV
Iron Triangle, The 406
GREATREX, RICHARD
For Queen and Country
[1988] 139
GREEN, JACK N.
Pink Cadillac 417
Race for Glory 418
GREENBERG, ADAM
Turner and Hooch 428
Worth Winning 431
GRIBBLE, DAVID
Tap 344
GUTHE, MANFRED
Buying Time 391

HAITKIN, JACQUES
Cage 392
Shocker 423
HAMMER, VICTOR
Lean on Me 209
HAMOU, LUC BEN
American Stories 389
HANNAN, PETER
How to Get Ahead in
Advertising 404
HARRIS, MARK
Ministry of Vengeance 412
HINTON, JIM
Identity Crisis 405
HOCHSTATTER, ZORAN
Return of the Swamp Thing,
The 419
HOLENDER, ADAM
Dream Team, The 397
HORA, JOHN
Loverboy 410
HUME, ALAN
Shirley Valentine 423

IMI, TONY
Wired 384
IRVING, LOUIS
Communion 78

JAMES, PETER
Driving Miss Daisy 99
Echoes of Paradise 397
JENSEN, PETER
Night Visitor 414
JEWETT, THOMAS
Trust Me 428
JONES, ALAN
Chorus of Disapproval, A 393
JUR, JEFF
Big Picture, The 391

KARPICK, AVI
River of Death 420

KATZ, STEPHEN M.
Who's Harry Crumb? 430
KEMPER, VICTOR J.
See No Evil, Hear No Evil 302
KENNEY, FRANCIS
Heathers 168
KEYZER, BRUNO DE
Life and Nothing But 408
KIESSER, JAN
Dad 86
KOENEKAMP, FRED
Listen to Me 409
Welcome Home 429
KOLTAI, LAJOS
Hanussen 403
KOVACS, LASZLO
Say Anything 287
KRANHOUSE, JON
Kickboxer 407

LAMKIN, KEN
Riverbend 420
LANE, SHELDON
Perfect Model, The 416
LARSON, DALE
Sexbomb 422
LASHELLE, JOSEPH
Obituaries 438
LASKUS, JACK
Stepfather II 425
LASZLO, ANDREW
Star Trek V 319
LAU, BART
It Had to Be You 406
LEMMO, JAMES
Hit List 404
Relentless 419
LEONETTI, MATTHEW F.
Johnny Handsome 407
LEVY, PETER
Nightmare on Elm Street V 414
LEWIS, DAVID
UHF 428
LHOMME, PIERRE
Camille Claudel [1988] 68
LINDLEY, JOHN W.
Field of Dreams 131
Immediate Family 185
True Believer 356
LLOYD, WALT
sex, lies and videotape 306
LONDON, JAMES
Toxic Avenger, Part II, The 427
Toxic Avenger, Part III, The 427
LUTIC, BERNARD
Return of the Musketeers,
The 419

MCALPINE, DONALD
Parenthood 267
See You in the Morning 422
MACAT, JULIO
Out of the Dark 416
MCCALMONT, JAMES
Escape from Safehaven 398

MCKINNEY, AUSTIN
Lords of the Deep 410
MACMILLAN, KENNETH
Henry V 173
MCPHERSON, JAMES
Fletch Lives 135
MAEDA, YONEZO
Taxing Woman's Return, A
[1988] 348
MAINTIGNEUX, SOPHIE
Four Adventures of Reinette and
Mirabelle [1986] 143
MANKOFSKY, ISIDORE
Skin Deep 424
MATHIAS, HARRY
Beverly Hills Brats 390
MEHEUX, PHILIP
Criminal Law 394
Renegades 419
MILLS, ALEC
Licence to Kill 221
MILLS, BILL
Fast Food 399
MOKRI, AMIR
Eat a Bowl of Tea 111
Life Is Cheap 408
MOLLOY, MIKE
Scandal 291
MONTI, FÉLIX
Old Gringo 262
MORRIS, MARK H. L.
True Blood 428
MÜLLER, ROBBY
Mystery Train 249
MURPHY, FRED
Enemies, A Love Story 119
Night Game 414

NARITA, HIRO
Honey, I Shrunk the Kids 181
NEYMAN, YURI
Ginger Ale Afternoon 401
NUSBAUM, WILLIAM
God's Will 402
NYKVIST, SVEN
Crimes and Misdemeanors 82
New York Stories 257

OHASHI, RENE
Millennium 412
OMENS, WOODY
Harlem Nights 164
ONDRICEK, MIROSLAV
Valmont 368
OPP, ALEXANDER
Sunday's Child 426

PAPAMICHAEL, PHEDON
After Midnight 388
Dance of the Damned 395
Stripped to Kill II 425
PAYNTER, ROBERT
When the Whales Came 430
PENNEY, JULIAN
Everlasting Secret Family,
The 398

463

PETERMAN, DONALD
  She's Out of Control   422
PETERSEN, CURTIS
  Food of the Gods II   400
PIE, EDWARD
  Masque of the Red Death   411
PIERCE-ROBERTS, TONY
  Out Cold   415
  Slaves of New York   424
PIKE, KELVIN
  Dry White Season, A   107
PINTER, TOMISLAV
  Manifesto   411
PIWKOWSKI, JOZEF
  Lodz Ghetto   410
POPE, DICK
  Wonderland   431
PORATH, GIDEON
  Kinjite   408
POSTER, STEVEN
  Next of Kin   414
PRATT, ROGER
  Batman   40
  High Hopes [1988]   177
PROTAT, FRANÇOIS
  Speed Zone   424
  Weekend at Bernie's   429
  Winter People   430
PRUSAK, JOHN
  Roger and Me   283

RABIER, JEAN
  Story of Women [1988]   332
RAFFERTY, KEVIN
  Roger and Me   283
RAGALYI, ELEMER
  Hungarian Fairy Tale, A   405
  Phantom of the Opera, The   417
REIFF, MANFRED
  Suitors, The   426
RESHOVSKY, MARC
  Teen Witch   426
REVENE, LARRY
  Bad Blood   390
REZNIKOV, YEFIM
  Little Vera   409
RICHARDSON, ROBERT
  Born on the Fourth of July   60
RIGOLEUR, DOMINIQUE LE
  Lectrice, La [1988]   213
RINZLER, LISA
  True Love   360
RIVAS, RAY
  Heart of Midnight   403
ROLL, GERNOT
  Rose Garden, The   421
ROSHER, CHARLES, JR.
  Police Academy VI   417
ROTUNNO, GIUSEPPE
  Adventures of Baron Munchausen,
    The   23
ROUSSELOT, PHILIPPE
  Bear, The [1988]   44
  We're No Angels   376
RUIZ-ANCHIA, JUAN
  Lost Angels   410

RUSH, MARVIN
  Meet the Hollowheads   411
RUTH, THOMAS DEL
  Look Who's Talking   229
RYAN, DOUG
  Best of the Best   390

SAAD, ROBERT
  Speed Zone   424
SAKS, ERIC
  Fun Down There   401
SALOMON, MIKAEL
  Abyss, The   19
  Always   32
SALZMANN, BERNARD
  Riding the Edge   420
SANDE, THEO VAN DE
  Miracle Mile   413
SARIN, VIC
  Cold Comfort   393
SCHERMER, BRUCE
  Roger and Me   283
SCHMIDT, RONN
  Catch Me If You Can   392
  Terror Within, The   426
SEALE, JOHN
  Dead Poets Society   90
SELLARS, RANDOLPH
  Mutant on the Bounty   413
SEMLER, DEAN
  Dead Calm   395
  Farewell to the King   399
  K-9   205
SHAPIRO, MARK
  Amanda   388
SIGEL, TOM
  Rude Awakening   421
SIMPSON, GEOFFREY
  Navigator, The [1988]   253
SINCLAIR, PETER
  Dealers   395
SLOCOMBE, DOUGLAS
  Indiana Jones and the Last
    Crusade   193
SMOOT, REED
  Gleaming the Cube   401
SOHLBERG, KARI
  Talvisota   336
SONNENFELD, BARRY
  When Harry Met Sally   380
SOPANEN, JERI
  Luckiest Man in the World,
    The   411
SOUTHON, MIKE
  Queen of Hearts   275
SOVA, PETER
  Sing   424
SPELLVIN, DAVID
  Animal Behavior   389
SPRATLING, TONY
  Edge of Sanity   397
SQUIRES, EUGENE
  Lodz Ghetto   410
STAPLETON, OLIVER
  Cookie   394

Earth Girls Are Easy   397
  She-Devil   310
STEIN, PETER
  Pet Sematary   271
STEINBERG, DAVID MAX
  Severance   422
STEVENS, ROBERT
  'Burbs, The   65
STEYN, JACQUES
  Kill Me Again   407
  Mighty Quinn, The   412
STORARO, VITTORIO
  New York Stories   257
SUHRSTEDT, TIMOTHY
  Bill and Ted's Excellent
    Adventure   48
SUNARA, IGOR
  Misplaced   413
SUSLOV, MISHA
  Prancer   418

TAKABA, TETSUO
  Tora-San Goes to Vienna   427
TAYLOR, RONNIE
  Sea of Love   299
THOMSON, ALEX
  Leviathan   408
  Rachel Papers, The   418
THORIN, DONALD E.
  Lock Up   409
  Tango and Cash   340
  Troop Beverly Hills   427
TICKNER, CLIVE
  Getting It Right   147
TIDY, FRANK
  Package, The   416
TOMITA, SHINJI
  Adventures of Milo and Otis,
    The   388

VAN DAMME, CHARLIE
  I Want to Go Home   405
VAN DE SANDE, THEO
  Rooftops   421
VERZIER, RENE
  Eddie and the Cruisers II   397
VIDGEON, ROBIN
  Fly II, The   400
  Parents   416
VILLALOBOS, REYNALDO
  Major League   233
VON STERNBERG, NICHOLAS
  No Retreat, No Surrender II   415

WATERS, PHILIP ALAN
  Cyborg   395
WEAVER, KATHIE
  Miracle Mile   413
WEHR, CURTIS J.
  Let It Ride   408
WEINCKE, JAN
  Penn and Teller Get Killed   416
WEST, BRIAN
  Jacknife   197
WEST, JONATHAN
  Sinful Life, A   423

CINEMATOGRAPHER INDEX

WEXLER, HASKELL
Blaze   56
Three Fugitives   426

WEXLER, HOWARD
Savage Beach   421

WILLIAMS, BILLY
Rainbow, The   279

WILSON, IAN
Checking Out   392
Erik the Viking   398

YACONELLI, STEVE
Karate Kid III, The   407
Gross Anatomy   402

YASUDA, KOSUKE
Free and Easy   400

YEOMAN, ROBERT
Drugstore Cowboy   103
Wizard, The   430

ZIELINSKI, JERZY
January Man, The   406
Valentino Returns   429

ZSIGMOND, VILMOS
Fat Man and Little Boy   399

ZURINAGA, MARCOS
Tango Bar   426

EDITOR INDEX

ADELMAN, SAM
  Midnight 411
AKERS, GEORGE
  Erik the Viking 398
ALBERTSON, ERIC
  Cheetah 393
ALLEN, DEDE
  Let It Ride 408
ALLEN, JOHN D.
  Fast Food 399
ANDERSON, WILLIAM
  Dead Poets Society 90
  Old Gringo 262
  Signs of Life 423
ANTON, EDWARD
  Horrow Show, The 404
ARAKI, GREGG
  Long Weekend, The 410
AUDSLEY, MICK
  We're No Angels 376
AUSTIN, PETER
  Fear, Anxiety and
    Depression 400
AVILDSEN, JOHN G.
  Karate Kid III, The 407
  Lean on Me 209

BAIRD, STUART
  Lethal Weapon II 217
BARNES, CHRIS
  Chorus of Disapproval, A 393
BARNETTA, PAM
  Everlasting Secret Family,
    The 398
BARRERE, ROBERT
  Night Game 414
BARRIENTOS, DANIEL
  Game, The 401
BARTON, SEAN
  Fly II, The 400
BEDFORD, RICHARD
  Wonderland 431
BEMAN, JENNIFER
  Roger and Me 283
BERENBAUM, MICHAEL
  Misplaced 413
BERGER, PETER
  Star Trek V 319
BIGGERSTAFF, CAROLINE
  Renegades 419
BLOOM, JOHN
  Jacknife 197
BLUMENTHAL, ANDY
  Shocker 423
BOCK, LARRY
  Bill and Ted's Excellent
    Adventure 48
BOISSON, NOELLE
  Bear, The [1988] 44
BONNOT, FRANÇOISE
  Fat Man and Little Boy 399

BORNSTEIN, CHARLES
  Phantom of the Opera, The 417
BORNSTEIN, KEN
  River of Death 420
BOUILLERIE, HUBERT DE LA
  Tango and Cash 340
BOULTON, ANDREW
  When the Whales Came 430
BOWERS, GEORGE
  Harlem Nights 164
  True Believer 356
BOYLE, PETER
  Queen of Hearts 275
BRADSEL, MICHAEL
  Henry V 173
BRANDON, MARYANN
  All's Fair 388
  Race for Glory 418
BRENNER, DAVID
  Born on the Fourth of July 60
BRETHERTON, DAVID
  Sea of Love 299
BROCHU, DONALD
  Lock Up 409
BROWN, BARRY ALEXANDER
  Do the Right Thing 94
BROWN, ROBERT
  Cousins 394
BUBA, PASQUALE A.
  Stepfather II 425
BURNETT, JOHN F.
  Leviathan 408

CAMBERN, DONN
  Ghostbusters II 151
CANDIB, RICHARD
  Eat a Bowl of Tea 111
CARNOCHAN, JOHN
  Little Mermaid, The 225
CARR, JOHN K.
  All Dogs Go to Heaven 27
CARTER, JOHN
  Karate Kid III, The 407
  Lean on Me 209
CASEY, RICHARD
  Hellbent 403
CHAPMAN, JOAN E.
  Weekend at Bernie's 429
CHIATE, DEBRA
  Look Who's Talking 229
CHIZUKO OSADA
  Adventures of Milo and Otis,
    The 388
CLAYTON, CURTISS
  Drugstore Cowboy 103
COATES, ANNE V.
  Farewell to the King 399
  Listen to Me 409
COBURN, ARTHUR
  Triumph of the Spirit 351

COLE, STAN
  Office Party 415
COLTON, CRAIG A.
  Mutant on the Bounty 413
CONNER, MICHAEL D.
  To Die For 427
COOKE, MALCOLM
  Edge of Sanity 397
CORRAO, ANGELO
  Signs of Life 423
COSTELLOE, JON
  Dealers 395
COX, JOEL
  Pink Cadillac 417
CRAFFORD, IAN
  Field of Dreams 131
CRAVEN, GARTH
  Turner and Hooch 428

DANOVIC, NENA
  Valmont 368
DAUGHTON, BILL
  Astonished 389
DAVALOS, JAMES
  Bad Blood 390
DAVIES, PETER
  Rainbow, The 279
DAVIS, FREEMAN
  Johnny Handsome 407
DAY, LISA
  Great Balls of Fire! 160
DEDIEU, ISABELLE
  Jesus of Montreal 201
DE LA BOUILLERIE, HUBERT
  Police Academy VI 417
DE STEFANO, LORENZO
  Ginger Ale Afternoon 401
DUCSAY, BOB
  Catch Me If You Can 392
DUFFNER, J. PATRICK
  My Left Foot 245
DUTHIE, MICHAEL J.
  American Ninja III 388

EBRAHIMIAN, GHASEM
  Suitors, The 426
ECONOMOU, MIKE
  Speed Zone 424
ELLIS, MICHAEL
  Breaking In 391
ENDLER, HELGA
  Sunday's Child 426
ERICKSON, GLENN
  Night Visitor 414

FARDOULIS, MONIQUE
  Story of Women [1988] 332
FARR, GLENN
  Old Gringo 262
  Physical Evidence 417

466

FEHR, KAJA
How I Got into College   404
FELDMAN, ETTIE
Purgatory   418
FELKER, TODD
Sexbomb   422
FERRETTI, ROBERT
Tango and Cash   340
FINAN, TOM
It Had to Be You   406
Wizard, The   430
FINFER, DAVID
Warlock   429
FINKLE, CLAUDIA
Crack House   394
My Mom's a Werewolf   413
FRANCIS-BRUCE, RICHARD
Dead Calm   395
FRANK, PETER C.
Miss Firecracker   237
FREEMAN-FOX, LOIS
K-9   205
FREUND, JAN
Sons   424
FRIEDMAN, PETER
Astonished   389
FRIZELL, JERRY
Beverly Hills Brats   390

GARCIA, MIRIA-LUISA
Four Adventures of Reinette and
Mirabelle [1986]   143
GIBBS, ANTONY
In Country   189
GILBERTI, NINA
Lords of the Deep   410
GILROY, JOHN
Luckiest Man in the World,
The   411
GLADWELL, DAVID
Lost Angels   410
GOODMAN, JOEL
Abyss, The   19
GOURSAUD, ANNE
Her Alibi   404
GREEN, BRUCE
Three Fugitives   426
GREENBERG, JERRY
National Lampoon's Christmas
Vacation   413
GREENE, DANFORD B.
Who's Harry Crumb?   430
GREGORY, JON
High Hopes [1988]   177
GROSSMAN, MARC
Far from Home   399
GROVER, JOHN
Licence to Kill   221
GUYOT, RAYMONDE
Lectrice, La [1988]   213

HACHE, JOELLE
Camille Claudel [1988]   68
HAIGHT, MAC
True Blood   428

HAIGHT, MICHAEL
Ministry of Vengeance   412
Savage Beach   421
HAIGIS, JACK
Fakebook   398
HALSEY, RICHARD
Earth Girls Are Easy   397
HANDMAN, DAVID
Deepstar Six   396
HANLEY, DANIEL
Parenthood   267
Pet Sematary   271
HARRIS, RICHARD A.
Fletch Lives   135
HARRISON, MATTHEW
Hellbent   403
HARVEY, MARSHALL
'Burbs, The   65
HEIM, ALAN
Valmont   368
HERRING, PEMBROKE
Great Balls of Fire!   160
HILL, DENNIS M.
Major League   233
Out Cold   415
HILL, MICHAEL
Parenthood   267
Pet Sematary   271
HIRSCH, PAUL
Steel Magnolias   328
HOENIG, DOV
She's Out of Control   422
HOLLYN, NORMAN
Heathers   168
HOLLYWOOD, PETER
Adventures of Baron Munchausen,
The   23
HONESS, PETER
Next of Kin   414
HORN, KAREN
Bloodfist   391
HOY, WILLIAM
Best of the Best   390
HUGGINS, JERE
Sing   424
HUTSHING, JOE
Born on the Fourth of July   60

JIMENEZ, FRANK
Kill Me Again   407
JOCHEM, MARY E.
Kinjite   408
JONES, ROBERT C.
See No Evil, Hear No Evil   302
JURGENSON, ALBERT
I Want to Go Home   405
Little Thief, The   409
JYMPSON, JOHN
Mighty Quinn, The   412

KAHN, MICHAEL
Always   32
Indiana Jones and the Last
Crusade   193
KAHN, SHELDON
Ghostbusters II   151

KANEFSKY, VICTOR
Identity Crisis   405
KATZ, ROBIN
Warm Summer Rain   429
KEF, JEANNE
Camille Claudel [1988]   68
KELLY, CHRIS
Getting It Right   147
KENNEDY, PATRICK
Tap   344
KERAMIDAS, HARRY
Back to the Future Part II   36
Chances Are   392
KERN, DAVID
Hit List   404
Relentless   419
Wicked Stepmother   430
KLINGMAN, LYNZEE
War of the Roses, The   372
KNUE, MICHAEL N.
Lock Up   409
KOEHLER, BONNIE
Heart of Dixie   403
KRAVETZ, CAROLE
Dance of the Damned   395
KRESS, CARL
Meet the Hollowheads   411
KURSON, JANE
Immediate Family   185

LANDIS, EVAN
Babar   389
LANE, CHARLES
Sidewalk Stories   315
LAWSON, TONY
Manifesto   411
LEIGHTON, ROBERT
Blaze   56
When Harry Met Sally   380
LIBIN, CHARLES
Distribution of Lead, The   396
LINDHORST, KEES
Rose Garden, The   421
LINK, JOHN
Road House   420
LINSON, PHILLIP
After Midnight   388
LIVINGSTONE, RUSSELL
Dream a Little Dream   396
LOEWENTHAL, DANIEL
Red Scorpion   418
LOMBARDO, LOU
In Country   189
January Man, The   406
Uncle Buck   364
LOMBARDO, TONY
Uncle Buck   364
LONDON, MELODY
Mystery Train   249
LOTTMAN, EVAN
See You in the Morning   422
LOVEJOY, RAY
Batman   40
LOVITT, BERT
Great Balls of Fire!   160

467

LOW, WARREN
Obituaries 440

MCDERMOTT, DEBRA
Cold Feet 393
MCGIRR, JOSEPH
Toxic Avenger, Part III, The 427
MACIAS, JUAN CARLOS
Old Gringo 262
MCKAY, CRAIG
She-Devil 310
MCMAHON, PATRICK
Little Monsters 409
Personal Choice 417
MALKIN, BARRY
New York Stories 257
MANOS, MARL
Out of the Dark 416
MANTON, MARCUS
I, Madman 405
Riverbend 420
MARI, PABLO
Tango Bar 426
MARK, STEPHEN
Masque of the Red Death 411
Stripped to Kill II 425
MARKS, RICHARD
Say Anything 287
MARTIN, DAVID
Rachel Papers, The 418
MARTIN, QUINNIE, JR.
After Midnight 388
MELNICK, MARK
Troop Beverly Hills 427
MERLIN, CLAUDE
Chocolat 393
MEYER, JEFF
Amanda 388
MILLER, JIM
Let It Ride 408
MILLER, TOM
Perfect Model, The 416
MIMOUNI, PATRICK
American Stories 389
MIRKOVICH, STEVE
Friday the 13th Part VIII 401
MOLIN, BUD
Bert Rigby, You're a Fool 390
MONDSHEIN, ANDREW
Cookie 394
Family Business 127
MONTPETITE, JEAN-GUY
Eddie and the Cruisers II 397
MORA, MARIO
Cinema Paradiso 74
MORRISS, FRANK
Disorganized Crime 396
MORSE, SUSAN E.
Crimes and Misdemeanors 82
New York Stories 257
MURRAY, JOHN
Ice House 405
MYERS, STEPHEN
976-EVIL 415

NADERI, AMIR
Suitors, The 426
NERVIG, SANDY
Life Is Cheap 408
NEWTON, ANGUS
Scandal 291
Vampire's Kiss 429
NICHOLSON, MARTY
Big Picture, The 391
NOBLE, THOM
Winter People 430
NYZINK, BRUCE
Milk and Honey 412

O'CONNOR, DENNIS
Prancer 418
UHF 428
O'HARA, BRIAN
Escape from Safehaven 398
O'MEARA, C. TIMOTHY
Dream Team, The 397
Farewell to the King 399
O'STEEN, SAM
Dry White Season, A 107

PAINE, EMILY
Fear, Anxiety and
Depression 400
PANKOW, BILL
Casualties of War 71
Parents 416
PAPPÉ, STUART
Enemies, A Love Story 119
PERCY, LEE
Checking Out 392
PERGAMENT, ROBERT
Skin Deep 424
POON, ALLEN
No Retreat, No Surrender II 415
PRIOR, PECK
Uncle Buck 364
PRYOR, TOM
No Holds Barred 415
PSENNY, ARMAND
Life and Nothing But 408
PUENTE, CARLOS
Licence to Kill 221
PUETT, DALLAS
Disorganized Crime 396
PURVIS, STEPHEN
Eighty-Four Charlie MoPic 115

RAND, PATRICK
Bill and Ted's Excellent
Adventure 48
RAWLINS, DAVID
Cold Feet 393
RAY, DAVID
Second Sight 422
REINER, JEFFREY
Sinful Life, A 423
REYNOLDS, WILLIAM
Rooftops 421
RODINELLA, THOMAS R.
Severance 422

ROLF, TOM
Black Rain 52
ROSELLA, GAIL KAPPLER
Amanda 388
ROSENBLUM, STEVEN
Glory 155
ROSENTHAL, LESLIE
Return of the Swamp Thing,
The 419
ROSS, ANGELO
Obituaries 443
ROTHCHILD, PAUL
Rude Awakening 421
ROTHKOWITZ, ED
Silent Night, Deadly
Night III 423
Warm Summer Rain 429
ROTTER, STEPHEN A.
Innocent Man, An 406
ROTUNDO, NICK
Cold Comfort 393
ROWAN, DENINE
Valentino Returns 429
RUBINOW, BARRY
Fear, Anxiety and
Depression 400
RUXIN, JAMES
Riding the Edge 420

SANBORN, KEITH
Fun Down There 401
SANDERSON, CHRIS
Life Is Cheap 408
SCHARF, WILLIAM S.
Innocent Man, An 406
SCHMIDT, ARTHUR
Back to the Future Part II 36
SCHOENFELD, BRENT
Nightmare on Elm Street V 414
Terror Within, The 426
SCHOONMAKER, THELMA
New York Stories 257
SCHWEITZER, MICHAEL
Toxic Avenger, Part II, The 427
SCOTT, JOHN
Navigator, The [1988] 253
SEARS, ERIC
Dad 86
Wired 384
SELAKOVICH, DAN
Season of Fear 421
SEMEL, STEPHEN
Miracle Mile 413
SEWELSON, KEVIN
No Retreat, No Surrender II 415
SHAH, SANJIV
Spices 425
SHAINE, RICH
Loverboy 410
SHAW, JONATHAN
Kill Me Again 407
SHAW, PENELOPE
Heart of Midnight 403
SHELDON, GREG
Hell High 403

SHUGRUE, ROBERT F.
Dead Bang 395
SILLIMAN, DRAKE
Fistfighter 400
SILVI, ROBERTO
Leviathan 408
SIMPSON-CROZIER, CLAIRE
Hell High 403
SINGLETON, STEPHEN
For Queen and Country
[1988] 139
SIVO, JULIA
Hungarian Fairy Tale, A 405
SMITH, BUD
Gross Anatomy 402
Sing 424
SMITH, HOWARD
Big Man on Campus 390
SMITH, JOHN VICTOR
Return of the Musketeers,
The 419
SMITH, LEE
Communion 78
SMITH, SCOTT
Gross Anatomy 402
Sing 424
SODERBERGH, STEVEN
sex, lies and videotape 306
STANZLER, WENDEY
Roger and Me 283
STEIN, ANNE
Sidewalk Stories 315
STEINBERG, DAVID MAX
Severance 422
STEINKAMP, WILLIAM
Fabulous Baker Boys, The 123
STEVENSON, MICHAEL A.
Honey, I Shrunk the Kids 181
STEVENSON, SCOTT
Cyborg 395
STEYN, JACQUES
Kill Me Again 407
STIGLIANO, ROGER
Fun Down There 401

STRACHAN, ALAN
How to Get Ahead in
Advertising 404
SUZUKI, AKIRA
Taxing Woman's Return, A
[1988] 348
SWINK, BOB
Welcome Home 429

TAVERNA, KATHRYN
Lodz Ghetto 410
TETONI, CHARLES
Halloween V 402
THOMPSON, PETER LEE
Kinjite 408
TINTORI, JOHN
True Love 360
TODD, MICHAEL
Buying Time 391
TONIOLO, CAMILLA
Bloodhounds of Broadway 391
TOOMAYAN, ALAN
Scenes from the Class Struggle
in Beverly Hills 295
TRAMER, SONYA SONES
How I Got into College 404

URIOSTE, FRANK
Road House 420

VANDENBURG, FRANS
Echoes of Paradise 397
Romero 420
VAN EFFENTERRE, JOELE
Music Box 241
VAN PEEBLES, MELVIN
Identity Crisis 405
VAN WIJK, JOKE
We're No Angels 376
VASQUEZ, JOSEPH B.
Street Story 425
VIRTANEN, KEIJO
Talvisota 336

WAHRAM, WAYNE
Kickboxer 407
WALKER, LESLEY
Shirley Valentine 423
WARNER, MARK
Driving Miss Daisy 99
WATTS, ROY
Iron Triangle, The 406
WEBER, BILLY
Package, The 416
WEINTRAUB, JOSEPH
Animal Behavior 389
WEISS, CHUCK
Nightmare on Elm Street V 414
WENNING, KATHERINE
Slaves of New York 424
Staying Together 323
WESTMORE, MARK S.
Cage 392
WHITTEMORE, GLORIA
Game, The 401
WIMBLE, CHRISTOPHER
Criminal Law 394
WISMAN, RON
Millennium 412
WOLF, JEFFREY
Penn and Teller Get Killed 416
WOLINSKY, SIDNEY
Worth Winning 431
WRIGHT, JOHN
Gleaming the Cube 401

ZABOLOCKAJA, ELENA
Little Vera 409
ZAHAVI, NATAN
Teen Witch 426
ZANUSO, CECILIA
Severance 422
ZETLIN, BARRY
Trust Me 428
ZIMMERMAN, DON
Package, The 416
ZINGALE, ROZANNE
Cyborg 395

ART DIRECTOR INDEX

ABEL, GENE
Relentless 419
Wicked Stepmother 430

ACKLAND-SNOW, TERRY
Batman 40

ADAM, KEN
Dead Bang 395

ADAMS, CHARMIAN
For Queen and Country
[1988] 139

ADAMS, JERRY
Lock Up 409

AHMAD, MAHER
Miss Firecracker 237

AHRENS, ANNE H.
Fabulous Baker Boys, The 123

AIRD, GILLES
Eddie and the Cruisers II 397
Jacknife 197
Speed Zone 424

ALLEN, ARAM
Stepfather II 425

ALLEN, REG
Obituaries 433

ALTADONA, JOSEPH M.
Cage 392

AMIES, CAROLINE
Getting It Right 147

ANDERSON, JOHN
'Burbs, The 65
Dead Poets Society 90

APPEL, LYNN RUTH
Ice House 405

ARNOLD, BILL
Music Box 241

ARNONE, JOHN
Penn and Teller Get Killed 416

ARRIGHI, LUCIANA
Rainbow, The 279

ARRONDO, GIL
Return of the Musketeers,
The 419

ATKINSON, ADRIENNE
Breaking In 391

AUSTIN, SHAY
Kickboxer 407

AZZARI, THO E.
Police Academy VI 417

BARBASSO, TERESA
Adventures of Baron Munchausen,
The 23

BARCLAY, WILLIAM
Jacknife 197

BARRECA, CHRIS
Astonished 389

BARRETT, KEITH
Crack House 394

BASTIEN, TED
Babar 389

BAYLISS, JAMES R.
Black Rain 52

BEARD, JOHN
Erik the Viking 398

BECK, WILLIAM
True Believer 356

BECKMAN, JOHN
Obituaries 434

BECROFT, MIKE
Navigator, The [1988] 253

BENOIT-FRESCO, FRANÇOIS
Story of Women [1988] 332

BERGER, RICHARD
Indiana Jones and the Last
Crusade 193
Lethal Weapon II 217
Tango and Cash 340

BERTALAN, TIVADAR
Edge of Sanity 397
Phantom of the Opera, The 417

BERTOTTO, MARIA JULIA
Tango Bar 426

BILOWIT, WILLIAM
Hell High 403

BIRDSALL, DAVID
We're No Angels 376

BIRNIE, CAMERON
Fletch Lives 135

BISHOP, DAN
Mystery Train 249

BISSELL, JAMES
Always 32

BLATT, STUART
Catch Me If You Can 392

BLOCK, SUSAN
Fear, Anxiety and
Depression 400

BLOOM, LESLIE
Black Rain 52
Cookie 394

BLUTH, DON
All Dogs Go to Heaven 27

BLY, JIMMIE
Fletch Lives 135

BOCQUET, GAVIN
Erik the Viking 398

BODE, SUSAN
Crimes and Misdemeanors 82
Fletch Lives 135
New York Stories 257

BOLTON, MICHAEL S.
Fly II, The 400

BOND, OLIVIA
Romero 420

BOOTH, NANCY
976-EVIL 415

BOURNE, MEL
Rude Awakening 421

BOWIN, CLAIRE J.
Wizard, The 430

BOYLE, ROBERT F.
Troop Beverly Hills 427

BRADBURY, CAROL
Babar 389

BRADEN, HUB
Steel Magnolias 328

BRADETTE, JACQUES
Physical Evidence 417

BRANDENBURG, ROSEMARY
Blaze 56

BRANDES, PHILLIP MICHAEL
Season of Fear 421

BRIGGS, KATHARIN
Pet Sematary 271

BRINK, GARY
Family Business 127

BRISBIN, DAVID
Animal Behavior 389
Drugstore Cowboy 103

BROCKHURST, DAVID
Wonderland 431

BROCKSCHMIDT, JOAN
Hell High 403

BROLLY, BARRY W.
Look Who's Talking 229

BUMSTEAD, HENRY
Her Alibi 404

BURIAN-MOHR, CHRIS
Always 32
Karate Kid III, The 407

BURKHARDT, JAY
Beverly Hills Brats 390
K-9 205

BUTCHER, CHAS
Winter People 430

BUTLER, CHRIS A.
Innocent Man, An 406

BUTLER, JOHANNA
Stepfather II 425

CAIN, ROGER
Erik the Viking 398

CALLAHAN, GENE
Steel Magnolias 328

CAMPBELL, JAN
Navigator, The [1988] 253

CAPRA, BERNT
Cold Feet 393

CARASIK, CHERYL
Ghostbusters II 151

CARFAGNO, EDWARD C.
Pink Cadillac 417

CARPENTER, R. W.
Weekend at Bernie's 429

CARR, JACKIE
Always 32

CARTER, FRED
Edge of Sanity 397

CARTER, RICK
Back to the Future Part II 36
Three Fugitives 426

470

CASEY, DONNA
Race for Glory 418
CASO, MARLA
Beverly Hills Brats 390
K-9 205
CAULEY, EVE
Drugstore Cowboy 103
CAVEDON, JANE
Cheetah 393
CERAOLO, FRANCO
Leviathan 408
CESARI, BRUNO
Leviathan 408
CHADWICK, PAUL
After Midnight 388
CHAMPION, ANN
Loverboy 410
CHARETTE, CYNTHIA KAY
Race for Glory 418
Shocker 423
CHARNLEY, DIANA
High Hopes [1988] 177
CHAUVIGNY, EMMANUEL DE
Camille Claudel [1988] 68
CHIARI, MARIO
Obituaries 436
CHILDS, PETER
Abyss, The 19
CHORNEY, JO-ANN
Cold Comfort 393
CHRISTIAN, RUSSELL
Abyss, The 19
CLAY, JIM
Queen of Hearts 275
CLOUDIA
Turner and Hooch 428
COBB, ROB
Leviathan 408
COCHRANE, SANDY
Fly II, The 400
COHEN, LESTER W.
True Love 360
COLLIS, JACK T.
Next of Kin 414
CONLEY, DAN
Dream Team, The 397
COOLWIJK, ROBERT VAN DER
Purgatory 418
COOPER, DORREE
Fat Man and Little Boy 399
Honey, I Shrunk the Kids 181
COOPER, KATHLEEN B.
Terror Within, The 426
CORSO, JOHN W.
Uncle Buck 364
COSTELLO, GEORGE
Beverly Hills Brats 390
K-9 205
COURT, KEN
Licence to Kill 221
CRISANTI, ANDREA
Cinema Paradiso 74
CRONE, RUSSELL B.
Harlem Nights 164

CUMMINGS, HOWARD
Signs of Life 423
DABE, MARC
Prancer 418
DANIELSON, CHAVA
Halloween V 402
DANIELSON, DINS
Pet Sematary 271
DAVENPORT, DENNIS
Physical Evidence 417
Welcome Home 429
DAVIES, TESSA
Old Gringo 262
DAY, MICHAEL
Big Man on Campus 390
DEAN, LISA
Eat a Bowl of Tea 111
DEARBORN, RICHARD
Trust Me 428
DECUIR, JOHN, JR.
Turner and Hooch 428
DEDIEU, JEAN CHARLES
Edge of Sanity 397
DEGAWA, MITSUO
Tora-San Goes to Vienna 427
DEGOVIA, JACKSON
Dad 86
In Country 189
DESCENNA, LINDA
Back to the Future Part II 36
DESPOTOVIC, VELJKO
Manifesto 411
DETITTA, GEORGE, JR.
New York Stories 257
See No Evil, Hear No Evil 302
She-Devil 310
DICK, DOUGLAS
Eighty-Four Charlie MoPic 115
DICK, JARO
Dream Team, The 397
DIERS, DON
Deepstar Six 396
DIETZ, GEORG
Bear, The [1988] 44
DILLEY, LESLIE
Abyss, The 19
DI SANTO, BYRNADETTE
Stepfather II 425
DJURKOVIC, MARIA
Scandal 291
DOBROWOLSKI, MAREK
Fear, Anxiety and
Depression 400
DORME, NORMAN
Henry V 173
DUFFIELD, TOM
Ghostbusters II 151
DUFFY, JIM
Next of Kin 414
DUNLOP, CHARLES
Millennium 412
DWYER, JOHN M.
Black Rain 52

EATWELL, BRIAN
Wired 384
ELLIS, PATRICIA
Warm Summer Rain 429
ELTON, PHILIP
Queen of Hearts 275
EMSHWILLER, SUSAN
Gleaming the Cube 401
ETCHEGARAY, FRANÇOISE
Four Adventures of Reinette and
Mirabelle [1986] 143
EYTH, ED
Meet the Hollowheads 411
FABUS, MARK
War of the Roses, The 372
FELLMAN, FLORENCE
Disorganized Crime 396
FENNER, JOHN
Dry White Season, A 107
FERNANDEZ, BENJAMIN
Indiana Jones and the Last
Crusade 193
FERRETTI, DANTE
Adventures of Baron Munchausen,
The 23
FETTIS, GARY
Fletch Lives 135
FIELDS, VIRGINIA
Sons 424
FISCHER, DAVID
Friday the 13th Part VIII 401
FISCHER, LISA
Animal Behavior 389
Great Balls of Fire! 160
National Lampoon's Christmas
Vacation 413
Out Cold 415
FISCHER, MARGARET C.
Kinjite 408
FISHGOYT, MIKHAIL
Escape from Safehaven 398
FLAMAND, THIERRY
Chocolat 393
FLEMING, BILL
Buying Time 391
FONSECA, GREGG
Fat Man and Little Boy 399
Honey, I Shrunk the Kids 181
FORD, MICHAEL
Licence to Kill 221
FORD, ROGER
Romero 420
FOREMAN, RON
Winter People 430
FOSSER, BILL
Music Box 241
FRANCO, JOHN, JR.
Bert Rigby, You're a Fool 390
FRANCO, ROBERT J.
Jacknife 197
FRANÇOIS, GUY-CLAUDE
Life and Nothing But 408
FREAS, DIANNA
Mystery Train 249

FREDERICKS, KATHARINE
  Fakebook 398
FREEBORN, MARK
  Cousins 394
  Immediate Family 185
FULTON, LARRY E.
  Deepstar Six 396
  Fat Man and Little Boy 399
FURST, ANTON
  Batman 40

GAFFIN, LAURI
  Big Man on Campus 390
GALLINE, FRANK
  Return of the Swamp Thing,
    The 419
GALVIN, TIM
  Lean on Me 209
  Lock Up 409
GANIS, GLENDA
  Heart of Dixie 403
GANZ, ARMIN
  Blaze 56
GARRITY, JOSEPH
  Big Picture, The 391
GARWOOD, NORMAN
  Glory 155
GASSNER, DENNIS
  Earth Girls Are Easy 397
  Field of Dreams 131
GAUGER, KURT
  Race for Glory 418
GEAGHAN, STEPHEN
  Who's Harry Crumb? 430
GIBESON, BRUCE
  She's Out of Control 422
GINSBURG, GERSHON
  Abyss, The 19
GLASS, TED
  Enemies, A Love Story 119
GODDARD, RICHARD C.
  Black Rain 52
  Three Fugitives 426
GOLDSMITH, MARGARET
  Drugstore Cowboy 103
GORFINE, PAUL W.
  Second Sight 422
GORTON, ASSHETON
  Lost Angels 410
GOULD, ROBERT
  Leviathan 408
GRAHAM, W. STEVEN
  Fletch Lives 135
  New York Stories 257
  Staying Together 323
GRAY, PERRY
  War of the Roses, The 372
GRAY, TIM
  Nightmare on Elm Street V 414
GREENBERG, STEPHEN
  Dance of the Damned 395
  Ministry of Vengeance 412
GREENGROW, ANTONY
  Bear, The [1988] 44

GREY, ALEXIS
  Toxic Avenger, Part II, The 427
  Toxic Avenger, Part III, The 427
GRIMES, BRUCE
  When the Whales Came 430
GROOM, BILL
  Cookie 394
  Lock Up 409
GROPMAN, DAVID
  Slaves of New York 424
GUERRA, ROBERT
  Family Business 127
  See You in the Morning 422
GUFFROY, PIERRE
  Valmont 368
GUNDLACH, ROBERT
  See No Evil, Hear No Evil 302
GUZMAN, PATO
  Enemies, A Love Story 119

HADDER, JIMMY
  Savage Beach 421
HAIGH, NANCY
  Field of Dreams 131
HALL, PATTI
  Speed Zone 424
HALLER, MICHAEL
  Cookie 394
HALLOWELL, TODD
  Dream Team, The 397
  Parenthood 267
HAMPTON, PETER J.
  Dealers 395
HANAN, MICHAEL Z.
  Pet Sematary 271
HARRIS, HENRY
  How to Get Ahead in
    Advertising 404
HARRIS, MICHAEL
  Dream Team, The 397
  Parents 416
  Sing 424
HARRISON, RICHARD
  We're No Angels 376
HARVEY, TIM
  Henry V 173
HAUSMANIS, ANDRIS
  Parents 416
HEGNEY, YVONNE
  Cyborg 395
HELFRITZ, RICHARD
  Licence to Kill 221
HELLER, CARYL
  Lean on Me 209
HELMY, MICHAEL
  Ginger Ale Afternoon 401
HELO, RICHARD
  Warm Summer Rain 429
HENDRICKSON, STEPHEN
  Fletch Lives 135
HENRY, CHRIS
  After Midnight 388
HICKS, JOHN ALAN
  Black Rain 52
  Dream Team, The 397

HIDES, BERNARD
  Farewell to the King 399
HIGGINS, DOUGLAS
  Personal Choice 417
HILKAMO, PERTTI
  Talvisota 336
HILL, DEREK R.
  Born on the Fourth of July 60
HOLLAND, SIMON
  Scandal 291
HOPKINS, SPEED
  Crimes and Misdemeanors 82
  New York Stories 257
HORNER, CHRISTOPHER
  Miracle Mile 413
HOWARD, JEFFREY
  Major League 233
HOWITT, PETER
  Indiana Jones and the Last
    Crusade 193
HUBBARD, MARTIN G.
  Harlem Nights 164
HUDOLIN, RICHARD
  Dead Bang 395
  Speed Zone 424
HUGHES, CHARLES L.
  'Burbs, The 65
HUGON, J. M.
  Race for Glory 418
HUNTER, CLARK
  Mutant on the Bounty 413
HUTMAN, JON
  Heathers 168
  Worth Winning 431
HYDES, BERNARD
  Casualties of War 71

IACOVELLI, JOHN
  Honey, I Shrunk the Kids 181

JACOBS, MATTHEW
  Dream a Little Dream 396
  I, Madman 405
JACQUES, SERGE
  Jacknife 197
JAMES, PETER
  Dry White Season, A 107
JAMES, ROBERT
  Dream Team, The 397
JAMISON, PETER
  Weekend at Bernie's 429
JENKINS, GEORGE
  See You in the Morning 422
JENSEN, JOHN R.
  Dad 86
  In Country 189
JOB, ANN
  Relentless 419
JOCKINSEN, JOHN
  Nightmare on Elm Street V 414
JOHNSON, RICHARD L.
  Born on the Fourth of July 60
JONSTON, P. MICHAEL
  Gross Anatomy 402
JORDAN, STEVEN J.
  Enemies, A Love Story 119

JORGENSON, WALTER
Game, The   401

KACZENSKI, CHESTER
Prancer   418

KALINOWSKI, WALDEMAR
Disorganized Crime   396

KAPLAN, CORY
Cold Feet   393

KAYE, ALAN S.
Black Rain   52

KEADING, HILJA
Mutant on the Bounty   413

KEEN, GREG
Dream Team, The   397

KELLY, ERROL
Iron Triangle, The   406

KELTER, JERIE
Big Picture, The   391
Weekend at Bernie's   429

KEMPSTER, VICTOR
Born on the Fourth of July   60
Driving Miss Daisy   99

KENNEY, BILL
Lock Up   409

KENNEY, ELENA
Dream Team, The   397

KENSINGER, ROBERT
Lost Angels   410
Scenes from the Class Struggle
   in Beverly Hills   295

KILVERT, LILLY
Worth Winning   431

KING, BYRON LANCE
Immediate Family   185

KING, ROBB WILSON
Return of the Swamp Thing,
   The   419

KLASSEN, DAVID
Leviathan   408
Tango and Cash   340

KLOPP, KATHE
How I Got into College   404

KOHUT-SVELKO, JEAN-PIERRE
Little Thief, The   409

KOIVISTO, AARRE
Talvisota   336

KOO, COLLETE
Life Is Cheap   408

KRANER, DOUG
Lean on Me   209

KROEGER, WOLF
Casualties of War   71
Let It Ride   408
We're No Angels   376

KUHN, BETH
Misplaced   413

KULJIAN, ANNE
Abyss, The   19

LAGOLA, CHARLES
Fakebook   398

LAGRANDE, DANIELE
Camille Claudel [1988]   68

LAMONT, MICHAEL
Licence to Kill   221

LAMONT, PETER
Licence to Kill   221

LANDO, PETER
We're No Angels   376

LANIER, JESSICA
True Love   360

LAWSON, PETA
Everlasting Secret Family,
   The   398

LEACH, SHAD
Fast Food   399

LEE, CELESTE
Major League   233

LEE, STEVE
Halloween V   402

LEE, VIRGINIA
Stripped to Kill II   425

LEIGH, DAN
Loverboy   410

LEKER, LARRY
All Dogs Go to Heaven   27

LEONARD, DOUGLAS
Cyborg   395

LEONARD, PHIL M.
Road House   420

LEPROUST, THIERRY
Lectrice, La [1988]   213

LEVESQUE, MICHAEL
Package, The   416

LEWIS, GARRETT
Glory   155
Steel Magnolias   328

LINDSTROM, KARA
Heathers   168

LING, BARBARA
Checking Out   392

LONERGAN, ARTHUR
Obituaries   440

LOQUASTO, SANTO
Crimes and Misdemeanors   82
New York Stories   257
She-Devil   310

LO SCHIAVO, FRANCESCA
Adventures of Baron Munchausen,
   The   23

LUBIN, DAVID
Disorganized Crime   396

LUDI, HEIDI
Bear, The [1988]   44

LUDI, TONI
Bear, The [1988]   44

LYNCH, SHIRLEY
My Left Foot   245

MCALPINE, ANDREW
For Queen and Country
   [1988]   139
Rachel Papers, The   418

MCATEER, JAMES
Renegades   419
Sing   424

MCCULLEY, ANNE
Troop Beverly Hills   427
War of the Roses, The   372

MCDONALD, ED
Indiana Jones and the Last
   Crusade   193

MCDONALD, LESLIE
Field of Dreams   131

MCKERNIN, KATHLEEN
Great Balls of Fire!   160

MCLANE, WILLIAM D.
Let It Ride   408

MCLARNEY, REGINA
It Had to Be You   406

MCSHERRY, ROSE MARI
Fly II, The   400

MCSHIRLEY, MARGIE STONE
Back to the Future Part II   36
Three Fugitives   426

MADDY, ROBERT
Black Rain   52

MAGALLON, FRANCISCO
Fistfighter   400

MAHER, GREG
Stripped to Kill II   425

MALM, JULIE
Fast Food   399

MANN, CATHERINE
Gross Anatomy   402
Karate Kid III, The   407

MANSBRIDGE, MARK
Say Anything   287
War of the Roses, The   372

MANZER, ALAN
Dead Bang   395

MARCH, MARVIN
Lethal Weapon II   217
Skin Deep   424
Tango and Cash   340

MARCOTTE, PAMELA
Hit List   404

MARSH, STEPHEN
National Lampoon's Christmas
   Vacation   413

MARSH, TERENCE
Bert Rigby, You're a Fool   390

MARTY, CHARLES
Camille Claudel [1988]   68

MARTY, JACK
Riverbend   420

MASLOWSKA, JERZY
Triumph of the Spirit   351

MASLOWSKA, KRYSTYNA
Triumph of the Spirit   351

MATEOS, JULIAN
Indiana Jones and the Last
   Crusade   193

MATTHEWS, WILLIAM F.
Gross Anatomy   402
Karate Kid III, The   407

MAUS, RODGER
Skin Deep   424

MAY, DAN
Uncle Buck   364

MAYER, MICHAEL
Wizard, The   430

MAYHEW, INA
Sidewalk Stories   315

MESTRONI, VALLY
  Ginger Ale Afternoon 401
MIKKOLA, RAIMO
  Talvisota 336
MILLER, DAVID BRIAN
  976-EVIL 415
MILLER, LAWRENCE
  True Believer 356
MINCH, MICHELLE
  Kill Me Again 407
MITCHELL, JOE
  Say Anything 287
MOORE, JOHN JAY
  Black Rain 52
  Personal Choice 417
  Sea of Love 299
MOORE, RANDY
  Shocker 423
MORALES, LESLIE
  Tap 344
  Winter People 430
MORIN, LOULA
  Valmont 368
MURRAY, GRAEME
  Look Who's Talking 229
MURRAY-LEACH, ROGER
  Mighty Quinn, The 412
MUSKY, JANE
  When Harry Met Sally 380
MUTO, JOHN
  Gleaming the Cube 401
MYERS, TROY
  Lords of the Deep 410
  Masque of the Red Death 411
  Ministry of Vengeance 412

NAKAMURA, SHUJI
  Taxing Woman's Return, A
    [1988] 348
NAST, CAROL
  Rude Awakening 421
NEEL, BEALA B.
  National Lampoon's Christmas
    Vacation 413
NELSON, GEORGE R.
  Harlem Nights 164
  When Harry Met Sally 380
NEMEC, JOSEPH, III
  Abyss, The 19
NICHOLS, DAVID
  Great Balls of Fire! 160
NORRIS, PATRICIA
  Tap 344
NOVOTNY, MICHAEL
  Weekend at Bernie's 429
NOWAK, CHRISTOPHER
  Dream Team, The 397
  Parenthood 267
  Vampire's Kiss 429

O'DONNELL, ELAINE
  Staying Together 323
OEHLER, GREG
  To Die For 427
OKOWITA, MICHAEL
  Steel Magnolias 328

OPPEWALL, JEANNINE
  CLAUDIA
  Animal Behavior 389
  Music Box 241
  Rooftops 421

PAIN, KEITH
  Glory 155
PAPROCKA, IZABELA
  Triumph of the Spirit 351
PARKER, ART
  Dead Bang 395
PARRONDO, GIL
  Farewell to the King 399
PASTERNAK, VLADIMIR
  Little Vera 409
PATTERSON, CLARISSA
  Echoes of Paradise 397
PAUL, VICTORIA
  Far from Home 399
PAULL, LAWRENCE G.
  Harlem Nights 164
PAYNE, JAMES W.
  Her Alibi 404
PEARL, LINDA
  Communion 78
  Out Cold 415
PERAZA, MICHAEL A., JR.
  Little Mermaid, The 225
PETERS, PAUL
  Little Monsters 409
PHELPS, NIGEL
  Batman 40
PHILLIPS, MIKE
  Dry White Season, A 107
PICKRELL, GREGORY
  Listen to Me 409
PICKWOAD, MICHAEL
  How to Get Ahead in
    Advertising 404
PINEZICH, LYN
  Sidewalk Stories 315
PISONI, EDWARD
  Jacknife 197
  Steel Magnolias 328
POHL, JIM
  True Believer 356
POLIZZI, LAUREN
  Great Balls of Fire! 160
POLL, LEE
  Steel Magnolias 328
POST, LAURIE
  Silent Night, Deadly
    Night III 423
POWSEY, CLIVE
  Babar 389
POYNTER, JIM
  True Believer 356
PRECHT, ANDREW
  Abyss, The 19
PRESTON, WARD
  UHF 428

RAINERI, ANNA RITA
  Teen Witch 426

RAJAU, ALBERT
  Valmont 368
RAMSEY, NINA
  New York Stories 257
  Parenthood 267
RANDOLPH, VIRGINIA
  Lethal Weapon II 217
RANDOM, IDA
  How I Got into College 404
  War of the Roses, The 372
RAU, GRETCHEN
  Rooftops 421
REES, KIM
  Best of the Best 390
REINHART, JOHN KRENZ, JR.
  Deepstar Six 396
  Major League 233
REYNOLDS, RICHARD
  How I Got into College 404
RICARD, DOMINIC
  Eddie and the Cruisers II 397
RICE, STEPHEN
  Teen Witch 426
RICHARDS, ETHEL ROBINS
  Loverboy 410
RICHARDSON, EDWARD
  Blaze 56
RICHARDSON, KIMBERLEY
  Immediate Family 185
RICHWOOD, FRANK
  Innocent Man, An 406
RITENOUR, SCOTT
  Old Gringo 262
RIVA, J. MICHAEL
  Lethal Weapon II 217
  Tango and Cash 340
ROBERTS, PHILLIPE
  Perfect Model, The 416
RODIS-JAMERO, NILO
  Star Trek V 319
ROGALLA, ERICA
  Music Box 241
ROMANEC, NICK
  Luckiest Man in the World,
    The 411
ROMINE, WOODY
  Valentino Returns 429
ROSENBERG, PHILIP
  Family Business 127
  January Man, The 406
ROSEWARNE, JOHN
  River of Death 420
ROSSE, STEVE
  Do the Right Thing 94
ROTH, DENA
  Communion 78
ROTHSCHILD, ANDREW
  High Hopes [1988] 177
ROTHSCHILD, JON
  Night Visitor 414
ROYSDEN, THOMAS L.
  Dad 86
  In Country 189
  Pink Cadillac 417
RUBEO, BRUNO
  Born on the Fourth of July 60

Driving Miss Daisy   99
Old Gringo   262

RUBINO, BETH
Signs of Life   423

RUDOLF, GENE
Heart of Midnight   403
Johnny Handsome   407
Millennium   412

SAKLAD, STEVE
Old Gringo   262

SALLIS, CRISPIAN
Driving Miss Daisy   99

SALSILLI, GUIDO
Indiana Jones and the Last
Crusade   193

SAMSON, KIM
Listen to Me   409

SANDIN, JUDI
Prancer   418

SANTACRUZ, SETH
Fistfighter   400

SASAKI, KYOJI
Black Rain   52

SAUINIER, JACQUES
I Want to Go Home   405

SCAIFE, HUGH
Casualties of War   71

SCHLUBACK, JAN
Rose Garden, The   421

SCHMIDT, JOANNE
sex, lies and videotape   306

SCHNELL, CURTIS
Criminal Law   394

SCHOPPE, JAMES L.
Second Sight   422

SCHULENBERG, ROBERT
Out of the Dark   416

SCHULTZ, KAREN
Slaves of New York   424

SCHUTT, DEBRA
Miss Firecracker   237

SCOTT, ELLIOT
Indiana Jones and the Last
Crusade   193

SCOTT, JEANETTE
Signs of Life   423

SCOTT, STEPHEN
Indiana Jones and the Last
Crusade   193

SCOTT, WALTER
Obituaries   443

SCULLY, RICHARD
Hellbent   403

SÉGUIN, FRANÇOIS
Jesus of Montreal   201
Milk and Honey   412

SENEGHAL, ANNIE
Race for Glory   418

SEYMOUR, SHARON
Heart of Dixie   403

SHANAHAN, JAMES
No Holds Barred   415
Riding the Edge   420

SHAPIRO, JOHN
Stripped to Kill II   425

SHEPARD, MAXINE
Best of the Best   390

SHIGETA, SHIGEMORI
Free and Easy   400

SHOHAN, NAOMI
Shocker   423

SILVA, FRANK
Tap   344

SIM, GORDON
Sea of Love   299

SIMAKIS, LIZ
Sexbomb   422

SIMON, MARK
Midnight   411

SINGELIS, JAMES T.
See No Evil, Hear No Evil   302

SISSMAN, ROB
Wizard, The   430

SKALA, MARTINA
Valmont   368

SKINNER, WILLIAM LADD
Lock Up   409

SMITH, PETER LANDSDOWN
Fat Man and Little Boy   399

SMITH, ROY FORGE
Bill and Ted's Excellent
Adventure   48
Warlock   429

SNYDER, DAVID L.
She's Out of Control   422

SPADER, VICTORIA
sex, lies and videotape   306

SPENCER, JAMES
'Burbs, The   65

SPENCER, NORRIS
Black Rain   52

SPHEERIS, LINDA
Worth Winning   431

SPIER, CAROL
Renegades   419
Sing   424

SPIRSON, JON
Great Balls of Fire!   160

SPISAK, NEIL
Night Game   414

SPRIGGS, AUSTEN
My Left Foot   245

STEELE, GARY
Warlock   429

STENSEL, CARL
Always   32

STEVENS, JOHN WRIGHT
Rooftops   421

STIGLIANO, ROGER
Fun Down There   401

STITES, WENDY
Dead Poets Society   90

STOLL, JOHN
Shirley Valentine   423

STRACK, EVA
Purgatory   418

STRAWN, C. J.
Nightmare on Elm Street V   414

STRIMLING, RUTH
American Ninja III   388

SWIFT, BRENTON
Halloween V   402

TAGLIAFERRO, PATRICK
Big Picture, The   391

TAKEHARU SAKAGUCHI
Adventures of Milo and Otis,
The   388

TAKENAKA, KAZUO
Black Rain   52

TAUCHER, DEAN
Weekend at Bernie's   429

TAVOULARIS, ALEX
Lost Angels   410
Scenes from the Class Struggle
in Beverly Hills   295

TAVOULARIS, DEAN
New York Stories   257

TAYLOR, JACK G., JR.
Troop Beverly Hills   427

TAYLOR, MICHAEL J.
Blaze   56

THETFORD, BRYAN
Second Sight   422

THOMAS, PHILIP
Silent Night, Deadly
Night III   423

THOMAS, WYNN
Do the Right Thing   94

THRASHER, HAROLD
When Harry Met Sally   380

TINGLOF, SIG
Turner and Hooch   428

TOMKINS, ALAN
Dry White Season, A   107

TORREY, DANA
Teen Witch   426

TOTH, ILDIKO
Lords of the Deep   410

TOWNS, DONALD A.
Little Mermaid, The   225

TOWNSEND, CHRIS
Scandal   291

TOWNSEND, JEFFREY
Fabulous Baker Boys, The   123

TROPP, STAN
War of the Roses, The   372

VAN WERSCH-COT, YSABELLE
Lectrice, La [1988]   213

VEGA, DONNA
Distribution of Lead, The   396

VENEZIANO, SANDY
Dead Poets Society   90

VEZAT, BERNARD
Camille Claudel [1988]   68

VIPOND, LINDA
Cousins   394
Friday the 13th Part VIII   401

VOLZ, CHRISTINA
Deepstar Six   396

WAGER, DIANNE
Bert Rigby, You're a Fool 390
WALKER, GRAHAM (GRACE)
Dead Calm 395
WALKER, STEVE
Her Alibi 404
WALSH, FRANK
Getting It Right 147
WARGA, MICHAEL
Hit List 404
WARREN, TOM
Old Gringo 262
She-Devil 310
WASHINGTON, DENNIS
Chances Are 392
WASSER, FRED
Hellbent 403
WATELET, MARILYN
American Stories 389
WEBSTER, DAN
Gleaming the Cube 401
Glory 155
WEILER, FREDERICK
Licence to Kill 221
WEINMAN, DAVE
New York Stories 257
WELCH, BO
Ghostbusters II 151
WHEELER, W. BROOKE
Kinjite 408

WHITE, GORDON
Bill and Ted's Excellent
Adventure 48
WILCOX, ELIZABETH
Who's Harry Crumb? 430
WILHEIM, LADISLAV
Red Scorpion 418
WILKINS, TOM
Abyss, The 19
WILLETT, JOHN
Breaking In 391
WILLIAMS, JENNIFER
Bill and Ted's Excellent
Adventure 48
WILLIAMS, SIMMIE
Perfect Model, The 416
WILLIAMS, TREVOR
Who's Harry Crumb? 430
WILLSON, DAVID
Immediate Family 185
WILSON, RON
I, Madman 405
WOLFF, STEVEN
It Had to Be You 406
Steel Magnolias 328
WOLVERTON, LYNN
No Holds Barred 415
WOOD, JOE
She's Out of Control 422
WOODBRIDGE, PAMELA
True Love 360

WOODRUFF, DONALD B.
Fletch Lives 135
WRIGHT, HILARY
Bad Blood 390
WRIGHT-BASILE, SABRINA
When Harry Met Sally 380
WURTZEL, STUART
Innocent Man, An 406
Old Gringo 262
Staying Together 323

YARHI, DAN
Physical Evidence 417
Welcome Home 429
YIP, TIMMY
Eat a Bowl of Tea 111
YOUNG, PETER
Batman 40

ZAK, LUCINDA
Sea of Love 299
ZEA, KRISTI
Miss Firecracker 237
New York Stories 257
ZENTIS, ROBERT
Sinful Life, A 423
ZIEMBICKI, ROBERT
Eat a Bowl of Tea 111
ZIMMERMAN, HERMAN
Black Rain 52
Star Trek V 319

MUSIC INDEX

ADLER, MARK
  Eat a Bowl of Tea 111
  Life Is Cheap 408
ANDREA, OSWALD D'
  Life and Nothing But 408
ANTONELLI, PAUL F.
  Out of the Dark 416
ARONSON, LEON
  Eddie and the Cruisers II 397
ATHERTON, SONIA WIEDER
  American Stories 389

BADALAMENTI, ANGELO
  Cousins 394
  National Lampoon's Christmas
  Vacation 413
BAHLER, TOM
  Cold Feet 393
BAKER, JAMES
  Fun Down There 401
BASSINSON, KEVIN
  Cyborg 395
BEETHOVEN, LUDWIG VAN
  Lectrice, La [1988] 213
BENOIT, JEAN-MARIE
  Jesus of Montreal 201
BERENHOLTZ, JIM
  Lords of the Deep 410
BERLIN, IRVING
  Obituaries 434
BERNSTEIN, ELMER
  My Left Foot 245
BLACKSTONE, WENDY
  Lodz Ghetto 410
BODDICKER, MICHAEL
  Adventures of Milo and Otis,
  The 388
BOLDT, SALLY
  Great Balls of Fire! 160
BROUGHTON, BRUCE
  Jacknife 197
BRYANS, BILLY
  Office Party 415
BURK, GREG
  Hellbent 403
BURNS, RALPH
  All Dogs Go to Heaven 27
  Bert Rigby, You're a Fool 390
BURR, STEVE
  Long Weekend, The 410
BURROWS, EDWARD W.
  Street Story 425
BURWELL, CARTER
  Checking Out 392

CAMERON, CHRISTOPHER
  "HAMBONE"
  God's Will 402
CARPENTER, JOHN
  Halloween V 402

CHABROL, MATTHIEU
  Story of Women [1988] 332
CHANG, GARY
  Dead Bang 395
CHASE, THOMAS
  976-EVIL 415
CHATTAWAY, JAY
  Red Scorpion 418
  Relentless 419
CHIHARA, PAUL
  Penn and Teller Get Killed 416
CIRINO, CHUCK
  Return of the Swamp Thing,
  The 419
CLAPTON, ERIC
  Communion 78
  Lethal Weapon II 217
CLINTON, GEORGE S.
  American Ninja III 388
COLEMAN, CY
  Family Business 127
COLOMBIER, MICHEL
  Loverboy 410
  Out Cold 415
  Who's Harry Crumb? 430
CONRAD, RICK
  Terror Within, The 426
CONTI, BILL
  Karate Kid III, The 407
  Lean on Me 209
  Lock Up 409
CONVERTINO, MICHAEL
  Queen of Hearts 275
COODER, RY
  Johnny Handsome 407
COPELAND, STEWART
  See No Evil, Hear No Evil 302
COPPOLA, CARMINE
  New York Stories 257

DAMAMME, QUENTIN
  Lectrice, La [1988] 213
D'ANDREA, JOHN
  Iron Triangle, The 406
DANNA, JEFF
  Cold Comfort 393
DANNA, MYCHAEL
  Cold Comfort 393
DAVID, HAL
  It Had to Be You 406
DAVIS, CARL
  Rainbow, The 279
  Scandal 291
DEBELLES, GREG
  Kinjite 408
DELERUE, GEORGES
  Her Alibi 404
  Steel Magnolias 328
DEMARCO, CHRISTOPHER
  Toxic Avenger, Part III, The 427

DEXTER, JOHN WILLIAM
  Dream a Little Dream 396
DHOLAKIA, RAJAT
  Spices 425
DIRT TRIBE
  Long Weekend, The 410
DIXON, ANDREW
  High Hopes [1988] 177
DIXON, WILLIE
  Ginger Ale Afternoon 401
DOMPIERRE, FRANÇOIS
  Jesus of Montreal 201
DONAGGIO, PINO
  Night Game 414
DONAHUE, MARC
  After Midnight 388
DONOVAN
  Eighty-Four Charlie MoPic 115
DORFF, STEVE
  Pink Cadillac 417
DOYLE, PATRICK
  Henry V 173
DROSVEV, P.
  Little Vera 409
DUDLEY, ANNE
  Mighty Quinn, The 412
  Say Anything 287
DUNDAS, DAVID
  How to Get Ahead in
  Advertising 404
DU PREZ, JOHN
  Chorus of Disapproval, A 393
  UHF 428

EDELMAN, RANDY
  Ghostbusters II 151
  Troop Beverly Hills 427
EIDELMAN, CLIFF
  Animal Behavior 389
  Triumph of the Spirit 351
ELFMAN, DANNY
  Batman 40
ELIAS, JONATHAN
  Far from Home 399
  Parents 416
  Rude Awakening 421
ELLIOT, RICHARD
  Teen Witch 426
ENO, ROGER
  Warm Summer Rain 429
ERBE, MICKY
  Milk and Honey 412

FAIN, SAMMY
  Obituaries 437
FALTERMEYER, HAROLD
  Fletch Lives 135
  Tango and Cash 340
FASMAN, BARRY
  My Mom's a Werewolf 413
FENTON, GEORGE
  We're No Angels 376

FERGUSON, JAY
  Gleaming the Cube 401
  Nightmare on Elm Street V 414
  Race for Glory 418
FIEDEL, BRAD
  Immediate Family 185
  True Believer 356
FIELDS, STEVEN
  Long Weekend, The 410
FOLK, ROBERT
  Police Academy VI 417
  Wicked Stepmother 430
FORTUNA, TONY
  Ice House 405
FOSTER, DAVID
  Listen to Me 409
FOX, CHARLES
  It Had to Be You 406
FRED'S CRASHSHOP
  Long Weekend, The 410
FULLER, PARMER
  Night Visitor 414

GALE, JACK
  Luckiest Man in the World,
    The 411
GIBBS, MICHAEL
  Breaking In 391
  Riding the Edge 420
GIBBS, RICHARD
  Say Anything 287
GILLON, IRIS
  Fast Food 399
GILMAN, PAUL
  Best of the Best 390
GIRRE, RONAN
  Four Adventures of Reinette and
    Mirabelle [1986] 143
GOLDBERG, BARRY
  Beverly Hills Brats 390
GOLDENBERG, SIMON
  For Queen and Country
    [1988] 139
GOLDENTHAL, ELLIOT
  Drugstore Cowboy 103
  Pet Sematary 271
GOLDSMITH, JERRY
  'Burbs, The 65
  Criminal Law 394
  Leviathan 408
  Star Trek V 319
GOLDSTEIN, WILLIAM
  Shocker 423
GOODMAN, MILES
  K-9 205
  Staying Together 323
GOVERNOR, MARK
  Masque of the Red Death 411
GREEN, JOHNNY
  Obituaries 438
GRISSETTE, STEVE
  Perfect Model, The 416
GROSS, CHARLES
  Turner and Hooch 428
GRUSIN, DAVE
  Dry White Season, A 107
  Fabulous Baker Boys, The 123

GRUSKA, JAY
  Sing 424
GUARD, BARRIE
  Toxic Avenger, Part II, The 427
GUNNING, CHRISTOPHER
  When the Whales Came 430

HADJINASSIOS, GEORGE
  Shirley Valentine 423
HAMLISCH, MARVIN
  January Man, The 406
HAMMOND, WAYNE
  Fun Down There 401
HANCOCK, HERBIE
  Harlem Nights 164
HAREPEACE
  Long Weekend, The 410
HARTLEY, RICHARD
  Dealers 395
HARTZOP, PAUL
  Kickboxer 407
HAYDEN, TODD
  Sinful Life, A 423
HOENIG, MICHAEL
  I, Madman 405
HOLDRIDGE, LEE
  Old Gringo 262
HONDA, TOSHIYUKI
  Taxing Woman's Return, A
    [1988] 348
HORNER, JAMES
  Dad 86
  Field of Dreams 131
  Glory 155
  Honey, I Shrunk the Kids 181
  In Country 189
HOWARD, JAMES NEWTON
  Major League 233
  Package, The 416
  Tap 344
HOWARTH, ALAN
  Halloween V 402
HYANS-HART, CHRISTOPHER
  Hell High 403

IBRAHIM, ABDULLAH
  Chocolat 393
ICEPICK, TROTSKY
  Hellbent 403
INNES, NEIL
  Erik the Viking 398
IRON CURTAIN
  Long Weekend, The 410

JANKEL, CHAZ
  Rachel Papers, The 418
JARED, GABRIEL
  Romero 420
JARRE, MAURICE
  Chances Are 392
  Dead Poets Society 90
  Enemies, A Love Story 119
  Prancer 418
JOHNSTON, JIM
  No Holds Barred 415
JOMY, ALAIN
  Little Thief, The 409

JONES, TREVOR
  Sea of Love 299
JORDAN, GLENN
  Meet the Hollowheads 411

KAMEN, MICHAEL
  Adventures of Baron Munchausen,
    The 23
  For Queen and Country
    [1988] 139
  Lethal Weapon II 217
  Licence to Kill 221
  Renegades 419
  Road House 420
  Rooftops 421
KANDER, JOHN
  I Want to Go Home 405
KEAN, NICHOLAS
  Suitors, The 426
KID CREOLE AND THE
  COCONUTS
  New York Stories 257
KIMBALL, JEFFREY
  True Love 360
KITAY, DAVID
  Look Who's Talking 229
KLINGMAN, MOOGY
  Fear, Anxiety and
    Depression 400
KRYSTAL, DAVID
  Buying Time 391
KYMLICKA, MILAN
  Babar 389

LAFERRIERE, YVES
  Jesus of Montreal 201
LAXTON, JULIAN
  Purgatory 418
LEE, BILL
  Do the Right Thing 94
LEVIN, GOEFF
  Personal Choice 417
LLOYD, MICHAEL
  Iron Triangle, The 406
LOOMIS, PAUL
  Riverbend 420
LURIE, JOHN
  Mystery Train 249

MACAR, RICH
  Hell High 403
MACCHI, EGISTO
  Rose Garden, The 421
MACCORMACK, GEOFF
  For Queen and Country
    [1988] 139
MCHUGH, DAVID
  Dream Team, The 397
  Three Fugitives 426
MADER
  Sons 424
MALIN, JOE
  Crimes and Misdemeanors 82
MANCINI, HENRY
  Physical Evidence 417
  Welcome Home 429

MUSIC INDEX

MANFREDINI, HARRY
  Cameron's Closet 392
  Deepstar Six 396
  Horrow Show, The 404
MANSFIELD, DAVID
  Miss Firecracker 237
MANZIE, JIM
  Stepfather II 425
MARCEL, LEONARD
  Sexbomb 422
MARDER, MARC
  Sidewalk Stories 315
MARTHA, ISTVAN
  Hungarian Fairy Tale, A 405
MARTINEZ, CLIFF
  sex, lies and videotape 306
MATSON, SASHA
  Bloodfist 391
  River of Death 420
MAY, DANIEL
  Severance 422
MENKEN, ALAN
  Little Mermaid, The 225
MENNONNA, JOEY
  Bad Blood 390
MOLLIN, FRED
  Friday the 13th Part VIII 401
MONFAREDZADEH,
  ESFANDIAR
  Guests of Hotel Astoria,
  The 402
MORODER, GIORGIO
  Let It Ride 408
MORRICONE, ENNIO
  Casualties of War 71
  Cinema Paradiso 74
  Fat Man and Little Boy 399
MORRIS, JOHN
  Second Sight 422
MOTZIG, BILL
  Echoes of Paradise 397
MYERS, BILL
  All's Fair 388
MYERS, STANLEY
  Scenes from the Class Struggle
  in Beverly Hills 295

NEWBORN, IRA
  Uncle Buck 364
NEWMAN, DAVID
  Bill and Ted's Excellent
  Adventure 48
  Disorganized Crime 396
  Gross Anatomy 402
  Heathers 168
  Little Monsters 409
  War of the Roses, The 372
NEWMAN, LIONEL
  Obituaries 441
NEWMAN, RANDY
  Parenthood 267
NEWMAN, THOMAS
  Cookie 394
NICHTERN, DAVID
  Big Picture, The 391

NITZSCHE, JACK
  Next of Kin 414

OLVIS, WILLIAM
  Kill Me Again 407

PALMER, CHRISTOPHER
  Valmont 368
PARSONS/HAINES
  Food of the Gods II 400
PEARSON, E.
  Identity Crisis 405
PERLMAN, LAURA
  To Die For 427
PETIT, JEAN-CLAUDE
  Return of the Musketeers,
  The 419
PICCIRILLO, MICHAEL
  Crack House 394
PIOVANI, NICOLA
  Manifesto 411
POLEDOURIS, BASIL
  Farewell to the King 399
  Wired 384
PRAY FOR RAIN
  Trust Me 428

RACHTMAN, KARYN
  Fear, Anxiety and
  Depression 400
REDONDO, EMILIANO
  Fistfighter 400
REVILL, GRAEME
  Dead Calm 395
ROBBINS, RICHARD
  Slaves of New York 424
ROBERTSON, ERIC N.
  Millennium 412
ROBINSON, J. PETER
  Wizard, The 430
RODGERS, NILE
  Earth Girls Are Easy 397
ROEWE, SCOTT
  Ministry of Vengeance 412
  True Blood 428
ROMANO, JOE
  Fear, Anxiety and
  Depression 400
ROWLAND, BRUCE
  Cheetah 393
RUCKER, STEVE
  976-EVIL 415
RUSSELL, WILLY
  Shirley Valentine 423

SANBORN, DAVID
  Lethal Weapon II 217
SARDE, PHILIPPE
  Bear, The [1988] 44
  Lost Angels 410
  Music Box 241
SCHANKER, LARRY
  Fakebook 398
SCHYMAN, GARY
  Hit List 404

SCOTT, JOHN
  Winter People 430
SEGAL, MISHA
  Phantom of the Opera, The 417
SHAHBAZIAN, F.
  Suitors, The 426
SHAIMAN, MARC
  When Harry Met Sally 380
SHEFFNER, JONATHAN
  Bloodhounds of Broadway 391
SHORE, HOWARD
  Innocent Man, An 406
  She-Devil 310
  Signs of Life 423
SILVESTRI, ALAN
  Abyss, The 19
  Back to the Future Part II 36
  She's Out of Control 422
SIMON, MARTY
  Eddie and the Cruisers II 397
SMALL, MICHAEL
  See You in the Morning 422
SMART, CHRIS
  Personal Choice 417
SOLES, STEVEN
  Silent Night, Deadly
  Night III 423
SOLOMON, MARIBETH
  Milk and Honey 412
SPEAR, DAVID
  No Retreat, No Surrender II 415
STAMPONE, ATILIO
  Tango Bar 426
STEWART, DAVID A.
  Rooftops 421
STOCKDALE, GARY
  Dance of the Damned 395
  Savage Beach 421
  Stripped to Kill II 425
STRIMPLE, NICK
  Iron Triangle, The 406
SUMMERS, ANDY
  Weekend at Bernie's 429

TABRIZI, DAVOOD A.
  Navigator, The [1988] 253
TAJ
  Escape from Safehaven 398
TALGORN, FREDERIC
  Edge of Sanity 397
TANGERINE DREAM
  Catch Me If You Can 392
  Miracle Mile 413
THOMAS, JOE
  Perfect Model, The 416
TIKKA, JUHA
  Talvisota 336
TORRANCE, TIM
  Mutant on the Bounty 413
TOWNS, COLIN
  Getting It Right 147
  Vampire's Kiss 429

URBANIAK, MICHAEL
  Astonished 389
  Misplaced 413

VACHE, WARREN
    Luckiest Man in the World,
        The 411
VALERO, JEAN-LOUIS
    Four Adventures of Reinette and
        Mirabelle [1986] 143
VANCE, KENNY
    Heart of Dixie 403
VASEGHI, A.
    Suitors, The 426
VITARELLI, JOSEPH
    Big Man on Campus 390
    How I Got into College 404

WALDEN, DANA
    My Mom's a Werewolf 413
WALLACE, BENNIE
    Blaze 56
WECKER, KONSTANTIN
    Sunday's Child 426

WENTWORTH, RICK
    How to Get Ahead in
        Advertising 404
WETHERWAX, MICHAEL
    Cage 392
    Midnight 411
WHEATLEY, DAVID
    Out of the Dark 416
    Speed Zone 424
WHEATON, MARK
    Hellbent 403
WILLIAMS, JOHN
    Always 32
    Born on the Fourth of July 60
    Indiana Jones and the Last
        Crusade 193
WILLIAMS, PATRICK
    Worth Winning 431
WILSON, JULIA
    Game, The 401

WOLINSKI, DAVID
    Season of Fear 421

YAMAMOTO, NAOZUMI
    Tora-San Goes to Vienna 427
YARED, GABRIEL
    Camille Claudel [1988] 68
YATES, CARMEN
    Ice House 405
YOUNG, CHRISTOPHER
    Fly II, The 400

ZAVOD, ALLAN
    Communion 78
ZIMMER, HANS
    Black Rain 52
    Driving Miss Daisy 99
    Wonderland 431
ZORN, JOHN
    Distribution of Lead, The 396

PERFORMER INDEX

ABRAHAM, F. MURRAY
Innocent Man, An 406
Personal Choice 417

ACKLAND, JOSS
Lethal Weapon II 217

ADELIN, JEAN-CLAUDE
Chocolat 393

ADJANI, ISABELLE
Camille Claudel [1988] 68

AGHADASHLOO, SHOHREH
Guests of Hotel Astoria,
The 402

AGRESTA, DAVID
Best of the Best 390

AGUILAR, KRIS
Bloodfist 391

AIELLO, DANNY
Do the Right Thing 94
Harlem Nights 164
January Man, The 406

ALAIMO, MARC
Tango and Cash 340

ALBERT, EDDIE
Big Picture, The 391

ALBERT, EDWARD
Fistfighter 400

ALDA, ALAN
Crimes and Misdemeanors 82

ALDA, RUTANYA
Gross Anatomy 402
Prancer 418

ALEANDRO, NORMA
Cousins 394

ALEONG, AKI
Farewell to the King 399

ALEXANDER, TERRY
Horrow Show, The 404

ALEXIO, DENNIS
Kickboxer 407

ALICIA, ANA
Romero 420

ALLEN, JO HARVEY
Checking Out 392

ALLEN, JOAN
In Country 189

ALLEN, KAREN
Animal Behavior 389

ALLEN, STEVE
Great Balls of Fire! 160

ALLEN, WOODY
Crimes and Misdemeanors 82
New York Stories 257

ALLEY, KIRSTIE
Look Who's Talking 229
Loverboy 410

ALLISON, MAY
Obituaries 433

ALMAGOR, GILA
Rose Garden, The 421

ALONSO, MARIA CONCHITA
Vampire's Kiss 429

AL-SHEHAIL, ALSSARI
Teen Witch 426

ALTAMURA, JOHN
Toxic Avenger, Part II, The 427
Toxic Avenger, Part III, The 427

ALVARADO, TRINI
Fakebook 398

ALYSIA, NICOLE
Sidewalk Stories 315

AMANDOLA, VITTORIO
Queen of Hearts 275

AMITIN, MARK
American Stories 389

AMOS, JOHN
Lock Up 409

ANDERSEN, DANA
Ginger Ale Afternoon 401

ANDERSON, DION
Rude Awakening 421

ANDERSON, ERIKA
Nightmare on Elm Street V 414

ANDERSON, HASKELL
Kickboxer 407

ANDERSON, KEVIN
In Country 189

ANDERSON, LONI
All Dogs Go to Heaven 27

ANDERSON, MELODY
Speed Zone 424

ANDRADE, SORAYA
Street Story 425

ANDREEFF, STARR
Dance of the Damned 395
Out of the Dark 416
Terror Within, The 426

ANDREOZZI, JACK
Hit List 404

ANDREU, SIMON
Fistfighter 400

ANDREWS, HARRY
Obituaries 433

ANDREWS, REAL
Food of the Gods II 400

ANGELIS, GINA DE
Cousins 394

ANT, ADAM
Trust Me 428

ANTUNES, MICHAEL (TUNES)
Eddie and the Cruisers II 397

APPLEBY, NOEL
Navigator, The [1988] 253

APPOLLONIA
Ministry of Vengeance 412

APREA, JOHN
Savage Beach 421

ARGENZIANO, CARMEN
Red Scorpion 418

ARGO, VICTOR
Her Alibi 404

ARMENDARIZ, PEDRO, JR.
Old Gringo 262

ARMSTRONG, BESS
Second Sight 422

ARMSTRONG, VALORIE
Nightmare on Elm Street V 414

ARNOLD, TICHINA
How I Got into College 404

ARQUETTE, LEWIS
Horrow Show, The 404

ARQUETTE, ROSANNA
New York Stories 257

ASHANA, ROCHELLE
Kickboxer 407

ASHBROOK, DANA
She's Out of Control 422

ASHLEY, ELIZABETH
Vampire's Kiss 429

ASHTON, JOHN
I Want to Go Home 405

ASSANTE, ARMAND
Animal Behavior 389

ASTIN, SEAN
Staying Together 323

ATKIN, HARVEY
Eddie and the Cruisers II 397

ATKINS, CHRISTOPHER
Listen to Me 409

ATSUMI, KIYOSHI
Tora-San Goes to Vienna 427

ATTILI, ANTONELLA
Cinema Paradiso 74

AUDRAN, STEPHANE
Sons 424

AUFFRAY, JACQUES
Four Adventures of Reinette and
Mirabelle [1986] 143

AUSTIN, KAREN
Far from Home 399

AVEDON, LOREN
No Retreat, No Surrender II 415

AVELLANA, JOE MARIE
Bloodfist 391

AVERY, MARGARET
Riverbend 420

AVILES, RICK
Identity Crisis 405
Mystery Train 249

AXELROD, ROBERT
Midnight 411

AXTON, HOYT
Disorganized Crime 396
We're No Angels 376

AYKROYD, DAN
Driving Miss Daisy 99
Ghostbusters II 151

AZEMA, SABINE
Life and Nothing But 408

AZIZIAN, ALI
Suitors, The 426

481

BABBAR, RAJ
Spices 425
BABCOCK, BARBARA
Heart of Dixie 403
BABILA, ASSURBANIPAL
Suitors, The 426
BACKUS, JIM
Obituaries 433
BACON, KEVIN
Big Picture, The 391
Criminal Law 394
BAILEY, G. W.
Police Academy VI 417
BAIN, BARBARA
Trust Me 428
BAIRD, ANTHONY
Cheetah 393
BAISHO, CHIEKO
Tora-San Goes to Vienna 427
BAKER, GEORGE
For Queen and Country
[1988] 139
BAKER, JOE DON
Criminal Law 394
BAKER, KATHY
Dad 86
Jacknife 197
BAKER, RAY
Physical Evidence 417
BAKER, SCOTT
Bad Blood 390
BAKKE, BRENDA
Fistfighter 400
BALABAN, BOB
Dead Bang 395
BALDWIN, ADAM
Next of Kin 414
BALDWIN, ALEC
Great Balls of Fire! 160
BALINT, ESZTER
American Stories 389
BALINT, STEFAN
American Stories 389
BALK, FAIRUZA
Valmont 368
BALL, LUCILLE
Obituaries 433
BALSAM, TALIA
Trust Me 428
BALTZ, KIRK
American Stories 389
BAMBER, DAVID
High Hopes [1988] 177
BANCROFT, ANNE
Bert Rigby, You're a Fool 390
BANKOLÉ, ISAACH DE
Chocolat 393
BANLIER, CHANTAL
Little Thief, The 409
BANSAGI, ILDIKO
Hanussen 403
BARBER, GLYNIS
Edge of Sanity 397
BARI, LYNN
Obituaries 433

BARKIN, ELLEN
Johnny Handsome 407
Sea of Love 299
BARNES, CHRISTOPHER
DANIEL
Little Mermaid, The 225
BARNES, PRISCILLA
Licence to Kill 221
Lords of the Deep 410
BARR, ROSEANNE
She-Devil 310
BARRES, MICHAEL DES
Pink Cadillac 417
BARRETTO, AMBER
Little Monsters 409
BARRIER, MAURICE
Life and Nothing But 408
BARRON, ROBERT V.
Bill and Ted's Excellent
Adventure 48
BARRYMORE, DREW
Far from Home 399
See You in the Morning 422
BARSI, JUDITH
All Dogs Go to Heaven 27
BARTEL, PAUL
Out of the Dark 416
Scenes from the Class Struggle
in Beverly Hills 295
BARTENIEFF, GEORGE
American Stories 389
BARTHOLOMEW, JOANNA
When the Whales Came 430
BARTLETT, ROBIN
Lean on Me 209
BARTY, BILLY
UHF 428
BASINGER, KIM
Batman 40
BASKIN, ELYA
Enemies, A Love Story 119
BASKIN, MICHAEL
Sidewalk Stories 315
BASTIANI, BILL
American Stories 389
BATES, KATHY
Signs of Life 423
BATSON, TERRIE
Cyborg 395
BAUER, AMBER
Cold Feet 393
BAUER, STEVEN
Gleaming the Cube 401
BAVIER, FRANCES
Obituaries 434
BAXLEY, BARBARA
Sea of Love 299
BAYSER, CLOTILDE DE
Little Thief, The 409
BEACH, MICHAEL
Lean on Me 209
BEACHAM, STEPHANIE
Troop Beverly Hills 427
BEALS, JENNIFER
Sons 424
Vampire's Kiss 429

BEANE, ANDREA
Long Weekend, The 410
BEATON, NORMAN
Mighty Quinn, The 412
BEATTY, NED
Ministry of Vengeance 412
Physical Evidence 417
BEAUMONT, CAROLINA
Game, The 401
BECK, ISHA MANNA
American Stories 389
BECKEL, GRAHAM
Lost Angels 410
True Believer 356
BECKER, HARTMUT
Triumph of the Spirit 351
BECKER, JACOB
American Stories 389
BECKWITH, WILLIAM
Escape from Safehaven 398
BEDELIA, BONNIE
Fat Man and Little Boy 399
BEER, DANIEL
Hell High 403
BEERS, MORRI
Trust Me 428
BEGLEY, ED, JR.
Scenes from the Class Struggle
in Beverly Hills 295
She-Devil 310
BELACK, DORIS
Luckiest Man in the World,
The 411
BELAFONTE, SHARI
Speed Zone 424
BELTRAN, ALMA
Trust Me 428
BELTRAN, ROBERT
Scenes from the Class Struggle
in Beverly Hills 295
BELUSHI, JAMES
K-9 205
BENING, ANNETTE
Valmont 368
BENJAMIN, PAUL
Do the Right Thing 94
BENNETT, ROSALIND
Dealers 395
BENSON, DEBORAH
Mutant on the Bounty 413
BENSON, JODI
Little Mermaid, The 225
BENSON, LAURA
I Want to Go Home 405
BENTON, STUART
Sexbomb 422
BERDAHL, BLAZE
Pet Sematary 271
BERENGER, TOM
Major League 233
BERG, PETER
Heart of Dixie 403
Race for Glory 418
Shocker 423
BERKENBLIT, ELLEN
Distribution of Lead, The 396

BERMAN, SHELLY
Teen Witch 426
BERNSEN, CORBIN
Bert Rigby, You're a Fool 390
Disorganized Crime 396
Major League 233
BERRY, RAYMOND J.
Born on the Fourth of July 60
BESCH, BIBI
Kill Me Again 407
BEYER, TROY
Rooftops 421
BEYMER, RICHARD
Silent Night, Deadly
Night III 423
BEZACE, DIDIER
Little Thief, The 409
BHAKOO, KULDEEP
Cheetah 393
BIEHN, MICHAEL
Abyss, The 19
BIEL, DICK
Game, The 401
BIKEL, THEODORE
Lodz Ghetto 410
BILLERY, RAOUL
Little Thief, The 409
BILLINGSLEY, PETER
Beverly Hills Brats 390
BINGHAM, BARBARA
Friday the 13th Part VIII 401
BIRDSALL, JESSE
Getting It Right 147
BIRKIN, DAVID
Return of the Musketeers,
The 419
BISSET, JACQUELINE
Scenes from the Class Struggle
in Beverly Hills 295
BLACK, KAREN
Out of the Dark 416
BLACQUE, TAUREAN
Deepstar Six 396
BLADES, RUBEN
Disorganized Crime 396
BLAIR, LINDA
Bad Blood 390
BLAKE, AMANDA
Obituaries 434
BLAKE, NOAH
Teen Witch 426
BLAKELY, SUSAN
My Mom's a Werewolf 413
BLANC, DOMINIQUE
Story of Women [1988] 332
BLANC, MEL
Obituaries 434
BLANC, MICHEL
Story of Women [1988] 332
BLANKS, BILLY
Bloodfist 391
BLESSED, BRIAN
Henry V 173
BLIER, BERNARD
Obituaries 435

BLISS, CAROLINE
Licence to Kill 221
BLOCK, J. S.
Music Box 241
BLOMMAERT, SUSAN J.
Pet Sematary 271
BLOMMFIELD, DON
Lost Angels 410
BLOOM, CLAIRE
Crimes and Misdemeanors 82
BLOUNT, LISA
Great Balls of Fire! 160
Out Cold 415
BLUM, MARK
Worth Winning 431
BLUMENFELD, ALAN
Out Cold 415
Worth Winning 431
BLUTEAU, LOTHAIRE
Jesus of Montreal 201
BLYRD, TOM
Out Cold 415
BOCHNER, LLOYD
Millennium 412
BOEPPLE, BEATRICE
Nightmare on Elm Street V 414
BOLOGNA, GABRIEL
It Had to Be You 406
BOLOGNA, JOSEPH
It Had to Be You 406
BONAKI, LOU
Severance 422
BOND, SAMANTHA
Erik the Viking 398
BOND, STEVE
To Die For 427
BOORMAN, KATRINE
Camille Claudel [1988] 68
BOREGO, JESSE
New York Stories 257
BORGES, STAN
Luckiest Man in the World,
The 411
BOSCHI, GIULIA
Chocolat 393
BOSCO, PHILIP
Dream Team, The 397
Luckiest Man in the World,
The 411
BOSLEY, TOM
Wicked Stepmother 430
BOUQUET, CAROLE
New York Stories 257
BOUTSIKARIS, DENNIS
Dream Team, The 397
BOWDEN, ANN
Amanda 388
BOWE, DAVID
UHF 428
BOWEN, MICHAEL
Season of Fear 421
BOWER, TOM
True Believer 356
BOWMAN, RILEY
Bloodfist 391

BOYDEN, PETER
Rude Awakening 421
BOYLE, LARA FLYNN
How I Got into College 404
BOYLE, PETER
Dream Team, The 397
Speed Zone 424
BRACCO, ELIZABETH
Mystery Train 249
BRACCO, LORRAINE
Dream Team, The 397
Sing 424
BRADFORD, RICHARD
Heart of Dixie 403
Night Game 414
BRADLEY, DAVID
American Ninja III 388
BRADSHAE, CARL
Mighty Quinn, The 412
BRADSHAW, CATHRYN
Bert Rigby, You're a Fool 390
BRANAGH, KENNETH
Henry V 173
BRANDAUER, KLAUS MARIA
Hanussen 403
BRANDIS, JONATHAN
Stepfather II 425
BRANDO, MARLON
Dry White Season, A 107
BRANDON, CLARK
Fast Food 399
BRANDT, MAX
American Stories 389
BRASCHI, NICOLETTA
Mystery Train 249
BRAUGHER, ANDRE
Glory 155
BRAY, THOM
Horrow Show, The 404
BRENNAN, EILEEN
It Had to Be You 406
BRENNER, DAVID
Worth Winning 431
BRENNER, MAURICE
American Stories 389
BRIDGES, BEAU
Fabulous Baker Boys, The 123
Iron Triangle, The 406
Signs of Life 423
Wizard, The 430
BRIDGES, JEFF
Cold Feet 393
Fabulous Baker Boys, The 123
See You in the Morning 422
BRIDGES, LLOYD
Cousins 394
Winter People 430
BRIERS, RICHARD
Henry V 173
BRIGGS, BUNNY
Tap 344
BRIGGS, JOE BOB
Great Balls of Fire! 160
BRILL, JASON
Hell High 403

BRILL, STEVEN
  sex, lies and videotape 306
BRINKMAN, BO
  Ice House 405
BRITTON, SHOTGUN
  Meet the Hollowheads 411
BROADY, ELOISE
  Weekend at Bernie's 429
BROCK, STANLEY
  UHF 428
BRODERICK, MATTHEW
  Family Business 127
  Glory 155
BROMFIELD, VALRI
  Who's Harry Crumb? 430
BROMKA, ELAINE
  Uncle Buck 364
BRONSON, CHARLES
  Kinjite 408
BROOKS, AMY
  Say Anything 287
BROOKS, JOEL
  Skin Deep 424
BROOKS, RICHARD
  Eighty-Four Charlie MoPic 115
  Shocker 423
BROSSE, SIMONE DE LA
  Little Thief, The 409
BROWN, CLANCY
  Season of Fear 421
BROWN, CURTIS
  Game, The 401
BROWN, DWIER
  Field of Dreams 131
BROWN, ERIC
  Stepfather II 425
BROWN, GARRETT M.
  Uncle Buck 364
BROWN, HENRY
  Stepfather II 425
BROWN, JIM
  Crack House 394
BROWN, JULIE
  Earth Girls Are Easy 397
BROWN, REB
  Cage 392
BROWN, ROBERT
  Licence to Kill 221
BROWN, THOMAS
  Honey, I Shrunk the Kids 181
  Welcome Home 429
BRUCE, CHERYL LYNN
  Music Box 241
BRUCHIM, BENNY
  Riding the Edge 420
B'TISTE, IILANA
  Iron Triangle, The 406
BUDA, CRYSTAL
  Animal Behavior 389
BUETEL, JACK
  Obituaries 435
BUHAY, KEN
  We're No Angels 376
BUNDY, BROOKE
  Riding the Edge 420

BUNEL, MARIE
  Story of Women [1988] 332
BUNTING, GARLAND
  Blaze 56
BUNTZMAN, DAVID
  American Stories 389
BURCH, SHELLY
  Identity Crisis 405
BURGARD, CHRISTOPHER
  Eighty-Four Charlie MoPic 115
BURKHART, JULI
  Warlock 429
BURMESTER, LEO
  Abyss, The 19
BURNETTE, AMELIA
  Winter People 430
BURNS, JERE
  Hit List 404
BURRALL, ALEX
  Parenthood 267
BURROUGHS, JACKIE
  Food of the Gods II 400
BURROUGHS, WILLIAM S.
  Drugstore Cowboy 103
BURROWS, DARREN
  976-EVIL 415
BURROWS, EDWARD W.
  Street Story 425
BUSCEMI, STEVE
  Heart of Midnight 403
  Mystery Train 249
  Slaves of New York 424
BUSFIELD, TIMOTHY
  Field of Dreams 131
BUTLER, MICHAEL
  Slaves of New York 424
BUZZI, RUTH
  My Mom's a Werewolf 413
BYRNE, MICHAEL
  Indiana Jones and the Last
    Crusade 193
BYRNES, EDD
  Troop Beverly Hills 427

CADY, GARY
  Erik the Viking 398
CAGE, NICOLAS
  Vampire's Kiss 429
CAILLOT, HAYDÉE
  Four Adventures of Reinette and
    Mirabelle [1986] 143
CALDERON, PAUL
  Sea of Love 299
CALFA, DON
  Weekend at Bernie's 429
CALLOW, SIMON
  Manifesto 411
CAMERON, KIRK
  Listen to Me 409
CAMERON-SCORSESE,
  DOMENICA
  God's Will 402
CAMILLERI, TERRY
  Bill and Ted's Excellent
    Adventure 48

CAMP, COLLEEN
  Wicked Stepmother 430
CAMP, JOANNE
  Luckiest Man in the World,
    The 411
CAMPBELL, GRAEME
  Office Party 415
CAMPBELL, TISHA
  Rooftops 421
CANDY, JOHN
  Speed Zone 424
  Uncle Buck 364
  Who's Harry Crumb? 430
CANFIELD, GENE
  Sea of Love 299
CANNAVALE, ENZO
  Cinema Paradiso 74
CANOFF, MITCHELL
  God's Will 402
CANTOR, MAX
  Fear, Anxiety and
    Depression 400
CAPOTORTO, CARL
  Fakebook 398
CAPRIOLI, VITTORIO
  Obituaries 435
CAPSHAW, KATE
  Black Rain 52
CARDONE, NATHALIE
  Little Thief, The 409
CARDUNO, ANNA CRAY
  Trust Me 428
CAREY, HARRY
  Breaking In 391
CARHART, TIMOTHY
  Pink Cadillac 417
CARLIN, GEORGE
  Bill and Ted's Excellent
    Adventure 48
CARLO, JOHANN
  Slaves of New York 424
CARLTON, HOPE MARIE
  Savage Beach 421
CARMINE, MICHAEL
  Leviathan 408
CARPENTER, DAVID
  Warlock 429
CARRADINE, KEITH
  Cold Feet 393
CARRADINE, ROBERT
  All's Fair 388
  Rude Awakening 421
CARRERA, BARBARA
  Loverboy 410
  Wicked Stepmother 430
CARREY, JIM
  Earth Girls Are Easy 397
CARRIERE, MAREIKE
  Rose Garden, The 421
CARROLL, JANET
  Family Business 127
CARROLL, PAT
  Little Mermaid, The 225
CARSON, JOEL
  Communion 78

CARTER, ALICE
Gross Anatomy 402

CARTER, FINN
How I Got into College 404

CARTER, HELENA BONHAM
Getting It Right 147

CARTWRIGHT, VERONICA
Valentino Returns 429

CARVALHO, BETTY
Halloween V 402

CARVER, BRENT
Millennium 412

CASARES, MARIA
Lectrice, La [1988] 213

CASCIO, SALVATORE
Cinema Paradiso 74

CASCONE, NICHOLAS
Eighty-Four Charlie MoPic 115

CASEY, BERNIE
Bill and Ted's Excellent
Adventure 48

CASPARY, KATRINA
My Mom's a Werewolf 413

CASPARY, TINA MARIE
Teen Witch 426

CASSAVETES, JOHN
Obituaries 435

CASSEL, JEAN-PIERRE
Return of the Musketeers,
The 419

CASSIDY, JOANNA
Package, The 416

CASTILLO, GERALD
Kinjite 408

CASTLE, JOHN
Dealers 395

CATES, PHOEBE
Heart of Dixie 403

CATLIN, VICTORIA
Mutant on the Bounty 413

CATTRALL, KIM
Return of the Musketeers,
The 419

CHALK, GARY
Fly II, The 400

CHAMBERLAIN, RICHARD
Return of the Musketeers,
The 419

CHAMMAH, LOLITA
Story of Women [1988] 332

CHAN, DENNIS
Kickboxer 407

CHAN, JOHN K.
Life Is Cheap 408

CHAN, MICHELE
American Ninja III 388

CHANDLER, KAREN MAYO
Stripped to Kill II 425

CHANNING, STOCKARD
Staying Together 323

CHAPLIN, GERALDINE
I Want to Go Home 405
Return of the Musketeers,
The 419

CHAPMAN, DANIEL
Bad Blood 390

CHAPMAN, GRAHAM
Obituaries 436

CHAPMAN, SEAN
For Queen and Country
[1988] 139

CHARLES, EMILE
Wonderland 431

CHARLES, JOSH
Dead Poets Society 90

CHASE, CHEVY
Fletch Lives 135
National Lampoon's Christmas
Vacation 413

CHATINOVER, MARVIN
New York Stories 257

CHAU, MR. KAI-BONG
Life Is Cheap 408

CHAU, MRS. KAI-BONG
Life Is Cheap 408

CHAYKIN, MAURY
Cold Comfort 393

CHEN, ERIC
Savage Beach 421

CHESNAIS, PATRICK
Lectrice, La [1988] 213

CHIEN, YU
Life Is Cheap 408

CHIKLIS, MICHAEL
Wired 384

CHILDS, KIRSTEN
See No Evil, Hear No Evil 302

CHING, WILLIAM
Obituaries 436

CHRIS, MARILYN
American Stories 389

CHRISTIAN-JONES, LINDA
Severance 422

CHRISTOPHER, DENNIS
Sinful Life, A 423

CHRISTOPHER-MYERS, BILL
Fakebook 398

CHUDABALA, ART
Gleaming the Cube 401

CHUNG, LAM
Life Is Cheap 408

CIMAROSA, TANO
Cinema Paradiso 74

CIMINO, LEONARDO
Penn and Teller Get Killed 416

CIMO, VALENTINO
Next of Kin 414

CINNANTE, KELLY
True Love 360

CLARK, BLAKE
Fast Food 399

CLARK, MATT
Horrow Show, The 404

CLARKE, CAITLIN
Penn and Teller Get Killed 416

CLARKE, DAMON
Escape from Safehaven 398
Game, The 401

CLARKE, J. D.
Luckiest Man in the World,
The 411

CLARKE, KENNETH R.
Fun Down There 401

CLARKE, RICHARD
Identity Crisis 405

CLEESE, JOHN
Big Picture, The 391
Erik the Viking 398

CLEVENOT, PHILLIPPE
Camille Claudel [1988] 68

CLOSE, DEL
Next of Kin 414

CLOSE, GLENN
Immediate Family 185

CLOUGH, JOHN SCOTT
Gross Anatomy 402

CLUZET, FRANÇOIS
Chocolat 393
Story of Women [1988] 332

COBB, RANDALL "TEX"
Fletch Lives 135

COBBS, BIL
January Man, The 406

CODY, PAUL
Savage Beach 421

COFFIN, FREDERICK
Out Cold 415

COHEN, J. J.
Back to the Future Part II 36

COHEN, JULIE
Lodz Ghetto 410

COHEN, LYNN
Lodz Ghetto 410

COLBERT, CATERO
Perfect Model, The 416

COLE, BEN
Edge of Sanity 397

COLEMAN, ERICK
Game, The 401

COLEMAN, NOEL
Edge of Sanity 397

COLEMAN, RENEE
Who's Harry Crumb? 430

COLIN, MARGARET
True Believer 356

COLLINS, PAULINE
Shirley Valentine 423

COLLINS, RICK
Toxic Avenger, Part II, The 427
Toxic Avenger, Part III, The 427

COLLINS, STEPHEN
Big Picture, The 391

COLON, ALEX
Mighty Quinn, The 412
Red Scorpion 418

COLTRANE, ROBBIE
Bert Rigby, You're a Fool 390
Henry V 173
Wonderland 431

COLVIN, NORM
Riverbend 420

COMDEN, BETTY
Slaves of New York 424

CONDOS, STEVE
Tap 344
CONNER, CHAZ
Meet the Hollowheads 411
CONNERY, SEAN
Family Business 127
Indiana Jones and the Last
Crusade 193
CONNORS, MIKE
Fistfighter 400
CONSTANTINE, MICHAEL
Prancer 418
CONTI, TOM
Shirley Valentine 423
CONTRERAS, PATRICIO
Old Gringo 262
COOGAN, KEITH
Cheetah 393
Cousins 394
COOK, PETER
Getting It Right 147
COOK, RANDALL WILLIAM
I, Madman 405
COOKIE
Street Story 425
COOLEY, ISABEL
Silent Night, Deadly
Night III 423
COOPER, CAMI
Shocker 423
COOPER, JACK
Toxic Avenger, Part II, The 427
CORBIN, BARRY
Who's Harry Crumb? 430
CORNELL, ELLIE
Halloween V 402
CORRI, NICK
Slaves of New York 424
CORT, BUD
Out of the Dark 416
CORTESE, VALENTINA
Adventures of Baron Munchausen,
The 23
COSTALLOS, SUZANNE
True Love 360
COSTNER, KEVIN
Field of Dreams 131
COUFOS, PAUL
Food of the Gods II 400
COULOURIS, GEORGE
Obituaries 436
COULSON, BERNIE
Eddie and the Cruisers II 397
COURANT, GÉRARD
Four Adventures of Reinette and
Mirabelle [1986] 143
COUSINS, CHRISTOPHER
Hell High 403
COX, VEANNE
Miss Firecracker 237
COYOTE, PETER
Heart of Midnight 403
CRANHAM, KENNETH
Chocolat 393

CRENNA, RICHARD
Leviathan 408
CRONYN, TANDY
January Man, The 406
CROSBY, DENISE
Miracle Mile 413
Pet Sematary 271
CROSS, HARLEY
Fly II, The 400
CROUSE, LINDSAY
Communion 78
CRUICKSHANK, LAURA
Buying Time 391
CRUISE, TOM
Born on the Fourth of July 60
CRUZ, ALEXIS
Rooftops 421
CRUZET, LIZA
Perfect Model, The 416
CRYER, JON
Penn and Teller Get Killed 416
CRYSTAL, BILLY
When Harry Met Sally 380
CULKIN, MACAULAY
Uncle Buck 364
CULP, ROBERT
Silent Night, Deadly
Night III 423
CUMMINGS, QUINN
Listen to Me 409
CUMMINS, MARTIN
Friday the 13th Part VIII 401
CUNY, ALAIN
Camille Claudel [1988] 68
CURTIS, SCOTT
Cameron's Closet 392
CURTIS, TONY
Midnight 411
CUSACK, CYRIL
My Left Foot 245
CUSACK, JOHN
Fat Man and Little Boy 399
Say Anything 287
CUYONNET, CLAUDE
Little Thief, The 409
CYPHERS, CHARLES
Major League 233
CZYZEWSKA, ELZBIETA
Misplaced 413

D'ABO, OLIVIA
Personal Choice 417
DAE KYU CHANG
Best of the Best 390
DAFOE, WILLEM
Born on the Fourth of July 60
Triumph of the Spirit 351
DAGGETT, JENSEN
Friday the 13th Part VIII 401
DALTON, TIMOTHY
Licence to Kill 221
D'AMBOISE, CHARLOTTE
Fakebook 398
D'AMICO, MARCUS
Long Weekend, The 410

D'ANGELO, BEVERLY
National Lampoon's Christmas
Vacation 413
D'ANGERIO, JOSEPH
Lost Angels 410
DANIELLI, ISA
Cinema Paradiso 74
DANIELS, ALEX
Cyborg 395
DANIELS, JEFF
Checking Out 392
DANIELS, WILLIAM
Her Alibi 404
DANIELSON, LYNN
Out of the Dark 416
DANSON, TED
Cousins 394
Dad 86
DANTE, MICHAEL
Cage 392
DANZA, TONY
She's Out of Control 422
DANZIGER, CORY
'Burbs, The 65
D'ARBANVILLE, PATTI
Wired 384
DA RE, ERIC
Silent Night, Deadly
Night III 423
DARLOW, LINDA
Immediate Family 185
DAVI, ROBERT
Licence to Kill 221
DAVID, CLIFFORD
Bill and Ted's Excellent
Adventure 48
DAVIDA, BROOKE
Trust Me 428
DAVIDOVICH, LOLITA
Blaze 56
DAVIDSON, FOZIAH
River of Death 420
DAVIES, STEVEN
Lords of the Deep 410
DAVIS, BETTE
Obituaries 437
Wicked Stepmother 430
DAVIS, DANIEL
K-9 205
DAVIS, DON
Personal Choice 417
DAVIS, GEENA
Earth Girls Are Easy 397
DAVIS, LISA
Edge of Sanity 397
DAVIS, OSSIE
Do the Right Thing 94
DAVIS, PHILIP
High Hopes [1988] 177
DAVIS, SAMMI
Rainbow, The 279
DAVIS, SAMMY, JR.
Tap 344
DAY-LEWIS, DANIEL
My Left Foot 245

DEACUTIS, WILLIAM
Trust Me 428
DEAKINS, LUCY
Cheetah 393
DEANE, LEZLIE
976-EVIL 415
DEBENNING, BURR
Nightmare on Elm Street V 414
DECIO, LEIGH
Hellbent 403
DEE, RUBY
Do the Right Thing 94
DEFELICE, J. GREG
Out of the Dark 416
DELIA, SHEPPARD,
Sexbomb 422
DELUISE, DOM
All Dogs Go to Heaven 27
DEMORNAY, REBECCA
Dealers 395
DEMPSEY, JEROME
Race for Glory 418
DEMPSEY, PATRICK
Loverboy 410
DEMUNN, JEFFREY
Blaze 56
DENCH, JUDY
Henry V 173
DE NIRO, ROBERT
Jacknife 197
We're No Angels 376
DENIS, JACQUES
Chocolat 393
DENNIS, SANDY
976-EVIL 415
Parents 416
DENNIS, WINSTON
Adventures of Baron Munchausen,
The 23
DEPARDIEU, GÉRARD
Camille Claudel [1988] 68
I Want to Go Home 405
DEPLANCHE, PHILIPPE
Little Thief, The 409
DEPREIST, JAMES
New Year's Day 414
DERN, BRUCE
'Burbs, The 65
DERN, LAURA
Fat Man and Little Boy 399
DESHORES, ERICK
Little Thief, The 409
DESIDERIO, ROBERT
Gross Anatomy 402
DESOTO, ROSANA
Family Business 127
DEVINE, MARGARET
Fakebook 398
DEVITO, DANNY
War of the Roses, The 372
DEVORKIN, DANIEL W.
Hellbent 403
DEVORKIN, STEVE
Hellbent 403

DE YOUNG, CLIFF
Rude Awakening 421
DIAMOND, BARRY
Midnight 411
DIAZ, EDITH
Scenes from the Class Struggle
in Beverly Hills 295
DIAZ, SULLY
True Believer 356
DIAZ, VIC
Bloodfist 391
DICENZO, GEORGE
Sing 424
DIDDLEY, BO
Eddie and the Cruisers II 397
DIGNAM, ARTHUR
Everlasting Secret Family,
The 398
DIGNAM, MARK
Obituaries 437
DILLENBERG, NICOLE
Long Weekend, The 410
DILLMAN, BRADFORD
Lords of the Deep 410
DILLON, KEVIN
Immediate Family 185
DILLON, MATT
Bloodhounds of Broadway 391
Drugstore Cowboy 103
DILLON, MELINDA
Staying Together 323
DIMITRI, NICK
Kill Me Again 407
DINGLE, JANE
Milk and Honey 412
DI PINTO, NICOLO
Cinema Paradiso 74
DISKIN, SHARON
American Stories 389
DIVINE
Out of the Dark 416
DIXON, DONNA
It Had to Be You 406
Speed Zone 424
DIXON, MACINTYRE
Dream Team, The 397
DJOLA, BADJA
Innocent Man, An 406
DOAZAN, AURELLE
Camille Claudel [1988] 68
DOBSON, PETER
Sing 424
DOE, JOHN
Great Balls of Fire! 160
DOHERTY, SHANNEN
Heathers 168
DOLENZ, AMI
She's Out of Control 422
DON, CARL
American Stories 389
DONAHUE, SHAWN
Wicked Stepmother 430
DONAHUE, TROY
Bad Blood 390

DONDANVILLE, MAUREEN
Long Weekend, The 410
D'ONOFRIO, VINCENT PHILIP
Signs of Life 423
DONOHOE, AMANDA
Rainbow, The 279
DONOVAN, TATE
Dead Bang 395
DOODY, ALISON
Indiana Jones and the Last
Crusade 193
DOOHAN, JAMES
Star Trek V 319
DOQUI, ROBERT
Miracle Mile 413
DORE, EDNA
High Hopes [1988] 177
DORNAN, KEVIN
Rude Awakening 421
DOROFF, SARAH ROWLAND
Three Fugitives 426
DOUGLAS, MICHAEL
Black Rain 52
War of the Roses, The 372
DOUGLAS, SARAH
Return of the Swamp Thing,
The 419
DOUGLAS, SUZZANNE
Tap 344
DOWNEY, ROBERT, JR.
Chances Are 392
True Believer 356
DOYLE-MURRAY, BRIAN
National Lampoon's Christmas
Vacation 413
DRAGO, BILLY
True Blood 428
DRAKE, FABIA
Valmont 368
DRESCHER, FRAN
Big Picture, The 391
UHF 428
DREYFUSS, RICHARD
Always 32
Let It Ride 408
DUBLIN, JESSICA
Escape from Safehaven 398
Toxic Avenger, Part II, The 427
Toxic Avenger, Part III, The 427
DUBOIS, JEAN-POL
Life and Nothing But 408
DUCASSE, CÉCILE
Chocolat 393
DUCHAUSSOY, MICHEL
Life and Nothing But 408
DUCHOVNY, DAVID
New Year's Day 414
DUCOMMUN, RICK
'Burbs, The 65
Little Monsters 409
DUCREUX, LOUIS
Story of Women [1988] 332
DUDA, JOHN JOSEPH
Prancer 418

DUDIKOFF, MICHAEL
  River of Death 420
DUFFEK, PATTY
  Savage Beach 421
DUGAN, DENNIS
  Parenthood 267
DUKAKIS, OLYMPIA
  Dad 86
  Look Who's Talking 229
  Steel Magnolias 328
DUKES, DAVID
  See You in the Morning 422
DUMMONT, DENISE
  Heart of Midnight 403
DUNBAR, ADRIAN
  Dealers 395
DUNCAN, ARTHUR
  Tap 344
DUNCAN, CATHERINE
  Shirley Valentine 423
DUNCAN, LINDSAY
  Manifesto 411
DUNFORD, CHRISTINE
  Slaves of New York 424
DUPREE, V. C.
  Friday the 13th Part VIII 401
DURAN, ROBERTO
  Harlem Nights 164
DURANG, CHRISTOPHER
  Penn and Teller Get Killed 416
DURBIN, JOHN
  Checking Out 392
  Mutant on the Bounty 413
DUROCK, DICK
  Return of the Swamp Thing,
    The 419
DUSE, VITTORIO
  Queen of Hearts 275
DUTTON, CHARLES
  Jacknife 197
DUTTON, ROCK
  Astonished 389
DWYER, DAVID
  Winter People 430
DYE, CAMERON
  Out of the Dark 416
DYE, JOHN
  Best of the Best 390

EASTERBROOK, LESLIE
  Police Academy VI 417
EASTON, RICHARD
  Henry V 173
EASTWOOD, CLINT
  Pink Cadillac 417
EASTWOOD, JAYNE
  Office Party 415
EBRAHIMIAN, CHASEN
  Distribution of Lead, The 396
EDMOND, LINDA
  God's Will 402
EDSON, RICHARD
  Do the Right Thing 94
EDWARDS, ANTHONY
  How I Got into College 404
  Miracle Mile 413

EDWARDS, JENNIFER
  All's Fair 388
EDWARDS, KENNETH
  Crack House 394
EDWARDS, LUKE
  Wizard, The 430
EDWARDS, PADDI
  Little Mermaid, The 225
EFRONI, YEHUDA
  American Ninja III 388
EGAN, RICHARD, JR.
  Kinjite 408
EGGERT, NICOLE
  Kinjite 408
EILBACHER, LISA
  Leviathan 408
EISENBERG, ARON
  Horrow Show, The 404
EKLAND, BRITT
  Scandal 291
ELDARD, RON
  True Love 360
ELIZONDO, HECTOR
  Leviathan 408
ELLIOTT, DENHOLM
  Indiana Jones and the Last
    Crusade 193
ELLIOTT, SAM
  Prancer 418
  Road House 420
ELMES, ROWAN
  Dry White Season, A 107
ELWES, CARY
  Glory 155
EMERSON, JONATHAN
  Eighty-Four Charlie MoPic 115
EMIL, MICHAEL
  New Year's Day 414
EMOTO, AKIRO
  Tora-San Goes to Vienna 427
ENGEL, GEORGIA
  Signs of Life 423
ENGLUND, ROBERT
  Nightmare on Elm Street V 414
  Phantom of the Opera, The 417
EPERJES, KAROLY
  Hanussen 403
EPSTEIN, PIERRE
  American Stories 389
ERLAND, CYNTHIA
  River of Death 420
ERMEY, R. LEE
  Fletch Lives 135
ESPOSITO, GIANCARLO
  Do the Right Thing 94
ESRAFILY, POURAN
  Distribution of Lead, The 396
ESTABROOK, CHRISTINE
  Second Sight 422
ESTEVEZ, RENEE
  Heathers 168
EVANS, AL
  Riverbend 420
EVANS, ART
  Mighty Quinn, The 412

EVERETT, TOM
  Best of the Best 390
EVERHARD, NANCY
  Deepstar Six 396
EVIGAN, GREG
  Deepstar Six 396
EWING, BARBARA
  When the Whales Came 430
FAHEY, JEFF
  True Blood 428
FAIRBRASS, CRAIG
  For Queen and Country
    [1988] 139
FAISON, FRANKIE
  Do the Right Thing 94
FALK, LISANNE
  Heathers 168
FALK, PETER
  Cookie 394
FANCY, RICHARD
  Identity Crisis 405
FANN, AL
  To Die For 427
FARENTINO, JAMES
  Her Alibi 404
FARGO, JAMES
  Riding the Edge 420
FARR, JAMIE
  Speed Zone 424
FARROW, MIA
  Crimes and Misdemeanors 82
  New York Stories 257
FAURE, RENEE
  Little Thief, The 409
FAUST, NICK
  God's Will 402
FAWCETT, FARRAH
  See You in the Morning 422
FAZIO, RON
  Toxic Avenger, Part II, The 427
  Toxic Avenger, Part III, The 427
FECHT, OZAY
  Rose Garden, The 421
FELDER, CLARENCE
  Nightmare on Elm Street V 414
FELDMAN, COREY
  'Burbs, The 65
  Dream a Little Dream 396
FENN, SHERILYN
  True Blood 428
FENTON, LANCE
  Heathers 168
FERNANDES, MIGUEL
  True Believer 356
FERNANDEZ, JUAN
  Kinjite 408
FERRELL, TYRA
  Mighty Quinn, The 412
FERRER, MIGUEL
  Deepstar Six 396
  Valentino Returns 429
FERRIGNO, LOU
  All's Fair 388
  Cage 392

FIELD, CHELSEA
Skin Deep 424
FIELD, SALLY
Steel Magnolias 328
FIELD, TODD
Gross Anatomy 402
FINKEL, HOWARD
No Holds Barred 415
FINLAY, FRANK
Return of the Musketeers,
The 419
FINLEY, EVELYN
Obituaries 438
FINNEGAN, JOHN
Big Man on Campus 390
FIRTH, COLIN
Valmont 368
FISHER, CARRIE
'Burbs, The 65
Loverboy 410
When Harry Met Sally 380
FISHER, JASEN
Parenthood 267
FISHER, YVONNE
Fun Down There 401
FLAHERTY, JOE
Back to the Future Part II 36
Speed Zone 424
FLAHERTY, LANNY
Winter People 430
FLEA
Back to the Future Part II 36
FLECK, JOHN
Mutant on the Bounty 413
FLEISCHER, CHARLES
Back to the Future Part II 36
FLETCHER, DEXTER
Rachel Papers, The 418
When the Whales Came 430
FLETCHER, LOUISE
Best of the Best 390
FLETCHER, PAGE
Buying Time 391
FLOWER, GEORGE (BUCK)
Relentless 419
FLUEGEL, DARLANNE
Lock Up 409
FLYNN, MIRIAM
National Lampoon's Christmas
Vacation 413
FONDA, BRIDGET
Scandal 291
FONDA, JANE
Old Gringo 262
FONDA, PETER
Rose Garden, The 421
FONG, ALLEN
Life Is Cheap 408
FORBES, LEONIE
Milk and Honey 412
FORD, HARRISON
Indiana Jones and the Last
Crusade 193

FORD, MARIA
Dance of the Damned 395
Stripped to Kill II 425
FORD, MICK
How to Get Ahead in
Advertising 404
FORD, STEVEN
When Harry Met Sally 380
FORD, TOMMY
Harlem Nights 164
FORDE, JESSICA
Four Adventures of Reinette and
Mirabelle [1986] 143
FOREE, KEN
True Blood 428
FORMAN, MILOS
New Year's Day 414
FORREST, FREDERIC
Music Box 241
Valentino Returns 429
FORREST, WILLIAM H.
Obituaries 438
FORSYTH, TONY
Wonderland 431
FORSYTHE, DREW
Amanda 388
FORSYTHE, WILLIAM
Dead Bang 395
Sons 424
FOSTER, AMI
Troop Beverly Hills 427
FOSTER, MEG
Leviathan 408
Relentless 419
Stepfather II 425
FOUTRIER, GUILLAUME
Story of Women [1988] 332
FOUTRIER, NICOLAS
Story of Women [1988] 332
FOX, COLIN
Food of the Gods II 400
FOX, JAMES
Farewell to the King 399
Mighty Quinn, The 412
FOX, MICHAEL J.
Back to the Future Part II 36
Casualties of War 71
FOXWORTH, ROBERT
Personal Choice 417
FOXX, REDD
Harlem Nights 164
FRANCIS, GEFF
For Queen and Country
[1988] 139
FRANK, TONY
Riverbend 420
FRANKFATHER, WILLIAM
Valentino Returns 429
FRANKLIN, DON
Big Picture, The 391
FRANZ, DENNIS
Package, The 416
FRAZIER, RON
Fat Man and Little Boy 399
Lost Angels 410

FREEMAN, MORGAN
Driving Miss Daisy 99
Glory 155
Johnny Handsome 407
Lean on Me 209
FRENCH, ARTHUR
Luckiest Man in the World,
The 411
FRESSON, BERNARD
Sons 424
FREWER, MATT
Far from Home 399
Honey, I Shrunk the Kids 181
Speed Zone 424
FRICKER, BRENDA
My Left Foot 245
FROME, MILTON
Obituaries 438
FRY, ED
Rude Awakening 421
FRYE, VIRGIL
Trust Me 428
FULGER, HOLLY
God's Will 402
FULLER, KURT
Miracle Mile 413
No Holds Barred 415
FULLER, LISA
Teen Witch 426
FULLER, SAMUEL
Sons 424
FUN, HUI
Eat a Bowl of Tea 111
FUREY, JOHN
Mutant on the Bounty 413
FURST, STEPHEN
Dream Team, The 397
FUWA, MANSAKU
Taxing Woman's Return, A
[1988] 348

GABLE, CHRISTOPHER
Rainbow, The 279
GAGO, JENNY
Old Gringo 262
Valentino Returns 429
GAINS, COURTNEY
'Burbs, The 65
GAINSBOURG, CHARLOTTE
Little Thief, The 409
GALECKI, JOHNNY
National Lampoon's Christmas
Vacation 413
GALLAGHER, PETER
sex, lies and videotape 306
GALLIVAN, MEGAN
Teen Witch 426
GAM, RITA
Midnight 411
GAMBON, MICHAEL
Rachel Papers, The 418
GAMMON, JAMES
Major League 233
GANZ, LOWELL
Parenthood 267

GARCIA, ANDY
  Black Rain   52
GARDENIA, VINCENT
  Skin Deep   424
GARDNER, ASHLEY
  Heart of Dixie   403
GARDNER, LEONARD
  Valentino Returns   429
GARFIELD, ALLEN
  Let It Ride   408
  Night Visitor   414
GARR, TERI
  Let It Ride   408
  Out Cold   415
GARRETT, SUSIE
  Wicked Stepmother   430
GAUTHIER, DAN
  Teen Witch   426
GAUVIN, AURORE
  Story of Women [1988]   332
GAVICH, SAMMI
  Escape from Safehaven   398
GAYE, LISA
  Toxic Avenger, Part II, The   427
  Toxic Avenger, Part III, The   427
GAYLE, JACKIE
  Bert Rigby, You're a Fool   390
GAYNES, GEORGE
  Police Academy VI   417
GAZELLE, WENDY
  Triumph of the Spirit   351
GAZZARA, BEN
  Road House   420
GAZZO, MICHAEL V.
  Cookie   394
GEARY, ANTHONY
  Crack House   394
  UHF   428
GEDRICK, JASON
  Rooftops   421
GEE, KEVIN JOHN
  Slaves of New York   424
GENDRON, FRANÇOIS-ERIC
  I Want to Go Home   405
GEOFFREYS, STEPHEN
  976-EVIL   415
GERMAIN, DONNA
  New Year's Day   414
GERSTEN, ALEXANDRA
  Fear, Anxiety and
    Depression   400
GERTZ, JAMI
  Listen to Me   409
  Renegades   419
GETZ, JOHN
  Fly II, The   400
GHAHREMANY, VIDA
  Guests of Hotel Astoria,
    The   402
GIAMBALVO, LOUIS
  Weekend at Bernie's   429
GIANASI, RICK
  Escape from Safehaven   398
GIANNINI, GIANCARLO
  New York Stories   257

GIBSON, HENRY
  'Burbs, The   65
GIBSON, MEL
  Lethal Weapon II   217
GIELGUD, JOHN
  Getting It Right   147
GIFFORD, ALAN
  Obituaries   438
GIFT, ROLAND
  Scandal   291
GILBERT, MELISSA
  Ice House   405
GILPIN, JACK
  Dream Team, The   397
GINTY, ROBERT
  Loverboy   410
GIRARD, RÉMY
  Jesus of Montreal   201
GLASER, LISA
  Stripped to Kill II   425
GLEASON, PAUL
  Night Game   414
GLENN, SCOTT
  Miss Firecracker   237
GLOVER, CRISPIN
  Back to the Future Part II   36
GLOVER, DANNY
  Lethal Weapon II   217
GLOVER, JOHN
  Meet the Hollowheads   411
GLOVER, JULIAN
  Indiana Jones and the Last
    Crusade   193
GLOVER, SAVION
  Tap   344
GLYNN, CARLIN
  Night Game   414
GLYNN, TAMARA
  Halloween V   402
GODDARD, PAUL
  Everlasting Secret Family,
    The   398
GODRECHE, JUDITH
  Sons   424
GOLDBLUM, JEFF
  Earth Girls Are Easy   397
GOLDFINGER, MICHAEL
  Harlem Nights   164
GOLDIN, MARTIN
  Fun Down There   401
GOLDSTEIN, MINDEL
  Distribution of Lead, The   396
GOODMAN, JOHN
  Always   32
  Sea of Love   299
GORDON, GALE
  'Burbs, The   65
GORDON, GREGORY
  Lodz Ghetto   410
GORMAN, BREON
  Cheetah   393
GORSHIN, FRANK
  Midnight   411
GORTNER, MARJOE
  American Ninja III   388

GOTTLIEB, MATTHEW
  Luckiest Man in the World,
    The   411
GOUGH, MICHAEL
  Batman   40
GOULD, ELLIOT
  Big Picture, The   391
  Night Visitor   414
GOULD, HAROLD
  Romero   420
GOULD, JASON
  Big Picture, The   391
  Listen to Me   409
GRAF, DAVID
  Police Academy VI   417
GRAFF, TODD
  Abyss, The   19
  Innocent Man, An   406
GRAHAM, GERRIT
  Big Man on Campus   390
  Police Academy VI   417
GRAHAM, HEATHER
  Drugstore Cowboy   103
GRANBERY, DON
  Physical Evidence   417
GRANGER, PHILIP
  To Die For   427
GRANT, FAYE
  January Man, The   406
GRANT, MICAH
  To Die For   427
GRANT, NORA
  Welcome Home   429
GRANT, RICHARD E.
  How to Get Ahead in
    Advertising   404
  Warlock   429
GRECO, PAUL
  Next of Kin   414
GREEN, ADOLPH
  I Want to Go Home   405
GREEN, JOEY
  Crack House   394
GREENQUIST, BRAD
  Pet Sematary   271
GREENSTEIN, PAUL
  Hellbent   403
GREER, JANE
  Immediate Family   185
GREVILL, LAURENT
  Camille Claudel [1988]   68
GREY, JENNIFER
  Bloodhounds of Broadway   391
GRIES, JONATHAN
  Kill Me Again   407
GRIFASI, JOE
  Chances Are   392
GRIFFITH, THOMAS IAN
  Karate Kid III, The   407
GRIFFITH, TRACY
  Fast Food   399
GRIMAULT, MARION
  Little Thief, The   409
GRIMES, TAMMY
  Slaves of New York   424

GRODENCHIK, MICHAEL
  American Stories 389
GRODY, KATHRYN
  Parents 416
GROOMES, GARY
  Wired 384
GROSS, EDAN
  Best of the Best 390
GROSS, MARY
  Troop Beverly Hills 427
GROSS, PAUL
  Cold Comfort 393
GROSSBERG, BRUCE
  Game, The 401
GUASTAFERRO, VINCENT
  Next of Kin 414
GUEST, NICHOLAS
  National Lampoon's Christmas
    Vacation 413
GUGINO, CARLA
  Troop Beverly Hills 427
GUILFOYLE, PAUL
  Dealers 395
GUILLAUME, ROBERT
  Lean on Me 209
GUINESS, TIM
  Fakebook 398
GULLOTTA, LEO
  Cinema Paradiso 74
GUNN, MOSES
  Luckiest Man in the World,
    The 411
GUNTON, BOB
  Cookie 394
GUSS, LOUIS
  Fakebook 398
  Slaves of New York 424
GUTTMAN, RONALD
  Her Alibi 404
GUY, JASMINE
  Harlem Nights 164
GWALTNEY, JACK
  Casualties of War 71
GWYNNE, FRED
  Disorganized Crime 396
  Pet Sematary 271

HAAS, LUKAS
  Music Box 241
  See You in the Morning 422
HABER, MARTIN
  Severance 422
HACKETT, BUDDY
  Little Mermaid, The 225
HACKMAN, GENE
  Package, The 416
HADDON, DAYLE
  Cyborg 395
HAGERTY, JULIE
  Bloodhounds of Broadway 391
  Rude Awakening 421
HAILEY, RICHARD
  Fun Down There 401
HAIM, COREY
  Dream a Little Dream 396

HALL, ARSENIO
  Harlem Nights 164
HALL, HARRIET
  Hit List 404
  Relentless 419
HALL, JERRY
  Batman 40
HALL, PHILIP BAKER
  How I Got into College 404
HALLAHAN, CHARLES
  True Believer 356
HALLAM, JOHN
  When the Whales Came 430
HALLYDAY, JOHNNY
  Iron Triangle, The 406
HALPERN, TIMOTHY L.
  Rude Awakening 421
HAMILTON, JANE
  Bad Blood 390
HAMILTON, RICHARD
  In Country 189
HAMMER, BEN
  American Stories 389
HAMPER, JANE
  Fear, Anxiety and
    Depression 400
HANAUER, TERRI
  Communion 78
HANCOCK, LOU
  Miracle Mile 413
HANEY, DARYL
  Lords of the Deep 410
HANEY, TONY
  True Believer 356
HANKS, TOM
  'Burbs, The 65
  Turner and Hooch 428
HANNA, ELIZABETH
  Babar 389
HANNAH, DARYL
  Steel Magnolias 328
HANSEN, (THE LARIAT)
  No Holds Barred 415
HANSEN, GALE
  Dead Poets Society 90
HARA, RICK
  Slaves of New York 424
HARDIN, JERRY
  Blaze 56
  Valentino Returns 429
HARDIN, MELORA
  Big Man on Campus 390
HARKINS, JOHN
  Slaves of New York 424
HARMON, MARK
  Worth Winning 431
HARPER, JESSICA
  Big Man on Campus 390
HARPER, TESS
  Criminal Law 394
  Her Alibi 404
HARRELL, REBECCA
  Prancer 418
HARRIS, DANIELLE
  Halloween V 402

HARRIS, ED
  Abyss, The 19
  Jacknife 197
HARRIS, MEL
  Cameron's Closet 392
  K-9 205
HARRIS, ROBIN
  Do the Right Thing 94
  Harlem Nights 164
HARSINI, MANUCHEHR
  Suitors, The 426
HARVEY, DON
  Casualties of War 71
HARVEY, TERENCE
  Phantom of the Opera, The 417
HASKELL, PETER
  Riding the Edge 420
HASSEL, DANNY
  Nightmare on Elm Street V 414
HATCHER, TERI
  Big Picture, The 391
  Tango and Cash 340
HATFIELD, HURD
  Her Alibi 404
HATHAWAY, AMY
  Kinjite 408
HAUER, RUTGER
  Bloodhounds of Broadway 391
HAURY, YASMINE
  Four Adventures of Reinette and
    Mirabelle [1986] 143
HAVERS, NIGEL
  Farewell to the King 399
HAVEY, ALLAN
  Checking Out 392
HAWKE, ETHAN
  Dad 86
  Dead Poets Society 90
HAWKES, IAN
  Queen of Hearts 275
HAWKINS, SCREAMIN' JAY
  Mystery Train 249
HAYAKAWA, KUMIKO
  Kinjite 408
HAYNES, JAYNE
  January Man, The 406
HAYNIE, JIM
  Staying Together 323
HAYSBERT, DENNIS
  Major League 233
HAYWOOD, CHRIS
  Navigator, The [1988] 253
HEALEY, JEFF
  Road House 420
HEALY, DORIAN
  For Queen and Country
    [1988] 139
HEARD, JOHN
  Package, The 416
HEDISON, DAVID
  Licence to Kill 221
HEE IL CHO, MASTER
  Best of the Best 390
HEFFNER, KYLE T.
  Mutant on the Bounty 413

HELGENBERGER, MARG
 After Midnight 388
HELM, LEVON
 Staying Together 323
HEMMINGS, DAVID
 Rainbow, The 279
HENDERSON, BILL
 No Holds Barred 415
HENDERSON, SAFFRON
 Fly II, The 400
HENRIKSEN, LANCE
 Hit List 404
 Horrow Show, The 404
 Johnny Handsome 407
HENRY, BUCK
 Rude Awakening 421
HEPBURN, AUDREY
 Always 32
HERD, RICHARD
 Gleaming the Cube 401
HERMAN, PAUL
 Next of Kin 414
HERRING, LAURA
 Silent Night, Deadly
  Night III 423
HERTFORD, WHITBY
 Nightmare on Elm Street V 414
HESLOV, GRANT
 Catch Me If You Can 392
HEUBECK, WENZEL
 Sunday's Child 426
HEWETSON, NICHOLAS
 Dealers 395
HEYWOOD, PAT
 Getting It Right 147
HICKEY, WILLIAM
 It Had to Be You 406
 National Lampoon's Christmas
  Vacation 413
 Sea of Love 299
 Sons 424
HICKS, CATHERINE
 She's Out of Control 422
HIGGINS, CLARE
 Wonderland 431
HILL, BERNARD
 Shirley Valentine 423
HINCHLEY, TOMMY
 Terror Within, The 426
HINES, DESI ARNEZ, II
 Harlem Nights 164
HINES, GREGORY
 Tap 344
HINGLE, PAT
 Batman 40
HO, ROCKY
 Life Is Cheap 408
HO SIK PAK
 Best of the Best 390
HOAK, CLARE
 Masque of the Red Death 411
HODDER, KANE
 Friday the 13th Part VIII 401
HODGE, STEPHANIE
 I, Madman 405

HOFFMAN, BASIL
 Communion 78
HOFFMAN, DUSTIN
 Family Business 127
HOFFMAN, ELIZABETH
 Silent Night, Deadly
  Night III 423
HOFFMAN, GABY
 Field of Dreams 131
 Uncle Buck 364
HOGAN, HULK
 No Holds Barred 415
HOLBROOK, HAL
 Fletch Lives 135
HOLDEN, MARJEAN
 Stripped to Kill II 425
HOLLIS, TOMMY
 Astonished 389
HOLLIT, RAYE
 Skin Deep 424
HOLM, IAN
 Henry V 173
HOLMES, MARK
 Eddie and the Cruisers II 397
HOLVOE, MARIA
 Worth Winning 431
HONG, JAMES
 Tango and Cash 340
HOOSIER, TRULA
 Sidewalk Stories 315
HOPKINS, ANTHONY
 Chorus of Disapproval, A 393
HOPKINS, JERMAINE
 Lean on Me 209
HOPPER, HEATHER
 Troop Beverly Hills 427
HOPPER, TIM
 God's Will 402
HORN, LANNY
 Fast Food 399
HORNE, J. R.
 Hell High 403
HOROVITZ, ADAM
 Lost Angels 410
HORROCKS, JANE
 Getting It Right 147
HOUSSEAU FAMILY, THE
 Four Adventures of Reinette and
  Mirabelle [1986] 143
HOWARD, ADAM COLEMAN
 Slaves of New York 424
HOWARD, ALAN
 Return of the Musketeers,
  The 419
HOWARD, CLINT
 Parenthood 267
HOWELL, C. THOMAS
 Return of the Musketeers,
  The 419
HUBBARD, PAUL
 Physical Evidence 417
HUBNER, KURT
 Rose Garden, The 421

HUDSON, ERNIE
 Ghostbusters II 151
 Leviathan 408
HUDSON, GARY
 Cameron's Closet 392
HUES, MATTHIAS
 Fistfighter 400
 No Retreat, No Surrender II 415
HUGHES, BRENDAN
 To Die For 427
HUGHES, MIKO
 Pet Sematary 271
HUGHES, STUART
 Food of the Gods II 400
HUGHES, WENDY
 Echoes of Paradise 397
HUHTAMO, MARKKU
 Talvisota 336
HUI, CINDA
 Life Is Cheap 408
HULCE, TOM
 Parenthood 267
HUMAN, MARIE
 Purgatory 418
HUNT, HELEN
 Next of Kin 414
HUNT, LINDA
 She-Devil 310
HUNTER, FRANCINE
 Slaves of New York 424
HUNTER, HOLLY
 Always 32
 Animal Behavior 389
 Miss Firecracker 237
HUNTER, RION
 Cage 392
HUNTER, TAB
 Cameron's Closet 392
 Out of the Dark 416
HUPPERT, ISABELLE
 Story of Women [1988] 332
HURLOCK, MADELINE
 Obituaries 438
HURT, JOHN
 Scandal 291
HURT, MARY BETH
 Parents 416
 Slaves of New York 424
HUSAK, FRANTISEK
 Hungarian Fairy Tale, A 405
HUSTON, ANJELICA
 Crimes and Misdemeanors 82
 Enemies, A Love Story 119
HUW, RICHARD
 Getting It Right 147
HYDE-WHITE, ALEX
 Kinjite 408
 Phantom of the Opera, The 417

IDLE, ERIC
 Adventures of Baron Munchausen,
  The 23
INGBER, MANDY
 Teen Witch 426
INNOCENT, RICHARD
 Henry V 173

PERFORMER INDEX

IRONS, JEREMY
  Chorus of Disapproval, A   393
IRONSIDE, MICHAEL
  Office Party   415
ISBELL, TOM
  Jacknife   197
ISHIDA, ERI
  Free and Easy   400
ISHIDA, JAMES
  Iron Triangle, The   406
ISHIMATSU, "GUTS"
  Black Rain   52
ISLER, SETH
  Valentino Returns   429
IVEY, JUDITH
  In Country   189
IVEY, LELA
  Welcome Home   429

JACK, WOLFMAN
  Midnight   411
JACKSON, DEAN
  American Stories   389
JACKSON, GLENDA
  Rainbow, The   279
JACKSON, JOHN M.
  Ginger Ale Afternoon   401
JACKSON, KATE
  Loverboy   410
JACKSON, LAMAR
  Physical Evidence   417
JACKSON, PHILIP
  High Hopes [1988]   177
JACKSON, SAM
  Do the Right Thing   94
JACKSON, STONEY
  Perfect Model, The   416
JACKSON, VICTORIA
  Family Business   127
  UHF   428
JACOBI, DEREK
  Henry V   173
JACOBS, STEVEN
  Echoes of Paradise   397
JACOBY, SCOTT
  To Die For   427
JACQUES, YVES
  Jesus of Montreal   201
JAGLOM, HENRY
  New Year's Day   414
JAKOBSON, MAGGIE
  New Year's Day   414
JAMES, BRION
  Horrow Show, The   404
  Red Scorpion   418
  Tango and Cash   340
JAMES, GRANT
  UHF   428
JAMES, JESSICA
  Immediate Family   185
JAMES, KEN
  Physical Evidence   417
JAMES, STEVE
  American Ninja III   388
  Riverbend   420

JANELL, CLAIRE
  Amanda   388
JANOWITZ, TAMA
  Slaves of New York   424
JARVIS, GRAHAM
  Parents   416
JASPER, STAR
  True Love   360
JEFFREY, PETER
  Adventures of Baron Munchausen,
    The   23
JENKINS, DAN
  In Country   189
JENKINS, RICHARD
  Blaze   56
  Sea of Love   299
JENNEY, LUCINDA
  Wired   384
JENSEN, GUNTHER
  976-EVIL   415
JERRY LEE
  K-9   205
JEWERS, RAY
  Edge of Sanity   397
JILLETTE, PENN
  Penn and Teller Get Killed   416
J. J.
  Welcome Home   429
JODDER, KANE
  Best of the Best   390
JOHANSEN, DAVID
  Let It Ride   408
JOHNSON, BRAD
  Always   32
JOHNSON, CHIP
  Warlock   429
JOHNSON, DON
  Dead Bang   395
JOHNSON, REGINALD VEL
  Turner and Hooch   428
JOHNSTON, JOHN DENNIS
  Pink Cadillac   417
JONES, ANDRAS
  Far from Home   399
JONES, CLYDE R.
  Crack House   394
JONES, DUANE
  To Die For   427
JONES, FREDDIE
  Erik the Viking   398
JONES, GILLIAN
  Echoes of Paradise   397
JONES, JAMES EARL
  Best of the Best   390
  Field of Dreams   131
  Three Fugitives   426
JONES, JAMIE
  Welcome Home   429
JONES, JEFFREY
  Valmont   368
  Who's Harry Crumb?   430
JONES, JOHN MARSHALL, JR.
  See J. J.
JONES, L. Q.
  River of Death   420

JONES, NICHOLAS
  When the Whales Came   430
JONES, O-LAN
  Miracle Mile   413
JONES, TERRY
  Erik the Viking   398
JONES, TOMMY LEE
  Package, The   416
JORDAN, RICHARD
  Romero   420
JOSEPH, JUDY
  Fun Down There   401
JOSEPHSON, ERLAND
  Hanussen   403
JOURDAN, LOUIS
  Return of the Swamp Thing,
    The   419
JOY, ROBERT
  Millennium   412
JUAREZ, RUBEN
  Tango Bar   426
JULIA, RAUL
  Romero   420
  Tango Bar   426
JULIANO, AL
  True Love   360
JUNG, CALVIN
  American Ninja III   388

KACZMAREK, JANE
  All's Fair   388
KAHAN, STEVE
  Lethal Weapon II   217
KAMAN, ROB
  Bloodfist   391
KANAN, SEAN
  Karate Kid III, The   407
KAPELOS, JOHN
  All's Fair   388
KAPLAN, WENDY
  Halloween V   402
KARIN, RITA
  Enemies, A Love Story   119
KARYO, TCHEKY
  Bear, The [1988]   44
KATARINA, ANNA
  Slaves of New York   424
KATIMS, ROBERT
  American Stories   389
KATSULAS, ANDREAS
  Communion   78
  Next of Kin   414
KATSURAGI, MAYAKO
  Toxic Avenger, Part II, The   427
KATZ, ALLAN
  Big Man on Campus   390
KAVA, CAROLINE
  Born on the Fourth of July   60
KAVNER, JULIE
  New York Stories   257
KAY, CHARLES
  Henry V   173
KAY, CHERYL
  Crack House   394

493

KAYE, CAREN
Teen Witch   426
KEARNEY, GILLIAN
Shirley Valentine   423
KEATON, MICHAEL
Batman   40
Dream Team, The   397
KEE, LEE SAU
Eat a Bowl of Tea   111
KEITEL, HARVEY
January Man, The   406
KEITH, BRIAN
Welcome Home   429
KELLERMAN, SALLY
All's Fair   388
KELLEY, DEFOREST
Star Trek V   319
KELLEY, SHEILA
Breaking In   391
Staying Together   323
KELLY, DAVID PATRICK
Penn and Teller Get Killed   416
KELLY, JEAN
Uncle Buck   364
KEMP, JEREMY
When the Whales Came   430
KENIN, ALEXA
Animal Behavior   389
KENNEDY, ARTHUR
Signs of Life   423
KENNEDY, GEORGE
Ministry of Vengeance   412
Terror Within, The   426
KENNEDY, JIHMI
Glory   155
KENNEDY, T. J.
Riverbend   420
KENSEI, KEN
Slaves of New York   424
KENSIT, PATSY
Lethal Weapon II   217
KEPROS, NICHOLAS
Identity Crisis   405
Lodz Ghetto   410
KERR, CHARLES
Babar   389
KEYES, EVELYN
Wicked Stepmother   430
KIDD, MICHAEL
Skin Deep   424
KIDMAN, NICOLE
Dead Calm   395
KIGADA, LYDIA
Cheetah   393
KILMER, VAL
Kill Me Again   407
KING, ALAN
Enemies, A Love Story   119
KING, ERIK
Casualties of War   71
KING, JEROME
Game, The   401
KING, LARRY
Eddie and the Cruisers II   397

KINNEAR, ROY
Return of the Musketeers,
The   419
KINSEY, LANCE
Police Academy VI   417
KIRBY, BRUNO
We're No Angels   376
When Harry Met Sally   380
KIRCH, REMY
Little Thief, The   409
KIRK, KEITH
Riverbend   420
KIRKLAND, SALLY
Best of the Best   390
Cold Feet   393
KISER, TERRY
Weekend at Bernie's   429
KITT, EARTHA
Erik the Viking   398
KLINE, KEVIN
January Man, The   406
KLISSER, EVAN J.
American Ninja III   388
KLYN, VINCENT
Cyborg   395
KNEPPER, ROB
Renegades   419
KOENIG, WALTER
Star Trek V   319
KOMOROWSKI, LILIANA
Astonished   389
KONG, GARY
Life Is Cheap   408
KORFF, HANS PETER
Sunday's Child   426
KOSINSKI, JERZY
Lodz Ghetto   410
KOTCHEFF, TED
Weekend at Bernie's   429
KOTLISKY, MARGE
God's Will   402
KOTTO, YAPHET
Ministry of Vengeance   412
KOVE, MARTIN L.
Karate Kid III, The   407
KOVERO, ESKO
Talvisota   336
KOYAMA, SHIGERU
Black Rain   52
KOZAK, HARLEY
Parenthood   267
KRABBE, JEROEN
Scandal   291
KRIGE, ALICE
See You in the Morning   422
KRISTOFFERSON, KRIS
Millennium   412
Welcome Home   429
KUDOH, YOUKI
Mystery Train   249
KUSE, RICHARD
Warlock   429
KUSSMAN, DYLAN
Dead Poets Society   90

KUZYK, MIMI
Speed Zone   424
KWOUK, BRUT
Race for Glory   418

LABELLE, PATTI
Sing   424
LABYORTEAUX, PATRICK
Heathers   168
LACOMBE, ANDRÉ
Bear, The [1988]   44
LADD, CHERYL
Millennium   412
LADD, DIANE
National Lampoon's Christmas
Vacation   413
LAFAYETTE, JOHN
Terror Within, The   426
LAHTI, CHRISTINE
Gross Anatomy   402
Miss Firecracker   237
LAKE, RICKI
Cookie   394
LAMB, DEBRA
Stripped to Kill II   425
LAMPERT, ZOHRA
Fakebook   398
LAMPKIN, CHARLES
Obituaries   438
LAN, LAW
Eat a Bowl of Tea   111
LANCASTER, BURT
Field of Dreams   131
LANDAU, MARTIN
Crimes and Misdemeanors   82
LANDFIELD, TIMOTHY
Cheetah   393
LANDHAM, SONNY
Lock Up   409
LANDMAN, JEFFREY
Halloween V   402
LANDON, HAL, JR.
Bill and Ted's Excellent
Adventure   48
LANDON, LAURENE
Wicked Stepmother   430
LANE, CHARLES
Sidewalk Stories   315
LANGDON, SUE ANE
UHF   428
LANGE, JESSICA
Music Box   241
LANGRICK, MARGARET
Cold Comfort   393
LANKFORD, KIM
Cameron's Closet   392
LARESE, KIM
Slaves of New York   424
LARKIN, BRYAN
She-Devil   310
LARROQUETTE, JOHN
Second Sight   422
LASSER, LOUISE
Rude Awakening   421
Sing   424

LATTANZI, MATT
Catch Me If You Can 392
LATZEN, ELLEN HAMILTON
National Lampoon's Christmas
Vacation 413
LAUDENBACH, PHILIPPE
Four Adventures of Reinette and
Mirabelle [1986] 143
LAURANCE, MATTHEW
Eddie and the Cruisers II 397
LAURANCE, MITCHELL
Stepfather II 425
LAURIE, PIPER
Dream a Little Dream 396
LAVIN, LINDA
I Want to Go Home 405
LAVOY, ZACHARY
Parenthood 267
LAWNER, MORDECAI
American Stories 389
LAWRENCE, STEPHANIE
Phantom of the Opera, The 417
LAYNE, RANDI
Fast Food 399
LAZARO, EUSEBIO
Return of the Musketeers,
The 419
LE, THUY THU
Casualties of War 71
LE TUAN
Gleaming the Cube 401
LEA, RON
Criminal Law 394
LEACHMAN, CLORIS
Prancer 418
LEARY, TIMOTHY
Rude Awakening 421
LEBRUN, DANIELE
Camille Claudel [1988] 68
LEE, ANN MARIE
Fly II, The 400
LEE, BILLY
Obituaries 439
LEE, CHRISTOPHER
Return of the Musketeers,
The 419
LEE, CINQUÉ
Mystery Train 249
LEE, DANA
Cage 392
LEE, JOIE
Do the Right Thing 94
LEE, MARK
Everlasting Secret Family,
The 398
LEE, SPIKE
Do the Right Thing 94
LEE, TIGER CHUNG
Cage 392
LEEDS, PHIL
Enemies, A Love Story 119
LEEWAY, JOE
Slaves of New York 424

LEGERE, PHOEBE
Toxic Avenger, Part II, The 427
Toxic Avenger, Part III, The 427
LE GROS, JAMES
Drugstore Cowboy 103
LEGUIZAMO, JOHN
Casualties of War 71
LEHMANN, FRIEDHELM
Rose Garden, The 421
LEIGH, JENNIFER JASON
Big Picture, The 391
Heart of Midnight 403
LEMBECK, MICHEL
Dream Team, The 397
LEMMON, JACK
Dad 86
LEMMONS, KASI
Vampire's Kiss 429
LENA, ROBERTA
Cinema Paradiso 74
LENKOWSKY, PHILIP
Slaves of New York 424
LENZ, KAY
Physical Evidence 417
LEONARD, ROBERT SEAN
Dead Poets Society 90
LEONARDI, MARCO
Cinema Paradiso 74
LEONG, AL
Bill and Ted's Excellent
Adventure 48
Cage 392
Savage Beach 421
LEPAGE, ROBERT
Jesus of Montreal 201
LERNER, KEN
Hit List 404
Relentless 419
LERNER, MICHAEL
Harlem Nights 164
LEROUX, MAXIME
Camille Claudel [1988] 68
LESKIN, BORIS
American Stories 389
LETTS, NIKKI
Ice House 405
LEVAND, LYN
Hellbent 403
LEVEQUE, EDWARD
Obituaries 439
LEVEY, JAY
UHF 428
LEVIN, CHARLES
No Holds Barred 415
LEVINE, ANNA
Warlock 429
LEVINE, ELLIOTT
American Stories 389
LEVINE, JERRY
Born on the Fourth of July 60
LEVINE, TED
Next of Kin 414
LEVITT, ZANE W.
Out of the Dark 416

LEVY, DENNA
Rude Awakening 421
LEVY, EUGENE
Speed Zone 424
LEW, JAMES
Best of the Best 390
LEWIS, CARL
Speed Zone 424
LEWIS, GEOFFREY
Catch Me If You Can 392
Out of the Dark 416
Pink Cadillac 417
LEWIS, JENNY
Troop Beverly Hills 427
Wizard, The 430
LEWIS, JERRY
Cookie 394
LEWIS, JULIETTE
Meet the Hollowheads 411
National Lampoon's Christmas
Vacation 413
LEWIS, LIGHTFIELD
Meet the Hollowheads 411
LEWIS, MICHAEL
Signs of Life 423
LEWIS, NATHAN
Phantom of the Opera, The 417
LIBERTINI, RICHARD
Animal Behavior 389
Fletch Lives 135
LIBIN, PAUL
Distribution of Lead, The 396
LIEH, LO
Life Is Cheap 408
LILLIE, BEATRICE
Obituaries 439
LILLY, HEATHER
See You in the Morning 422
LINCOLN, TONY
God's Will 402
LINDFORS, VIVECA
Misplaced 413
LINDLEY, AUDRA
Troop Beverly Hills 427
LINDSAY, ROBERT
Bert Rigby, You're a Fool 390
LINKE, PAUL
Parenthood 267
LINNEA
Sexbomb 422
LINVILLE, LARRY
Earth Girls Are Easy 397
LIOTTA, LOU
Severance 422
LIOTTA, RAY
Field of Dreams 131
LIPTON, PEGGY
Kinjite 408
LISKA, STEPHEN
Sexbomb 422
LISTER, TOM (TINY), JR.
Midnight 411
No Holds Barred 415
LITHGOW, JOHN
Out Cold 415

LITTLE, CLEAVON
  Fletch Lives 135
LIVELY, ROBYN
  Karate Kid III, The 407
  Teen Witch 426
LIVINGSTON, PAUL
  Navigator, The [1988] 253
LLEWELYN, DESMOND
  Licence to Kill 221
LLOYD, CHRISTOPHER
  Back to the Future Part II 36
  Dream Team, The 397
LLOYD, EMILY
  Cookie 394
  In Country 189
LLOYD, JOHN BEDFORD
  Abyss, The 19
LLOYD, NORMAN
  Dead Poets Society 90
LOCANE, AMY
  Lost Angels 410
LOCHTMAN, JUSTINE
  American Stories 389
LOCKHART, JUNE
  Big Picture, The 391
LOCKLEAR, HEATHER
  Return of the Swamp Thing,
    The 419
LOCKLIN, LORYN
  Catch Me If You Can 392
LODER, JOHN
  Obituaries 439
LODGE, DAVID
  Edge of Sanity 397
LOGGIA, ROBERT
  Relentless 419
  Triumph of the Spirit 351
LOM, HERBERT
  River of Death 420
LOMBARD, MICHAEL
  Pet Sematary 271
  Second Sight 422
LOMBARDI, LUCA
  Sunday's Child 426
LONDON, LISA
  Savage Beach 421
LONE, JOHN
  Echoes of Paradise 397
LONG, JOSEPH
  Queen of Hearts 275
LONG, SHELLEY
  Troop Beverly Hills 427
LONGO, TONY
  Worth Winning 431
LONGSTRETH, EMILY
  Big Picture, The 391
LOOMIS, ROD
  Bill and Ted's Excellent
    Adventure 48
LOONG, BLAISE
  Cyborg 395
LOPEZ, ANGELO
  Street Story 425
LOPEZ, GERRY
  Farewell to the King 399

LOPEZ, PERRY
  Kinjite 408
LORDS, TRACI
  Fast Food 399
LOTTIMER, EB
  Lords of the Deep 410
  Stripped to Kill II 425
LOUIS-DREYFUS, JULIA
  National Lampoon's Christmas
    Vacation 413
LOVE, DARLENE
  Lethal Weapon II 217
LOWE, CHAD
  True Blood 428
LOWELL, CAREY
  Licence to Kill 221
LUCHINI, FABRICE
  Four Adventures of Reinette and
    Mirabelle [1986] 143
LUCIANO, MICHAEL
  Rude Awakening 421
LUCKINBILL, LAURENCE
  Star Trek V 319
LUDWIG, PAMELA
  Race for Glory 418
LUJAN, BOB
  Vampire's Kiss 429
LUKE, KEYE
  Mighty Quinn, The 412
LUMLEY, JOANNA
  Shirley Valentine 423
LUND, JORDAN
  Jacknife 197
LUNDGREN, DOLPH
  Red Scorpion 418
LUNDY, JESSICA
  Vampire's Kiss 429
LUPONE, PATTI
  Driving Miss Daisy 99
LYMAN, WILL
  Office Party 415
LYNCH, DEREK
  Distribution of Lead, The 396
LYNCH, KATE
  Eddie and the Cruisers II 397
LYNCH, KELLY
  Drugstore Cowboy 103
  Road House 420
  Warm Summer Rain 429
LYNCH, VALERIA
  Tango Bar 426
LYNN, BILL
  Welcome Home 429
LYNN, CARRIE
  Heathers 168
LYONS, BRUCE
  Navigator, The [1988] 253

MCANALLY, RAY
  My Left Foot 245
  We're No Angels 376
MCARTHUR, ALEX
  Race for Glory 418
MACARTHUR, ROY
  Escape from Safehaven 398

MCCABE, RUTH
  My Left Foot 245
MCCALMAN, MACON
  Cold Feet 393
  Valentino Returns 429
MCCANN, CHUCK
  Cameron's Closet 392
MCCARTHY, ANDREW
  Weekend at Bernie's 429
MCCARTHY, KEVIN
  Fast Food 399
  UHF 428
MCCAUGHAN, CHARLES
  Slaves of New York 424
MACCHIO, RALPH
  Karate Kid III, The 407
MCCLOSKEY, LEIGH
  Cameron's Closet 392
MCCLURE, MARC
  After Midnight 388
MCCOMB, HEATHER
  New York Stories 257
MCCOO, MARILYN
  My Mom's a Werewolf 413
MCCOWEN, ALEC
  Henry V 173
MCCOY, MATT
  Deepstar Six 396
  Police Academy VI 417
MCDERMOTT, BRIAN
  For Queen and Country
    [1988] 139
MCDERMOTT, DYLAN
  Steel Magnolias 328
MCDONALD, CHRISTOPHER
  Chances Are 392
MCDONALD, MARIA
  Mighty Quinn, The 412
MCDONOUGH, KIT
  Valentino Returns 429
MCDOWALL, RODDY
  Big Picture, The 391
MACDOWELL, ANDIE
  sex, lies and videotape 306
MCEWAN, GERALDINE
  Henry V 173
MCFARLANE, HAMISH
  Navigator, The [1988] 253
MCGANN, PAUL
  Dealers 395
  Rainbow, The 279
MCGILL, BRUCE
  Out Cold 415
MCGILL, EVERETT
  Licence to Kill 221
MCGILLIS, KELLY
  Winter People 430
MCGINLEY, JOHN C.
  Fat Man and Little Boy 399
MCGINLEY, TED
  Physical Evidence 417
MCGOVERN, ELIZABETH
  Johnny Handsome 407
MCGRATH, DEREK
  She's Out of Control 422

MCGUANE, TOM
Cold Feet 393
MCINNERNY, TIM
Erik the Viking 398
MCINTIRE, JOHN
Turner and Hooch 428
MACK, MARION
Obituaries 440
MCKAY, ANTHONY NORMAN
Perfect Model, The 416
MCKEAN, MICHAEL
Big Picture, The 391
Earth Girls Are Easy 397
MCKELLAN, IAN
Scandal 291
MCKENNA, T. P.
Red Scorpion 418
MCKENZIE, JULIA
Shirley Valentine 423
MCKEOWN, CHARLES
Adventures of Baron Munchausen,
The 23
Erik the Viking 398
MCKINNEY, BILL
Kinjite 408
MACLAINE, SHIRLEY
Steel Magnolias 328
MCMILLAN, KENNETH
Obituaries 440
Three Fugitives 426
MCMURRAY, SAM
Wizard, The 431
MCNAMARA, WILLIAM
Dream a Little Dream 396
MACNEE, PATRICK
Masque of the Red Death 411
MACNEIL, PETER
Physical Evidence 417
MACNICOL, PETER
Fakebook 398
Ghostbusters II 151
MCQUEEN, ARMELIA
No Holds Barred 415
MCQUEEN, SIMON
Trust Me 428
MCRAE, FRANK
Farewell to the King 399
Licence to Kill 221
Lock Up 409
MACVITTIE, BRUCE
January Man, The 406
MCWHIRTER, JILLIAN
After Midnight 388
MADDALENA, JULIE
To Die For 427
MADIGAN, AMY
Field of Dreams 131
Uncle Buck 364
MADONNA
Bloodhounds of Broadway 391
MADORSKY, BRYAN
Parents 416
MADSEN, MICHAEL
Kill Me Again 407

MADSEN, VIRGINIA
Heart of Dixie 403
MAEDA, GIN
Tora-San Goes to Vienna 427
MAGGIO, PUPELLA
Cinema Paradiso 74
MAGHSOUDLOU, BAHMAN
Suitors, The 426
MAGNUSON, ANN
Checking Out 392
MAGRATH, GAVIN
Babar 389
MAHLER, BRUCE
Police Academy VI 417
MAHONEY, JOCK
Obituaries 440
Say Anything 287
MÄKELA, KONSTA
Talvisota 336
MÄKELA, TANELI
Talvisota 336
MALIKYAN, KEVORK
Indiana Jones and the Last
Crusade 193
MALINA, JUDITH
American Stories 389
Enemies, A Love Story 119
MALONEY, MICHAEL
Henry V 173
MALSON, TERE
Escape from Safehaven 398
MAN, WU KIN
Life Is Cheap 408
MANDEL, HOWIE
Little Monsters 409
MANDYLOR, COSTAS
Triumph of the Spirit 351
MANES, GINA
Obituaries 440
MANGANO, SILVANO
Obituaries 440
MANGASARIAN, VACHEH
Guests of Hotel Astoria,
The 402
MANN, LEONARD
Silent Night, Deadly
Night III 423
MANN, WESLEY
Who's Harry Crumb? 430
MANOFF, DINAH
Staying Together 323
MANOLIKAKIS, ANDREAS
Ice House 405
MANTELLO, JOE
Cookie 394
MANVILLE, LESLIE
High Hopes [1988] 177
MARCIANO, DAVID
Hellbent 403
MARGOLIS, LAURA
God's Will 402
MARIE, MADELEINE
Camille Claudel [1988] 68
MARIN, CHEECH
Rude Awakening 421

MARIN, JASON
Little Mermaid, The 225
MARISCHKA, GEORGE
Rose Garden, The 421
MARKLE, PAUL
Eddie and the Cruisers II 397
MARS, KENNETH
Little Mermaid, The 225
Police Academy VI 417
MARSHALL, CLARE
Purgatory 418
MARSHALL, E. G.
National Lampoon's Christmas
Vacation 413
MARTELL, LEON
Stepfather II 425
MARTIN, ANDREA
Rude Awakening 421
Worth Winning 431
MARTIN, DAN
Casualties of War 71
MARTIN, NAN
Animal Behavior 389
MARTIN, PEPPER
Mutant on the Bounty 413
MARTIN, SHARLENE
Friday the 13th Part VIII 401
MARTIN, STEVE
Parenthood 267
MARTINE, DANIEL
Cage 392
MARTINEZ, A
She-Devil 310
MARZBAN, MOHSEN
Guests of Hotel Astoria,
The 402
MASK, ACE
Return of the Swamp Thing,
The 419
MASSEY, DANIEL
Scandal 291
MASSEY, MARISOL
Second Sight 422
MASTERSON, MARY STUART
Chances Are 392
Immediate Family 185
MASTRANTONIO, MARY
ELIZABETH
Abyss, The 19
January Man, The 406
MASTROIANNI, ARMAND
Relentless 419
MASUOKA, TORU
Taxing Woman's Return, A
[1988] 348
MASUR, RICHARD
Far from Home 399
MATHESON, DAVID
Eddie and the Cruisers II 397
MATHESON, TIM
Speed Zone 424
MATHEWS, JON
Animal Behavior 389

MATSUDA, YUSAKU
  Black Rain   52
  Obituaries   440
MATZ, JERRY
  American Stories   389
  Lodz Ghetto   410
MAUDE-ROXBY, RODDY
  How to Get Ahead in
    Advertising   404
MAUR-THORP, SARAH
  Edge of Sanity   397
MAYER, CHARLES
  American Stories   389
MAYRON, GALE
  Heart of Midnight   403
MAYRON, MELANIE
  Checking Out   392
MAZURSKY, PAUL
  Enemies, A Love Story   119
  Scenes from the Class Struggle
    in Beverly Hills   295
MEBS, GUDRUN
  Sunday's Child   426
MEEK, JEFFREY
  Winter People   430
MEILLON, JOHN
  Everlasting Secret Family,
    The   398
MELE, NICK
  Nightmare on Elm Street V   414
MELFORD, JILL
  Edge of Sanity   397
MEMEL, STEVEN
  I, Madman   405
MENDELSOHN, BOB
  Cold Feet   393
MERRITT, THERESA
  Astonished   389
METCALF, LAURIE
  Uncle Buck   364
METTE, NANCY
  Meet the Hollowheads   411
METZLER, JIM
  976-EVIL   415
MEYER, JEFF
  Amanda   388
MIANO, ROBERT
  Midnight   411
  Ministry of Vengeance   412
MIAO, CORA
  Eat a Bowl of Tea   111
  Life Is Cheap   408
MICHAELS, JULIE
  Road House   420
MICHEL, ALBERT, JR.
  Crack House   394
MIDKIFF, DALE
  Pet Sematary   271
MIKASA, MICHAEL
  Savage Beach   421
MIKUNI, RENTARO
  Free and Easy   400
  Taxing Woman's Return, A
    [1988]   348
MILER, DICK
  Far from Home   399

MILES, SYLVIA
  She-Devil   310
MILFORD, PENELOPE
  Heathers   168
MILITARY, FRANK
  Dead Bang   395
MILLER, DENNIS
  Everlasting Secret Family,
    The   398
MILLER, HARVEY
  New Year's Day   414
MILLER, JOSHUA
  Meet the Hollowheads   411
  Teen Witch   426
MILLER, LYNN
  Ice House   405
MILLER, MAGGIE MAE
  Cage   392
MILLER, PENELOPE ANN
  Dead Bang   395
MILLS, RICHARD
  Milk and Honey   412
MILLS-COCKELL, JUNO
  Parents   416
MIN, CHENG KWAN
  Life Is Cheap   408
MIN LUONG
  Gleaming the Cube   401
MING, LAU SIU
  Eat a Bowl of Tea   111
MINTER, KELLY
  Miracle Mile   413
  Nightmare on Elm Street V   414
MIOU-MIOU
  Lectrice, La [1988]   213
MIQUEL, JOELLE
  Four Adventures of Reinette and
    Mirabelle [1986]   143
MIRANDA, ROBERT
  Sons   424
MIRKOVICH, TIMOTHY BURR
  Friday the 13th Part VIII   401
MIRREN, HELEN
  When the Whales Came   430
MITCHELL, HEATHER
  Everlasting Secret Family,
    The   398
MITCHELL, JOHN CAMERON
  Misplaced   413
MITCHELL, WILLIAM
  Amanda   388
MITCHELL-SMITH, ILAN
  Identity Crisis   405
MIYAMOTO, NOBUKO
  Taxing Woman's Return, A
    [1988]   348
MIYORI, KIM
  Big Picture, The   391
  Loverboy   410
MODINE, MATTHEW
  Gross Anatomy   402
MOFFAT, DONALD
  Music Box   241
MOKAE, ZAKES
  Dad   86

  Dry White Season, A   107
  Gross Anatomy   402
MOLINA, ALFRED
  Manifesto   411
MOLL, RICHARD
  Wicked Stepmother   430
MOONEY, LAURA
  She's Out of Control   422
MOONEY, MAUREEN
  Hell High   403
MOORE, ALVY
  Horrow Show, The   404
MOORE, DEMI
  We're No Angels   376
MOORE, DUDLEY
  Adventures of Milo and Otis,
    The   388
MOORE, FRANK
  Food of the Gods II   400
MOORE, IRENE
  New Year's Day   414
MOORE, MATTHEW
  Fly II, The   400
MOORE, MELBA
  All Dogs Go to Heaven   27
MOORE, MICHAEL
  Roger and Me   283
MOORE, TERRY
  Beverly Hills Brats   390
MOPHID, SORAYA
  Guests of Hotel Astoria,
    The   402
MORALES, ESAI
  Bloodhounds of Broadway   391
MORAN, MICHAEL P.
  Physical Evidence   417
MORANIS, RICK
  Ghostbusters II   151
  Honey, I Shrunk the Kids   181
  Parenthood   267
MORITA, NORIYUKI "PAT"
  Karate Kid III, The   407
MOROFF, MIKE
  Cage   392
MORRIS, ALEX
  Riverbend   420
MORRIS, ANITA
  Bloodhounds of Broadway   391
  Sinful Life, A   423
MORRISON, ERNIE
  Obituaries   441
MORRISON, GLORIA
  Midnight   411
MORRISSETTE, BILLY
  Catch Me If You Can   392
MORSHOWER, GLENN
  Eighty-Four Charlie MoPic   115
MORTON, JOE
  Tap   344
MOSELEY, BILL
  Silent Night, Deadly
    Night III   423
MOSS, ARNOLD
  Obituaries   441

MOSTEL, JOSH
Animal Behavior 389
MOTHUPI, COLLIN
Cheetah 393
MOUNTEN, LIBERTY
Bert Rigby, You're a Fool 390
MOYNIHAN, MAURA
Slaves of New York 424
MPOFU, BEKHITHEMBA
Dry White Season, A 107
MUELLER-STAHL, ARMIN
Music Box 241
MULLER, KATARINA LENA
Rose Garden, The 421
MULLER, ROLF
Cyborg 395
MULLIGAN, PAT
Kill Me Again 407
MULLINAR, ROD
Echoes of Paradise 397
MULRONEY, DERMOT
Staying Together 323
MURPHY, CHARLES Q.
Harlem Nights 164
MURPHY, EDDIE
Harlem Nights 164
MURPHY, MICHAEL
Game, The 401
Shocker 423
MURRAY, BILL
Ghostbusters II 151
MURRAY, BRIAN-DOYLE
How I Got into College 404
MUZA, MELVIN
Street Story 425

NAGASE, MASATOSHI
Mystery Train 249
NAGAYAMA, KEN
Best of the Best 390
NAGOURNEY, NICHOLAS B.
Fun Down There 401
NAKASAKO, SPENCER
Life Is Cheap 408
NANO, AGNESE
Cinema Paradiso 74
NAPIER, CHARLES
Hit List 404
NAPIER, MARSHALL
Navigator, The [1988] 253
NASSAR, DEBORAH ANN
Dance of the Damned 395
NATH, RAGHU
Spices 425
NATHANSON, ROY
American Stories 389
NAVAB, SHAHAB
Suitors, The 426
NAVAL, DEEPTI
Spices 425
NAYYAR, HARSH
Slaves of New York 424
NAZAROV, YURI
Little Vera 409

NEESON, LIAM
Next of Kin 414
NEGODA, NATALYA
Little Vera 409
NEILL, SAM
Dead Calm 395
NEJAD, NASER RAHMANY
Guests of Hotel Astoria,
The 402
NELSON, CRAIG T.
Troop Beverly Hills 427
Turner and Hooch 428
NELSON, JUDD
Relentless 419
NEUMAN, FRED
Astonished 389
NEVILLE, JOHN
Adventures of Baron Munchausen,
The 23
NEWLAND, JOHN
Purgatory 418
NEWMAN, PAUL
Blaze 56
Fat Man and Little Boy 399
NEWMANN, FREDERICK
Lodz Ghetto 410
NEWTON, WAYNE
Licence to Kill 221
NGAI, BONNIE
Life Is Cheap 408
NGOR, HAING S.
Iron Triangle, The 406
NGUYEN, KIEU CHINH
Welcome Home 429
NICHOLAS, HAROLD
Tap 344
NICHOLS, NICHELLE
Star Trek V 319
NICHOLSON, JACK
Batman 40
NICKLAS, JAN
Rose Garden, The 421
NIEMEIER, MIRJAM
Sunday's Child 426
NIGHY, BILL
Phantom of the Opera, The 417
NIKKARI, ESKO
Talvisota 336
NIMOY, LEONARD
Star Trek V 319
NISHIDA, TOSHIYUKI
Free and Easy 400
NOBLE, JAMES
Chances Are 392
NOIRET, PHILIPPE
Cinema Paradiso 74
Life and Nothing But 408
Return of the Musketeers,
The 419
NOLTE, NICK
Farewell to the King 399
New York Stories 257
Three Fugitives 426
NOONAN, TOM
Mystery Train 249

NORGAARD, CARSTEN
Wonderland 431
NORMAN, JOHN
Riverbend 420
NORTH, ALAN
Lean on Me 209
Penn and Teller Get Killed 416
See No Evil, Hear No Evil 302
NOVELLO, DON
New York Stories 257
NOZAD, KAMRAN
Guests of Hotel Astoria,
The 402
NOZIK, BRUCE
American Stories 389
NTSHINGA, THOKO
Dry White Season, A 107
NTSHONA, WINSTON
Dry White Season, A 107
NUNEZ, MIGUEL
Harlem Nights 164
NUNN, BILL
Do the Right Thing 94

OBEROI, SURESH
Spices 425
OBERON, ELAN
Farewell to the King 399
OBREGON, RODRIGO
Savage Beach 421
O'BRIEN, KEVIN
Warlock 429
O'BRIEN, TOM
Physical Evidence 417
O'BRYAN, PATRICK
976-EVIL 415
Relentless 419
O'CONNELL, DEIRDRE
Misplaced 413
O'CONNOR, DERRICK
Dealers 395
Lethal Weapon II 217
O'CONNOR, KEVIN J.
Signs of Life 423
Steel Magnolias 328
O'CONOR, HUGH
My Left Foot 245
OFFNER, DEBORAH
American Stories 389
OKERLUND, GENE
No Holds Barred 415
OKUMOTO, YUJI
True Believer 356
OLDMAN, GARY
Criminal Law 394
O'LEARY, JOHN
Stepfather II 425
O'LEARY, WILLIAM
Lost Angels 410
OLIN, LENA
Enemies, A Love Story 119
OLIVER, BARRET
Scenes from the Class Struggle
in Beverly Hills 295

OLIVERI, ROBERT
  Honey, I Shrunk the Kids   181
OLIVIER, LAURENCE
  Obituaries   441
OLMOS, EDWARD JAMES
  Triumph of the Spirit   351
O'MARA, MOLLIE
  Escape from Safehaven   398
O'NEAL, PATRICK
  New York Stories   257
O'NEAL, RYAN
  Chances Are   392
O'NEILL, AMY
  Honey, I Shrunk the Kids   181
O'NEILL, DICK
  She's Out of Control   422
O'NEILL, ED
  Disorganized Crime   396
  K-9   205
O'NEILL, REMY
  To Die For   427
ONNISMAA, MATTI
  Talvisota   336
ONO, MIYUKI
  Black Rain   52
ONSONGO, PAUL
  Cheetah   393
ONSUM, GARY
  Fun Down There   401
O'QUINN, TERRY
  Stepfather II   425
ORBACH, JERRY
  Crimes and Misdemeanors   82
O'REILLY, CYRIL
  Dance of the Damned   395
ORLANDINI, HAL
  Purgatory   418
ORR, JAMES
  Hellbent   403
ORSINI, MARINA
  Eddie and the Cruisers II   397
O'SHEA, MILO
  Dream Team, The   397
OSTERHAGE, JEFF
  Masque of the Red Death   411
OSTRICHE, MURIEL
  Obituaries   441
OUIMETTE, STEPHEN
  Babar   389
OVERTON, RICK
  Earth Girls Are Easy   397
  Sinful Life, A   423

PAAVILAINEN, HEIKKI
  Talvisota   336
PACINO, AL
  Sea of Love   299
PACKER, DAVID
  Trust Me   428
PADDOCK, CAROLINE
  Fun Down There   401
PAGE, KEN
  All Dogs Go to Heaven   27

PALANCE, JACK
  Batman   40
  Tango and Cash   340
PALMER, DAVID
  No Holds Barred   415
PALOMINO, CARLOS
  Silent Night, Deadly
    Night III   423
PANKIN, STUART
  Second Sight   422
PARAGON, JOHN
  UHF   428
PARE, MICHAEL
  Eddie and the Cruisers II   397
PARFITT, JUDY
  Getting It Right   147
PARKER, COREY
  Big Man on Campus   390
  How I Got into College   404
PARKER, DAVID
  Valentino Returns   429
PARKER, MARY LOUISE
  Signs of Life   423
PARKER, SUNSHINE
  Road House   420
PARKES, GERARD
  January Man, The   406
PARKS, CATHERINE
  Weekend at Bernie's   429
PARRISH, STEVE
  Midnight   411
PARTON, DOLLY
  Steel Magnolias   328
PASDAR, ADRIAN
  Cookie   394
PASMUR, IRINA
  American Stories   389
PASTORE, VINNY
  True Love   360
PATERSON, BILL
  Adventures of Baron Munchausen,
    The   23
PATIL, SMITA
  Spices   425
PATON, LAURIE
  Physical Evidence   417
PATRICK, GREGORY
  Bad Blood   390
PATRICK, RANDAL
  Fast Food   399
PATTERSON, BILL
  Rachel Papers, The   418
PAUL, ADRIAN
  Masque of the Red Death   411
PAUL, DON MICHAEL
  Heart of Dixie   403
  Winter People   430
PAULIN, SCOTT
  Turner and Hooch   428
PAULL, MORGAN
  Out Cold   415
PAWLICK, AMBER
  Friday the 13th Part VIII   401
PAX, JAMES
  Kinjite   408

PAXTON, BILL
  Next of Kin   414
PAYNE, ALLEN
  Rooftops   421
PAYNE, BRUCE
  For Queen and Country
    [1988]   139
  Wonderland   431
PAYNE, JOHN
  Obituaries   442
PEARCE, ADRIENNE
  American Ninja III   388
  Purgatory   418
PEARCE, HELEN
  When the Whales Came   430
PEARCE, JACQUELINE
  How to Get Ahead in
    Advertising   404
PECK, GREGORY
  Life Achievement Award   1
  Old Gringo   262
PECORARO, JOE
  Harlem Nights   164
PEEL, DAVID
  Rude Awakening   421
PEEPLES, NIA
  Deepstar Six   396
PELLEGRINO, MARK
  No Holds Barred   415
PELLETIER, GILLES
  Jesus of Montreal   201
PENHALL, BRUCE
  Savage Beach   421
PENN. See JILLETTE, PENN
PENN, CHRISTOPHER
  Best of the Best   390
PENN, SEAN
  Casualties of War   71
  We're No Angels   376
PERETZ, SUSAN
  Sing   424
PEREZ, ROSIE
  Do the Right Thing   94
PERKINS, ANTHONY
  Edge of Sanity   397
PERLICH, MAX
  Drugstore Cowboy   103
PERRIER, MIREILLE
  Chocolat   393
PERRIN, JACQUES
  Cinema Paradiso   74
PERROT, FRANÇOIS
  Life and Nothing But   408
PERRY, BARBARA
  Trust Me   428
PERRY, FELTON
  Checking Out   392
PERRY, MATTHEW L.
  She's Out of Control   422
PERSKY, LISA JANE
  When Harry Met Sally   380
PESCE, FRANK
  Relentless   419

PESCE, FRANK
  Relentless 419
PESCI, JOE
  Lethal Weapon II 217
PETERS, BERNADETTE
  Pink Cadillac 417
  Slaves of New York 424
PETERS, ELISEBETH
  She-Devil 310
PETERS, JOEY
  Ministry of Vengeance 412
PETERS, VIRGINIA
  Stripped to Kill II 425
PETERSEN, WILLIAM
  Cousins 394
PETERSON, AMANDA
  Listen to Me 409
PETERSON, HALEY
  Cyborg 395
PFEIFFER, DEDEE
  Horrow Show, The 404
PFEIFFER, MICHELLE
  Fabulous Baker Boys, The 123
PHILIPS, EMO
  UHF 428
PHILLIPS, ETHAN
  Bloodhounds of Broadway 391
  Lean on Me 209
PHILLIPS, JULIANNE
  Fletch Lives 135
  Skin Deep 424
PHILLIPS, LESLIE
  Scandal 291
PHILLIPS, LOU DIAMOND
  Disorganized Crime 396
  Renegades 419
PHILLIPS, SIAN
  Valmont 368
PHILLIPS, WENDY
  Wizard, The 431
PHOENIX, LEAF
  Parenthood 267
PHOENIX, RIVER
  Indiana Jones and the Last
    Crusade 193
PICCARDO, ROBERT
  976-EVIL 415
PICKETT, CINDY
  Deepstar Six 396
PIERSE, SARAH
  Navigator, The [1988] 253
PILEGGI, MITCH
  Shocker 423
PINCHOT, BRONSON
  Second Sight 422
PINSENT, GORDON
  Babar 389
PISTILLI, CARL
  Severance 422
PLANA, TONY
  Romero 420
PLANCHON, ROGER
  Camille Claudel [1988] 68

PLEASENCE, DONALD
  Halloween V 402
  River of Death 420
PLIMPTON, MARTHA
  Parenthood 267
PO, TONG
  Kickboxer 407
PODEWELL, CATHY
  Beverly Hills Brats 390
POLIZOS, VIC
  Harlem Nights 164
POLLARD, MICHAEL J.
  Fast Food 399
  Next of Kin 414
  Night Visitor 414
  Season of Fear 421
  Tango and Cash 340
POLLEY, SARAH
  Adventures of Baron Munchausen,
    The 23
  Babar 389
POP, JULIE
  Purgatory 418
PORIZKOVA, PAULINA
  Her Alibi 404
PORTER, ALISAN
  Parenthood 267
PORTNOW, RICHARD
  Meet the Hollowheads 411
PORTSER, MARY
  True Love 360
POTTER, MADELEINE
  Slaves of New York 424
POTTS, ANNIE
  Ghostbusters II 151
  Who's Harry Crumb? 430
POURAN
  Suitors, The 426
POWELL, MARCUS
  Escape from Safehaven 398
PRESLE, MICHELINE
  I Want to Go Home 405
PRESTON, GRANT
  American Ninja III 388
PREZIOSO, MILLIE
  Hell High 403
PRINCE, WILLIAM
  Second Sight 422
PRINGLE, AILEEN
  Obituaries 442
PRINGLE, BRYAN
  Getting It Right 147
PROCHNOW, JURGEN
  Dry White Season, A 107
PROVAL, DAVID
  UHF 428
PRYCE, JONATHAN
  Adventures of Baron Munchausen,
    The 23
  Rachel Papers, The 418
PRYOR, RICHARD
  Harlem Nights 164
  See No Evil, Hear No Evil 302
PULLMAN, BILL
  Cold Feet 393

PURI, OM
  Spices 425
PURVIS, JACK
  Adventures of Baron Munchausen,
    The 23

QUAID, BUDDY
  Ice House 405
QUAID, DENNIS
  Great Balls of Fire! 160
QUAID, RANDY
  Bloodhounds of Broadway 391
  National Lampoon's Christmas
    Vacation 413
  Out Cold 415
  Parents 416
QUAYLE, ANTHONY
  Obituaries 442
QUESTEL, MAE
  National Lampoon's Christmas
    Vacation 413
  New York Stories 257
QUILL, TIM
  Listen to Me 409
  Staying Together 323
QUINE, RICHARD
  Obituaries 442
QUINN, J. C.
  Abyss, The 19
  Gross Anatomy 402
  Turner and Hooch 428
QUINN, MARTHA
  Eddie and the Cruisers II 397

RAAB, ELLIE
  Fabulous Baker Boys, The 123
RADELL, DANIEL
  Ministry of Vengeance 412
RADNER, GILDA
  Obituaries 442
RAIMI, THEODORE
  Shocker 423
RAIVIO, ANTTI
  Talvisota 336
RALPH, SHERYL LEE
  Mighty Quinn, The 412
RAMIREZ, LYDIA
  Street Story 425
RAMIS, HAROLD
  Ghostbusters II 151
RAMSEY, ANNE
  Meet the Hollowheads 411
RAMSEY, LOGAN
  Meet the Hollowheads 411
RAMSEY, MARION
  Police Academy VI 417
RANDALL, TONY
  It Had to Be You 406
RANDOLPH, JOHN
  National Lampoon's Christmas
    Vacation 413
RAPP, ANTHONY
  Far from Home 399
RASCHE, DAVID
  Innocent Man, An 406
  Wicked Stepmother 430

RASHAD, AHMAD
  Best of the Best   390
RATCHFORD, JEREMY
  Welcome Home   429
RATRAY, DEVIN
  Little Monsters   409
  Worth Winning   431
RAVENSCROFT, CHRISTOPHER
  Henry V   173
RAWSON, EMMA
  Phantom of the Opera, The   417
RAY, UNCLE
  Harlem Nights   164
RAYMOND, BILL
  How I Got into College   404
RAYSON, BEN
  Cookie   394
REA, PEGGY
  In Country   189
REDGRAVE, LYNN
  Getting It Right   147
  Midnight   411
REDMAN, AMANDA
  For Queen and Country
  [1988]   139
REED, ALYSON
  Skin Deep   424
REED, OLIVER
  Adventures of Baron Munchausen,
    The   23
  Return of the Musketeers,
    The   419
REESE, DELLA
  Harlem Nights   164
REEVES, KEANU
  Bill and Ted's Excellent
    Adventure   48
  Parenthood   267
REEVES, SCOTT
  Friday the 13th Part VIII   401
REGION, DANIEL
  God's Will   402
REGISTER, MEG
  Ministry of Vengeance   412
REGOPSTAAN
  Red Scorpion   418
REID, FIONA
  Milk and Honey   412
REID, KATE
  Signs of Life   423
REID, TIM
  Dead Bang   395
REILLY, CHARLES NELSON
  All Dogs Go to Heaven   27
REILLY, JOHN C.
  Casualties of War   71
  We're No Angels   376
REINER, TRACY
  Masque of the Red Death   411
  New Year's Day   414
REMAR, JAMES
  Dream Team, The   397
REMSEN, BERT
  Miss Firecracker   237
RENNIE, MAX
  When the Whales Came   430

REX, GREG
  Rude Awakening   421
REY, REYNALDO
  Harlem Nights   164
REYNOLDS, BURT
  All Dogs Go to Heaven   27
  Breaking In   391
  Physical Evidence   417
REYNOLDS, LARRY
  Physical Evidence   417
RHAMES, VING
  Casualties of War   71
RHEE, PHILLIP
  Best of the Best   390
RHEE, SIMON
  Best of the Best   390
RHOADES, BARBARA
  Out Cold   415
RHOADES, MICHAEL
  Eddie and the Cruisers II   397
RHYS-DAVIES, JOHN
  Indiana Jones and the Last
    Crusade   193
RICHARD, JUNIOR
  Hit List   404
RICHARDS, ARIANA
  Prancer   418
RICHARDS, MICHAEL
  UHF   428
RICHARDSON, LEE
  Fly II, The   400
RICHARDSON, NATHASHA
  Fat Man and Little Boy   399
RICHARDSON, PATRICIA
  Lost Angels   410
RICHARDSON, SY
  Kinjite   408
  Mystery Train   249
RICHMAN, PETER MARK
  Friday the 13th Part VIII   401
RICHMOND, BRANSCOMBE
  Cage   392
RICHTER, DEBORAH
  Cyborg   395
RICHWINE, MARIA
  Ministry of Vengeance   412
RICKMAN, ALAN
  January Man, The   406
RICO, PAT
  Tap   344
RIDDICK, GEORGE
  Sidewalk Stories   315
RIDINGS, RICHARD
  Erik the Viking   398
RIGNACK, ROGER
  True Love   360
RITTER, JOHN
  Skin Deep   424
RIVERO, GEORGE
  Fistfighter   400
RIVIERE, MARIE
  Four Adventures of Reinette and
    Mirabelle [1986]   143
RIZACOS, ANGELO
  Physical Evidence   417

ROARKE, JOHN
  Mutant on the Bounty   413
ROBARDS, JASON
  Dream a Little Dream   396
  Parenthood   267
ROBARDS, SAM
  Casualties of War   71
ROBBINS, TIM
  Erik the Viking   398
  Miss Firecracker   237
ROBERT, QUARRY
  Sexbomb   422
ROBERTS, DARRYL
  Perfect Model, The   416
ROBERTS, DORIS
  National Lampoon's Christmas
    Vacation   413
ROBERTS, ERIC
  Best of the Best   390
  Rude Awakening   421
ROBERTS, FRANCESCA
  Heart of Dixie   403
ROBERTS, JULIA
  Steel Magnolias   328
ROBERTS, TANYA
  Purgatory   418
ROBERTSON, GEORGE R.
  Police Academy VI   417
ROBERTSON, JENNY
  Heart of Dixie   403
ROBINS, LAILA
  Innocent Man, An   406
ROBINSON, MADELEINE
  Camille Claudel [1988]   68
ROCHON, LELA
  Harlem Nights   164
ROCKET, CHARLES
  Earth Girls Are Easy   397
  How I Got into College   404
ROCKSAVAGE, DAVID
  Four Adventures of Reinette and
    Mirabelle [1986]   143
ROEBUCK, DANIEL
  Disorganized Crime   396
ROESKE, FIONA
  Who's Harry Crumb?   430
ROGERS, MIMI
  Mighty Quinn, The   412
ROHNER, CLAYTON
  I, Madman   405
ROLLE, ESTHER
  Driving Miss Daisy   99
  Mighty Quinn, The   412
ROLSTON, MARK
  Sinful Life, A   423
ROMAND, BÉATRICE
  Four Adventures of Reinette and
    Mirabelle [1986]   143
ROMANO, ANDY
  Major League   233
ROOKER, MICHAEL
  Music Box   241
  Sea of Love   299
ROONEY, MICKEY
  Erik the Viking   398

ROSE, KATHERINE
  Distribution of Lead, The   396
ROSELLA, GAIL KAPPLER
  Amanda   388
ROSEN, HERSCHEL
  American Stories   389
ROSENBLAT, BARBARA
  Lodz Ghetto   410
ROSENFELS, JOAN
  American Stories   389
ROSS, CHELCIE
  Major League   233
ROSS, RICHARD LEE
  Game, The   401
ROSSELLINI, ISABELLA
  Cousins   394
ROSSETTER, KATHY
  Hell High   403
ROSSI, LEO
  Hit List   404
  Relentless   419
ROTHROCK, CYNTHIA
  No Retreat, No Surrender II   415
ROUNDTREE, RICHARD
  Crack House   394
  Night Visitor   414
ROURKE, MICKEY
  Johnny Handsome   407
ROUSE, HUGH
  Purgatory   418
ROWE, ELY
  Distribution of Lead, The   396
ROXS, HOWARD
  Fun Down There   401
ROYER, RÉGIS
  Lectrice, La [1988]   213
RUBELL, MARIA
  976-EVIL   415
RUBEN, TOM
  Dance of the Damned   395
  Stripped to Kill II   425
RUBENS, HERBERT
  American Stories   389
RUBIN, JERRY
  Rude Awakening   421
RUBINSTEIN, ZELDA
  Teen Witch   426
RUCHÉ, CHRISTIAN
  Lectrice, La [1988]   213
RUCK, ALAN
  Three Fugitives   426
RUEHL, MERCEDES
  Slaves of New York   424
RUGGIERO, ALLELON
  Dead Poets Society   90
RUPPEL, ACHIM
  Rose Garden, The   421
RUSCIO, AL
  Cage   392
RUSH, DEBORAH
  Parents   416
RUSHTON, JARED
  Honey, I Shrunk the Kids   181

RUSS, WILLIAM
  Disorganized Crime   396
RUSSELL, KAREN
  Hell High   403
RUSSELL, KURT
  Tango and Cash   340
  Winter People   430
RUSSELL, THERESA
  Physical Evidence   417
RUSSO, AARON
  Rude Awakening   421
RUSSO, DANIEL
  Life and Nothing But   408
RUSSO, JAMES
  We're No Angels   376
RUSSO, RENE
  Major League   233
RUTTAN, SUSAN
  Chances Are   392
RYAN, EILEEN
  Parenthood   267
  Winter People   430
RYAN, FRAN
  Chances Are   392
  Out Cold   415
RYAN, JOHN P.
  Best of the Best   390
RYAN, KEN
  Astonished   389
RYAN, MEG
  When Harry Met Sally   380
RYAN, MITCHEL
  Winter People   430
RYANE, MELODY
  Lords of the Deep   410
RYDALL, DEREK
  Night Visitor   414
RYDELL, CHRISTOPHER
  How I Got into College   404
RYDER, WINONA
  Great Balls of Fire!   160
  Heathers   168
RYU, CHISHU
  Tora-San Goes to Vienna   427

SAA, YVONNE
  Terror Within, The   426
SACHS, ADRIANNE
  Best of the Best   390
SAGAL, JOEY
  Return of the Swamp Thing,
    The   419
SÄGEBRECHT, MARIANNE
  War of the Roses, The   372
SAINDON, PAUL
  Fun Down There   401
SALATA, GREGORY
  Weekend at Bernie's   429
SALAZAR, LEONARD PORTER
  Lost Angels   410
SALEM, KARIO
  Triumph of the Spirit   351
SALENGER, MEREDITH
  Dream a Little Dream   396

SALMELA, TOMI
  Talvisota   336
SALMI, ALBERT
  Breaking In   391
SAMAAN, NURITH-HAYAT
  Sunday's Child   426
SANDS, JULIAN
  Warlock   429
SAN GIACOMO, LAURA
  sex, lies and videotape   306
SARANDON, CHRIS
  Slaves of New York   424
SARANDON, SUSAN
  Dry White Season, A   107
  January Man, The   406
SARFATI, ASHER
  Riding the Edge   420
SARGENT, DICK
  Teen Witch   426
SARNE, MICHAEL
  Riding the Edge   420
SARTAIN, GAILARD
  Blaze   56
SAVAGE, BEN
  Little Monsters   409
SAVAGE, FRED
  Little Monsters   409
  Wizard, The   430
SAVAGE, JOHN
  Do the Right Thing   94
SAWYER, CONNIE
  Far from Home   399
SAXON, JOHN
  My Mom's a Werewolf   413
SBARGE, RAPHAEL
  Riding the Edge   420
SCALES, PRUNELLA
  Chorus of Disapproval, A   393
SCHAAL, WENDY
  'Burbs, The   65
SCHACHT, SAM
  Heart of Midnight   403
SCHAEFFER, REBECCA
  Obituaries   443
  Scenes from the Class Struggle
    in Beverly Hills   295
SCHEIDER, ROY
  Listen to Me   409
  Night Game   414
SCHELL, MAXIMILIAN
  Rose Garden, The   421
SCHIAVELLI, VINCENT
  Cold Feet   393
SCHICKEL, ERIKA
  Toxic Avenger, Part II, The   427
SCHILLER, DANNY
  Erik the Viking   398
SCHMIDINGER, WALTER
  Hanussen   403
SCHNABBE, TIMM
  Sunday's Child   426
SCHNEIDER, DAN
  Big Picture, The   391

SCHNEIDER, JOHN
  Ministry of Vengeance   412
  Speed Zone   424
SCHOEFFING, MICHAEL
  Slaves of New York   424
SCHOELEN, JILL
  Phantom of the Opera, The   417
SCHRAGE, LISA
  Food of the Gods II   400
SCHUCK, JOHN
  My Mom's a Werewolf   413
  Second Sight   422
SCHULTZ, DWIGHT
  Fat Man and Little Boy   399
SCHULTZ, JEFF
  Buying Time   391
SCHWAN, IVYANN
  Parenthood   267
SCIORRA, ANNABELLA
  True Love   360
SCOFIELD, PAUL
  Henry V   173
  When the Whales Came   430
SCOTT, KIMBERLY
  Abyss, The   19
SCOTT, RENATA
  Stepfather II   425
SCOTT, TASHA
  Troop Beverly Hills   427
SCULLY, SAMANTHA
  Best of the Best   390
  Silent Night, Deadly
    Night III   423
SEALE, BOBBY
  Rude Awakening   421
SEARS, DJANET
  Milk and Honey   412
SECOR, KYLE
  Heart of Dixie   403
SEDGWICK, KYRA
  Born on the Fourth of July   60
SEEGER, MINDY
  Relentless   419
SEELY, JOE
  Nightmare on Elm Street V   414
SEGAL, GEORGE
  All's Fair   388
  Look Who's Talking   229
SEGALL, PAMELA
  After Midnight   388
SEKI, DANN
  Savage Beach   421
SEKINE, TSUTAMU
  Toxic Avenger, Part II, The   427
  Erik the Viking   398
SELLECK, TOM
  Her Alibi   404
  Innocent Man, An   406
SELTZER, WILL
  Wizard, The   430
SENTIER, JEAN-PIERRE
  Camille Claudel [1988]   68
SERATO, MASSIMO
  Obituaries   443
SEROTTI, KAYLA
  Fun Down There   401

SEVERANCE, JOAN
  No Holds Barred   415
  See No Evil, Hear No Evil   302
SHADIX, GLENN
  Heathers   168
SHAFF, COREY
  Distribution of Lead, The   396
SHAH, NASEERUDDIN
  Spices   425
SHAHINIAN, SHARON
  Escape from Safehaven   398
SHAKMAN, MATT
  Meet the Hollowheads   411
SHANER, MICHAEL
  Bloodfist   391
  Savage Beach   421
SHANKS, DONALD L.
  Halloween V   402
SHANNON, MOLLY
  Phantom of the Opera, The   417
SHAPIRO, RICK
  True Love   360
SHARKEY, BILLY RAY
  After Midnight   388
SHARKEY, RAY
  Scenes from the Class Struggle
    in Beverly Hills   295
  Wired   384
SHARP, LESLEY
  Rachel Papers, The   418
SHARRETT, MICHAEL
  Kill Me Again   407
SHATNER, WILLIAM
  Star Trek V   319
SHAW, FIONA
  My Left Foot   245
SHAW, HELEN
  Parenthood   267
SHAW, STAN
  Harlem Nights   164
SHAW, VANESS
  Game, The   401
SHAWN, ERICK
  Game, The   401
SHAWN, WALLACE
  Scenes from the Class Struggle
    in Beverly Hills   295
  She's Out of Control   422
  We're No Angels   376
SHEEDY, ALLY
  Heart of Dixie   403
SHEEN, CHARLIE
  Major League   233
SHEEN, MARTIN
  Beverly Hills Brats   390
  Personal Choice   417
SHEEN, RAMON
  Beverly Hills Brats   390
SHEEN, RUTH
  High Hopes [1988]   177
SHELTON, SLOANE
  Jacknife   197
SHEPARD, SAM
  Steel Magnolias   328
SHEPHERD, CYBILL
  Chances Are   392

SHEPHERD, SUZANNE
  Uncle Buck   364
SHER, ANTHONY
  Erik the Viking   398
SHERWOOD, ANTHONY
  Eddie and the Cruisers II   397
SHERWOOD, DAVID
  Purgatory   418
SHIELDS, BROOKE
  Speed Zone   424
SHIGETA, JAMES
  Cage   392
SHIMOJO, MASSAMI
  Tora-San Goes to Vienna   427
SHINDLER, MERRILL
  Eddie and the Cruisers II   397
SHINOBURYU
  Toxic Avenger, Part II, The   427
SHIRE, TALIA
  New York Stories   257
SHOR, DAN
  Bill and Ted's Excellent
    Adventure   48
SHORT, MARTIN
  Big Picture, The   391
  Three Fugitives   426
SHRAPNEL, JOHN
  How to Get Ahead in
    Advertising   404
SHUE, ELISABETH
  Back to the Future Part II   36
SIEGEL, HARVEY
  Bad Blood   390
SIEMASZKO, CASEY
  Back to the Future Part II   36
  Breaking In   391
SIHOL, CAROLINE
  I Want to Go Home   405
SILER, RICK
  Escape from Safehaven   398
  Game, The   401
SILVA, TRINIDAD
  UHF   428
SILVER, CLAUDIA
  American Stories   389
SILVER, RON
  Enemies, A Love Story   119
SILVERMAN, JONATHAN
  Weekend at Bernie's   429
SIMON, JOSETTE
  Milk and Honey   412
SIMS, HOWARD "SANDMAN"
  Harlem Nights   164
  Tap   344
SIMS, SYLVIA
  Shirley Valentine   423
SINCLAIR, JOHN GORDON
  Erik the Viking   398
SINGER, LORI
  Warlock   429
SIZEMORE, TOM
  Lock Up   409
SKERRITT, TOM
  Big Man on Campus   390
  Steel Magnolias   328

SKYE, IONE
Rachel Papers, The 418
Say Anything 287
SLATER, CHRISTIAN
Gleaming the Cube 401
Heathers 168
Personal Choice 417
Wizard, The 430
SLEAN, CHERYL
Hellbent 403
SLOAN, RON
Warm Summer Rain 429
SLUE, ERROL
January Man, The 406
Milk and Honey 412
SLYDE, JIMMY
Tap 344
SMITH, BUBBA
Police Academy VI 417
SMITH, COTTER
Cameron's Closet 392
SMITH, JEANNE
Fun Down There 401
SMITH, KURTWOOD
Dead Poets Society 90
Heart of Dixie 403
True Believer 356
SMITH, LANE
Race for Glory 418
SMITH, ROGER GUENVEUR
Do the Right Thing 94
SMITH, SHAWNEE
Who's Harry Crumb? 430
SMITH, YEARDLY
Ginger Ale Afternoon 401
SMITROVICH, BILL
Renegades 419
SMITS, JIMMY
Old Gringo 262
SMOTHERS, DICK
Speed Zone 424
SMOTHERS, TOM
Speed Zone 424
SNIPES, WESLEY
Major League 233
SNYDER, DREW
Misplaced 413
SNYDER, JOHN
K-9 205
True Believer 356
SOBECK, GREG
Lords of the Deep 410
SOEBERG, CAMILLA
Manifesto 411
SOEHNGEN, SANDRA
Severance 422
SOKOLOV, ANDREI
Little Vera 409
SOLONDZ, TODD
Fear, Anxiety and
Depression 400
SOLTANI, BAHMAN
Suitors, The 426
SOMBART, NICOLAUS
Rose Garden, The 421

SOMERVILLE, GRETSCHEN
Fun Down There 401
SOMMER, JOSEF
Bloodhounds of Broadway 391
Chances Are 392
SORIANO, AQUILINA
Troop Beverly Hills 427
SOTO, TALISA
Licence to Kill 221
SPACEY, KEVIN
Dad 86
See No Evil, Hear No Evil 302
SPADER, JAMES
Rachel Papers, The 418
sex, lies and videotape 306
SPEIR, DONA
Savage Beach 421
SPELVIN, GEORGINA
Bad Blood 390
SPENCER, JOHN
Black Rain 52
SPENCER, PRINCE C.
Harlem Nights 164
SPINELL, JOE
Obituaries 443
SPINKS, MICHAEL
Speed Zone 424
SPRINGSTEEN, PAMELA
Fast Food 399
STALLONE, FRANK
Heart of Midnight 403
STALLONE, SYLVESTER
Lock Up 409
Tango and Cash 340
STANDER, LIONEL
Cookie 394
Wicked Stepmother 430
STANLEIGH, KATHRYN
Sexbomb 422
STANTON, HARRY DEAN
Dream a Little Dream 396
STARR, BEAU
Halloween V 402
Relentless 419
STARR, MIKE
Uncle Buck 364
STARRETT, JACK
Obituaries 443
STEADMAN, ALISON
Shirley Valentine 423
STECKLER, DOUG
Who's Harry Crumb? 430
STEEDMAN, TONY
Bill and Ted's Excellent
Adventure 48
STEEN, JESSICA
Sing 424
STEENBURGEN, MARY
Miss Firecracker 237
Parenthood 267
STEIGER, ROD
January Man, The 406
STEIN, MARGARET SOPHIE
Enemies, A Love Story 119

STEPHENS, ROBERT
Henry V 173
Wonderland 431
STERN, AMANDA
Leviathan 408
STERN, DANIEL
Leviathan 408
Little Monsters 409
STERNHAGEN, FRANCES
Communion 78
See You in the Morning 422
STEVENS, ANDREW
Terror Within, The 426
STEWART, CATHERINE MARY
Riding the Edge 420
Weekend at Bernie's 429
STILLER, BEN
Next of Kin 414
STING
Adventures of Baron Munchausen,
The 23
STOCKER, JOHN
Babar 389
STOCKWELL, DEAN
Buying Time 391
STOLLER, SHIRLEY
Sons 424
STOLTZ, ERIC
Fly II, The 400
Manifesto 411
STONE, SHARON
Personal Choice 417
STOWE, MADELEINE
Worth Winning 431
STRASSMAN, MARCIA
Honey, I Shrunk the Kids 181
STREEP, MERYL
She-Devil 310
STRITZEL, OLIVER
Race for Glory 418
STRUMMER, JOE
Mystery Train 249
STRYKER, CHRISTOPHER
Hell High 403
STUBBS, IMOGEN
Erik the Viking 398
SUCHET, DAVID
When the Whales Came 430
SUGARMAN, SARA
Dealers 395
SUMMER, ROREN
Terror Within, The 426
SUOSALO, MARTTI
Talvisota 336
SURGES, PAT
Nightmare on Elm Street V 414
SUTHERLAND, DONALD
Dry White Season, A 107
Lock Up 409
Lost Angels 410
SUTHERLAND, KIEFER
Renegades 419
SUTHERLAND, KRISTINE
Honey, I Shrunk the Kids 181

SUZMAN, JANET
  Dry White Season, A   107
SWART, RUFUS
  Purgatory   418
SWAYZE, PATRICK
  Next of Kin   414
  Road House   420
SWEENEY, D. B.
  Sons   424
SWEET, RACHEL
  Sing   424
SWOPE, TRACY BROOKS
  Big Picture, The   391
SYLVESTER, HAROLD
  Hit List   404
SZIGETI, CYNTHIA
  Sinful Life, A   423

TAGGART, RITA
  Horrow Show, The   404
TAKAKURA, KEN
  Black Rain   52
TAKEI, GEORGE
  Star Trek V   319
TALMADGE, VICTOR
  American Stories   389
TAN, BIRKE
  Stripped to Kill II   425
TANAMI, YATSUKO
  Free and Easy   400
TANBA, TETSURO
  Taxing Woman's Return, A
    [1988]   348
TANDY, JESSICA
  Driving Miss Daisy   99
TANI, KEI
  Free and Easy   400
TARANTINA, BRIAN
  January Man, The   406
  Uncle Buck   364
TATE, VANESSA
  Riverbend   420
TAVERNIER, NILS
  Story of Women [1988]   332
TAYBACK, VIC
  All Dogs Go to Heaven   27
TAYLOR, LILI
  Say Anything   287
TAYLOR, RENEE
  It Had to Be You   406
TAYLOR, RON
  Relentless   419
TAYLOR, VERN
  Amanda   388
TEAGUE, MARSHALL
  Road House   420
TEFKIN, BLAIR
  Sinful Life, A   423
TELLER
  Penn and Teller Get Killed   416
TENNON, JULIUS
  Riverbend   420
TERRY, JOHN
  In Country   189

TERZO, NINO
  Cinema Paradiso   74
TESH, JOHN
  Shocker   423
THACKER, TAB
  Identity Crisis   405
THAMES, BYRON
  Eighty-Four Charlie MoPic   115
THAYER, MAX
  No Retreat, No Surrender II   415
THEODORE, BROTHER
  'Burbs, The   65
THERRIEN, PHIL
  Hellbent   403
THEUS, REGGIE
  Perfect Model, The   416
THIEBAUD, JIM
  976-EVIL   415
THIGPEN, LYNNE
  Lean on Me   209
THOMAS, BETTY
  Troop Beverly Hills   427
THOMAS, HEIDI
  Crack House   394
THOMAS, HENRY
  Valmont   368
THOMERSON, TIM
  Who's Harry Crumb?   430
THOMPSON, EMMA
  Henry V   173
THOMPSON, LEA
  Back to the Future Part II   36
THOMSEN, GREGG GOMEZ
  Crack House   394
THOMSON, DAVIDSON
  Rude Awakening   421
THORP, SARAH MAUR
  River of Death   420
THRELFALL, DAVID
  When the Whales Came   430
THURMAN, UMA
  Adventures of Baron Munchausen,
    The   23
TIERNEY, LAWRENCE
  Horrow Show, The   404
TIGHE, KEVIN
  K-9   205
  Road House   420
TILLY, JENNIFER
  Fabulous Baker Boys, The   123
  Far from Home   399
  Let It Ride   408
TILLY, MEG
  Valmont   368
TIMM, CHARLES
  Game, The   401
TOBIAS, HEATHER
  High Hopes [1988]   177
TOBOLOWSKY, STEPHEN
  Great Balls of Fire!   160
  In Country   189
TODD, BEVERLY
  Lean on Me   209
TOKUDA, MARILYN
  Cage   392

Farewell to the King   399
  Trust Me   428
TOLBERT, BERLINDA
  Harlem Nights   164
TOLKAN, JAMES
  Back to the Future Part II   36
  Ministry of Vengeance   412
  Second Sight   422
  True Blood   428
TOMLINS, JASON
  Eighty-Four Charlie MoPic   115
TOMPKINS, ANGEL
  Crack House   394
  Relentless   419
TONG, JACQUELINE
  How to Get Ahead in
    Advertising   404
TOPPANO, PETA
  Echoes of Paradise   397
TORIKKA, TIMO
  Talvisota   336
TORN, RIP
  Cold Feet   393
  Hit List   404
TOTH, LESLIE
  Buying Time   391
TOUSSAINT, LORRAINE
  Breaking In   391
TOUZI, HOOSHANG
  Guests of Hotel Astoria,
    The   402
TOUZI, MARIYAM
  Suitors, The   426
TOWNSEND, ROBERT
  Mighty Quinn, The   412
TRACY, ARTHUR
  American Stories   389
TRAVANTI, DANIEL J.
  Millennium   412
TRAVOLTA, JOHN
  Look Who's Talking   229
TREAS, TERRI
  Terror Within, The   426
TREEN, MARY
  Obituaries   443
TREMBLAY, JOHANNE-MARIE
  Jesus of Montreal   201
TRIESTE, LEOPOLDO
  Cinema Paradiso   74
TRINTIGNANT, MARIE
  Story of Women [1988]   332
TSOUSOUVAS, SAM
  Lodz Ghetto   410
TSUGAWA, MASAHIKO
  Taxing Woman's Return, A
    [1988]   348
TUBB, BARRY
  Valentino Returns   429
  Warm Summer Rain   429
TUCCI, STANLEY
  Fear, Anxiety and
    Depression   400
  Slaves of New York   424
TUCKER, MICHAEL
  Checking Out   392

TUMBTZEN, TATIANA
Perfect Model, The   416
TURNER, FRANK
Fly II, The   400
TURNER, KATHLEEN
War of the Roses, The   372
TURTURRO, AIDA
True Love   360
TURTURRO, JOHN
Do the Right Thing   94
TYRRELL, SUSAN
Far from Home   399

UCHIDA, YUYA
Black Rain   52
UECKER, BOB
Major League   233
UEDA, KOICHI
Taxing Woman's Return, A
[1988]   348
ULLMANN, LIV
Rose Garden, The   421
UNDERWOOD, JAY
Uncle Buck   364

VACCARO, BRENDA
Cookie   394
VAIL, BRETTON
Long Weekend, The   410
VALEN, NANCY
Loverboy   410
VAN BELLINGHEN, CAROLYN
Bad Blood   390
VAN CLEEF, LEE
Obituaries   444
Speed Zone   424
VAN DAMME, JEAN-CLAUDE
Cyborg   395
Kickboxer   407
VAN DER VELDE, NADINE
After Midnight   388
VANEL, CHARLES
Obituaries   444
VAN PATTEN, JOYCE
Trust Me   428
VAN PEEBLES, MARIO
Identity Crisis   405
VARGA, MARIA
Hungarian Fairy Tale, A   405
VARNEY, JIM
Fast Food   399
VATANPARAST, BAHRAM
Guests of Hotel Astoria,
The   402
VAUGHN, ROBERT
River of Death   420
VAWTER, RON
Fat Man and Little Boy   399
sex, lies and videotape   306
VELEZ, EDDIE
Rooftops   421
VENTURA, JESSE (THE BODY)
No Holds Barred   415
VERMES, DAVID
Hungarian Fairy Tale, A   405

VERNON, KATE
Office Party   415
VERONICA, CHRISTINA
Bad Blood   390
VIERIKKÖ, VESA
Talvisota   336
VIGNAL, PASCALE
Life and Nothing But   408
VIGODA, ABE
Look Who's Talking   229
Prancer   418
VINCE, PRUITT TAYLOR
K-9   205
VINCENT, JAN-MICHAEL
Hit List   404
VINTAS, GUSTAV
Midnight   411
VRANA, VLASTA
Eddie and the Cruisers II   397
VUCKOVICH, PETE
Major League   233
VUNDLA, KA
Cheetah   393

WAGNER, BRUCE
I, Madman   405
WAHL, JOANNA
Game, The   401
WAI, ERIC TSANG CHI
Eat a Bowl of Tea   111
WAI, LO
Life Is Cheap   408
WAITE, BETTY
Fun Down There   401
WAITE, HAROLD
Fun Down There   401
WAITE, MICHAEL
Fun Down There   401
WAITS, TOM
Cold Feet   393
Mystery Train   249
WAKAYAMA, TOMISABURO
Black Rain   52
WALKEN, CHRISTOPHER
Communion   78
WALKER, ARNETIA
Scenes from the Class Struggle
in Beverly Hills   295
WALKER, GREG
January Man, The   406
WALKER, JOHN
Vampire's Kiss   429
WALKER, JONATHAN
Fakebook   398
WALKER, KIM
Heathers   168
WALKER, LINWOOD
Riverbend   420
WALLACE, JACK
Bear, The [1988]   44
WALLACE, LEE
Batman   40
WALLACE, MARCIA
My Mom's a Werewolf   413

WALSH, CHARLES HUNTER
Loverboy   410
WALSH, ED
Let It Ride   408
WALSH, J. T.
Big Picture, The   391
Dad   86
Wired   384
WALSH, KEN
January Man, The   406
WALSH, M. EMMET
Catch Me If You Can   392
Mighty Quinn, The   412
Red Scorpion   418
WALSH, SYDNEY
To Die For   427
WALSKI, STEPHANIE
Far from Home   399
WALTER, TRACEY
Batman   40
Out of the Dark   416
WAN, CHAN KIM
Life Is Cheap   408
WARD, LYMAN
Milk and Honey   412
Riding the Edge   420
WARD, PHIL
Hellbent   403
WARD, RACHEL
How to Get Ahead in
Advertising   404
WARNER, DAVID
Office Party   415
WARREN, LESLEY ANN
Worth Winning   431
WARRILOW, DAVID
Lodz Ghetto   410
WASHINGTON, DENZEL
For Queen and Country
[1988]   139
Glory   155
Mighty Quinn, The   412
WATANABE, GEDDE
UHF   428
WATERS, CLAIRE
Game, The   401
WATERS, HARRY, JR.
Back to the Future Part II   36
WATERSTON, JAMES
Dead Poets Society   90
WATERSTON, SAM
Crimes and Misdemeanors   82
Welcome Home   429
WATZDORF, DIETRICH VON
Sunday's Child   426
WAY, EILEEN
Queen of Hearts   275
WAYANS, DAMON
Earth Girls Are Easy   397
WAYNE, PATRICK
Her Alibi   404
WEAVER, SIGOURNEY
Ghostbusters II   151
WEBBER, ROBERT
Obituaries   444

WEDGEWORTH, ANN
Miss Firecracker 237
WEIGEL, TERI
Far from Home 399
Savage Beach 421
WEINBERGER, UDO
Sunday's Child 426
WEISS, WILLIAM MURRAY
Little Monsters 409
WEISSMAN, JEFFREY
Back to the Future Part II 36
WELKER, FRANK
Prancer 418
WELLER, PETER
Leviathan 408
WELLES, GWEN
New Year's Day 414
WELLISZ, EVA
Lodz Ghetto 410
WELLS, STANLEY
Hellbent 403
WELSH, KENNETH
Physical Evidence 417
WEST, RED
Road House 420
WESTERMAN, FLOYD
Renegades 419
WESTON, CELIA
Lost Angels 410
WEYERS, MARIUS
Deepstar Six 396
Farewell to the King 399
WHALEY, FRANK
Born on the Fourth of July 60
Field of Dreams 131
Little Monsters 409
WHALLEY-KILMER, JOANNE
Kill Me Again 407
Scandal 291
WHATLEY, LIEM
Iron Triangle, The 406
WHINERY, WEBSTER
Hell High 403
WHITAKER, FOREST
Johnny Handsome 407
WHITE, AL
Red Scorpion 418
WHITE, CHRISSIE
Obituaries 444
WHITE, KAREN MALINA
Lean on Me 209
WHITE, SUNNY JOE
Eddie and the Cruisers II 397
WHITTON, MARGARET
Little Monsters 409
Major League 233
WIEDLIN, JANE
Bill and Ted's Excellent
Adventure 48
WIEST, DIANNE
Cookie 394
Parenthood 267
WIGGINS, CHRIS
Babar 389
WILBRINK, JOHANNES
Sunday's Child 426

WILCOX, LISA
Nightmare on Elm Street V 414
WILDE, CORNEL
Obituaries 444
WILDER, GENE
See No Evil, Hear No Evil 302
WILKENING, CATHERINE
Jesus of Montreal 201
WILKERSON, LAURNEA
Sing 424
WILLIAMS, BILLY
Game, The 401
WILLIAMS, BILLY DEE
Batman 40
WILLIAMS, CAROLINE
Stepfather II 425
WILLIAMS, CINDY
Big Man on Campus 390
Rude Awakening 421
WILLIAMS, DARNELL
Sidewalk Stories 315
WILLIAMS, DICK ANTHONY
Tap 344
WILLIAMS, GUY
Obituaries 444
WILLIAMS, JOBETH
Welcome Home 429
WILLIAMS, ROBIN
Adventures of Baron Munchausen,
The 23
Dead Poets Society 90
WILLIAMS, SPICE
Sexbomb 422
WILLIAMS, TREAT
Heart of Dixie 403
WILLIAMSON, MYKEL T.
Miracle Mile 413
WILLIAMSON, SCOTT
Mutant on the Bounty 413
WILLIS, BRUCE
In Country 189
Look Who's Talking 229
WILSON, DON
Bloodfist 391
WILSON, RICHARD
How to Get Ahead in
Advertising 404
WILSON, SANDYE
Sidewalk Stories 315
WILSON, SCOTT
Johnny Handsome 407
WILSON, THOMAS F.
Back to the Future Part II 36
WILSON, TREY
Great Balls of Fire! 160
Miss Firecracker 237
Welcome Home 429
WING, CHOY CHAN
Farewell to the King 399
WINNINGHAM, MARE
Miracle Mile 413
Turner and Hooch 428
WINSLOW, MICHAEL
Police Academy VI 417

WINTER, ALEX
Bill and Ted's Excellent
Adventure 48
WINTER, MELANIE
New Year's Day 414
WINTERS, ROLAND
Obituaries 444
WISE, RAY
Race for Glory 418
Season of Fear 421
WISE, WILLIAM
Farewell to the King 399
WITTENBAUER, JOHN
Escape from Safehaven 398
WITTER, KAREN
Midnight 411
WOLF, KELLY
Triumph of the Spirit 351
WOLFE, IAN
Checking Out 392
WOLFE, MICHAEL J.
True Love 360
WOLFE, TRACI
Lethal Weapon II 217
WOLPE, LISA NICOLE
Severance 422
WONG, IRIS
Obituaries 444
WONG, MICHELLE
Kinjite 408
WONG, RUSSELL
Eat a Bowl of Tea 111
WONG, VICTOR
Eat a Bowl of Tea 111
Life Is Cheap 408
WOODARD, ALFRE
Miss Firecracker 237
WOODBURY, AL
Obituaries 444
WOODBURY, JOAN
Obituaries 445
WOODS, JAMES
Immediate Family 185
True Believer 356
WOODS, LANCE
Long Weekend, The 410
WOOLDRIDGE, KAREN
Criminal Law 394
WOOLDRIDGE, SUSAN
How to Get Ahead in
Advertising 404
WORONOV, MARY
Scenes from the Class Struggle
in Beverly Hills 295
WORTHY, ATHEN
Dance of the Damned 395
WREN, CLARA
Season of Fear 421
WRIGHT, AMY
Miss Firecracker 237
WRIGHT, BEN
Little Mermaid, The 225
WRIGHT, JENNY
I, Madman 405
Valentino Returns 429

PERFORMER INDEX

WRIGHT, SAMUEL E.
Little Mermaid, The 225
WU, PING
Iron Triangle, The 406
WUHL, ROBERT
Batman 40
Blaze 56
WYMAN, NICHOLAS
Rude Awakening 421
WYNER, GEORGE
Fletch Lives 135
Listen to Me 409
WYSS, AMANDA
To Die For 427

YANKOVIC, WEIRD AL
UHF 428
YASOUKA, RIKIYA
Toxic Avenger, Part II, The 427
YORK, KATHLEEN
Checking Out 392
Cold Feet 393
YORK, MICHAEL
Return of the Musketeers,
The 419

YOUNG, BRUCE PETER
Slaves of New York 424
YOUNG, BURT
Beverly Hills Brats 390
YOUNG, KAREN
Criminal Law 394
Night Game 414
YOUNG, RICHARD
Indiana Jones and the Last
Crusade 193
Innocent Man, An 406
Lords of the Deep 410
YOUNG, SEAN
Cousins 394
YU, WU MING
Eat a Bowl of Tea 111
YUE, MARION KODAMA
Kinjite 408

ZADE, RAMY
After Midnight 388
ZAGARIA, ANITA
Queen of Hearts 275
ZAITZEVA, LUDMILA
Little Vera 409

ZANE, BILLY
Back to the Future Part II 36
Dead Calm 395
ZANE, LISA
Heart of Dixie 403
ZENTARA, EDWARD
Triumph of the Spirit 351
ZENTNER, RENA
Street Story 425
ZERBE, ANTHONY
Licence to Kill 221
Listen to Me 409
See No Evil, Hear No Evil 302
ZEROCKS
Street Story 425
ZISCHLER, HANNS
Rose Garden, The 421
ZOMER, NILI
Riding the Edge 420
ZUNIGA, DAPHNE
Fly II, The 400
Gross Anatomy 402
Staying Together 323

SUBJECT INDEX

The selection of subject headings combines standard Library of Congress Subject Headings and common usage in order to aid the film researcher. Cross references, listed as *See* and *See also*, are provided when appropriate. While all major themes, locales, and time periods have been indexed, some minor subjects covered in a particular film have not been included.

ABORTION
  Camille Claudel [1988] 68
  Story of Women [1988] 332
ACTORS AND ACTRESSES (*See also* FILMMAKERS AND FILMMAKING *and* THEATER)
  Jesus of Montreal 201
  Wired 384
ADOLESCENTS
  Back to the Future Part II 36
  Cinema Paradiso 74
  Dead Poets Society 90
  Lean on Me 209
  Lectrice, La [1988] 213
  Parenthood 267
  Say Anything 287
  Staying Together 323
ADULTERY
  Crimes and Misdemeanors 82 •
  Eat a Bowl of Tea 111
  Getting It Right 147
  Look Who's Talking 229
  sex, lies and videotape 306
  She-Devil 310
  Story of Women [1988] 332
AFRICAN AMERICANS (*See also* APARTHEID *and* RACIAL PREJUDICE)
  Do the Right Thing 94
  Glory 155
  Harlem Nights 164
  Lean on Me 209
  Tap 344
AGING (*See also* MATURING)
  Cinema Paradiso 74
  Dad 86
  Driving Miss Daisy 99
  High Hopes [1988] 177
  Queen of Hearts 275
AIRPLANES
  Always 32
ALCOHOLISM
  Mystery Train 249
ALIENATION (*See also* ISOLATION *and* LONELINESS)
  Lethal Weapon II 217
ALIENS
  Abyss, The 19
  Communion 78
ALLEGORY
  Abyss, The 19
AMBITION (*See also* SUCCESS)
  Blaze 56
  Miss Firecracker 237
AMERICAN SOUTH (*See also* GEORGIA; LOUISIANA;

MEMPHIS; MISSISSIPPI; *and* NEW ORLEANS)
  Blaze 56
  Driving Miss Daisy 99
  Great Balls of Fire! 160
  Staying Together 323
  Steel Magnolias 328
ANIMALS
  All Dogs Go to Heaven 27
  Bear, The [1988] 44
  K-9 205
ANTI-SEMITISM (*See also* JEWS AND JEWISH LIFE *and* NAZIS AND NAZISM)
  Driving Miss Daisy 99
APARTHEID
  Dry White Season, A 107
ARCHAEOLOGY
  Indiana Jones and the Last Crusade 193
ART AND ARTISTS
  Camille Claudel [1988] 68
  Four Adventures of Reinette and Mirabelle [1986] 143
  Ghostbusters II 151
  My Left Foot 245
  New York Stories 257
  Sidewalk Stories 315
ASIANS AND ASIAN AMERICANS (*See also* CHINA *and* JAPAN)
  Eat a Bowl of Tea 111
AUTHORS AND WRITERS (*See also* JOURNALISTS AND JOURNALISM)
  Communion 78
  Enemies, A Love Story 119
  She-Devil 310
AUTOMOBILES AND AUTOMOBILE RACING
  Driving Miss Daisy 99

BASEBALL
  Field of Dreams 131
  Major League 233
  Parenthood 267
BEVERLY HILLS
  Scenes from the Class Struggle in Beverly Hills 295
BIG-CITY LIFE
  Batman 40
  Black Rain 52
  Do the Right Thing 94
  Eat a Bowl of Tea 111
  Enemies, A Love Story 119
  Fabulous Baker Boys, The 123
  Four Adventures of Reinette and Mirabelle [1986] 143

  Getting It Right 147
  Harlem Nights 164
  Look Who's Talking 229
  Navigator, The [1988] 253
  See No Evil, Hear No Evil 302
  Sidewalk Stories 315
  Taxing Woman's Return, A [1988] 348
  Uncle Buck 364
  When Harry Met Sally 380
BIGAMY
  Enemies, A Love Story 119
BIOGRAPHY
  Camille Claudel [1988] 68
  Great Balls of Fire! 160
  My Left Foot 245
  Story of Women [1988] 332
  Triumph of the Spirit 351
  Wired 384
BLACK COMEDY
  Heathers 168
  She-Devil 310
  War of the Roses, The 372
BLINDNESS
  Cinema Paradiso 74
  Crimes and Misdemeanors 82
  See No Evil, Hear No Evil 302
BOSTON
  Field of Dreams 131
BOXING AND FIGHTS
  Triumph of the Spirit 351
BROTHERS AND SISTERS
  Back to the Future Part II 36
  Camille Claudel [1988] 68
  Fabulous Baker Boys, The 123
  Honey, I Shrunk the Kids 181
  Navigator, The [1988] 253
  Parenthood 267
  Staying Together 323
BUREAUCRACY
  Roger and Me 283
BUSINESS EXECUTIVES (*See also* CAREER WOMEN)
  Roger and Me 283
  Taxing Woman's Return, A [1988] 348

CANADA
  Jesus of Montreal 201
CAREER WOMEN
  Four Adventures of Reinette and Mirabelle [1986] 143
  Lectrice, La [1988] 213
  Steel Magnolias 328
  Taxing Woman's Return, A [1988] 348
  When Harry Met Sally 380

SUBJECT INDEX

CATHOLICS AND CATHOLICITY
  Jesus of Montreal 201
  We're No Angels 376
CENTRAL AMERICA
  Licence to Kill 221
CHILD ABUSE
  Sidewalk Stories 315
CHILDBIRTH
  Immediate Family 185
  Look Who's Talking 229
  Parenthood 267
  Steel Magnolias 328
CHILDREN AND CHILD
    REARING
  All Dogs Go to Heaven 27
  Cinema Paradiso 74
  Dad 86
  Family Business 127
  Ghostbusters II 151
  Honey, I Shrunk the Kids 181
  Look Who's Talking 229
  My Left Foot 245
  Navigator, The [1988] 253
  New York Stories 257
  Parenthood 267
  Queen of Hearts 275
  Sidewalk Stories 315
  Uncle Buck 364
CHINA
  Eat a Bowl of Tea 111
CHRISTIANITY (See also
    CATHOLICS AND
    CATHOLICITY)
  Jesus of Montreal 201
CIVIL WAR (See also
    REVOLUTION)
  Glory 155
CLASS CONFLICT
  For Queen and Country [1988] 139
  Getting It Right 147
  Valmont 368
CLEVELAND
  Major League 233
COMMUNITY
  Always 32
  Do the Right Thing 94
CONCENTRATION CAMPS
  Triumph of the Spirit 351
CONNIVERS
  Batman 40
CORRUPTION
  Harlem Nights 164
  Taxing Woman's Return, A
    [1988] 348
COUNTRYSIDE
  Four Adventures of Reinette and
    Mirabelle [1986] 143
  In Country 189
CRIME (See also BIGAMY;
    DRUGS AND DRUG ABUSE;
    KIDNAPING; MURDER;
    PROSTITUTES AND
    PROSTITUTION; RAPE; and
    ROBBERY)
  Batman 40
  Black Rain 52
  Drugstore Cowboy 103
  For Queen and Country [1988] 139
  Ghostbusters II 151

Harlem Nights 164
K-9 205
Licence to Kill 221
Music Box 241
See No Evil, Hear No Evil 302
Story of Women [1988] 332
Tango and Cash 340
Tap 344
Taxing Woman's Return, A
  [1988] 348

DANCERS AND DANCING
  Tap 344
DEATH AND DYING (See also
    SUICIDE)
  All Dogs Go to Heaven 27
  Always 32
  Cinema Paradiso 74
  Crimes and Misdemeanors 82
  Dad 86
  Do the Right Thing 94
  Glory 155
  In Country 189
  Jesus of Montreal 201
  Navigator, The [1988] 253
  Pet Sematary 271
  Steel Magnolias 328
  Story of Women [1988] 332
  Talvisota 336
  Triumph of the Spirit 351
  Wired 384
DECADENCE
  Getting It Right 147
DESERTS
  Indiana Jones and the Last
    Crusade 193
DESPAIR
  Drugstore Cowboy 103
  Sidewalk Stories 315
DETECTIVES
  Fletch Lives 135
  Sea of Love 299
  Tango and Cash 340
  Taxing Woman's Return, A
    [1988] 348
DIVORCE
  Parenthood 267
  Sea of Love 299
  War of the Roses, The 372
DOCTORS AND MEDICINE
  Crimes and Misdemeanors 82
  Dad 86
DOCUMENTARY
  Roger and Me 283
DOMESTIC VIOLENCE
  Sidewalk Stories 315
  War of the Roses, The 372
DREAMS
  Field of Dreams 131
  Getting It Right 147
  Lectrice, La [1988] 213
  Navigator, The [1988] 253
DRUGS AND DRUG ABUSE (See
    also ALCOHOLISM)
  Drugstore Cowboy 103
  K-9 205
  Lethal Weapon II 217
  Licence to Kill 221
  Tango and Cash 340

True Believer 356
Wired 384

ECONOMICS
  Do the Right Thing 94
EDUCATION (See also SCHOOLS
    AND SCHOOL LIFE and
    TEACHERS AND
    TEACHING)
  Bill and Ted's Excellent
    Adventure 48
  Lean on Me 209
EIGHTEENTH CENTURY
  Adventures of Baron Munchausen,
    The 23
  Valmont 368
EMIGRATION AND
    IMMIGRATION
  Enemies, A Love Story 119
  Music Box 241
ENVIRONMENTALISM
  Do the Right Thing 94
ENVY
  Do the Right Thing 94
  Miss Firecracker 237
ESCAPE
  Eighty-Four Charlie MoPic 115
  We're No Angels 376
ESPIONAGE
  Licence to Kill 221
ETHNOLOGY
  Do the Right Thing 94
EUROPE AND EUROPEANS (See
    also FINLAND; FRANCE;
    GREAT BRITAIN; GREECE;
    IRELAND; ITALY; and THE
    SOVIET UNION)
  Enemies, A Love Story 119
EXILE
  Enemies, A Love Story 119
  Mystery Train 249

FAILURE
  Fabulous Baker Boys, The 123
FAMILIES AND FAMILY LIFE
    (See also BROTHERS AND
    SISTERS; CHILDREN
    AND CHILD REARING;
    DIVORCE; MARRIAGE;
    MOTHERS; and
    PATRIARCHY)
  Back to the Future Part II 36
  Communion 78
  Crimes and Misdemeanors 82
  Dad 86
  Driving Miss Daisy 99
  Eat a Bowl of Tea 111
  Family Business 127
  Field of Dreams 131
  High Hopes [1988] 177
  Honey, I Shrunk the Kids 181
  Immediate Family 185
  In Country 189
  Indiana Jones and the Last
    Crusade 193
  Lethal Weapon II 217
  Music Box 241
  My Left Foot 245
  Parenthood 267
  Queen of Hearts 275

Say Anything 287
Staying Together 323
Triumph of the Spirit 351
Uncle Buck 364
War of the Roses, The 372
FANTASY
Lectrice, La [1988] 213
Parenthood 267
FARMS AND FARMING (See also
RURAL AMERICA)
Field of Dreams 131
FEAR
Enemies, A Love Story 119
Lectrice, La [1988] 213
FEMINISM
Camille Claudel [1988] 68
Look Who's Talking 229
She-Devil 310
Story of Women [1988] 332
War of the Roses, The 372
FILMMAKERS AND
FILMMAKING (See also
ACTORS AND ACTRESSES
and THEATER)
Cinema Paradiso 74
Crimes and Misdemeanors 82
Eighty-Four Charlie MoPic 115
When Harry Met Sally 380
FINLAND
Talvisota 336
FIREMEN AND FIRES
Always 32
FLIGHT
Always 32
FOOD
Eat a Bowl of Tea 111
Staying Together 323
FORESTS
Always 32
FRANCE (See also PARIS)
Henry V 173
Story of Women [1988] 332
Valmont 368
FRIENDSHIP
All Dogs Go to Heaven 27
Always 32
Bill and Ted's Excellent
Adventure 48
Black Rain 52
Driving Miss Daisy 99
Four Adventures of Reinette and
Mirabelle [1986] 143
Ghostbusters II 151
Harlem Nights 164
Henry V 173
Honey, I Shrunk the Kids 181
Immediate Family 185
In Country 189
Jacknife 197
Lethal Weapon II 217
Queen of Hearts 275
Sea of Love 299
sex, lies and videotape 306
Star Trek V 319
Steel Magnolias 328
Tango and Cash 340
When Harry Met Sally 380
Wired 384

FUNERAL RITES AND
CEREMONIES
Driving Miss Daisy 99
FUTURE
Back to the Future Part II 36
Navigator, The [1988] 253
Star Trek V 319

GAMBLING
All Dogs Go to Heaven 27
Harlem Nights 164
GENERATION GAP
Dad 86
Parenthood 267
GEORGIA
Driving Miss Daisy 99
GHOSTS
Field of Dreams 131
Ghostbusters II 151
Indiana Jones and the Last
Crusade 193
Mystery Train 249
Pet Sematary 271
GOLD, GOLD MINES, AND
MINING
Navigator, The [1988] 253
GREAT BRITAIN (See also
LONDON)
For Queen and Country [1988] 139
Getting It Right 147
Henry V 173
Indiana Jones and the Last
Crusade 193
Mystery Train 249
Scandal 291
GREECE
Triumph of the Spirit 351
GREED
Fletch Lives 135
High Hopes [1988] 177
Taxing Woman's Return, A
[1988] 348
GRIEF
Always 32
Steel Magnolias 328
GUILT
Born on the Fourth of July 60
Casualties of War 71
Drugstore Cowboy 103
In Country 189
Music Box 241
Star Trek V 319
GYPSIES
Triumph of the Spirit 351

HEDONISM
Family Business 127
HEROISM
All Dogs Go to Heaven 27
Ghostbusters II 151
Glory 155
K-9 205
Licence to Kill 221
Navigator, The [1988] 253
Sidewalk Stories 315
HISTORY
Bill and Ted's Excellent
Adventure 48
Born on the Fourth of July 60

Dry White Season, A 107
Glory 155
Henry V 173
Triumph of the Spirit 351
HORROR
Pet Sematary 271
HOTELS, MOTELS, AND
TAVERNS
Mystery Train 249
HOUSING
Sidewalk Stories 315
War of the Roses, The 372
HUNTERS AND HUNTING
Bear, The [1988] 44
HYPOCRISY
Taxing Woman's Return, A
[1988] 348

ILLNESS (See also MENTAL
ILLNESS)
High Hopes [1988] 177
IMMIGRATION (See
EMIGRATION AND
IMMIGRATION)
IMPOTENCE
sex, lies and videotape 306
INDIVIDUALISM
Batman 40
Black Rain 52
Great Balls of Fire! 160
Jesus of Montreal 201
Lectrice, La [1988] 213
IOWA
Field of Dreams 131
IRELAND
My Left Foot 245
ISOLATION (See also
ALIENATION and
LONELINESS)
Casualties of War 71
Jacknife 197
ITALIAN AMERICANS
True Love 360
ITALY
Cinema Paradiso 74
Mystery Train 249
Queen of Hearts 275
JAPAN
Black Rain 52
Mystery Train 249
Taxing Woman's Return, A
[1988] 348
JESUS CHRIST
Jesus of Montreal 201
JEWS AND JEWISH LIFE
Crimes and Misdemeanors 82
Driving Miss Daisy 99
Enemies, A Love Story 119
JOURNALISTS AND
JOURNALISM (See also
AUTHORS AND WRITERS)
Blaze 56
Dry White Season, A 107
Fletch Lives 135
When Harry Met Sally 380
Wired 384

SUBJECT INDEX

KABUKI
  Jesus of Montreal 201
KIDNAPING
  Ghostbusters II 151
KINGS, QUEENS, AND ROYALTY
  Henry V 173
KNIGHTS AND KNIGHTHOOD
  Henry V 173
  Indiana Jones and the Last
    Crusade 193

LAW, LAWYERS, AND TRIALS
  Dry White Season, A 107
  Immediate Family 185
  Jesus of Montreal 201
  Music Box 241
  New York Stories 257
  True Believer 356
  War of the Roses, The 372
LESBIANISM
  Rainbow, The 279
LITERATURE
  Dead Poets Society 90
  Lectrice, La [1988] 213
  My Left Foot 245
LONDON
  Queen of Hearts 275
LONELINESS (See also
    ALIENATION and
    ISOLATION)
  Four Adventures of Reinette and
    Mirabelle [1986] 143
LOS ANGELES
  Lethal Weapon II 217
LOUISIANA
  Blaze 56
  Fletch Lives 135
LOVE
  Abyss, The 19
  All Dogs Go to Heaven 27
  Always 32
  Cinema Paradiso 74
  Drugstore Cowboy 103
  Eat a Bowl of Tea 111
  Enemies, A Love Story 119
  Getting It Right 147
  Heathers 168
  Jacknife 197
  K-9 205
  Little Mermaid, The 225
  My Left Foot 245
  New York Stories 257
  Queen of Hearts 275
  Rainbow, The 279
  Say Anything 287
  sex, lies and videotape 306
  Tap 344
  True Love 360
  Valmont 368

MACHISMO
  Casualties of War 71
  K-9 205
  True Love 360
MARDI GRAS
  All Dogs Go to Heaven 27
MARRIAGE (See also DIVORCE)
  Abyss, The 19
  Communion 78
  Crimes and Misdemeanors 82

Dad 86
  Eat a Bowl of Tea 111
  Family Business 127
  Immediate Family 185
  Miss Firecracker 237
  Parenthood 267
  Queen of Hearts 275
  sex, lies and videotape 306
  She-Devil 310
  Staying Together 323
  Steel Magnolias 328
  True Love 360
  War of the Roses, The 372
  When Harry Met Sally 380
  Wired 384
MATURING (See also AGING)
  Born on the Fourth of July 60
  Casualties of War 71
  Dead Poets Society 90
  Drugstore Cowboy 103
  Getting It Right 147
  Immediate Family 185
  In Country 189
  Music Box 241
  My Left Foot 245
  Steel Magnolias 328
  Uncle Buck 364
MEDIEVAL TIMES
  Navigator, The [1988] 253
MEMORIES (See also
    NOSTALGIA)
  Casualties of War 71
  Enemies, A Love Story 119
  In Country 189
  Music Box 241
  Star Trek V 319
MEMPHIS
  Mystery Train 249
MENTAL ILLNESS (See also
    NEUROSES and OBSESSION)
  Abyss, The 19
  Camille Claudel [1988] 68
  Communion 78
  Dad 86
  Heathers 168
MEXICO
  Born on the Fourth of July 60
  Old Gringo 262
MILITARY LIFE (See also
    SOLDIERS; VIETNAM WAR;
    WAR; and WORLD WAR II)
  Abyss, The 19
  Born on the Fourth of July 60
  Casualties of War 71
  Glory 155
  Talvisota 336
MISSISSIPPI
  Miss Firecracker 237
MISTAKEN OR SECRET
    IDENTITY
  Batman 40
  Music Box 241
  See No Evil, Hear No Evil 302
  We're No Angels 376
MORALITY
  All Dogs Go to Heaven 27
  Black Rain 52
  Casualties of War 71
  Dry White Season, A 107
  Family Business 127

Great Balls of Fire! 160
  Jesus of Montreal 201
  Miss Firecracker 237
  Rainbow, The 279
  Story of Women [1988] 332
  Taxing Woman's Return, A
    [1988] 348
  Valmont 368
MOTHERS
  High Hopes [1988] 177
  Look Who's Talking 229
  New York Stories 257
  Steel Magnolias 328
MOTION PICTURES (See
    FILMMAKERS AND
    FILMMAKING)
MOUNTAINS AND MOUNTAIN
    CLIMBING
  Star Trek V 319
MURDER
  Batman 40
  Black Rain 52
  Crimes and Misdemeanors 82
  Dry White Season, A 107
  Fletch Lives 135
  Heathers 168
  Licence to Kill 221
  Sea of Love 299
  See No Evil, Hear No Evil 302
  Sidewalk Stories 315
  Taxing Woman's Return, A
    [1988] 348
MUSIC AND MUSICIANS (See
    also SINGERS AND
    SINGING)
  Fabulous Baker Boys, The 123
  Great Balls of Fire! 160
  Harlem Nights 164
  Mystery Train 249
  Tap 344
MYTHS, LEGENDS, AND
    FOLKLORE
  Adventures of Baron Munchausen,
    The 23
  Batman 40
  Indiana Jones and the Last
    Crusade 193
  Little Mermaid, The 225
  Mystery Train 249

NAZIS AND NAZISM
  Indiana Jones and the Last
    Crusade 193
  Music Box 241
  Triumph of the Spirit 351
NEIGHBORS
  'Burbs, The 65
  High Hopes [1988] 177
NEUROSES
  Fabulous Baker Boys, The 123
  Lectrice, La [1988] 213
  Wired 384
NEW ENGLAND
  Pet Sematary 271
NEW JERSEY
  Lean on Me 209
NEW ORLEANS
  All Dogs Go to Heaven 27
  Blaze 56

NEW YORK
Black Rain 52
Crimes and Misdemeanors 82
Do the Right Thing 94
Enemies, A Love Story 119
Ghostbusters II 151
Harlem Nights 164
New York Stories 257
Sea of Love 299
Sidewalk Stories 315
Tap 344
True Believer 356
True Love 360
When Harry Met Sally 380
NEWSPAPERS AND REPORTERS
(See JOURNALISTS AND
JOURNALISM)
NIGHTCLUBS
Blaze 56
Fabulous Baker Boys, The 123
Great Balls of Fire! 160
Harlem Nights 164
1900'S
Old Gringo 262
1960'S
Scandal 291
True Believer 356
NOSTALGIA (See also
MEMORIES)
Back to the Future Part II 36
Eat a Bowl of Tea 111
Jacknife 197
NUCLEAR POWER
Abyss, The 19

OBSESSION
Batman 40
Star Trek V 319

PARIS
Camille Claudel [1988] 68
Four Adventures of Reinette and
Mirabelle [1986] 143
PATRIARCHY
Family Business 127
Indiana Jones and the Last
Crusade 193
Parenthood 267
PATRIOTISM
Born on the Fourth of July 60
PHILOSOPHY
Crimes and Misdemeanors 82
Four Adventures of Reinette and
Mirabelle [1986] 143
PHYSICAL HANDICAPS
Born on the Fourth of July 60
My Left Foot 245
See No Evil, Hear No Evil 302
PLAGUES
Navigator, The [1988] 253
POETS
Dead Poets Society 90
POLICE
Batman 40
Black Rain 52
Drugstore Cowboy 103
Dry White Season, A 107
K-9 205
Lethal Weapon II 217
Sea of Love 299

See No Evil, Hear No Evil 302
Tango and Cash 340
POLITICS AND POLITICIANS
Blaze 56
Scandal 291
When Harry Met Sally 380
POPULAR CULTURE
Batman 40
Blaze 56
Eat a Bowl of Tea 111
Fabulous Baker Boys, The 123
Ghostbusters II 151
Great Balls of Fire! 160
Roger and Me 283
See No Evil, Hear No Evil 302
sex, lies and videotape 306
Tap 344
When Harry Met Sally 380
PORNOGRAPHY
Jesus of Montreal 201
POVERTY
High Hopes [1988] 177
My Left Foot 245
Sidewalk Stories 315
PRIESTS
We're No Angels 376
PRISONS AND PRISONERS
True Believer 356
We're No Angels 376
PROSTITUTES AND
PROSTITUTION
Black Rain 52
Harlem Nights 164
Scandal 291
PSYCHOLOGISTS AND
PSYCHOLOGY
Communion 78

QUEENS (See KINGS, QUEENS,
AND ROYALTY)

RACIAL PREJUDICE (See also
APARTHEID)
Blaze 56
Do the Right Thing 94
Driving Miss Daisy 99
Dry White Season, A 107
For Queen and Country [1988] 139
Glory 155
Lethal Weapon II 217
RAPE
Casualties of War 71
RELIGION AND SPIRITUALITY
(See also CATHOLICS AND
CATHOLICITY and
CHRISTIANITY)
Field of Dreams 131
Fletch Lives 135
Great Balls of Fire! 160
Indiana Jones and the Last
Crusade 193
Jesus of Montreal 201
Navigator, The [1988] 253
Star Trek V 319
We're No Angels 376
RESTAURANTS
Eat a Bowl of Tea 111
RESURRECTION
Pet Sematary 271

REVENGE
Batman 40
Black Rain 52
Dry White Season, A 107
Licence to Kill 221
Queen of Hearts 275
She-Devil 310
REVOLUTION (See also
CIVIL WAR)
Old Gringo 262
ROADS, STREETS, AND
HIGHWAYS
K-9 205
Licence to Kill 221
Mystery Train 249
ROBBERY
Family Business 127
ROMANCE
Always 32
Batman 40
Black Rain 52
Blaze 56
Cinema Paradiso 74
Crimes and Misdemeanors 82
Fabulous Baker Boys, The 123
Ghostbusters II 151
Great Balls of Fire! 160
Henry V 173
In Country 189
Indiana Jones and the Last
Crusade 193
Jacknife 197
K-9 205
Lectrice, La [1988] 213
Licence to Kill 221
Little Mermaid, The 225
Look Who's Talking 229
Major League 233
Mystery Train 249
Old Gringo 262
Say Anything 287
She-Devil 310
Sidewalk Stories 315
Staying Together 323
Uncle Buck 364
Valmont 368
When Harry Met Sally 380
ROYALTY (See KINGS, QUEENS,
AND ROYALTY)
RURAL AMERICA
Field of Dreams 131
In Country 189
RUSSIA (See THE SOVIET
UNION)

SAILORS
Abyss, The 19
SATIRE
Taxing Woman's Return, A
[1988] 348
SCHOOLS AND SCHOOL LIFE
(See also EDUCATION and
TEACHERS AND
TEACHING)
Dead Poets Society 90
Heathers 168
Lean on Me 209
Say Anything 287
SCIENCE AND SCIENTISTS
Abyss, The 19
Back to the Future Part II 36

Honey, I Shrunk the Kids 181
Star Trek V 319
SCIENCE FICTION
Abyss, The 19
Communion 78
Star Trek V 319
SEATTLE
Say Anything 287
SELF-DISCOVERY
Casualties of War 71
Dad 86
Getting It Right 147
Lectrice, La [1988] 213
Little Mermaid, The 225
My Left Foot 245
Rainbow, The 279
Say Anything 287
Sea of Love 299
Uncle Buck 364
SERVANTS
Driving Miss Daisy 99
SEX AND SEXUALITY
Abyss, The 19
Always 32
Back to the Future Part II 36
Blaze 56
Crimes and Misdemeanors 82
Drugstore Cowboy 103
Eat a Bowl of Tea 111
Enemies, A Love Story 119
Fabulous Baker Boys, The 123
Getting It Right 147
Great Balls of Fire! 160
Harlem Nights 164
Heathers 168
Immediate Family 185
In Country 189
Jesus of Montreal 201
K-9 205
Lectrice, La [1988] 213
Licence to Kill 221
Look Who's Talking 229
Mystery Train 249
New York Stories 257
Parenthood 267
Rainbow, The 279
Say Anything 287
Scandal 291
Scenes from the Class Struggle
   in Beverly Hills 295
Sea of Love 299
See No Evil, Hear No Evil 302
sex, lies and videotape 306
Staying Together 323
Story of Women [1988] 332
Tango and Cash 340
True Love 360
Uncle Buck 364
Valmont 368
When Harry Met Sally 380
Wired 384
SINGERS AND SINGING (See also
   MUSIC AND MUSICIANS)
Back to the Future Part II 36
Fabulous Baker Boys, The 123
SISTERS (See BROTHERS AND
   SISTERS)
SMALL-TOWN LIFE
Back to the Future Part II 36
Born on the Fourth of July 60
Cinema Paradiso 74

Miss Firecracker 237
Roger and Me 283
Staying Together 323
Story of Women [1988] 332
We're No Angels 376
SOCIAL REFORM
Born on the Fourth of July 60
Dry White Season, A 107
Roger and Me 283
Sidewalk Stories 315
SOLDIERS (See also MILITARY
   LIFE; VIETNAM WAR;
   WAR; and WORLD WAR II)
Born on the Fourth of July 60
Casualties of War 71
Eighty-Four Charlie MoPic 115
In Country 189
Talvisota 336
SOLITUDE
Born on the Fourth of July 60
New York Stories 257
SOUTH AFRICA (See also
   APARTHEID)
Dry White Season, A 107
Lethal Weapon II 217
THE SOVIET UNION
Talvisota 336
SPORTS AND SPORTS FIGURES
   (See also BASEBALL and
   BOXING AND FIGHTS)
Field of Dreams 131
Major League 233
STORMS AND NATURAL
   DISASTERS
Abyss, The 19
STUDENTS (See SCHOOLS AND
   SCHOOL LIFE)
SUBMARINE BOATS
Abyss, The 19
SUCCESS (See also AMBITION)
Cinema Paradiso 74
Fabulous Baker Boys, The 123
SUICIDE
Heathers 168
SUPERNATURAL (See also
   GHOSTS)
Field of Dreams 131
Ghostbusters II 151
Navigator, The [1988] 253
Pet Sematary 271
SUPERSTITION
Navigator, The [1988] 253
SWINDLERS AND SWINDLING
Four Adventures of Reinette and
   Mirabelle [1986] 143
TEACHERS AND TEACHING
   (See also EDUCATION and
   SCHOOLS AND
   SCHOOL LIFE)
Dead Poets Society 90
Dry White Season, A 107
Lean on Me 209
My Left Foot 245
TELEVISION
Crimes and Misdemeanors 82
Wired 384

THEATER
Adventures of Baron Munchausen,
   The 23
Jesus of Montreal 201
TIME TRAVEL
Back to the Future Part II 36
Bill and Ted's Excellent
   Adventure 48
Navigator, The [1988] 253
TURN OF THE CENTURY
Camille Claudel [1988] 68
Rainbow, The 279
VACATIONS
'Burbs, The 65
VETERANS (See also SOLDIERS)
For Queen and Country [1988] 139
VIETNAM WAR
Born on the Fourth of July 60
Casualties of War 71
Eighty-Four Charlie MoPic 115
In Country 189
Jacknife 197
VIOLENCE
Batman 40
Black Rain 52
Born on the Fourth of July 60
Casualties of War 71
Do the Right Thing 94
Indiana Jones and the Last
   Crusade 193
K-9 205
Lethal Weapon II 217
Mystery Train 249
Tango and Cash 340
Valmont 368
WAR (See also VIETNAM WAR
   and WORLD WAR II)
Adventures of Baron Munchausen,
   The 23
WEALTH
Roger and Me 283
Scenes from the Class Struggle
   in Beverly Hills 295
She-Devil 310
Valmont 368
WITCHCRAFT
Little Mermaid, The 225
WORKING CLASS
My Left Foot 245
Roger and Me 283
True Love 360
WORLD WAR II
Eat a Bowl of Tea 111
Enemies, A Love Story 119
Indiana Jones and the Last
   Crusade 193
Music Box 241
Story of Women [1988] 332
Talvisota 336
Triumph of the Spirit 351
WRITERS (See AUTHORS AND
   WRITERS)
WYOMING
Always 32
YOUTH
Four Adventures of Reinette and
   Mirabelle [1986] 143
My Left Foot 245